INFORMATION SYSTEMS ANALYSIS AND MODELING

An Informational Macrodynamics Approach

THE KLUWER INTERNATIONAL SERIES IN ENGINEERING AND COMPUTER SCIENCE

INFORMATION SYSTEMS ANALYSIS AND MODELING

An Informational Macrodynamics Approach

by

Vladimir S. Lerner

National University, U.S.A.

KLUWER ACADEMIC PUBLISHERS

Boston / Dordrecht / London

Distributors for North, Central and South America:
Kluwer Academic Publishers
101 Philip Drive
Assinippi Park
Norwell, Massachusetts 02061 USA
Telephone (781) 871-6600
Fax (781) 871-6528
E-Mail <kluwer@wkap.com>

Distributors for all other countries:
Kluwer Academic Publishers Group
Distribution Centre
Post Office Box 322
3300 AH Dordrecht, THE NETHERLANDS
Telephone 31 78 6392 392
Fax 31 78 6546 474
E-Mail <orderdept@wkap.nl>

Electronic Services <http://www.wkap.nl>

Library of Congress Cataloging-in-Publication Data

Lerner, Vladimir S., 1931-
Information systems analysis and modeling : an information macrodynamics approach/ by Vladimir S. Lerner.
p. cm.--(The Kluwer international series in engineering and computer science; SECS 532)
Includes bibliographical references and index.
ISBN 0-7923-8683-3 (alk. paper)
1. Management information systems. 2. System analysis. I. Title. II. Series

T58.6 .L45 1999
003--dc21

99-048108

Printed on acid-free paper.

Printed in the United States of America

This book is dedicated to my lovely wife, Sanna, for her love, kindness, patience, and support.

In memory of my parents, Semion and Maria Lerner.

CONTENTS

PREFACE

Information Macrodynamics (IMD) presents the **unified** informational systemic approach with **common information language** for modeling, analysis and optimization, of a variety of the **interactive** processes, such as physical, biological, economical, social, and informational, including human activities.

Comparing it with **Thermodynamics**, which deals with transformation energy and represents a theoretical foundation of Physical Technology, **IMD** deals with transformation information, and can be considered a theoretical foundation of **Information Computer Technology** (ICT).

ICT includes but is not limited to applied computer science, computer information systems, computer and data communications, software engineering, and artificial intelligence.

In ICT, information flows from different data sources, interacts to create new information products. The information flows may interact physically or via their virtual connections initiating an information dynamic process that can be distributed in space.

As in **Physics**, an actual problem is understanding general *regularities* of the information processes in terms of information law, for their engineering and technological design, control, optimization, the development of computer technology, operations, manipulations, and management of real information objects.

The IMD mathematical formalism is transformed into corresponding informational mechanisms, analytical and algorithmic procedures implemented by IMD software packet, which has been applied for constructive solution of actual practical problems.

This book belongs to an interdisciplinary science that represents the new theoretical and computer-based methodology for system informational description and improvement, including various activities in such interdisciplinary areas as thinking, intelligent processes, management, and other nonphysical subjects with their mutual interactions, informational superimpositions, and the information transferred between interactions.

The book reflects the author's style of working with original results rather than studying well-known theories.

The mathematical formalism of revealing regularities is an essential attribute of the IMD modeling mechanisms and their correctness.

Part Descriptions

Part 1 contains the Mathematical IMD foundation including

- Informational Microlevel Statistics
- Informational Macrolevel Dynamics
- Informational Hierarchical Concentrated and Distributed Models with Informational Network as a upper model level.

A reader who is interested in applications, may start reading the book from

Part 2, which includes a short review of the basic (Part 1) results.

Part 2 contains Elements of Information Systems Theory with an essential analysis of IMD cooperative macrostructures, their dynamics and geometry, stability, self-organization, evolution, adaptation, genetic mechanism, and coding language, and the optimal model's time duration.

Informational-physical models, with connections to information technologies, are considered in Part 3.

Theoretical IMD results and analytical methods are transformed into numerical procedures, computer algorithms, and software packages in Part 4, Chapters 4.1-4.7.

Chapter 4.1 describes the analytical and numerical solutions of IMD problems for different model's examples.

Chapters 4.2-4.7 describe the solution of IMD problems and the applications of IMD for information technology, including

- Data modeling and communications with applications to optimal data encoding, encryption, classification, and modeling of space visual informational structures
- Cognitive models in artificial intelligence with information mechanisms of learning, knowledge acquisition, evaluation, and representation
- Informational macroeconomic models with evaluation of human contributions and analysis of optimal macrosystem organization
- Biological IMD models with examples that reveal the information mechanisms of concrete biological and medical processes
- Manufacturing Applications, including the informational modeling and optimization of some industrial technological processes with implementation of the optimal control systems and Computer-Aided Design.

IMD information mechanism analyses of the creation of complex phenomena (at the macrolevel) caused by random contributions (at the microlevel).

The *specific features* of IMD consist of

- the unified informational description of the different interconnected interdisciplinary fields (as innovative technologies with human participation; human cognitive processes, knowledge acquisition, educational processes; environmental, macroeconomical, biological, and medical processes, social relations) with their system modeling, analysis, optimization, computer modeling, and simulation
- revealing the informational superimposing phenomena of a variety of interactive processes (of different nature) that cannot be discovered by traditional approaches
- building a macroscopic informational model that reflects the informational macrodynamic regularities of the complex object created by the large number of random interactions, considered as a microlevel stochastic model
- modeling the many level hierarchical informational network of the cooperative macrostructures with computer methodology of identification and restoration, each particular model based on the object observations
- revealing the dynamic order and self-organization of the analyzed system, and possible chaotic behavior as well
- determining the informational control functions (as an inherent part of macromodeling) with the optimal controls applying to the object, for their optimization, automatic operations, manipulations, management, and

improvement

- IMD brings a united systemic formalism for a successive object's modeling, algorithmization, and software programming.

Most of the book can be read independently, referring to Part 1 for proofs and details.

Students can study the IMD problems, solutions, and practical applications as well.

The cited formulas within each paragraph or chapter start with a paragraph or chapter number, for example 1.12; for the outside references, we use the complete number starting with part, chapter, and paragraph (for example, 1.1.12).

IMD represents a new science field with its specific object and research methodology, and with prospective results for a number of sciences.

This book provides new ideas for both theory and applications that would be interesting for a wide audience, including professional, scholars, researchers, students, and information technology users.

This book would also be useful as an IMD Introductory Course (starting from Part 2).

The author has taught "Information Macrodynamics" for graduate students at the University of California at Los Angeles (UCLA) and at West Coast University.

This book could be used in computer science, engineering, business and management, education, psychology, and for different interdisciplinary fields.

ACKNOWLEDGMENTS

Many thanks to my colleagues with whom I have been collaborating on the IMD research and academic activities for several years:
In the former Soviet Union : Professors R.Truchaev, V. Portougal, P. Husak, my brother, Professor Yury Lerner, programmer analysts A. Gorbanev, B. Roychel, A. Zaverchnev, I. Risel, E.Kogan
latter on collaborating in the USA:
Drs. J. Abedi, R. Dennis, H. Herl, D. Niemi, W. Happ, Professors L.Preiser, W. Van Snyder, W. Van Vorst, W. Makovoz, D. Scully, C. Kattemborough.

My great appreciation to Professors Achim Sydow and Yi Lin for reviewing this manuscript and ma king the valuable comments, and also to the anonymous reviewers who contributed to the book improvements.

The author thanks Dr. Michael Talyanker for developing the AutoCAD simulation procedure with IMD examples.

I am indebted to Dr. Robert Dennis, my colleague and a former UCLA graduate, who has not only participated in our collaborative research but also contributed in the manuscript shaping and formatting.

Active student participation has helped me refine various lecture notes, examples, and computer solutions.

The author wishes to thank Mr. Lance Wobus and Mrs. Sharon Palleschi at Kluwer Academic Publishers for supporting the IMD project.

My family deserves great appreciation for permitting my preoccupation with this work for so long. I remain indebted to my lovely wife Sanna, my children Alex, Tatyana, Olga, sons- and daughter-in-law Alex, Michael, Natalia, and my grandchildren Dina, Sacha, Jeffrey, Daniel.

INTRODUCTION

Modeling of complex systems in techniques, technology, biology, economics, sociology is based on revealing the behavioral regularities created by a large number of interactive processes. Computer Technology (CT) deals with various data that generally are random reflecting object activities at the microlevel as the elementary informational exchanges between interactions.

A great many interactions of a random nature, in turn, can generate new dynamic processes and structures that enable for systemic integrations. Dynamic behavior of random elements possesses new features that are basically distinct from their statistic behavior. The considered information object has a bilevel structure with the stochastic process at the microlevel and dynamic processes at the macrolevel.

Formal revealing of the *informational dynamic regularities* created by microlevel stochastic processes (independent on their nature), represents an essential interest. Informational language is the most suitable for such general description.

Informational MacroDynamics (IMD) contains formal mathematical and computer methodology to describe the transformation of random information processes (at the microlevel) into a system of dynamic processes (at the macrolevel) to model the observed processes on the basis of both the discovery of their information dynamic regularities and the identification of their macrodynamic equations with restoration the model during the object observations.

The IMD model consists of three main layers: microlevel stochastics, macrolevel dynamics, and a dynamic network of information flows, that by interacting, are able to produce new information. The CT input data is transformed into the format of initial information flows for that network, and the output network flows are represented in the required database format. The general hierarchical structures are concretized with the use of a formal procedure for the observed process's identification.

Integrating *the microlevel stochastics into a new macrolevel dynamics is an essential object's quality.*

The systemic informational dynamic description reveals the information mechanism of the initial object processes, their mathematical modeling, information data exchanges, control, optimization, and computation processes (as a process transforming information). It represents most general approach for any existing and designed objects. It brings common information methodology and a computer solution for actual systemic problems to a wide diversity of nonphysical and physical complex objects. The IMD scientific subject defines *regularities of transformation of information involving a human being*. As distinct from physics, informational regularities are represented not only in mathematical or corresponding verbal forms, but even more useful are *algorithmical structures, computer programs, and information networks*. As in physics, mathematical substantiation of regularities and obtaining the equations of certain laws can be based on an *extremal* principle formulated by some functional. Principles of minimal action in mechanics, electrodynamics, optics, and minimal entropy production are the different forms of a variational principle (VP).

According to VP, the actual trajectories of a physical system are not arbitrary but can be found from an equation that results from the solution of a corresponding variational problem. For example, the equation of Newton's second law can be obtained from variation principle for the energy functional:

$$E = \int_t L dt \text{, where } L = T + U$$

is the Lagrange function that includes the kinetic energy $T = 1/2 \sum_i m_i v_i^2$ depending on speeds v_i and mass m_i, and the potential energy $U = U(r_i)$ depending on state coordinates r_i.

Using Euler's partial equation , Calculus of Variations, for that functional:

$$\frac{d}{dt}\frac{\partial L}{\partial v_i} - \frac{\partial U}{\partial r_i} = 0,\ i = 1,\dots,n,$$

we obtain the equation of its extremals: $m_i a_i = F_i$, with $F_i = -\frac{\partial U}{\partial r_i}$ as a force, and $a_i = \frac{dv_i}{dt}$ as an acceleration. That equality, in particular, at $\frac{dx_1}{dt} = v$, $\frac{dx_2}{dt} = a$, can be represented by the controllable system of differential equation:

$$\dot{x} = Ax + u,\ A = \begin{bmatrix} 0,1 \\ 0,0 \end{bmatrix},\ \frac{dx_1}{dt} = x_2,\ \frac{dx_2}{dt} = u,\ u = \frac{F}{m}$$

where u is the control function, and $(x_1, x_2) = x$ are the components of the state vector x. Solving that equation defines the extremal trajectories depending on control. By it analogy, other minimal principles can be applied to define the evolution of physical systems. Natural laws allow only certain object movements with admissible trajectories. The actual problem is to find a generalized informational form of VP for an observed information process that can be characterized by some unknown proper functional with random observed trajectories. Mathematical foundation of the VP principle is very important not only for IMD and traditional information theory, but also for systems theory, statistics, ans mathematical physics. The observed process is represented by a set of random interactions connected via a Marcovian chain with a probabilistic path integral evaluation. This functional accumulates the integral *informational* contributions from the local functionals of interacting microlevel processes that evaluate a cooperative result of interactive dynamics as a collective (macro) functional. A dynamic macromodel follows from the solution of the VP minimax problem for the *entropy* form of this functional. The entropy *functional,* as a measure of information *process,* marks a major departure of IMD from traditional information approaches that use an entropy *function.*

The traditional maximal, minimal, or minimax principles for the entropy function are able to select the optimal *states* and create a *static* information model.

Applying the VP to the entropy functional allows us to obtain the irreversible *macrodynamic* model and to reveal the informational regularities of macrodynamics. The macrofunctional is able to accumulate and extract order from microlevel randomness and transfer it to the macrolevel. Initial microlevel sources of information can generate a new secondary level informational macrodynamics through the micro- macrolevel information channel. Macromovement occurs along segments of the initial n-dimensional extremal of the entropy functional. These segments are successively joint at discrete points effectively shortening the initial dimension and ultimately leading to the renovation of dynamic process.

The problem of extremization of the entropy functional by the applied control functions formulates also the performance criteria in the optimal control problem.

Informational macro modeling operating with the control functions, enables us to analyze the information transfer mechanisms in the corresponding dynamic structures with feedback synthesis, which is useful in Optimal Control Systems. The IMD control functions are not given from outside but are the attributes of the problem solution, and include within the dynamics the hidden (invisible) variables.

The IMD creates essentially new *systemic* results with regard to the Shannon Information Theory. The macromodel is able to bind the initial states into a *process* that originates from the collectivization of many dimensional microlevel stochastics into cooperative macrodynamics.

An Information System is an interconnected set of interactions exchanging information, and capable of integrating them into a common information unit.

An ordered chain of mutually coordinated dynamics, informational geometry of the cooperative structures, carries out such phenomena as aggregation and hierarchy; stability under environmental disturbances; structural stability to preserve the integrated structure; adaptability in expansive progressive development and improvement (in the process of cyclic functioning); reproductivity (by accepting and creating new information and other cooperative structures and processes). Figure 1 presents an initial sketch-diagram of the interacting processes $(\tilde{x}_t^i, \tilde{x}_t^k, \tilde{x}_t^j)$, which are superimposing in a common environment, and exchanging the information contributions $(w_t^{kj}, w_t^{ik}, w_t^{ij})$. The processes $(\tilde{x}_t^i, \tilde{x}_t^k, \tilde{x}_t^j)$ are mutually connected. Each process $\tilde{x}_t^i$ might generate other processes $(\tilde{x}_t^k, \tilde{x}_t^j)$, and interacts with them. The informational exchanges can also be a result of transformation $\tilde{x}_t^k$ into $\tilde{x}_t^i, \tilde{x}_t^j$ and back. This primary interacting set we consider to be the microlevel processes of an observed object. Each trajectory of an element's movement represents a random process. The contributions (w_t^{kj}, w_t^{ik}, w_t^{ij}) are the sources of the second level macroprocesses (x_t) with a possibility of creation the new effects and new structures (e_t) that are not inherent to any of the processes before interacting. The interaction of superimposing processes can be considered to be their mutual cross-self-control, and as a result, it transfers information between them. An information functional responsible for regularities accumulates the contributions both from initial microlevel statistics and macrolevel dynamics. In Figure 1, a simple form of information law defines the following macromodel as a matrix relation between information flow, $I = \dot{x}_t$, and corresponding information force, $X = \frac{\partial S}{\partial x}$ (that depends on the applied control): $I = \hat{l} X$, where the operator $\hat{l}$ depends on statistical characteristics of the interacting microlevel process $\tilde{x}_t$ and the inner control; the functional S is defined by a set random information contributions w_t, and the n-dimensional operator $\hat{l}$ is successively identified at discrete points of changing the operator structure, which brings a new effect, e_t, in solution of the above equation.

The ranged spectrum of the operator $\hat{l}$ defines the sequence of the initial macrolevel quantities information $\{h_i\}$ in information network IN (Figure 2).

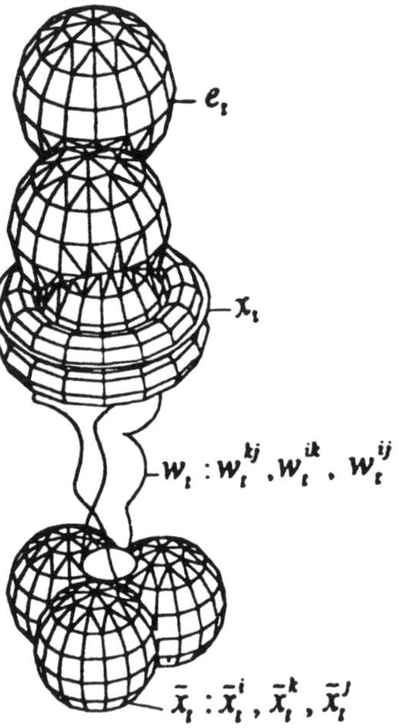

Figure 1. An initial sketch-diagram of the set of interacting processes $\tilde{x}_t : \tilde{x}_t^i, \tilde{x}_t^k, \tilde{x}_t^j$ $\tilde{x}_t : \tilde{x}_t^i, \tilde{x}_t^k, \tilde{x}_t^j$ created the informational contributions $w_t : w_t^{kj}, w_t^{ik}, w_t^{ij}$, and the macrolevel process x_t with generation of new effects and new structures, e_t.

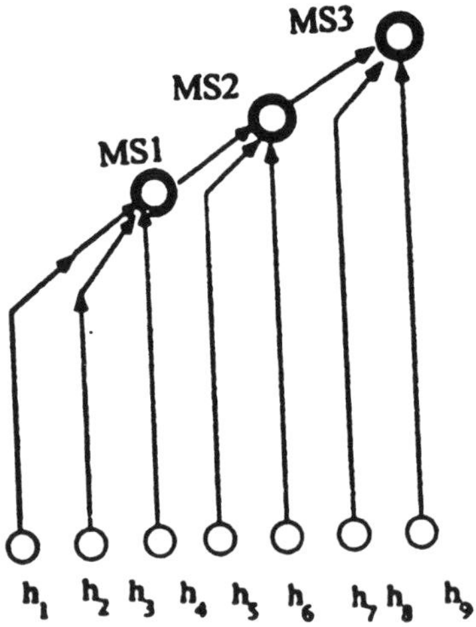

Figiure 2. Dynamic network of hierarchical informational macrostructures (MS).

The dynamic form of informational transformations (reflecting the VP regularities) as in physics, requires mathematical expression as a *group of invariant transformations preserving some measure*.

Mathematical foundation of IMD is based on the same approach, using an information measure. The VP for the entropy path functional defines the relative Shannon measure of uncertainty as an invariant of the group transformations. That automatically includes Shannon's information theory (SIT) as a *static* information model into the IMD. The SIT defines the capacity of a communication channel and was developed as a strategy to combat noise interference in a physical channel of communications.

According to SIT, the quantity information of a symbol is measured by the probabilistic measure of uncertainty (or surprise) that the symbol carries among a considered set of the equal potential symbols.

This number defines a minimal bit of an information content of the set of symbols (to convey this set). To evaluate a random sequence of symbols (forming a message), the SIT needs to measure the multidimensional correlation's between the message symbols. It requires a full dynamic correlation analysis of the message with unknown probability distributions. Existing correlation techniques mostly evaluate the *static* connections in *linear* approximations between the message symbols. The STI provides a mathematical basis for quantifying the information content of a message symbol but is not ready for direct measuring an actual Shannon's quantity information of the *message*.

The IMD introduces an integral information measure that evaluates a random chain of symbols by an information functional (as a function of the total chain sequence), which is a single number (for each of the chain connections) that measures the Shannon's quantity of information for the total chain.

The IMD evaluates an optimal connection within the chain of symbols and enables it to choose the chain with a minimum of a total uncertainty. For the optimal chain connections, the minimum bit of an information content is a common information measure useful for a comparison of different chains by a unique measurement methodology.

The IMD identification techniques enable the restoring of the function of quantity Shannon's information for each symbol connected into the optimal IN chain. IMD extends the SIT by utilizing the notion of channel capacity as a fundamental characteristic of information systems.

The IMD methodology evaluates the quantity, quality, and complexity of information reflecting *the regularities*. Using other than Marcovian measures in the uncertainty function (including for example, fuzzy set measure and various others) essentially extends the definition and application of information functional and IMD methodology.

Constructive results in the solution of an appropriate VP problem is based on chosen classes of micro- macrolevel models or their corresponding analogies.

The considered path integral is a mathematical tool for evaluating the observations and building a mathematical model of ordered phenomena. Informational regularities are described by the IMD analogy of Hamiltonian equations with specific dynamic constraint (DC) that stochastics impose on macrodynamics. The DC is responsible for mechanism of cooperation creating inner control functions that lead to forming the hierarchical information structures.

An optimal cooperating mechanism consists of successfully joining the triplet structures within the hierarchy. Each triplet models a consolidation of three three-dimensional space distributed macro processes. The moment of their cooperating is accompanied with forming (at some conditions) the Collective Chaotic Attractors.

The synthesized macrodynamics give rise to the self-organized structures becoming ordered in the process of optimal motion. A dynamic space distributed *network* of information macronodes are enclosed as an unification of the structural stable attractors. The information network models the system structure and architecture. The information functional is used for measuring a complexity of the dynamic model and the corresponding network.

The minimization procedure of the entropy functional leads to a constructive methodology of creation of a *computer program of a minimal complexity* (for a given model). Such a program expresses an application of the information law for the object model. The bound dynamic macrostructure creates their intrinsic Informational Geometry.

Function of Information Macrosystemic Complexity [MC] evaluates the hierarchy and structural complexity, of both the network dynamics and of the geometry.

A sequence of the macronodes represented by discrete control logics creates some coding information language. The MC defines a minimal code of optimal algorithm that accumulates an integral network information and can be used for the network restoration.

Within the optimal IN, the upper node encapsulates a total network information into this node. The IN is squeezed into one final IN node carrying nonredundant information that accumulates not only the entire network with its space spiral geometrical structures but also statistical microlevel.

That quality can be used for a data compression and encryption in communication technology. Identifying an observed *random process*, the methodology enables us to compress it into one macro state, and transmit the node information with a subsequent restoration of all nonredundant data.

By representing a *visual* information via a sequence of the triplet's geometry *fractions* , it is possible to squeeze up the fractions into one final IN node.

Information superhighway, learning, cognitive processes, and others are examples of such information integration for particular objects into the systems.

The IN node structure can be considered to be a base for storing and sequential retrieving the identifying data. The final IN node accumulates the complex of the IMD mathematical operations, including the logics of control functions. Information is located and distributed in a geometrical field in the form of information macrostructures (MS). The regularities reveal the MS geometrical form and the process of their creation. The geometrical space of MSs represent a place for storing and memorizing information generated by macrodynamics.

The geometry acquires the system category as a bound hierarchical information structure. A curvature of geometrical space is a source of the rotating transformation of the dynamic operator toward a subsequent integration, memorization, and forming the macrostructures. The geometrical space is a supplementary source of information that is capable of carrying control functions and mechanisms of ordering. In the process of generating macrostructures, the dynamics (stable) and geometry compete by contributing an opposite sign of entropies. In a growing dimension, integrated dynamics are memorized in a corresponding geometry by increasing the MS curvature that could be an additional (to nonstable dynamics) source of self-organization.

As distinct from physics, which deals with a material substance, IMD deals with both material (hardware) and nonmaterial information substance creation (software, in particular). It is important to understand the informational relations of such substances, and because of human involvement, to study connections between memory, cognition, and their material carriers in Artificial Intelligence (AI), and so on. Both human beings and nature interact (between and within each other's domain) using a common informational language (for example DNA code, antigene-antibodies, odor and sound receptors, and other complementary formations). IMD intends to understand the principles of building this information language and communicating with it. Understanding information regularities has a diversity of computer applications: design of optimal algorithms, networks, optimal control strategies, systems analysis, decision making, data modeling, software engineering (requires analysis and specifications), cognitive and learning processes, and algorithms. The actual IMD problem is the identification of a dynamic informational macromodel based on observations of random processes. A correct mathematical macromodel can be obtained only in a process of restoration of undivided interactions of complex object and the identification of its equations.

A series of well-known identification methods are based on the approximation of an observed process by some class of equations (operators). The choice of an approximating operator is more often defined not by the physical law equations. An approximating criterion as a measure of closeness between both observation process and a solution of identification equation, usually are not associated with the object's physical regularities, and in general, is *arbitrary*. At such a formal approximation, some superimposing cross phenomena would not be taken into consideration. The quantitative effect of that phenomena could be insignificant in terms of the accepted operator and the approximating criteria, but it is important from the physical and application viewpoints. Applied mathematical models are mostly reversible, for the irreversible observed processes, and have been developed, basically, for "simple objects" without the consideration of a two-level structure of complex objects, their macroscopic characteristics, and interacting processes.

The IMD identification methodology is based on restoring the model operator at each discrete interval defined by the object's observation. The macromodel is irreversible as a real object. Renovating the initial macro operator is directed on the minimizing uncertainty (with increasing order) and is predictable by the object regularities. IMD applications include information modeling, simulation, and optimal control of nonequilibrium thermodynamic and biological processes; the restoration of IN dynamics and geometry; optimal prognosis, filtering, and synthesis of optimal macrostructures associated with a particular information form of the model criterion; universal code for the macromodel description, transformation and communication; comparison of different objects by their information complexity, and the IN's of enclosed information, creating a compressed algorithmical representation of the object. IMD contains not only the theory but also the effective computer-based methodology with applied software packages and the results of applications and implementations.

Computer methodology of system modeling, simulation, and control with the IMD software package is instrumental for the practical solution of real problems in technology, engineering, and artificial intelligence.

The dynamic form of informational transformations (reflecting the VP regularities) as in physics, requires mathematical expression as a *group of invariant transformations preserving some measure.*

Mathematical foundation of IMD is based on the same approach, using an information measure. The VP for the entropy path functional defines the relative Shannon measure of uncertainty as an invariant of the group transformations. That automatically includes Shannon's information theory (SIT) as a *static* information model into the IMD. The SIT defines the capacity of a communication channel and was developed as a strategy to combat noise interference in a physical channel of communications.

According to SIT, the quantity information of a symbol is measured by the probabilistic measure of uncertainty (or surprise) that the symbol carries among a considered set of the equal potential symbols.

This number defines a minimal bit of an information content of the set of symbols (to convey this set). To evaluate a random sequence of symbols (forming a message), the SIT needs to measure the multidimensional correlation's between the message symbols. It requires a full dynamic correlation analysis of the message with unknown probability distributions. Existing correlation techniques mostly evaluate the *static* connections in *linear* approximations between the message symbols. The STI provides a mathematical basis for quantifying the information content of a message symbol but is not ready for direct measuring an actual Shannon's quantity information of the *message*.

The IMD introduces an integral information measure that evaluates a random chain of symbols by an information functional (as a function of the total chain sequence), which is a single number (for each of the chain connections) that measures the Shannon's quantity of information for the total chain.

The IMD evaluates an optimal connection within the chain of symbols and enables it to choose the chain with a minimum of a total uncertainty. For the optimal chain connections, the minimum bit of an information content is a common information measure useful for a comparison of different chains by a unique measurement methodology.

The IMD identification techniques enable the restoring of the function of quantity Shannon's information for each symbol connected into the optimal IN chain. IMD extends the SIT by utilizing the notion of channel capacity as a fundamental characteristic of information systems.

The IMD methodology evaluates the quantity, quality, and complexity of information reflecting *the regularities*. Using other than Marcovian measures in the uncertainty function (including for example, fuzzy set measure and various others) essentially extends the definition and application of information functional and IMD methodology.

Constructive results in the solution of an appropriate VP problem is based on chosen classes of micro- macrolevel models or their corresponding analogies.

The considered path integral is a mathematical tool for evaluating the observations and building a mathematical model of ordered phenomena. Informational regularities are described by the IMD analogy of Hamiltonian equations with specific dynamic constraint (DC) that stochastics impose on macrodynamics. The DC is responsible for mechanism of cooperation creating inner control functions that lead to forming the hierarchical information structures.

An optimal cooperating mechanism consists of successfully joining the triplet structures within the hierarchy. Each triplet models a consolidation of three three-dimensional space distributed macro processes. The moment of their cooperating is accompanied with forming (at some conditions) the Collective Chaotic Attractors.

The synthesized macrodynamics give rise to the self-organized structures becoming ordered in the process of optimal motion. A dynamic space distributed *network* of information macronodes are enclosed as an unification of the structural stable attractors. The information network models the system structure and architecture. The information functional is used for measuring a complexity of the dynamic model and the corresponding network.

The minimization procedure of the entropy functional leads to a constructive methodology of creation of a *computer program of a minimal complexity* (for a given model). Such a program expresses an application of the information law for the object model. The bound dynamic macrostructure creates their intrinsic Informational Geometry.

Function of Information Macrosystemic Complexity [MC] evaluates the hierarchy and structural complexity, of both the network dynamics and of the geometry.

A sequence of the macronodes represented by discrete control logics creates some coding information language. The MC defines a minimal code of optimal algorithm that accumulates an integral network information and can be used for the network restoration.

Within the optimal IN, the upper node encapsulates a total network information into this node. The IN is squeezed into one final IN node carrying nonredundant information that accumulates not only the entire network with its space spiral geometrical structures but also statistical microlevel.

That quality can be used for a data compression and encryption in communication technology. Identifying an observed *random process*, the methodology enables us to compress it into one macro state, and transmit the node information with a subsequent restoration of all nonredundant data.

By representing a *visual* information via a sequence of the triplet's geometry *fractions* , it is possible to squeeze up the fractions into one final IN node.

Information superhighway, learning, cognitive processes, and others are examples of such information integration for particular objects into the systems.

The IN node structure can be considered to be a base for storing and sequential retrieving the identifying data. The final IN node accumulates the complex of the IMD mathematical operations, including the logics of control functions. Information is located and distributed in a geometrical field in the form of information macrostructures (MS). The regularities reveal the MS geometrical form and the process of their creation. The geometrical space of MSs represent a place for storing and memorizing information generated by macrodynamics.

The geometry acquires the system category as a bound hierarchical information structure. A curvature of geometrical space is a source of the rotating transformation of the dynamic operator toward a subsequent integration, memorization, and forming the macrostructures. The geometrical space is a supplementary source of information that is capable of carrying control functions and mechanisms of ordering. In the process of generating macrostructures, the dynamics (stable) and geometry compete by contributing an opposite sign of entropies. In a growing dimension, integrated dynamics are memorized in a corresponding geometry by increasing the MS curvature that could be an additional (to nonstable dynamics) source of self-organization.

As distinct from physics, which deals with a material substance, IMD deals with both material (hardware) and nonmaterial information substance creation (software, in particular). It is important to understand the informational relations of such substances, and because of human involvement, to study connections between memory, cognition, and their material carriers in Artificial Intelligence (AI), and so on. Both human beings and nature interact (between and within each other's domain) using a common informational language (for example DNA code, antigene-antibodies, odor and sound receptors, and other complementary formations). IMD intends to understand the principles of building this information language and communicating with it. Understanding information regularities has a diversity of computer applications: design of optimal algorithms, networks, optimal control strategies, systems analysis, decision making, data modeling, software engineering (requires analysis and specifications), cognitive and learning processes, and algorithms. The actual IMD problem is the identification of a dynamic informational macromodel based on observations of random processes. A correct mathematical macromodel can be obtained only in a process of restoration of undivided interactions of complex object and the identification of its equations.

A series of well-known identification methods are based on the approximation of an observed process by some class of equations (operators). The choice of an approximating operator is more often defined not by the physical law equations. An approximating criterion as a measure of closeness between both observation process and a solution of identification equation, usually are not associated with the object's physical regularities, and in general, is *arbitrary*. At such a formal approximation, some superimposing cross phenomena would not be taken into consideration. The quantitative effect of that phenomena could be insignificant in terms of the accepted operator and the approximating criteria, but it is important from the physical and application viewpoints. Applied mathematical models are mostly reversible, for the irreversible observed processes, and have been developed, basically, for "simple objects" without the consideration of a two-level structure of complex objects, their macroscopic characteristics, and interacting processes.

The IMD identification methodology is based on restoring the model operator at each discrete interval defined by the object's observation. The macromodel is irreversible as a real object. Renovating the initial macro operator is directed on the minimizing uncertainty (with increasing order) and is predictable by the object regularities. IMD applications include information modeling, simulation, and optimal control of nonequilibrium thermodynamic and biological processes; the restoration of IN dynamics and geometry; optimal prognosis, filtering, and synthesis of optimal macrostructures associated with a particular information form of the model criterion; universal code for the macromodel description, transformation and communication; comparison of different objects by their information complexity, and the IN's of enclosed information, creating a compressed algorithmical representation of the object. IMD contains not only the theory but also the effective computer-based methodology with applied software packages and the results of applications and implementations.

Computer methodology of system modeling, simulation, and control with the IMD software package is instrumental for the practical solution of real problems in technology, engineering, and artificial intelligence.

PART I. MATHEMATICAL FOUNDATIONS OF INFORMATIONAL MACRODYNAMICS

1.1. INFORMATION VARIATIONAL PRINCIPLE

1.1.1. Initial Mathematical Models: Minimax Principle

Model of microlevel process

The processes of interaction of microlevel stochatsic elements are modeled by solving the n-dimensional controlled stochastic Ito equation (given in the random process theory [1] with regular limitations), which is considered as an initial *object* :

(1.1) $d\,\tilde{x}_t = a\,t, \tilde{x}_t,\, u_t)\,dt + \sigma(t, \tilde{x}_t)d\,\xi_t,\;\; \tilde{x}_s = \eta$, $t \in (s,T)$,

$\eta: (\Omega^1, \Psi^1, P^1) \rightarrow (R^n, \beta, G)$; $P^1 = P^1(B^1)$, $B^1 \subset \Psi^1$,

$P_s = P_s(D) = P^1\{\omega^1 : \eta(\omega^1) \in D\} = P^1\{\eta \in D\}$, $\omega^1 \in \Omega^1$, $D \subset \beta$,

$\{\eta \in D\} \subset \Psi^1$, $P_s(x) = P^1\{\eta = x\}$, $x \in R^n$, $d\,P_s(x)/d\,x = p_s(x)$;

$\xi_t = U_t - U_o$; $U_t : (\Omega'', \Psi'', P'') \rightarrow (C, U, \mu^o)$; $P'' = P''(B'')$, $B'' \in \Psi''$;

$M''[\cdot] = \int_{\Omega'} [\cdot] P''(d\omega'')$, $\omega'' \in \Omega''$, $\omega \in \Omega$, $\mu(C) = 1$, $\{\tilde{x}_t \in A\} \subset \Psi$,

$\mu^o = \mu^o(A) = P''\{\omega'' : U_t(\omega'') \in A\} = P''\{U_t \in A\}$,

$A \subset U$, $\{U_t \in A\} \in \Psi''$; $\mu^o(C) = 1$; $\tilde{x}_t : (\Omega, \Psi, P) \rightarrow (C, U, \mu)$,

$\Omega = \Omega^1 \times \Omega''$, $\Psi = \Psi^1 \times \Psi''$, $P(B'' \times D) = \int_D P''(B'')g(x)\,dx$,

$\mu = \mu(A) = P\{\omega : \tilde{x}_t(\omega) \in A\} = P\{\tilde{x}_t \in A\}$, $\sigma : \Delta \times R^n \rightarrow \angle(R^n)$,

$\det\sigma \neq 0$; $a : \Delta \times R^n \times U \rightarrow R^n$, $U \subset R^r$, $r \leq n$,

where U_t is the n-dimensional Wiener's process, $C = C(\Delta, R^n)$ is the space of the continuous on Δ, n-dimensional vector-functions with operations in R^n; U is σ- algebra in C, created by all possible opened (in C metric) sets; $\angle(R^n)$ is the space of linear operators in R^n. The functions shift $a(t, \tilde{x}_t, u_t) = \overline{a^u}(t, x)$ and diffusion $\sigma(t, \tilde{x}_t)$ satisfy the following conditions of smoothness:

(1.2) $a(\mathrm{t},\cdot,\cdot) \in \mathrm{KC}'(\Delta, R^n)$; $\mathrm{KC}'(\Delta, R^n) = \mathrm{C}(\Delta, R^n) \cap (\mathrm{C}^1, \Delta^o)$,

$$\Delta^o = \Delta \setminus \bigcup_{k=1}^{m} \tau_k,\ \tau_k \in \Delta,\ \sigma_{ij}(\mathrm{t}, \cdot) \in \mathrm{C}^1(\Delta^o, \mathrm{R}^1),\ \sigma_{ij}(x, \cdot) \in \mathrm{C}^1(R^n, \mathrm{R}^1),$$

for example, $\mathrm{C}^1(\Delta^o, \mathrm{R}^1)$ and $\mathrm{C}^2(R^n, R^n)$ are the space of continuous differential functions, and the continuous and twice differential functions accordingly. Control (u_t) is formed as a function of time and macro variables ($\bar{x}_t$), which are nonrandom with respect to set Ω'', and are measured by some physical instruments.

Model of the macrolevel processes

is a set of probabilistic trajectories $\bar{x}_t \overset{def}{=} \bar{x}(\mathrm{t}, \eta)$, in the space state with $\bar{x}_s = \eta$:

(1.3) $\bar{x}_t : \Delta \times (R^n, \beta, P_s) \rightarrow (R^n, \beta)$,

$\bar{x}'(\mathrm{t},.) \overset{def}{\in} \mathrm{KC}^1(\Delta^o, R^n) \subset \mathrm{C}(\Delta, R^n)$ (modP'),

KC' is a space of the continuous piece-wise differential on Δ, n-dimensional vector functions. The control law is defined by the following feed-back equation :

(1.4) $u_t \overset{def}{=} u(\mathrm{t}, \bar{x}_t)$, $u : (\Delta \times R^r) \rightarrow \mathrm{U}$; $u(\mathrm{t}, \cdot) \in \mathrm{KC}'(\Delta, U)$,

$u(\cdot, x) \in C^2(R^n, U)$, $u_t \in \mathrm{KC}'(\Delta, U)$,

$u_{+-} = \lim (u(\mathrm{t}, x(\tau_k)))$ $(\mathrm{t} \rightarrow (\tau_k + \text{-o}))$ (modP1); k=0,...,n, $\tau_k \in \Delta$,

where KC'(Δ,U), KC(Δ,U) are the piecewise differential and piecewise continuous on Δ functions accordingly; mod P' is defined with probability P'=1.

The control u_t is nonrandom with respect to Ω''. From (1.2) it follows that the Lipchitz conditions, the linear growth by $x \in R^n$, and the uniformity with respect to $(\mathrm{t}, u) \in \Delta \times \mathrm{U}$, are satisfied with necessity; and the limitations (1.4) are correct. Therefore, according to [1], the solution (1.1) exists and is a unique on (Ω'', Ψ'', P''), (Ω, Ψ, P), and at these spaces exist the moments of different orders. The vector $a = a(\mathrm{t}, x, u)$ of the stochastic equation in physical problems defines the macroscopic speed (drift) of a medium (with diffusing Brownian particles), which has a meaning of reqular flow:

(1.5) $d\, \bar{x}_t / dt = a(\mathrm{t}, x, u)$, $\bar{x}_s = \eta$.

Matrix $\sigma = \sigma(\mathrm{t}, x)$ characterizes the pecularities of a medium to conduct flow (1.5).

The model of the programmable trajectories (as a task) at microlevel

is given by the process $\tilde{x}_t'$ that satisfies the corresponding stochastic equation

(1.7) $d\, \tilde{x}_t' = a'(\mathrm{t}, \tilde{x}_t')\, dt + \sigma(\mathrm{t}, \tilde{x}_t') d\, \xi_t$, $\quad \tilde{x}_s' = \eta'$,

η': $(\Omega^1, \Psi^1, P^1) \rightarrow (R^n, \beta, P_s')$; $d\,P_s'(x)/d\,x = p_s'(x)$;

$\tilde{x}_t'$: $(\Omega, \Psi, P) \rightarrow (C, U, \mu')$, $\mu'(A) = P\{\tilde{x}_t' \in A\}$, $\mu'(C) = 1$;

$a'(t, \cdot) \in C^1(\Delta^o, R^n)$, $a'(\cdot, x) \in C^2(R^n, R^n)$.

The model of the programmable trajectories (as a task) at macrolevel

is defined by the process

(1.8) $\bar{x}_t \overset{def}{=} \bar{x}'(t, \eta), \bar{x}': \Delta \times (R^n, \beta, P_s) \rightarrow (R^n, \beta), \bar{x}'(t,) \overset{def}{\in} C^1(\Delta^o, R^n)$(modP')

$\bar{x}'(t,\cdot) \overset{def}{\in} C^1(\Delta^o, R^n)$ (modP'), where $C^1(\Delta^o, R^n)$ is the space of continuous differential n- dimensional vector-functions. The corresponding regular flow at macro level is defined by the equation similar to (1.5):

(1.9) $d\,\bar{x}_t'/dt = a(t, \bar{x}_t')$, $\bar{x}_t' = \eta'$.

The difference in the distributions for the macroprocesses $\bar{x}_t$ and $\bar{x}_t'$ has a simple physical interpretation: both the object and the control tasks are measured by the different instruments.

The equations in deviations

The micro-and macrotrajectories we consider in deviations from the programmable movements are given for the two-level model by appropriate tasks:

(1.10) $\tilde{x}_t^* = \tilde{x}_t - \tilde{x}_t'$, $x_t = \bar{x}_t - \bar{x}_t'$

for the micro-and macrolevel processes accordingly. Selection of u_t is limited by the requirements: 1) each of processes' $\tilde{x}_t^*$, $\tilde{x}_t$ measured on (C,U) are absolutely continuous with respect to other; 2) measure x_t coincides with $\tilde{x}_t^*$. According to first one, $\tilde{x}_t^*$ is found as a solution of stochastic equation with the same function $\sigma(t, x)$, $(t, x) \in \Delta \times R^n$ as in (1.1), and with unknown drift $a^*(t, \tilde{x}_t^*, u_t)$ from

(1.11) $d\tilde{x}_t^* = a^*(t, \tilde{x}_t^*, u_t)\,dt + \sigma(t, \tilde{x}_t^*)d\xi_t$, $\tilde{x}_s^* = \eta^*$,

$\eta^* = \eta - \eta'$; η^*: $(\Omega^1, \Psi^1, P^1) \rightarrow (R^n, \beta, P_s^*)$; $dP_s^*(x)/dx = p_s^*(x)$;

$p_s^*(x) = \int_{R^n} p_s(x+y)\, p_s'(y)dy$; $M''[\cdot] = \int_{R^n} [\cdot]\, p_s^*(x)dx$, $M''[\cdot] = \int_{R^n} [\cdot]\, p_s^*(x)dx$;

$\tilde{x}_t^*$: $(\Omega, \Psi, P) \rightarrow (C, U, \mu^*)$, $\mu^*(A) = P\{\tilde{x}_t^* \in A\}$, $\mu^*(C) = 1$.

Function $a^*(t, \tilde{x}_t^*, u_t) = a^u(t, x)$ via $(t, x, u) \in \Delta \times R^n \times U$ satisfies the same relations as $a(t, x, u)$; $u_t = u(t, x_t + \overline{x}_t')$. According to (1.10) we have

(1.12) $x_t = x(t, \eta^*)$, $x(t, \cdot) \in KC'(\Delta \times R^n)$ (modP').

The points of discontinuity of vector-functions $\overline{x}(t, \cdot)$, $x(t, \cdot)$ are defined by the set $\{\tau_k\}$, k=1,..., m points of the control switching.

At these points, we consider the one-sided derivatives:

$$\dot{x}_- \overset{def}{=} \lim_{t \to \tau_k - o} \dot{x}(t, \cdot) \; ; \dot{x}_+ \overset{def}{=} \lim_{t \to \tau_k + o} \dot{x}(t, \cdot).$$

Lacking the explicit macrolevel description, brings us a wide class of dynamic macroprocesses as a subset of the piecewise differential n-dimensional vector -functions $x_t \in KC'(\Delta \times R^n)$ on $\Delta = [s, T)$, $x \in R^n$.

Model of disturbances

is considered as an auxiliary random process (that is chosen as the standard one) $\zeta_t = \zeta(t, \omega); \zeta : \Delta \times (\Omega, F, P_x) \to (R^n, \beta)$ which models the perturbations $\zeta_t = \tilde{\xi}_t$ at the macrolevel. The standard process is defined by solving the equation

(1.13) $\zeta_t = \int_0^t \sigma(\upsilon \xi_\upsilon) d\zeta_\upsilon$,

and satisfies the conditions

$M_s[\zeta_t] = M[\zeta_t] = 0$, where $M_s[\cdot] = \int_\Omega [\cdot] P_x d\omega$; $M[\cdot] = \int_\Omega [\cdot] P' d\omega'$.

An essence of the extremal principle .

By Feinman's ideology [2], a measured process $\overline{x}_t$ has to reflect some regularities of the controlled object. Numerous examples from physics show that regularities of deterministic and stochastic systems are formulated and formalized by some extremal principles [3]. It allows to assume that an extremal principle can express regularities of a considered system. Hence, the measured object's process might disclose the object regularities, as an identification tool, subordinated to the extremal problem. Modeling is based on disclosing the regularities by minimization of uncertainties in the observed object. For a random object, the most probable trajectories may approximate the extremals as the object's macrotrajectories.

We formulate the considered extremal principle as a probability problem of approximating microlevel processes ($\tilde{x}_t$) by macrolevel processes ($\overline{x}_t$):

(1.14) $P_1 = P\{\rho_{L_2}(\tilde{x}_s, \overline{x}_t) < \delta\} \to \underset{\overline{x}_t}{Sup}$, $L_2 = L_2(\Delta, R^n)$,

$$\rho_{L_2}(\varphi,\psi)=(\int_0^T|\varphi-\psi|^2 dt)^{1/2}, \quad (\varphi,\psi)\in L_2,$$

$$|\varphi-\psi|^2=\sum_{i=1}^{n}(\varphi_i-\psi_i)^2; \delta>0, \quad \overline{x}_t \overset{def}{=} \overline{x}_t(t,\eta), \quad \overline{x}_t \overset{def}{\in} KC'(\Delta, R^n)(\mathrm{modP}_1),$$

where $L_2(\Delta, R^n)$, $KC'(\Delta, U)$, $KC(\Delta, U)$ are the spaces of square-summed, piecewise differential, piecewise continuous on Δ functions accordingly (mod P', P'=1).

The approximation of the problem for the programmable trajectories analogous to (1.14) has the form:

(1.15) $P_2=P\{\rho_{L_2}(\tilde{x}_s', \overline{x}_t')<\delta\}\rightarrow \underset{\overline{x}_t}{Sup}$.

The problem statement

The problem is to synthesize the controllable macro model $\overline{x}_t(u_t)$ that satisfies the equations (1.14, 1.15) and these requirements for the probabilities:

(1.16) $P_3=P\{\rho_{L_2}(\tilde{x}_t, \tilde{x}_t')<\delta\}\rightarrow \underset{\overline{x}_t}{Sup}$, $\underline{m}(P_3)\rightarrow \underline{m}(P_4)$

$P_4=P\{\rho_{L_2}(\overline{x}_t'+\tilde{\xi}_t, \tilde{x}_t)<\delta\}$,

where $\underline{m}(P_i)$ is the lowest limit of the probabilities P_i, i=1-4.

The equation $P'\{|\overline{x}_T - \overline{x}'_T| > \varepsilon\}$, $\varepsilon>0$ is an additional condition, depending on the requirements to the object. The relation (1.16) expresses the closeness of the control object to the task at macrolevel, and (1.14, 1.15) establishes the connections between the deviations from the tasks for the micro- and macrolevel processes.

With some limitations (see ch.1.1.2), the fulfillment of (1.16) leads to the following maximal conditions for the probabilities:

(1.17) $P_4=P\{\rho_{L_2}(\tilde{\xi}_t, x_t)<\delta\}\rightarrow \underset{x_t}{Sup}$,

(1.18) $P_5=P\{\rho_{L_2}(\tilde{x}_t^*, x_t)<\delta\}\rightarrow \underset{x_t}{Sup}$.

1.1.2. The probabilistic evaluation of the micro- and macrolevel processes

Definition. The trajectory φ_t passes a locality of the trajectory ψ_t with the maximal probability if the lowest probability limit of their closeness reaches the maximum:

(2.1) $P\{\rho_\Delta(\psi_t, \varphi_t) < \delta\} \rightarrow \underset{\varphi_t}{Sup}$; $\forall\, \delta>0, \varphi_t \in KC'(\Delta, R^n), \varphi_t \in C(\Delta, R^n)$

and the upper probability limit of their distantness (as a measure of the process's separateness) reaches the minimum:

(2.1') $P\{\rho_\Delta(\psi_t, \varphi_t) \geq \delta\} \rightarrow \underset{\varphi_t}{Inf}$; $\forall\, \delta>0$,

$\rho_\Delta(\psi_t, \varphi_t) = \| \psi_t - \varphi_t \|_{(\bullet)} = \rho_{(\bullet)}(\psi_t, \varphi_t)$.

Depending on the considered distance in the C- or L_2 metrics (ρ_C, ρ_{L_2}), the evaluation (2.1) has meaning of the C- or L_2 closeness, and the evaluation (2.1') has a meaning of the C- or L_2 distantness.

The relationship between the considered probabalistic evaluations is the following:

$$\rho_{L_2}(\psi_t, \varphi_t) = [\int_s^T \sum_{i=1}^n (\psi_i(t) - \varphi_i(t))^2 dt]^{1/2} =$$

$$= [\int_s^T (\sum_{i=1}^n (\psi_i(t) - \varphi_i(t))^2)^{1/2} \sum_{i=1}^n ((\psi_i(t) - \varphi_i(t))^2)^{1/2} dt]^{1/2} \leq$$

$$\leq [\int_s^T \max_{t\in\Delta} (\sum_{i=1}^n (\psi_i(t) - \varphi_i(t))^2)^{1/2} \times (\sum_{i=1}^n (\psi_i(t) - \varphi_i(t))^2)^{1/2} dt]^{1/2} \leq$$

$$\leq [\int_s^T \max_{t\in\Delta} (\sum_{i=1}^n (\psi_i(t) - \varphi_i(t))^2)^{1/2}) \times \max_{t\in\Delta} (\sum_{i=1}^n (\psi_i(t) - \varphi_i(t))^2)^{1/2} dt]^{1/2} =$$

$$= \max_{t\in\Delta} (\sum_{i=1}^n (\psi_i(t) - \varphi_i(t))^2)^{1/2} \times (T-s)^{1/2} = \rho_C(\psi_t, \varphi_t)(T-s)^{1/2},$$

$$\rho_C(\psi_t, \varphi_t) \leq \rho_{L_2}(\psi_t, \varphi_t)(T-s)^{-1/2}, \{\rho_C(\psi_t, \varphi_t) < \delta\} \subseteq$$

$$\subseteq \rho_{L_2}(\psi_t, \varphi_t)(T-s)^{-1/2} < \delta\}, P\{\rho_{L_2}(\psi_t, \varphi_t) < \delta\} \geq P\{\rho_C(\psi_t, \varphi_t)(T-s)^{1/2} < \delta\}.$$

Because the C-closeness is stronger than L_2-closeness, we consider for the evaluation (2.1) the C-closeness, and for the evaluation (2.1') the L_2 -distantness.

Using the relations (1.11, 12), (2.1,1') and the triangle inequalities, we arrive at

Lemma 2.1. The problem of evaluation of the lowest probability limit of closeness of the controlled process ($\tilde{x}_t$(u)) to standard process (ζ_t) at the microlevel is reduced to following evaluations relating the micro- and macrolevel processes to each other:

(2.2) $P_1 = P\{\rho_\Delta(\tilde{x}_t, \zeta_t) < \delta\} \rightarrow \underset{\tilde{x}_t(u)}{Sup}$,

(2.3) $P_2 = \mathrm{P}\{\rho_\Delta(\tilde{x}_t, x_t) < \delta\} \rightarrow \underset{\tilde{x}_t(u)}{Sup}$,

(2.4) $P_3 = \mathrm{P}\{\rho_\Delta(\zeta_t, x_t) < \delta\} \rightarrow \underset{\tilde{x}_t(u)}{Sup}$.

The *proof* follows from the triangle inequality for the relations at the condition
$\rho_\Delta(\tilde{x}_t, \zeta_t) \le \rho_\Delta(\tilde{x}_t, x_t) + \rho_\Delta(\zeta_t, x_t); \{\rho_\Delta(\tilde{x}_t, x_t) < \delta\} \supseteq$
$\{(\rho_\Delta(\tilde{x}_t, x_t) + \rho_\Delta(\zeta_t, x_t)) < \delta\} \supseteq \{\rho_\Delta(\tilde{x}_t, x_t) < \delta/2\} \times \{\rho_\Delta(\zeta_t, x_t) < \delta/2\}$.
For the independent events $\{\rho_\Delta(\tilde{x}_t, x_t) < \delta/2\}$, $\{\rho_\Delta(\zeta_t, x_t) < \delta/2\}$ and an arbitrary $\delta > 0$, we come to $P_1 = P_2 \cdot P_3$, and then the conditions of maximization each of the probabilities (2.3,4) follows: ●

Lemma 2.2. Let's introduce function $y_t = y(t, x): \Delta \times (R^n, \beta, \overline{P}_s) \rightarrow (R^n, \beta)$, $y(t,\cdot) \in KC'(\Delta, R^n)$ (modP'), assuming that is true

(2.5) $y_s = y_s(\omega'): (\Omega', F', P') \rightarrow (R^n, \beta, \overline{P}_s)$; $\omega' \in \Omega'$, $d\overline{P}_s/dx = \overline{p}_s(x)$,

and the function $\tilde{y}_t$ that satisfies the equation

$$\tilde{y}_t = \tilde{y}_s + \int_s^t q(v, \tilde{y}_v, u_v)\,dv + \int_s^t \sigma(v, \tilde{y}_v)\,d\zeta_v,$$

where $\tilde{y}_s = \tilde{y}_s(\omega'): (\Omega', F', \hat{P}_s) \rightarrow (R^n, \beta, \hat{P}_s)$, $d\hat{P}_s/dx = \hat{p}_s(x)$, $\tilde{y}_t = \tilde{y}(t, \omega, x)$,
$\tilde{y}(\cdot, \omega, x): (\Omega, F, P_x) \rightarrow C(U, \mu^3{}_x)$, $\mu^3{}_x = \mu^3{}_x(C) = 1$,
$\tilde{y}(\cdot, \omega''): (\Omega'', F'', P) \rightarrow (C, U, \mu^3{}_x)$, $\omega'' \in \Omega''$, and the function $q(t, x, u)$ with $q: \Delta \times R^n \times U \rightarrow R^n$ satisfies the conditions analogous to (1.2) for $a^u = a^u(t, x)$.
Then the following probabilitistic evaluations are satisfied:

(2.6) $\mathrm{P}\{\rho_\Delta(\tilde{y}_t, y_t) < \delta\} = P_x\{\rho_\Delta(\tilde{y}_t, y_t) < \delta\}$; $y_s = \tilde{y}_s$,

(2.7) $\mathrm{P}\{\rho_\Delta(\tilde{y}_t, y_t) < \delta\} = \hat{P}_s{}^* P_x\{\rho_\Delta(\tilde{y}_t - y_t, \tilde{y}_s - y_s) < \delta\}$; $y_s \ne \tilde{y}_s$,

(2.8) $\hat{P}_s{}^* = \hat{P}_s{}^*(D_\delta) \int_{D_\delta} (\int_{R^n} \overline{P}_s(y) \hat{P}_s(x+y)\,dy)\,dx$;

$D_\delta \subset \beta$, $D_\delta = K(0, \delta) = \{x \in R^n: \|x\| < \delta\}$.

Proof. Using the Marcovian property for $y_s = \tilde{y}_s$, we have

$$\mathrm{P}\{\rho_\Delta(\tilde{y}_t, y_t) < \delta\} = \int_{K(y_s,\delta)} d\,\hat{P}_s(\tilde{y}_s) \hat{P}_s\{\rho_\Delta(\tilde{y}_t, y_t) < \delta\} =$$

$$= \int_{K(x,\delta)} \hat{P}_s(y) P_y\{\rho_\Delta(\tilde{y}_t, y_t) < \delta\}\,dy =$$

$$= \int_{K(x,\delta)} \hat{\delta}(y - x) P_y\{\rho_\Delta(\tilde{y}_t, y_t) < \delta\}\,dy = P_x\{\rho_\Delta(\tilde{y}_t, y_t) < \delta\};\ (x, y) \in R^n,$$

where $\hat{\delta}(x)$ is the n-dimensional delta-function with its center in $x \in R^n$, $K(x, \hat{\delta}) = \{ y \in R^n : \| y - x \| < \delta \}$, with $\| y - x \| = (\sum_{i=1}^{n} (y_i - x_i)^2)^{1/2}$.

For $y_s \neq \tilde{y}_s$, $\overline{P}_s \neq \hat{P}_s$, using the triangle inequality, we have
$\rho_\Delta(\tilde{y}_t, y_t) \leq \rho_\Delta(\tilde{y}_t, y_t + \tilde{y}_s - y_s) + \rho_\Delta(y_t, y_t + \tilde{y}_s - y_s) = \rho_\Delta(\tilde{y}_t, y_t + \tilde{y}_s - y_s) +$

$+ \rho_\Delta(\tilde{y}_s - y_s, 0)$, $O = \|O_i\|_{i=1}^{n}$, $\rho_\Delta(\tilde{y}_s - y_s, 0) = \|y - x\|_{R^n} = (\sum_{i=1}^{n} (\tilde{y}_{is} - y_{is})^2)^{1/2}$,

$\{\rho_\Delta(\tilde{y}_t, y_t) < \delta\} \supseteq \{(\rho_\Delta(\tilde{y}_t, y_t + \tilde{y}_s - y_s) + \rho_\Delta(y_t, y_t + \tilde{y}_s - y_s)) < \delta\} \supseteq$
$\supseteq \{\{\rho_\Delta(\tilde{y}_t, y_t + \tilde{y}_s - y_s) < \delta/2\} \{\rho_\Delta(\tilde{y}_s - y_s, 0) < \delta/2\}\}$.
$P\{\rho_\Delta(\tilde{y}_t, y_t) < \delta\} \geq P\{\{\rho_\Delta(\tilde{y}_t, y_t + \tilde{y}_s - y_s) < \delta/2\} \{\rho_\Delta(\tilde{y}_s - y_s, 0) < \delta/2\}\}$.

The events $\{\rho_\Delta(\tilde{y}_t, y_t + \tilde{y}_s - y_s) < \delta/2\}$ and $\{\rho_\Delta(\tilde{y}_s - y_s, 0) < \delta/2\}$ are independent because the first one does not depend on β, and the second one has been defined on β. Then, because $\delta > 0$ is chosen arbitrary, the relation follows:
$P\{\rho_\Delta(\tilde{y}_t, y_t) < \delta\} \geq P'(B_\delta') P_x\{\rho_\Delta(\tilde{y}_t, y_t + \tilde{y}_s - y_s) < \delta\}$; $y_s \neq \tilde{y}_s$,
where $B_\delta' = \{\omega' : \{\rho_\Delta(\tilde{y}_s - y_s, 0) < \delta\} \subset F'$. According to [11] we have the equality $P'(B_\delta') = \hat{P}_s^*(D_\delta)$, where last probability satisfies (2.8). Finaly we get (2.7). •
The lowest evaluations (2.6,7) are different only by the multiplicator responsible for closeness of the initial conditions. We need to evaluate the right side of (2.6,7).

Theorem 2.1. The probabilty of the evaluation of closeness φ_t to ζ_t is defined by

(2.9) $P\{\rho_\Delta(\zeta_t, \varphi_t) < \delta\} = P_{x=0}\{\rho_\Delta(\zeta_t, \varphi_t) < \delta\} =$

$= P_0\{\rho_\Delta(\zeta_t, \varphi_t) < \delta\} \geq P_0(B_\delta)\, \varepsilon \exp - \{(S(\varphi_t) + [2S(\varphi_t)(1-\varepsilon)^{-1}]^{1/2}\}$,
$\varphi_t \in KC'(\Delta, R^n)$, $\zeta_t \in C(\Delta, R^n)$.

(2.10) $S(\varphi_t) = 1/2 \int_s^T \dot{\varphi}_t^T \dot{\varphi}_t \, dt = \int_s^T |\dot{\varphi}_t|^2 dt$; $\varphi_s = 0$, $\zeta_s = 0$,

where $|\dot{\varphi}_t|^2 = \sum_{i=1}^{n} \dot{\varphi}_i^2(t)$, $\varepsilon \in (0,1)$, $B_\delta = \{\omega : \{\rho_\Delta(\zeta_s, 0) < \delta\}\} \subset F$.

Proof. Let $\tilde{\varphi}_t = -\varphi_t + \zeta_t$ and assume that the measures (μ_o, μ_o^4) of corresponding functions $(\tilde{\varphi}_t, \zeta_s)$ on (C,U) are absolutely continuous with respect to each other. Then according to (2.6) we get the following relations
$P_0\{\rho_\Delta(\zeta_t, \varphi_t) < \delta\} = P_{x=0}\{\rho_\Delta(\zeta_t, \varphi_t) < \delta\} = P_{x=0}\{\rho_\Delta(\varphi_t, 0) < \delta\} =$
$= P_0\{\rho_\Delta(\varphi_t, 0) < \delta\}$.

Using the Radon-Nikodim theorem [1] and the relation for the density measures

[4], we come to the equality for considered probability

$$P_0\{\rho_\Delta(\varphi_t\ ,0)<\delta\}=\int_{B_\delta}\frac{d\mu_0^4}{d\mu_0}(\zeta(\cdot,\omega))P_0d\omega=$$

$$=\int_{B_\delta}\exp[-(S(\varphi_t)+\int_s^T\dot{\varphi}_t d\zeta_t]P_0d\omega\ .$$

The last relation is equal to the following expression

$$(2.11)\ \exp\text{-}(S(\varphi_t)\int_{B_\delta}\exp[-\sum_{i=1}^{n}\int_s^T\dot{\varphi}_i(t)d\zeta_i(t,\omega)]<\delta\}P_0d\omega,$$

where $B_\delta=\{\omega:\{\rho_\Delta(\zeta_s,0)<\delta\}\subset F$, and μ_0^3 , μ_0 are the measures for ζ_t,φ_t on (C,U) , $S(\varphi_t)=1/2\int_s^T|\dot{\varphi}_t|^2\,dt$.

We evaluate the second comultiplier in (2.11) by Chebyshev's inequality:

$$(2.12)\ \ P_0\{\eta(\omega)\le a\}\le M_0[f(\eta)]/f(a),$$

where $\eta(\omega)$ is a nonnegative random variable, $\omega\in\Omega$, $a\in R^1_+$,

$$M_0[\cdot]=M_{x=0}[\cdot]=\int_\Omega[\cdot]\,P_0d\omega,\ f(s)$$

is a monotonous increasing on R^1_+ function, $s\in R^1_+$. Let us assume

$$(2.13)\ \eta(\omega)=\exp[-\int_s^T(\dot{\varphi}_t d\zeta_t)]\lambda(B_\delta)\ ;\ a=\exp[-(2S(\varphi_t))^{1/2}(1-\varepsilon)^{-1/2}],$$

$$f(\eta)=\eta\,\lambda(B_\delta),\ \lambda(B_\delta)=\begin{cases}1,\omega\in B_\delta\\0,\omega\notin B_\delta\end{cases}.$$

Then it is fulfilled $f(a)=a$, and according to the relations (2.12,13) we have

$$\int_{B_\delta}\eta(\omega)\ P_0d\omega\ge a\ P_0\{\lambda(B_\delta)\ \eta(\omega)\ge a\},$$

$$\{\lambda(B_\delta)\ \eta(\omega)\ge a\}\overset{def}{=}\{\omega:\omega\in B_\delta;\ \eta(\omega)\ge a\}=$$
$$=\{\omega:\omega\in B_\delta\}\cap\{\omega:\eta(\omega)\ge a\},$$

$$P_0\{\lambda(B_\delta)\ \eta(\omega)\ge a\}\overset{def}{=}P_0(B_\delta)P_0\{\eta(\omega)\ge a\,|\,B_\delta\},$$

where $P_0\{\eta(\omega)\ge a\,|\,B_\delta\}$is the conditional probability of the event $\eta(\omega)\ge a$ at the condition B_δ (the independence of events $\{\omega:\omega\in B_\delta\}$ and $\{\omega:\eta(\omega)\ge a\}$ is not assumed). Then, taking into account the relation (2.13), we have :

$$(2.14)\int_{B_\delta}\exp[\int_s^T\dot{\varphi}_i(t)d\zeta_i]P_0d\omega\ge P_0(B_\delta)\exp[-(2S(\varphi_t))^{1/2}(1-\varepsilon)^{-1/2}]\times$$

$$\times P_0\{\exp[-\int_s^T \dot{\psi}_i(t)d\zeta_i] \geq \exp[-(2S(\psi_t))^{1/2}(1-\varepsilon)^{-1/2}] | B_\delta\}.$$

Since $\forall B \subset F$: $P_0(B | B_\delta) = 1 - P_0(\overline{B} | B_\delta)$, $\overline{B} = \Omega | B$, we assume

$$B = \{\exp[-\int_s^T \dot{\varphi}_i(t)d\zeta_i] \geq \exp[-(2S(\varphi_t))^{1/2}(1-\varepsilon)^{-1/2}]\} = \{-\int_s^T \dot{\varphi}_i(t)d\zeta_i \geq$$

$$\geq -(2S(\varphi_t))^{1/2}(1-\varepsilon)^{-1/2}\}.$$ Then we obtain

$$(2.15)\ \overline{B} = \{\exp[-\int_s^T \dot{\varphi}_i(t)d\zeta_i] \leq \exp[-(2S(\varphi_t))^{1/2}(1-\varepsilon)^{-1/2}]\} =$$

$$= \{-\int_s^T \dot{\varphi}_i(t)d\zeta_i \leq -(2S(\varphi_t))^{1/2}(1-\varepsilon)^{-1/2}\}.$$

$$P_0(B | B_\delta B G_x^{-1}) = 1 - P_0\{[-\int_s^T \dot{\varphi}_i(t)d\zeta_i] \leq [-(2S(\varphi_t))^{1/2}(1-\varepsilon)^{-1/2}] | B_\delta\}.$$

For the evaluation of $P_0(\overline{B} | B_\delta)$, we are using a generalized Kolmogorov's inequality for martingals, and also the pecularities of the stochastic integral [1]:

$$(2.16)\ P_0(\overline{B} | B_\delta) \geq P_0\{|\int_s^T \dot{\varphi}_i(t)d\zeta_i| \geq (2S(\varphi_t))^{1/2}(1-\varepsilon)^{-1/2}] | B_\delta\} \leq$$

$$\leq (1-\varepsilon)/2S(\varphi_t) M_0\{[\int_s^T \dot{\varphi}_i(t)d\zeta_i]^2 | B_\delta\} = (1-\varepsilon)/2S(\varphi_t) M_0\{1/2\int_s^T |\dot{\varphi}_t|^2 dt. | B_\delta\} =$$

$$= 1-\varepsilon;\ M\{1 | B_\delta\} = 1-\varepsilon.$$

From that, by using the equation (2.15) we obtain

$$(2.17)\ P_0(\overline{B} | B_\delta) = P_0\{\exp[-\int_s^T \dot{\varphi}_i(t)d\zeta_i] \geq \exp[-(2S(\varphi_t))^{1/2}(1\varepsilon)^{-1/2}] | B_\delta\} \geq \varepsilon.$$

By the subsequent substitutions the obtained relations we come to (2.9). •

Let us use the equations (2.9,10) for the evaluation of the lowest probabilities limit (2.6,7). Assume we might construct an operator (or a family of operators):

$$(G_x : C(\Delta, R^n) \rightarrow C(\Delta, R^n); G_x : KC(\Delta, R^n) \rightarrow KC(\Delta, R^n)$$

that reflects ζ_t on $\tilde{y}_t$, and φ_t on y_t accordingly and satisfies these relations

$$(2.18)\ G_x : \zeta_t \rightarrow \tilde{y}_t,\ P_x\{G_x \zeta_t = \tilde{y}_t\} = 1,$$

$$(2.19)\ G_x : \varphi_t \rightarrow y_t,\ G_x \varphi_t = y_t,\ G_x^{-1} x : y_t \rightarrow \varphi_t,\ G_x^{-1} y_t = \varphi_t,$$

where G_x^{-1} is an inverse operator on $KC(\Delta, R^n)$, at $(G_x^{-1} y_t)_{t=s} = \varphi_s$.

Then the following is true:

Lemma 2.3. If the transformation (2.18) exists, then the lowest probabilities limit

(2.6,7) can be evaluated by the following relations:

(2.20) $P\{\rho_\Delta(\tilde{y}_t, y_t) < \delta\} \geq P_0(B_\delta)\varepsilon \exp\{-S(y_t) + [2S(y_t)(1-\varepsilon_1)^{-1}]^{1/2}\}, y_s = \tilde{y}_s$,

(2.21) $P\{\rho_\Delta(\tilde{y}_t, y_t) < \delta\} \geq P_s^*(B_\delta)\varepsilon \exp\{-S(y_t) + [2S(y_t)(1-\varepsilon_1)^{-1}]^{1/2}\}, y_s \neq \tilde{y}_s$

(2.22) $S(y_t) = 1/2 \int_s^T (G_x^{-1} y_t)^T (G_x^{-1} y_t)\, dt$.

Proof. Using the relations (2.18,19) we may write (2.6) in the form:
$P_x\{\rho_\Delta(\tilde{y}_t, y_t) < \delta\} = P_x\{\rho_\Delta(G_x\varphi_t, G_x\varphi_t) < \delta\}$, $\rho_\Delta(G_x\varphi_t, G_x\varphi_t) \leq$
$\leq \|G_x\|_c\, \rho_\Delta(\varphi_t, \zeta_t) = \|G_x\|_c\, \rho_\Delta(G_x^{-1} y_t, \zeta_t)$; $\{\rho_\Delta(G_x\varphi_t, G_x\varphi_t) < \delta\} \supseteq$
$\supseteq \{\|G_x\|_c\, \rho_\Delta(G_x^{-1} y_t, \zeta_t) < \delta\} = \{\rho_\Delta(G_x^{-1} y_t, \zeta_t) < \delta / \|G_x\|_c\}$,
where $\|G_x\|_c$ is the norm of G_x in subspace C=$C(\Delta, R^n)$. Because $\delta > 0$ is chosen arbitrary, we have $\{\rho_\Delta(G_x^{-1} y_t, \zeta_t) < \delta / \|G_x\|_c\} \supseteq \{\rho_\Delta(G_x^{-1} y_t, \zeta_t) < \delta\}$,
(2.23) $P_x\{\rho_\Delta(\tilde{y}_t, y_t) < \delta\} \geq P_x\{\rho_\Delta(G_x^{-1} y_t, \zeta_t) < \delta\} = P_0\{\rho_\Delta(G_x^{-1} y_t, \zeta_t) < \delta\}$.
From that, by applying relations (2.9,10) for evaluation of the right-hand side of equation (2.23), and taking into account relations(2.6,7), we come to (2.20-22) ●.

Because the C-closeness is stronger than L_2-closeness, the obtained lowest probability limits (2.20,22) are also satisfied for the evaluation of L_2-closeness.

Lemma 2.4. The operator, created by the solution (2.5), satisfies the relations (2.18,19), and the function (2.22) has a view:

(2.24) $S(y_t) = 1/2 \int_s^T (\dot{y}_t - q(t, y_t, u_t))^T (2b(t, y_t)^{-1} (\dot{y}_t - q(t, y_t, u_t))\, dt$, $2b = \sigma\sigma^T$.

Proof. It is naturally to choose G_x as an operator that is created by solution (2.5). The solution is continuous with probability 1, which exists and is a unique.

Then G_x reflects $C(\Delta, R^n)$ on itself with probability 1, and relation (2.18) is fulfilled (because any two solutions (2.5) at the same initial conditions coincide with probability 1). On the subspace $C(\Delta, R^n)$ of the space KC'(Δ, R^n), the operator G_x defines the reflection $\varphi_t \in$KC' into $y_t \in$KC' as a solution of the Volterra second order integral equation [1]:

(2.25) $y_t = y_s + \int_s^t [q(\upsilon, y_\upsilon, u_\upsilon) + \sigma(\upsilon, y_\upsilon)\dot{\varphi}_\upsilon] d\upsilon$,

that exists and is a unique on KC' at the introduced limitations of the considered functions of drift and diffusion.

The G_x has also inverse operator on KC' ; its explicit form follows from (2.25):

(2.26) $G_x^{-1} y_t = \varphi_t = \int_s^t \sigma^{-1}(\upsilon, y_\upsilon)(\dot{y}_t - q(t, y_t, u_t)) d\upsilon$.

Therefore, the relations (2.19) are satisfied with the operator G_x, created by the initial object's stochastic equation. ●

Assuming the sequential fulfillment $y_t = x_t$, $\tilde{y}_t = \tilde{x}_t$, and $\tilde{y}_t = \zeta_t$, we obtain from relations (2.20, 21, 22), as a result, the following estimators (2.3,4) in the forms

(2.27) $P_2 \geq P_0(B_\delta)\varepsilon \exp\{-S_2(x_t) + [2S_2(x_t)(1-\varepsilon)^{-1}]^{1/2}\}$, $S_2(x_t) = \int_s^T L_2 \, dt$,

(2.27') $L_2 = 1/2(\dot{x} - a^u(t,x))^T (2b(t,x))^{-1} (\dot{x} - a^u(t,x))$,

(2.28) $P_3 \geq P_s{*}(D_\delta)\, P_0(B_\delta)\varepsilon \exp\{-S_3(x_t) + [2S_3(x_t)(1-\varepsilon)^{-1}]^{1/2}\}$,

$$S_3(x_t) = \int_s^T L_3 \, dt, \quad L_3 = 1/2\, \dot{x}^T (2b(t,x))^{-1} \dot{x} .$$

<u>Theorem</u> <u>2.2.</u> The lowest probability limit of the evaluation probability (2.2) is defined by the relations:

(2.29) $P_1 \geq P_s{*}(D_\delta)\, P_0(B_\delta)\varepsilon \exp\{\{-S_1\, x_t) + [2S_1(x_t)(1-\varepsilon)^{-1}]^{1/2}\}$,

(2.30) $S_1 = M_x[\int_s^T \tilde{L}_1 \, dt] = \int_s^T M_x[\tilde{L}_1]\, dt$,

$\tilde{L}_1 = 1/2 a^u(t,\tilde{x})^T (2b(t,\tilde{x}))^{-1} a^u(t,\tilde{x})$,

moreover, the (2.30) coincides with the conditional entropy of the processes $\tilde{x}_t$ related to ζ_t (or with the entropy of the controlled processes defined with the respect to standard one by the transformation $\tilde{x}_t \rightarrow \zeta_t$):

(2.31) $S(\tilde{x}_t / \zeta_t) = M_x\{\ln[\frac{d\mu_0^2}{d\mu_x^*}(\tilde{x}_s(\cdot,\omega,x))]^{-1}\} = S_1$.

Proof. By analogy with the relations of Lemma 2.1, we may write:

(2.32) $P_1 = P\{\rho_\Delta(\tilde{x}_t, \zeta_t) < \delta\} = P\{\rho_\Delta(\tilde{x}_t{*}, 0) < \delta\} \geq$

$\geq P_s{*}(D_\delta)\, P_x\{\rho_\Delta(\tilde{x}_t{*} - \tilde{x}_s{*}, 0) < \delta\}$; $\tilde{x}_t{*} = \tilde{x}_t - \zeta_t$.

Because the measures μ_x^* and μ_0^2 of the processes $(\tilde{x}_t, \zeta_t)$ are mutually continuous, we may apply the Radon-Nicodim theorem for the last multiplier in (2.32):

(2.33) $P_x\{\rho_\Delta(\tilde{x}_t{*} - \tilde{x}_s{*}, 0) < \delta\} = \int_{B_{2\delta}} \frac{d\mu_0^2}{d\mu_x^*}(\tilde{x}_s{*}(\cdot,\omega,x))\, P_x(d\omega)$;

$B_{2\delta} = \{\omega : \rho_\Delta(\zeta_t, 0) < \delta\}$.

According to [8,11] and previous results, the following relations are fulfilled

(2.34) $\frac{d\mu_0^2}{d\mu_x^*} = \exp[-(\tilde{S}_1 + \int_s^T (\sigma(t,\tilde{x}_t^*))^{-1} a^u(t,\tilde{x}_t^*)\, d\zeta_t)]$; $\tilde{S}_1 = \tilde{S}_1(\tilde{x}_t{*})$,

(2.35) $\tilde{S}_1=1/2\int_s^T a^u(t,\tilde{x})^T(2b(t,\tilde{x}))^{-1}a^u(t,\tilde{x})\,dt$; $2b=\sigma\,\sigma^T$.

For the evaluation of (2.33,34), we use the relations (2.12,13) by exchanging the symbols P_0, M_0 with P_x, M_x accordingly, and assuming

(2.36) $\int_{B_{2\delta}}\eta(\omega)=\dfrac{d\mu_0^2}{d\mu_x^*}(\tilde{x}_s(\cdot,\omega,x))$, a=exp$\{S_1(x_t)+[2S_1(x_t)(1-\varepsilon)^{-1}]^{1/2}\}$,

(2.37) $S_1=M_x[\tilde{S}_1]$, f(η)= η.

Then by analogy with (2.14) we obtain for (2.36,37) the inequalities:

(2.38) $P_x\{\rho_\Delta(\tilde{x}_t{}^*-\tilde{x}_s{}^*,0)<\delta\}\geq P_x(B_{2\delta})\exp\{S_1(x_t)+$

$+[2S_1(x_t)(1-\varepsilon)^{-1}]^{1/2}\}\times P_x\{\exp[-(\tilde{S}_1+\int_s^T(\sigma(t,\tilde{x}_t^*))^{-1}a^u(t,\tilde{x}_t^*)d\zeta_t)]\geq$

$\geq\exp\{S_1(x_t)+[2S_1(x_t)(1-\varepsilon)^{-1}]^{1/2}\}$.

For the evaluation of the first co-muliplier in (2.38), we are using the equalities

$P_x(B_{2\delta})=P_x\{\rho_\Delta(\tilde{\xi}_t,0)<\delta\}$=P$\{\rho_\Delta(\tilde{\xi}_t,0)<\delta\}$.

Let $G_{x=0}=G_0$ is created by transformation $G_0\,\zeta_t=\tilde{\xi}_t$. Then we have

$\rho_\Delta(\tilde{\xi}_t,0)=\rho_\Delta(G_0\,\zeta_t,G_0\,0)\leq\|G_0\|_c\,\rho_\Delta(\zeta_t,0)$;

$\{\rho_\Delta(\tilde{\xi}_t,0)<\delta\}\supseteq\{\|G_0\|_c\,\rho_\Delta(\zeta_t,0)<\delta\}=$

$=\{\rho_\Delta(\zeta_t,0)<\delta/\|G_0\|_c\}\supseteq\{\rho_\Delta(\zeta_t,0)<\delta\}$, and the equality follows

(2.39) $P_x(B_{2\delta})\geq$P$\{\rho_\Delta(\zeta_t,0)<\delta\}=P_0\{\rho_\Delta(\zeta_t,0)<\delta\}=P_0(B_\delta)$.

For the evaluation of the last co-muliplier in (2.38), we apply the following inequalities

(2.40) D=$\{\exp[-(\tilde{S}_1+\int_s^T(\sigma(t,\tilde{x}_t^*))^{-1}a^u(t,\tilde{x}_t^*)d\zeta_t)]\geq$

$\geq\{\exp-\{S_1(x_t)+[2S_1(x_t)(1-\varepsilon)^{-1}]^{1/2}\}=$

$=-[(\tilde{S}_1+\int_s^T(\sigma(t,\tilde{x}_t^*))^{-1}a^u(t,\tilde{x}_t^*)d\zeta_t)]\geq$

$\geq-\{S_1+[2S_1(1-\varepsilon)^{-1}]^{1/2}\}\supseteq\{-\tilde{S}_1\geq-S_1\}\cap$

$\cap\{-\int_s^T(\sigma(t,\tilde{x}_t^*))^{-1}a^u(t,\tilde{x}_t^*)d\zeta_t)\}\geq-[2S_1(1-\varepsilon)^{-1}]^{1/2}$=AB,

(2.41) P_x(D)$\geq P_x$(AB)=1-$P_x(\overline{AB})$, (A,B, D)$\subset$F, $\overline{AB}=\Omega\backslash AB$,

using the duality principle in theory of sets in the form

(2.42) $\overline{AB}=\{\overline{\{\omega\in A\}\cap\{\omega\in B\}}=\overline{\{\omega\in A\}}\cup\overline{\{\omega\in B\}}=\overline{A}+\overline{B}$

and the relation (2.42) in the form

(2.43) $P_x(\bar{A}+\bar{B})=P_x(\bar{A}+P_x(\bar{B})-P_x(\bar{A},\bar{B})$, where

(2.44) $\bar{A}=\{-\tilde{S}_1\geq -S_1\}$, $\bar{B}=\{-\int_s^T (\sigma(t,\tilde{x}_t^*))^{-1} a^u(t,\tilde{x}_t^*)d\zeta_t)\}\leq$

$\leq -[2S_1(1-\varepsilon)^{-1}]^{1/2}$.

From the relations (2.41-43), it follows that

(2.45) $P_x(D)\geq 1-[P_x(\bar{A})+P_x(\bar{B})-P_x(\bar{A},\bar{B})]$.

Using the initial equation (1.1) and the (2.35,44), we obtain

$$\int_s^T (\sigma^{-1}a^u)d\zeta_t=\int_s^T (\sigma^{-1}a^u)[\sigma^{-1}(d\tilde{y}_t-a^u dt)]=\int_s^T ((2b)^{-1}a^u)d\tilde{y}_t-2\tilde{S}_1;$$

$\sigma=\sigma(t,\bullet)$, $a^u=a^u(t,\bullet)$, $b=b(t,\bullet)=1/2\,\sigma(t,\bullet)\sigma^T(t,\bullet)$,

$$\bar{B}=\{-\int_s^T ((2b)^{-1}a^u)d\tilde{y}_t+2\tilde{S}_1 \leq -[2\tilde{S}_1(1-\varepsilon)^{-1}]^{1/2}\}\supseteq\{\bar{N}\,|\,\bar{A}\}\supseteq\bar{A},$$

$$\bar{N}=\{(-\int_s^T ((2b)^{-1}a^u)d\tilde{y}_t)\leq -\{2\tilde{S}_1+[2\tilde{S}_1(1-\varepsilon)^{-1}]^{1/2}\},\ \bar{N}\subset F.$$

From that, these relations follow:

(2.46) $\bar{A}\bar{B}=\{\omega\in\bar{A}\}\cap\{\omega\in\bar{B}\}=\{\omega\in\bar{A}\}=\bar{A}$; $\bar{B}=\bar{A}$; $P_x(D)\geq 1-P_x(\bar{B})$.

For the upper evaluation of $P_x(\bar{B})$ we are using (2.43, 36, 35) and the Chebychev inequalities in the form

(2.47) $P_x(\bar{B})\leq P_x\{|\int_s^T (\sigma^{-1}a^u)d\zeta_t|\geq[2S_1(1-\varepsilon)^{-1}]^{1/2}\}\leq(1-\varepsilon)\times$

$\times M_x[|\int_s^T (\sigma^{-1}a^u)d\zeta_t|^2]/2S_1=(1-\varepsilon)M_x[|\int_s^T (\sigma^{-1}a^u)|^2 dt]/2S_1=(1-\varepsilon)$.

After the substitution (2.47) in (2.46) we obtain $P_x(D)\geq\varepsilon$.

From this and according to (2.32-35, 38-40) the result (2.29-30) follows. The functional (2.30) coincides with a definition of the conditional entropy [5]:(2.31).

Using relations (2.34, 35) and $M_x[\int_s^T (\sigma^{-1}a^u)d\zeta_t]=0$, we get $S(\tilde{x}_t/\zeta_t)=S_1$. ●

Theorem 2.3. If the transformations (2.18, 19) are satisfied (2. 23), then the minimum of the upper limit of the probabilistic evaluation of the L_2-distancy:

(2.48) $P\{\rho_{L_2}(\tilde{y}_t,y_t)\geq\delta\}\to\underset{\varphi_t}{Inf}$, $\forall\,\delta>0$,

is reached at the solution of the equation

(2.49) $\dot{y}_t=q(t,y,u)$.

Proof. To evaluate the relation (2.48) we apply the inequality (2.12), which according to the transformations (2.18, 19) has a view:

(2.50) $P\{\rho_{L_2}(\tilde{y}_t, y_t) \geq \delta\} \leq 1/\delta^2 M[\rho_{L_2}{}^2(\tilde{y}_t, y_t)] =$

$= 1/\delta^2 M[\rho_{L_2}{}^2(G_y \zeta_t, G_y \varphi_t)] \leq 1/\delta^2 M_s[K_y^2] M_0[\rho_{L_2}{}^2(\zeta_t, \varphi_t)]$,

$t \in \Delta = (s,T)$; $\delta > 0$, $G_y = G_{y=0}$, $y_s = \tilde{y}_s = 0$;

where K_y is the Lipshiz constant for operator G_y.

At the limitation imposed on the stochastic equation, the K_y can be expressed via the Lipshiz constant for q, σ, and the following equalities, where the last one $(T-s) = mes(\Delta)$; $M_0[\cdot] = M_{y=0}[\cdot]$ is an operator of mathematical expectation (M) corresponding to the probability mesure $\hat{P}_s$ on the σ-algebra F' created by the deviations ($\tilde{y}_s - y_s$)(mod $\hat{P}_s$)

The fulfillment of (2.48) at conditions (2.18, 19) leads to the problem:

(2.51) $M_0[\rho_{L_2}{}^2(\tilde{y}_t, y_t)] \to \underset{\varphi_t}{Inf}$.

For solution the problem (2.51), we are using the relations:

(2.52) $M_{\zeta_s}[\cdot] = \lim_{h \to 0} M_{\zeta_{s+h}}[\cdot]$; $M_{\zeta_s}[\rho_{L_2}{}^2(\zeta_t, \varphi_t)] =$

$= \int_\Omega \rho_{L_2}{}^2(\zeta_t, \varphi_t) P_{\zeta_s}(d\omega) = \int_\Omega \rho_{L_2}{}^2(\zeta_t, \varphi_t) P_0(d\omega) =$

$= M_0[\rho_{L_2}{}^2(\zeta_t, \varphi_t)] = \lim_{h \to 0} M_{\zeta_{s+h}}[\rho_{L_2}{}^2(\zeta_\upsilon, \varphi_\upsilon)]$, $\upsilon \in [s+h, T]$.

Then the problem (2.51) consists of minimizing the right-hand side of the last equality. Since h is arbitrary chosen, let us assume $s+h = t \in \Delta$. Then we get

$M_{\zeta_t}[\rho_{L_2}{}^2(\zeta_\Theta, \varphi_\Theta)] = M_\zeta[\rho_{L_2}{}^2(\zeta_\Theta, \varphi_\Theta)] =$

$= M_\zeta[\int_s^T |\zeta_\Theta - \varphi_\Theta|^2 d\Theta] = \tilde{u}(\zeta_t, t)$; $\Theta \in [t,T]$, $\zeta = \zeta_t$,

where the function $\tilde{u}(\zeta_t, t)$ satisfies the equation [8]:

(2.53) $-\partial \tilde{u} / \partial t = 1/2 \nabla \tilde{u} + |\varphi_t - \zeta|^2$; $\nabla = \sum_{i=1}^n \partial^2 / \partial \zeta_i^2$, $\lim_{t \to T} \tilde{u}(\zeta_t, t) = 0$,

$(\zeta_t, t) \in (R^n \times \Delta)$, $|\bullet|^2 = ||\bullet||^2_{R^n}$.

This equation for the function $\tilde{u}(\zeta_t, t)$ is connected with the problem (2.51, 52)

(2.54) $M_0[\rho_{L_2}{}^2(\zeta_\Theta, \varphi_\Theta)] = \lim_{t \to s} \tilde{u}(\zeta_t, t) = \tilde{u}(s,0) \to \underset{\varphi_t}{Inf}$; $\zeta(t=s) = 0$.

For the execution (2.54), it should be obtained from the solution of equation (2.53). The solution of this equation (that is not considered here in details) has a view:

(2.55) $\tilde{u}(\zeta_t, t) = \int_s^T \sum_{i=1}^n (\varphi_i(\tau) - \zeta_i)^2 d\tau + n/2(T-t)^2$.

(2.56) $\lim_{t \to s} \tilde{u}(\zeta_t, t) = \tilde{u}(s,0) \int_s^T \sum_{i=1}^n (\varphi_i(\tau) - \zeta_i)^2 d\tau + n/2(T-t)^2 = \| \varphi_t \|_{L_2}^2 + n/2(T-t)^2$

and the problem (2.55) is reduced to the condition $\| \varphi_t \|_{L_2}^2 \to \underset{\varphi_t}{Inf}$.

From this it follows that $\varphi_t = 0$, $\forall t \in (s,T)$. The last equality (according to (2.26)) can be executed on the solutions (2.49). To *prove* this result it is not necessary to obtain a solution (2.53) if we write the condition (2.54) in the form:

(2.57) $\lim_{t \to s} M_0[\rho_{L_2}{}^2(\zeta_t, \varphi_t)] = M_0[\| \varphi_t \|_{L_2}^2] = \| \varphi_t \|_{L_2}^2$.

We will show that at the condition $y_s \neq \tilde{y}_s = 0$, we obtain the same result.

Indeed, using the triangle inequality we have

$\{\rho_{L_2}(\tilde{y}_t, y_t) < \delta\} \supseteq \{\rho_{L_2}(\tilde{y}_t, y_t + \tilde{y}_s - y_s) < \delta/2\} \times \{\rho_{L_2}(\tilde{y}_s - y_s, 0) < \delta/2\} =$

$= \{A\}\{B\}; \{\rho_{L_2}(\tilde{y}_t, y_t) < \delta\} \subseteq \overline{\{A\}\{B\}}$; $\overline{\{A\}\{B\}} \overset{def}{=} \Omega \times \Omega' \setminus \{A\}\{B\}$;

$\overline{\{A\}} = \{\rho_{L_2}(\tilde{y}_t, y_t + \tilde{y}_s - y_s) \geq \delta/2\} \subset F$, $\overline{\{B\}} = \{\rho_{L_2}(\tilde{y}_s - y_s, 0) \geq \delta/2\} \subset F'$.

Using the relations (2.42,43) at $P_x = P$, we obtain

$P\{\rho_{L_2}(\tilde{y}_t, y_t) \geq \delta\} \leq P\{\overline{A + B}\} = P\{\overline{A}\} + P\{\overline{B}\} - P\{\overline{A, B}\}$.

From that, because F and F' are independent, it follows that

(2.58) $P\{\rho_{L_2}(\tilde{y}_t, y_t) \geq \delta\} \leq P\{\overline{B}\} + (1 - P\{\overline{B}\}) P\{\overline{A}\}$,

where $P\{\overline{A}\}$ is the probability of the considered event ($\tilde{y}_s = y_s = 0$, mod $\hat{P}_s$). Since the function (2.58) is increasing monotonous with respect to $P\{\overline{A}\}$, then its upper estimator is defined by the upper estimator for $P\{\overline{A}\}$, and this estimator can be found from (2.58). Beside this, the only y_t is covered by $P\{\overline{A}\}$, and because of that, finding the $\underset{y_t}{Inf}$ of the upper limit of the probability (2.50) is reduced to the $\underset{y_t}{Inf}$ of the upper limit of $P\{\overline{A}\}$. (At that case, $G_y = G_{y=0}$, $K_y = K_{y=0}$). Therefore, the upper limit of the probability (2.50) has a minimum on the solutions (2.49) independently on the values $\tilde{y}_s, y_s$. (The numerical values of these limitations are different in the cases of $y_s \neq \tilde{y}_s$, and $y_s = \tilde{y}_s$ accordingly). •

Corollary 2.1. The solutions of equation (2.49) pass the locality of function $\tilde{y}_t \in C(\Delta, R^n)$ with maximal probability (according to the considered definition).

Indeed, the maximization of the estimator (2.27) is reduced to the condition

(2.59) $\min_{y_t} S_2(y_t) = \min_{y_t} \int_s^T L_2 \, dt$, $L_2 = 1/2(\dot{y} - q)^T (2b)^{-1} (\dot{y} - q)$,

that is fulfilled at $\dot{y} = q$ (t,y,u). As a result we obtain the relation

$P\{\rho_{L_2}(\tilde{y}_t, y_t) \geq \delta\} \geq \underline{m} \to \underset{\dot{y}=q}{Sup}$; $P\{\rho_{L_2}(\tilde{y}_t, y_t) \geq \delta\} \geq \overline{m} \to \underset{\dot{y}=q}{Inf}$;

i.e., the solutions (2.49) become the nearest to the most probable solutions (in the L_2-metric) by the upper evaluation ($\overline{m}$) as well as by the lower ($\underline{m}$) evaluation of the above probabilities. •

Comments 2.1. Using the relations

$$P_o\{\rho_\Delta(\tilde{\varphi}_t, 0) < \delta\} \overset{def}{=} \int_{B'_\delta} P_o^4(d\omega), B'_\delta = \{\rho_\Delta(\tilde{\varphi}_t, 0) < \delta\},$$

$\mu_o^4(A) = P_o^4\{\omega: \tilde{\varphi}_t(., \omega) \in A\}$, $A \subset U$, and the formula of changing the measure in integrals [8], we get the following representation of the above relation

$$\int_{B'_\delta} P_o^4(d\omega) = \int_\Omega \lambda(B'_\delta) P_o^4(d\omega) = \int_\Omega \lambda(B'_\delta) \frac{d\mu_o^4}{d\mu_o}(\tilde{\varphi}_t(., \omega)). \bullet$$

The evaluator (2.3) reaches a maximum on the solutions equation $\dot{x} = a^u$, and because of that, the problem (2.2), (2. 28) consists of the execution of the condition

(2.60) $\min_{x_t} S_1(x_t) = \min_{x_t} \int_s^T L_3 \, dt$, $L_3 = 1/2 \dot{x}^T (2b)^{-1} \dot{x}$, $\dot{x} = a^u(t,x) \neq 0$.

The condition (2.60) expresses the problem of minimizing the entropy functional, defined on the macroprocess. According to the relations (2.31, 2-4), the problem (2.2) is reduced to minimizating the object's functional of uncertainty. That leads to revealing the regularities of an observed object by modeling the object's macroprocesses using the functional's extremals.

The essence of the problem P_2 and P_3 nearness consists of linking of the micro- and macrolevel processes by their abilities of approximating the disturbance (ζ_t). The P_2 and P_3 nearness is executed as the probability closeness to some lowest limits. As a result, the macrolevel process that approximates the microlevel process with a maximal probability (2.60), enables us to minimize the entropy functional for the bilevel structure of the object's processes.

The problem is solved by forming the dynamic macro model of a random object. •

Lemma 2.5. Execution of the conditions (2.2-2.27-2.29) leads to the equation

(2.61) $(1 - x)^3 = \frac{Sx^2}{2}$,

that at $x \in (0,1)$, S>0 corresponds to the maximum of the function

(2.62) $f(x=\varepsilon)\,\varepsilon \exp[-(\frac{2S_i}{1-\varepsilon})^{1/2}] \rightarrow \max_{\varepsilon \in (0,1)}$ for $S_i>0$, i=1,2,4.

Proof. Let us introduce the function

(2.62a) $f(x) = x\exp[-(\frac{2S}{1-x})^{1/2}]$, $x \in (0,1)$, S>0,

and to analyze its maximum: $f'(x) = \exp[-(\frac{2S}{1-x})^{1/2}] + x\exp[-(\frac{2S}{1-x})^{1/2}] \times$

$(-1) \times (2S)^{1/2}(-\frac{1}{2})\ -(\frac{1}{1-x})^{-3/2}(-1) = 0$, $1 = (2S)^{1/2}(\frac{1}{2})\frac{x}{(1-x)^{3/2}}$.

We come to the equation $(1-x)^3 = \frac{Sx^2}{2}$, $x \in (0,1)$, $S>0$

that has a unique real root. Let us determine f"(x) at the point $x \in (0,1)$ that is defined by the solution of the equation (2.61):

$$f''(x) = \exp[-(\frac{2S}{1-x})^{1/2}](2S)^{1/2}(\frac{1}{2})\ (-1)\frac{1}{(1-x)^{3/2}} -$$

$$-(2S)^{1/2}(\frac{1}{2})\ \exp[-(\frac{2S}{1-x})^{1/2}]\frac{1}{(1-x)^{3/2}} - (2S)^{1/2}(\frac{1}{2}) \times$$

$$\times\ x\frac{d}{dx}\{\frac{\exp[-(\frac{2S}{1-x})^{1/2}]}{(1-x)^{3/2}}\} = -\frac{(2S)^{1/2}}{(1-x)^{3/2}}\exp[-(\frac{2S}{1-x})^{1/2}] - (2S)^{1/2}(\frac{1}{2}) \times$$

$$\times\ x\frac{d}{dx}\{\frac{\exp[-(\frac{2S}{1-x})^{1/2}]}{(1-x)^{3/2}}\};\ \frac{d}{dx}\{\frac{\exp[-(\frac{2S}{1-x})^{1/2}]}{(1-x)^{3/2}}\} = \frac{\exp[-(\frac{2S}{1-x})^{1/2}]}{2(1-x)^3} \times$$

$(-(2S)^{1/2} + 3(1-x)^{1/2})$. At the extremal point of the solution, we come to the

relation $f''(x) = \frac{(2S)^{1/2}\exp[-(\frac{2S}{1-x})^{1/2}]}{(1-x)^{3/2}}(\frac{1}{2} + \frac{3}{2(2S)^{1/2}}(1-x)^{1/2} - (2S)^{1/2}) =$

$$= -\frac{(2S)^{1/2}\exp[-(\frac{2S}{1-x})^{1/2}]}{(1-x)^{3/2}}(\frac{1}{2} + \frac{3}{2(2S)^{1/2}}(1-x)^{1/2}) < 0,$$

that satisfies the maximum of (2.62a). Therefore, the execution of (2.62) at $x = \varepsilon$, leads to (2.61), with the following roots of the equation: ε_i at $S = S_i$, i=1,2,4. •

Comments 2.2 . The evaluation $P_0(B_\delta)$ in (2.29). According to [8] we may express the above probability in the form

$$P_o\{\xi_t \in \overline{A}\} \geq 1 - 2\, P_o\{\xi_T \notin \overline{A}\},$$

where $\overline{A} \subset U$ is an arbitrary closed concave set.

Let us introduce the balls $\overline{A}(0,\delta_o)$, $A(0,\delta)$, $\overline{K}(0,\delta_o)$ in (C,U) and (R^n,β) accordingly, with a fixed value $\delta_o < \delta$: $\overline{A}(0,\delta_o) = \{\varphi_t \in C{:}\rho_\Delta(\varphi_t, 0) \leq \delta_o\}$,

$$A(0,\delta) = \{\varphi_t \in C{:}\rho_\Delta(\varphi_t, 0) < \delta\}, \overline{K}(0,\delta_o) = \{x \in R^n{:}(\sum x_i^2 \leq \delta_o\}.$$

Let us assume $\overline{A} = \overline{A}(0,\delta_o)$. and use the following relations

$$B_\delta \overset{def}{=} \supset\{\xi_t \in \overline{A}(0,\delta)\} \supset \{\xi_t \in \overline{A}(0,\delta_o)\}$$

$$\{\xi_T \notin \overline{A}(0,\delta_o)\} = \{\xi_T \notin \overline{K}(0,\delta_o)\} = \{|\xi_T| > \delta\}, |\xi_T| = (\sum_{i=1}^{n} \xi_i^2(T,\omega))^{1/2},$$

According to the evaluation of the problem in [8], we get the representation

$$P_o\{|\xi_T| > \delta\} = K_n \int_{\delta_o/(T)^{1/2}} r^{n-1} \exp(-r^2/2)dr,$$

where $K_n^{-1} = \Gamma(\frac{n}{2}) \times 2^{\frac{n-2}{2}}$, $\Gamma(\alpha)$, α>0 is the Euler gamma-function.

Finally, we come to the evaluation of the probability

$$P_o(B_\delta) \geq P_o\{\xi_T \in \overline{A}(0,\delta_o)\} \geq 1 - 2P_o\{\xi_T \notin \overline{A}(0,\delta_o)\} =$$

$$= 1 - 2K_n \int_{\delta_o/(T)^{1/2}} r^{n-1} \exp(-r^2/2)\, dr \quad (2.63).$$ •

At given trajectories (1.11) and corresponding functionals (2.30) on them, it is possible to determine a such $\varepsilon_i \in (0,1)$, i=1-3 in (2.27-29) at which is executed

$$\varepsilon \exp[-(\frac{2S_i}{1-\varepsilon})^{1/2}] \to \max_{\varepsilon \in (0,1)}.$$

Then by the lowest evaluation of $P_0(B_\delta)$ and P_s^* in (2.27-29), we obtain the numerical evaluations for the corresponding probabilities [11].

Analysis of the microlevel process

Let us define a numerical evaluation of the transformation of the processes $\tilde{x}(\cdot) \rightarrow \tilde{x}'(\cdot)$ by the considered entropy functional in the form

$$S(s,T,\tilde{x}(\cdot)) \overset{def}{=} M_{\tilde{x}_s,B}[\ln(q_{sT}^{-1}(\tilde{x}(\cdot)))] \geq 0 \overset{def}{=} M_{\tilde{x}_s,B}[\ln(q_{sT}^{-1}(\tilde{x}(\cdot)))] \geq 0,$$

$$M_{\tilde{x}_s,B}[\cdot] = \int_B [\cdot] P_{\tilde{x}_s,B}(d\omega), \tilde{x}(\cdot) \in \tilde{B} \subset \beta(C)$$

where $\beta(C)$ is the Borele algebra in metric C, and

$$q_{s,T}^{-1}(\tilde{x}(\cdot)) = \frac{dP_{s,T}}{dP'_{s,T}}(\tilde{x}(\cdot)) = \frac{P(s,\tilde{x}_s,T,dy)}{P'(s,\tilde{x}_s,T,dy)}$$

is Radon-Nicodim's density measure of transformation of the probability P into P' [8]. For the Marcovian process with the additive functional

$$\omega_\Delta = \omega_s^T = \int_s^T \sigma^{-1}(t,\tilde{x}_t)\,\hat{a}^u(t,\tilde{x}_t)\,d\xi_t + \frac{1}{2}\int_s^T |\sigma^{-1}(t,\tilde{x}_t)\hat{a}^u(t,\tilde{x}_t)|^2\,dt \geq 0,$$

and the corresponding equations in deviations:

$$d\tilde{z}_t = d\tilde{x}_t - a^1(t,\tilde{x}_t)\,dt\,,\ \hat{a}^u = a(t,x,u) - a^1(t,x),$$

$$d\xi\,(t) = \sigma^{-1}(t,\tilde{x}_t)(d\tilde{x}(t) - a(t,\tilde{x}_t,u)\,dt) = \sigma^{-1}(t,\tilde{x}_t)(d\tilde{z}(t) - \hat{a}^u(t,\tilde{x}_t)\,dt),$$

the following relations are true

$$\int_s^T (\sigma^{-1}(t,\tilde{x}_t)\hat{a}^u(t,\tilde{x}_t))d\xi(t) = \sum_{i=1}^n \int_s^T (\sigma^{-1}(t,\tilde{x}_t)\hat{a}^u(t,\tilde{x}_t))_i\,d\xi_i(t) =$$

$$= \sum_{i=1}^n \int_s^T \sum_{j=1}^n (\sigma_{ij}^{-1}(t,\tilde{x}_t)\hat{a}_j^u(t,\tilde{x}_t))_i d\xi_i(t);$$

$$\int_s^T |\sigma^{-1}(t,\tilde{x}_t)\hat{a}^u(t,\tilde{x}_t)|^2\,dt = \int_s^T (\sigma^{-1}(t,\tilde{x}_t)\hat{a}^u(t,\tilde{x}_t))^T \sigma^{-1}(t,\tilde{x}_t)\hat{a}^u(t,\tilde{x}_t)d\,t =$$

$$= \int_s^T (\hat{a}^u(t,\tilde{x}_t))^T (2b(t,\tilde{x}_t))^{-1} \hat{a}^u(t,\tilde{x}_t)dt =$$

$$= \int_s^T \sum_{i,j=1}^n (2b(t,\tilde{x}_t)^{-1})_{ij}\,\hat{a}_i^u(t,\tilde{x}_t)\hat{a}_j^u(t,\tilde{x}_t)_i dt\ ;\ 2b(t,x) = \sigma(t,x)\sigma^T(t,x)\ ;$$

$$\frac{dP'}{dP}(\tilde{x}(\cdot)) \overset{def}{=} \frac{dP_s'}{dP_s}(\tilde{x}_s)\exp(-\omega_\Delta) = q_{s,T}(x(\cdot));$$

$$\omega_\Delta = \int_s^T \sigma^{-1}(t,\tilde{x}_t)\,\hat{a}^u(t,\tilde{x}_t)\,(\sigma^{-1}(t,\tilde{x}_t)(d\tilde{z}(t) - \hat{a}^u(t,\tilde{x}_t)\,dt))+$$

$$+\frac{1}{2}\int_s^T |\sigma^{-1}(t,\tilde{x}_t)\hat{a}^u(t,\tilde{x}_t)|^2\,dt = \int_s^T (\hat{a}^u(t,\tilde{x}_t))^T(2b(t,\tilde{x}_t))^{-1}(d\tilde{z}(t) -$$

$$-\hat{a}^u(t,\tilde{x}_t)\,dt) + \frac{1}{2}\int_s^T |\sigma^{-1}(t,\tilde{x}_t)\hat{a}^u(t,\tilde{x}_t)|^2\,dt =$$

$$=\sum_{j=1}^n \int_s^T \sum_{i=1}^n (2b(t,\tilde{x}_t)^{-1}{}_{ij}\,\hat{a}_i^u(t,\tilde{x}_t)d\tilde{z}_j(t) -$$

$$-\sum_{j=1}^n \int_s^T \sum_{i=1}^n (2b(t,\tilde{x}_t)^{-1}{}_{ij}\,\hat{a}_i^u(t,\tilde{x}_t)\hat{a}_j^u(t,\tilde{x}_t)\,dt +$$

$$+\frac{1}{2}\sum_{j=1}^n \int_s^T \sum_{i=1}^n (2b(t,\tilde{x}_t)^{-1}{}_{ij}\,\hat{a}_i^u(t,\tilde{x}_t)\hat{a}_j^u(t,\tilde{x}_t)\,dt =$$

$$=\sum_{j=1}^n \int_s^T \sum_{i=1}^n (2b(t,\tilde{x}_t)^{-1}{}_{ij}\,\hat{a}_i^u(t,\tilde{x}_t)d\tilde{z}_j(t) -$$

$$-\frac{1}{2}\sum_{j=1}^n \int_s^T \sum_{i=1}^n (2b(t,\tilde{x}_t)^{-1}{}_{ij}\,\hat{a}_i^u(t,\tilde{x}_t)\hat{a}_j^u(t,\tilde{x}_t)\,dt.$$

Then we obtain the entropy functional in the form

$$\Delta S(s,T,x(\cdot)) = S(s,T,x(\cdot)) - M_{\tilde{x}_s,B}[\ln\frac{dP_s}{dP'_s}(\tilde{x}_s)] =$$

$$= M_{\tilde{x}_s,B}[\sum_{i=1}^n \int_s^T \sum_{j=1}^n (\sigma^{-1}(t,\tilde{x}_t))_{ij}\hat{a}_j^u(t,\tilde{x}_t)\,d\xi_i(t) +$$

$$+\frac{1}{2}\sum_{j=1}^n \int_s^T \sum_{i=1}^n (2b(t,\tilde{x}_t)^{-1}{}_{ij}\,\hat{a}_i^u(t,\tilde{x}_t)\hat{a}_j^u(t,\tilde{x}_t)\,dt] =$$

$$= M_{\tilde{x}_s,B}[\int_s^T \hat{L}(t,\tilde{x}_t,u(t,\overline{x}_t)dt],\ \hat{L}(t,\tilde{x},u) = \frac{1}{2}(\hat{a}^u)^T(2b)^{-1}\hat{a}^u\ .$$

Considering $s \in \tilde{B}$, $M_{s,\tilde{x}_s}[\cdot] = \int_{\tilde{B}} [\cdot] P_{s,\tilde{x}_s}(d\omega)$, we come to particular form of the entropy functional :

$$S(s,T,\tilde{x}(\cdot)) = M_{s,\tilde{x}_s}[\ln q_{s,T}^{-1}(\tilde{x}(\cdot))] \geq 0,$$

$$\Delta S(s,T,\tilde{x}(\cdot)) \overset{def}{=} S(s,T,\tilde{x}(\cdot)) - M_{s,\tilde{x}_s}[\ln \frac{dP_s}{dP'_s}(\tilde{x}_s)] =$$

$$= \int_s^T M_{s,\tilde{x}_s} \hat{L}(t,\tilde{x}_t,u(t,\bar{x}_t))dt, \text{ where } \hat{L}(t,x,u) = \frac{1}{2}\sum_{i,j=1}^{n}(2b_{ij})^{-1}\hat{a}_i^u \hat{a}_j^u,$$

$$\Delta S(s,T,\tilde{x}(\cdot)) = M_{s,\tilde{x}_s}(\sum_{j=1}^{n}\int_s^T \sum_{i=1}^{n}(2b_{ij}(t,\tilde{x}_t)^{-1}\hat{a}_i^u dz_j(t) - \int_s^T \hat{L}(t,\tilde{x}_t,u(t,\bar{x}_t))dt).$$

Using the indications

$$\tilde{x}_t^* = \tilde{x}_t - \tilde{x}'_t, \; x_t = M_{s,\tilde{x}_s}[\tilde{x}_t^*] = \bar{x}_t - \bar{x}_t^1,$$

$$\tilde{x}_t^* = \tilde{x}_s^* + \int_s^t a^u(\upsilon,\tilde{x}_\upsilon^*)d\upsilon + \int_s^t \sigma(\upsilon,\tilde{x}_\upsilon^*)d\xi(\upsilon), \; \tilde{x}_s^* = \tilde{x}_s - \tilde{x}_s^1$$

for the transformation

$$\tilde{x}_t^*(\cdot) \to \varsigma(\cdot), \varsigma_t = \zeta_s + \int_s^t \sigma(\upsilon,\zeta_\upsilon)d\xi(\upsilon),$$

we come to the equalities:

$$\Delta S(s,T,\tilde{x}^*(\cdot)) = \int_s^T M_{s,\tilde{x}^*_s} L(t,\tilde{x}_t^*,u(t,x_t))dt, \; L = \frac{1}{2}(a^u)^T(2b)^{-1}a^u,$$

$$\Delta S(s,T,\tilde{x}^*(\cdot)) = M_{s,\tilde{x}^*_s}[\sum_{j=1}^{n}\int_s^T \sum_{i=1}^{n}(2b_{ij}(t,\tilde{x}_t^*)^{-1}a_i^u(t,\tilde{x}_t^*)d\tilde{x}_j^*(t) -$$

$$-\int_s^T L(t,\tilde{x}_t^*,u(t,x_t))dt].$$

The control function is applied to obtain the equivalent probabilities at the transformation P into P'. Such transformation consists of discontinuing (cutting off) the process $\tilde{x}_t$ at the moment of exiting the process $\tilde{x}_t$ from a given set B.

The cutting off procedure is defined by the following transformation for the additive functional: $\omega_s^T = \begin{Bmatrix} 0, t \leq \tau \\ \infty, t > \tau \end{Bmatrix}$. The corresponding transitional probability

$$P'(s,\tilde{x},\tau,B)=M_{s,\tilde{x}}[\exp(-\omega_s^T)] = \int_B q_{s,T} P_{s,\tilde{x}}[d\tilde{x}_t],$$

satisfies the relations: $q_{s,T}=\begin{Bmatrix} 0, t\leq\tau \\ 1, t>\tau \end{Bmatrix}$, and at $t>\tau$, $P'(s,\tilde{x},t,B)=0$,

at $t\leq\tau$, $P'(s,\tilde{x},t,B)=\int_B q_{s,T}P_{s,\tilde{x}}[d\tilde{x}_t]$, $P'(s,\tilde{x},t,B)=\int_B q_{s,T}P_{s,\tilde{x}}[d\tilde{x}_t]$.

The trajectory $\tilde{x}_t$ is cutting off at a random moment τ ,for which the conditional probability is defined by the formula $P(\tau>t)=\exp(-\omega_s^T)$.

The obtained relations lead to the two forms of representation the functionals:

$\Delta S(s,T,\tilde{x}^*(\cdot))=M_{s,B}[\omega_s^T]$ and

$$\omega_s^T=-\frac{1}{2}\sum_{j=1}^{n}\int_s^T\sum_{i=1}^{n}(2b_{ij}(t,\tilde{x}_t)^{-1})a_i^u(t,\tilde{x}_t)a_j^u(t,\tilde{x}_t)dt+$$

$$+\sum_{j=1}^{n}\int_s^T\sum_{i=1}^{n}(\sigma_{ij}(t,\tilde{x}_t)^{-1}a_j^u(t,\tilde{x}_t)d\xi_j(t).\Delta S(s,T,\tilde{x}^*(\cdot))=$$

$$=M_{s,\tilde{x}^*_s}[\int_s^T\sum_{i,j=1}^{n}(2b_{ij}(t,\tilde{x}_t)^{-1}a_i^u(t,\tilde{x}_t)a_j^u(t,\tilde{x}_t)dt(t)] = \int_s^T W(t,\tilde{x}_t)dt.$$

The first one turns to zero at $\omega_s^T=0$, the second one turns to zero at $a_i^u(t,\tilde{x}_t)=0$.

This contradiction is eliminated by using the formula

$$\Delta S(s,T,\tilde{x}^*(\cdot))=\begin{Bmatrix} M_{s,B}[\omega_s^T], \omega_s^T\neq 0 \\ 0, \omega_s^T=0 \end{Bmatrix}.$$

The condition $\omega_s^T=0$ is executed if is true the equality

$$\frac{1}{2}\int_s^T\sum_{i,j=1}^{n}(2b_{ij}(t,\tilde{x}_t)^{-1}a_i^u(t,\tilde{x}_t)a_j^u(t,\tilde{x}_t)dt=$$

$$=-\sum_{j=1}^{n}\int_s^T\sum_{i=1}^{n}(\sigma_{ij}(t,\tilde{x}_t)^{-1}a_j^u(t,\tilde{x}_t)d\xi_j(t).$$

According to that, $\Delta S=M_{s,\tilde{x}}[\omega_s^T]$, and if, for example $\det b(t,\tilde{x}_t)|_{t=\tau+0}=0$, and $a^u(t,\tilde{x}_t)|_{t=\tau+0}\neq 0$, $\Delta S=\lim_{\varepsilon\to 0} M_{s,\tilde{x}}[\omega_s^{\tau+\varepsilon}]=\infty$, then the above conditions for both the additive functional and the cutting off the process can be satisfied.

The execution of the equality $\omega_s^T = 0$ is also possible when the controlled drift is changing its sign at the moment τ of the object model renovation. At that moment, if the informational entropy $\Delta S(\tilde{x}_t)$ turns into δ-function, then the corresponding (macro level) function of action, $\Delta S(t,x)$ (ch.1.1.3) undergoes to analogous jump.

If the right side of the equality at $a_i^u(\tau + o) < 0$ becomes more than the left side, then $\omega_s^\tau(\tau + o) \to -\infty$, and the entropy can reach an infinite negative value, that could be useful for the subsequent process consolidation (ch.1.2.6).

Another kind of the cutting off moment τ is executed when each trajectory of the transformed process $\tilde{x}_t$ is discontinuing at the following τ interval time $\Delta\tau$ with the probability $W(\tau,\tilde{x})\Delta\tau + o(\Delta\tau)$, where $W(t,\tilde{x}) \geq 0$ is the cutting off probability density. In this case, process $\tilde{x}_t$ is cutting off with the same density that $\tilde{x}_t$ is transformed into $\tilde{x}_t'$. Functional $\Delta S(s,T,\tilde{x}^*(\bullet))$ defines the conditional probability of the existence of the process on the interval (s, τ):

$$\exp(-\int_s^\tau W(t,\tilde{x}_t)dt) = 1 - W(\tau,\tilde{x})\Delta\tau + o(\Delta\tau),\ s = \tau - \Delta\tau,$$

that at the density $W(\tau,\tilde{x}) = 0$, approaches $1 + o(\Delta\tau)$.

The corresponding transitional probability

$$\tilde{P}(s,\tilde{x}_s,t,B) = \tilde{P}_{s,\tilde{x}}(\tilde{x}_t \in B) = \int_B \exp(-\omega_s^t) \to \int_B \tilde{P}_{s,\tilde{x}}[d\tilde{x}_t],\ \text{at } B = \Omega$$

approaches 1, and at $\omega_s^T \to \infty$, $\tilde{P}(s,\tilde{x}_s,t,B) \to 0$. The probability of the existence of the process outside of the interval (s,τ) also approaches zero. The probability of cutting off $\tilde{x}_t$ on the interval (s,τ) is determined by knowing the function $W(t,\tilde{x}_t)$. The functional ω_s^τ defines the probability of the existence of the moment $\tau \in [s,T]$ that reaches the maximum at $\omega_s^T = 0$, $\Delta S(\tilde{x}_t) = 0$. The condition of the moment τ existence (with probability 1) is defined by the optimal control function minimizing the entropy functional . Such control "cuts off "the process at moment τ , and it is getting $\omega_s^T = 0$. The transitional probability for the transforming state $(s,\tilde{x} \to \tau, B)$ according to the Jensen inequality [8]::

$$P(s,\tilde{x},\tau,B) = M_{s,\tilde{x}}[\exp(-\omega_s^T)] \geq \exp(-M_{s,\tilde{x}}[\omega_s^T]) = \exp(-\Delta S(x_T))$$

reaches the maximum value equal to 1 at $\Delta S(x_T) = 0$.

It means, the extremal principle formulates the regularities that minimize uncertainty.

The result $\Delta S(x_T) = 0$ follows also from the relations defining the entropy

$\Delta S(\tilde{x}(\bullet)) \overset{def}{=} M_{s,\tilde{x}} [\ln \frac{P_{t,\tilde{x}}[d\tilde{x}_T]}{P'_{t,\tilde{x}}[d\tilde{x}_T]}]$, assuming that the probabilities $P_{t,\tilde{x}}[d\tilde{x}_T], P'_{t,\tilde{x}}[d\tilde{x}_T]$ obtained from Jensen's inequality have meaning of the corresponding transitional probabilities. We get

$$\Delta S(\tilde{x}_T) = M_{s,\tilde{x}} [\ln \frac{P_{t,\tilde{x}}[d\tilde{x}_T]}{P'_{t,\tilde{x}}[d\tilde{x}_T]}] = \Delta S(x_T) = \ln \frac{P_{t,\tilde{x}}[dx_t]}{P'_{t,\tilde{x}}[dx'_t]}.$$

Because x_t, x'_t are nonrandom trajectories, the corresponding probabilities are $P_{t,\tilde{x}}[dx_T]=1, P'_{t,\tilde{x}}[dx_T]=1$, and therefore $\Delta S(x_T)=0$. Transitional probability satisfies the differential equation $-\frac{\partial P}{\partial t} = a\frac{\partial P}{\partial x} + b\frac{\partial^2 P}{\partial x^2} - \mathrm{WP}$, that at $b\frac{\partial^2 P}{\partial x^2}=\mathrm{WP}$ leads to Liouville's equation. At these conditions, the corresponding transitional probability $P(s,\tilde{x}_s,\tau,\tilde{x}_t)$ is defined on the extremals, and $\exp(-\Delta S(x_t))$ has a meaning of the transitional probability on the extremals.

Therefore, the extremals are the trajectories of the maximal equal probable states that satisfy the Liouville theorem (about preservation of the phase volume) at any moment $t \le \tau$. At the execution of the above equations, the transitional probability of the control process coincides with the corresponding transitional function for the extremal ensemble $P(s,\tilde{x}_s,\tau,\tilde{x}_t) = P(s,\tilde{x}_s,\tau,x_t)$.

At this meaning, the extremal ensemble and the controlled diffusion process are stochastically equivalent.

Because of this, Liouville's theorem is true for the diffusion process only at the moments $t = \tau$ preceding to the cutting off moment.

About the minimum condition for the microlevel entropy functional

Let us consider a closed measured set $\overline{B}_\tau=[s,\tau]\times\overline{B}$ where $[s,\tau]\subset\Delta$, $\overline{B}\subset\beta(\Omega)$, B=int $\overline{B}$, $\Gamma \overset{def}{=} \overline{B} \setminus B$, $B_\tau=(s,\tau)\times B$, $\Gamma_\tau \overset{def}{=} \overline{B}_\tau \setminus B_\tau$.

The distribution of the entropy functional $S(\tilde{x}(\bullet))$ on the set B_τ as a function of time $t\in(s,\tau)$ and the current random state $x\in B$, can be found by solving the following boundary problem:

$$-\frac{\partial S(t,x)}{\partial t}=\sum_{i=1}^{n} a_i^u(t,x)\frac{\partial S(t,x)}{\partial x_i}+\sum_{i,j=1}^{n} b_{ij}(t,x)\frac{\partial^2 S(t,x)}{\partial x_i \partial x_j}+W(t,x),$$

$(t,x)\in B_\tau$, $W(t,x)\geq 0$,

(2.64) $S(s,x)=f_1(x)$, $f_1(x)\in C(B,R_+^{'})$, or

(2.64a) $S(\tau,x)=f_2(x)$, $f_2(x)\in C(B,R_+^{'})$

(2.64b) $S(t,y)=f_3(t,y)$, $y\in\Gamma$, $f_3(t)\in C([s,\tau],R_+^{'})$.

Using the concept of proving the maximum principle (for the heat transfer problem [5]), we get the following result.

The solution of the problem (2.64, 2.64a,b) reaches the maximal value on the border of the set $\overline{B}_\tau$: e.g., at t=s, or t=τ ; or on the border Γ of the set $\overline{B}$.

It means, for $\forall(t_o,x_o)\subset B_\tau$, the following inequality is satisfied:

$$S(t_o,x_o)\geq \inf_{x\in B, y\in\Gamma}\ \min_{t\in(s,\tau)}[f_1(x),\ f_2(x), f_3(t,y)].$$

To *prove* this, let us assume the opposite. Let us consider such a moment $\exists(t_o,x_o)\subset B_\tau$ that the inequality is satisfied in the form:

(2.65) $S(t_o,x_o)-\inf_{x\in B, y\in\Gamma}\ \min_{t\in(s,\tau)}[f_1(x),\ f_2(x), f_3(t,y)]\leq -\varepsilon$, $\varepsilon>0$.

Let us form an auxiliary function

(2.65a) $V(t,x)=S(t,x)+\dfrac{\varepsilon(t_o-t)}{2\tau}$

and show that it takes a minimal value on the set B_τ.

Because the set $\overline{B}_\tau$ is closed and limited, and the fulfillment of the second Weierstrass theorem for continuous functions [12], the function $V(t,x)$ reaches a precise lower limit on $\overline{B}_\tau$.

Using the inequality (2.65)and the function (2.65a) we have

$$V(s,x)\geq f_1(x)-\frac{\varepsilon t}{2\tau}\geq f_1(x)-\frac{\varepsilon}{2}\geq \inf_{x\in B} f_1(x)-\frac{\varepsilon}{2};$$

$$V(t,x)\geq f_2(x)-\frac{\varepsilon t}{2\tau}\geq f_2(x)-\frac{\varepsilon}{2}\geq \inf_{x\in B} f_2(x)-\frac{\varepsilon}{2};$$

(2.65b) $V(t,y)\geq f_3(t,y)-\dfrac{\varepsilon t}{2\tau}\geq f_3(t,y)-\dfrac{\varepsilon}{2}\geq \inf_{y\in\Gamma}\ \min_{t\in(s,\tau)} f_3(t,y)-\dfrac{\varepsilon}{2}$.

From the equation (2.64) it follows :

(2.66) $\inf_{x\in B} f_1(x)-S(t_o,x_o)\geq\varepsilon$; $\inf_{x\in B} f_2(x)-S(t_o,x_o)\geq\varepsilon$;
$\inf_{y\in\Gamma}\min_{t\in(s,\tau)} f_3(t,y)-S(t_o,x_o)\geq\varepsilon$.

According to equation (2.65a), we have $S(t_o,x_o)=V(t_o,x_o)$.

After the joint solution of the systems (2.65b) and (2.66), we get

(2.67) $V(s,x)\geq V(t_o,x_o)+\frac{\varepsilon}{2}$; $V(\tau,x)\geq V(t_o,x_o)+\frac{\varepsilon}{2}$;
$V(t,y)\geq V(t_o,x_o)+\frac{\varepsilon}{2}$.

From this system of the inequalities it follows that the function $V(t,x)$ does not get a minimal value on Γ_τ. Because the minimum on $\overline{B}_\tau$ does exist, it means, the minimum can be reached at some inner points of $\overline{B}_\tau$, and therefore, on the set B_τ.

At the points (t^*,x^*) of minimum of function $V(t,x)$ are executed the relations

(2.68) $\frac{\partial V}{\partial t}(t^*,x^*)=0$; $\frac{\partial V}{\partial x_i}(t^*,x^*)=0$, i=1,..., n;

(2.68a) $\frac{1}{2}\sum_{i,j=1}^{n}h_{ij}\Delta x_i\,\Delta x_j\geq 0,\ h_{ij}=\frac{\partial^2 V}{\partial x_i\partial x_j}(t^*,x^*),\ \Delta x_i=x_i-x_i^*$.

For x as the current state of the diffusion process, and for any $\delta>0$, the following relation is satisfied [8]:

(2.69) $\int_{|x-x^*|\leq\delta}\Delta x_i\,\Delta x_j\,P(t^*,x^*,t^*+\Delta t,dy)=2b_{ij}(t^*,x^*)\,\Delta t+o(\Delta t)$.

Because δ is an arbitrary, we may choose it from the condition
$B_\delta=\{|x-x^*|\geq\delta\}\subset B$.

Let us integrate the inequality (2.69) by the probability measure
$P(t^*,x^*,t^*+\Delta t,B_\delta)$ on the set B_δ and then divide its both sides on $\Delta t\to 0$.

Considering the condition $\lim_{\Delta t\to 0}\frac{O(\Delta t)}{\Delta t}=0$, $\forall t^*\in(s,\tau)$, we get

(2.70) $\sum_{i,j=1}^{n}h_{ij}(t^*,x^*)b_{ij}(t^*,x^*)=\sum_{i,j=1}^{n}\frac{\partial^2 V}{\partial x_i\partial x_j}(t^*,x^*)b_{ij}(t^*,x^*)\geq 0$

From the joint equalities (2.68, 270) we may write the following inequality (2.70a)

$$\frac{\partial V}{\partial t}(t^*,x^*)+\sum_{i=1}^{n}\frac{\partial V}{\partial x_i}(t^*,x^*)a_i^u(t^*,x^*)+\sum_{i,j=1}^{n}\frac{\partial^2 V}{\partial x_i\partial x_j}(t^*,x^*)b_{ij}(t^*,x^*)\geq 0.$$

Using the relations (2.67, 2.70a) we have

(2.71) $$\frac{\partial V}{\partial t}(t,x)=\frac{\partial S(t,x)}{\partial t}-\frac{\varepsilon}{2\tau},\ \frac{\partial V}{\partial x_i}(t,x)=\frac{\partial S(t,x)}{\partial x_i},\ i=1,\dots,n,$$

$$\frac{\partial^2 V}{\partial x_i \partial x_j}(t,x)=\frac{\partial^2 S(t,x)}{\partial x_i \partial x_j},\ i,j=1,\dots,n\ .$$

After substituting (2.71) into (2.70a) at t=t*, $x=x^*$ we come to the inequality

$$\frac{\partial S(t^*,x^*)}{\partial t}+$$

$$+\sum_{i,j=1}^{n}\frac{\partial^2 S}{\partial x_i \partial x_j}(t^*,x^*)b_{ij}(t^*,x^*)+\sum_{i=1}^{n}\frac{\partial S}{\partial x_i}(t^*,x^*)a_i^u(t^*,x^*)\ \geq \frac{\varepsilon}{2\tau}.$$

Using the equations (2.64) and (2.70a) we come to the inequality

$$-W(t^*,x^*)\geq\frac{\varepsilon}{2\tau}>0,\ W(t^*,x^*)<0.$$

Because the inequality $W(t,x)\geq 0$ is correct by definition, we come to a contradiction that proves the initial statement. In particular, considering τ=T in (2.64b) and taking the t=T as a moment of cutting off the process, according to [8], we have $f_2(x)=f_3(t,y)$=0. Therefore, the absolute minimum of S (t, x)-function ($S(\tilde{x}(\cdot))$ =0) will be reached at the moment of the exit $\tilde{x}_t$ on the border of the set $B\times[s,T]$. The extremal value of S (t, x)-function can be found for such $x=\tilde{x}(\tau)$ that belongs to the border of the B region. To fix these values, the random process should be cut off at the moment following the first exit of the process on the border of set Γ. Cutting off the microprocess is an operation that selects the extremal solution of the given boundary problem. Execution of that operation can perform the control that enables us to keep the random process within a given set.

Many dimensional Marcovian process generally has n such the first exits on Γ. The moment of the execution of equality for the transitional probabilities:

(2.72) $$P(s,\tilde{x},\tau,B)-P^*(s,\tilde{x},\tau,B)\Rightarrow\int_B(P(s,\tilde{x},\tau,dy)-P^*(s,\tilde{x},\tau,dy))=0$$

is the moment of cutting off the random process. The execution of condition ($S(\tilde{x}(\cdot))$ =0) for an arbitrary B leads to the equality $q_s^\tau=\frac{P_{s,\tilde{x}}[d\tilde{x}_t]}{P^*_{s,\tilde{x}}[d\tilde{x}_t]}=1$ for the density measure at "almost everywhere" in B. If τ is the moment of the first exit $\tilde{x}_t$ on Γ, then the operation of cutting off at that $\tilde{x}(\tau)\in\Gamma$ is freezing the process $\tilde{x}_t$ on the set Γ, where the condition $S(\tau,x)$=0 is satisfied, and the relation (2.72) takes place. Cutting off is a specific method of the random processes theory that connects the parabolic equation boundary problem to the Marcovian diffusion processes. Executing the condition $S(\tilde{x}(\cdot))$ =0 solves the problem of transferring (in a probabilistic meaning) the initial random process on some assigned process. •

1.1.3. Solution of the variational problem

Let us formulate the variational problem (VP) using the Lagrange method of eliminating constraints [6] and the Pontryagin maximum principle [7]:

(3.1) $S_p = \int_s^T L^o(t,x,dx/dt,u(t,x))\,dt \rightarrow extr$,

(3.2) $L_p = \mu_o L(t,x,dx/dt) + p^T(dx/dt - a^u);\ a^u = a^u(t,x)$,

(3.3) $L_p^u = \mu_o L(t,x,a^u) + p^T(dx/dt - a^u),\ L^o = (L_p, L_p^u)$,

(3.4) $L(t,x,dx/dt) = 1/2(dx/dt)^T(2b)^{-1}dx/dt$,

$L(t,x,a^u) = 1/2(a^u)^T(2b)^{-1}a^u = L^u,\ b = b(t,x)$;

(3.5) $\varphi(t,x,u) = 0;\ t \in \Gamma_\varphi,\ \varphi : (\Gamma_\varphi, R^n, U) \rightarrow R^1,\ \Gamma_\varphi \subset \Delta;\ a^u(t,x) \neq 0$,

where μ_o, p are the Lagrangian multipliers: $\mu_o \in R_+^1$, $p(t,\cdot) \in KC^1(\Delta, R^n)$, Γ_φ is a discrete set of $t \in \Delta$, where the equalities of costraint (3.5) (imposed on (3.1-3.4) is defined. The Lagrangian L^o is written in the classic (3.2), and the Pontryagin's (3.3) forms. Let's build the field of the functional on S_p on the set

$\tilde{Q} = (\Delta \setminus (\bigcup \tau_k \bigcup \Gamma_\varphi) \times R^n;\ \Delta^o = \Delta \setminus \bigcup_{k=1}^{m} \tau_k$,

with τ_k as the points of the control discontinuity (1.4). The field is defined by the execution of conditions [6] for Hamiltonian H_p and conjugate variables X_p, X :

(3.6) $dX_p/dt\,(t,x,a^u(t,x)) = -\partial H_p/\partial x;\ H_p = H_p(t,x,X_p)$,

(3.7) $\partial X_i/\partial x_j(t,x,a^u(t,x)) = \partial X_j/\partial x_i(t,x,a^u(t,x)),\ i,j = 1,\dots,n$

(3.8) $X_p = \partial L_p/\partial(dx/dt) = \mu_o X + p$;

$X = \partial L(t,x,dx/dt)/\partial(dx/dt) = (2b(t,x))^{-1}\,dx/dt$,

(3.9) $\mu_o X + p = \mu_o(2b(t,x))^{-1}\,dx/dt + p,\ \ dx/dt = a^u(t,x) = 2b\,t,x)X$,

(3.10) $H_p(t,x,X_p) = (dx/dt)^T X - L_p =$

$= \mu_o(X_p - p)^T b(t,x)(X_p - p) + p^T a^u(t,x)$,

(3.11) $H_p(t,x,X) = \mu_o X^T b(t,x)X + p^T a^u(t,x)$,

(3.12) $dx/dt = \partial H_p(t,x,X_p)/\partial X_p = \mu_o 2b(t,x)X = \mu_o\ a^u(t,x)$,

(3.13) $\partial H_p/\partial X_p = \partial X/\partial X_p \cdot \partial H_p/\partial X = E \cdot \partial H_p/\partial X = \partial H_p(t,x,X)/\partial X$,

(3.14) $p = \partial L_p^u/\partial(dx/dt),\ \ H_p^u(t,\cdot) = (dx/dt)^T p - L_p^u(t,\cdot) =$

$= -\mu_o L^u(t,x) + p^T a^u(t,x),\ \mu_o = 1$.

(3.15) $dp/dt = -\partial H_p^u / \partial x = (\partial (a^u(t,x))/\partial x)^T p +$
$+ \partial (1/2 (a^u)^T (2b)^{-1} a^u)/\partial x$.
The last relation is a stationary condition of maximum principle [7].

<u>*Lemma* 3.1 (L1)</u>. Let us have the field of functional on $\tilde{Q}$ as a result of the solution of problem (3.1) with the equations (3.8,9) and with the corresponding function of action $S_p(t,x)$; let us define a function $\tilde{S}_p(t,x)$, which satisfies the Kolmogorov equation (K)[1] at each point of the set $(t,x) \in Q$, and on a certain set $Q^o \subset \tilde{Q}$ in the field of the functional's extremals it satisfies the equation

(3.16) $(a^u)^T \partial \tilde{S}_p / \partial x + \sum_{i,j=1}^{n} b_{ij} \partial^2 \tilde{S}_p / \partial x_i \partial x_j = p^T a^u, \; a^u = a^u(t,x)$,

$b=b(t,x)>0$. Then, the above function $\tilde{S}_p$ exists and satisfies the equations

(3.17) $\partial \tilde{S}_p / \partial x = X_p, \quad -\partial \tilde{S}_p / \partial t = H_p$,
hence, it satisfies also the functional field equations, as well as the equation:
(3 18) $\partial X_p / \partial x = \partial X / \partial x = -2 X X^T$,

that defines the $N=n^2$ equations of the differential constraints in (3.5).
Proof. The function of action $S_p(t,x)$ on $\tilde{Q}$ satisfies the Hamilton-Jacobi (HJ) equations: $-\partial \tilde{S}_p / \partial t = 1/2 (a^u)^T (2b)^{-1} a^u + p^T a^u, \; \partial \tilde{S}_p / \partial x = X_p(t,x)$,
$-\partial \tilde{S}_p / \partial t = H_p, \; \tilde{Q} = (\Delta \setminus (\bigcup \tau_k \bigcup \Gamma_\varphi) \times R^n$.
The distribution of the functional
$\tilde{S}(t, T, x) = \tilde{S}(t, x)$ on $Q = \Delta^0 \times R^n$ satisfies the K equation:
$-\partial \tilde{S} / \partial t = (a^u)^T \partial \tilde{S} / \partial x + b \, \partial \tilde{S} / \partial x^2 + \tilde{L}, \; \tilde{L} = 1/2 (a^u)^T (2b)^{-1} a^u$,
$\tilde{S} = \tilde{S}(t, x), \; a^u = a^u(t, x), \; b = b(t, x)$.

Let us consider the function $\tilde{S}_p(t,x)$ that satisfies the condition of L1, i.e., the K equation and it satisfies the equation (3.16) on the set $Q^0 \subset \tilde{Q}$ in the field of extremals. Then the above mentioned HJ equations and, hence (3.17) hold true for this function as well. Since (3.16) is a linear elliptic (for $\tilde{S}_p$) equation solvable under the given boundary conditions ((3.16) on the right-hand side), then the function $\tilde{S}_p(t,x)$ exists, and equation (3.16) along with (3.8, 17) acquires the form

$$(a^u)^T X + (a^u)^T p + \sum_{i,j=1}^{n} b_{ij} \partial X_{ip} / \partial x_j = p^T a^u, \; X^T 2bX + \sum_{i,j=1}^{n} b_{ij} \partial X_{ip} / \partial x_j = 0$$

$$\varphi=\sum_{i,j=1}^{n} b_{ij}(\partial X_{ip} / \partial x_j + 2 X_i X_j)=0,\ b>0;\ \det b \neq 0.$$

The last relation is true for the constraint φ if it satisfies the equality (3.18).

To implement condition $\tilde{S}_p(t,x)=extr S(t,x)$, $(t,x)\in \tilde{Q}$, the above HJ and K equations have to be considered in a single and the same region. We assume that the equality Q= $\tilde{Q}$ is fulfilled. From which it follows $\Gamma_\varphi=\bigcup_{k=1}^{m}\tau_k$, i.e., the set Γ_φ where (3.20, 33) holds true, coincides with the moments of the control discretizations. For implemention of the equation (3.16) by applying the controls, let us assume

$$Q^0=Q^0_- \cup Q^0_+ \ ,\ Q^0_{+-}=\bigcup_{k=1}^{m}\tau_{k+-0}\times X(\tau_k)\ ,$$

i.e., the constraint (3.5,18) is imposed in the vicinity of the hyperplanes of the space $R^1_+ \times R^n$ defined by the set $\bigcup_{k=1}^{m}\tau_k$, which will be selected constructively later on. •

Theorem 1 (T1). The equations for the field of functional (3.6,7) and for the differential constraint (3.18) of the variational problem are executed jointly when the following equations for the macromodel and controls hold true:

(3.19) a^u=A(t)($x+v$), A(t)= $A_t \in$CC(Δ , $\angle(R^n)$) $\cap$ C^1(Δ^0, $\angle(R^n)$);

$(t,x)\in \Delta\times R^n$, $\Gamma_\varphi=\bigcup_{k=1}^{m}\tau_k$

(3.20) $v_t=v(t,\cdot)\in$CC(Δ,V)$\cap$ C^1(Δ^0,V), $v_t:\Delta\rightarrow$ V, V $\subset R^n$

where v is the control vector, reduced to a state vector x.

Proof. The equality (3.6) is a conjugate Hamilton equation (3.13) satisfying the Lagrangian in the form of (3.2). The equality (3.15) is the stationary condition of the maximum principle satisfying the Lagrangian in the form of (3.3). These equations are the consequences of the single and the same variational principle being represented in two forms. Threfore, either (3.6,7) or (3.6, 15) must be equivalent at $\tilde{Q}=Q$. That involves a joint consideration of the field equations (3.6,7), the differential equation for the conjugate vector in the field for Haminltonian (3.10):

(3.21) $\partial X_p(t,x) / \partial t=-\partial H_p(t,x,X_p(t,x)) / \partial x=-\partial H / \partial x -$

$\partial H_p / \partial X_p \cdot \partial X_p / \partial x$, $\partial H_p / \partial X_p=\partial H / \partial X$, $\partial H_p / \partial X_p=a^u$,

$\partial X_p / \partial x=\partial X / \partial x$,

the equation of differential constraint in the form (3.18), and the equation

(3.22) $\partial(\partial X_p / \partial t) / \partial x$=-2[$(\partial X / \partial t)\ X^T+X(\partial X / \partial t)^T$], $(t,x)\in \tilde{Q}$.

The right side of (3.22) for H_p(3.10) upon substitution of (3.18) assumes the form:

(3.23) $\partial H_p / \partial x$ =1/2$(\partial a^u / \partial x)^T X$+2$X X^T b X$+$(\partial a^u / \partial x)^T p$.

The equations (3.22) and (3.23) can be written in the form

(3.24) $\partial X_p / \partial t = -1/2(\partial a^u / \partial x)^T X + X X^T a^u - (\partial a^u / \partial x)^T p$;

$\partial [-1/2(\partial a^u / \partial x)^T X - X X^T a^u - (\partial a^u / \partial x)^T p] / \partial x =$

$= -1/2\, \partial (\partial a^u / \partial x)^T / \partial x : (X + 2p) +$

$+ (\partial a^u / \partial x)^T X X^T + X X^T \partial a^u / \partial x - 2 X X^T (X^T a^u)$.

Since the functional (3.1) reaches its extremum on solutions of equations (3.8,9), the variational conditions of coordination in the functional field [6] are satisfied:

$\partial X(t, x\; a^u(t,x)) / \partial t = -\partial H(t, x, a^u(t,x)) / \partial t$,

$H = 1/2(a^u)^T (2b)^{-1} a^u = 1/2 X^T a^u$. From that, using equation (3.25), we obtain

$-\partial H / \partial x = -1/2[(\partial X / \partial x)^T a^u + (\partial a^u / \partial x)^T X] =$

$= -1/2[-2 X X^T a^u + (\partial a^u / \partial x)^T X]$, and the equality (3.23) takes the form

(3.25) $2[(\partial X / \partial) X^T + X(\partial X / \partial)^T] = 2 X X^T (a^u) X^T -$

$-(\partial a^u / \partial x)^T X X^T + 2 X (a^u)^T X X^T - X X^T \partial a^u / \partial x = 4 X (X^T a^u) X^T -$

$-(\partial a^u / \partial x)^T X X^T - X X^T \partial a^u / \partial x$.

From the joint consideration of (3.23, 24) and (3.23, 25), we get the equality

$1/2\, \partial (\partial a^u / \partial x)^T / \partial x : (X + 2p) = \| o_{ij} \|_{i,j=1}^n = O$,

which is an identical at $\tilde{Q} = (\Delta \setminus (\mathbf{U} \tau_k \times R^n)$, if $\partial^2 a_k^u (t,x) / \partial x_i \partial x_j \equiv O$;

i,j, k=1,...,n , $(t, x) \in \tilde{Q}$, from which the equations (3.19, 20) follows. Operator A=A(t) does not depend on the randomness of $\omega' \in \Omega'$ by its definition. ●

Comment 3.1. From the last conclusion, in particular, this realtion follows: $M[d\tilde{x}_t] = M[A(t)(\tilde{x}_t + v_t)]dt$, $M[d x_t] = M[A(t)(x_t + v_t)]dt$, and we obtain

(3.26a) $x_t = M[\tilde{x}_t]$. ●

Corollary 3.1.

Lagrangian of the functional that satisfies both the K and HJ equations has a view:

$L_p = -1/2[(dx / dt - a^u)^T X_p - b\, \partial X_p / \partial x]$,

that follows directly from

$-L_p + (dx / dt)^T X_p = (a^u)^T X_p + b\, \partial X_p / \partial x + \tilde{L}$, at $L_p = \tilde{L}$. ●

Corollary 3.2.

The conjugate vector p of Pontryagin's optimization problem satisfies the equation $C_o p = (b + C_o/2) X$, where C_o is an independable on time constant vector.

Indeed, by applying the maximum principle to the Hamiltonian (3.14), we get

$dH_p^u / dt = d(-L + p^T a^u) / dt = 0$; $L = 1/2\, X^T a^u$,

$X^T d a^u / dt + d X^T / dt\, a^u = 2 (p^T d a^u / dt + d p^T / dt\; a^u)$,

$(X - 2p)^T d a^u / dt = -d[(X - 2p)^T a^u] / dt$.

From that, the equation follows: $(X - 2p)^T, C_o = -a^u$, $dx / dt = 2 b X$

that defines vector p via vector X at given C_o . •

Comment 3.2. In particular, at the execution of the equations

C_o=-3$(2b)^{-1}$, p=1/2$(2b)^{-1}(dx/dt - 3a^u)$, p=-$(2b))^{-1} a^u$, $dx/dt = a^u$,

X_p=3/2$(2b)^{-1}(dx/dt - a^u)$,

the Lagrangian satisfying both the K and HJ equations acquires a view:

L_p=3/8[$(dx/dt - a^u)^T (b)^{-1}(dx/dt - a^u) + b^{-1} \partial b / \partial x (dx/dt - a^u) +$

$+ \partial a^u / \partial x$].

The last form, in particular, at constant diffusion, coincides with the Onsager-Machlup Lagrangian [8]. We note, that at $X_p = X + p = 0$ (as one of the conditions of $dx/dt = a^u$, C_o =- 3$(2b)^{-1}$), the expression for $L_p = dS_p / dt$ turns to zero, that corresponds to the constant value of the total entropy S_p on its extremals. (The total entropy contains the components delivered outside by the controls, and generated by the microlevel stochastics). The entropy functional that satisfies the VP, we call the proper functional (PF).

The Lagrangian of the proper functional

L_p=-1/2[$(dx/dt)^T (2b^{-1})(dx/dt) + p^T (dx/dt - a^u)$], with (3.16,18):

$p^T a^u = (X + p)^T a^u + b\, \partial X / \partial x - (2b X)^T X$, $dx/dt = a^u$, $2bX = dx/dt$

takes the form L_p= -1/2[$(a^u)^T (2b^{-1})(a^u) - X^T dx/dt + (dx/dt)^T X$)]. •

<u>*Corollary* 3.3.</u> From (3.8,19, 20) the explicit relations for vector X and the differential constraint (3.18) follow in the form

(3.26) $X(t,x)$=$(2b(t,x))^{-1}$A(t)(x+v), A=A^T, $b = b^T$, $(2b)^{-1}$A=A$(2b)^{-1}$,

(3.27) $\partial X_i / \partial x_j$=- $(2b)^{-1} \partial (2b) / \partial x_j (2b)^{-1} a^u + (2b)^{-1} \partial a^u / \partial x_j$=

=-2$X X_j$=-2$(2b)^{-1} a^u X_j$, $(t, x) \in \tilde{Q}$.

(3.28) - $\sum_{k,v=1}^{n} \partial (2b_{ik}) / \partial x_j (2b)_{kv}^{-1} a_v^u + A_{ij}$ =-2$a_i^u \sum_{k=1}^{n} (2b)_{jk}^{-1} a_k^u$, i,j=1,...,n,

which along with (3.12) define the dynamic model of random object satisfying the VP. The form (3.9, 26) coincides with the equation of nonequilibrium thermodynamics, where the function b =b(t, x) defines its kinetic operator [9]. •

Comments 3.3. Informational macro model (3.12, 26, 28) contains the control (3.20) which, unlike the maximum principle, appears in the conjugate vector expression, and therefore, participates in the constraint equation (3.27, 28). That connects the functions of drift and diffusion, and represents an initial equation for identification of the macromodel operator by measuring the nonlinear matrix of diffusion. If the matrix A depends on time, this matrix might also be used for the identification the diffusion matrix b=b(t).

In this case, the equation of differential constraint takes the form

(3.29) A_t [E+2$(x + v)(x + v^T$ $A_t (2b_t)$]= $\| o_{ij} \|_{i,j=1}^{n} = O$, $(t, x) \in \tilde{Q}$, which with $\det(x+v)(x+v)^T A_t(2b_t)^{-1} \equiv O$, can be satisfied only when $A_t = \| o_{ij} \|_{i,j=1}^n = O$.

The last condition confirms dx/dt $(t \in \Delta)=0$ for (3.12), while departing from the condition (3.3). When b= b(t) = b_t this condition is satisfiable at the "punched" points of the set $\tilde{Q}$: $Q^0 = (\bigcup \tau_k \times R^n)$, and when $b = b(t, x)$, it satisfies within the "couple region" $\tilde{Q}$. The equation of constraint (3.18) at $b = b_t$ can be satisfied at

(3.30) $\partial X / \partial x + 2XX^T = \varepsilon$, $\varepsilon = \varepsilon(t, x) = \forall (t, x) \in \Delta \times R^n$, $\varepsilon = \angle(R^n)$;

(3.31) $\rho(\varepsilon) \rightarrow \min$, $\rho(\varepsilon) = (\sum_{i,j=1}^{n} \varepsilon_i^{2})^{1/2}$,

$$\rho_1(\varepsilon) = (\sum_{i,j=1}^{n} M\varepsilon_j^{2}), \quad \rho_2(\varepsilon) = (\sum_{i,j=1}^{n} (M\varepsilon_j)^{2})^{1/2} = 0$$

whith some accuracy ε , that is getting minimal in the sense of (3.31) with the accuracy estimation in the different measures ($\rho(\varepsilon)$, $\rho_1(\varepsilon)$, $\rho_2(\varepsilon)$)

By using the last estimation we come to the equality

(3.32) $M[\partial X / \partial x + 2XX^T] = \| o_{ij} \|_{i,j=1}^n = O$,

Considering it with (3.29) we obtain the relation for identification A_t:

(3.33) $A = -r_v^{-1} b = -b\, r_v^{-1}$, $r_v = M[(x+v(x+v)^T]$,

using the matrices A and r_v, where r_v^{-1} and b commutate at the joint execution of the equations of the functional field (3.7) and of the constraint (3.32).

The condition (3.31) is satisfiable at the set $\tilde{Q}$ if the following relations are true:

(3.34) $\partial \varepsilon_{ij}(\tau, x_\tau) / \partial t = 0$, $\partial \varepsilon_{ij}(\tau, x_\tau) / \partial x_v = 0$, i, j, v=1,..., n, $\tau \in \bigcup_{k=1}^{m} \tau_k$;

with the equation of constraint (3.29) that according to (3.30) takes the form:

(3.35) $1/2E + (x+v)X^T = A^{-1} b\, \varepsilon$, $(t, x) \in \tilde{Q}$, $b = b_t$. •

<u>Theorem 3.2 (T2)</u>. The equations of the functional field (3.6,7) and of the differential constraints (3.30, 34, 35) of the VP are consistent if (3.20) is fulfilled, and the equation of identification of operator on $Q^0 = (\bigcup \tau_k \times R^n)$ has the form:

(3.36) $A(\tau_k + -o) = A_{+-} = r_{1+-} r^{-1}_{v+-} = r^{-1}_{v+-} r_{1+-}$; $r_{v+-} = r_v(\tau_k + -o)$,

$$r_{1+-} = r_1(\tau_k + -o) = r_1^*(\tau_k + -o), \quad r_1 = M\{\frac{dx}{dt}(x+v)^T\}.$$

To *prove* T2 we use jointly the equations (3.22,30) and (3.31) in the forms

$\partial(\partial X / \partial t) / \partial x = -2[(\partial X / \partial t) X^T + X(\partial X / \partial t)^T] + \partial \varepsilon / \partial t$,

$\partial \varepsilon / \partial t = \partial \varepsilon / \partial x = \| o_{ij} \|_{i,j=1}^n = O$, $(t, x) \in \tilde{Q}$,.

Following the methodology of proving T1, we write down the equations

(3.37) $\partial H_p / \partial x = 1/2\, (\partial a^u / \partial x)^T X + X X^T a^u - 1/2\, \varepsilon^T a^u + (\partial a^u / \partial x)^T p$,

(3.38) $\partial X_p / \partial t = -1/2 (\partial a^u / \partial x)^T X + X X^T a^u - 1/2\, \varepsilon^T a^u - (\partial a^u / \partial x)^T p$.

From that, after substitution into (3.22) we obtain

$$\partial (1/2\, \partial a^u / \partial x)^T) / \partial x : (X + 2p) - (\partial a^u / \partial x)^T X X^T$$
$$+ 1/2 (\partial a^u / \partial x)^T \varepsilon - X X^T \partial a^u / \partial x + 4 X X^T (X^T a^u)$$

(3.39) $-2\varepsilon (X^T a^u) + 1/2\, (\partial \varepsilon / \partial x)^T : a^u + 1/2\, \varepsilon^T \partial a^u / \partial x$.

Similarly to the relations (3.24, 25) after substitution of (3.30, 31) we get

$$1/2\, \partial (\partial a^u / \partial x)^T / \partial x : (X + 2p) + 1/2\, \varepsilon^T \partial a^u / \partial x +$$

(3.40) $1/2 (\partial a^u / \partial x)^T \varepsilon - 2\varepsilon (X^T a^u) = -\varepsilon^T a^u X^T - (\varepsilon^T a^u X^T)^T$.

The last relation has to be an identical on $\tilde{Q}$ irrespectively of the explicit form of the function $\varepsilon(t, x)$. This condition is fulfilled if it holds true on $\tilde{Q}$ both the representation (3.19), and the relations

(3.41) $\varepsilon = \varepsilon^T$, $\det \varepsilon \neq 0$, $\varepsilon^T \partial a^u / \partial x = (\partial a^u / \partial x)^T \varepsilon$,

$$\varepsilon^T a^u X^T = (\varepsilon^T a^u X^T)^T.$$

From the equations (3.19,40,41) we obtain the following relations:

(3.42) $2\, \varepsilon^T a^u X^T + \varepsilon^T \partial a^u / \partial x = 2\, \varepsilon X^T a^u$,

$$A + 2 a^u X^T = 2 X^T a^u \mathrm{E},\ \varepsilon \varepsilon^{-1} = \mathrm{E},$$

$$(2b)^{-1} A + 2X X^T = X^T a^u (2b)^{-1} 2,\ b = b(t),\ (t, x) \in \tilde{Q},$$

$$\partial X / \partial x + 2 X X^T = (2b)^{-1} 2 \mathrm{Sp}(a^u X^T),\ \varepsilon = b^{-1} \mathrm{Sp}(a^u X^T),$$

$$A (2b)^{-1} A^{-1} + 2 a^u (x + v)^T = 2b\, 2 A^{-1} (X^T a^u),\ X^T a^u = \mathrm{Sp}(a^u X^T),$$

$$A^{-1} 2b A + 2(x + v)(a^u)^T = 2 A^{-1} 2b (X^T a^u).$$

The relations (3.42), (3.20), and (3.26) lead to the equations

(3.43) $a^u (x + v)^T = (x + v)(a^u)^T$;

$$(\mathrm{d}x/\mathrm{d}t)_{+-} (x + v_{+-})^T = (x + v_{+-})(\mathrm{d}x/\mathrm{d}t)_{+-}^T,\quad t \in (\tau_k + -o), k = 1, \dots, n.$$

After taking the mathematical expectation we arrive at the relation (3.36) for the identification of the operator A_{+-} (on $Q^0 = (\bigcup \tau_k \times R^n)$) through the covariance function and its derivative.at the discrete intervals of applying control . ●

Comments 3.4. Operator M[•], applied directly to the dynamic model (3.12), leads to the relation for identifcation matrix A_t ($t \in \Delta^0$), and we arrive at the equations

(3.44) $A(t)=r_1(t)r_v^{-1}(t) = A^T = r_v^{-1}(t)r_1(t);(t\in\Delta^0)$,

(3.45) $r_v(t)=r_1(t)+r_1(t)^T+M[(dv/dt)(x+v)^T+(x+v)(dv/dt)^T]$

where the covariance matrices are defined via the observed macro variables, or via continuos functions $b_t=-r_1(t)$ and $r_v(t)$, with respect to validity of (3.33).

From the equations (3.32,33) we get $X=-1/2r_v^{-1}(x+v)$, and the Lagrangian $L_p=1/2(a^u)^T(2b)^{-1}(a^u)-1/2((dx/dt)^T r_v^{-1}(x+v)-(x+v)^T(dx/dt))$. •

For *optimal synthesis of the control* (3.20) we formulate and solve *Boltz's problem*:

$$(3.46)\quad \min_{v\in V} S_{pl}=\min_{v\in V}\{\int_s^T L^o{}_p dt+l(x,v)\}=S^o_{pl}$$

where $L_p{}^o$ is defined according to (3.2,3), and the terminal part of (3.46) contains the equation of constraint on $Q^0=(\bigcup \tau_k\times R^n)$ in the form

$$(3.47)\quad l=\sum_{k=1}^m l_k^+ +\sum_{k=1}^m l_k^-,\ l_k^{+-}=\sum_{i,j=1}^n \tilde{\mu}_{ijk}^{+-}\varphi_{ijk}^{+-},\ l_k^{+-}\in Q^0{}_{-+},(\tilde{\mu}_k^+,\tilde{\mu}_k^-)\in\angle(R^n);$$

$$(3.48)\quad \varphi_{ijk}^{+-}=\delta_{ij}/2+(x_i(\tau_{kj})+v_i)(\tau_k+-o))X_j((\tau_k+-o),x_i(\tau_{kj}))-$$

$$-\sum_{v=1}^n (A(\tau_k+-o)^{-1}b(\tau_k+-o))_{iv}\varepsilon_{vj}((\tau_k+-o),x(\tau_{kj})),\ \delta_{ij}=\begin{cases}1, i=n\\ 0, i\neq n\end{cases},$$

where $\tilde{\mu}_k^{+-}$ are the matrices of the Lagrangian multipliers; the indices + – correspond to matrice values at $t=(\tau_k+-o)$, $k=1,...,m$ accordingly.

The equalities (3.47,48) considered with respect to the equations

$$(3.49)\quad \sum_{i,j=1}^n \tilde{\mu}_{ij}^{+-}(x+v_{-+})_i\sum_{v=1}^n (2b_{+-})^{-1}A_{+-})_{jv}(x+v_{-+})_v=$$

$$=\sum_{i,j=1}^n(\sum_{j=1}^n \tilde{\mu}_{ij}^{+-}((2b_{+-})^{-1}A_{+-})_{jv})(x+v_{-+})_i(x+v_{-+})_v=$$

$$=\sum_{i,v=1}^n(\tilde{\mu}^{+-}((2b_{+-})^{-1}A_{+-})_{iv}(x+v_{-+})_i(x+v_{-+})_v;$$

$$l_k^{+-}=(\sum_{i,v=1}^n(\tilde{\mu}(2b)^{-1}A)_{iv}(x+v)_i(x+v)_v)|_{t=\tau_k+-o}+$$

$$+1/2Sp\ \mu\ |_{t=\tau_k+-o}\left(\sum_{i,v=1}^{n}\tilde{\mu}_{ij}\sum_{v=1}^{n}(A^{-1}b)_{iv}\varepsilon_{vj}\right)|_{t=\tau_k+-o}\,.$$

and applying the equations (3.34,35) jointly with the equality

$$(3.50)\ \partial\, l_k^{+-}/\partial\, x_q=\{2[\sum_{i,\,v=1}^{n}(\tilde{\mu}((2b)^{-1}A)_{iv}(x+v)_v\,\delta_{iq}]-$$

$$-\ [\sum_{i,j=1}^{n}\tilde{\mu}_{ij}\sum_{v=1}^{n}(A^{-1}b)_{iv}\partial\varepsilon_{vj}/\partial x_q]\ \}|_{t=\tau_k+-o}=\ 2(\tilde{\mu}\,(2b)^{-1}A(x+v))_q\,|_{t=\tau_k+-o},$$

$q=1,..,n$ lead to the following relations for the function $l(x,v)$ in (3.46):

$$(3.51)\ \partial\, l_k^{+-}/\partial\, x=2\tilde{\mu}_k^{+-}\ X^{+-},\ \ X^{+-}=X(\tau_k+-o)\ ,$$

$$(3.52)\ \partial\, l_k^{+-}/\partial\,\tau_k=0\ ,\ k=o,\ldots,m.$$

The combination of equations (3.51), (3.52), (3.50) redefines fully the function $l(x,v)$ expressed in terms of sought optimal controls in Boltz's problem •

<u>*Theorem 3.3* (T3)</u> The problem (3.46-52) has a solution under (1) piecewise constant controls (3.20); (2) the controls are switching at the moments $\tau\in\bigcup_{k=1}^{m}\tau_k$, defined by the conditions of equalization of relative phase speeds of dynamic model:

$$(3.53)\ dx_i/dt\ (\tau_k-o)\ \ x_i^{-1}(\tau_k)=dx_j/dt\ (\tau_k-o)\ \ x_j^{-1}(\tau_k),\qquad i,j=1,\ldots,n,$$

$k=1,\ldots,m$, and (3) the controls are renovating the matrix $A_+=A(\tau_k+o)$ at those moments which are identifiable by the relation

$$(3.54)\ A_+=1/2(dr/dt)_-\,r_-^{-1}(1+\mu_v^2),\ r=M[x\,x^T],\ \mu_v^2\in R^1\ ;$$

and (4) the optimal reduced controls are determined by the equations:

$$(3.55a)\ \ v_+=-\,v_-+\mu_v^1\ E(x+v_-)\ ,\ \mu_v^1\in R^1\ \ ,\ \ x_T=0;$$

$$(3.55b)\ \ v_+=\angle_v^2\,x\ \ ,\ \ \angle_v^2=\mu_v^2\,E\ \ ,\ \ \mu_v^2=(0,\,-\,2)\,.$$

Poof of T3 (1) is based on the equality for two expressions for X, one in the form: (3.56) $\partial X(t,x,a^u(t,x))/\partial t=-A(2b)^{-1}A(x+v);\ b=b_t$.

It follows from (3.8) for H_p (3.10) and from the equation (3.15) at

$$dp/dt-\partial L/\partial(dx/dt)=-(\partial a^u/\partial x)^T p=\partial X_p/\partial t=dp/dt+dX/dt\,.$$

The other form we derive by differentiating directly the expression

$$(3.57)\ X=(2b)^{-1}r_1r_v^{-1}(x+v)=M[(2b)^{-1}dx/dt\,(x+v)^T]r_v^{-1}(x+v):$$

$$dX / dt = d\{M[(2b)^{-1} dx / dt (x+v)^T] r_v^{-1}(x+v)\}/dt +$$
$$+M[(2b)^{-1} dx / dt (x+v)^T]\, d(r^{-1}_v (x+v)/dt \; +$$
$$+M[(2b)^{-1} dx / dt (x+v)^T] r^{-1}_v\, d(x+v)/dt\,.$$

Let us uncovered each of the components of the considering expressions for X:

(3.58) $d\{M[(2b)^{-1} dx / dt (x+v)^T] r_v^{-1} (x+v)\}/dt = M[dX / dt (x+v)^T] +$

$+M[(2b)^{-1} A(x+v)(x+v)^T A] + M[(2b)^{-1} A(x+v)(dv / dt)^T] r_v^{-1} (x+v)$.

We substitute into the first component the expression following from (3.56):

(3.59) $M[\partial X (t, x, a^u(t,x))(x+v)/ \partial t] = -A(2b)^{-1} A r_v$,

and taking the mathematical expectation for the second component, we get

(3.60) $d\{M[(2b)^{-1} dx / dt (x+v)^T] r_v^{-1} (x+v)\}/dt =$

$$= -A(2b)^{-1}(x+v) + (2b)^{-1} A r_v A r_v^{-1} (x+v) +$$
$$+(2b)^{-1} A\, M[(x+v)(dv / dt)^T] r_v^{-1} (x+v).$$

For the second and third components of (3.57) this equality follows:

$M[(2b)^{-1} dx / dt (x+v)^T] d((r_v^{-1})/dt (x+v)) =$

$= M[A(x+v)(x+v)^T](-1)\, r_v^{-1}\; d(r_v)/dt\; r_v^{-1} (x+v) =$

$= -(2b)^{-1} A\{r_1 + M[dv / dt\; (x+v)^T] + M[(x+v)(dv / dt)^T + r_1{}^T\} r_v^{-1} (x+v)$;

$M[(2b)^{-1} dx / dt (x+v)^T] r_v^{-1}\; d(x+v)/dt =$

$= (2b)^{-1} AA(x+v) + (2b)^{-1} A dv / dt$.

By substitution the obtained relations into (3.57) we reduce it to the form

$dX / dt = -A(2b)^{-1} A(x+v) + (2b)^{-1} A(dv / dt\;$ -

$-M[dv / dt (x+v)^T]) r_v^{-1}(x+v)$. From that, due to the validity of (3.56), we get

(3.61) $(2b)^{-1} A(dv / dt - M[dv / dt (x+v)^T]) r_v^{-1} (x+v) = \|o_{ij}\|_{i,j=1}^{n} = O$.

At the execution of the inequalities $2b \neq \|o_{ij}\|_{i,j=1}^{n} = O$; $A \neq \|o_{ij}\|_{i,j=1}^{n} = O$,

when $a^u = A(x+v) \neq \|o_{ij}\|_{i,j=1}^{n} = O$, the equality (3.61) can be identically true at

(τ_k, τ_{k-1}), k=1,...,m only if control satisfies the equality $dv / dt = \|o_{ij}\|_{i,j=1}^{n} = O$.

From that, due to an arbitrariness of chosen $(\tau_k, \tau_{k-1}) \in \Delta^0$, we have

(3.62) $dv / dt = \| o_{ij} \|_{i,j=1}^{n} = O, \ \forall (\tau_k, \tau_{k-1}) \in \Delta^0, \quad v_t \in CC(\Delta, \subset R^n)$.

To *prove* T3 (2), let us apply the Erdmann-Weierstrass condition [6] for the Boltz problem (3.46) at the points of the control discretization:

(3.63) $X_p(\tau+o) + \partial l / \partial x(\tau+o) = X_p(\tau-o) - \partial l / \partial x(\tau-o)$;

$H_p(\tau+o) - \partial l / \partial \tau(\tau+o) = H_p \tau-o) + \partial l / \partial \tau(\tau+o)$.

Whence by using the equations (3.51, 52), we obtain

(3.64) $X^+ + p^+ + 2\tilde{\mu}^+ X^+ = X^- + p^- - 2\tilde{\mu}^- X^-, \quad H_p^+ = H_p^-$.

Because at $\forall (X^+, p^+, X^-, p^-)$, the coefficients $(D^+, D^-) \in \angle(R^n)$, holds true

(3.65) $p^{+-} = D^{+-} X^{+-}$.

From that we come to the following equations:

(3.66) $H_p = X^T b X + (a^u)^T p =$

$= 1/2 \sum_{ij=1}^{n} (A(E+2D)(2b)^{-1} A)_{ij} (x+v)_i (x+v)_j, \ t \in \tau_k\text{-o}$,

$M[X^T bX] = 1/4 \sum_{i=1}^{n} (A(2b)^{-1} d\, r_v / dt)_{ii} = 1/4\ Sp\,[A(2b)^{-1}\, d\, r_v / dt]$,

$dX / dt = -AX, \quad M[p^T a^u] = 1/2\ Sp\,[AD(2b)^{-1}\, d\, r_v / dt]$,

$M[H_p] = 1/4 Sp\,[A(E+D)(2b)^{-1}\, d\, r_v / dt]$,

(3.67) $H_p(\tau+o) - H_p(\tau-o) =$

$= 1/4 \sum_{ij=1}^{n} [(\Theta_+ (dr_v / dt)_+)_{ij} (r_{v_+}^{-1} (x+v_+)(x+v_+{}^T)_{ij} -$

$- (\Theta_- dr_v / dt)_-)_{ij} (r_{v_-}^{-1} (x+v_-)(x+v_-)_{ij})^T] = 0, \ \Theta_{+-} = A_{+-}(E+2D^{+-})(2b_{+-})^{-1}$,

$r_{v_+} = M[(x+v_+)(x+v_+)^T], \ r_{v-} = M[(x+v_-)(x+v_-)]$,

(3.68) $M_-[\cdot] = M_x(\tau_{k-1})[\cdot]$.

From the equations (3.64,65,67), by applying the operator (3.68) to (3.67) we get

(3.69) $(E + 2\tilde{\mu}^+ + D^+)\, X^+ = (E - 2\tilde{\mu}^- + D^-)\, X^-$,

(3.70) $Sp\, \Theta_+ (dr_v / dt)_+ - Sp\, \Theta_- (dr_v / dt)_- = 0$.

(3.70) $Sp\,\Theta_+(dr_v / dt)_+ - Sp\,\Theta_-(dr_v / dt)_- = 0$.

Since the matrix trace (Sp) and the matrix continuity are invariant under the linear transformations, the equality (3.70) must be satisfiable independently on the selected coordinate system, that is possible at the fulfillment of equation

(3.71) $A_+(E+2D^+)(2b_+)^{-1}(dr_v / dt)_+ = A_-(E+2D^-)(2b_-)^{-1}(dr_v / dt)_-$.

The relation (3.70) is the condition of continuity for equation (3.66) by the probability measure consistent with the operator (3.68). Since $D^{+-} \in \angle(R^n)$ are the auxiliary matrices, which are not imposed by the variational principle, it is expedient to eliminate them from the subsequent analysis by selecting the Lagrange's multipliers in the equation (3.47). To this end we assume

(3.72) $(E+2\tilde{\mu}^+ + D^+) \overset{def}{=} -+(E+2D^+)$, $(E-2\tilde{\mu}^- + D^-) \overset{def}{=} -+(E+2D^-)$.

Therefore the equality (3.69) takes the form

(3.73) $(E+2D^+)X^+ = -+(E+2D^-)X^-$, $\tilde{\mu}^{+-} = +-1/2D^{+-}$, $\tilde{\mu}^{+-} = -+E-+3/2D^{+-}$,

and from the equations (3.71,73) we get the following relations

(3.74) $E+2D^+ = (A_+)^{-1}A_-(E+2D^-)(2b_-)^{-1}((2b_+)^{-1}(dr_v / dt)_+)^{-1}$,

$X^+ = 1/2(2b_+)^{-1}(dr_v / dt)_+ r_{v+}^{-1}(x+v_+)$, $X^- = 1/2(2b_-)^{-1}(dr_v / dt)_- r_{v_-}^{-1}(x+v_-)$

(3.75) $(A_+)^{-1}A_-(E+2D^-)(2b_-)^{-1}(dr_v / dt)_-)\, r_{v+}^{-1}(x+v_+) =$

$= +-(E+2D^-)((2b_-)^{-1}(dr_v / dt)_-) r_{v_-}^{-1}(x+v_-)$ ·

By multiplying the equality (3.75) on $(x+v_+)^T$ and applying (3.68) we obtain

(3.76) $\underline{(A_+)^{-1}A_-}\ \underline{(E+2D^-)(2b_-)^{-1}(dr_v / dt)_-} =$

$= +-(E+2D^-)(2b_-)^{-1}(dr_v / dt)_- r_{v_-}^{-1} M_-[(x+v_-)(x+v)^T]$.

After eliminating D^- the equality (3.76) serves for the identification of the matrix A_+. The matix A_+, renovated at the moment of applying the control, is determined as the A_- matix. It requires the satisfaction of the following natural equalities:

(3.77) $D^{+-} \overset{def}{=} (D^{+-})^T$, $(E+2D^{+-})(2b_{+-})^{-1}(dr_v / dt)_{+-} \overset{def}{=}$

$\overset{def}{=} ((E+2D^{+-})(2b_{+-})^{-1} dr_v / dt)_{+-})^T$,

$[(E+2D^+)(2b_+)^{-1}(dr_v / dt)_+)((E+2D^-)(2b_-)^{-1}(dr_v / dt)_-))^{-1}] \overset{def}{=}$

$\overset{def}{=} [(E+2D^+)(2b_+)^{-1}(dr_v / dt)_+)((E+2D^-)(2b_-)^{-1}(dr_v / dt)_-))^{-1}]^T$.

Taking into account the execution of the equations (3.71,77), the left side of (3.76) represents a symmetric matrix equal to the product of the underlined symmetric matrices. From the equality (3.76) the identification equation follows

(3.78) $A_+=+-A_-[M_-[(x+v)(x+v)_+^T]]^{-1} r_{v_-}$,

as well as the relation (3.75) in the form

(3.79) $M_-[(x+v)(x+v)_+^T]r_{v+}^{-1}(x+v)_+=(x+v)_-$.

Let us consider two forms of the controls (3.62) satisfying the accepted assumptions, i.e., the relations (3.79, 67, 77) and the identification equation (3.78) for each of them. The following relations for the controls

(3.80) $v_+=-v_-+\angle_v^1(x+v_-)$, $\angle_v^1\in\angle(R^n)$, $\angle_v^1=(\angle_v^1)^T$,

$r_{v_+}=(\angle_v^1+E)\, r_{v_-}(\angle_v^1+E)^T$, $r_{v+}^{-1}=(\angle_v^1+E)^{-1} r_{v_-}^{-1}((\angle_v^1+E)^{-1})^T$,

$(x+v_-)(x+v_-)^T(\angle_v^1+E)\overset{def}{=}(\angle_v^1+E)(x+v_-)(x+v_-)^T$

satisfying identically (3.79, 67) and are verifiable by the direct substitution.

The condition (3.79) is satisfied identically by $\angle_v^1=\mu_v^1 E$, $\mu_v^1\in R^1$.

By applying the last equalities, the equation (3.79) acquires the form

(3.81) $A_+=+-A_-(\angle_v^1+E)^{-1}$, $A_+=+-A_-(1+\mu_v^1)^{-1}$.

The second form of the controls, according to the equations

(3.82a) $v_+=\angle_v^2 x$, $v_+-v_-=\angle_v^2 x-v_-$, $\angle_v^2\in\angle(R^n)$, $\angle_v^2=(\angle_v^2)^T$,

$\angle_v^2=\mu_v^2 E$, $\mu_v^2=(0,-2)$.

(3.82b) $(xx^T)(\angle_v^2+E)\overset{def}{=}(\angle_v^2+E)(xx^T)$,

$r_{v_+}=(\angle_v^2+E)\, r\, (\angle_v^2+E)$, $r=M(xx^T)$,

we also subordinate to the relation (3.79). After substitution we get the equalities

(3.83) $M_-[(x+v_-)x^T](\angle_v^2+E)(\angle_v^2+E)^{-1} r^{-1}(\angle_v^2+E)^{-1}(\angle_v^2+E)x=$

$=M_-(x+v_-)x^T]r^{-1}x=x+v_-$;

(3.84) $r^{-1}x=\{M_-[(x+v)_-x^T]\}^{-1}(x+v_-)$.

By multiplying both sides of (3.83) on $(dr_v/dt)_-$, we obtain (dx/dt) on the left side and the equality $(dr_v/dt)_- r_{v_-}^{-1} M_-[(x+v_-)x^T]r^{-1}x=$

$$=M_{-}[(dr_v/dt)_{-} r_{v-}^{-1}(x+v)_{-} x^T] r^{-1} x = M_{-}[(dx/dt)_{-} x^T] r^{-1} x$$

on the right side. From whence the equation follows

(3.85) $(dx/dt)_{-} = M_{-}[(dx/dt)_{-} x^T] r^{-1} x$.

The equalities (3.83-85) are equivalent. By writing the model in the form

(3.86) $(dx/dt)_{-} = A^v(t,x)x$, $A^v = A\left(E + \left\|\frac{v_j(\tau,.)}{x_i(t,.)}\delta_{ij}\right\|_{i,j=1}^{n}\right)$; $x_i(t,\bullet) \neq 0$

and comparing (3.86) with (3.85), we arrive at the equality

(3.87) $M_{-}[(A^v)_{-}(x\ x^T)] = M_{-}(A^v)_{-} r$,

which is identically satisfied if the following equality is fulfilled

(3.88) $\angle_v^2 = \left\|\angle_v^2 \delta_{ij}\right\|_{i,j=1}^{n}$.

In this case, the matrix A^v $(\tau - 0) = A^v(\tau_k - 0)$ is independent of the initial random conditions $x(\tau_k - 0)$, k=1, ..., (m-1). According to (3.68), the matrix gets averaged by these variables. From the relations (3.86-88) the equality follows

(3.89) $M_{-}(A^v)_{-} = A^v_{-} = M_{-}[(dx/dt)_{-} x^T] r^{-1}$

and equation (3.85) is satisfied identically. From that, follows the execution of (3.75-76). After substituting the obtained relations with the controls (3.82a) into the equation (3.67) we arrive at the equality

(3.90) $\{M_{-}[(x+v_{-})x^T]\}^{-1}(x+v_{-})x^T = \{M_{-}[(x+v_{-})x^T]\}^{-1} x(x+v)^T$

From that, we get the condition to which the considered controls should satisfy

(3.91) $M_{-}[(x\,x^T)](v_{-}x^T + x\,v_{-}^T) + [M_{-}(x\,v_{-}^T) - M_{-}(v_{-}x^T)](x\,x^T) +$
$+ M_{-}(x\,v_{-}^T)v_{-}\,x^T - M_{-}(v_{-}x^T)x\,v_{-}^T = \|o_{ij}\|_{i,j=1}^{n} = O$.

Both equations (3.91) and (3.90) are satisfiable identically if the following is valid:

(3.92) $v_{-}x^T = x\,v_{-}^T$, $\tau \in \{\tau_k\}$, k=1,...,m .

From the equation (3.55) the relation $(dx_i/dt)_{-}(x+v_{-})^T = (x+v_{-})(dx_i/dt)_{-}^T$ follows, which at $x_i(\tau_k) \neq 0$, can be written in the following form

(3.93) $(dx_i/dt)_{-} x_j\,(1 + v_{j-}/x_j) = (dx_j/dt)_{-} x_i\,(1 + v_{i-}/x_i)$, i, j=1,..,n.

That equation with respect to condition (3.92) assumes the form

(3.94) $(dx_i/dt)_{-} x_j = (dx_j/dt)_{-} x_i$, $\tau \in \{\tau_k\}$, k=1,...,m.

The validity of the last equation is provided by the corresponding selection of the moments $\{\tau_k\}$, k=1,...m of applying control.

Let us write the equality (3.89) with consideration of (3.94) in the form

(3.95) $(A^v)_- = 1/2(dr/dt)_- r^{-1} = 1/2\, r^{-1} (dr/dt)_-$.

The relation (3.82b) is satisfiable identically if the following relation is true :

(3.96) $\angle_v^2 = \mu_v^2 E \quad , \quad \mu_v^2 \in R^1$.

Taking into account the equalities (3.82a,b), the equation (3,78) acquires the form

(3.97) $A_+ = +-1/2(\angle_v^2 + E)^{-1}\, r^{-1}(dr/dt)_- = +-1/2(\angle_v^2 + E)^{-1}\, (dr/dt)_-\, r^{-1}$,

or can be represented in other form consistent with relation (3.96):

(3.98) $A_+ = +-1/2A(1+\mu_v^2)^{-1} r r^{-1}(dr/dt) = +-1/2(1+\mu_v^2)^{-1}\, (dr/dt) r r^{-1}$.

The values of μ_v^2, μ_v^1 for the controls (3.80) or (3.82) are obtainable from the additional conditions (e.g., μ_v^1 from the condition $x(T) = x_T = \|o_j\|_{i,j=1}^n = O$).

Since the feedback control is applied to the closed system, it is natural to assume the equality $A_+ = (A^v)_-$, which in accordance with (3.94, 98) is fulfilled with $\mu_v^2 = (0,-2)$.

The first part ($\mu_v^2 = 0$) is inconsistent with the application of new controls. Hence the remaining part: $\mu_v^2 = -2$, brings us to resulting equality for synthesis the control

(3.99) $v_+ = -2x(\tau)$,

(3.100) $\delta v = v_+ - v_- = -2x(\tau) - v_-$.

The last equation determines the control jump (a "needle"control's action), as the control applied to the closed system.

The formula of identification of the model operator at the moment τ is

(3.101) $A_+ = (A_+)^T = 1/2(dr/dt)(\tau - o)\, r^{-1}(\tau)$, $(dr/dt)_- = 1/2(dr/dt)(\tau - o)$.

The relations (3.80, 82a,b) coincide when the control $v_- = \|o_j\|_{i,j=1}^n = O$.

Under this condition $A_+ = +-A_- \equiv (A^v)_-$.

At the moments of applying the controls, the initial macro model is renovated, and its operator cannot retain its previous value, i.e., for $\tau_1 = 0$ we have A(+0)=-A(-0). •

Comments 3.5. The relations (3.53-55) determine the values of the discrete controls, under whose action the identification of unknown operator takes place in process of the optimal motion; the time of the identification it the part of optimal process.

This is an essence of the joint process of optimal control and identification [17, 20].

The reduced control presents a projection of the initial control on each of the state macro coordinates; that is fulfilled in case of controllability and identifiability of the object. The initial control, according to equation (1.1.1) (dimension r≤n), is derived a^u=A($x+v$) at the given structure of the drift vector and the corresponding identifiable operator (3.54,44). This control provides also satisfaction of the equality (3.21). The reduced controls in (3.99,100) have a specific meaning for macro systems, because they reflect a mechanism of self-control via the macro coordinates, that are useful for a direct programming and prognosis of the macro movement. •

Comments 3.6 The "needle" control functions

The "needle" controls (3.100) select the macro trajectory pieces where the variational principle, in the form of equality $\tilde{S}(\tilde{x}_t) = extr S(x_t) = S^o$, are violated. The extremal values of $\tilde{S}(\tilde{x},t) = S^o(x,t)$ for all moments $t \le \tau$ are defined by such state variables (x,t) that belong to given set Q^o. At the moments τ +o, after applying the needle controls, the variables $x(\tau$ +o) are leaving this set, being on the border of Q^o at the moment τ. The additive functional $\tilde{\omega}_s^T$ (for $\tilde{S}$ =M[$\tilde{\omega}_s^T$]) is defined on solution of the microlevel stochastic equation at this set. The moment of exiting from the set Q^o is determined via the additive functional by using the equation:

$$\omega_s^T = \begin{Bmatrix} 0, t < \tau + o \\ \infty, t \ge \tau + o \end{Bmatrix}.$$

The corresponding multiplicative functional is

$$q_s^T = \exp(-\omega_s^T) = \begin{Bmatrix} 0, t < \tau + o \\ 1, t \ge \tau + o \end{Bmatrix}$$

and defines the probability density of breaking (cutting) off the process $\tilde{x}_t$.

At the moment of preceding the breaking off, the state vector x is located on the border of Q^o with probability 1, and at the next following moment (when x leaves Q^o), the probability of x belonging to Q^o becomes equal to zero. After discontinuing the needle control, at the moment ($\tau + o + \varepsilon$), the state vector x is returns back to the set Q^o, and the additive functional satisfies the relation $\omega_s^T = \begin{Bmatrix} \infty, t < \tau + o + \varepsilon \\ 1, t \ge \tau + o + \varepsilon \end{Bmatrix}$. On the time interval ($\tau + o, \tau + o + \varepsilon$), the additive functional acquires the form of the δ - function: $\omega_{\tau+o}^{\tau+o+\varepsilon} = \delta(\varepsilon)$.

The corresponding increment of the microlevel entropy is defined on the extended set

$$Q \supset Q^o:\ \Delta\tilde{S}(\varepsilon) = M[\omega_{\tau+o}^{\tau+o+\varepsilon}] = \int_{Q^o} \delta(\omega) P_{\varepsilon,\omega}(d\omega) = \begin{Bmatrix} 0, x \in Q^o \\ 1, x \notin Q^o \end{Bmatrix},$$

at the condition of an uninterrupted probability measure $P_{x,t}$. Therefore, the above entropy makes a jump at applying the needle control. Because the additive functional is continuous, the distribution $P_{x,t}(d\omega)$ exists, and it is also continuous. The moment of jump of the additive functional is a Marcovian moment that corresponds to the moment of reaching the given set and breaking off the initial process. For the Marcovian moment, the probability distributions before and after the jump are independent. Uncoupling the time correlations, we get

$$M[x_i(\tau+o)x_i(\tau+o+\varepsilon)]=M[x_i(\tau+o)]M[x_i(\tau+o+\varepsilon)], \text{ i=1,...,n.}$$

This takes place at the Marcovian moment. The necessity of breaking off the stochastic process follows directly from the condition of keeping this process within the set Q^o, to satisfy both micro- and macro equations. The jump of the micro level entropy starts from entropy $\tilde{S}(\tau-o)$. Because the entropy $S^o(\tau-o)$ takes a minimum on the set Q^o, and the entropy $\tilde{S}(\tau-o)$ has a maximum on Q^o, the increment entropy $\Delta\tilde{S}(\varepsilon)$ decreases the value of $\tilde{S}(\tau-o)$ and increases the value of $S^o(\tau-o)$. A more sufficient comparison of the functions $\tilde{S}(\tau+o)$ and $S^o(\tau+o)$ is not possible because the entropy function is not defined outside of set Q^o. Thus, the needle control brings some negative increment to the macrolevel entropy with respect to microlevel entropy.

Let us show, that the debalance generates the macrovariable defined by the microvariables. At the moments $(\tau, \tau+o+\varepsilon)$, the macrotrajectories x_t are transferring into the microtrajectories $\tilde{x}_t$. At moment t=τ, on the Q^o border, the micro- and macrotrajectories are undistinguished. Taking into account the relations

$$L(\tau)=M_{s,\tilde{x}}[\tilde{L}(\tau)]=H(\tau),$$

$$M[L(\tau)]=M[M_{s,\tilde{x}}[\tilde{L}(\tau)]]=\hat{H}(\tau), \hat{H}(\tau)=\frac{1}{2}Sp(\dot{r}r^{-1}(\tau)),$$

and a similar form for the functions $\tilde{L}(\bullet)$, $L(\bullet)$, we have

$$Sp(\dot{r}r^{-1}(\tau))=Sp(\dot{\tilde{r}}\tilde{r}^{-1}(\tau)),\ r(\tau)=\tilde{r}(\tau)=M_{s,\tilde{x}}[x'(\tau)x'^{T}(\tau)],$$

for $x_i^2(\tau)=r_{ii}(\tau)$, the connection of the micro- and macrovariables follows: :

$$x_i(\tau)=\{\int_{Q^o}p(\tilde{x}'(\tau))(\tilde{x}_i'(\tau))^2(d\tilde{x}'(\tau))\}^{\frac{1}{2}}.$$

They can be determined only for the moments of applying the controls. Because this relation is satisfied on the border of the region Q^o at the moment τ, when $p(\tilde{x}'(\tau))=\delta(\tilde{x}'(\tau))$, the values of the macrovariables $x'(\tau)=\tilde{x}'(\tau)_{|Q^o}$ are limited and defined by the above set of microvariables. The microvariables are associated with the border values for the set of microvariables where both micro- and macroequations satisfy simultaneously. The problem of the macroscopic averaging of random functional has been reduced to the solution of the variation problem for the corresponding nonrandom functional being defined on the border of some region (Q^o). The problem gets solution by breaking off the controlled random process at the moments τ, and by keeping the process within the given set Q^o where the conditions $x'(\tau) = \tilde{x}'(\tau)_{|Q^o}$ are satisfied. •

Let us consider a *simultaneous solution of the problem of the optimum control and identification* of the object, discretely observed at the moments of applying $\tau \in \{\tau_k\}$, k=1,..., m, and transformed by the control (3.55) into the terminal state x_T=0. For the object model in the diagonal form:

$$(3.102)\ dz/dt = \bar{A}(z+\bar{v}),\ \bar{A}=G^{-1}AG,\ G=\|G_{ij}\| \in \angle(R^n),$$

$$\det G \neq 0, \forall t \in \Delta,\ z=Gx,\ \bar{v}=Gv,$$

$$x_T=\|o_i\|^n_{i,j=1} = O \Leftrightarrow z_T=\|o_i\|^n_{i,j=1} = O,\ \bar{v}=-2z(\tau),$$

$$\bar{A}^v = \bar{A}\left(E+\left\|\frac{v_j(\tau,\bullet)}{z_i(t,\bullet)}\delta_{ij}\right\|^n_{i,j=1}\right)=\|\lambda_i(t)\|^n_{i=1},$$

the piecewise matrices are fixed inside the intervals of the control discretization and are identifiable precisely according to equations (3.44, 54) at each discrete interval.

<u>*Theorem* 3.4 (T4)</u>. Transfer system (3.102) to origin of its coordinate system by the controls (3.55), applicable at moments when the equation (3.53) is satisfied, requires the existence of two eigenvalues that at each of the moments satisfy to the equality

$$(3.103)\ \lambda_i^k=\lambda_j^k,\ t\in(\tau_{k-1},\tau_k);\ \lambda_i^k=\lambda_i(t=\tau_{k-1}),\quad i,j=1,\dots,n,\ k=1,\dots,m$$

with the number of the control discretization intervals being equal to n.

Proof. By applying the relation (3.53) to (3.102) with the v-controls from (3.55):

$$(3.104)\ \bar{A}(\tau_k+o)=\bar{A}^v(\tau_k-o)=d\bar{r}/dt(\tau_k-o)(\bar{r}(\tau_k))^{-1};\ A(+0)=-A(-0)=A^v(-0);$$

$$\bar{A}^v(\tau_k-o)=\|\lambda_i(t)\|^n_{i=1},\ k=1,\dots,m,\ \bar{r}_{ii}=M[z_i^2(t,\bullet)],\ \bar{v}=-2z(\tau_{k-1}),$$

we arrive at the equality (3.103), where λ_i^k, λ_i^{k-1} are connected by the recurrent relations $\lambda_i^k=-\lambda_i^{k-1}\exp(\lambda_i^{k-1}\tau_k)(2-\exp(\lambda_i^{k-1}\tau_k))^{-1}$ obtained as a result of substitution of the solutions of (3.102) into (3.104) with the controls from (3.104): $z_i(t,\cdot)=(2-\exp(\lambda_i^{k-1}\tau_k))z_i(\tau_{k-1})$, $t\in(\tau_{k-1},\tau_k)$.

By writing the solution at a last control discretization interval $(\tau_{m-1}, \tau_m), \tau_m = T$:

(3.105) $z_i(T,\bullet) = (2-\exp(\lambda_i^{m-1}T))\, z_i(\tau_{m-1},\cdot) = 0, \quad z_i(\tau_{m-1},\cdot) \neq 0$, i = 1,..,n,

we come to the relation defining T at the preceding equalization of the eigenvalues::

(3.106) $T = \tau_{m-1} + \ln 2/\lambda_i^{m-1}, \quad \lambda_i^{m-1} > 0, \quad \lambda_1^{m-1} = \lambda_2^{m-1} \ldots = \lambda_n^{m-1} > 0.$

At other discretization moments (applying the conditions of the pairwise equalization of (3.104) and (3.106)) we get two chains of the equalities for $n \geq m$:

(3.107)
$$\lambda_1^{m-1} = \lambda_2^{m-1} = \ldots = \lambda_n^{m-1}$$
$$\lambda_1^{m-2} = \lambda_2^{m-2} = \ldots = \lambda_{n-1}^{m-2}$$
$$\ldots\ldots\ldots$$
$$\lambda_1^{m-i-1} = \lambda_2^{m-i-1} = \ldots = \lambda_{n-i}^{m-i-1}$$
$$\ldots\ldots\ldots$$

(3.108) $\lambda_1^1 = \lambda_2^1 = \ldots = \lambda_{n-m+2}^1$,

and for $n \leq m$ accordingly we get the following chain of the equalities:

(3.109)
$$\lambda_1^{m-1} = \lambda_2^{m-1} \ldots = \lambda_n^{m-1}$$
$$\lambda_1^{m-2} = \lambda_2^{m-2} = \ldots = \lambda_{n-1}^{m-2}$$
$$\ldots\ldots\ldots$$
$$\lambda_1^{m-i-1} = \lambda_2^{m-i-1} = \ldots = \lambda_{n-i}^{m-i-1}$$
$$\ldots\ldots\ldots$$
$$\lambda_1^{m-n+1} = \lambda_2^{m-n+1} .$$

The system of the equations (3.107, 109) defines the sought (m-1), (n-1) moments of the controls discretization. From equation (3.107), in a particular, the equation (3.108) follows. It is inconsistent with the condition of pairwise equalization of eigenvalues (3.103) at n>m. The system (3.109) is well defined, it agrees with (3.102), and coincides with (3.107) if the number of its equations is equal to the number of the unknowns, i.e., (3.107,109) have a meaning when n = m. ●

Theorem 3.5 (T5). Execution of the conditions (3.103) leads to indistinguishability in time of the corresponding variables in some coordinate system of states:

(3.110) $$\hat{z}_i = \hat{z}_j\,;\ \hat{z}_i = \hat{G}_{ij}\,\hat{z}_j\,;\ \hat{G}_{ij} = \begin{Vmatrix} \cos\varphi_{ij}, -\sin\varphi_{ij} \\ \sin\varphi_{ij}, \cos\varphi_{ij} \end{Vmatrix},\ \varphi_{ij} = \mathrm{arctg}\left(\frac{z_j(\tau_k) - z_i(\tau_k)}{z_j(\tau_k) + z_i(\tau_k)}\right).$$

To prove this we consider the geometrical meaning of the condition of equalizing of the eigenvalues, as a result of the solutions of the equation (3.102).

Applying the relations (3.53) to the solutions of equation (3.102), we get:

$$(3.111)\quad \frac{dz_i}{z_i dt}=\frac{dz_j}{z_j dt}\ ;\quad z_j(t,\bullet)=\frac{z_j(\tau_k.)}{z_i(\tau_k.)}z_i(t,\bullet),\quad i,j=1,..,n,\ k=1,...,(n-1)$$

where the last equality defines a hyper plane being in parallel to the axis $z_i=0$, $z_j=0$, $i\neq j$, $i,j=1,..,n$. By rotating the system of coordinates $(o\,z_i \dots z_n)$ with respect to that axis, it is found a coordinate system where the equations (3.111) are transformed into the equalities for the state variables $\hat{z}_i$ in the form (3.110).

The corresponding angle of rotation of the coordinate plane $(o\,z_i\ z_j)$ is determined by the relation (3.110). Due to the arbitrariness of k=1,..., (n-1), i, j=1,..,n, the foregoing holds true for any two components of the state vector and for each interval of discretization. By carrying out the sequence of such (n-1) rotations, we come to the system $(o\,\hat{z}_1 \cdots \hat{z}_n)$, where all the state variables are indistinguishable in time. ●

Comments 3.6. If a set of the discretization moments $(\overset{1}{\tau_k}, \overset{i}{\tau_k}, \overset{N_k}{\tau_k})$ exists (for each optimal control v_k) then a unique solution of the optimization problem is reached by choosing a minimal interval $\overset{i}{\tau_k}$ for each v_k that accomplishes the transformation of the system to the origin of coordinate system during a minimal time. The macrovariables are derived as a result of memorizing the states $z_i(\tau_k)$; i,k = 1,..,n in the relations (3.111), which constitutes an attribute of the applied controls equation (3.102).

The transformation $(G\times \hat{G})$ transfers $\{x_i\}$ to new macrovariables $\{\hat{z}_i\}$, whose pairwise indistinguishibility at the successive moments $\{\tau_k\}$ agrees with the reduction of numbers of independent macrocoordinates, referred to as the states consolidation.

The successive equalization of the relative phase speed (3.53), accompanied by memorization of $z_i(\tau_k)$, determines the content of the ordering mechanism [10].

Therefore, the problem of forming a sequentially consolidated macromodel is solved simultaneously in the process of optimal motion combined with identification of the renovated operator. The macromodel is reversible within discretization intervals and is irreversible out of them. According to the extremal properties of the information entropy, the segments of the extremals approximate the stochastic process with a maximum probability, i.e., without losing information about it.

This allows us to get the optimal and nonlinear filtration of the stochastic process within the discretization intervals. ●

Comment 3.7. Solution of the equation of differential constraint (3.18)

Let us consider the equation of the constraint (3.18) in a more general form:

$$\frac{\partial A}{\partial x} + A^T F A = 0 \text{ at } x = \{x_i\}, i = 1,..,n \ , \ A = A(x), A = A^T, F = F(x).$$

Applying matrix A^{-1} on both sides of the equation and using the symmetry of A, we get

$$A^{-1}\frac{\partial A}{\partial x}A^{-1} + F = 0.$$

Applying the chain rule for differentiation to the matrix $A^{-1}A = E$ and then multiplying on the left side by A^{-1} gives us

$$A^{-1}\frac{\partial A}{\partial x}A^{-1} = -\frac{\partial A^{-1}}{\partial x},$$

which after substitution in the previous equation gives $-\dfrac{\partial A^{-1}}{\partial x} + F = 0$.

By the integration the last equation with respect to all x components, we obtain the solution

$$A^{-1} = \int F dx_i + A^{-1}(x_1, \dots, x_{i-1}, 0, x_{i+1}, \dots).$$

In particular, considering the simplified equation for one dimensional x,

$$F = 2E, \ \frac{\partial A}{\partial x} + 2A^T A = 0,$$

where $A^T(x) = A(x) = \begin{bmatrix} a(x), b(x) \\ b(x), c(x) \end{bmatrix}$

and substituting into the previous matrix equation, we get the solution

$$\int F dx = 2xE\begin{bmatrix} 2x, 0 \\ 0, 2x \end{bmatrix}, \qquad A^{-1}(O) = \begin{bmatrix} \dfrac{c}{ac-b^2}, & -\dfrac{b}{ac-b^2} \\ -\dfrac{b}{ac-b^2}, & \dfrac{a}{ac-b^2} \end{bmatrix},$$

$$A = \begin{bmatrix} \dfrac{2x(ac-b^2)+a}{4x^2(ac-b^2)+2x(a+c)+1}, & \dfrac{b}{4x^2(ac-b^2)+2x(a+c)+1} \\ \dfrac{b}{4x^2(ac-b^2)+2x(a+c)+1}, & \dfrac{2x(ac-b^2)+c}{4x^2(ac-b^2)+2x(a+c)+1} \end{bmatrix}.$$

The last solution can be directly applied to the equation (3.18) for

$$A = X = \begin{bmatrix} X_{11}, X_{12} \\ X_{21}, X_{22} \end{bmatrix} = \begin{bmatrix} a(x), b(x) \\ b(x), c(x) \end{bmatrix}, A(0) = X(x=0) = \begin{bmatrix} X_{11}(0), X_{12}(0) \\ X_{21}(0), X_{22}(0) \end{bmatrix}.$$

The above solutions can be equal at the state coordinate points

$$x^* = \left[\frac{a(0) - b(0)}{2(a(0)c(0) - b^2(0))} \right]$$

with the following equalities for the conjugate coordinates determined by x^*:

$$X_{11}(0) \neq X_{12}(0), \quad X_{11}(x^*) = X_{12}(x^*) = X_{21}(x^*) =$$

$$= \frac{b(0)}{4x^{*2}(a(0)c(0) - b^2(0)) + 2x^*(a(0) + c(0)) + 1}.$$

There is also the possibility of the equalization of the solutions

$X_{12}(x) = X_{21}(x)$, $X_{22}(x)$, or all of the solutions $X(x) = X_{ij}(x)$, i,j=1,2 for the initial conjugate coordinates $X_{11}(0) = X_{22}(0) \neq 0, X_{12}(0) \neq 0$.

REFERENCES

1. Gihman I.I., Scorochod A.V. *Theory of Stochastic Processes*, Vol. 3, Moscow: Nauka, 1975.

2. Feynman R. *The character of physical law*, London: Cox and Wyman LTD, 1963.

3. Kac M. (Ed.). *Probability and related topics in physical science*, NY: Inter science Publ., 1957.

4. Fredlin M.I., and Wentzell A.D. *Random Perturbations of Dynamical Systems*, N.Y: Springer-Verlag, 1984.

5. Stratonovich R.L. *Theory of Information*, Moscow: Soviet Radio, 1975.

6. Gelfand I.M., and Fomin S.V. *Calculus of Variations*, N.Y.: Prentice Hall, 1963.

7. Alekseev V.M., Tichomirov V.M., Fomin S.V. *Optimal Control*, Moscow: Nauka, 1979.

8. Durr D., Bach A. "The Onsager-Machlup Function as Lagrangian for the Most Probable Path of Diffusion Process", *Communications in Mathematical Physics*, 1978; 60, 2:153-170.

9. De Groot S.R. (Ed.) *Thermodynamics of Irreversible Processes*, International Physic School "Enrico Fermi", Bologna, 1960.

10. Lerner V.S. Mathematical Foundation of Information Macrodynamics, Journal Systems Analysis-Modeling-Simulation, 1996; 26, 1-4:119-184.

11. Lerner V.S. "Mathematical Foundation of Information Macrodynamics: Dynamic Space Distributed Macromodel", *Journal Systems Analysis-Modeling-Simulation*, 1999; 35: 297-336.

1.2. THE SPACE DISTRIBUTED MACROMODEL

1.2.1. The information macrofunctional and the equations of its extremals

The controlled bi-level model of distributed object contains the distributed random process $\tilde{x}_t(l) = \tilde{x}(\omega'',t,l)$ at the microlevel depending on the nonrandom space parameter $l \in R^\nu$, ν=1, 2, 3.

The process is considered to be a solution to the controlled stochastic equation

(1.1) $d\ \tilde{x}_t(l) = a(\mathrm{t},\tilde{x}_t(l),\ u_t(l))\ dt + \sigma(\mathrm{t},\tilde{x}_t(l))d\ \xi_t,\ \tilde{x}_s = \eta(\omega',l)$,

where $x(\cdot,\cdot,l) \in C^2(R^\nu,R^n)$, $\overline{x}_t(l) = \mathrm{M}'[\tilde{x}_s] = x(\omega',\mathrm{t},l)$; $2b = \sigma\sigma^T$

$\mathrm{M}'[\cdot] = \int_{\Omega'}[\cdot]P'(d\omega')$, $\omega' \in \Omega'$, $a(\mathrm{t},\cdot,\cdot)$, $\sigma(\mathrm{t},\cdot)$, $u(\mathrm{t},x,\cdot)$, $\eta(\omega',\cdot)$,

satisfy the requirements for the concentrated model (1.1.1, 1.2).

It means both the drift (a) (as a regular distributed flow) and the diffusion conductivity of a medium (σ) depend parametrically on the non random the ν-dimensional vector $\overline{l} = \overline{e}l$, that characterize the geometrical coordinates of a point in some selected affine space system. A given microlevel process $\tilde{x}_t^{\,1}(l) = \tilde{x}^1(\omega'',t,l)$ represents a task by analogy with task in the concentrated model. The controlled microlevel process $\tilde{x}_t(l) = \tilde{x}(\omega'',t,l)$ is considered in a derivation of the some programmed process $\tilde{x}_t^{\,1}(l)$, where $l = \{l_1, l_2, l_3\}$.

The functional of corresponding variation problem: $\overline{S} = \int_s^T M'[\tilde{L}]$ dt depends on the space variables. The entropy functional that averages $\overline{S}$ by $\Sigma \subset R^\nu$ is

(1.2) $\overline{S}^l = \int_\Sigma \int_s^T M'[\tilde{L}]dtdv$, $\mathrm{d}v = \mathrm{d}l_1 \mathrm{d}l_2 \mathrm{d}l_3$,

serves as a measure of closeness of the considered random fields ($\tilde{x}_t, \tilde{x}_t^{\,1}$) that model the local interactions. The corresponding proper functional at the macrolevel:

(1.3) $S^l = \int_{G^4} L(x_i(t,l), \partial x_i(t,l)/\partial t)d\overline{v}$, $d\overline{v} = dvdt$,

$$L = 1/2 \sum_{i,j=1}^{n} (2b)_{ij}^{-1}\ \partial x_i(t,l)/\partial t\ \partial x_j(t,l)/\partial t;\ \ x: \Delta \times R^3 \to R^n,\ \Delta \subset R_+^1$$

where G^4 is the four-dimensional space time region of ($\overline{l}$,t), and satisfies the principle of local stability in the field theory [1-2]. The problem is to find the extremals of the functional (1.3). The macromodel obtained as the Euler-Ostrogradsky equation [2] of extremals for the Lagrangian (1.3), has a view

(1.4) $\sum_{j=1}^{n}\{\partial^2 x_i / \partial t^2 (2b)^{-1}{}_{kj} + \partial x_j(t,l) / \partial t[\partial(2b)^{-1}{}_{kj} / \partial t -$

$- 1/2 \sum_{i=1}^{n} \partial(2b)^{-1}{}_{kj} / \partial x_i \, \partial x_i(t,l) / \partial t]\}=0;$

$\partial x_m / \partial t = a_m(\mathrm{t}, x, u)$, $a_m = \mathrm{A}(x + v(\tau, l))$, $\mathrm{A}=\mathrm{A}^T$, m=1,...,n;

$b = b(\mathrm{t}, x)$, b, A: $\Delta \times R^3 \rightarrow \angle(R^n)$; u: $\Delta \times R^3 \rightarrow R^r$, $\tau \in \Delta$, r≤n.

In particular, for the diagonalized matrix model with the Lagrangian

$\mathrm{L}= \sum_{i=1}^{n} (\sigma_{ii}^{-1} \partial x_i / \partial t)^2$, we obtain the equation of extremals in the form

(1.5) $\partial x^2{}_i / \partial t^2 = \sigma_{ii}^{-1} \partial \sigma_{ii} / \partial t \; \partial x_i / \partial t$, i=1,...,n.

1.2.2. The transformation of the space coordinates and the invariant conditions for the proper functional

The space motion in a field is presented by a transformation of coordinates $\bar{l}^o = \{l_k^{\,o}\}$, that are given initially in the immobile system, connected with an observer, and are transformed into the mobile coordinate system $\bar{l} = \{l_k\}$, k=1, 2, 3:

(1.6) $\bar{l} = \bar{A}\,\bar{l}^o + \bar{L}$, $\bar{L} = \bar{L}(\mathrm{t})$,

with an orthogonal matrix of rotation $\bar{A} = \|\bar{a}_{ij}\|_{i,j=1}^{3}$ and a vector $\bar{L} = \{\bar{L}_k\}$, k=1,2,3 reflecting an appropriate shift of the origin of the initial coordinate system. (1.6) represents a continuous, simple, single-parametrical (of t) family of Euclid's space transformations, that allows of changing a scale in each of the space points, and is the most general in the theory of Solid-State Matter. Extremal principle provides an invariance of the proper functional (PF) (1.3) on the family of transformations (1.6), that enables system to preserve the macrodynamic laws in all observed mobile systems at deterministic movements of the object (1.4). The process, defined by Lagrangian (1.3) and the transformation, determines the object's natural space coordinate system. The problem consists of application Noether's theorem [2] for PF, transformed by (1.6), and determination of the parameters of the transformation.

Lemma 1. The invariance conditions for the functional (1.3) at transformation is

(1.7) $Z_0 = \begin{cases} t = t, \\ \bar{l}^o = \bar{A}(t)^{-1}(\bar{l} - \bar{L}) \end{cases}$

and is equivalent to the invariance conditions at transformation

(1.8) $Z_* = \begin{cases} t^* = t^*, t^* = t + \delta t, \\ \bar{l}^o = \bar{A}(t^*)^{-1}(\bar{l}^* - \bar{L}(t^*)) \end{cases}$

Indeed. Let us consider the vector

$$\bar{l}^*(t,\bar{l}^o) = \bar{l}(t+\delta t) = \bar{A}(t+\delta t)\bar{l}^o + \bar{L}(t+\delta t)$$

at fixed t* defined by the space shift $\delta\bar{l}^o$. According to Noether's theorem, for the functional, which is invariant at transformations (1.7), the conservation laws hold true at small deviations of parameter δt. It defines: $Z_* S^l = S^l{}_o = S^l$; $Z_o S^l = S^l{}_*$. From that, we get $S^l{}_o = S^l{}_*$. Besides, for the shift $\delta\bar{l}^o$, that can be observed only in an immobile system, the invariance conditions must be preserved during a time. ●

Theorem 1. The execution of model's equations in the form

(1.9) $\partial x_j / \partial t\,(t, \bar{l}) = -1/2\, \partial x_i / \partial \bar{l} \cdot \bar{Y}$,

(1.10) $\bar{Y} = \{Y_k\}$, $\partial \bar{Y} / \partial t = 0$, k=1,2,3;

$$\bar{Y} = \lim_{\delta t \to 0} = \frac{\bar{l}(t+\delta t) - \bar{l}(t)}{\delta t} = \frac{\partial \bar{l}}{\partial t} = \dot{\bar{A}}(\bar{A})^{-1}(\bar{l} - \bar{L}) + \dot{\bar{L}} ,$$

represents the sufficient condition of invariance of the functional (1.3) at transformation (1.8) for the twice continuous differentiating function $x_i = x_i(t, \bar{l})$ satisfying the equation of exremals (1.4) (with non zero derivatives $\frac{\partial x_i}{\partial t} \neq 0$).

Proof. The functional (1.3) is invariant at transformation (8) if the following equality is true:

$$(1.11)\ \int_{G^4} L(x_i, \partial x_i / \partial t) d\bar{v} + \int_{G^4} L'(\partial x_i / \partial t, \partial x_i / \partial \bar{l}) d\bar{v} =$$

$$= \int_{G^4} L(x_i^o, \partial x_i^o / \partial t) d\bar{v}_o \text{ , L'=0, } d\bar{v} = dvdt \ ,$$

where the states x_i^o, x_i, given accordingly in the immobile and in mobile coordinate systems, are connected by the relations (with a symbol of scalar multiplication<>)

(1.12) $x_i^o = x_i(t, \bar{A}\,\bar{l}^o + \bar{L})$,

$$(1.13)\ \partial x_i^o / \partial t = \partial x_i / \partial t\,(t, \bar{A}\,\bar{l}^o + \bar{L}) + <\partial x_i / \partial \bar{l}, \partial \bar{l} / \partial t> =$$

$$= \partial x_i / \partial t\,(t, \bar{A}\,\bar{l}^o + \bar{L}) + <\partial x_i / \partial \bar{l},\ \dot{\bar{A}}(\bar{A})^{-1}(\bar{l} - \bar{L}) + \dot{\bar{L}}>.$$

The last equation follows directly from considering below the gradient form of the equation, determined in the coordinate systems, connected by transformation (1.8):

$$\partial x_i / \partial l_j = \sum_{k=1}^{3} \partial x_i / \partial l_k^o \bar{a}_{kj},\ \|\bar{a}_{kj}\| = \bar{A}^{-1};\ \text{k,j=1,2,3};\ grad x_i = \bar{A} grad^o x_i .$$

From this equation, at the execution of $\bar{A}^{-1} = \bar{A}^T$, we obtain

$$(1.14) <\partial x_i / \partial \bar{l}, \partial \bar{l} / \partial t> = <\bar{A} grad\, x_i^o, \partial \bar{l} / \partial t> = (\partial x_i / \partial t)^T \partial \bar{l} / \partial t =$$

$$= (\bar{A} grad^o x_i)^T \partial \bar{l} / \partial t = (\partial x_i / \partial \bar{l}^o)^T \bar{A}^T \partial \bar{l} / \partial t = (\partial x_i / \partial \bar{l}^o)^T \bar{A}^{-1} \partial \bar{l} / \partial t .$$

The condition (1.11) after substituting (1.12,13) leads to the relation for Lagrangian

$$(1.15)\ L' = 1/2 \sum_{i,j=1}^{n} (2b)_{ij}^{-1} \{<\partial x_j / \partial \bar{l}, \dot{\bar{A}}(\bar{A})^{-1}(\bar{l} - \bar{L}) + \dot{\bar{L}}> \times$$

$$\times <[\partial x_i \ / \ \partial t + 1/2 < \partial x_i \ / \ \partial \bar{l} \, , \dot{\bar{A}}(\bar{A})^{-1}(\bar{l} - \bar{L}) + \dot{\bar{L}} > +$$

$$+ < \partial x_i \ / \ \partial \bar{l} \, , \dot{\bar{A}}(\bar{A})^{-1}(\bar{l} - \bar{L}) + \dot{\bar{L}} > [\partial x_i \ / \ \partial t + 1/2 < \partial x_i \ / \ \partial \bar{l} \, ,$$

$$\dot{\bar{A}}(\bar{A})^{-1}(\bar{l} - \bar{L}) + \dot{\bar{L}} >]\} = 0,$$

which is executed if one of the following equations is true :

$$(1.16)\ \partial x_i \ / \ \partial \bar{l} + < (\partial x_i \ / \ \partial \bar{l} \,)^{T} , (\dot{\bar{A}}(\bar{A})^{-1}(\bar{l} - \bar{L}) + \dot{\bar{L}}) > = 0,$$

$$(1.17)\ < (\partial x_i \ / \ \partial \bar{l} \,)^{T} , (\dot{\bar{A}}(\bar{A})^{-1}(\bar{l} - \bar{L}) + \dot{\bar{L}}) > = 0.$$

At $\dfrac{\partial x_i}{\partial t} \neq 0$, only equation (1.16) is left. Besides (1.16), the sufficient condition of the functional (1.3) invariance represents the equality for first variation: $\delta S^l = 0$, that at the variable domain of integration G^4 for $\delta S^l = \delta S_1^l + \delta S_2^l$ has a view:

$$(1.18)\ \delta S_1^l = \int_{G^4} (\sum_{i=1}^{n} [\frac{\partial L}{\partial x_i} - \sum_{k=1}^{4} \frac{\partial}{\partial l_k} (\frac{\partial L}{\partial (\partial x_i \ / \ \partial l_k)}] \bar{\delta} x_i) d\bar{v} \ ,$$

$$\bar{\delta} x_i = \delta \ x_i - \sum_{k=1}^{4} \frac{\partial x_i}{\partial l_k} y_k \, ,$$

$$\delta S_2^l = \int_{G^4} \sum_{i,k=1}^{n,4} [\frac{\partial}{\partial l_k} (\frac{\partial L}{\partial (\partial x_i \ / \ \partial l_k)} \bar{\delta} x_i) + \frac{\partial (L y_k)}{\partial l_k}] d\bar{v} \, , \quad \bar{y}_o = \{ y_k \}, \ k=1,..,4,$$

where the last component in δS_2^l, that represents the integral of divergence, can be reduced to integral at the border of the domain G^4. The parametrs y_k according to [2] are defined by the transformation of the coordinate system (1.8).

After decomposition (1.8) in Maclaurin's series we have

$$\bar{l}(t + \delta t) \cong \bar{l}(t) + \delta t [\dot{\bar{A}}(\bar{A})^{-1}(\bar{l} - \bar{L}) + \dot{\bar{L}}] \, .$$

From this equation follows the equality for the auxiliary function

$$(1.19)\ \bar{y} = \lim_{\delta t \to 0} \frac{\bar{l}(t + \delta t) - \bar{l}(t)}{\delta t} = \frac{\partial \bar{l}}{\partial t} = \dot{\bar{A}}(\bar{A})^{-1}(\bar{l} - \bar{L}) + \dot{\bar{L}} \, , \quad y_4 = 1 \, .$$

The condition $\delta S_1^l = 0$ defines the equation of extremal (1.4), (1.5).

The remained equation is $\delta S_2^l = 0$ from which (at an arbitrary G^4) the relation follows:

$$\sum_{k=1}^{4} \frac{\partial}{\partial l_k} (\sum_{i=1}^{n} \frac{\partial L}{\partial (\partial x_i \ / \ \partial l_k)} (- \sum_{k=1}^{3} \frac{\partial x_i}{\partial l_k} y_k)) + \sum_{k=1}^{4} \frac{\partial (L y_k)}{\partial l_k} = 0, \ i=1,\dots,n.$$

Because L does not depend on $\dfrac{\partial x_i}{\partial l_k}$, k=1,2,3, we arrive at the equation

(1.20) $$\frac{\partial}{\partial t}\left(\sum_{i=1}^{n}\frac{\partial L}{\partial(\partial x_i/\partial t)}\left(-\sum_{k=1}^{4}\frac{\partial x_i}{\partial l_k}y_k\right)\right)+\sum_{k=1}^{4}\frac{\partial(Ly_k)}{\partial l_k}=0.$$

From that, taking into account the relations

(1.21) $$\frac{\partial L}{\partial(\partial x_i/\partial t)}=X_i^l \quad ,\frac{\partial L}{\partial x_i}=\frac{\partial X_i^l}{\partial t} \quad ,$$

we have

(1.22) $$\frac{\partial}{\partial t}\left(\sum_{k=1}^{4}X_i^l\left(-\sum_{k=1}^{3}\frac{\partial x_i}{\partial l_k}y_k\right)\right)=\sum_{i=1}^{n}\left[\frac{\partial X_i^l}{\partial t}\left(-\sum_{k=1}^{4}\frac{\partial x_i}{\partial l_k}y_k\right)+\right.$$

$$\left.+X_i^l\left(-\sum_{k=1}^{3}\frac{\partial^2 x_i}{\partial l_k\partial t}y_k\right)+X_i^l\left(-\sum_{k=1}^{4}\frac{\partial x_i}{\partial l_k}\frac{\partial y_k}{\partial t}\right)\right];$$

(1.23) $$\frac{\partial L}{\partial l_k}=\sum_{i=1}^{n}\left(\frac{\partial L}{\partial x_i}\frac{\partial x_i}{\partial l_k}+\frac{\partial L}{\partial(\partial x_i/\partial t)}\frac{\partial^2 x_i}{\partial l_k\partial t}\right)=\sum_{i=1}^{n}\left(\frac{\partial X_i^l}{\partial t}\frac{\partial x_i}{\partial l_k}+X_i^l\frac{\partial^2 x_i}{\partial l_k\partial t}\right)$$

(1.24) $$\sum_{k=1}^{4}\frac{\partial(Ly_k)}{\partial l_k}=<gradL,\bar{y}>\sum_{i=1}^{n}\left(\frac{\partial X_i^l}{\partial t}\left(\sum_{k=1}^{4}\frac{\partial x_i}{\partial l_k}y_k\right)+X_i^l\left(\sum_{k=1}^{4}\frac{\partial^2 x_i}{\partial l_k\partial t}y_k\right)\right).$$

After substituting equations (1.22-24) into condition (1.20) we obtain

(1.25) $$\sum_{i=1}^{n}\left[\frac{\partial X_i^l}{\partial t}\left(-\sum_{k=1}^{4}\frac{\partial x_i}{\partial l_k}y_k\right)+X_i^l\left(-\sum_{k=1}^{4}\frac{\partial^2 x_i}{\partial l_k\partial t}y_k\right)+X_i^l\left(-\sum_{k=1}^{4}\frac{\partial x_i}{\partial l_k}\frac{\partial y_k}{\partial t}\right)+\right.$$

$$\left.+\frac{\partial X_i^l}{\partial t}\left(\sum_{k=1}^{4}\frac{\partial x_i}{\partial l_k}y_k\right)+X_i^l\left(\sum_{k=1}^{4}\frac{\partial^2 x_i}{\partial l_k\partial t}y_k\right)\right]+L\,div\bar{y}=0;$$

$$\bar{y}=(y_1,y_2,y_3),\quad div\bar{y}_o=div\bar{y}.$$

For the twice differentiating function $x_i=x_i(t,\bar{l})$ of the arguments $(t,\bar{l})$ on $\Delta\times R^3$, the relation:

(1.26) $$\frac{\partial^2 x_i}{\partial l_k\partial t}=\frac{\partial^2 x_i}{\partial t\partial l_k};\quad i=1,\dots,n,\ k=1,2,3,4$$

is correct. Then equality (1.25) leads to the equation

$$\sum_{i=1}^{n}X_i^l\left(-\sum_{k=1}^{4}\frac{\partial x_i}{\partial l_k}\frac{\partial y_k}{\partial t}\right)+L\,div\bar{y}=0,$$

from which at $L=1/2\sum_{i=1}^{n}(\sigma_{ii}^{-1}\partial x_i/\partial t)^2=1/2\sum_{i=1}^{n}X_i^l\frac{\partial x_i}{\partial t}$ we arrive at

(1.27) $$\sum_{i=1}^{n}X_i^l\left[\left(-\sum_{k=1}^{4}\frac{\partial x_i}{\partial l_k}\frac{\partial y_k}{\partial t}\right)+1/2\,div\bar{y}\,\frac{\partial x_i}{\partial t}\right]=0.$$

Because the matrix $\dot{\bar{A}}(\bar{A})^{-1}=C$ is a skew-symmetric, it is fulfilled $div\bar{y}=0$. The remaining equation is

$$(1.28)\ \sum_{i=1}^{n} X_i^l \left(-\sum_{k=1}^{4} \frac{\partial x_i}{\partial l_k}\frac{\partial y_k}{\partial t}\right)=0,$$

which is executed at the condition

$$(1.29)\ \partial\bar{y} / \partial t = \partial(y_1, y_{2,} y_3) / \partial t = 0 .$$

The last result is also true for the general Lagrangian form (1.3), because the equations (1.17,21) are satisfied for functional (1.3). If a functional is invariant, then the first of its variation turns to zero automatically on the extremals. Because of that, the equation (1.28) must be satisfied. This is an additional requirement for the execution of (1.29) .The identical execution of (1.28) by means of condition (1.29) (that is fulfilled by an appropriate choice of the functions $\bar{A} = \bar{A}(t), \bar{L} = \bar{L}(t)$), corresponds to the condition of the conservation for the informational laws.

Considering the fulfillment of the Noether theorem at an arbitrary (nonextremal) surface, we may write the first variation of functional (1.18) in the form

$$\delta S^l = \int_{G^4}\{\sum_{i=1}^{n}(\frac{\partial L}{\partial x_i}\bar{\delta} x_i + \sum_{k=1}^{4}\frac{\partial L}{\partial(\partial x_i / \partial l_k)}\frac{\partial}{\partial l_k}\bar{\delta} x_i) + \sum_{k=1}^{4}\frac{\partial(Ly_k)}{\partial l_k}\}d\bar{v} =$$

$$\int_{G^4}\{\sum_{i=1}^{n}(\frac{\partial L}{\partial x_i}\bar{\delta} x_i + \frac{\partial L}{\partial(\partial x_i / \partial l_k)}\frac{\partial}{\partial t}(-\sum_{k=1}^{4}\frac{\partial x_i}{\partial l_k}y_k))+\sum_{k=1}^{4}\frac{\partial(Ly_k)}{\partial l_k}\}d\bar{v}\ ;$$

$$\bar{\delta} x_i = (-\sum_{k=1}^{4}\frac{\partial x_i}{\partial l_k}y_k).$$

At the condition of arbitrariness of the integrating domain, we obtain

$$(1.30)\ \sum_{i=1}^{n}(\frac{\partial L}{\partial x_i} + \frac{\partial L}{\partial(\partial x_i / \partial l_k)}\frac{\partial}{\partial t}(-\sum_{k=1}^{4}\frac{\partial x_i}{\partial l_k}y_k))+\sum_{k=1}^{4}\frac{\partial(Ly_k)}{\partial l_k}=0.$$

The last component of equation (1.30) can be reduced to the form

$$(1.31)\ \sum_{k=1}^{4}\frac{\partial(Ly_k)}{\partial l_k} = < gradL, \bar{y} > + Ldiv\bar{y} = < gradL, \bar{y} > =$$

$$=2\sum_{i=1}^{n}\frac{\partial x_i}{\partial t}\sigma_{ii}^{-3}(\sum_{k=1}^{4}\frac{\partial^2 x_i}{\partial t\partial l_k}y_k\sigma_{ii} - \sum_{k=1}^{4}\frac{\partial x_i}{\partial l_k}y_k\frac{\partial\sigma_{ii}}{\partial t}).$$

By substituting equations (1.21,31) into the equation (1.30) we get the relation

$$(1.32)\ \sum_{i=1}^{n}2[(-\frac{\partial x_i}{\partial t}\sigma_{ii}^{-3}\frac{\partial\sigma_{ii}}{\partial t})(-\sum_{k=1}^{4}\frac{\partial x_i}{\partial l_k}y_k)+2\frac{\partial x_i}{\partial t}\sigma_{ii}^{-2}\frac{\partial}{\partial t}(-\sum_{k=1}^{4}\frac{\partial x_i}{\partial l_k}y_k)]+$$

$$+\sum_{i=1}^{n}2\frac{\partial x_i}{\partial t}\sigma_{ii}^{-3}(\sum_{k=1}^{4}\frac{\partial^2 x_i}{\partial t\partial l_k}y_k\sigma_{ii} - \sum_{k=1}^{4}\frac{\partial x_i}{\partial l_k}y_k\frac{\partial\sigma_{ii}}{\partial t})=$$

$$=\sum_{i=1}^{n}2\frac{\partial x_i}{\partial t}\sigma_{ii}^{-3}[\sum_{k=1}^{4}(\frac{\partial x_i}{\partial l_k}y_k\frac{\partial\sigma_{ii}}{\partial t} - \frac{\partial^2 x_i}{\partial t\partial l_k}y_k\sigma_{ii} - \frac{\partial x_i}{\partial l_k}\frac{\partial y_k}{\partial t}\sigma_{ii} + \frac{\partial^2 x_i}{\partial t\partial l_k}y_k\sigma_{ii} -$$

$$-\frac{\partial x_i}{\partial l_k}\frac{\partial\sigma_{ii}}{\partial t})]=0.$$

From whence taking into account relation (1.26), we arrive at equation

$$\sum_{i=1}^{n} 2\frac{\partial x_i}{\partial t}\sigma_{ii}^{-2}\left(\sum_{k=1}^{4} -\frac{\partial x_i}{\partial l_k}\frac{\partial y_k}{\partial t}\right)=\sum_{i=1}^{n} X_i^l\left(\sum_{k=1}^{4} -\frac{\partial x_i}{\partial l_k}\frac{\partial y_k}{\partial t}\right)=0,$$

that coincides with the considered equation (1.28).

This means the identity $\frac{\partial y_k}{\partial t} \equiv 0$ is executed, and the condition (1.29) is satisfied.

Therefore, if the functional is invariant, its first variation turns to zero by the transformation that executes the condition (1.29). ●

Corollary 1. The sufficient condition of the functional invariance is the execution of the equation (1.16), i.e., it requires the fulfillment of the equation

$$(1.33)\quad \sum_{k=1}^{4}\frac{\partial x_i}{\partial l_k} y_k = -\frac{\partial x_i}{\partial t};\ i=1,2,\ldots,n.$$

Indeed. By substituting the equations (1.33) and (1.21,31) into (1.30) we obtain

$$\sum_{i=1}^{n}\left[\left(-2\frac{\partial x_i}{\partial t}\sigma_{ii}^{-3}\frac{\partial \sigma_{ii}}{\partial t}\right)\frac{\partial x_i}{\partial t}+2\frac{\partial x_i}{\partial t}\sigma_{ii}^{-2}\frac{\partial^2 x_i}{\partial t^2}\right]+$$

$$+\sum_{i=1}^{n}2\frac{\partial x_i}{\partial t}\sigma_{ii}^{-3}\left(\sum_{k=1}^{4}\frac{\partial^2 x_i}{\partial t\partial l_k}y_k\sigma_{ii}+\frac{\partial x_i}{\partial t}\frac{\partial \sigma_{ii}}{\partial t}\right)=$$

$$=\sum_{i=1}^{n}2\frac{\partial x_i}{\partial t}\sigma_{ii}^{-3}\left(\frac{\partial^2 x_i}{\partial t^2}\sigma_{ii}+\sum_{k=1}^{4}\frac{\partial^2 x_i}{\partial t\partial l_k}y_k\sigma_{ii}\right)=0;$$

$$(1.34)\quad \sum_{i=1}^{n}2\frac{\partial x_i}{\partial t}\sigma_{ii}^{-2}\left(\frac{\partial^2 x_i}{\partial t^2}+\frac{\partial}{\partial t}\left(\sum_{k=1}^{4}\frac{\partial x_i}{\partial l_k}y_k\right)-\right.$$

$$\left.-\sum_{k=1}^{4}\frac{\partial x_i}{\partial l_k}\frac{\partial y_k}{\partial t}\right)=\sum_{i=1}^{n}2\frac{\partial x_i}{\partial t}\sigma_{ii}^{-2}\left(\frac{\partial^2 x_i}{\partial t^2}-\frac{\partial^2 x_i}{\partial t^2}-\sum_{k=1}^{4}\frac{\partial x_i}{\partial l_k}y_k\right)=$$

$$=\sum_{i=1}^{n}2\frac{\partial x_i}{\partial t}\sigma_{ii}^{-2}\left(-\sum_{k=1}^{3}\frac{\partial x_i}{\partial l_k}\frac{\partial y_k}{\partial t}\right)=\sum_{i=1}^{n}X_i^l\left(-\sum_{k=1}^{3}\frac{\partial x_i}{\partial l_k}\frac{\partial y_k}{\partial t}\right)=0.$$

Thus, the relation (1.29) has been obtained without using condition (1.26) and the extremal equations. It is the result of execution (1.33), that guarantees the zero equality for the first variation of the functional . But from this fact it is not possible to obtain directly the sought transformation (1.7).

Only after transforming the first variation into the form (1.33), does it become clear that the identical equalization of this variation to zero must be executed by the fulfillment relation (1.29), which is a consequence of the initial variation principle.

Moreover, the result (1.29) represents a condition of the constant space velocity in an arbitrary coordinate system. ●

The equations (1.9,10) we consider as the differential constraints, imposed on the field equations by the variation principle.

1.2.3. The parameters of the space transformation

We will use the equation (1.10) for determinaing the parameters of the space coordinates transformation at the following conditions

(1.35) $\overline{y}=\overline{y}(t,\overline{l})=\dot{\overline{A}}(\overline{A})^{-1}(\overline{l}-\overline{L})+\dot{\overline{L}}=C(\overline{l}-\overline{L})+\dot{\overline{L}}$;

$\frac{\partial \overline{y}}{\partial t}=\dot{C}(\overline{l}-\overline{L})+C\dot{\overline{L}}+\ddot{\overline{L}}+0.$

The last equality has to be true identically at any $\overline{l}$.
From whence the equation for the angular rotation follows:

(1.36) $\dot{C}(t)=0$, $C=\|C_{ij}\|$, C_{ij}=Const, $i\neq j, C_{ij}=-C_{ji}$; $C_{jj}=0$,

and the equality (1.35) is divided on two equations:

(1.37) $\dot{\overline{A}}(\overline{A})^{-1}=C$, $\dot{\overline{A}}=C\overline{A}$; $C=1/2(C-C^{T})$; $C^{T}=\|C_{ji}\|$;

(1.38) $\ddot{\overline{L}}-C\dot{\overline{L}}=0$; $\ddot{\overline{L}}=C\dot{\overline{L}}$,
where C is the angular constant of the speed rotation.
By integrating (1.37) we obtain the equation for the space coordinate transformation
(1.39) $\overline{A}(t)=\exp[(t-t_o)C]\overline{A}(t_o)$, t_o=s.

For the considered plan movement with the transformation matrix:

$$\overline{A}=\begin{Vmatrix}\cos\phi,\sin\phi\\ -\sin\phi,\cos\phi\end{Vmatrix};\ \overline{A}^{-1}=A^{T},$$

the equality (1.37) is executed at the fulfillment of the equations:

(1.40) $$\frac{d\phi}{dt}\begin{Vmatrix}-\sin\phi,\cos\phi\\ -\cos\phi,-\sin\phi\end{Vmatrix}\begin{Vmatrix}\cos\phi,-\sin\phi\\ \sin\phi,\cos\phi\end{Vmatrix}=C;\ \frac{d\phi}{dt}=\text{Const}.$$

Thus, (1.40) is the necessary and sufficient condition for fulfillment (1.36) at the plan movement. From whence, taking into account the requirement

$$\overline{y}=\frac{d\overline{l}}{dt}=\frac{\partial\overline{y}}{\partial t}\frac{d\phi}{dt}=C,\ \overline{l}=\overline{l}((\phi(t)),$$

we arrive at the condition

(1.41) $$\frac{\partial\overline{l}}{\partial\phi}=\text{Const}.$$

Fulfillent of this condition is not enough for the general case of space movement. Equation (1.38) admits reducing the order, it is represented by the solution of system of regular differential equations with constant coefficients at given initial conditions:

(1.42) $\dot{R}=CR$; $\dot{\overline{L}}=R$; $\overline{L}(t_o)=\overline{L}_o$; $\dot{\overline{L}}(t_o)=R_o$.

1.2.4. Equations of the distributed systems and their identification

The fulfillment of the extremal principle leads to the following equations

(1.43) $\frac{\partial x}{\partial t}=-1/2<\frac{\partial x}{\partial\overline{l}},(\dot{\overline{A}}(\overline{A})^{-1}(\overline{l}-\overline{L})+\dot{\overline{L}})>=0$, $\dot{\overline{A}}(\overline{A})^{-1}=C$,

$\ddot{\overline{L}}-C\dot{\overline{L}}=0$, $C=1/2(C-C^{T})$.

The joint consideration of the equations for extremals (1.4) and differential constraint (1.16) leads to the following forms of the distributed macromodels.

By substituting equation (1.33) into equality (1.5), we arrive at the model

$$(1.44)\ \sigma_{ii}\frac{\partial^2 x_i}{\partial t^2}+1/2(\sum_{k=1}^{3}\frac{\partial x_i}{\partial l_k}y_k)\frac{\partial \sigma_{ii}}{\partial t}=0;\ i=1,\dots,n.$$

After differentiating the equality (1.33), we come to the equation

$$(1.45)\ 2\frac{\partial^2 x_i}{\partial t^2}+\sum_{k=1}^{3}\frac{\partial^2 x_i}{\partial l_k \partial t}+\sum_{k=1}^{3}\frac{\partial x_i}{\partial l_k}\frac{\partial y_k}{\partial t}=0;$$

$$\frac{\partial^2 x_i}{\partial t^2}=-1/2\sum_{k=1}^{3}\frac{\partial^2 x_i}{\partial l_k \partial t}y_k;i=1,\dots,n.$$

By substituting the last one into (1.5), we have $\frac{\partial \sigma_{ii}}{\partial t}\frac{\partial x_i}{\partial t}+1/2\,\sigma_{ii}\sum_{k=1}^{3}\frac{\partial^2 x_i}{\partial l_k \partial t}y_k=0$

And finally, after substituting equation (1.33) into (1.45), we obtain the model

$$(1.46)\ \sum_{k=1}^{3}(\frac{\partial^2 x_i}{\partial l_k \partial t}\sigma_{ii}-\frac{\partial x_i}{\partial l_k}\frac{\partial \sigma_{ii}}{\partial t})y_k=0;\quad \frac{\partial x_i}{\partial l_k}\frac{\partial \sigma_{ii}}{\sigma_{ii}\partial t}=\frac{\partial(\partial x_i/\partial t)}{\partial l_k};\ y_k\neq 0.$$

The controllable distributed macromodel with the reduced controls v is

$$(1.47)\ \frac{\partial x}{\partial t}=A(t,\bar{l})(x+v);\ C\frac{\partial x}{\partial l}=A(t,\bar{l})(x+v),$$

and can be represented also in the form (as the right side of (1.47)):

$$\sum_{j=1}^{n}A_{ij}(x_j+v_j)=\sum_{k,m}^{3}\sum_{v=1}^{3}(\frac{\partial x_j}{\partial l_v}\bar{A}_{vk}^{-1}\bar{A}_{km}^{-1}(\bar{A}\dot{\bar{l}}^{o})_m+\dot{L}_m(t))\ .$$

If each of phase vector's component x performs a single-dimension movement in the direction of the space axis $l_i=l$, then (1.47) acquires the diagonal form

$$(1.48)\ \frac{\partial x}{\partial t}=\lambda\,(x+v);\ c\frac{\partial x}{\partial l}=\lambda\,(x+v);$$

$$x=x(t,l),\ v=v_s(l)=-2x(s,l),\ \lambda=\lambda\,(t,l).$$

Within this system, the parameter $\lambda=\lambda\,(t,l)$, that defines the matrix A, is identified by an analogy with the concentrated model:

$$(1.49)\ \lambda\,(t,l)=cM[\frac{\partial x}{\partial l}(x+v)^T]r_v^{-1};\ r_v=M[(x+v)(x+v)^T],$$

$$\lambda_i=1/2r_{vi}r_{vi}^{-1}=\dot{\sigma}_{ii}\sigma_{ii}^{-1}\ .$$

The jumps of the model's control and operator are

(1.50) $\delta v=v(\tau+o,l)-v(\tau-o,l)$, $\delta A=A(\tau+o,l)-A(\tau-o,l)$,

and also the set $\tau=\bigcup_k \tau_k\subset\Delta$ is determined from the Erdman-Weierstrass conditions [2]. As a result, we obtain the optimal control, particularly in the form

(1.51) $v(\tau+o,l)=-2x(\tau+o,l)$

and the following equation for the matrix renovation:

(1.52) $A(\tau+o,l)=1/2\frac{\partial r}{\partial t}(\tau\text{-}o,l)r^{-1}(\tau,l),\ r(\tau,l)=M[x+v)(x+v+)^T]$

at the moments of equalization of the relative phase speeds of the state vector:

(1.53) $\frac{\partial z_i}{\partial t}(\tau-o,l)\ z_i^{-1}(\tau,l)=\frac{\partial z_j}{\partial t}(\tau-o,l)\ z_j^{-1}(\tau,l),\ z=Gx,$

$G:\Delta\times R^3\rightarrow\angle(R^n)$.

The relation (1.53) identifies the points of the control application and the matrix A renovation.

The Lagrangian, in a more general case than (1.2), admits the representation

$$L=\sum_{i,j=1}^{n}B_{ij}\hat{y}_i\hat{y}_j*\text{-}1/2\sum_{i=1}^{n}(x_i*\frac{\partial x_i}{\partial t}\text{-}x_i\frac{\partial x_i}{\partial t}*),$$

$$\hat{y}_i=\sum_{k=1}^{3}G_{ik}\frac{\partial x_i}{\partial l_k},\ \hat{y}_i*=\sum_{k=1}^{3}G_{ik}*\frac{\partial x_i}{\partial l_k}*,$$

where the vector $\hat{y}$ is proportional to gradient of the state vector, and it is analogous with a general force [3] and the conjugate vector X.

The corresponding Euler-Ostrogradsky equations lead to the equation of extremals for the main $(x,\hat{y})$ and the conjugate variables $(x*,\hat{y}*)$ in the above equations:

(1.54) $\frac{\partial x_i}{\partial t}=\sum_{j=1}^{n}B_{ij}(\sum_{k,m=1}^{3}G_{jm}G_{ik}*\frac{\partial^2 x_j}{\partial l_m\partial l_k}),\ i=1,\dots,n.$

In a particular, at the conditions

$G_{jm}=g_jG_m,\quad G_{ik}*=g_i*G_k,\quad G_kG_m=G_{km}=\delta_{km},\ k,m=1,2,3,$

the equations of the extremals acquire a view

(1.55) $\frac{\partial x_i}{\partial t}=\sum_{j=1}^{n}D_{ij}\sum_{m=1}^{3}\frac{\partial^2 x_j}{\partial l_m^2};\ i,j=1,\dots,n,\ \|D_{ij}\|_{i,j=1}^{n}=D;\ D_{ij}=B_{ij}g_ig_i*.$

This last equation leads to the matrix diffusion equation in the form

(1.56) $\frac{\partial x}{\partial t}=D\Delta\ x$

with the generalized diffusion matrix D and the Laplace operator $\Delta=\nabla^2$.

The macromodel in the form of the nonequilibrium thermodynamic equation follows from (1.55), using the definition of the generalized flow [3]: $I=\frac{\partial x}{\partial t}$.

From equation (1.54) we get the connection between the flows and forces $\bar{X}$:

(1.57) $I_i=\sum_{j=1}^{n}\bar{l}_{ij}\bar{X}_j,\ \bar{l}_{ij}=B_{ij}g_i;\ \bar{X}_i=g_i\sum_{m=1}^{3}\frac{\partial^2 x_j}{\partial l_m^2}.$

The equation of extremals takes the nonequilibrium thermodynamic form

$$\frac{\partial x}{\partial t}=2b\,\overline{X}^{l}\;;\;\overline{X}^{l}=\frac{\partial\Delta\overline{S}^{l}}{\partial\nabla x},\quad \nabla x=\text{grad}\,x\;,$$

and follows directly from the entropy form of the macrofunctional for the local homogenous fields: $\Delta\overline{S}^{l}=1/2\nabla x^{T}g\nabla x$.

The macromodels of the distributed systems described by the integral equations

$$(1.58)\quad \frac{\partial x_i}{\partial t}(t,l)=\sum_{j=1}^{n}\int_{\tilde v}\hat{l}_{ij}(l,\tilde{l},t)\overline{X}_i(\tilde{l},t)d\tilde{l}\;,$$

depend on the kinetic operator $\hat{l}\,(l,\tilde{l},t)=1/2\dfrac{\partial\hat{r}}{\partial t}(l,\tilde{l},t)$ that is identifiable by the correlation vector- function $\hat{r}$ of the initial random field.

The optimization problem is formulated as a maximum condition for the Hamiltonian

$$H=\int_{v}\frac{\partial x}{\partial t}(t,\bar{l})^{*}\,X(t,\bar{l})\,d\bar{l}\,.$$

For the space distributed system, the generalized flow I=a^{u} depends on the gradients $a^{u}=g_{o}\dfrac{\partial x}{\partial l}$; $g_o=g_o(x,t,v)$. At this case, the random field is averaged with respect to some piecewise space curves, defined from equation (1.1), with the shift-vector depending on the generalized flow. Among those curves, the variational principle is able to select the extremals of the proper functional.

For the proper functional and its Lagrangian in the form:

$$S=\iint L\,dt\,dl\;;\;L=1/2\,(a^{u})^{T}(2b)^{-1}a^{u}\;-$$

$$-\,1/2(\frac{\partial x}{\partial t}^{T}r_{v}^{-1}(x+v)+(x+v)^{T}\,r_{v}^{-1}\frac{\partial x}{\partial t});\;\; l=(l\text{x},\,l\text{y},l\text{z})\,,$$

the Euler-Ostrogradsky equation has a view:

$$\frac{\partial L}{\partial x^{*}}-\frac{\partial}{\partial t}\frac{\partial L}{\partial\dot{x}_{t}}-\frac{\partial}{\partial l}\frac{\partial L}{\partial\dot{x}_{l}}=$$

$$=1/2[r_{v}^{-1}\frac{\partial x}{\partial t}+\frac{\partial}{\partial t}(r_{v}^{-1}(x+v))-(2b^{-1})\frac{\partial}{\partial l}(g_{o}\frac{\partial x}{\partial l})]=0,$$

from which the equation of extremals follows:

$$1/2r_{v}^{-1}\frac{\partial x}{\partial t}+1/2r_{v}^{-1}\frac{\partial x}{\partial t}+1/2\frac{\partial}{\partial t}(r_{v}^{-1}(x+v))=1/2(2b^{-1})g_{o}\frac{\partial^{2}x}{\partial l^{2}}\,,$$

$$r_{v}^{-1}\frac{\partial x}{\partial t}+1/2(x+v)^{T}\frac{\partial}{\partial t}(r_{v}^{-1})=1/2(2b^{-1})g_{o}\frac{\partial^{2}x}{\partial l^{2}}^{T}\,.$$

We receive the controlled diffusion form of macroequation, identified by microlevel

$$\frac{\partial x}{\partial t}=1/2r_{v}\,(2b)^{-1}g_{o}\frac{\partial^{2}x}{\partial l^{2}}+\frac{\partial r_{v}}{\partial t}r_{v}^{-1}(x+v)^{T});r=M\{(x+v)(x+v)^{T}\};$$

$g_o = r\, r_v^{-1}(x+v)$; $g_o = M\{\frac{\partial x}{\partial t}(x+v)^T\} \times [M\{\frac{\partial x}{\partial l}(x+v)^T\}]^{-1}$, $M = M_{t',x}$,

which represents a known form of the diffusion equation:

$$\frac{\partial x}{\partial t} = f(t, b(t)) \frac{\partial^2 x}{\partial l^2} + f'(t)(x+v) ,$$

with the controls v(τ,l) and the relations for identification the functions:

$$f = 1/2 r_v (2b)^{-1} g_o ; f' = 1/2 \frac{\partial r_v}{\partial t} r_v^{-1},\ g_o(t) = r_1 (r_1^l)^{-1},\ r_1^l = M\{\frac{\partial x}{\partial l}(x+v)^T\}.$$

The considered macro dynamic models have these common peculiarities:

- the natural connection with the random microlevel processes
- the unity of the macrodescription and identification
- the formulation and solution of a particular control problem by a general form of proper functional (that is concretized for specific object).

The choice of the concrete macromodel depends on specific characteristics of the identified object, the particular task, and the methodology of the model application as well. The identified macroequations, that reflect the informational regularities of complex systems (represented by the variational principle) are more substantial than approximatiing of the observed processes by a prior chosen class of operators.

1.2.5. The macromodel singular points and the singular trajectories

For the considered concentrated and distributed macromodels, the analysis of existence and the uniqueness of singular points or the singular trajectories represents the principal and sufficient interest. The equation for a pair equalization of the relative phase speeds at each discrete point t' for the concentrated model :

$$(5.1)\ \lambda_{it} = \frac{dx_i}{x_i dt}(t'-0) = \frac{dx_k}{x_k dt}(t'-0) = \lambda_{kt},\ \text{or}\ \lambda_{it}\lambda_{it}^* = \lambda_{kt}\lambda_{kt}^*$$

leads to singularities of the dynamic operator, that follows from [4].

We will show that the dynamics and geometry at each of the singular points of the spatial macromodel are bound.

Such analysis is provided for the model of the pair interacted distributed subsystems in a basic form of independable equations in partial derivations of the first order, with phase variable (x_1, x_2), spatial coordinate (l), and time (t) :

(5.2) $A_i\, \partial x_i / \partial t = B_i\, \partial x_i / \partial l + V_i$; i=1, 2 ,

where $A_i = A_i(t, l, x_i)$, $B_i = B_i(t, l, x_i)$ are the coeficients, and $V_i = V_i$ (t, l, x_i), are the controls. Initial conditions are given by the distributions:

(5.3) $x_i\ (l, t_o) = x_i\ (l, t = t_o)$, or $x_i\ (l_o, t) = x_i(t, l = l_o)$.

The equations (5.2-3) characterize a reflection of some region of plane (t,l) on the region of space (S,x_i). The peculiarities and class of the surface are completely defined by specific equations of the reflection. At a known solution of the problem according to equations (5.2-3), the surface can be defined in the parametric form

(5.4) S=S(x_i(t, l)).

The singular point of the second order on the considered surface is determined by the matrix condition:

(5.5) rank $\left| \frac{\partial x_i / \partial t, \partial S / \partial t}{\partial x_i / \partial l, \partial S / \partial l} \right| \neq 2$, i=1, 2

which corresponds to the identical turning to zero of all minors (Mi, i=1,2,3) of the second order (of above matrix). By introducing the radius-vector

R= $x_1\, e_1 + x_2\, e_2 +$ S e_3

where e_i (i=1,2,3) are the orths of the basic vectors $\bar{e}$ and Rt= $\partial R / \partial t$, Rl= $\partial R / \partial l$ are the corresponding derivatives,
we come to the equation (5.4) in form of the condition
(5.6) [Rt × Rl]=0.
The equation of the normal to the surface (5.4) has a view [5]:

(5.7) $\vec{n} = \frac{\det|x_i|}{\det|t,l|}$ where $\vec{n} = \frac{\vec{N}}{N}$ is the orth of the normal $\vec{N}$.

Because Rt , Rl are the tangent vectors to the coordinate lines, the execution of the relation (5.5) or (5.6) is equivalent to the condition of non existence of the normal (5.7) at the given singular points. Since a normal to surface is determined independently on a method of the surface parametrization, we come to the following conditions of existence of considering singular points:

(5.8) $\vec{N} = \sum_{i=1}^{3} M_i e_i$ =0; M_i=0, i=1,2,3;

$$M_1 = \det \begin{vmatrix} \partial x_1 / \partial t, \partial x_2 / \partial t \\ \partial x_1 / \partial l, \partial x_2 / \partial l \end{vmatrix} = J = \frac{\det|x_i|}{\det|t,l|} = 0,\ M_i = \det \begin{vmatrix} \partial x_i / \partial t, \partial S / \partial t \\ \partial x_i / \partial l, \partial S / \partial l \end{vmatrix},$$

that corresponds to the degeneracy of the Jacobean J. This leads to a strong connection of geometrical coordinates (l, $\bar{e}$) with the state vector dynamics (x_i(t)).

It is known that for system (5.2) in the diagonalized form (with $|\lambda_i(t)|, |\lambda_i(l)|$ as the corresponding eigenvalues) the following equalities are executed :
(5.9) $(|\lambda_i(t)|^{-1})\partial x_i / \partial t = (|\lambda_i(l)|^{-1}) \cdot \partial x_i / \partial l + V_i(\mathrm{t}, l)$.
It is possible to build such a system of ordinary differential equations in a symmetrical form:
(5.10) $dt / (\lambda_i(t)|^{-1}) = - dl / (|\lambda_i(l)|^{-1}) = d\, x_i / d\, V_i$ i=1, 2,
that its common integral: $\Phi^i = \Phi^i(\phi_1^i, \phi_2^i)$=0 together with the first integrals:

$$\phi_1^i = \int \lambda_i(l)\, dl + \int \lambda_i(t) dt ; \phi_2^i = x_i + \int \lambda_i(l) V dl$$

will be the solutions of the equations (5.9, 10).
The concrete form of the common integral is defined by (5.3) and (5.9,10):

(5.11) $\Phi = \phi_2 - \int \lambda(l)[f(\phi)]V[f(\phi)]\partial f / \partial \phi \} d\phi + x(t_0, l)[f(\phi)]$

where $\phi = \phi_1 - \int \lambda(\tau) d\tau = \int \lambda\ (l) dl + \int \lambda(t)\, dt - \int \lambda\ (\tau) d\tau$, and f is the root of the equation $f = l(\phi_1(\tau), \tau)$ solved for l and fixed $t=\tau$:

(5.12) $\int \lambda(l) dl = \phi_1(\tau) - \int \lambda(\tau) d\tau$, $\phi_1(\tau) = \phi_1|_{t=\tau}$.

The special solution of equation (5.8) has the view

(5.13) $x = -\int \lambda(l) V dl + \int \lambda(l)[f(\phi))] V[f(\phi))] \partial f / \partial \phi \} d\phi + x(\text{to}, l)[f(\phi)]$.

At these conditions, the corresponding partial derivations have a view

(5.14) $\partial x_i / \partial t = -\int \lambda_i(l) \partial V_i / \partial t dl + \Phi_i \lambda_i(t)$,

(5.15) $\partial x_i / \partial l = -\lambda_i(l) V_i + \Phi_i \lambda_i(l)$;

(5.16) $\Phi_i = [\partial x_i(t_o, l) / \partial f_i(\phi_i) + \lambda_i(l) V_i(\phi_i)] \partial f_i / \partial \phi_i$

By imposing the condition (5.8) on (5.14-16), we come for (x_1, x_2) to the equation:

$$(\int \lambda_1(l) \partial V_1 / \partial t dl - \lambda_1(t)\Phi_1)(\lambda_2(l) V_2 - \Phi_2 \lambda_2(l)) =$$

$$(\int \lambda_2(l) \partial V_2 / \partial t dl - \lambda_2(t)\Phi_2)(\lambda_1(l) V_1 - \Phi_1 \lambda_1(l)),$$

which is executed if $\lambda_1(l)=0$, or $\lambda_2(l)=0$,

and at different combinations of the following pairs of the relations:

(5.17) $V_1 = \Phi_1$, or $V_2 = \Phi_2$, $(\int \lambda_1(l) \partial V_1 / \partial t dl - \lambda_1(t)\Phi_1)=0$,

or

$(\int \lambda_2(l) \partial V_2 / \partial t dl - \lambda_2(t)\Phi_2)=0$, where the last ones are correct for

(5.18) $\lambda_1(t) \neq 0$; $\lambda_2(t) \neq 0$, or in a particular, at $\lambda_1(t)=0$, $\Phi_1=0$, $\partial V_1 / \partial t=0$; or at $\lambda_2(t)=0$; $\Phi_2=0$; $\partial V_2 / \partial t=0$, or at

(5.19) $$\frac{\int \lambda_1(l) \partial V_1 / \partial t dl - \lambda_1(t)\Phi_1}{\lambda_1(l)(V_1 - \Phi_1)} = \frac{\int \lambda_2(l) \partial V_2 / \partial t dl - \lambda_2(t)\Phi_2}{\lambda_2(l)(V_2 - \Phi_2)} = \text{Ko}.$$

This means the invariant Ko (that is not dependable on indexes in (5.19)) exists on the solutions of the system of i-equations; Ko could also take the constant value for some of the pairs of the indexes. Therefore, the singular points, defined by the conditions (5.5) and (5.17-18) do exist, and they are not singles.

The geometrical place of the singular points can be represented by isolated states of the system (5.2), as well as by singular trajectories. The invariant Ko corresponds to the equalization of the local subsystems speeds at transferring via a singular curve. The condition (5.19) (as an analogy of the invariant form of (5.1) for distributed model) defines the singular curve, created by the process interaction. At the singular points, the rank of the expended matrix is decreased, and the eigenvectors of dynamic operator and the space orths of basic vectors (in space) become orthogonal (as it follows from (5.6-8)). At the singular points, the state consolidation takes place. The alteration of the space coordinates can be expressed by a function of dynamic variable, as it is defined by the function (5.4), and it follows from the condition of invariance (5.19) at the discrete points (t_1, t_2): $l(t_1) = T(x(t_1)))$; $l(t_2) = T(x(t_2))$.

If we will not consider some trivial cases, then our conditions lead to the equations: $\partial x_i / \partial t = \partial x_i / \partial l = 0$, or in a particular to $\partial x_1 / \partial t = \partial x_1 / \partial l = 0$, $\partial x_1 / \partial t = \partial x_2 / \partial l = 0$, $\partial x_2 / \partial t = \partial x_1 / \partial l = 0$, and $\frac{\det|x_i|}{\det|t,l|} = 0$. The relation

$\Phi_i = \partial f_i(\phi_i) / \partial \phi_i + [\partial x_i(t_o, l)(f_i) / \partial f_i + \lambda_i(l)(f_i)V(f_i)] = V_i$

along the singular trajectory, in particular at the fulfillment of the condition

$\lambda_i(t) = \text{const}; \phi_i = \lambda_i(t)t + \lambda_i(l)l - \lambda(\tau)\tau;\ f_1 = \phi_i(\lambda_i(l))^{-1} =$

$= l + (\lambda_i(t) / \lambda_i(l))(t - \tau)$, $\partial f_i / \partial \phi_i = (\lambda_i(l))^{-1}$ is satisfied if

$\partial x_i(t = t_0) / \partial f_i = \partial x_i(t = t_0) / \partial l|_{l = f_i} = \lambda_i(l)(V_i(t,l) - V_i(t, f_i))$.

This condition binds $l = l(x)$ and $\lambda_i(t) / \lambda_i(l)$, or the geometrical coordinates and eigenvectors, and also connects the current controls with the initial distribution (5.3). Therefore, the singular points and the trajectories carry out the additional information about the connection between geometry, dynamics, and controls.

1.2.6. The macromodel's space movement directed toward the state consolidation

The essence of the problem

The nondistinguished states in the concentrated system could be formed at the discrete moments within the optimal control process. The identicalness of these states we call *state consolidation.* The discrete moments are identifiable by the condition of the relative phase speeds equalization, which is responsible for the consolidation (as an equivalence of the pair's eigenvalues), only if the macro model is reduced to the diagonal form. The successful equalization of the eigenvalues represents an essential part of the optimal movement toward a given terminal state.

Let us consider the possible solution of the consolidation problem during the model space movement. The most general is the distributed macromodel, moving in the space with a constant speed and transforming the coordinates according to equation (1.6). The space speed and the initial matrix of transformation should be given from the additional to the problem requirements (1.42). It is natural to consider the relations that lead toward the diagonalization of the controlled macromodel matrix at the discrete moments, as the additional conditions that redefine the VP optimization problem. The consolidated states enable to form the model's macrolevel if they can be selected, memorized, and stored at the fixed space points. According to that, the space distributed macromodel (1.43) we subordinate into the state consolidation problem: to find such a geometrical locality in R^3 space where some of the macrodistributions are nondistinguished:

(6.1) $\hat{z}_i(t, \bar{l}) = \hat{z}_j(t, \bar{l})$.

That means the states are selected at the discrete moments with equal relative speeds:

(6. 2) $\frac{\partial z_i}{\partial t}(\tau - o, \bar{l}) z_i^{-1}(\tau, \bar{l}) = \frac{\partial z_j}{\partial t}(\tau - o, \bar{l}) z_j^{-1}(\tau, \bar{l})$

and are assumed to be transformed into the nondistinguished states. The considered space movement is directed toward the geometrical joining of the nondistinguished phase states, that leads to their consolidation and identicalness, which decreases the macro model dimension. The integrated model is formed by the successive joining of the equations with the equalized states (6.1), and their memorizing at the discrete control points in the process of the space movement. That movement is able of ordering the macromodel and reducing the number of the independent distributions by forming the cooperative hierarchical structures. The changes of the space vector create the specific geometrical constraints that govern the inner peculiarities of the distributed model. These peculiarities are not only the results of mathematical transformations, but represent important characteristics of real macrosystems that are able to change their geometry toward optimizing of the proper functional.

The consolidation leads to reducing the number of components of the positive defined Lagrangian (1.3). At other equal conditions, it decreases the numerical value of the proper functional and the corresponding entropy functional at the microlevel. The consolidation can be considered as an *additional mechanism* for the functional minimization that integrates the initial minimax principle to the principle minimum of uncertainty (PM), responsible for the informational space and time cooperations. The regularities of the process are defined by the movement along the extremals of the proper functional, and by the macrobehavior directed toward the state consolidation.

The considered modeling problem consists of the execution of the space movement with such a matrix $\overline{A}=\overline{A}$ (t) that provides the transformation T=T(t) to the matrix **A**=A(t,·), changing it into the diagonal form:

(6.3) $T^{-1}\mathbf{A}\cdot T=\Lambda$; $\Lambda = |\Lambda_i|, \Lambda_i = |\lambda^i_j|$, i=1,.., n, .

To execute that, it is necessary to connect the transformation T=T(t) with the matrix of rotation $\overline{A}$, which defines the parameters C and L according to (1.37,42).

Diagonalization of Dynamic Operator by the Space Transformation

The controled model (1.47) can be written in the form

(6.4) $\dfrac{\partial x}{\partial t}=\mathbf{A}\,x$, $x{:}\,\Delta\times R^3\rightarrow R^n$, $t\in\Delta\subset R^1{+}$, $\bar{l}\in R^3$,

$\mathbf{A}=\mathbf{A}(t,v)$; $v{:}\ \Delta\times R^3\rightarrow R^n$.

<u>*Theorem* 2.</u> Let us have the macromodel (6.4) with the vector variables x, defined in the moving 3×n-dimensional spatial systems of coordinates $\bar{l}=\bar{e}^i_j l^i_j$, i=1,..., n; j=1,2,3, that are built on eigenvectors of the 3n×3n dimensional matrix A(t,·), and let us exist the transformation of this matrix to diagonal form (6.3) with the eigenvalues{λ^i_j}, the eigenvectors $z=\{\bar{z}^i_j\}$, so it is **fulfilled** the realtion:

(6.5) $x(\bar{l})$=T(t)· $z(\bar{l}\,*)$; $\bar{l}\,*=\{\bar{l}^*_{ik}\}$, i=1,.., n; j=1,2,3,

in the spatial coordinate system $\bar{l}\,*=\bar{e}^{*i}_j l^{*i}_j$,

where the vector of the states $z=\{z_i)\}$ is defined with the matrix Λ . **Then**

1). the 3n×3n dimensional matrix of rotation of 3n spatial coordinates: G=$|g^i|$, i=1, ... , n with the 9th-dimensional matrix of rotation g^i, that is defined by the transformation T:

(6.6) $G=T;\ \frac{dG}{dt}\cdot G^{-1}=\mathrm{inv}(t)$,

and satisfies the condition of invariance of the proper functional;

2. at the transformation of each of the n-dimensional local spatial coordinate: $\bar{l}^i = g^i \bar{l}^{*i}$, the condition of invariance of the proper functional acquires the form

$$\frac{dg^i}{dt}(g^i)^{-1} = c_i = \mathrm{inv}(t, i),\ c_j = c_i = \ldots = c(t,i,j),\ |c_j| = C,\ i,j=1,..,n$$

with the execution of the following equations

(6.7) $\frac{dx_i}{x_i}(\tau_i) = \frac{dx_j}{x_j}(\tau_i),\ \frac{dx_i}{dt} = a_i x_i,\ a_i = |a_i^k|,\ i=1,\ldots,n,\ k=1,2,3$

at each discretization moment $\{\tau_i\}$.

Proof. 1) For the state vector z, considering in some mobile coordinate system $\bar{l}^*$, the following equations, that satisfy the extremal principle for the proper functional, hold true:

(6.8) $\frac{\partial z}{\partial t} = \Lambda z,\ \frac{\partial z}{\partial t} = \bar{l}^* \mathrm{Cgrad}^* z,\ \Lambda z = \bar{l}^* \mathrm{Cgrad}^* z$.

The analogous equations hold true for the state vector x, defined in the other mobile coordinate system $\bar{l}$ by the relations:

(6.9) $\frac{\partial x}{\partial t} = \bar{l}\ \mathrm{Cgrad}\, x,\ \frac{\partial x}{\partial t} = \mathbf{A} x,\ \mathbf{A} x = \bar{l}\ \mathrm{Cgrad}\, x$.

Let us transform the last equation into the form (6.8), with the matrix $C = \frac{dG}{dt}\cdot G^{-1}$ holding constant at transformation (6.3), which preserves the proper functional. Using the transformation (6.3), we have

(6.10) $T^{-1}\mathbf{A}T z T = G\bar{l}^* \mathrm{C\,grad}^* z T G^T,\ \Lambda z = T^{-1} G\, \bar{l}^* \mathrm{Cgrad}^* z\, T G^T$.

The equations (3.10,3) are identical at the execution of $T^{-1}G = TG^T$. At this condition, the matrix T is equal to the orthogonal matrix of rotation, for which it is true that $G^{-1} = G^T$. The last equality must be also fulfilled for T:$T^{-1} = T^T$. ●

2) Considering the diagonalization of the matrix $\mathbf{A}$ by using of the n-blocks matrix of rotation G of the n-local coordinate systems, we arrive at the relations

$$(g^i)^{-1} a_i g^i = \Lambda_i,\ g^i (g^i)^{-1} a_i g^i (g^i)^{-1} (g^i)^{-1} = g^i \Lambda_i (g^i)^{-1} = \Lambda_i,$$

$c_i a_i (c_i)^{-1} = \Lambda_i,\ c_j a_j (c_j)^{-1} = \Lambda_j$, i,j=1,...,n , that are connected at the discrete moments $\{\tau_i\}$by the equations $\Lambda_j(\tau_i) = \Lambda_i(\tau_i),\ a_j(\tau_i) = a_i(\tau_i)$, i,j=1,...,n.

From that, the equality follows $c_j = c_i = \ldots = c(t,i,j)$, which is responsible for the independent on time equalization of all local invariants for each of the n-mobile coordinate systems. ●

Therefore, all matrixes $|a_i|$ can be diagonalized by using the single constant matrix C, that corresponds to the equal matrixes of rotation for all n- coordinate systems.
Corollary 2 . **If** matrix **A** is represented by the n-blocks of the 3×3 dimensional normal, the pair-commutative real matrixes $\overline{a}_j^i$, i=1,...,n, j=1,2,3, for each of the state variables{ x_i }, defined in their three-dimensional geometrical coordinate system $\overline{l}_j^i = \overline{e}_j^i l^i$, and the matrixes ($\overline{a}_j^i$, $\overline{a}_j^{i-1}$) are the pair-commutative, forming the Abel's group [6], **then** matrix **A** is transformed to the canonical form

$$\text{(6.11)}\ \mathbf{K} = K_i,\quad K_i = \begin{Vmatrix} 1,0,0 \\ 0,\cos\varphi_i,\sin\varphi_i \\ 0,-\sin\varphi_i,\cos\varphi_i \end{Vmatrix},\ i=1,\dots,n$$

with the eigenvalues represented in the form

$$\text{(6.12)}\ \Lambda_i = \begin{Vmatrix} 1,0,0 \\ 0,\exp(j\varphi_i),0 \\ 0,0,\exp(-j\varphi_i) \end{Vmatrix},\ \lambda_1^i=1;\ \lambda_{2,3}^i=\exp(+-j\varphi_i),$$

by using the single real transformation To, that brings each matrix $\overline{a}_j^i$, j=1, 2, 3 to the canonical form:

$$\text{(6.13)}\ \text{To}^{-1}\cdot\overline{a}_j^i\cdot\text{To}=K_i,$$

and it determines the matrix of rotation G^o =To which is common for all of the three-dimensional system of coordinates.

Proof. Because the normal real matrixes $\overline{a}_j^i$, i=1,...,n, j=1, 2, 3 , are commutative, they can be reduced to the diagonal form (6.12) by using a single common Unitarian transformation (6.12) into (6.11) [6]. Each of the block-matrix $a_i=\|a_j^i\|$ characterizes the space coordinates of each of the states { x_i } in the three-dimensional orthonormal coordinate system of the Euclid space. According to this, the $a_i=\|a_j^i\|$ is the orthogonal matrix with the determinant equal to 1. The characteristic equation for this matrix has the component equal to 1 as the multiplicator of the equation's roots. Because the characteristic equation has the real coefficients, only two options are possible: one root is equal to 1, and other two roots are equal $\exp(+-j\varphi_i)$, or both other roots are equal -1. The second option is a partial case of the first one, at $\varphi_i = \pi$. For that, according to the Theorem 2, we get transformation To=G^o with G^o as the matrix of rotation, determined by the transformation To. ●

Comments. The eigenvectors of the matrix K_i: $\overline{z}_i^\lambda = (\overline{z}_i^1, \overline{z}_i^2, \overline{z}_i^3)$ we consider in its own three-dimensional space coordinate system, that is defined by the matrix G^o (t), and it is rotated independently. The starting $9n^2$-dimensional matrix **A** contains the 2n-complex conjugate eigenvalues $\lambda^{i}_{2,3} = \cos\varphi_{io} + -\sin\varphi_{io}$.

The equalization of the matrix eigenvalues K_i is performed by the rotation of conjugate eigenvectors $(\bar{z}_i^2, \bar{z}_i^3)$ of each of the triple $\bar{z}_i^{\lambda} = (\bar{z}_i^1, \bar{z}_i^2, \bar{z}_i^3)$, on the angle $+ - \varphi_{i1}(\tau_1^i)$ respectively to the axis of the eigenvector $\bar{z}_i^1$, that corresponds to the eigenvalue λ_1^i=1. The moments of time, $\tau_i = t_1^i$, i=1,...,n, are defined by the condition of disappearance of the imaginary part in each of the conjugate eigenvalues: $\mathrm{Im}\,\lambda^{i}_{2,3}(t_1^i) = \beta^{i}_{2,3}(t_1^i) = 0$,i=1,..,n, following from (3.7).

At the moments t_1^i , the matrix (3.11) transforms each triple to the form $K_i(t_1^i) = K_i^o = \cos\varphi_{ij}\mathrm{E}$; the matrix A($t_1^i$) reduces the rank from 3n to n, and it is characterized by the n real eigenvalues $\alpha_i(t_1^i) = \alpha_{i1} = \cos\varphi_{i1}$, i=1,...,n (that define the dimension of the nonsingular matrix A(t_1^i)). •

The space movement in direction of i-th eigenvector is described by the equation

$$(6.14) \quad \frac{\partial z_i}{\partial t} = -1/2\, y_i \frac{\partial z_i}{\partial l_i},$$

where y_i is the constant speed of rotation of the i-th coordinate system, l_i is the scalar space coordinate, measuring in direction of the vector $\bar{z}_i^{\lambda}$, that is defined in this i-th coordinate system. The solution of the differential equation

$$(6.15) \quad \frac{\partial z_i}{\partial t} = \lambda_t^i z_i \ , \quad \lambda_t^i = \lambda_o^i \exp(\lambda_o^i t)(2-\exp(\lambda_o^i t))^{-1}; \quad \lambda_t^i = \alpha_t^i + -\beta_t^i,$$

(considered in the direction of each of the i-th eigenvalue),which defines the moments $\{t_1^i\}$that take non less, than n numerical values (for different eigenvalues $\{\lambda_o^i\}$, i=1,...,n); that characterize the successive time intervals of reducing the number of the nonequal **A**-eigenvectors (from 3n to n). The subsequent decreasing of their numbers occurs as the result of the equalization of the real eigenvalues $\{\alpha_i(t_1^i)\}$, forming the n^2-dimensional nonsingular matrix A(t_1^i), i.e., at the following discrete intervals: t_2^i, t_3^i. In the process of the eigenvector's indicalness, the space movement (3.14), considered at the ranged moments of time $\{t_1^i, t_2^i, t_3^i, ...,\}$, transfers successively from one eigenvalue to other, and the movement is characterized by the transformation of rotation that preserves the proper functional.

At this transformation, the equality y_i = Const holds true within any of the rotating local space coordinate systems. In particular, the matrixes of rotation around an arbitrary and fixed axis are commutative.

The commutativeness is also fulfilled at the multiplication of the matrix of rotation and some transformation of symmetry with respect to the origin of the coordinate system. Both cases are essential for modellng of crystallite structures.

Example. Let the pair-commuting matrixes have a form $\bar{a}^i_j = \begin{Vmatrix} v^i_{11}, v^i_{12}, v^i_{13} \\ v^i_{21}, v^i_{22}, v^i_{23} \\ v^i_{31}, v^i_{32}, v^i_{33} \end{Vmatrix}$, i=1,...,n

with the determinant and the module of all eigenvectors equal to 1, moreover, $\lambda^i_1=1$ and $\lambda^i_{2,3}=\exp(+-j\varphi_{io})$. The matrix $\bar{a}^i_j$ has the real eigenvectors $\bar{z}^i_1 = (\bar{z}^i_{11}, \bar{z}^i_{12}, \bar{z}^i_{13})$ corresponding to the eigenvalue $\lambda_1=1$; and the complex conjugated eigenvectors $\bar{z}^i_2 = (\bar{z}^i_{21}, \bar{z}^i_{22}, \bar{z}^i_{23})$, $\bar{z}^i_3 = (\bar{z}^i_{31}, \bar{z}^i_{32}, \bar{z}^i_{33})$, corresponding to the eigenvalues $\lambda^i_{2,3} = \cos\varphi_{io} + -\sin\varphi_{io}$. The $\bar{z}^i_1$-components, that define the direction of rotation of the axis with the angle φ_{io}, are connected by the relations $\bar{z}^i_1 = \bar{z}^i_{11}:\bar{z}^i_{12}:\bar{z}^i_{13} = (v^i_{23} - v^i_{32}):(v^i_{31} - v^i_{13}):(v^i_{12} - v^i_{21})$. The value of the angle φ_{io} follows from the equality $\varphi_{io}=\arccos(1/2(Sp\bar{a}^i_j - 1))$, and the coordinates of the eigenvectors $(\bar{z}^i_2, \bar{z}^i_3)$ are found from the equations $\bar{a}^i_j \bar{z}^i_2 = \exp(j\varphi_{io})\bar{z}^i_2$ and $\bar{a}^i_j = \exp(-j\varphi_{io})\bar{z}^i_3$.

The unitary matrix $U = \begin{Vmatrix} 1,0,0 \\ 0, 2^{-1/2}, j2^{-1/2} \\ 0, 2^{-1/2}, -j2^{-1/2} \end{Vmatrix}$

transfers each of the diagonal matrixes (3.12) to the canonical form (3.11).

The real matrix To, that transfers the initial matrix $\bar{a}^i_j$ to the canonical form, is determined by multiplication of two unitary matrixes UUo, i .e., it is the orthogonal matrix with columns, equal to the real components of the eigenvectors: To=$\| \bar{z}^i_1, (\bar{z}^i_2 + \bar{z}^i_3)2^{-1/2}, (\bar{z}^i_2 - \bar{z}^i_3) j2^{-1/2} \| = \| \bar{z}^i_{10}, \bar{z}^i_{20}, \bar{z}^i_{30} \|$.

In particular, for the orthogonal real matrix

$\bar{a}^{11}_{13} = \begin{Vmatrix} -2^{-1/2}, -3^{-1/2}, -6^{-1/2} \\ 0, 3^{-1/2}, -2 \bullet 6^{-1/2} \\ 2^{-1/2}, -3^{-1/2}, -2 \bullet 6^{-1/2} \end{Vmatrix}$, $\det\bar{a}^{11}_{13}=1$, $Sp\bar{a}^{11}_{13}=-0.538$, $\cos\varphi_{io}=-0.769$,

$\sin\varphi_{io}=0.639$, $\lambda^1_{1,2}=-0.769+-j0.639$, $\varphi_{io}=-0.69+-2\pi N$, N=0,1,... we find the components of the eigenvectors: $z^1_{11}=0.414$, $z^1_{11}=0.414$, $z^1_{12}=-1.932$, $z^1_{13}=1$;

$z^1_{21}=(-0.148-j1.543)2^{-1/2}$, $z^1_{22}=(0.698-j0.33)2^{-1/2}$, $z^1_{23}=1$;

$z^1_{31}=(-0.148+j1.543)2^{-1/2}$, $z^1_{32}=(0.698+j0.33)2^{-1/2}$, $z^1_{33}=1$;

and sought the orthogonal matrix of the transformation:

$$(6.16)\ T_o = \begin{Vmatrix} 0.414, -0.148, -1.548 \\ -1.932, 0.698, -0.33 \\ 1, 2^{-1/2}, 0 \end{Vmatrix},\ T_o^{\,o} = \begin{Vmatrix} 0.187, -0.0934, -0.978 \\ -0.873, 0.440, -0.209 \\ 0.459, 0.895, 0 \end{Vmatrix}.$$

The columns of (3.16) as the coordinates of the vectors $\{\bar{z}^i_{jo}\}$, j=1,2,3, determine the space coordinate system;where $T_o^{\,o}$ is the unitary matrix corresponding to T_o. The orthogonality of T_o can be checked directly as well as the unitarity of $T_o^{\,o}$.

The others matrixes $\{\bar{a}^i_2, \bar{a}^i_3\}$ are reduced by the same transformation to the form

$$K_2 = \begin{Vmatrix} 1, 0, 0 \\ 0, \cos\varphi_{2o}, \sin\varphi_{2o} \\ 0, -\sin\varphi_{2o}, \cos\varphi_{2o} \end{Vmatrix},\ K_3 = \begin{Vmatrix} 1, 0, 0 \\ 0, \cos\varphi_{3o}, \sin\varphi_{3o} \\ 0, -\sin\varphi_{3o}, \cos\varphi_{3o} \end{Vmatrix}.$$

Assuming $\varphi_{2o} = 1.2, \varphi_{3o} = 1.05, \cos\varphi_{2o} = 0.355, \sin\varphi_{2o} = 0.93$, $\sin\varphi_{3o} = 0.866, \cos\varphi_{3o} = 0.5$, we consider the equal and mobile space coordinate systems with the matrixes K_1, K_2, K_3, defined in each of them accordingly.

The transformation from the initial coordinate system (where the matrixes $\bar{a}^i_j$ and the vectors $\bar{z}^i_{jo}$ are defined) into the coordinate system, which is built on the vectors $\bar{z}^i_{jo}$ (where the matrixes K_i are determined), corresponds to the space rotation of the initial coordinate system until it will coincide with the vectors' $\bar{z}^i_{jo}$ directions.

At the rotation of the mobile coordinate system on the angle ($-\varphi_{io}$) (with respect to the eigenvector $\bar{z}^i_1$ that corresponds to the eigenvalue λ^i_1=1), two of its axis's will coincide with the direction of the eigenvectors, $\bar{z}^i_2$ and $\bar{z}^i_3$, that correspond to the eigenvalues $\lambda^i_{2,3} = \cos\varphi_{io} + -\sin\varphi_{io}$; and the matrix K_i is transformed into $K_{io} = E$. The space movement, considered along the direction of the above vectors, is described by considered equations (6.14,15).

The consolidation of this process consists of the pair equalization of the eigenvalues, starting with the complex conjugated pairs: $\lambda^i_2(t^i_1) = \lambda^i_3(t^i_1)$.

At the discrete moments t^i_1, the imaginary components of the eigenvalues turn to zeros that correspond to execution of the equation

$$(6.17)\ \operatorname{Re}\lambda_i(t^i_1) = \operatorname{Re}\lambda_{i+1}(t^i_1) = \alpha_{i1},\ \operatorname{Im}\lambda_i(t^i_1) = \operatorname{Im}\lambda_{i+1}(t^i_1)$$

and to rotating of the mobile coordinate system on the angle $\varphi_{i1} = \arccos\alpha_{i1}$.

Because of the disappearance of the imaginary component of $\bar{z}^i_{23}(t^i_1)$, the rotation on the angle $-\varphi_{io} + \varphi_{i1} = \Delta\varphi_{i1}$ has to be finalized up to the moment t^i_1.

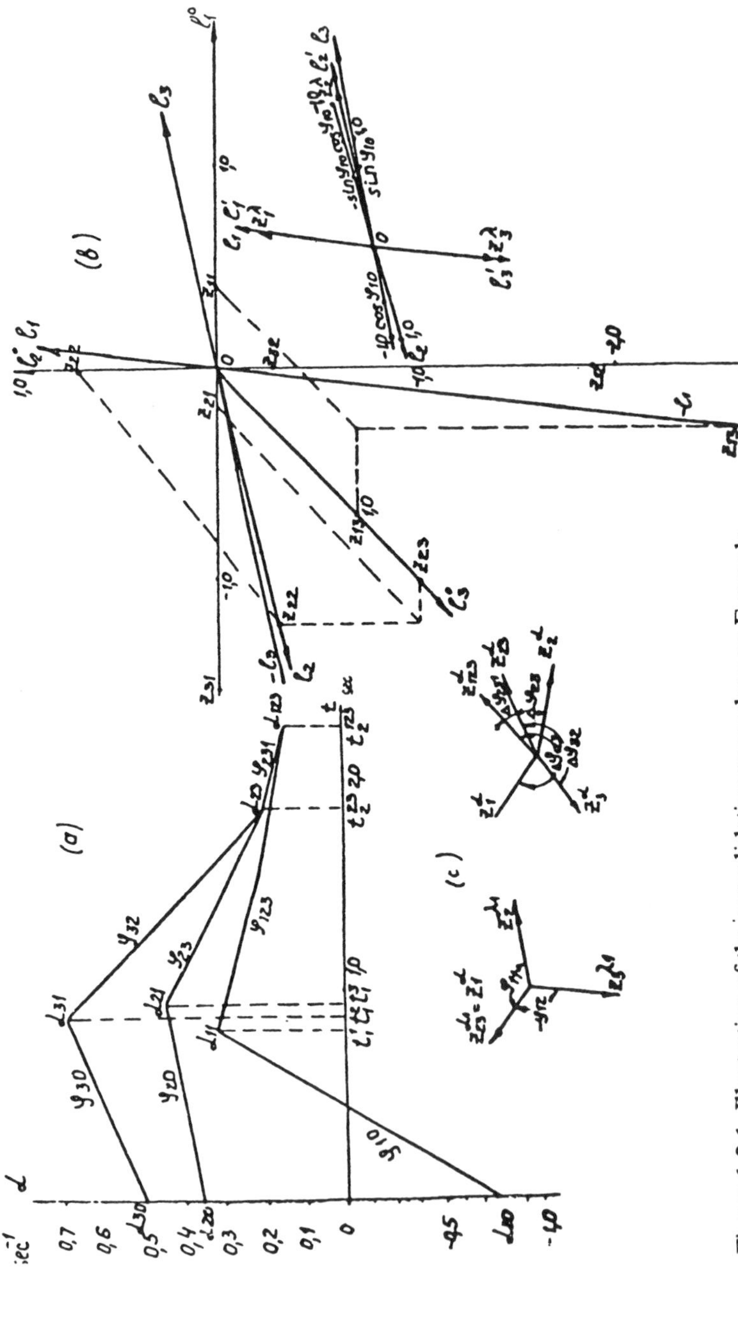

Figure 1.2.1. Illustration of the consolidation procedure on Example.

In the rotated coordinate system, the canonical matrix is transformed into the form K_{io}. For the considered example, we have α_{11}=0.325, α_{21}=0.425, α_{31} = 0.70; φ_{11}= 1,25, φ_{21}= 1.13, φ_{31}= 0.79; t_1^i= 0.82, t_2^i =0.94, t_3^i = 0.88.

The following consolidation procedure contains the equalization of the components $\alpha_{ijm}(t_j^{ikm})$ (Figure 1.2.1) in the process of the independent rotations of each of the coordinate systems.

So, up to the moment t_2^{23} in the partitioned matrixes K_1, K_2, the components $\alpha_{21}(t_2^{23})=\alpha_{31}(t_2^{23})=\alpha_{23}$, α_{23}=0.2, t_2^{23}=1.88 become an equal.

The space coordinate system, connected with the matrix K_2, has to be rotated on the angle φ_{23}=arccos α_{23} – arccos α_{21}= 0.23, and the coordinate system, connected with K_3, should be rotate on the angle φ_{32}=arccos α_{23} – rccos α_{31}=0.57 until their coincidence at the moment t_2^{23}. After that, the obtained coordinate system, connected with the matrix K_1, is rotating on the angles $\Delta\varphi_{231}$=arccos α_{123}-- arccos α_{23}=1.42-1.36= 0.06, and $\Delta\varphi_{123}$=arccos α_{123}– $\Delta\varphi_{11}(t_1^1)$ = 1.42-0.20=1.22. The coincidence of these coordinate systems is achieved simultaneously with the equalization of the eigenvalues at the moment t_2^{123} = 2.27.

The procedural sequence is shown in Figure 1.2.1(a-b).

To get the nondistinguished states at each of the discrete moments, the additional rotations of the space coordinate axises on the angles (defined by the equations (3.1)) should be applied.

The considered space movement represents a single-dimensional motion along the vector $\bar{z}_i^{\lambda}$, defined in the corresponding mobile coordinate system, that has been built on the eigenvectors of the matrix $\bar{a}_j^i$. In the consolidated process, the above motion successively transfers from one such eigenvector to another, and is modeled by the scalar equations (6.14,15) with the variable parameter $\alpha_{ij} = \alpha_i(t_j^i)$.

It is not essential to set up the initial position for the mobile coordinate system with respect to the immobile one. The relative motion of the mentioned system on the angles $\Delta\varphi_{ij}$ is the definitive condition. It is important that the existence of the common three-dimensional coordinate system for the vector $\bar{z}_i^{\lambda}$, where all commutative matrixes $\bar{a}_j^i$ acquire the canonical form. The conditions of its fulfillment represents an essential practical interest.

Corollary 3. **If** in the equation

$\dot{z} = \Lambda(t)\, z$,

the state coordinates are connected by the relations

$\dot{z}_i = z_{i+1}$, $\dot{z}_i = \lambda_i(t) z$, i=1,...,n,

then the matrix $\Lambda(t)$ can be presented in the form

$$(6.18)\ \Lambda = \begin{vmatrix} \lambda_1 \\ 0, \lambda_2 = \dfrac{\dot{\lambda}_1 + \lambda_1^2}{\lambda_1} \\ 0, 0, \lambda_3 = \dfrac{\dot{\lambda}_2 + \lambda_2^2}{\lambda_2} \\ 0, 0, \ldots, \lambda_n = \dfrac{\dot{\lambda}_{n-1} + \lambda_{n-1}^2}{\lambda_{n-1}} \end{vmatrix}$$

The *proof* follows directly from the relations

$\dot{z}_{i+1} = \dot{\lambda}_i z_i + \lambda_i \dot{z}_i = (\dot{\lambda}_i + \lambda_1^2) z_i = \lambda_{i+1} z_{i+1}, z_{i+1} = \dot{\lambda}_i z_i$. In particular, at $\dot{\lambda}_i$ (t)=0, the above matrix acquires a form, $\Lambda = \lambda_1 E$ that can be checked directly.

The relation $\dot{\lambda}_i = \dfrac{d}{dt}(\dfrac{\dot{z}_i}{z_i}) = 0$, as a condition of the local equilibrium, executed by the equalization of $\lambda_1(\tau_1) = \lambda_2(\tau_1) = \lambda_3(\tau_1)$, leads toward to such relations for the state coordinates, that they become the phase coordinates at these moments. •

Corollary 4. **If** in the system

(6.19) $\dot{z} = \Lambda z$,

the state coordinates are connected by the relations

(6.20) $\dot{z}_i = z_{i+1}$, i =1,2; $\dot{z}_k = z_{k+1}$, k = 4,5; $\dot{z}_m = z_{m+1}$, m = 7, 8; $\dot{z}_l = z_{l+1}$, l=n-2, n-1; $\dot{z}_j = \lambda_j z_j$, j=1,...,3n,

then at $\dot{\lambda}_i(t) = \dot{\lambda}_k(t) = \dot{\lambda}_m(t) = 0$, the matrix Λ is represented in the block form:

(6.21) $\Lambda = |\lambda^i_j|$;

(6.22) $\lambda^i_j = \begin{vmatrix} \lambda^1_j \\ 0, \lambda^k_j, \\ 0, 0, \lambda^m_j \end{vmatrix}$, j=1,3; k=4,5; m=7,8; i=1,...,k,...,m.

To *prove* the first one, we are writing this matrix in the form (6.21), and then successively reducing it to the form (6.22). •

Corollary 5. **If** together with the differential equation (6.19), that satisfies the Corollary 4, is given the transformation $x = T^{-1} z$, where x is the state vector, defined by the differential equation $\dot{x} = Ax$, A is the 3n× 3n- dimensional matrix, **then** the matrix A is represented by the n block-matrixes in the form A=$|\overline{a}^i_j|$,i=1,...,n , j =1,2,3 having the n-common eigenvectors.

The *proof* follows from the similarity of the matrixes $|\overline{a}^i_j|$ and $|\lambda^i_j|$.

The last matrixes also have the n multiple (repeated) eigenvalues.

Because of this, the n- common eigenvectors of the matrix $|\overline{a}_j^i|$ exist.

The physical meaning of this result is that if the vector's state coordinates are divided on the phase coordinates that satisfy the relations (6.19), then matrix A can be reduced to the block form with the pairwise commutative partitioned matrixes.

The last matrixes can be represented by the matrixes of rotation with the common basis. As it follows from [6], the system (6.19) with optimal controls, switching at the points of the eigenvalues equalization, according to the equalities $\lambda_i^t(\tau) = \lambda_j^t(\tau); \lambda_i^{t=0} = \lambda_{i0} = \alpha_{i0} + -\beta_{i0}$,

satisfying the relations $\dot{z}_i = z_{i+1}$, i=1,...,n-1, should have the elementary common denominator of the eigenvalues: $\gamma_i^\alpha = \dfrac{\alpha_{io}}{\alpha_{i+1,0}}$.

At the consolidation of the controlled subsystems by 3, the two elementary denominators exist for each of these eigenvalues triple [6].

From the above relations, the existence of elementary denominators of the matrix A follows:

(6.23) $\lambda_{20} = \lambda_{10} / \gamma_1^\alpha,\ \lambda_{30} = \lambda_{20} / \gamma_2^\alpha,$

$\lambda_{40} = \lambda_{30} / \gamma_1^\alpha, \lambda_{50} = \lambda_{40} / \gamma_2^\alpha, \lambda_{60} = \lambda_{50} / \gamma_1^\alpha, \ldots$

The eigenvectors, corresponding to the different eigenvalues (in a particular, for the first triple: $(\lambda_{10}, \lambda_{20}, \lambda_{30})$) form the basis of the three-dimensional subspace.

The eigenvectors, corresponding to the denominative eigenvalues (for example, $\lambda_{20}, \lambda_{40}, \lambda_{60}, \ldots$) form the basis's of the cyclic subspaces at which the n-dimensional space of the operator A is divided.

The existence of the elementary denominators of the eigenvalues is a consequence of the preservation of the common denominator γ_i^α for all n-local equations of the systemic model (6.15-16).

Corollary 6. The matrix T, that transfers **A** to the diagonal form Λ, is defined by the covariation matrix r of the object (1.1.1) in the form T=$r\ d$, where d is an arbitrary diagonal nonsingular matrix.

The *proof* follows from the relations

(6.24) $\hat{H} = 1/2Sp(\dot{r}r^{-1}),\ \dot{r} = Ar + rA^T,\ r = M(xx^T),$

$\hat{H} = 1/2Sp(A + rA^T r^{-1}) = Sp\Lambda;\ Sp(A) = Sp(A^T) = Sp\Lambda,$

$Sp(T^{-1}AT + T^{-1}rA^T r^{-1}T) = 2Sp\Lambda, Sp(T^{-1}rA^T r^{-1}T) = SpA^T, T^{-1}r = Ed.$

From this, the object state coordinates $\{\hat{y}_i\}$ at the control discrete points are proportional to the conjugate Hamiltonian model's coordinates $\{X_i\}$.

Indeed. Using the relations $\hat{y} = T^{-1}x,\ X(\tau) = r^{-1}(\tau)x(\tau),$

we come to the realation $\hat{y}(\tau) = d^{-1}X(\tau)$ ●.

Comments. For the object, that is consolidated in the process of the space movement, the covariation matrix assumes the representation

$$(6.25)\ r=\begin{vmatrix} 1,0,0 \\ 0,\cos\varphi_o,\sin\varphi_o \\ 0,-\sin\varphi_o,\cos\varphi_o \end{vmatrix} d,$$

that follows from the connections of the matrixes of transformation and rotation for the considered objects.

The considered class of the objects undergoes the consolidation during the space movement, if one of the group's peculiarities is fulfilled:

- the covariation matrix of the state vector can be represented in the form (6.25), or
- the state coordinates are connected by the relations (6.20).

The structural symmetry is a consequence of variational principle and the field equations. The consolidation leads to the dynamic asymmetry of the macrostructures. The matrix of rotation, applied to the ranged three eigenvectors keeps the function of the spatial density of probability being invariant before the execution of consolidations. The jump of the macromodel dimension at its integration changes the symmetry order. The asymmetry of integrated structures creates their new peculiarities and morphology. The states, that are bound "by three" represent an analogy of the "three critical" identical phases at the translations of the second order, with a typical connection of kinetics, diffusion, and symmetry of ordering in crystals. The controllability of the macromodel depends on its evolution which includes the mechanisms of the renovated dynamics, geometry, and consolidation. Selection and memorization of positive eigenvalues violates the spatial-time symmetry, creating irreversibility and local non stability.

Consolidation by fixing the irreversible phase translations counteracts fluctuations and nonstability, and creates the hierarchy of global stable macromodels and macrostructures. The considered macromodel is a linear approximation of nonlinear movements. This model can create bifurcation solutions at odd multiplicities of the eigenvalues of the linear operator. At random interactions of two macromodels, it is possible that the chaotic resonance [7] arising with the discrete time spectrum (when some of the continuous time values acquire a probability equal to zero).

Such resonance can be a result of mutual acceptance information by these models, and the discrete time is a consequence of these interactions.

Therefore, we may consider the discrete time as an attribute of the interacting systems.

The IMD approach introduces the systemic methodology of obtaining both the ordinary and partial differential equations from statistics.

REFERENCES

1. Glansdorf P., Prigogine J. *Thermodynamic Theory of Structure, Stability and Fluctuations*, N.Y.: Wiley, 1971.
2. Gelfand I.M., Fomin S.V. *Calculus of Variations*, N.Y.: Prentice Hall, 1963.
3.DeGroot S.R, Mazur P. *Non-Equilibrium Thermodynamics*, Amsterdam: North-Holland Publ.,1962.
4.Poston T., Stewart I. *Catastrophe Theory and Its Applications*, London: Pitman, 1978.
5. Norden A.P. *Short Course of Differential Geometry*, Moscow: Nauka, 1958.
6.Hantmacher, F.R. *Theory of Matrixes*, Nauka: Moscow, 1967.
7. Ippen E., Linder J., and Dito W.L. "Chaotic Resonance: A Simulation." *Journal of Statistical Physics*, 1993; 70, 1-2: 437-450.

1.3. THE OPTIMAL TIME-SPACE DISTRIBUTED MACROMODEL WITH CONSOLIDATED STATES (OPMC)

The OPMC is the integrated macromodel that includes the analytical synthesis and optimal prognosis of the joint macrodynamics and the space movement, the sequence of state consolidation, the strategy of controls application, and the geometrical macromodel structure forming.

1.3.1. Local invariants and OPMC dynamic peculiarities

Theorem 1. The peculiarities of the OPMC characterizes the following system of local invariants:

- he indicators of the time (t_i) and space (l_i) discrete intervals (DI):

(1.1) $\cos(\gamma\alpha') + \gamma^{-1}\sin(\gamma\alpha') - 1/2\exp(\alpha') = 0$,

$\operatorname{Im}\lambda_i^t(t_i) = \operatorname{Im}\lambda_i^l(l_i) = 0$, $i = 1,\dots,n$,

(1.2) $2\cos(\gamma\beta') - \gamma\sin(\gamma\beta') - \exp(\beta') = 0$; $\operatorname{Re}\lambda_i^t(t_i) = \operatorname{Re}\lambda_i^l(l_i) = 0$,

(1.3) $$\alpha_{i+1}^t(t_{i+1}) = -\alpha_i^t(t_i)\exp(\alpha_i^t(t_i)(t_{i+1} - t_i)) \times (2 - \exp(\alpha_i^t(t_i)(t_{i+1} - t_i)))^{-1}, \alpha_i^t(t_i) = \alpha_k^t(t_i)$$

$\lambda_i^t = \alpha_i^t + j\beta_i^t$, $\lambda_i^l = \alpha_i^l + j\beta_i^t$, $A^t = \|\lambda_i^t\|$, $A^l = \|\lambda_i^l\|$, $\lambda_i^t(t_o) = \lambda_{io}^t$,

- the conditions of coordination and connection of the invariants:

(1.4) $\gamma = \gamma^t = \dfrac{\beta_i^t}{\alpha_i^t} = \dfrac{\beta_i^l}{\alpha_i^l} = \gamma^l = Const$;

(1.5) $\alpha_i^t(t_i)t_i = \alpha(\gamma) = Const$ (a); $\beta_i^t(t_i)t_i = \beta(\gamma) = Const$ (b);

(1.6) $\alpha_i^t(t_o)t_i = \alpha'(\gamma) = Const$,

$\beta_i^t(t_o)t_i = \beta'(\gamma) = Const$, $\alpha'(\gamma = 0) = 0.768$; $\alpha(\gamma = 0) = 0.232$

(1.7) $l_i = c_i t_i$, $c_i = \dfrac{\alpha_i^t}{\alpha_i^l} = c(n,\gamma)$ =Const;

(1.8) $\alpha' = \alpha\exp(-\alpha)(1-\gamma^2)^{1/2}(4 - 4\exp(-\alpha)\cos(\gamma\alpha) + \exp(-2\alpha))^{-1/2}$;

(1.9) $(\cos(\gamma\beta) - \gamma\sin\beta)(\sin(\gamma\alpha) - \gamma\cos(\gamma\alpha)) = \exp(\beta - \alpha)$;

- the conditions of forming the ranged spectrum of the eigenvalues:

(1.10) $\gamma_{i,m}^{\alpha^t} = \dfrac{\alpha_{i+1,m}^t}{\alpha_{i,m}^t} = \dfrac{\alpha_{i+1,m}^l}{\alpha_{i,m}^l} = \gamma_{i,m}^{\alpha^l} = \gamma_{i,m}^{\alpha}$ =Const (i,m) , m=0,1,...,n-1.

Proof. The relations (1.1) follow directly from the equalities

$\lambda_i^t(t_i) = \lambda_j^t(t_i)$, $\lambda_j^t(t_o) = \lambda_{jo}^t = \alpha_{jo}^t + \beta_{jo}^t$, $\lambda_i^t(t_o) = \lambda_{io}^t = \alpha_{jo}^t - \beta_{jo}^t$ i,j=1,...,n;

$$\lambda_i^t(t_i) = \lambda_j^t(t_o)\exp((\lambda_j^t(t_o)t_i)(2-\exp((\lambda_j^t(t_o)t_i))^{-1}, \gamma_{io} = \frac{\beta_{io}^t}{\alpha_{io}^t} = \frac{\beta_{io}}{\alpha_{io}}.$$

If the coordintes of state vector ($x=\{x_i\}$) are the phase coordinates, they satisfy the condition (1.11):

$\dot{x}_{io} = x_{i-1,o}$, $x_{io} = x_i(t_o)$ i=1,...,n,

and the relation

$$\frac{\partial x_i}{x_i \partial t}(t_i) = \frac{\partial x_j}{x_j \partial t}(t_i)$$

acquires the form

$$(1.12)\ (\frac{\partial x_i}{\partial t}(t_i))^2 = +-x_i(t_i)\frac{\partial^2 x_i}{\partial t^2}(t_i),$$

from which equations (1.2), (1.3) follow at the imaginary eigenvalues, and at the real eigenvalues accordingly. Indeed. The relation (1.11) at the conditions

$$x_i = x_i(0)\exp(\int \lambda_i^t dt),$$

$$\lambda_i^t(t_i) = \lambda_j^t(t_o)\exp((\lambda_j^t(t_o)t_i)(2-\exp((\lambda_j^t(t_o)t_i))^{-1}$$

leads to the equation $\frac{d\lambda_i^t}{dt}\exp(2\int \lambda_i^t dt)|_{t=t_i}=0$,

which at the fulfillment of inequality $\exp(2\int \lambda_i^t dt) \neq 0$ acquires a view

$$(1.13)\ \frac{d\lambda_i^t}{dt}|_{t=t_i}=0.$$

The last one corresponds to the following system

$$h = [(\alpha_{io}^t \cos\beta' - \beta_{io}^t \sin\beta')(2-\exp\alpha'\cos\beta') -$$

$$-\exp\alpha'(\beta_{io}^t\cos\beta' + \alpha_{io}^t\sin\beta')]$$

$$hg_1 - gg_2 = 0,\ hg_2 - gg_1 = 0,\ g = 2(\gamma'\cos\beta' + \sin\beta') - \gamma\exp\alpha',$$

$$g_1 = [\alpha_{io}^t(2-\exp\alpha'\cos\beta') - \beta_{io}^t\exp\alpha'\sin\beta'],$$

$$g_2 = [\alpha_{io}^t\exp\alpha'\sin\beta' + \beta_{io}^t(2-\exp\alpha'\cos\beta')],$$

which at $\alpha_{io}^t \neq 0$ (**a**), $\beta_{io}^t \neq 0$ (**b**), $\beta' \neq 0 + -2\pi k, k = 1,2,..$ (**c**)

leads to the equality Im $\lambda_i^t(t_i)$=0, or Re$\lambda_i^t(t_i)$=0.

The condition $\alpha_{io}^t = \beta_{io}^t = 0$ is the trivial one, and (c) corresponds to (b).

Applying (1.1-3) for equations $\frac{\partial x_i}{\partial t} = \lambda_i^t x_i$; $\frac{\partial x_i}{\partial l} = \lambda_i^l x_i$,

we receive (1.5) and (1.6). From equation (1.1) we get the equality

$$\exp\alpha'(\gamma\to 0) = \lim_{\gamma\to 0} 2[\frac{\sin\gamma\alpha'}{\gamma} + \cos\gamma\alpha'] = 2(\alpha'(\gamma\to 0)+1),$$

whose solution leads to the right part of (1.5). The corresponding invariant $\alpha(\gamma \to 0)$ is found based on connection of the invariants (1.8).

Equations (1.4, 10) are a result of the joint solution of equations (1.1,3), and condition (1.6). The connection of the invariants is a consequence of the equations (1.5, 6), (1.3) and (1.2), (1.5, 6) accordingly. In particular, from (1.1) at the constant α', equation (1.4) follows. Because each of the invariants(1.5, 6) depends on the fixed γ, that defines $\alpha^t_{i,m}$, we arrive at (1.10). ●

Theorem 2. For OPMC with complex ranged eigenvalues $\{\lambda^t_{i,o}\}$at $|\alpha^t_{i,o}|>|\alpha^t_{i+1,o}|$, the joint execution of (1.1,3) leads to the minimal sum of the discrete intervals for each (i, i+1) couple of equations.

Indeed. For each of the OPMC couples with the complex $\{\lambda^t_{i,o}\}$, the relations (1.1,3) must be executed at the discrete points. For such equations, the sum of the discrete intervals is a minimal (at other equal conditions) if the discrete moment (found from (1.3)) for the one couple (for which $|\alpha^t_{i,o}|>|\alpha^t_{i+1,o}|$) coincides with the discrete moment (found from (1.1)) for the second couple (Figure 1.3.1), then the additional discrete interval is not required.

That result follows from the joint solutions (1.1,3) for the ranged eigenvalues spectrum at the condition $|\alpha^t_{i,o}|>|\alpha^t_{i+1,o}|$.

The requirement of coinciding (at t_i) the eigenvalue $\alpha^t_i(t_i) = \alpha^t_i(\gamma, \alpha^t_{i,o})$ with

$$\alpha^t_{i+1}(t_i) = \alpha^t_{i+1}(\gamma', \alpha^t_{i+1,o}),\ \gamma' = \frac{\beta^t_{i+1,o}}{\alpha^t_{i+1,o}} \text{ at the condition } \gamma^\alpha_i(\gamma) = \frac{\alpha^t_{i+1,o}}{\alpha^t_{i,o}},$$

leads to $\gamma = \gamma'$. The last one determines the preservation of the invariants (1.5,6,4) for the macromodel with the fixed eigenvalues spectrum. In particular, at γ =0.8, from joint solution (1.1,3), we get γ^α_i =6. ●

Theorem 3. For each of three OPMC couples with the complex eigenvalues$\{\lambda^t_{i,o}\}$ at $|\alpha^t_{i,o}|>|\alpha^t_{i+1,o}|>|\alpha^t_{i+2,o}|$ and the fulfillment (1.10,12), the minimal sum of the discrete intervals is accomplished at the joint solutions of the equations (1.10, 8, 6,5,3,1).

Indeed. In this case, the moment (t_{i+2}) of the disappearance of imaginary part of $\lambda^t_{i+2}(t_{i+2})$(according to (1.1)) coincides with the discretization moments found from the solution (1.3) of i- and (i+1)-couple equations when the real eigenvalues are equalized. The total consolidation time of the considered triple does not exceed the discrete interval of t_{i+2} defined from equation (1.1). ●

Implementation of this condition by the joint solutions of (1.10, 8, 6, 5, 3, 1) defines

(1.14) $\gamma^\alpha_{i+1,m} = 6^k (3.89)^i (2.21)^{m+1-i}$ for γ =0.5, m=0,1,...,n/2+1,

where k is the number of the switching pairwise controls, m is the number of

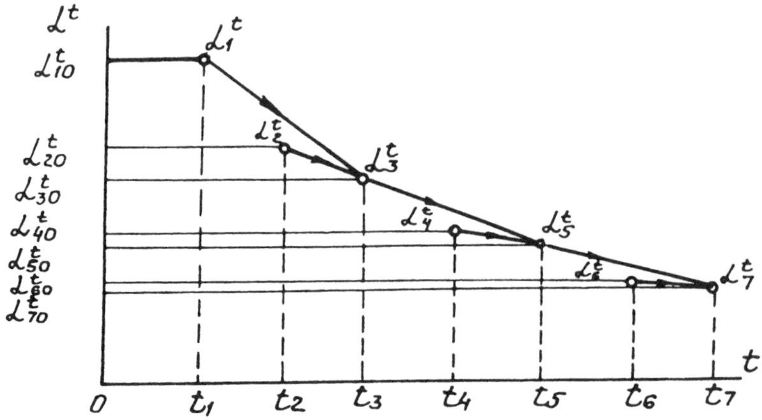

Figure 1.3.1. The equalization of the OPMC eigenvalues.

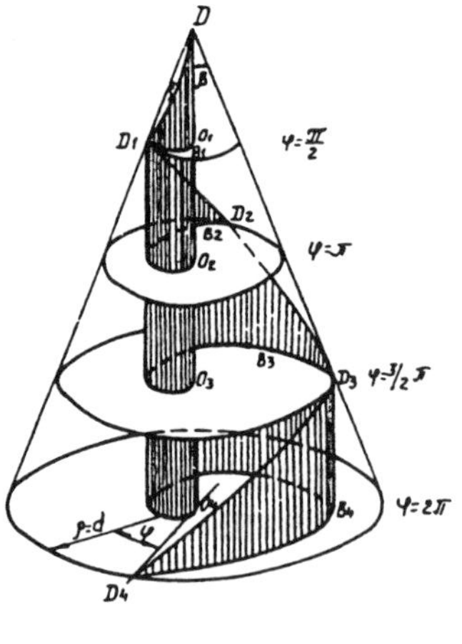

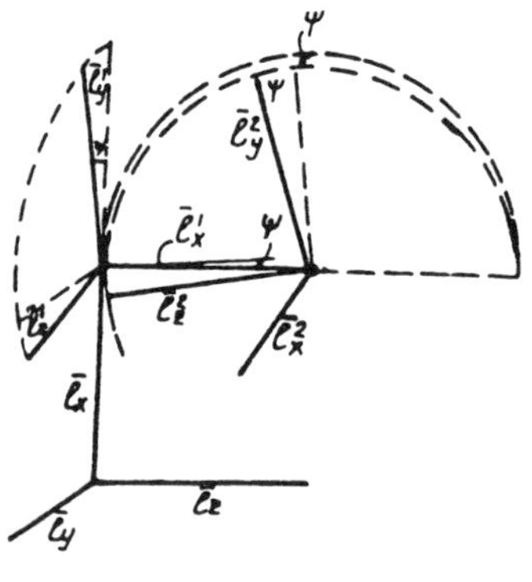

Figure 1.3.3. The OPMC space asym

Figure 1.3.2. The OPMC trajectories of the spiral-shaped curve $\rho = b\sin(\varphi \sin\beta)$ on a conic surface at the points D, D1, D2, D3, D4 with the spatial discretization intervals DD1= μ ,which correspond to the angle $\varphi = \pi k / 2$, \k=1,2,3,... of the projection of radius vector $\rho(\varphi,\beta)$ on the base of the cone (O,O1, O2, O3, O4) with a vertex angle β.

consolidations by three; and the admissible values of γ is 0-0.8.

At $\gamma \rightarrow$(0.9-3.5) the deviations of all coordinates are increasing without limitations indicating that the OPMC is losing stability.

The values of $\gamma^{\alpha}_{i+1,m}$, at other m>3 are found from the joint solution of the mentioned system equations.

The equation (1.14) at m>3 does not have solutions.

Because the OPMC also represents an optimal filter, the initial eigenvalues that are different from $\alpha^t_{i,o} = \alpha^t_{i,o} 6^{1-i}$ i=2,3,...,n, are a subject of filtering.

The control action of forming such a filter, consists of transferring the model coordinates on the switching line (1.5a) for the synthesis of the dissipative processes, or on the line (1.5b) for the synthesis of the oscillatory processes.

The implementation of (1.1,3,10) leads to creating the successively integrated dissipative macrostructures that accompany increasing t_i and decreasing the consolidated real eigenvalue

(1.15) $$\alpha^t_i(t_i) = \frac{t_{i+1} - t_{i-1} - 2t_i}{(t_{i+1} + t_{i-1})(t_i - t_{i-1})} \geq \frac{2\alpha^t_{i-1}(t_{i-1})\alpha^t_{i+1}(t_{i+1})}{\alpha^t_{i-1}(t_{i-1}) + \alpha^t_{i+1}(t_{i+1})} > 0.$$

The condition of positivity (1.15) is satisfied by switching the needle controls at the infinite nearest moments of time t_k, $t_k + \delta, \delta \sim o(t_k)$:

(1.16) $$\delta v(t_k) = v(t_k + \delta) - v(t_k),$$

changing the differential equation matrix $A^t = A(t_k + -o)$ sign

$$A(t_k + o) = -(2E - \exp(A(t_k - o)\delta))^{-1} A(t_k - o) \exp(A(t_k - o)\delta);$$
$$A(t_k + o) = -A(t_k - o), \delta \rightarrow 0.$$

The sequence of the applied controls we call the optimal OPMC strategy if it satisfies the maximum principle of Theorem 1.1.1 in the form

(1.17) max $\hat{H}(t_i)$=minSp $\lambda^t_i(t_i)$.

According to (1.10, 13, 14), this condition corresponds to min$|\alpha^t_i(t_i)| = \alpha^o_i$.

The optimal strategy (that is chosen from the set of possible strategies enabling us to transfer the process on the switching line (1.5a)) is a such one, at which the minimal $|\alpha^t_i(t_i)|$ will be achieved at each discrete moment.

<u>*Corollary* 1.</u> The optimal control strategy is satisfied by the simultaneous switching of each control's triple at points (t_{i+1}) for the OPMC ranged eigenvalues spectrum, obtained from the joint solution (1.10, 8, 6, 5, 3, 1).

The optimal strategy accompanies the consolidation of the eigenvalues by three with the total number of discrete points m = n/2+1, that is less (according to n-1-(n/2+1)=n/2-2) than the number of discretes for the eigenavalues which are not consolidating by three.

The procedure consists of joining the two eigenvalues at first, and then adding a third eigenvalue. Optimal triplet structure includes the doublet as a *primary* element. For the ranged spectrum, defined from the joint solution (1.1, 3, 15), the minimal sum of the discrete interval is a unique and a single.

This strategy is executed for the spectrum of the initial eigenvalues, defined by the multiplicators (1.14) with the maximal $\gamma_n^{\alpha_0}$=(2.21) $(3.89)^{n/2}$, which characterizes the optimal-minimal filter.

The values { α_{io}^t } that are different from the optimal set

(1.18) $\alpha_{i+1,o}^t=(0.2567)^i(0.4514)^{1-i}\alpha_{1o}^t$, $\alpha_{1o}^t=\alpha_{\max}$

do not affect the OPMC peculiarities and filter in the practical implementation. (ch.4.1,4.7.3). ●

<u>*Corollary 2.*</u> The minimumal condition (1.17), expressed via the dispersion of the synthesized process $D^o=\frac{(2.042)^{n/2}(3.896)^{n-2/2}}{0.758\bullet 2.21}t_1^n\, t_1=\frac{\alpha'}{\alpha}$, γ =0.5,

defines the initial OPMC dimension n is found from the eigenvalue equation

(1.19) $(\frac{\alpha'(\gamma)}{\alpha_{1o}^t})^n[(\frac{\alpha_{1o}^t}{\alpha_{3o}^t})(\frac{\alpha_{1o}^t}{\alpha_{2o}^t})(\frac{\alpha_{2o}^t}{\alpha_{3o}^t}-1)]^{n/2-1}(\frac{\alpha_{3o}^t}{\alpha_{1o}^t}-1)^{n/2}$=1

and relation (1.14) written for given γ . And vice versa, that is also true. ●

The OPMC dimension n can be expressed via the starting consolidating moment (t_1)of the triplet's time sequence (t_1,t_2,t_3) according to the formula

(1.20) $(2\ln\alpha-\ln t_1)n+0.6184825=0$, γ =0.5.

Changing t_1, even with the constant invariants $\alpha(\gamma)$and the ratios of $\gamma_2^\alpha=t_2/t_1(\gamma)$, $\gamma_3^\alpha=t_3/t_1(\gamma)$, leads to a new OPMC dimension.

The spectrum of the initial eigenvalues, the consolidation procedure, and the optimal strategy are found for the OPMC set with given (n, γ).

By the joint solution of the equations (1.19, 20,10,9,7-1), the following parameters γ_n^α, α_{1o}^t, α_{no}^t, $\gamma_{i,m}^\alpha$; $\{\alpha_i^t(t_i)\}_{i=1}^{n-1}$ $\{v_i(t_i), z_i(t)\}_{i=1}^n$ are obtained successively .

<u>*Corollary 3.*</u> In the OPMC, the macroprocesses $z_i(t), z_k(t)$ are ranged in such a way that the following relation is executed:

$$\frac{\partial^2 z_i}{\partial t^2}(t_i)[\frac{\partial z_i}{\partial t}(t_i)]^{-1}=\frac{\partial z_k}{\partial t}(t_i)z_k(t_i)^{-1}\ .\bullet$$

<u>*Theorem 4.*</u> **If** the phase coordinates { z_i } at the initial moment t_o are connected by the relations $z_{i-1}(t_o)=\lambda_i^t(t_o)\, z_i(t_o)$,

then at the moment t_i this equation holds true

(1.21) $z_{i-1}(t_i)$=-2 $\dot z_i(t_i)$

with the relative accuracy

(1.22) $\varepsilon_i=\frac{\delta z_i}{z_i}(t_{i-1})=\exp(-\alpha')(\gamma^\alpha\alpha')-2(1-\frac{\alpha'}{\alpha})$,

that at $\gamma=0.5$ does not exceed

(1.23) ε_i =0.0095-0.112.

Indeed. At the execution of the relations

(1.24) $\frac{x_i(t_i)}{x_{i-1}(t_{i-1})} = \frac{x_i(t_o)}{x_{i-1}(t_o)}$, $x_{i-1}(t_i) = x_{i-1}(t_{i-1})(2 - \exp\lambda^t_{i-1}(t_i - t_{i-1}))$,

$\alpha^t_{i-1}t_{i-1} = \alpha = \text{inv}$; $\frac{\lambda^t_i}{\lambda^t_{i-1}} = \gamma^{\alpha}_{i,i-1} = \text{inv}$,

the initial requirement regarding the condition (1.21) can be then fulfilled with the accuracy

(1.25) $\varepsilon_i = \frac{\delta x_i}{x_i}(t_{i-1})$, $\delta x_i(t_i) = 2\dot{x}_i(t_i) - x_{i-1}(t_i) = 2\ \lambda^t_i\ x_i(t_i)\ \text{-}2x_{i-1}(t_{i-1}) +$

$+ x_{i-1}(t_{i-1})\exp(-\lambda^t_{i-1}(t_i)t_{i-1})\exp(\lambda^t_{i-1}(t_i)t_i)$.

The last equation, after substituting (1.24, 25) is reduced to the form (1.22), and it defines the limited accuracy values (1.23) at $\gamma = 0.5$. ●

Theorem 5. The equality (1.21) is fulfilled with zero error, if the initial conditions are bound by the relations

(1.26) $\dot{x}_i(t_o) = k_i x_{i-1}(t_o)$, $k_i = \frac{\alpha'}{2\alpha}(2 - \exp(\gamma^{\alpha}_i \alpha')) = \text{inv}$,

or the discrete moments are defined from the condition

(1.27) $t_i^2 = t_{i-1}t_{i+1}$.

The result is proved by direct substitution of (1.25) into (1.21), (1.5). ●

Corollary 4. For the OPMC with t_i=2,21t_{i-1}, t_{i+1}=3.79t_{i-1}, γ=0.5, the admissible relative time accuracy of the fulfillment (1.26) is equal to $\Delta t_i{}^* = \frac{\delta t_i}{t_i}$.

With that accuracy (or 1.23), the self-forming of the optimal controls is possible

(1.28) $u(t_i) = \lambda^t_i(t_i)v_i(t_i) = -2\lambda^t_i(t_i)z_i(t_i) = z_{i-1}(t_i)$,

at the discretization moments of the process $z_{i-1}(t_i)$, if the fixed values of the initial $z_i(t_o)$ perform the function of the applied starting control $v(t_o)$. ●

1.3.2. The OPMC geometrical structure

The OPMC geometrical structure is a result of space transformations of the macro dynamic variables that satisfy the invariant condition for the entropy functional in the controlled process of the space-time motion, which accompanies the evolution of the consolidated macrostructures.

Theorem 6. The trajectory of each of the n three-dimensional OPMC movements represents the parametrical equation of a helix curve on the cone (Figure 1.3.2), with a radius-vector $\bar{r}(\rho, \varphi, \psi^o)$ projection on the cone base:

(2.1) $\rho_i = b_i \sin(\varphi_i \sin\psi_i^o)$;

and transferring from the one cone trajectory to another cone trajectory is executed at the points that satisfy the extreme condition of the equation (2.1) at

(2.2) $\varphi_i(l_i)\sin\psi_i^{\,o}=\pi/2$.

Proof. The trajectory of each of the n- three-dimensional movements, with a nonorthogonal, in general, the matrix of rotation $\overline{A}$ (at the fixed angle with respect to one of the coordinate axis) has a simple representation in the cylindrical space coordinate system $l(\bar{r})=l(\rho,\varphi,\psi^{o})$:

$$z=r\cos\psi^{o},\ z^{2}=r^{2}+\rho^{2},\ z=\rho(tg\psi^{o})^{-1},\ dl^{2}=d\rho^{2}+\rho^{2}d\varphi^{2}+dz^{2},$$

where φ is the angle's increment of the radius vector ρ; ψ^{o} is the fixed angle's increment with respect to the axis z.

At the zero increment, $d\,\psi^{o}=0$, the equality follows:

$$dl=[(\frac{d\rho}{d\varphi})^{2}\sin^{-2}\psi^{o}+\rho^{2}]^{1/2}d\varphi .$$

The condition (2. 2.6) (as a consequence of the VP execution for $Y\equiv\dfrac{dl}{dt}=c$)is imposed on that equality. From hence, this differential equation follows:

$$\bar{d}^{2}=(\frac{d\rho}{d\varphi})^{2}\sin^{-2}\psi^{o}+\rho^{2},\ \bar{d}=\frac{dl}{d\varphi}=\text{Const.}$$

The solution of this equation in the form (2.1) represents the parametrical equation of the spiral curve on the conic surface S:

$$\sum_{i,j=1}^{n}\frac{\partial^{2}S}{(\partial l_{j}^{i})^{2}}(\bar{l}_{j}^{i}-l_{j}^{i})^{2}=0,\ \bar{l}_{j}^{i}=\sum\bar{e}_{j}^{i}l_{j}^{i},$$

where $\bar{l}_{j}^{i}$ are the coordinates of the radius vector $\bar{r}$ of the fixed nonsingular point, l_{j}^{i} are the current point's coordinates on the cone with the angle $2\psi^{o}$ at the vertex with the $\bar{d}$ as the curve parameter and with the projection $\bar{\rho}$ of the radius vector $\bar{r}$ on the cone base. For the constant $\bar{d}$, this relation follows

$$\text{(2.3)}\quad \frac{\partial^{2}\rho}{\partial\varphi^{2}}\sin^{-2}\psi^{o}+\rho=0,\ \frac{\partial\rho}{\partial\varphi}\neq 0;$$

$$\frac{\partial^{2}\rho}{\partial\varphi^{2}}\sin^{-2}\psi^{o}+\rho^{2}\neq 0,\ \frac{\partial\rho}{\partial\varphi}=0.$$

The first of the relations (for (2.1)) is fulfilled automatically; the second part, at the fulfillment (2.2), corresponds to the extremal condition for $\rho=\rho(\varphi)$ at the existence of a singular point at which location the transformation from one cone trajectory (2.1) to the analogous trajectory of another cone occurs. Transformation $\overline{A}$ carries up the n spiral curves on the corresponding cones (Figure 1.3.2). •

<u>Theorem 7.</u> At the discretization moments, the parameters of the spiral curves (2.1, 2) are equal, and they satisfy the equations

(2.4) $\varphi_i(t_i) = k\pi$, $\psi_i^o = \arcsin(2k)^{-1}$, k=1,2,...

Indeed. From the orthogonal conditions for the vectors $\bar{l}_i(t_i)$, $\bar{l}_{i+1}(t_{i+1})$ that are written via the directional cosines of the normal on the cone:

(2.5) $\overline{\alpha}_1^i = \frac{d\bar{l}_1^i}{d\mu_i} = \frac{d\rho_i}{d\varphi_i tg\psi_i^o} = \cos\ \psi_i^o \cos(\varphi_i \sin\ \psi_i^o)$; $\varphi_i = \varphi(\tau_i)$,

$\overline{\alpha}_2^i = \frac{d\bar{l}_2^i}{d\mu_i} = \sin\ \psi_i^o \cos\varphi_i \cos(\varphi_i \sin\ \psi_i^o) - \sin\varphi_i \sin(\varphi_i \sin\ \psi_i^o)$,

$\overline{\alpha}_3^i = \frac{d\bar{l}_3^i}{d\mu_i} = \sin\ \psi_i^o \sin\varphi_i \cos(\varphi_i \sin\ \psi_i^o) + \cos\varphi_i \sin(\varphi_i \sin\ \psi_i^o)$

the equation connecting the above vectors follows

(2.6) $\bar{l}^i(\tau_i)\ \bar{l}^i(\tau_{i+1}) = 0$, $\overline{\alpha}_1^i \overline{\alpha}_1 + \overline{\alpha}_2^i \overline{\alpha}_2 + \overline{\alpha}_3^i \overline{\alpha}_3 = 0$,

where

(2.7) $\overline{\alpha}_1 = \cos\ \psi_i^o \cos(\varphi(\tau_i) \sin\ \psi_i^o)$,

$\overline{\alpha}_2 = \sin\ \psi_i^o \cos\varphi_i(\tau_i) \cos(\varphi_i(\tau_i) \sin\ \psi_i^o) -$

$- \sin\varphi_i(\tau_i) \sin(\varphi_i(\tau_i) \sin\ \psi_i^o)$,

$\overline{\alpha}_3 = \sin\ \psi_i^o \sin\varphi_i(\tau_i) \cos(\varphi_i(\tau_i) \sin\ \psi_i^o) +$

$+ \cos\varphi_i(\tau_i) \sin(\varphi_i(\tau_i) \sin\ \psi_i^o)$.

Considering the equations (2.6-7) at the initial angle $\varphi(\tau_i) = \varphi(0) = 0$, and with the substitution of (2.5,7) into (2.6) , we obtain

(2.8) $\cos^2 \psi_i^o \cos(\varphi_i \sin\ \psi_i^o) + \sin^2 \psi_i^o \cos(\varphi_i \sin\ \psi_i^o) -$

$\sin\psi_i^o \sin(\varphi_i) \cos(\varphi_i \sin\ \psi_i^o) = 0$.

The solution of the last equation at $\overline{\varphi} = \varphi_i \sin\ \psi_i^o = \pm \pi / 2$ leads to

(2.9) $\sin\varphi_i = 0$.

The joint solution (2.8, 9) defines the minimal real roots $\varphi_i = \pm 6\pi$, $\psi_i^o = \pm 0.08343$.

In general case we get the relations

$\varphi_i = k\pi$, $\sin\psi_i^o = (2k)^{-1}$, k=1,2,...and at k=1: $\varphi_i = \pi$, $\psi_i^o = \pi/6$.

The obtained relations hold true for each cone, and because of that, all cones have the same angle at the vertex $\psi_i^o = \psi^o$ and the extremal value of the radius vector $\rho_i = \rho_i(\mu_i)$ $(l_i \sim \mu_i)$ at that angle.

The parameters of the spiral $b_i = b(\mu_i) = \mu_i(\varphi_i)^{-1}$ for each cone are equal $\rho_i = \rho_i(\mu_i) = b_i \sin(\varphi_i \sin\ \psi_i^o) = b_i$. ●

Let us consider the directional cosines of the normal on the cones that are defined at the different discrete moments in the coordinate system constrained with

particular cone. In the cone vertex, defined at the discrete points, we obtain
(2.10) $l_i(\tau_i)=\mu_i$+o; i=n, n-1,...,1; φ(0)=0, $\overline{\alpha}_1^i = \overline{\alpha}_1 = \cos\psi^o$,
$\overline{\alpha}_2^i = \overline{\alpha}_2 = \sin\psi^o, \overline{\alpha}_3^i = \overline{\alpha}_3$=0;
in the cone base, defined at the discrete points:
$l_k(\tau_k)=\mu_k$+o, k=n-1, ..., 7,5,3,1 , we have
(2.11) φ_k=6π, $\overline{\alpha}_2^k$=0,$\overline{\alpha}_1^k$=0, $\overline{\alpha}_3^k$=1.

At the intermediate points, we get the relations
(2.12) $\Delta\overline{\overline{l}}^j = (l(t)-\overline{l}^j(\tau_j))(\overline{\alpha}_1^j\overline{l}_1^j+\overline{\alpha}_2^j\overline{l}_2^j+\overline{\alpha}_3^j\overline{l}_3^j)$; j=(i,k). •

Theorem 8. At the moments of the matrix A^t eigenvectors' consolidation, when this equation holds true
(2.13) $\lambda^t{}_i(t_k)=\lambda^t{}_j(t_k)=\lambda^t{}_m(t_k+o(t_k))$, k=1,3,5; i,j,m=1,2,...,n,
the vectors $\overline{l}^i(t_k), \overline{l}^j(t_k), \overline{l}^m(t_k)$, that coincide by their direction with the corresponding eigenvectors of the matrix A^t, have equal directions.
That result follows from the definition of vectors $\overline{l}^i$ and the equality of the eigenvalues. • Using (2.10,12) we write the result of the theorem 8 in the form

(2.14) $$\frac{\Delta\overline{l}^i(t_k)}{|\Delta\overline{l}^i(t_k)|}=\frac{\Delta\overline{l}^j(t_k)}{|\Delta\overline{l}^j(t_k)|}=\frac{\Delta\overline{l}^m(t_k+o(t_k))}{|\Delta\overline{l}^m(t_k+o(t_k))|},$$ i,j,m=1,2,...,n; k=1, 3, 5.

The condition of equality of directions for the vectors $\overline{l}^i(t_k)\ \overline{l}^j(t_k)$,
we may also express in the form

(2.15) $$\frac{\overline{l}^{i-1}(t_{i-1})+\Delta\overline{l}^i(t_k)}{|\overline{l}^i(t_k)|}=\frac{\overline{l}^{j-1}(t_{i-1})+\Delta\overline{l}^j(t_k)}{|\overline{l}^j(t_k)|},\quad \overline{l}^i=\overline{l}^{i-1}+b_i\varphi_i$$,i,j=1,...,n;

k=1, 3, 5,.

Considering at the discrete moments t_k, the equal modules in the form
$|\overline{l}^i(t_k)|=|\overline{l}^j(t_k)|=|\overline{l}\ (t_k)|$, $\mu_i=l_i(t_i)$ -$l_i(t_{i-1})$,
we obtain after differentiating (2.15) at $t\rightarrow t_k$, the relations

(2.16) $$\frac{d\Delta\overline{l}^i(t_k)}{dt}=\frac{d\Delta\overline{l}^j(t_k)}{dt},\ c^i{}_z=\frac{d\Delta\overline{l}_z^i(t_k)}{dt}=\frac{d\Delta\overline{l}_z^j(t_k)}{dt}=c^j{}_z\ .$$

Taking into account the condition $\frac{d\Delta\overline{l}^i(t_k)}{dt}\neq\frac{d\Delta\overline{l}^j(t_k)}{dt}$, the equaties (2.16) for the vectors $\Delta\overline{l}^m(t_k+o(t_k))$ and $\Delta\overline{l}^i(t_k)$, or $\Delta\overline{l}^j(t_k)$ are not fulfilled, in general.

The equality for the derivations (2.16) along the l_z-axis, characterizes the equal speeds in a chosen direction of the growing macrostructure, which is defined by the final discrete interval, where ($\frac{d\Delta\overline{l}_z^i(t_k)}{dt}\alpha_z^i$) is the projection of the linear vector speed; $\Delta \bar{l}_z^{\,i} \dfrac{d\alpha_z^i}{dt}$ is the projection of the angle speed for the vector $\Delta \bar{l}^{\,i}$.

The relations (2.14-16) hold true on the discrete intervals, that correspond to the movement along the hyperbola $\alpha = inv$.

Let us consider the increment of the angle η for vector $\bar{l}^{\,i} = \bar{l}^{\,i}(\eta)$ for the sector of the entrance on the hyperbola, i.e., for $t_0 \le t < t_i$.

Because $\bar{\bar{l}}^{\,i}(\eta)$ coincides by the direction with the corresponding eigenvector $\bar{z}^{\,i}(t) = z_\alpha{}^i(t\ ) + jz_\beta{}^i(t\ )$ of the matrix $A(t)=\| \alpha_i^t(t) + j\beta_i^t(t)\|_{i=1}^n$,
this task can be resolved using the condition of the zero-equality for the imaginary component of the eigenvector at the moment of entrance on the hyperbola.

We obtain the solution of the equation

$$z_\beta{}^i(t_0)(2\text{-}\exp(\alpha_i^t(t_0)\, t_i)\cos(\beta_i^t(t_0)\, t_i))=$$
$$= z_\alpha{}^i(t_0)\exp(\alpha_i^t(t_0)\, t_i)\sin(\beta_i^t(t_0)\, t_i),$$

(2.17) $$\operatorname{tg}\eta = \frac{z_\beta{}^i(t_0)}{z_\alpha{}^i(t_0)} = \frac{\exp(\alpha_i^t(t_0)t_i)\sin(\beta_i{}^t(t_0)t_i)}{2-\exp(\alpha_i^t(t_0)t_i)\cos(\beta_i{}^t(t_0)t_i)}.$$

For the optimal model, this relation represents the invariant

$$c_x^0 = \frac{\exp(\alpha')\sin(\gamma\alpha')}{2-\exp(\alpha')\cos(\gamma\alpha')}$$

that depends on $\alpha'(\gamma)$. At γ =0.5, α' =0.706, we get c_x^0 =7.0866, which determines the angle η=1.430611($\approx 82^o$).

The condition of the zero-equality for the real component of the eigenvector defines the angle η' at the moment t'=t_i- of reaching the process starting point :

$$tg\eta' = \frac{z'_\beta{}^i(t_0)}{z'_\alpha{}^i(t_0)} = \frac{2-\exp(\alpha_i^t(t_0)t_i-)\cos(\beta_i^t(t_0)t_i-)}{\exp(\alpha_i^t(t_0)t_i-)\sin(\beta_i{}^t(t_0)t_i-)} = c_x^{'0},$$

$$c_x^{'0} = \frac{2-\exp(b_o)\cos(\gamma b_o)}{\exp(b_o)\sin(\gamma b_o)}$$

which is defined by the invariant $b_o(\gamma) = \alpha_i^t(t_0)t_i-$. At γ =0.5, b_o=-0.517, we obtain $c_x^{'0}$=523.1, which defines $\eta' \approx \pi/2$..

Assume the optimal motion along a normal takes place on the surfaces of the corresponding cones with the spiral equation (2.1) at the discrete moments. The increment of the angle η of the spiral rotation, is determined from the condition

(2.18) $\bar{\alpha}_1^i(t_0)\,\bar{\alpha}_1^i(t_i) + \bar{\alpha}_2^i(t_0)\,\bar{\alpha}_2^i(t_i) + \bar{\alpha}_3^i(t_0)\,\bar{\alpha}_3^i(t_i) = \cos\eta$, i-1,...,n,

and holds the form

(2.19) $\varphi_\eta^i(t_i) = \varphi_\eta$.

At γ =0.5, α' =0.706, that angle is equal $\varphi_{\eta} \approx 18rad$.

The corresponding relation (2.18) (with cos η' on the right side) defines the space angle of a spiral rotation φ_{η}' to reach the cone vertex at the moment $t'=t_i -$.

At γ =0.5, b_o=-0.517 $\eta' \approx \pi / 2$, that angle takes on the value $\varphi_{\eta}' \approx 18.9rad$.

The condition (2.16) for the vector $\bar{\bar{l}}_k^{\,i}(t_k + o)$ on the k-cone with respect to the vector $\bar{\bar{l}}_k^{\,m}(t_k + o)$, defined on the cone at the μ_{i+1} discrete interval on the switching line, acquires a view:

(2.20) $$\frac{d\Delta \bar{l}_z(t_k + o(t))}{dt} = \frac{d\Delta \bar{l}_z^{\,m}(t_k + o(t))}{dt}$$, k=1,3,5; m=1,2,..

The fulfillment (2.14-19) leads to the coordination of the mutual positions of the considered cones in space and the determination of alterating of the vectors $\bar{\bar{l}}^{\,i}$(t) (i=n,n-1,...1) in the immobile coordinate system (l_x, l_y, l_z).

Let us form this coordinate system on the m -cone :

(2.21) $(\bar{l}_1^{\,m}, \bar{l}_2^{\,m}, \bar{l}_3^{\,m}) = (l_x, l_y, l_z)$,

at the discrete moment, that finalizes the consolidation procedure.

As a result of execution of (2.14), we arrive at the following equations of the normals in the immobile coordinate system, for example at n=6:

(2.22) $\Delta \bar{l}^{\,6} = (1-l^6)(\bar{\alpha}_1^6 l_x + \bar{\alpha}_2^6 l_y + \bar{\alpha}_3^6 l_z)$, $\bar{\alpha}_1^6 = \alpha_x$, $\bar{\alpha}_2^6 = \alpha_y$, $\bar{\alpha}_3^6 = \alpha_z$,

$$\Delta \bar{l}^{\,5} = (1-l^5)(-\bar{\alpha}_1^5 l_x + \bar{\alpha}_2^5 l_y + \bar{\alpha}_3^5 l_z),$$

$$\Delta \bar{l}^{\,4} = (1-l^4)[(\bar{\alpha}_1^4 \cos\psi \cos\psi^o + \bar{\alpha}_2^4 \sin\psi \cos\psi^o + \bar{\alpha}_3^4 \sin\psi^o) l_x +$$
$$+(\bar{\alpha}_1^4 \cos\psi \sin\psi^o + \bar{\alpha}_2^4 \sin\psi \sin\psi^o - \bar{\alpha}_3^4 \cos\psi^o) l_y +$$
$$+(\bar{\alpha}_1^4 \sin\psi - \bar{\alpha}_2^4 \cos\psi) l_z],$$

$$\Delta \bar{l}^{\,3} = (1-l^3)[(\bar{\alpha}_1^3 \sin\psi \cos\psi^o + \bar{\alpha}_2^3 \cos\psi \cos\psi^o +$$
$$+\bar{\alpha}_3^3 \sin\psi^o) l_x + (\bar{\alpha}_2^3 \cos\psi \sin\psi^o + \bar{\alpha}_1^3 \sin\psi \sin\psi^o - \bar{\alpha}_3^3 \cos\psi^o) l_y +$$
$$+(\bar{\alpha}_1^3 \cos\psi - \bar{\alpha}_2^3 \sin\psi) l_z],$$

where (ψ, ψ_1) are the angles of rotation of the local coordinate systems.

For the subsequent discretization points $\Delta \bar{l}^{\,2}$, $\Delta \bar{l}^{\,1}$, we introduce the indications that will simplify the equations form:

(2.23) $$A_x^2 = (\bar{\alpha}_1^2 \cos\psi_1 + \bar{\alpha}_2^2 \sin\psi_1) \sin\psi^o - \bar{\alpha}_3^2 \cos\psi^o,$$
$$A_y^2 = (-\bar{\alpha}_1^2 \cos\psi_1 + \bar{\alpha}_2^2 \sin\psi_1) \cos\psi^o + \bar{\alpha}_3^2 \sin\psi^o,$$
$$A_z^2 = \bar{\alpha}_1^2 \sin\psi_1 - \bar{\alpha}_2^2 \cos\psi_1,$$
$$A_x^1 = (\bar{\alpha}_1^1 \sin\psi_1 + \bar{\alpha}_2^1 \cos\psi_1) \sin\psi^o + \bar{\alpha}_3^1 \cos\psi^o,$$

$A_y^1 = \overline{\alpha}_1^1 (\cos\psi_1 - \sin\psi_1)\cos\psi^o - \overline{\alpha}_3^1 \sin\psi^o,$

$A_z^1 = \overline{\alpha}_1^1 \cos\psi_1 - \overline{\alpha}_1^2 \sin\psi_1.$

Generally, for the sequential set of discrete points we obtain

(2.24) $\Delta\bar{l}^{\,j} = (1 - l^{\,j})\,[(A_y^j \cos\psi_1 \cos\psi^o + A_x^j \sin\psi_1 \sin\psi^o + A_z^j \sin\psi^o) l_x$

$+(A_y^j \cos\psi_1 \sin\psi^o + A_x^j \sin\psi^o - A_z^j \cos\psi^o) l_y +$

$+(A_x^j \cos\psi_1 - A_y^j \sin\psi_1) l_z]$; j=2,1,

where $(\overline{\alpha}_1^i, \overline{\alpha}_2^i, \overline{\alpha}_3^i)$ are the directional cosines of the normal in the local coordinate system of the i-cone; i=1,..., 6; j=2,1. As it follows from (2.23, 24), the condition (2.14) can be executed with an accuracy of approximating the rotation of the local coordinate system on some angle (ψ, ψ_1). We choosie the values of the angles (ψ, ψ_1,..., ψ_k) from the condition (2.15) in the form

$$c_z^{3-5}(t_5) = \left(\frac{\partial \Delta l_z^{3-5}}{\partial\varphi}\frac{d\varphi}{dt}\right)(t_5) = \left(\frac{\partial \Delta l_z^{4-5}}{\partial\varphi}\frac{d\varphi}{dt}\right)(t_5) = c_z^{4-5}(t_5),$$

$l_z^{4-5} = l_z^4 + b_5\varphi(\overline{\alpha}_1^4 \cos\psi + \overline{\alpha}_2^4 \sin\psi)$;

$l_z^{3-5} = l_z^3 + b_3\varphi(\overline{\alpha}_2^3 \cos\psi - +\overline{\alpha}_1^3 \sin\psi)),$

where the signs in the last equation correspond to the different spiral directions on the considered cones (the "minus" for the right spiral direction and the "plus" for the left spiral direction). We arrive at the relations

$\dot{l}_z^{4-5} = c_z^{4-5} = b_3(c/b_3)(\overline{\alpha}_1^4 \cos\psi + \overline{\alpha}_2^4 \sin\psi) +$

$+ b_5\varphi(\dot{\overline{\alpha}}_1^4 \cos\psi + \dot{\overline{\alpha}}_2^4 \sin\psi),$

$\dot{l}_z^{3-5} = c_z^{3-5} = c(\overline{\alpha}_2^3 \cos\psi - +\overline{a}_1^3 \sin\psi) + b_3\varphi(\dot{\overline{\alpha}}_2^3 \cos\psi - +\dot{\overline{\alpha}}_1^3 \sin\psi),$

$\overline{\alpha}_1 = \cos\psi^o \cos(\varphi\sin\psi^o); \dot{\overline{\alpha}}_1 = -(c/b)\sin\psi^o \sin(\varphi\sin\psi^o),$

$\overline{\alpha}_2 = \sin\psi^o \cos\varphi\cos(\varphi\sin\psi^o) - \sin\varphi\cos(\varphi\sin\psi^o), b = b_3$

$\dot{\overline{\alpha}}_2 = -(c/b)[(1+\sin^2\psi^o)\cos(\varphi\sin\psi^o) + 2\sin\psi^o \sin\varphi\cos(\varphi\sin\psi^o)].$

From hence, because these relations hold true

$\varphi = 6\pi$, and $\varphi\sin\psi^o = \pi/2$

at the point of the triple consolidation, we obtain

(2.25) $\overline{\alpha}_1 = 0, \overline{\alpha}_2 = 0,\ \dot{\overline{\alpha}}_1 = -(c/b)\sin\psi^o\cos\psi,\ \dot{\overline{\alpha}}_2 = -c/b(1+\sin^2\psi^o)$;

$c_z^{4-5} = -6\pi c\,[\sin\psi^o \cos\psi^o \cos\psi + (1+\sin^2\psi^o)\sin\psi],$

$c_z^{3-5} = -6\pi c[(1+\sin^2\psi^o)\cos\psi + \sin\psi^o \cos\psi^o \sin\psi],$

or from $c_z^{4-5} = c_z^{3-5}$ we have $(1 - \sin\psi^o\cos\psi^o + \sin^2\psi^o)\cos\psi =$

$= (1 - +\sin\psi^o\cos\psi^o + \sin^2\psi^o)\sin\psi,$

(2.26) $$tg\,\psi = \frac{(1 - \sin\psi^o\cos\psi^o + \sin^2\psi^o)}{(1 + -\sin\psi^o\cos\psi^o + \sin^2\psi^o)},$$

at ψ^o =0.08343, ψ =0.70311; moreover, for the equal directed spirals at small angle ψ^o, we get $\psi = \pi/4 - \psi^o$.

For the spirals of the opposite directions, it follows that $\psi' = \pi/4$.

For the intervals t_1-t_3, t_2-t_3, we come to the analogous procedure for the definition of the angles ψ_1, ψ_3, which take the same values. We get

(2.27) $\psi = \psi_1 = \psi_2 = ... = \psi_k = \pi/4 - \psi^o$; $\psi_1' = \psi_2' = ... = \psi_k' = \pi/4$.

At the last interval of the optimal motion for example, for (t_5-t_7), (t_6-t_7), the following equations are executed

(2.28) $l_z^{5-7} = l_z^5 + b_5\varphi\alpha_z^5$; $l_z^{6-7} = l_z^6 + b_6\varphi\alpha_z^6$; $c_z^{5-7} = c\alpha_z^5 + b_5\varphi\dot{\alpha}_z^5$;

$c_z^{6-7} = c\alpha_z^6 + b_6\varphi\dot{\alpha}_z^6$,

where at $\varphi = 6\pi$, $\dot{\alpha}_z^j$=0, α_z^j=1, j=5,6, we get $c_z^{5-7} = c_z^{6-7} = c$.

This corresponds to the resulting macrosystem motion along the l_z axis with the constant speed c after finalizing the optimal process.

Because of this, the extremal condition for $\Delta\bar{l}_z(\psi)$ (2.28) (which is in agreement with the increments of this coordinate by other cones), defines its maximal increments. By analogy, we determine the conditions of the cones coordination (formed before the entrance on the hyperbola) with the cones that correspond to the movement along the hyperbola switching line.

The condition (2.14) leads to the equation in the form (2.22).

From condition (2.19), we find the angle ψ^o of the relative rotation of the above cones. Considering, for example, the cones between the points $(l_6 - l_7)$, $(l_0 - l_6)$ we come to the following equations:

(2.29) $c_z^6(t) = \dot{\varphi}(t)b_3\alpha_z^6(t) + b_3\varphi(t)\dot{\alpha}_z^j(t)$; t= $t_6 + o$, c_z^6=0; $\varphi(t_6 + o)$ =0;

t'=$t_6 - o$; $\varphi(t_6 - o)$ =6π;

$$c_z^6(t') = \dot{\varphi}(t')b_3(\alpha_x(t')\cos\psi^o - \alpha_y(t')\sin\psi^o) +$$

$$+ b_3\varphi(t')(\dot{\alpha}_x(t')\cos\psi^o - \dot{\alpha}_y(t')\sin\psi^o)$$

$$\dot{\alpha}_x = -(c/b)(\cos\psi^o\sin\psi^o), \dot{\alpha}_y = -(c/b)(1+\sin^2\psi^o);$$

$$\alpha_x(t') = \alpha_y(t') = 0,\ b = b_3,$$

$$c_z^6(t') = -6\pi c[(1+\sin^2\psi^o)\sin\psi^o) - \sin\psi^o\cos\psi^o\cos\psi'^o\sin\psi)].$$

By equalization of speeds c_z^6(t) =$c_z^6(t')$, we get $\mathrm{tg}\,\psi'^o = \dfrac{\sin\psi^o\cos\psi^o}{1+\sin^2\psi^o}$;

tg ψ'^o(γ =0.5)=0.0075 ≈ 0, $\psi'^o \approx 0$. The same relations follow from the consideration of the condition (2.19) for the cones between the points $(l_3 - l_5)$, $(l_0 - l_3)$.

Finally, we come to the following recurrent equations for the projection of the normals (defined by the n-cones) with respect to the immobile coordinate system:

(2.30) $l^i_x = l^i_x(t_j) + b_i\varphi_i(\Delta t_j)\alpha_x(\Delta t_j)$; $\Delta t_i \rightarrow \tau_i$, j=0,1,...,n, i=1,...,n;

$l^i_y = l^i_y(t_j) + b_i\varphi_i(\Delta t_j)\alpha_y(\Delta t_j)$; ψ^o=0, $\varphi(\tau_j) = 6\pi$, $\varphi(0) = 0$;

$l^i_z = l^i_z(t_j) + b_i\varphi_i(\Delta t_j)\alpha_z(\Delta t_j)$; $\eta = \eta^o$=6π , $\psi = \pi/4$.

Using the obtained results, for the OPMC we find (as a function of the model parameters (n, γ, k)) the relative angle of rotation of the local coordinate system:

- at the moment of the entrance on the hyperbola:

(2.31) $\overline{\psi}$=arctg[$\sin\psi^o\cos\psi^o(1+\sin^2\psi^o)^{-1}$]=Const ($n$, γ, k);

- at tdiscrete moments (on the macromovement along the hyperbola):

(2.32) $\overline{\psi}(t_i)$=arctg($1-\sin\psi^o\cos\psi^o+\sin^2\psi^o$)×

×$(1+-\sin\psi^o\cos\psi^o+\sin^2\psi^o)^{-1}$,

where the signs " +" and "-" are related to spirals of the opposite directions.

A different values of γ bring variations to the angles' values φ, ψ, η, ψ'^o, $\overline{\psi}$.

The execution of (2.23-32) coordinates the mutual positions of the cones in the space and determines the changes of the geometrical macromodel coordinates in the immobile system.

The obtained geometrical structure reflects the necessity of memorizing the macrodistributions in space, created by the undistinguished states in consolidation process.

1.3.4. The triplet's structure

The geometrical meaning of consolidation at the discrete points consists of an additivity of the cone volumes V^i_k, and their increments computed at these points for each triple:

(3.1) $V_k(t_k) = V^i_k + V^{i+1}_k + V^{i+2}_k$, $\Delta V^{i,i+2}_k = 2(3V^{i-2,i}_k + V^{i-1,i}_k)$, i=3,5,7

forming the triplet as a new macrostructure.

The ratio of the volume V^i_k to the surface F_k of the forming structure characterizes its relative strength Π (as a specific force of the pressure, measured by the ratio of the weight within the volume V^i_k to F^i_k):

$$(3.2)\ \Pi = \frac{V^i_k}{F^i_k} = b/3\sin(\varphi\sin\psi^o)\cos\psi^o,\quad F^i_k = \frac{\pi\rho_i^2}{\sin\psi^o} + \pi\rho_i^2.$$

The condition of the extreme for the relative strength ($\frac{\partial\Pi}{\partial\varphi} = 0$) is satisfied by the execution of the relation (2.2), i.e., with the maximum $\rho(\varphi)$.

Each triplet is a structure with the odd symmetry order following :

$$(3.3)\ \Pi_c = \frac{2\pi}{\pi/2+-(\pi/4-\arcsin(2k)^{-12})},\quad \Pi'_c = \frac{2\pi}{\pi/4-\arcsin(2k)^{-12}},$$

$\Pi_c(\psi^o) \cong 3, \Pi_c(-\psi^o) \cong 7, \Pi'_c(\psi^o)=9, k=1$.

Moreover, the positions of the triplet's local coordinate axes in the space are not repeated precisely (Figure 1.3.3), and any symmetrical transformations can not bring the above axes to an equivalent position. The transformation of local coordinates is preserved at $\varphi = + - \pi$ (k=1), and it possesses the symmetry of the reflection. The angle ψ^o as a third space coordinate depends on parameter k .

With growing k, the number of three-dimensional coordinates is increasing, and restricted relations take place that admit even symmetry order

(3.4) $\lim\limits_{k\to\infty} \Pi_c(+\psi^o)=2.66$; $\lim\limits_{k\to\infty} \Pi_c(-\psi^o)=8$; $\lim\limits_{k\to\infty} \Pi'_c(\psi^o)=8$

although, the "conditional " symmetry order is the odd at any limited k .

The considered space movement is accompanied with a rotary movement along each helix, and therefore it possesses a rotating moment $M(i)$ that is defined by the scalar multiplication of a system's impulse $imp(i)$ and the radius vector of the rotation $\bar{r}(i)$ for each local extremal piece (i) :

(3.5) $M(i) = imp(i) \bullet \bar{r}(i)$, $imp(i) = \dfrac{\partial L(x_i, \partial x_i / \partial t)}{\partial C_i}$, $C_i = \dfrac{dl_i}{dt}$.

The impulse is preserved for the Hamiltonian model, and at the vicinity of the discretization moment when the macrostructure is forming, the radius of rotation acquires a maximal value $\bar{r}(i) = b(i)$, where $b(i)$ is the radius of the i-cone base. This defines the maximal value of each local rotating moment for considered the i-piece of extremal movement around the corresponding coordinate axis: $M_{t=\tau}(i) = M_m(i) = imp(i) \bullet b(i)$.

The $M_m(i)$ is able of rotating the initial matrix eigenvalues for the eigenvector's space cooperation. This rotary moment of the macromodel movement exists independently on electrical and magnetic fields as an intrinsic information-geometrical characteristic of the process of informational structure forming. Applying the above results leads to the algorithmic software procedure that uses the IMD software packet for the restoration of the OPMC dynamic and geometrical structures for a given (γ ,c, k , α_{io}^t).

1.3.4. The OPMC classification and accuracy of the object modeling

The entropy function defined on the extremals

(4.1) $\Delta\hat{S} = M[(x+v)^T X] = 1/2M[(x+v)^T r_v^{-1}(x+v)] = n/2$

preserves the constant during all times of optimal motion, and under the coordinate transformations:

$$T = x(\tau)T_\tau(x(s)), T_\tau = \prod_{i=1}^{n}(2E - \exp(A(t_i)t_i), x(s) = x(t_o).$$

The piecewise function $\hat{H}(\tau)=1/2\,A(\tau)$ is changed by jumping at the matrix

$A(\tau)$ renovating points satisfying $\sum_{i=1}^{n} \hat{H}(\tau_i)\ \tau_i = \Delta\hat{S}$ and defining the entropy of transformation: Sup $\hat{H}(\tau_i)$=h(T_τ).

The local Hamiltonian has a meaning of the specific entropy of the OPMC: $h^v = \frac{\partial \Delta\hat{S}}{\partial V}$, and the entropy for the object: $h_o^{\ v} = \frac{\partial \Delta\hat{S}_o}{\partial V_o}$, where the function

$$(4.2)\ h^v = \frac{\partial \Delta\hat{S}}{\partial t} / \frac{\partial V}{\partial t} = -\hat{H} / \dot{V}, \dot{V} = c\,\hat{F},\ \hat{F} = \bigcup_{k=1}^{m} F^k,$$

$$h_o^{\ v} = \frac{\partial \Delta\hat{S}_o}{\partial V_o} = -\frac{\hat{H}_o}{\dot{V}_o}\quad \hat{H}_o = 1/4 \mathrm{Sp}\, \dot{r}r^{-1},\ c = c(n, \gamma, k),\ \dot{V}_o = c_o\, \hat{F}_o,$$

characterizes the peculiarities of a particular macrostructure.

This function is defined by the dynamics and geometry, and it determines the information unity of the superimposing processes as a numerical indicator of the similarity of the created macro structures. Objects with equal $h_o^{\ v}$ are similar (in terms of equal information measure), and have the corresponding OPMC's that form a system of interlinking processes. The measure of the object and OPMC equivalence is determined by the relative accuracy of modeling:

$$(4.3)\ \varepsilon_m^0 = \min_{n,\gamma} \varepsilon_m,\ \varepsilon_m = \frac{h^v{}_o}{h^v} - 1,\ \varepsilon_m' = \frac{1/4Sp(\dot{r}r^{-1})}{1/2Sp\alpha_{io}^t} - 1, \text{ at } \dot{V} = \dot{V}_o.$$

The identified extremal equations minimize ε_m, but it is not always possible to evaluate the exact equivalence of the real object and its model.

The execution of equation (4.3) with a given accuracy establishes a possibility of modeling an object by the OPMC; h_v^0 associates with the measuring of the information density of the diffusion process at the model's microlevel.

The dynamic indicator of the OPMC consolidation represents the ratio

$$(4.4)\ m(t_i)\alpha_i^t(t_i) / \sum_{i=1}^{n} \alpha_i^t(t_i) = h_\varepsilon^t,$$

where m is the number of consolidated processes, and n is the total number of the OPMC processes. The optimal controls select the structures with equal $\alpha_i^t(t_i)$ and join them. The methodology of optimal synthesis of the OPMC dynamics and geometrical structures have been implemented on computers with applied software packet that includes (but is not limited) model's parameters n=4-100, γ =(0.0-0.8) h^v serves as an indicator of the trajectories' complexity, and also characterizes the number of the renovating points, where the new information and structure are created. The optimal trajectory segments with the set of the discrete controls, represent a minimal code that can be restored if the function $h^v = h^v(n, \gamma, \mathrm{k})$ is known. The macromodel parameters with equivalent encoding control methods that preserves h^v are connected. Current model parameters (n, γ, k) can be determined by their relations with respect to some basic model parameters (n_o, γ_o, k_o):

$$(4.5)\quad \frac{Sp(\alpha_{io}(n,\gamma))}{Sp(\alpha_{io}(n_o,\gamma_o))} = \frac{c(n,\gamma,k_0)c^2(n_o,\gamma_o,k_o)F^3(n,\gamma,k)}{c^3(n,\gamma,k)F^2(n_o,\gamma_o,k_o)F(n,\gamma,k_o)},$$

$c(n_o,\gamma_o,k_o) = c_o$, $V(n_o,\gamma_o,k_o) = V_o$, $L(n_o,\gamma_o,k_o) = L_o$.

From hence, at given (n_o,γ_o,k_o), the parameters (n, γ, k) are found and then are computed: the dynamic parameters (t_i, T, $v_i(t_i)$, $x_i(t_i)$) and the geometrical OPMC characteristics (l_i, L, c, $v_i(l_i)$, $x_i(l_i)$, V^i_k}, which determine the kinetics of the interlinking processes and the sizes of the geometrical macro structures.

This methodology also leads to the macrostructure classification depending on both the chosen models' parametrs (n, γ, k) and (n_o,γ_o,k_o).

Based on this computation, the typical sequence of the OPMC models are built.

With increasing n and decreasing γ, the relative model parameters such as the geometrical sizes (L/L_0), the volumes (V/L_0), and the duration of functioning (T/T_0) are growing, while the relative speeds (c/c_0) are decreasing. With growing n, getting the lowest γ requires increasing k (decreasing ψ^o) that leads to an essential increasing of the macromodel complexity [1]. At small n, the OPMC with the nearest characteristics exist. As the OPMC dimensions and complexities grow, the nearest OPMC's (according to the classification) have more different characteristics that moves them far away with increasing n.

The macrocomplexity, defined by a sequence of the encoded macro states, is connected with the micro level randomness, representing an attribute of an entire macromodel. The macroprocess' irreversibility restricts repeating the model's dynamics and geometry with the same controls that are associated with nonreplacement of the optimal coding program as the code unexchangeability. The model's information value is characterized by the unexchangeability of the model coding program by another program at the model reconstruction. A macrostate has a different value depending on the accumulated information. With growing n, a given macrostate accumulates a new information and binds it into the triplet structures. Each following triplet encloses the preceding one and therefore, possess an increasing information value. The memorized sequence of encoding macro states according to their values and the time-space locations represents the macro model's structural information.

Comment. The OPMC has a more general meaning for revealing regularities of different sciences. Consider a science goal to be the knowledges of science approaching the truth by minimizing uncertainty between observations (as a contemporary justification of truth) and the actual truth, we can utilize OPMC as a common computerized scientific methodology.

REFERENCE

1. Lerner V.S. "Informational Systems Modeling of Space Distributed Macrostructures," *Proceedings of the 1998 Western Multiconference Conference on Mission Earth: Modeling and Simulation of Earth Systems,* January 1998; San Diego.

PART II. INFORMATION SYSTEMS MODELING

2.1. INFORMATION SYSTEMS THEORY AND IMD

2.1.1. Information Systems (IS)

Definition. *Information System (IS) is an interconnected set of interactions exchanging information capable of integrating them into a common informational unit.*

Information is everything that has a corresponding measure.

Some of information is available for observation.

The IS under observation is an *object*, which is *a selected part* of a real (space -time distributed) world (as a system) *that is subject of examination.*

The ability of the interacting set for integration is a fundamental quality that defines a system. For IS, the root source of integration is the information connections of the interactive sets via the mechanism of the information exchanges. Information connection includes but is not limited to physical interactions; important are the virtual interactions, whose *space-time* locations do not coincide. Cooperation could be considered as a result of the *interactive processes* generating the *elements* that are capable of creating *cooperative structures*. The interconnections and interactions carry out an inner *feedback* mechanism that, under some conditions, working concurrently with integration, enables the creation of *order*. At such consideration, the *ordered* interactive set is formed by the *cooperative elements*, while the *ordered cooperative structure* represents their integrated *unit*. IS spreads out to reach a limit that is restricted by the boundary of transmitting information from the interacting set. The informational connections in particular, via *observations* enable the generation of *randomness*. A single phenomenon, that is separated from the observer has a deterministic nature. The large number of interactive processes has a *random nature*, being sources of *behavioral dynamic* regularities. A great many interactions can generate new *dynamic* processes and *dynamic structures*.

Thus, the attributes of the IS are *randomness*, generating *information*, and *dynamic* processes extracting regularities and creating *ordered structures* that bind information. An ordered chain of mutually coordinated dynamics, a geometry of the cooperative structures, that carries out such phenomena as aggregation and hierarchy, stability, adaptability, evolutionary ability in the process of cyclic functioning, and reproductivity of information and cooperative structures, are the subjects of Information Systems Theory (IST).

2.1.2. Analytical and Informational Systems Models

The goal of Analytical Systems Model (ASM) is to reflect the above phenomena, with integration (cooperation) as a key characteristic of a systemic object. The ASM describes the specific object's regularities based on their particular laws, as physical, biological, economical, social, etc. The main difference between a regular mathematical model and ASM consists in the ability to represent a set of interactions integrating into a common unit (system, subsystem). The Information Systems Model (ISM) includes the analytical object's representation by a common information language (IL) that describes the systemic information interactions and cooperations in terms of information measure. According to Shannon's Information Theory, the quantity information of a symbol is measured by the probabilistic measure of uncertainty (or surprise), which the symbol carries among a considered set of equal potential symbols. This number defines an information code of the IL (as minimal bits of information content of the set of symbols, which convey this set). The IL may contain other measures of uncertainty as well as optimal information code of minimal complexity , with the language syntax and grammar. The ISM goal is to reflect general informational regularities of a wide diversity regarding the specific nature of the objects.

The object regularities should be expressed by some information law, which in a mathematical form is utilized for information modeling.

We consider an information order as a common characteristic of any specific regularity and law. The ISM compact form is an optimal algorithm of minimal program of the object regularities. Information Modeling includes a *human being* (as an observer, carrier, and producer of information), with restoration of the model during the object observations. No special hypotheses or statements are made about the system elements or their interconnections; no strict determinism and causality are supposed. Certain causes may or may not may produce such an effect with some probability; all elements' relations are unknown, uncertain.

The emergence of systemic elements and their selection depends upon a specific set of interactions. The main modeling problems are identification, discovery, and prognosis of regularities via system modeling; finding conditions for statistical or dynamic description, and the model specification (linear, nonlinear; concentrated, distributed, continuous, discrete, homogeneous, and so on); modeling the system's elements, as the selected system's parts that enable cooperation into common unit, and finding their relations to the system; creation, dissemination, transformation (between the elements), reproduction, and destruction of information in a system; prediction order, or disorder, stability, nonstability, systemic disintegration, self-organization, and adaptation.

2.1.3. Information Systems Analysis

To reflect the nature of systemic object phenomena, the Information Model requires current informative data from the initial interactive processes for model identification. It is essential for both object and model to possess such characteristics as observability and identifiability , the model input (IN) (to collect data and control) and output (OUT) (to estimate and evaluate the model functioning) with the possibility of feedback (FB) between them (Figure.2.1.1).

Both the input and output equations should be distributed in time-space and satisfy the conditions of controllability. The initial object data is transformed into the informational state space coordinates, controls, by the control filter (CF) that selects the most informative (nonredundant) data to feed the model .

That, in addition to controllability, is connected with the problem of informational control filtering. The interpreter (IP) transforms the model's outgoing informational space coordinates into the initial data format. Feedback deals with the information

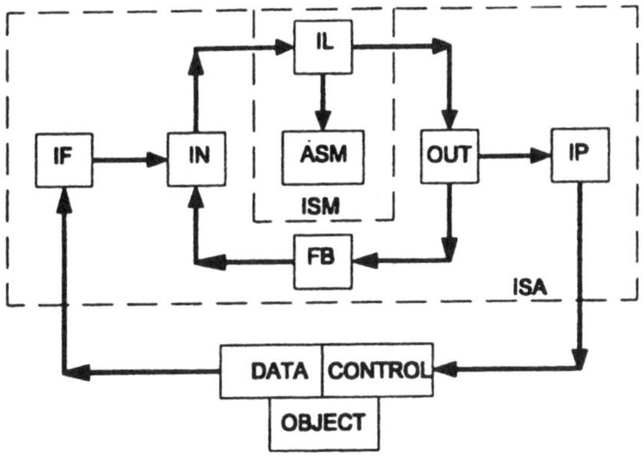

Figure 2.1.1. Schematic structure of ISM and ISA.

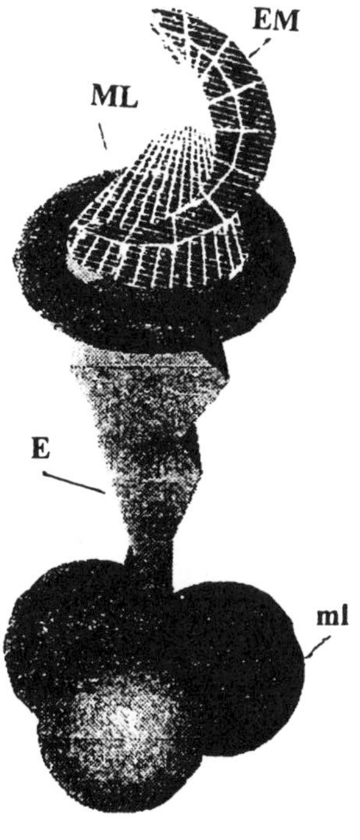

Figure 2.1a.
Computer drafted sketch-diagram representing the IS structure: interactive microlevel (ml) generating elements (E), and macrolevel (ML) forming evolutionary macrostructures (EM).

space coordinates. To analyze model performance and select the solutions that satisfy some criteria, the model needs computer simulation that requires transformation of the initial analytical model (ASM or/and ISM) into a numerical model, applying optimization methods toward a solution of the appropriate extremal criteria problems. Numerical modeling also includes equations of observation, identification, control strategy, feedback, input, output, transformations into informational variable and back to initial data.

The criteria can evaluate the quality of the model performance, feasibility of the solutions, simulation results, control and decision-making process, etc.

The ISM analysis, numerical modeling, computer simulation, and performance are the elements of Information Systems Analysis (ISA). The main ISA goal is to select the ISM solutions applicable to Information Technology. Implementation of ISA requires a software for numerical modeling, computer simulation, and a hardware for filters, sensors, and so on. The information language of ISM and ISA is capable of unifying the diversity of specific models and different nature of objects.

Such a general information description can bring a corresponding numerical representation and modeling with the possibility of creating a family of standard models (for different information objects) and associated standard software.

A specific software should transform a particular object data into an information data format and vice-versa applicable also for control and decision-making. ISA is an application of IST, and the ISA with its hardware and software is applied to ICT.

2.1.4. Collective stochastics in the IMD systemic model

Complex stochastic motions in many real objects enable creating some regular
Complex stochastic motions in many real objects enable of creating some regular dynamic processes as the sources of organization. For example, creation of physical structure in process of solidification and crystallization is accompanied with interactions of such phenomena as thermo conductivity, thermo diffusion, chemical reactions, kinetics, hydrodynamics; the Benar-Reley cells, generated in convective process of nonstable fluctuations; the autocatalic chemical reactions; the ecological Lotka-Volterra models, and others. Self-organizing biological structures of origin and growing organs, intelligent structures are the results of interactions of physical, chemical, and informational processes. The creation of human knowledge is a product of the interaction of a large number of informational processes, many of them are communicating virtually. The dissipative structures [1] are a large class of dynamic phenomena arising in the process of ordering of chaotic movements from nonstable dynamics. Such nonlinear dynamics are considered as a result of chaotization of nonstable regular motions. Nonlinear mechanics originates from Hamiltonian mechanics and the Canonical theory of small perturbances [2]. Nonstable motions in such a model lead to decreasing and then decoupling of the time correlations and mixing up the phase trajectories. Finally, global diffusion arises as a result collectivization of two-dimensional systems [2]. Another approach to creation of dynamic phenomena is based on Informational Macrodynamics (IMD) that originate from the process of collectivization of many dimensional stochastics considered as a microlevel source of arising macrolevel dynamics. The IMD microlevel generates new information and informational macrolevel structures. Regularities of creation of information and its structurization in both micro- and macrolevel processes are the IMD goal. An assumption of existence of initial

regular physical dynamics and condition of their nonstability is not required.

The microlevel stochastics can model the interactive information flows from different data sources connecting via physical or virtual communications. In particular, the collective stochastics could be a product of stochastization of the nonstable regular motions in nonlinear dynamics as well. In such a consideration, the IMD includes the nonlinear dynamics as a more general approach.

A system of interacting elements is modeled by statistical movement of an ensemble of the large number of Brownian particles. An example is the motion of a weighted particle under action of a large number of molecular forces.

The trajectories of Brownian movement form a Marcovian diffusion process with the function of probabilities as a solution of the Fokker-Plank-Kolmogorov equations [3]. Marcovian approximation is a well-known formalism for modeling a wide class of random processes.

The description of many dimensional interactions by such a model represents an unsolved problem. Even for a simple case of the "reflecting screen boundary's conditions," when the random mixing-up process starts, the solution of the problem is very difficult. It requires more general mathematical models of the microlevel process. For the above examples, the stochastic equation (1.1.1) describes a model of the n-dimensional components of the initial microlevel processes $\tilde{x}(t)$ before their collectivization. In the controlled stochastic equations (1.1.17), the applied controls may turn the many dimensional stochastics in direction of their collectivization or their separation. It would depend on chosen criterion of evaluating of the control performance and the task of control applications. The applied control can also transform the initial Macrovian process into non Marcovian. To extract order from random *observation*, the process $\tilde{x}(t)$ is transformed into Wiener's process $\xi(t)$ (considered as a standard process that models of a complete disorder).

This transformation represents the task of control action. A *relative* information model uses the additive functional (ω_s^T) connected with the density measure (1.2.33) of transformation of the process's probabilities. The conditional mathematical expectation of the additive functional defines the entropy *functional*

$$(1.1)\ S(s,T,x(\bullet)) \overset{def}{=} M_{\tilde{x}_s,B}[\omega_s^T],\ M_{\tilde{x}_s,B}[\bullet] = \int_B [\bullet] P_{\tilde{x}_s,B}(d\omega)$$

that represents the macroscopic information measure of the processes transformation. An informational difference between $\tilde{x}(t)$ and $\xi(t)$ is a numerical measures of a possible negentropy generation as an information source for such transformations. The entropy functional has an analogy with Feinman's Path integral [4] and can be written in Lagrange's form

$$(1.2)\ S = \int_s^T M_{s,\tilde{x}_s} \tilde{L}(t,\tilde{x}_t,u(t,\tilde{x}_t))dt\ .$$

The entropy functional characterizes a relative order (with respect to stochastic Wiener process) and includes the controls (as a function of macro coordinates) that are applied for both micro- and macrolevels. Such controls could minimize or maximize the informational closeness of the controlled process to the standard one depending on a chosen maximum or minimum of the entropy functional.

If the standard process is characterized only by the diffusion components, then the solution of minimization problem for the above entropy functional leads to stochastization of the initial object at microlevel. In the opposite case, when the standard process is characterized only by the drift vector, the solution of the control problem leads to regularization of the initial stochastics.

The minimization of the relative entropy functional (1.1,2) describes the ordered macrolevel process by disordering of the microlevel process, or minimum entropy functional with respect to the macrolevel and its maximum at the microlevel. The same control action leads to collectivization of microlevel stochastics into a global diffusion and to cooperation of macrolevel process finally into one-dimensional dynamics. Informational variation principle (VP) applied to Marcovian microlevel, is a mathematical tool for discovering the IMD regularities. Maximization of the VP functional represents the optimal criterion of collective processes which can also evaluate a maximal usefulness of an element functioning within collective medium.

2.1.5. Macrolevel dynamics

The minimax principle for the entropy functional enables to select the extremals of collective dynamics as the macrotrajectories and to join the local extremals into cooperative motion. Macrotrajectories are formed by a "cutting off" of an ensemble of the controlled microtrajectories at the discrete moments (ch.1.3).

The optimal problem introduces a proper (eigenfunctional) functional:

$$S(x(t)) = \underset{u(t)\in\Omega_u}{extr}\; S(x(t,u(t,x)))$$

as the extremal value for entropy functional that satisfies VP. The eigenfunctional is a characteristic of the process of joining trajectories into a collective for both macro- and microlevels. That distinguishes it from the entropy functional, as a more general characteristic of relative disorder of transformed random process.

The difference between the eigen- and entropy functionals characterizes a potential closeness of observed process to collective motion.

The eigenfunctional is preserved on its extremals as the macrotrajectories.

The solution of the VP problem defines the macrolevel dynamics in the form of Hamiltonian equations for conjugate informational macrocoordinates (x, X):

$$(1.3)\qquad \frac{dx}{dt} = \frac{\partial H}{\partial X}, \quad \frac{dX}{dt} = -\frac{\partial H}{\partial x}, \quad X = \frac{\partial S}{\partial x}$$

and the equation of the differential constraint (DC):

$$(1.4)\qquad e(x, X, t') = \frac{\partial X}{\partial x} + 2X\,X^T \geq 0,$$

that stochastics impose on Hamiltonian Dynamics. The equations (1.3,4) model the IMD regularities and describe the macromechanics of uncertainty as an informational analogy of irreversible physical mechanics. The DC equation is based on the joint solution of the Kolmogorov and Hamilton equations (Part 1); it accumulates a "deterministic effect " of the microlevel's stochastics imposed on the Hamiltonian mechanics and kinetics at the discrete points (DP). The DC changes the structure and value of the macromodel operator creating its dynamic dependency on observed data. The macrodynamic process is characterized by the discrete extremal's intervals (DI) t', selected from the Hamilton's solutions via DC and determined by VP's invariants. Hamilton's equations determine, in general, the reversible dynamic solutions, and the DC equation imposes (at DI) the dynamic connection with the Marcovian stochastics, characterized by the diffusion matrix $b=b(t,x)$:

(1.5) $H(t')= X^T(t')\dfrac{dx}{dt}(t')=-1/2\, b(t',x(t'))\dfrac{\partial X}{\partial x}(t')$.

The Hamiltonian acquires the entropy production meaning, but only at the DP. Within the DP (when the DC is absent) time is reversible.

The irreversibility arises at the moment of constraint imposture. Marcovian transformation ($\tilde{x}_t \rightarrow \xi_t$) represents the model of the irreversible transformation; at macrolevel that preserves the total entropy and generates the randomness (in the DP localities). Microlevel stochastics create the macrolevel informational forces X, and macrolevel dynamics could originate the microlevel stochastics (through diffusion). Transformation of information from micro- to macrolevel is most effective when the H-function of information losses (1.5) gets minimal (according to (1.4)). The optimal inner control

(1.6) $v(t')=-2\,x(t')$

is formed by the DC through the conjugate vector

(1.7) $X=(2b)^{-1}\,\mathbf{A}\,(x+v)$; $\mathbf{A}v=u$, $\mathbf{A}=\{\lambda_i(t)\}$, $\lambda_i(t)=\alpha_i\pm j\beta_i$, i=1,...,n,

that connects differential operator **A** to statistical characteristics of the random process in the form of nonlinear correlations, which leads to the precise and a simple identification equation as a function of diffusion matrix or conditional correlations

(1.8) $\mathbf{A}=1/2\, b(t')[\int_{t'} b(t)dt]^{-1}$; $\mathbf{A}=M_{t',x}\{x(t)\dfrac{dx}{dt}^T(t)\}[M_{t',x}\{x(t)x^T(t)\}]^{-1}$.

Under the optimal control action, the macrolevel extremals enable us to approximate the microlevel random trajectories with maximal probability (ch.1.2) that measures their closeness. The **A**-matrix of the differential IMD equation (in a simple form) is

(1.9) $\dfrac{dx}{dt}=\mathbf{A}(x+v)$, $\mathbf{A}=\mathbf{A}(t',x)$,

which in turn is a differential operator of the classic mechanical analogy, and it acquires the irreversible qualities only at the DP, due to the second law, and is generated by the stochastics. Elsewhere (within each DI), $\mathbf{A}(t',x)$ is preserved and changed in stepwise due to the constraint imposition. At the moments of preceding the cooperation, the ($r\times n$) dimensional time correlations are uncoupled.

The separation of the nonlinear connections at the moments of the uncoupling correlation, leads to the selection of nonlinear operator from the symbol of conditional mathematical expectation for the controlled correlation function (1.8). This phenomenon, connected with the jumpwise nonlinear effects in the locality of DP, is used for the essential nonlinear operator identification (ch. 4.1). Within a DI, for each piece of the model extremal, the identification uses only the pair correlation's techniques.

The inner nonlinearities model the bifurcations and chaotic activities at the points of interactions. The movement along inside or outside of the pieces of each extremal separates the linear and nonlinear parts of the model with reversible and irreversible processes. The IMD starts with the stochastic model, which through

Chaotic Dynamics (CD) and the inner controls of discrete action at the macrolevel, is able to initiate a new second level of stochastics. The points of the CD development are predictable by the PM informational law. Two scales of the macro process are considered: large time intervals (t, t' -0) (outside of the DP), when the macromovement is analogous to the classic one, and the small intervals (in the DP vicinity) $|t'$ -0, t' +0$|$, when the macromovement is defined by the DC equation.

For the spatial distributed system, the solution of the VP problem leads to a controlled diffusion form of macroequation, identified by the microlevel (ch. 2). In addition to the control functions (1.6) , the macromodel possesses the "needle" controls acting as δ -function at the DP localities, and selecting the macrotrajectory pieces where the VP and the Erdman-Weirstrass conditions could violate.

The joint consideration of micro-and macroequations leads to the information analogy of Schrodinger's equation for the function of action S [4]:

$$(1.10)\ -\frac{\partial S}{\partial t} + WS - 1/2\, b\, \frac{\partial^2 S}{\partial x^2} = 0\ ; WS = -\frac{dS}{dt},$$

at $S=jhS^*$, $W=-jhW^*$, $b=-\frac{h}{jm}$, $h=\frac{jt}{t'}$

with the conjugate operators S^*, W^*, and the analogies of quantum Hamiltonian $H^* = -jh\frac{\partial S}{\partial t}$, information mass ($m$), and the function of indeterminacy h. Forming a hidden self- generated and ordering control takes place at the quantum macromodel level with its inherent uncertainty representing the carrier of cooperative differential constraint (DC).

Solution of the DC equation describes the forces X=X(x), which the second law imposes on Hamiltonian equations.

In particular, for a two-dimensional model, the solution $X = \begin{vmatrix} X_{11}, X_{12} \\ X_{21}, X_{22} \end{vmatrix}$ has the property (ch. 1.13) that if $x = \frac{X_{21}(0) - X_{11}(0)}{2(X_{11}(0)X_{22}(0) - X_{12}^2(0))}$,

then three solutions $X_{11}(x) = X_{21}(x) = X_{21}(x)$ coincide. If in addition $X_{11}(0) = X_{22}(0)$, then all four solutions coincide at $x = -[X_{12}(0) + X_{22}(0)]^{-1}$.

This property is able of creating macrocooperation and a system hierarchy.

2.1.6. Hierarchy of the information model

The transfer on the quantum macrolevel and the DP vicinity is accompanied with the equalization of the relative phase velocities of the macrovariables:

$$(1.11)\ \lambda_{it} = \frac{dx_i}{x_i dt}(t' -0) = \frac{dx_k}{x_k dt}(t' -0) = \lambda_{kt}, \text{ or } \lambda_{it}\lambda^*_{it} = \lambda_{kt}\lambda^*_{kt}$$

and the selection of the extremals takes place, for which the condition (1.11) is satisfied. At the moments t' the differential operator **A** is diagonalized successively.

This procedure is accomplished upon the equalization of all $\lambda_{it}, \lambda_{jt}$ (at j=n-1).

At the moments t', the controls (1.6) are applied, which results in the transfer of the movement from the pair of the extremals to the joint extremal, with a new differential operator corresponding to equal eigenvalues (1.11).

The renovating operator is memorized at the moment (t' +0), and remains the same along the next DI. At the same time, the macrostate, carrying the information maximum, is memorized by its coping and doubling through the controls (1.6), on the basis of selection of the subsystem competing for the maximum information acceptation. This procedure corresponds to the successive macromodel cooperation during the process of optimal movement, concurrently forming the hierarchical structure, which is memorized at the DP. The information states, characterized dynamically by the same entropy and the same structure of proper functional, are bound through the general function of losses (1.5).

At the moment (t' -0), a local minima of information production

$$(1.12)\ \max H' = \min \frac{\partial S}{\partial t} = \min |-\frac{dx}{dt}(t')^T X(t')| > 0,$$

binds the dynamic macrostructures at the moments (t' +0). Each DP is the result of joint solution of the three equations that could be nonlinear; such points are singular with the possibility of all kinds of Chaotic Dynamic Phenomena. The dynamic model operator is renovated at the points of discretization, where the extremals are freely selected and stuck together by the rules related to quantum mechanics. The selected macrostates carry the information maximum about the observed random process, realizing its optimal discrete filtering. The renovated operator and macrostates are sources of the new information, new properties, and the structures at the points of consolidation. The procedure of changing the operator is directed on minimization uncertainty (with increasing order), and is predictable by the VP invariants. There exist two subregions (RS) of the complex initial eigenvalues (λ_{io}*) of the differential operator. One of them corresponds to a positive direction of time (RS+), another one to the negative direction (RS-). At the phase trajectories approaching the RS+, the imaginary part of the eigenfunction turns into zero (or the pure imaginary eigenvalue is transferred to the real one). At the phase trajectories approaching the RS-, the real eigenvalues turn into zeroes. The RS represents the geometrical subspace where the curvature and symmetry change by a step jumping.

Within RS+ the real eigenvalues cooperate; moreover, the optimal procedure is to join them by threes with the following addition of a new pair to those, which were cooperated before a three. Such an elementary information dynamic structure (triplet) can also be formed by the real eigenvalues (from RS+) cooperating with primary two-conjugate imaginary eigenvalues (from RS-), when those regions adjoin one another. A zone of uncertainty (UR) is spreading between RS+ and RS-. It is characterized by a constant parameter of indeterminacy h.

The quantum macromodel is the carrier of the trigger effect, which is evidenced in the stepwise control action (1.6), and via the existence of the needle controls, responsible for changing the operator sign.

Along the trajectories, ending in RS+, the invariant

$$(1.13)\ \mathbf{a} = |\alpha_{io}| t_i = \alpha'(\gamma),\quad \alpha_{io} = \mathrm{Re}\,\lambda_{io},\quad \beta_{io} = \mathrm{Im}\,\lambda_{io},\quad \mathbf{a_o} = |\alpha_{it}| t_i = \alpha(\gamma)$$

is preserved; along the trajectories, transferring into RS-, the invariant

$$(1.14)\ \mathbf{b}'_o = |\beta_{io}|\, t_i^-,\ \mathbf{b}'_o = \gamma\, |\alpha_{io}|\, t_i^-,\ \gamma = |\frac{\beta_{io}}{\alpha_{io}}|$$

is preserved; moreover, **a** has a meaning of the quantity of the real information, formed at the moment t_i, and **b**o represents the quantity of the imaginary information at moment t_i^- of the hitting in RS-. Considering here t' - as an imaginary time, and t' as a real time, we get the UR uncertainty parameter:

$$(1.15)\ h = \frac{jt}{t'} = \frac{t_i^-}{t_i}; h = \frac{\mathbf{b}_o'}{\gamma \mathbf{a}} = \frac{\mathbf{b}_o}{\mathbf{a}},\ \mathbf{b}_o(\gamma) = |\alpha_{io}| t_i^-.$$

At $\mathbf{a} = \mathbf{b}_o$, $h = 1$, and for the pure real eigenvalues, uncertainty is $h = 0$, taking into account the sphere of the admitted values of the invariants,
$\mathbf{a}(\gamma = 0-1) = 0.765 - 0.3$, $\mathbf{b}_o(\gamma = 0-1) = 0.698 - 0.3$.

The maximum value of the invariant $\mathbf{a} = \ln 2 = h_{oo}$ characterizes the elementary information quantity within a single discretization interval.

As long as a quantum macrolevel contains the imaginary information ($h \neq 0$), and its probabilistic description is preserved. While a quantum macromodel's description can be applied, the information coordinates and their derivatives, the flows (the impulses) cannot be determined simultaneously within the region RS. The controls symbolize the creation of order from stochastics by an input of negentropy into a closed system, for example, at the expense of high-quality energy or unstable stochastic dynamics. The macromodel with such controls is capable of integration of its states at the DP and shortening the dimension of phase space, which are accompanied by forming the hierarchical information macrostructures (MS), memorized at DP. The MSs accumulate a defect of information spending for binding of the integrated macrostates at DP. MS is characterized by an information mass.

Each new MS is the source of the controls for the next integration and ordering.

Information Structured Network of Macronodes (IN, Figure 2.1.2, 3) is formed as Unification of Chaotic Attractors that model the collectivization both micro- and macrolevels. Algorithmization of the network nodes' information determines the minimal discrete spectrum of the local quantities of information $\{h_{io}$, i=1,...,n $\}$ for which the systemic representationis is defined and the hierarchical network of the structured information is reconstructed. Finally, the IMD model has five-levels of hierarchy: statistical microlevel; quantum dynamic level; dynamical (classical) macrolevel (as a result of selection of the initial macrostates and macrotrajectories); hierarchical informational dynamic network of macrostructures; and a possibility of creation of the second stochasic level as a result of Chaotic Dynamics.

2.1.7. Forming informational structures

The trajectories moving to the locality of the RS+ (or RS-) correspond to the eigenvalue transformation of rotation T+ (or T-), which is reversible.
The goal of that transformation is to bring together the corresponding eigenvalues, which is necessary for hitting into the region of the quantum regularity's action.
The classic dynamics are responsible for the transfer in the locality of the quantum

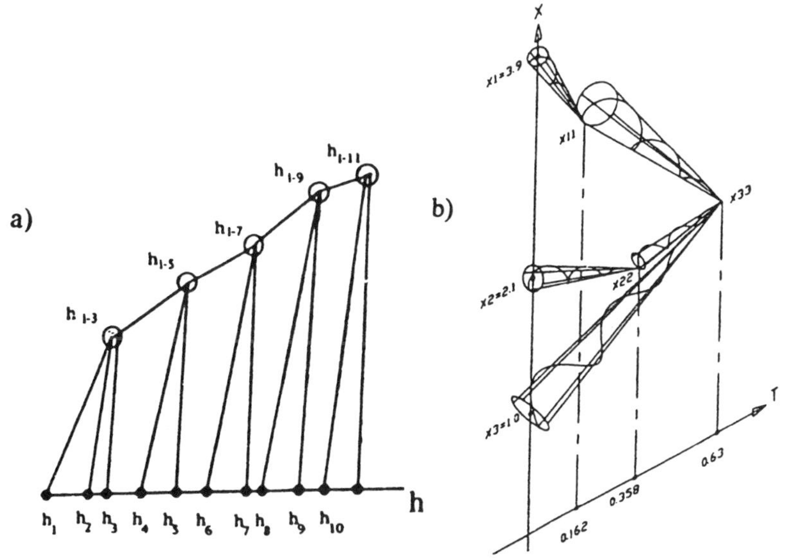

Figure 2.1.2. Forming the network of macrostructures: a) the network of the controlled nodes with the initial quantity information $\{h_{io}\}, i = 1,\ldots,n$; b) a triplet.

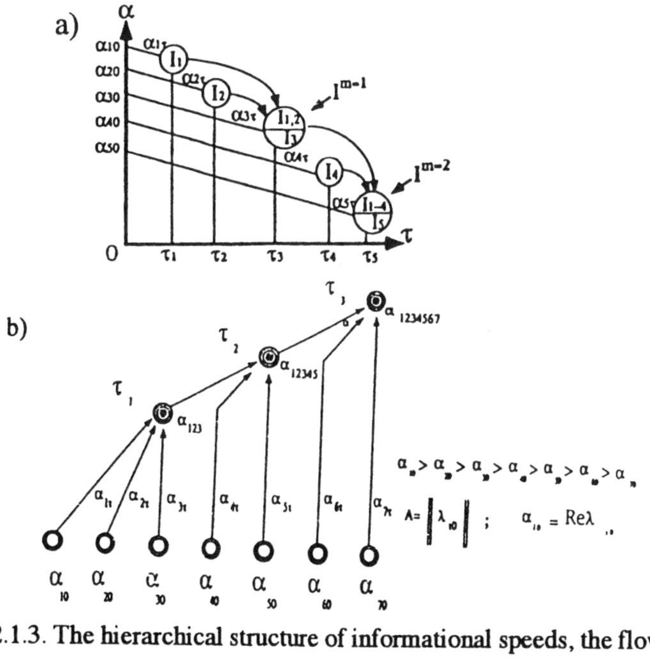

Figure 2.1.3. The hierarchical structure of informational speeds, the flows $I_i = \alpha_{i\tau}$ in process of optimal consolidation: a) the equalization of the model eigenvalues; b) the hierarchical model.

level, and the irreversible equation of the quantum macrodynamics describes the information interaction and binding of the macrostates into hierarchical structures.

When the condition **a** =**b**o is satisfied, the reversible transformation, by the separate action on the real (T+) and imaginary (T-) components, combines the regions RS+ and RS-, preparing the manifestation of the quantum regularities; that correspons to interaction of the imaginary eigenvalue pair (from RS-) with the doubled real eigenvalues (from RS+). At the combination of the RS+ and RS-, the above eigenvalues turn out to be infinitely closed, and their mutual transformation is performed. First, an elementary triplet is formed, with the conjugate imaginary information speed transformed into the real one:

(1.16) $(-j\beta_{it})(j\beta_{it}) = 2\alpha_{it}^2, \quad \beta_{it} = (2)^{1/2}\alpha_{it}$.

Then, a similar process takes place due to forming the information structure, which includes that real information and two new conjugate imaginary information speeds.

For this situation, the imaginary parts deliver the real information $2(2)^{1/2}\alpha_{it}t_i$, and the real part brings the information equal to $2\alpha_{it}t_i$.

Triplet accumulates the information difference, or the defect one:

(1.17) $d_{13}^o = 2\alpha_{it}((2)^{1/2} - 1)t_i) = 2$ **a**o $((2)^{1/2} - 1)$.

For the real relative informational speed: $\text{Re}\dfrac{dx_i}{x_i dt}(t') = \alpha_{it}$,

the corresponding real quantity of information is

$$(1.18) \qquad \mathbf{a}_o = \int_{t_{j-1}}^{t_j} \left(\frac{dx_i}{x_i dt}\right) dt = \ln\left(\frac{x_i(t_{j-1})}{x_i(t_j)}\right) = \alpha_{it} t_i .$$

At the considered border of RS+, RS-, we get the equalities **a** =**b**o; γ =1, and $\mathbf{a}_o$ has an admitted maximal value: $\mathbf{a}_o(\gamma=1)=0.295$. Because $\ln x(t')$ has the information meaning with the applied control (1.6), it turns out to be transferred to the relative real information measured $h_{oo} = \ln 2x(t') - \ln x(t') = \ln 2$, that is equal to the value of the invariant **a** (γ) on the single discretization interval.

Also, it is possible to form a triplet structure in a different way, by virtue of the existence of free real information when one of the eigenvalues is positive.

The defect of information for that regular triplet, formed at moment t_3 is

$$(1.19)\ d_{13} = \mathbf{a}_o\left(\left(\frac{t_3}{t_1}\right) - 1\right)/\left(\left(\frac{t_1}{t_3}\right) - 1\right) + \left(\left(\frac{t_3}{t_2}\right) - 1\right)/\left(\left(\frac{t_2}{t_3}\right) - 1\right) - 1)),$$

where the first two parts represent the increment information from α_{1t} and α_{2t} at moment t_3, and third one is $\alpha_{3t}t_3 = \mathbf{a}_o$. We may compare the information defects d_{13}^o, d_{13} for the same conditions : $\dfrac{t_3}{t_1}(\gamma=1)=2.25$, $\dfrac{t_2}{t_3}(\gamma=1)=1.825$. We obtain $d_{13}(\gamma=1)=0.066\mathbf{a}_o << d_{13}^o$. At $\gamma=0$, $\dfrac{t_3}{t_1}=4.48$; $\dfrac{t_2}{t_3}=1.813$; $\mathbf{a}_o(\gamma=0)= 0.23$ we get the higher value of $d_{13}(\gamma = 0)= 3.064\ \mathbf{a}_o$ and need to apply the controls that requires negentropy $3\mathbf{a}_o$ =0.69. The formed macromodel represents a system of the successively complicated information structures, for which geometrical sizes and intervals of interactions become larger at transferring to the upper levels of hierarchy. The action of the constrains at all hierarchical levels appears in the mutual attraction of the consolidated elements with accumulation of a constant quantity of the bound information at each consolidated point (that is $\mathbf{a}_o$ for doublet, and $\mathbf{a}$ for triplet). The entropy S of the **n**-dimensional initial information spectrum is S=$2\mathbf{a}_o\mathbf{n}$, at each moment the pair consolidation decreases by $2\mathbf{a}_o(\gamma)$. For the triplet structure, the dimension decreases by $2\mathbf{a}$ for each point of the triple consolidation at the triplet number **m** = (**n**-1)/2 (at odd **n**), and **m**=**n**/2 (at even **n**). For the last case, the remaining single state carries controls for consolidation of **n**/2-1 macrostates in triplets. The triplet is an optimal elementary structure that requires for its formation a minimal sum of the DIs, which is associated with a minimal bound information. Thus, the successive forming of two doublets with intermediate UR requires more negentropy than forming a single triplet at the intermediate UR coinciding with the UR of the third macrostate (Fig.2.1.3a,b). Within the first optimal discrete interval (for a triplet structure forming when the real eigenvalues equal zero and the Hamiltonian model works), only a potential of uncertainty h exists. The real h arises at those discrete moments when the DC is imposed. Within the second optimal DI (for a triplet, or a doublet, with cooperation of two eigenvalues) a real h exists.

The intrinsic uncertainty is not only a product of probabilistic theory, but also is a result of irreversibility, the creation of real information and a positive time course.

The multiplicity invariant is defined by the ratio of the eigenvalues and the corresponding DI according to the equation:

$$(1.20)\quad \frac{\alpha_k}{\alpha_{k-1}} = \frac{t_{k-1}}{t_k} = \gamma_i^{\alpha}(\gamma), \; .$$

The UR, where the set of the operator eigenvalues are distributed, is evaluated by its area F. By integrating the operator spectrum within the UR region, we obtain

$$(1.21)\quad F= 1/2\sum_{j}^{n} \ln R(t_j),$$

where $R(t_j)=r(t_j+0)\, r^{-1}(t_j-0)$ is the relative covariations generated locally at t_j.

If the relative covariation on the border of the local region (for a given j) is not changed ($R(t_j)=1$), then the corresponding elements of the considered sum become zeroes.

The uncertainty within the given region disappears, and the process is entirely determined within the considered time interval. The information generated by the UR, is defined by the measure that distinguishes the regularity from randomness. For a total random Wiener's process, with $R(t_j)= 0$ at $r(t_j+0)=\delta_o(t_j)$ (with δ_o as Dirac's function), the function $F \rightarrow -\infty$ approaches a negative infinity. For the integral evaluation of the possible URs, we consider a meaning of that function in a limit for growing dimensions n , at the conditional continuous operator spectrum:

$$(1.22)\ F(\infty)=1/2 \lim_{n\to\infty} \sum_{i=1}^{i=n} \ln R(t_j)=1/2 \int_{R(t_1)}^{R(t_n)} R(t_j)dR(t_j)=$$
i=1

$=1/2\, R(t_n)[(\ln R(t_n)-1)-R(t_1)(\ln R(t_1)-1)]\ ; t_n=T_o.$

Example1. Suppose the starting macromodel in the form (1.9) has two initial imaginary eigenvalues and the initial matrix equal to :

$$\text{Im}\ \lambda_{1,2}=\pm j \quad \text{with} \quad \mathbf{A}(t_0)=\begin{Vmatrix}0 & 1\\ -1 & 0\end{Vmatrix}.$$

After applying the controls (1.6) at the moment t_0+0, the modified eigenvalues satisfy the equation

$$\lambda_{1,2}\ (t)=2\sin(t)\pm j\left(\frac{2\cos(t)-1}{5-4\cos(t)}\right).$$

The positive time direction symbolizes coming to time $t'=\pi/3$, when $\text{Im}\ \lambda_{1,2}(t')=0$, and at the border of RS+ the real eigenvalue is equal to

$$\text{Re}\lambda_1(t')=\alpha_{1t}=\frac{2\sin(\pi/3)}{2-4\cos(\pi/3}=0.547\ .$$

For the negative time direction is fulfilled $\text{Re}\,\lambda_1(t'-)=0,\ t'+=0$, and at the border of RS- the pair of the imaginary eigenvalues is equal to

$$\text{Im}\ \lambda_{1,2}(t'-)=\beta_{1,2}(t'-)=\pm\left(\frac{2\cos(t'-)-1}{5-4\cos(t'-)}\right).$$

To determine $t'-$ in this case, we have to take into account the time interval ($\delta t'$) between RS+ and RS-. For the definition $\delta=\delta t'/t'$ as a relative interval of the control switching, we consider the increment of the eigenvalue at δ :

$$\delta\ \alpha_{1t}(\delta t')=\left(\frac{a_{1t}\exp(a_{1t}t'(1+\delta))}{2-\exp(a_{1t}t'(1+\delta))}\right)-\alpha_{1t}=\left(\frac{2\mathbf{a}_o(1-\exp(\mathbf{a}_o(1+\delta))}{t'(2-\exp(\mathbf{a}_o(1+\delta))}\right),$$

which we compare with the eigenvalue derivative

$$\alpha'_{it}=\frac{d(a_{it}(t))}{dt}\Big|_{t=t'}=\frac{d}{dt}\Big|\left(\alpha_{io}\left(\frac{\exp(a_{io}t)}{2-\exp(a_{io}t)}\right)\right)\Big|_{t=t'}=$$

$$=2\alpha_{io}^2\left(\frac{\exp(a_{io}t')}{(2-\exp(a_{io}t'))^2}\right)=\frac{2a_{it}^{\ 2}}{\exp(\mathbf{a})}\ ;\ \mathbf{a}_o=\alpha_{1t}t'.$$

Denoting $\delta\ \alpha_{1t}'=\alpha_{1t}'\delta t'$, we obtain thenthe following equation:

$$\delta=-\left(\frac{\exp(\mathbf{a})(1-\exp(\mathbf{a}_o(1+\delta))}{\mathbf{a}_o(2-\exp(\mathbf{a}_o(1+\delta))}\right),\ \mathbf{a}=\alpha_{io}t',$$

which determines δ for a given $\mathbf{a}_o(\gamma)$, $\mathbf{a}(\gamma)$. For the admitted $\mathbf{a}_o$, $\mathbf{a}$ in that model, the equation has the approximate solution $\delta \cong \mathbf{a}_o$. For $\mathbf{a}_o(\gamma=1)=0.29$, $\mathbf{a}(\gamma=1)\cong|-0.5|$, $\delta=0.29$, and for $\mathbf{a}(\gamma=0.5)=|\sim-0.7|$, $\delta=0.25$. This solution is a result of the entropy generation by stochastics within RS, where the local entropy is equal $2\mathbf{a}_o$. Hence $\delta t' = \mathbf{a}_o(\gamma)t'$, and for $\mathbf{a}_o(\gamma=1)=0.2$, $\delta t'=0.3$;

$$\beta_{it}=\frac{2\cos 0.3-1}{5-4\cos 0.3}=0.7725.$$

For these α_{it}, β_{it} the condition (1.16) is fulfilled with a sufficient approximation, and δ is defined by the defect of information (1.19) within the UR ($\delta \sim= de$), that means de, as well as $\mathbf{a}_o$, are responsible for the uncertainty of the moments of discretization. Hence, at the free information lacking, its source could be the triplet structure (formed by the interaction of the conjugate imaginary information speeds) with the maximal elementary defect equal to $2(2)^{1/2}\mathbf{a}_o(\gamma)\models\mathbf{a}(\gamma)$, or ln2 at $\gamma=0.5$; where $\mathbf{a}(\gamma)$ represents the information measure of degree of cooperation, with its maximum at $\gamma=0$. A direct connection between $\delta^*=\dfrac{t^+-t^-}{t^+}, t^+=t'$, as a measure of the time irreversibility, and the h-measure of UR leads to the formula: $\delta^*=1-h=\dfrac{\mathbf{a}(\gamma)-\mathbf{b}_o(\gamma)}{\mathbf{a}(\gamma)}$,

which defines the values for the relative δ^*: $\delta^*(\gamma\rightarrow 0)\approx 0.075$, $\delta^*(\gamma\rightarrow 0.5)\approx 0.186$, $\delta^*(\gamma\rightarrow 1)\approx 0.52$; and $h(\gamma\rightarrow 0)\approx 0.925$, $h(\gamma\rightarrow 0.5)\approx 0.814$, $h(\gamma\rightarrow 1)\approx 0.48$.

Both invariants $\mathbf{a}$ and $\mathbf{b}_o$ define δ^* and h, and the real and imaginary information as well. For the ranged eigenvalue spectrum, R(t_1) is formed by the most rapid component of this spectrum associated with the correlation $r_1(t_1)$. That spectrum's component carries the largest contribution in the uncertainty creation, evaluated by the square F of the above region. The rise of complexity of the information structure occurs by the extension of UR. The bound information during this process is created by the quantum macrolevel at the transformation of the imaginary information speed into real one according to (1.16).

Example 2. Applying the initial control $v=-2x(0)$ to the linear model, : $\dot{x}(t)=\lambda_o(x(t)+v)$, we may write this model in the form: $\dot{x}(t)=\lambda(t)x(t)$ with the eigenvalue $\lambda(t)=\lambda_o T=\alpha_i(t_i')+-j\beta_i(t_i')$ and the examined transformation $T=-\exp(\lambda_o t)/(2-\exp(\lambda_o t))$, where T can be represented by the discrete control changing the feedback action at the moment t_i', in a particular at $t_0=0$.

This control is able to change the sign of the feedback if $\alpha_o t_i' = \mathbf{a}>\ln 2$ at the real positive initial eigenvalue α_o, or at $\beta_o t_i'=\mathbf{b}_o'$ for the negative one.

The controllable model of the T-transformation is responsible for considered features. This model defines the entropy increment during time interval t_i':
$S(t_i')=-\lambda_o t_i'$ T. The model satisfies the VP if it preserves $S(t_i')$ at each interval t_i' or it preserves the local invariant $\alpha_i t_i'=\mathbf{a}_o$, at the execution $S(\mathbf{a}_o)=\mathbf{a}$.

The entropy production for this model, $H=\alpha_i(t_i')=\lambda_o T$, is positive at $\mathbf{a}_o<0$.

The question is, whether or not it ispossible for the creation of a negative real entropy within RS- (at the imaginary eigenvalues and imaginary time)?

To get the answer we consider the value of S (λ_o=j, $t_i'-=$ jt) for that model :

$$T(t,\lambda_o=j)=-\frac{\exp(jt)}{2-\exp(jt)};\ \lambda\,(t,\lambda_o=j)=2\frac{\sin(t)}{5-4\cos(t)}-j\frac{2\cos(t)-1}{5-4\cos(t)}.$$

Hence, within RS- at the imaginary λ and real time, it is possible to obtain the pure real and positive entropy production , H_a ($t=\pi/3$)=0.577.

For the imaginary time t$-$ = jt we may express λ by the hyperbolical functions:

$$\lambda\,(t-=jt,\ \lambda_o=j)=+-j\frac{2sh(t)+2ch(t)-1}{5-4ch(t)}$$

and gain the entropy increment equal to :

$$S(t-,j)=t\,\frac{2ch(t)+-2sh(t)-1}{5-4ch(t)}.$$

This function increases to S=$-\infty$ at t$-$ = jln2 , and at ch(t) = sh(t)$-$ 0.5 (t$\cong$ 0.7) it becomes zero. At t > 0.7, S changes sign again acquiring a positive value. So, the model can generate the negative and infinitive entropy only in a small region

$$\delta\,(t-):\ t-=j\ln 2+\delta\,(t-): \begin{cases} S(t<\ln 2)>0, \\ S(t=\ln 2)=-\infty, \\ S(t>\ln 2+\delta\,(t))>0. \end{cases}$$

This result supports a possibility of creation of the real and theoretically infinitive negentropy at RS-. Real increment S defines the real invariant $\mathbf{a}\sim\mathbf{b}_o$ in equation

$$T=-\frac{\exp(-j\mathbf{b}_o)}{2-\exp(-j\mathbf{b}_o)},\quad H=H_a+-jH_b$$

and the real entropy production (H_a), which triggers the RS-. Therefore, the explosion of the negative entropy (at δ -region of RS-) enables creation of the real physical processes (at RS+). The irreversible state's creation is accompanied with changing the symmetry of differential operator at the moments of its renovation and memorization. At the locality of the DP, the macromovement passes through the fractal separatrex saddles that separate the new formed structure from the nonstability region preceding its formation. The emerging information structure is a result of interaction of the information flows (with different speeds) at the various moments. On each discretization interval, the quantity of information I is created depending on the invariant value $\mathbf{a}$ (or $\mathbf{a}_o$), and on the quantity of the joint flows in triplets (**m**) or on the total number of the flows for macro system dimension **n** :
$I(\mathbf{m})=2\mathbf{a}(2\mathbf{m}+1)$; or $I(\mathbf{m})=2\mathbf{a}(3+2(\mathbf{m}-1)$, $I(\mathbf{n})=2\mathbf{a}_o(\mathbf{n}-1)$; $\mathbf{m}=\mathbf{n}/2-1$, $\mathbf{n}=2,4,6..$,

where each pair of interactions doubles the elementary invariant value.
The flow depending on some specific number n_o : $I(n_o)$=2**a** n_o (n_o=1,2..) defines not only the triplet but also the doublets, and others structures depending on n_o.

For the ranged flows, the discrete spatial time distribution of that information is shown in Figure 2.1.3 with the dynamic network of the information structures, and the geometrical network structure, Figure 1.3.2. Each fixed quantity of information in that network determines the position of the information structure as a carrier of this information, and in its dynamic connection with other macrostructures by assigning to it the vector of orientation of spiral-shaped curve on the cone: ρ (lx, ly, lz) , the moment of the macro structure forming t', and also the frequency of the initiating information flow (α_{it} =**a**$/t'$) . The I represents the information quantity evaluation of the states enclosed in the macrostructure. The macromodel memorizes the ordered information bound in the structure at the DP. The network (Figure 2.1.3) is a channel for propagating the information flow I(**m**), **m**=1,2,..., for which the notion of channel capacity C_p is applied. C_p= -PlnP-(1-P)ln(1-P), measured by an appropriate probability P for an elementary flow (of a minimal message), is equal to **a** . Crossing the cone's macrostructure of volume V by some surface, we determine its cross section F' on that surface. If the compared cross sections, F', F", are characterized by the suitable channel capacities C_p, C_p, then the equivalent radiuses R', R", defined by the geometric cone's parameter **k** (ch.1.1.3), are connected by the equation $\frac{R}{R''}=\frac{C'_p}{C''_p}$, which relates C_p to **k**.

2.1.8. Relation of the imaginary and real information to the model internal time

The relative time $\delta^* = \frac{t^+ - t^-}{t^+}$ that measures the difference between a creation of imaginary (t^-) and real information (t^+), is determined via the uncertainty parameter h: δ^*=1-h. During δ^* the imaginary eigenvalues, as a solution of a pure Hamiltonian model is transformed into the real eigenvalues generated by the differential constraint (DC). The Hamiltonian model enables continuously generating $j\beta_{it}$, which exists at δ-locality of each of the discrete moments t^+. At the δ-locality of t^-, the real eigenvalue $\alpha_{io}=\alpha_{it}$ (t=t_o) presumably enables to be transformed into the imaginary eigenvalue $j\beta_{it}$ according to the invariant equations $\alpha_{io}\, t^-$=**b**ₒ , $\beta_{io} t^-$=**b**ₒ' under the inverse time course t^- (which is prohibited by the second law, but is an admissible in the Hamiltonian model). Actual sources of imaginary eigenvalues are the instabilities creating oscillations. During the interval $t^+ - t^-$, the imaginary eigenvalue decreases from $\beta(t^-) = \beta^o$ to zero at $\beta(t^+)$, and the real eigenvalue increases from zero at $\alpha(t^-)$ to $\alpha(t^+) = \alpha'$. The initial

model eigenvalues at t=t_o: α_{io}, β_{io}, $\gamma = \frac{\beta_{io}}{\alpha_{io}}$, are formed within the interval $t^+ - t^-$, at some moment t_o, with the absolute values of $\alpha_{io} > \alpha(t^-) > 0, \beta_{io} < \beta^o$.
Assuming the linear dependencies in equations : $\frac{t^+}{t^- + t^+} = \frac{\beta_{io}}{\beta^o}$, $\frac{t^-}{t^+ + t^-} = \frac{\alpha_{io}}{\alpha'}$,
we get the equalities $\frac{\beta_{io}}{\beta^o} + \frac{\alpha_{io}}{\alpha'} = 1$, $\frac{t^+}{t^-} = \frac{\alpha'}{\alpha_{io}} - 1$, $\frac{t^-}{t^+} = \frac{\beta^o}{\gamma\alpha'} = h$.
Comparing with the previous formula for h, for that consideration, we assume $\beta(t{=}0) = \beta^o = \beta'_{io}$. Then we have $h = \frac{\alpha_{io}}{\Delta\alpha'}$, $\Delta\alpha' = \alpha' - \alpha_{io}$, $\frac{\beta^o}{g\alpha'}\frac{\Delta\alpha'}{\alpha_{io}} = 1$, where $\frac{\Delta\alpha'}{\alpha_{io}}$ measures an elementary relative entropy production during one DI: t'=$t^+ - t_o$, that is in inverse proportion to h. Let us consider a positive time direction $t^-{}_+ =$ $= - t^-$. Generation of the imaginary and real information $S_b = \beta^o t^-{}_+ = h\,\gamma\,\alpha'\,t^-{}_+$, $S'_a = \alpha'\,t^-{}_+$ is in direct proportion starting from t'=t^+ and during the same interval $t^-{}_+$. Using the equation $\beta_{io} t^-_+ = -b'_o = \beta^o t^-_+ (1 - \frac{\alpha_{io}}{\alpha'})$, where $S_b = \beta^o t^-{}_+$, $S_a = \alpha_{io}\, t^-{}_+$, we obtain the relationship between contributions of the imaginary S_b and real information S_a: $\frac{S_b}{S_a} = \gamma\,(1+h)$, or for S'_a, S_b, directly from $\frac{\beta^o}{\alpha'} = \gamma h$, $h = \frac{t^-}{t^+}$, we get $\frac{\beta^o}{\alpha'} = \frac{\beta_{io}}{\alpha_{io}}\frac{t^-}{t^+} = \frac{b_o}{a} =$inv , or $\frac{S_b}{S'_a} = \frac{b_o}{a} = h = \frac{t^-}{t^+}$.
It means, there exists the invariant relationship between the imaginary information contribution from Hamiltonian model and real information contribution from DC; and the parameters β^o, α' are determined by the model invariants. The imaginary component arises as a potential possibility of transformation it into the real one at the DP. Within the DI, that imaginary information exists (in a closed system) as a potential source of corresponding real information. Its value depends on the time interval, and on initial β^o that can be found at known $(t^+ - t^-)$ from the equation

$$\operatorname{Im}\lambda_{it} = \operatorname{Im}\{\frac{j\beta^o \exp((j\beta^o)(t^+ - t^-))}{2 - \exp((j\beta^o)(t^+ - t^-))}\} = 0 .$$

The value of α' follows from the known invariant $\mathbf{b_o} / \mathbf{a}$.

According to the DC contribution, is fullfilled : H=Sp$\mathbf{A}(t')$, at $\mathbf{A}(t')$=0, and the entropy production is equal to zero. At the final DP, the entropy production is equal to H(t_{n-1})=$\mathbf{a} / t_{n-1}$, or h_o=$\mathbf{a}$ is proportional to H: h_o =H $\bullet$ t_{n-1}.

Start to real entropy production gives the discrete control (applied at t=t'), which is a consequence of DC, as a formalized representation of interactions. The control transforms the initial eigenvalue λ_{io} into the current one at the discrete moment λ_{it} that enable it to generate a real eigenvalue component.

The positive time course is able to generate the real entropy, and the negative time course theoretically can generate the imaginary (potential) information.

The difference between a positive and negative time is a measure of the ratio of real and imaginary information according to equation:

$$(1.23)\quad \delta^* = \frac{t^+ - t^-}{t^+} = 1 - \frac{S_b}{S'_a},$$

where $t^- = -t^-_+$ is the interval of creation of initial real information $S_a = \alpha_{io} t^-_+$ $S_a = \alpha_{io} t^-_+$. During interval t^+, the stabilization of the initial entropy takes place via the procedure of the optimal cooperation. If δ^* =0, then $\frac{S_b}{S'_a} = 1$ and vice versa. For all other positive vales $\delta^* \geq 0$, we come to the condition $S'_a \geq S_b$.

2.1.9. Evolution of macromodel invariants

Under the action of random perturbations, the macromodel evolves to minimal $\gamma \rightarrow 0$. It leads to increasing the number **n** of consolidated subsystems. With increasing $\gamma \rightarrow 1$, the dimension **n** in decreasing. At $\gamma \geq 0.8$ the divergence of the dynamic trajectories takes place, as an opposite of their consolidation, and the macrosystem evolves to the disintegration. The consolidation process develops along the line of switching controls at a geometrical locality (RS+) of DPs and the chaotic attractors. Along this line, described by the equation :

(1.24) $\cos(\gamma\, \mathbf{a}) + \sin(\gamma\, \mathbf{a}) = 0.5\exp(-\mathbf{a})$,

all imaginary eigenvalues of the dynamic operator are equal zero. A macrosystem can evolve along this line at constant entropy S=Se+Si if its internal entropy (Si>0) is compensated by the external negentropy (Se<0) delivered from the environment. Each DP (t_i) is characterized for by the entropy invariant **a** and the entropy production H= Sp(h'_i); $h'_i = \alpha_i(t_i)$. Until the entropy production is positive the time direction (along the line (1.24)) is also positive. At the consolidation process, the joint macro states bind the entropy defect into the triplets. At the DP, the external negentropy is transferred into consolidated irreversible macrostates. Between the macrostates before and after consolidation, the entropy barrier exists at locality of DP. This barrier has a form of the considered δ-controls, as a source of the entropy of δ-impulse at each DP. The barrier is measured by the negentropy expenses for breaking symmetry of macrostates. Breaking symmetry is a result of selection of the states admitted for consolidation. The H(t_i) is positive at each DI.

The irreversible states create the systemic order. Another character of the macrosystemic dynamics takes place along the switching line with the equation

(1.25) $\cos(\gamma\ \mathbf{b_o}) - \gamma\ \sin(\gamma\ \mathbf{b_o}) = \exp(\mathbf{b_o})$,
where all real eigenvalues of the dynamic operator are equal zeroes. This line is a geometrical locality (RS-) of macro movement at the imaginary entropy S* =jS, and the entropy production $H^*(t^*)=jHb=jSp(h_i')$, $jh_i'=\beta_i(t_i)$, with imaginary time t*=t-.

The IN nodes have a physical analogy to macrostates in the nonequilibrium thermodynamic process of local stability [4].

According to Prigogine's theorem, this process is accompanied with a successive equalization of local flows $j_i^* = dx_i / x_i dt = \lambda_i$.

Gradient imaginary information (per UR): $j\partial\mathbf{b}_o / \partial h$ initiates the transfer information through UR. Because $\mathbf{b}_o$ and h are the minimal discrete values for these variables, we have $\partial\mathbf{b}_o = \mathbf{b}_o$, $\partial h = h$, and the gradient generates the real information: $j\mathbf{b}_o / h = \mathbf{a}$. At a vicinity of the transferring points $|\mathbf{a}| = \mathbf{b}_o$, and $|h|$ =1, which leads to t-= t', or to the phenomenon of time reversibility at these points.

For any other points at the lines (1.24, 25); $h<1$, and time is irreversible.

Transformation from the line (1.25) to the line (1.24) is accompanied with some jumps by overcoming the barrier of uncertainty h ; $\beta_{1t} = \beta_1(t-)$ is transforming into α_{1t} during some finite period t_o', that initiates the real time direction at the line (1.24). At the line (1.25), β_{1t} = 0, and the initial real time t_o' does not exist. At the line (1.24), we have $\beta_{1t} = \beta_1(t' = t_o')$ =0, and at $\alpha_{1t} = \alpha_1(t' = t_o')$ =0, γ =0. Strictly speaking, at the line (1.25), γ value does not exist at $|\mathbf{a}| = \mathbf{b}_o$. The two lines (1.24, 25) define the parametric curves on the real and imaginary spaces accordingly, as a result of VP, and therefore, they express some information law. The movement along line (1.25) preserves the invariant $\mathbf{b}_o'$, but the second law as well as any other real physical law is not fulfilled.

The imaginary entropy production is summarized at the consolidation of the successive resonance's along (1.25) with increasing invariant $\mathbf{b}_o'$ at decreasing γ .

Is it possible to transfer from one of the considered space to another one?

The answer depends on existing common solutions to the nonlinear equations (1.24), (1.25). Both of them have two equal solutions: at γ =0 and γ =+-1 with the invariants values $\mathbf{b_o}(\gamma=0) = -\mathbf{a}(\gamma=0) = \ln 2$, and $\mathbf{b_o}(\gamma=1) = -\mathbf{a}(\gamma=1) \cong 0.3$.

That means a theoretical possibility exists of transferring from RS+ to RS- and back at the parametrs values γ =0 and γ =1. Let us consider each of them.

The macrosystem can evolve approaching γ =1 in a process of disintegration at $\gamma \geq 0.8$, and then it is transfering to $\mathbf{b_o}(\gamma = 1) = 0.3$ at RS-. Another opportunity exists at the locality of γ =0 with $\mathbf{b_o} = -\mathbf{a} = \ln 2$. This transformation is accompanied with the infinite negentropy jump (see Examples) at the region of uncertainty (UR) between RS+ and RS-. Evolution along the line (RS-) at $\gamma \rightarrow 0$ is also accompanied with transferring to this UR. As a reflection of an information law, the

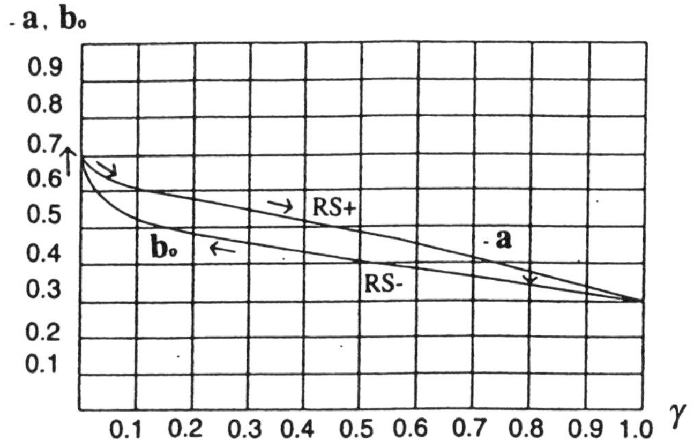

Figure 2.1.4. Evolution of the macromodel invariants (the loop between the information subspaces RS+ and RS-).

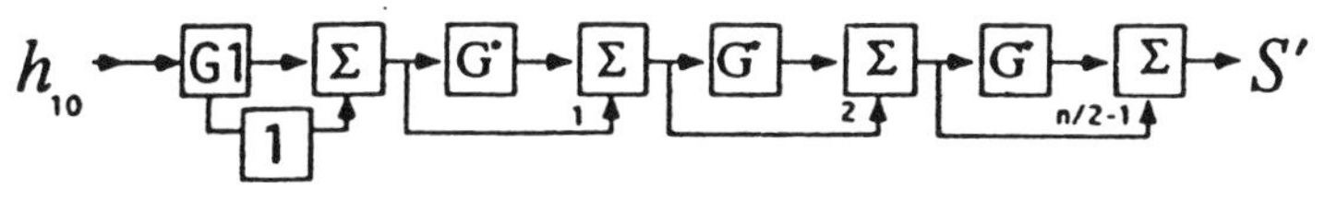

Figure 2.1.5. Scheme of the structured initial information.

parametric lines exhibit the evolution of possible macro states through some loop: γ =(0→1), (1→0) (Figure 2.1.4) with transferring over infinite negentropy bar at considered locality of γ =0. The macromodel admits the existence of the information structures in both real and imaginary subspaces.

Example 3. Let us consider the physical model of the transformation of the initial imaginary information into a real one. The information speed is modeled by a current in an electrical circuit with the initial zero active resistance R=1/A, A=Reλ , and $\lambda_1=j\beta_1$, $\lambda_2=j\beta_2$, with the inductivity L, capacity C, defined by λ_1=1/ jLw=- j/Lw, $\lambda_2=j$Cw, and the frequency spectrum equal to w=(LC)$^{1/2}$ at $\beta_1=\beta_1$=B=(L/C)$^{1/2}$.

Because the initial active resistance and the active current are zero, the value of initial real entropy, the entropy production are equal zero, and all information speeds are imaginary. At the interaction of L and C, arises the active resistance equal to R=(2C/ L)$^{1/2}$ with an initial parameter γ =(2)$^{1/2}$ that corresponds to systemic invariants **a** =0.499, $\mathbf{a}_o$=0.33, **b**o=0.481 and the uncertainty parameter h =0.964.

The relation $A = +- B/(2)^{1/2}$ following from the physical model, corresponds to an effective conductivity of the circuit for the entropy current. This equation also supports our results about the possibility of transformation of initial imaginary information into a real one. During the interaction, the imaginary information produces the real information speed equal to H=-dS/dt=$B/(2)^{1/2}$ =$(L/2C)^{1/2}$, and the inner macrosystem time starts with finite interval t' =**a** /A=**a** R. At B=0, we get H = 0, A = 0, R=∞, and the entropy current disappears. When the imaginary information is zero, the active information is also zero as a result of delivering outside the imaginary information. The systemic connections, that bind and join the macrostates, disappear at the zero of imaginary information, and the inner macrosystem time starts at the moment t' .

The generation of order starts from the delivery of an initial information wave. Invariant γ defines the negentropy N' in each triplet according to the formula: N'=-1/2 [2-ln**a** (γ)+ln(α_1/α_2)], or its numerical values: N'(γ =0.1)=1.583, N'(γ =0.5)=1.570. With decreasing γ , the negentropy increment as a source of cooperation, is increasing. Invariant **a** * corresponding the creation of a single information element (**n**=1) at increasing γ >0, can be found from the equation:

$$-\mathbf{a}^2(\gamma=0)/(\mathbf{a}^2(\gamma=0)-0.5)+\mathbf{a}^{*2}(\gamma)/(\mathbf{a}^{*2}(\gamma)-0.5)=1.$$

We obtain $\mathbf{a}'(\gamma) = (\mathbf{a}(\gamma = 0) - \mathbf{a}^*(\gamma)) / \mathbf{a}(\gamma = 0)$=1/137 as a minimal increment of invariant **a** (γ =0). Invariant **a**' evaluates a probability of creation a single element from the pair **a** , **a** *, and represents an analogy of structural constant in quantum mechanics [2]: $e^2/h^*C_o^*$=1/137 with e as an electrical charge of electron, h^* is Planck's constant, and C_o^* is the light speed; **a**' ~ E/m-E*/m* corresponds to a minimal difference between the ratios of inner energies (E, E*) related to corresponding information masses (m, m*)

2.1.10. Creation of information: Sources of consolidation and self-organization

The dynamic process, described by the equation of extremal (inside of each DI) does not create information but only preserves it. An initial stable model with negative eigenvalues possesses the positive entropy production $\frac{dS}{dt}$ =- Sp**A** .

To create the optimal macrodynamics, the model needs the controls (1.6) that change the sign of the dynamic operator, and therefore, supply the negative entropy production - 2dS/dt.

This situation is repeated at each DP to finish the optimal process. The initial model is self-creative if it generates the negentropy production

$-\frac{dS}{dt}(t')$=2Sp**A**(t')>0 at each DP. The macromodel creativeness measures an ability to create new macrostates that enable to accumulate a defect of information.

The optimal controls select the structures with an equal $\alpha_i^t(t_i)$ and join them.

The source of the consolidation is the negentropy ΔN_i that is generated at

- renovating the peculiarities at the applied control points: $\Delta N_i(t_i)$=- 1/2{SpA$(t_i+\delta)$- SpA$(t_i-\delta)$}δ, $\delta \sim o(t_i)$>0;
- applying of the needle controls: $\Delta N^{\delta}{}_i$=**a**$(\gamma)^2$ **n**; **a** $=\alpha_{io}^t t_i$;
- "diagonalizing" of superimposing processes during the space movement (ch.1.2.6):

$$\Delta N^l = \int \Delta L^l dt,\ \Delta L^l = -1/2\sum_{i,k=1}^{n}(\dot{x}_i\dot{x}_k(2b_{ik})^{-1} - \dot{z}^2{}_i(2b_i)^{-1}).$$

Analysis of the elementary consolidation process (**n**=2) leads to following relations:

$$\Delta N(\delta) = -1/2\int_{t_1-o-\delta}^{t_1-o} SpA^t dt = 1/2(\alpha_1^t(t_1-o)\delta + \alpha_2^t(t_1-o)\delta) =$$

$$= \alpha_1^t(t_1-o)\delta = \mathbf{n}/2,\ -\ \Delta N'(\delta) = -1/2\int_{t_1+o}^{t_1+o+\delta} SpA^t dt = -\alpha_1^t(t_1+o)\delta = -\mathbf{n}'/2.$$

If before the consolidation $\alpha_1^t(t_1+o)\delta$ =1 at **n**=2 is correct, then after the consolidation $\alpha_1^t(t_1+o)\delta$ =1/2 at **n**=1 holds true. From hence, it follows $\alpha_1^t(t_1+o)$=1/2$\alpha_1^t(t_1-o)$, which decreases the entropy production and the dissipative loses in consolidated system, defining a new process negentropy $\Delta N_1^{\delta} = 2\alpha_1^t(t_1-o) - \alpha_1^t(t_1+o) = 3\alpha_1^t(t_1+o)$, ΔN_1^{δ}=0.81, $\alpha_1^t(t_1)$=0.27, **a**=0.706, γ=0.5; and ΔN_1^{δ}=0.997 at $\gamma \rightarrow 0$.

The creation of information corresponds to transferring subregion RS- into subregion RS+ with the process unpredictability within the UR.

The transfer of RS- into RS+ is connected with the following peculiarities:

the jump-changing of the symmetry order (from the symmetry for the Hamilton's equations to the asymmetry, dictated by the constraint imposition); the discontinuity jump-changing of the initial space curving; the transference from the stability border (at $\lambda_{i,i+1}(t'-0)=\pm j\beta_{it}$) to the local nonstability (at $\lambda_i(t')=2\alpha_{it}>0$), characterized by the phase picture in a fractal separatrix form; the elementary act of origin of the interaction between the initial undependable latent information sources, which gives the rise to the initial dissipation; the reversible states transferring into irreversible ones, accompanied with the states binding; the start of the time and the geometry space, where the forming informational structure is distributed; the memorization of the forming structure.

Transformation of the imaginary information (from RS-) into a real one is accompanied with forming the informational structures' elements that possess the real *geometrical* sizes in RS+. The natural boundaries determine the geometrical coordinates that limit the sizes of the particular structure. The boundary surface (given by the VP natural boundaries) acts as a reflecting screen that breaks a further forming of the consolidated states in RS+. Each geometrical structure carries information about the future macromodel trajectories by the corresponding probabilities. The spatial-time movement of the macrolevel assumes the probabilistic description with the transitive probability of the future states relatively to the given ones. Each of the following macrotrajectory's pieces of discretization is defined by the random process of the microlevel at the locality of the preceding DP, which is a source of uncertainty, entropies, and the consolidated MS structures.

As a result of the principle minimum (PM), the local invariants in the form of preserved systemic parameters appear as

- ratio (G*) of the frequencies in the nearest neighboring pairs of the information spectrum: $G^*=\dfrac{\alpha_{k+1}/\alpha_k}{\alpha_k/\alpha_{k-1}}=\text{inv}$
- quantity of the real structure information stored in the points of pairs ($\mathbf{a}_o=\text{inv}$), or triples ($\mathbf{a}=\text{inv}$) interacting (as doublets and triplets)
- quantity of the imaginary structure information ($\mathbf{b}_o'$) within RS-
- number of the initial macroprocesses **n** defining a maximal model's dimension
- parameter of oscillation (γ) characterizing a measure of uncertainty for each structure element of the systemic model
- parameter of symmetry of the geometrical structure (**k**) responsible for a repeatability of the three-dimensional coordinate axes at the transition of the macrostructure to the next DP.

Indicated macroparameters (instead of initial conditions and local trajectories) define the information created in points of interaction of the systemic model.

Each macro structure is defined by three independent invariants (**n**, γ, **k**), defined by the functions of ($G^*=G^*(\gamma)$, $\mathbf{a}=\mathbf{a}(\gamma)$, $\mathbf{a}_o=\mathbf{a}_o(\gamma)$, $\mathbf{b}_o=\mathbf{b}_o(\gamma)$).

Only the complex eigenvalues create a negentropy increment at moment (t') of disappearance of its imaginary component. Generation of negentropy at real t' requires $\gamma\neq 0$, and only at $\gamma\neq 0$ is the consolidation of real macrostates possible. The initial source of the negentropy is the imaginary information that is created at the negative t- (imaginary time). In other words, at $\gamma \neq 0$ there exists an initial uncertainty $h \neq 0$, and the initial imaginary information cannot be equal to zero.

The process of negentropy generation requires existence of initial uncertainty created by the transformation of the imaginary information, (delivered outside) into the real one at a negative time. The states on the line (1.25) participate in the transformation into real states (on the line (1.24)); presumably, these states have been formed while the real eigenvalues were equal to zeroes; and consequently, the conjugate imaginary eigenvalues could emerge.

The triplet structure follows from VP if the $n \times n$ dimensional macromodel matrix can be represented by the rotation of the 3×3 matrix of the three-dimensional space coordinate systems, with the consolidation of the eigenvectors by three at each third moment of discretization, and this operation is repeated in the following triplets; the invariant (1.14) is preserved for all moments of consolidation. That repeats and preserves the transformation of three-dimensional rotations for all triplet's structures.

2.1.11. The informational macrodynamic complexity

The MS structure accumulates the information by its binding.

The information evaluation of DC (1.5) is a measure of the successive information binding at the moments of the cooperation and ordering. Because at these points the information is generated and forming hierarchical structure becomes progressively complicated, that measure evaluates the information complexity (MC) of a macrodynamic structure. The MC-function contains the successive summing up of the local entropy productions and determines the minimal hierarchical organization algorithm. Taking into account the positive additivity of the element's sum (1.5), the MC-function is increased successively at DP. Each of the hierarchical levels is characterized by a proper meaning of the MC, determining its upper limit of the minimal entropy production. As it follows from (1.5,8), the MC depends on the diffusion matrix of the initial random process, which brings its connection to the degree of process disordering, and according to (1.21), it is related to the increment the sums of relative covariations at the moments of the information generation. For each dynamic macromodel dimension, the optimal information description is established, which characterizes the admitted level of ordering. For the ranged eigenvalues of the macromodel matrix $\mathbf{A}$, the eigenvalue sum is preserved within the corresponding DP: $\mathrm{Sp}\mathbf{A}(t')\sim \mathrm{Sp}\mathbf{A}(t_o)$. In the spatial distributed macromodel, the elements of information volume, forming at DP, is characterized by the volume speed $dV / dt\,(t')$, and the MC function has the view:

$$(1.26)\quad \mathrm{MC}= \frac{SpA(t_o)}{dV / dt(t')}\,.$$

MC depends on the number of macrostates $\mathbf{n}$ and on parameter γ, which evaluates the information distance between $\mathbf{n}$, as a measure of uncertainty of each macrostate, equal to $2\mathbf{a}(\gamma)$. As γ becomes smaller, information difference between $\mathbf{n}$ grows. At growing γ, the information difference between the nearest macrostates (x_i, x_{i+1}) is decreased, and at $\gamma=3$, $x_i / x_{i+1}=1$, this difference disappears, which leads to decreasing $\mathbf{n}$. MC is the most complete characteristic of macrosystem, defined by dynamics ($\mathbf{n}, \gamma$) and geometry ($\mathbf{k}$).

The MC-complexity depends on both the algorithmic complexity, defined by the minimal discrete spectrum at the quantum level, and on a mutual closeness of the nearest discretes which is evaluated by $h = h(\gamma)$.

The MC complexity, in addition to dynamics, takes into account the space locations of the nearest discretes and the MS volumes. An external model (environment) via its space volume speed $\frac{dV(e)}{dt}$ is able to deliver an analogy of controls (as a volume speed $2\frac{dV}{dt}$) to initial model. Complexity MC(e) of such external model could be equal to the MC complexity for the initial internal model. MC-function measures complexity of initial information before it aggregation into IN structure.

2.1.12. The transformation of information: Inner communication language

The macromodel Hamiltonian at the fixed value of the invariant **a** :

$$(1.27)\ \mathrm{H}' = \mathbf{a} \sum_{i=1}^{m} (t_i)^{-1}; \quad \mathbf{m}=\mathrm{n}/2+1, \{t_i\}=t',$$

is characterized by a minimal discrete number of the **m**-triplet structures that are associated with discrete code. The code depends on the operator spectrum and the UR. Each irreversible transformation of information restricts the assigned precision of the code symbols. The operators with the same initial spectrum don't have the identical transformations because of the UR existence. The two transformations with the equal operators give rise to nonequal codes. An accomplishment of the successive transformation leads to extension of the UR, because the positive function of the losses H and the additive UR arise at each such transformations. The optimal code reflects the specific sequence of the memorized macrostates consolidated into the structured nodes (according to the initial information spectrum). The optimal code, transferred to the another macrosystem (for example by copying) is capable of producing duplicate similar macro systems. Each transformation, performed on the initial data, describes a certain dynamic process that is transformed at the discrete moments with its UR. The optimal code, corresponding to a given transformation is unchangeable; it is the unique code that evaluates the quality of the transferal information as it's value. The complexity, defined by a succesiveness of the coded macro states, is connected with the model randomness. The value of information is a measure of the coding program's nonsurplusage, as its unexchangeability with another coding program at the macromodel reconstructing. The macrostate has a different value depending on accumulated and memorized information into it. Each of the subsequent triplet accumulates more information than the previous one, and, therefore, possesses increasing value in the irreversible nonsymmetrical process. The unchangeable states with increasing values are memorized. The structured information that is transmitted by the sequence of the coded states eliminates a possible ambiguity of encoding the dynamics and geometry at the same controls, **k**, and C_p. A substantial meaning for the optimal dynamics has a *quality* of information that is characterized by its maximal information speed $\hat{H}_m = 1/2|\lambda^t{}_m|$, within the ranged eigenvalue spectrum $\lambda^t{}_m = \lambda^t_{1o}$. The concepts of complexity, valuele, and quality information arise in IMD by a natural way. The OPMC classification, obtained as a result of numerical computer simulation, enables us to place the models in order of increasing MC=$(h^\nu)^{-1}$, $\mathbf{n}, \gamma^{-1}$, and establishes a correspondence of the complexity with dynamics and geometry. The transformation of one code into another code is performed with the preservation of the function of complexity:

$$(1.28)\ \mathrm{MC}' = \frac{SpA'(t_o)}{dV'/dt(t')} = \frac{SpA''(t_o)}{dV''/dt(t'')} = \mathrm{MC}''; \quad \frac{dV'}{dt} = C'F'.$$

Preservation of the sequence of code symbols is possible even if the volume speed of the transferred information is changing. It leads to the connection of the linear speeds C,' C" of the transferring the signals through the information area of the cross sections F', F", with the corresponding channel capacities $C^{'}_p, C^{''}_p$:

$$(1.29)\ \frac{SpA'(t_o)'}{SpA''(t_o)} = \frac{C'F'(t')}{C''F''(t'')} = \frac{C'C^{'}_p}{C''C^{''}_p}.$$

One possibility appears to minimize transmitting code error. Information encoding with preservation of the code value demands the corresponding changes made to the transmitted volume speed , taking into account the concrete spectrum characteristics. Restoration of the optimal code with its information volume and the quality requires knowing the parameters $(\mathbf{n}, \gamma, \mathbf{k})$. Macrodynamics are responsible for the connection of the speed of the transmitted information with the information quantity in the MS forming during communication. The IN assumes an existence of the inverse transformation of the accumulated flows into the relative information speeds (the frequencies). The code is a part of the IN structure where each sign-symbol (letter or their combinations as terms) is characterized by its connection with an initial object. The informational content depends on the symbol ranging that defines the symbol place within the IN. The location of the specific symbol in such ranging reflects both its quantity of information and its measure of effectiveness in connection to the initial object within a language. Therefore, the IN symbol represents a *model of a language* where the symbol's position depends on its informational content, and the symbols' admissible combinations are defined by the rules of forming the enclosed triplet's structures (reflecting the language grammar). Because the signs' relations to the initial objects are determined by the language dictionary, it does not belong to the inner language structure and could be redetermined in the process of language usage. The same could be done with the initial symbol position, whose variation depends on the specific text content and on the symbol combination of the text terms. Thus, using the IN as a language model requires certain manipulations of the position of the initial assigned symbols to control the meaning of the obtained terms according to a dictionary. The MC defines the minimal code of the optimal algorithm, which can be restored by the dynamic model, and MC can be written through the successive times of the macrostate's memorization, carrying the maximum of information. As a specific integral evaluation of an object's intrinsic information, the MC-number represents a general information measure for the comparison, labeling, and the classification of a diversity of natural objects (physical, economic, social, and even a human being).

2.1.13. The length of optimal code

The optimal code represents the sequence of the double states (1.7) memorized at the discrete moment: t_i. So, each **n** dimensional model is encoded by **n** interval of DP. The states, memorized at each DP, have equal probability. And for each DP, the entropy of the microlevel ensemble is equal to S=1/2 (at γ =0.5) with a total entropy of **n** intervals equal to S=**n**/2. Suppose a total message carries **n** independent elementary messages, and each DP is characterized by an equal probability of each UR. So, the total message, carried by the control code, consists of **n** independent elementary units, that is used only once from exp(**n**/2) equally probability communications. If we transfer this message by sequence of L letters from W their total numbers, then, we get the probability of the Ws possible messages. Therefore, the optimal length of code is equal to L= $\dfrac{n}{2\ln W}$.

Each value of controls (1.7) at each DP is defined by the value of the same interval:

$$t_i=\left(\frac{\mathbf{a}}{a_{io}}\right),\quad \alpha_{it}=\frac{dx_i}{x_i dt}(t_i),\quad \ln\left(\frac{x_i(t_i)}{x_i(t_o)}\right)=\mathbf{a}(\gamma)\ln\left(\frac{\mathbf{a}}{\mathbf{b}_o}\right)(\gamma);\quad t_o=\left(\frac{\mathbf{b}_o}{a_{io}}\right).$$

Here each α_{io} has a different initial moment t_o, but all {α_{io}} satisfy the equations for above invariants at the same moment t_o=t_o' - t_o". Macromodel starts from moment t_o"=0, when $\alpha_i(t_o)$=0. If we encode the controls in the logarithmic units, then each control value is defined by the time interval $t_i(\gamma)$. The same letters can be used to encode the control (1.7) , and for encoding the time intervals. Then the possible numbers of alphabet necessarily to encode the controls are reduced to W=n.

The length of the sequence of those letters is equal to L*= $\dfrac{n}{2\ln(n)}$. For example, to encode n=20, we need W=20. Each word has length of L*=3.33-4 letters from that alphabet. This the length of optimal Lempel- Ziv coding procedure [7] where the information complexity and code entropy are defined by that length. The macromodel's L* is constant for a given **n** and γ . The effective length of optimal code, or the total time interval of that code transmission, is defined by the sum

(1.30) T*= $t_1+t_2 - t_1+t_3-t_2 + \quad +t_{n-1} - t_{n-2} \quad = t_{n-1}(\gamma, \mathbf{n})$,

which is equal to the (**n**-1) DI. For γ =0.5, each of **n** controls carries the entropy of the UR equal $2\mathbf{a}_o(\gamma)$, and each letter of optimal code from alphabet W carries information $2\mathbf{a}_o(\gamma)$ = lnW. The limited values of invariant $\mathbf{a}_o(\gamma)$: (0.23-0.4) at γ =(0-2.5), requires the code alphabet with W=exp($\mathbf{a}_o(\gamma)$)=2-3 letters. IMD defines the bi-level structure of optimal coding with the primary alphabet W'=**n**, and the second level alphabet W"=**m** of macrounits. The information distance between code letters preserves $\gamma=\gamma$ (G**=$\dfrac{t_3 t_1}{t_2^{\,2}}$). Each triplet is encoded by three symbols preserving the constant length of the macrounits L*=3. To encode **m**=n/2 triplets we need the alphabet with W=**m** letters. Such code has entropy S*=3ln(**n**/2), and the probability of each message P*=exp(S*), where **n**=2exp(S*/3). For example, the genetic code with L*=3 and W=**m**=4 corresponds to the macromodel with **n**=8, which forms 3 triplets with the average quantity of information S*=3ln4=4.15 bits, and encodes N=$\mathbf{m}^3$ =64 messages. The macromodel has the following possibilities for the optimal coding: **m**=**n**/2 triplets with constant three letters length L* and W=**n**/2; the **n**-DIs encoding by a constant L*=3, and W=**n**; random N messages by **m** triplets and L*=3 for macromodel dimension ln(**n**)= (1/L*)lnN+ln2, and W=**m**; random message with average entropy S* by numbers of triplets **m** =exp(S*/L*), W=**m**, L*=3; or the equal probability sequence of **n** random values by alphabet with n symbols and optimal L* for Lempel- Ziv procedure [7].*Computational complexity* as a minimal program length *running time*, is defined by the equation for T*.

2.1.14. The structure of initial information

Both the initial S' and current process' entropies S are represented by the sum of the local entropies:

$$S=\sum_i h_{it}\ ;\ h_{it}=\mathbf{a}_o(\gamma),\ S'=\sum_i h_{io}\ ,\ h_{io}=\mathbf{a}(\gamma)$$

where the initial eigenvalues of each triplet satisfy the relations of multiplication

$$\frac{a_{2o}}{a_{1o}}=G_1\ ;\ \frac{a_{3o}}{a_{2o}}=G_2\ ,\ \text{at}\ \ \frac{a_{2o}}{a_{1o}}=\frac{h_{2o}}{h_{1o}}\ ;\ \frac{a_{3o}}{a_{2o}}=\frac{h_{3o}}{h_{2o}}\ .$$

The local entropies h_{io} , measured at the moment t_o, are not equal, but are proportional to α_{io} forming the same sum S'=S, that is preserved in optimal process. We come to the conditions expressed by the invariant relations:

$$\frac{h_{2o}}{h_{1o}}=\frac{h_{4o}}{h_{3o}}=\frac{h_{6o}}{h_{5o}}=,.\ \ldots=\frac{h_{i+1,o}}{h_{io}}=G_1\ ,.\ \ldots\ \ i=1,3,5,7,..,n-1,$$

$$\frac{h_{3o}}{h_{2o}}=\frac{h_{5o}}{h_{4o}}=,.\ \ldots=\frac{h_{j+1,o}}{h_{jo}}=G_2\ \ ;\ j=2,4.6,\ldots,n,$$

$$S'=(h_{1o}+h_{3o}+h_{5o}+.,..+h_{io})(1+G_1)\ \text{where}$$

$$\frac{h_{3o}}{h_{1o}}=\frac{h_{3o}h_{2o}}{h_{2o}h_{1o}}=G_1G_2=G^*\ ;\ \frac{h_{5o}}{h_{1o}}=\frac{h_{5o}h_{4o}h_{3o}}{h_{4o}h_{3o}h_{1o}}=G_2\,G_1\,G_1\,G_2=(G^*)^2\ ;$$

$$\frac{h_{7o}}{h_{1o}}=\frac{h_{7o}h_{6o}h_{5o}}{h_{6o}h_{5o}h_{1o}}=(G^*)^3\ ;\ \frac{h_{k-1,o}}{h_{1o}}=(G^*)^{k/2-1}\ ;\ k=4,6,8,\ldots,n.$$

So, we can represent the initial entropy as a function of invariant G^*:

$$S'=h_{1o}(1+G^*+(G^*)^2+,\ \ \ldots+(G^*)^{n/2-1})(1+G_1)=S'(n,G^*,h_{1o}),$$

where the local invariants G_1 , G_2 are connected by the equations

$$G_1=\frac{\exp(\mathbf{a}_o/G^*)-0.5\exp(\mathbf{a}_o);}{\exp(\mathbf{a}_oG_1/G^*)-0.5\exp(\mathbf{a}_o)},\ G_1=G_1(G^*).$$

The initial Hamiltonian is expressed in the analogous form:

$H_o'(\mathbf{n},\gamma)=\mathrm{Sp}(\alpha_{io})=\alpha_{1o}(1+G_1+G_1G_2+(G_2)^2+(G_1G_2)^2+(G_1)^3(G_2)^2+\ldots$

By measuring $\alpha_{io}(\gamma)=1/2\,\frac{dr_{io}}{dt}(r_{io})^{-1}$ we can determine $(\mathbf{n},\gamma)$ from condition $|\mathrm{Sp}(1/2\,\frac{dr_{io}}{dt}(r_{io})^{-1})-H_o'(\mathbf{n},\gamma)|<\varepsilon$ The successive increase of the initial information corresponds to H': $S''=\frac{S'}{h_{1o}}=(1+G_1)(1+(G^*)^{i/2-1},\ )$; i=1,2,3,...,n and characterizes the capacity of the channel transferring the triplet code to the MS structure. Structuring is accompanied by the fixed ratio of the frequency spectrum: $\frac{a_{i+2,o}}{a_{io}}=G^*(\gamma)$, which can be identified by the initial entropy

The maximum value of the accumulated structural entropy:

(1.31) $S\#(\mathbf{n},\gamma)=\max S''=(1+G_1)(1+(G^*)^{i/2-1})$

is a quantitative evaluation of bound information, that contains the minimum necessary information to reconstruct S'. Being measured in logarithmic scale, it characterizes the complexity of the structurized information. The relation $h_{1o}(\gamma)=\frac{2\mathbf{a}_o(\gamma)n}{S''(n,\gamma)}$ connects the parameters $(\mathbf{n},\gamma)$ with structural entropy and the invariants. Parameter $G^{**}=G_2/G_1=\frac{h_{io}h_{i+2,o}}{(h_{i+1,o})^2}$ is constant for the optimal code evaluating its structure. For example, in the English alphabet with its most frequently used 19 letters (E,T,...,Y), this parameter has a limitation: G**=1.066-0.909 with γ=2.1-2.2. For the Russian alphabet at the same conditions G**=1.176-0.877. Surplusage (Sr) of message (language) is defined by the ratio of the initial (h_{1o}) and terminal quantity (h_n) of the bound information: $\mathrm{Sr}=1-\frac{h_n}{h_o}=$ $=1-(G^*)^{n/2-1}$. Then for English, at G*=0.75 , **n**=20, Sr=0.75; for Russian, at G*=0.83, **n**=20, Sr=0.60. To transmit the basic three parameters $(\mathbf{n},\gamma,\mathbf{k})$ we need the three letters code with $W=\exp(2\,\mathbf{a}_o(\gamma)\,\mathbf{n}/3)$. For the considered example we get h_{1o}=0.9345 and W=exp(4/3)≈4 (at γ =0.5). For **n**=16, γ =0.5 G_1=0.452, we obtain h_{1o}=1.324. Such a macromodel can bind **m**=**n**/2-1=7 triplets. As **n** grows, the numbers of the bound triplets is increased, but the correlation r_{1o} is decreased.

2.1.15. The negentropy creation in the spatial macromodel: Simulation of self- organization

For the Hamiltonian macromodel the classic entropy definition by phase volume can be used: $S=\ln \mathbf{G}(t_i)$, where **G** is a relative volume of the phase flows, changing at t_i according to the model's probability function connected with the parameters:

(1.32) $G=\frac{\exp(m_i a_{io} t_i)}{V*}$; $V*=\frac{Vm_i}{V_o}$,

where m_i is the number of the initial phase flows $\{a_{io}\}$ joined together at DP; Vm_i is the volume of those consolidated phase flows, considered comparatively to the volume of a single phase flow V_o at that moment. The total entropy increment

(1.33) $S_{dv} = S_d - S_v = m_i a_{io} t_i - \ln V*$,

is generated both by the macrodynamics changing the operator (S_d), and by geometry changing the information volume (S_v) in process of spatial movements. If V_o is equal to the initial triplet volume (V_{o3}), then the corresponding entropy is $S_d = \mathbf{a}$, and the total entropy of the macrosystem dimension **n** has the view :

(1.34) $S_{dv} = \mathbf{a}(\gamma)\mathbf{m} - \ln V_3^*(\mathbf{m}, \gamma, \mathbf{k})$; $V_3^* = \frac{V_{n+1}}{V_{o3}}$; $\mathbf{m}=\mathbf{n}/2-1$,

where V_3^* is the relative information volume, equal to the ratio of the total volume, formed during the (n+1) DI of the optimal movement (V_{n+1}), to the information volume (V_{o3}), considered as the initial one. The result of the macrostructures synthesizes and simulation by an applied program package are shown in Table 2.1.

Table 2.1. Results of Computer Simulation

No	1	2	3	4	5	6	7
n	6	6	8	8	10	12	8
γ	0.7997	0.59	0.5707	0.5273	0.5165	0.5142	0.7252
k	7	9	15	16	27	45	7
$\mathbf{n}_o$	4	4	4	4	4	4	6
$\mathbf{k}_o$	0.0001	0.0001	0.0001	0.0001	0.0001	0.0001	0.0001
$\mathbf{k}_o$	6	6	6	6	6	6	6
V_3^*	2.029	2.123	6.495354	6.565434	19.29426	55.58958	1.51149
S_{dv}	0.565	0.6112	0.8689	0.87418	1.1982	1.542	0.8669

No	8	9	10	11	12	13
n	10	12	18	18	18	50
γ	0.5896	0.5859	0.5773	0.5546	0.5323	0.522
k	10	13	28	29	30	1324
$\mathbf{n}_o$	6	6	6	6	6	8
$\mathbf{k}_o$	6	6	6	6	6	6
$\mathbf{k}_o$	0.0001	0.0001	0.0001	0.0001	0.0001	0.0001
$V*$	8.97	40.455	3697.6	4061.58	4447.89	28752271.0
S_{dv}	0.534	0.398	0.015	-0.0693	-0.13812	-2.051736

Total entropy S_{dv} increases with the rise of dimensions, and then decreases, changing its sign at **n**<18, γ <0.55. S_{dv} acquires the most negative values at the greatest dimensions (**n**>50). In these cases, the number of information states, defining informational volume, increases faster than the rise of the entropy in the macrodynamic process. So, the negentropy generated at **n**=50, γ =0.522, is enough to compensate for the total entropy that is necessary to form a single triplet: S_{3d}=0.684 (γ =0.522) 3=2.052.

Therefore, self-organization is possible at dimensions **n**> 50.

If we take into account the information bound into the triplet, then the entropy per dimension unit is decreased: **a** '= **a** $((2)^{1/2}$-1)=0.283, at **a** (γ =0.522)= 0.648.

The indicated entropy increments take this view for the same model's examples:

N	4	6	13
S_{3d}	-0.541	-1.005	-15.353

The most negentropy is generated with a defect entropy calculation, accumulated within the structure. The self-controllability for the macrosystem dimension **n**=48, containing the subsystem with the minimal dimension **n**=8, was established before [8] from other considerations. There exists a crucial limit of complexity that gives start of the jumpwise changing of the systemic characteristics, creating the extrernal negentropy production and self-organization. Because the natural macrostructures are distributed in space, the considered results represent sufficient interest. It means that ordering and self- organization are possible for the natural system and processes without violating the second law .

The IN structure represents a mathematical tool for aggregating of different models in form of differential equations, or dynamic flows, obtained also independently on the microlevel's statistics. The IMD determines the general methodology for systematic modeling and optimization.

REFERENCES

1. Nicolis G., Prigogine I. *Self-Organization in Nonequilibrium Systems*, N.Y.: John Wiley, 1977.

2. Lichtenberg A.J, Lieberman M.A. Regular and Stochastic Motion, N.Y.: Springer-Verlag, 1983.

3. Kac M.(Ed). *Probability and related topics in physical science*, N.Y.: Inter science Publishers, Inc., 1957.

4. Feynman R., Leighton R., Sands M. *The Feynman Lectures on Physics. Quantum Mechanics*, N.Y.: Addison-Wesley,1963.

6. Kolmogorov A.N. *Theory of Information and Theory of Algorithms*, Moscow: Nauka, 1987.

7. Ziv J., and Lempel A. "A universal algorithm for sequential data compression". *IEEE Transactions on Information Theory*, 1977; 23, 3: 337-343.

8. Lerner V.S. "Dynamic Model of the Origin of Order in Controlled Macrosystem." *Thermodynamics and Regulation of Biological Processes*, Berlin, New York: Walter de Gruyter & Co: 383-397, 1984.

9. Lerner V.S. "Information Systems Theory: A review of concepts, history, and applications," *Systems Analysis, Modelling and Simulation*, International Journal, 1999;35:175-190.

2. 2. SOME GENERAL INFORMATION MACROSYSTEMIC FUNCTIONS

2. 2.1. Macrosystem stability

A stability analysis is based on an accepted mathematical model of a system. The VP defines the equation for the macromodel function of action $S = \int_s^T L(\dot{x},x,t)dt$ and its derivative $\frac{dS}{dt} = L(\dot{x},x,t)$, that can be used as Liapunov's functions for the stability analysis. If sign$S$=-sign $\frac{dS}{dt}$, then the system is stable by Liapunov's criterion. For the considering Marcovian model, the macrolevel function of action along an extremal is $S = x(t)^T X(t)$. It can be represented in form $S = x(t)^T h(t) x(t)$, where the sign S=sign$h(t)$. The Lagrangian $L(\dot{x},x,t) = \dot{x}(2b(t,x))^{-1}\dot{x}$ satisfies the relation sign$L$=sign $b(t,x)$.

According to Liapunov's criterion the sign of sign$b(t,x)$=-sign$h(t)$ is an indicator of macromodel stability. Because of $h(t)=r(t)^{-1}$>0, the system stability requires sign < 0, or at $b = 1/2\dot{r}$, and we come to the condition sign$\dot{r}$<0 at sign r>0, that defines the negative sign of the macromodel matrix A=$1/2\dot{r}(t)^{-1}r(t)$, which satisfies this criterion. An interaction of two or three deterministic but instable trajectories can be described statistically [2]. Such an initially deterministic process can create stochastics at both micro and macroevels. The corresponding function $b(t,x)$ defines a divergence of the macro- or microlevel trajectories accordingly. The function $b(t,x)$ initiated by stochastics, is the same for both micro- and macrolevels. Applying the autonomous controls for each of the levels, or working with a single macro- or microlevel process independently, or acting on three and more microlevels, can bring a different $b(t,x)$ at each level.
The macrotrajectory satisfying the VP, is distinguished from an arbitrary trajectory (as a solution of equation $\dot{x} = a^u$, $a^u = Ax$) by the condition $A = 1/2\dot{r}r^{-1}$, which is not fulfilled automatically. The nearness to the extremal macro trajectory is measured by the difference of corresponding matrices: $\delta = Sp(A - 1/2\dot{r}r^{-1})$, or $\delta^* = \delta[Sp(A)]^{-1} = 1 - Sp(1/2\dot{r}r^{-1})[Sp(A)]^{-1}$, $Sp(1/2\dot{r}r^{-1}) = H$.

The balance equation of preservation of the entropy functional on the extremals is applicable for the analysis of cooperative motion, based on Liapunov's stability.

The DPs of the applying controls are the bifurcation points of possible changes of the macromovement. The character of the subsequent movement, starting from DP's, depends on the control function that symbolizes possible human activities.

For arbitrary control functions, the subsequent model movement and system stability, in general, are unpredictable.

Applying the optimal control function makes such prediction possible.

At DPs, the minimal entropy production as a condition of local equilibrium has the physical analogy of minimum of potential energy of the macroelements after their consolidation, or the Liapunov's function U for the condition of equilibrium:

$U=-\Delta S(\mathbf{n},\gamma)\geq 0;\ dU/d\tau=-H(i)<0,\ \tau=\tau_i,$

where the increment of function of action at the optimal control $v(\tau)=-2x(\tau)$ is

$\Delta S(\mathbf{n},\gamma)=\Delta S(\tau)=x(\tau)^T X(\tau)=-x(\tau)^T h(\tau)x(\tau),$

and the function $H(i)=Sp\,A(\tau_i)$ depends on the number (i) of the consolidated states. Therefore, the optimal cooperative model is stable by Liapunov's criterion.

The appearance of the new macromodel properties corresponds to bifurcations and possible local instability. The instability accompanied with the jumpwise transferring on other movements, is one of the reasons a chaotic motion. It leads to the divergence of phase trajectories following their compression at changing movements. Such phenomenon is especially true for the dynamic macromodel at the vicinity of DPs. The metric Kolmogorov-Sinai entropy represents the differential entropy for the macromodel that is defined by the relation [1]:

$$\hat{h}^a=\sum_{i=1}^{m}\sigma_i^+,$$

where σ_i^+ are positive Liapunov's indicators. The dimension of Chaotic Attractor at the DP locality, is determined by the Moiré formula [2]:

$$d_m=\frac{\sum_{i=1}^{m}\sigma_i^+}{\sum_{i=1}^{l}\sigma_i^-}+k,$$

where k is the number of nonnegative, m is the number of positive, and l is the number of negative σ_i^- Liapunov's indicators. For the optimal macromodel, we have $k=m=\frac{n}{2}+1,\ l=\frac{n}{2}$. From this, at $|\sigma_i^-|=|\sigma_i|$, we get $d_m=\frac{n}{2}+2$, which corresponds to the decreasing number of state variables for the n-dimensional model in the vicinity of DPs. At the final moment T, when the macromodel has a single dimension with one positive Liapunov's indicator, chaotic movement is possible.

The diffusion processes at the microlevel stabilize the macrosystem at DPs by conjungating diffusion and macrokinetics. At these points (except the final moment T), the Hessian matrix of the differential equation

$$\Gamma=\det\left\|\frac{\partial^2 S}{\partial x_i\partial x_j}\right\|,\ \Gamma(i)=\det r(i)>0,$$

defined by the diffusion $b(i)=1/2\dot{r}(i)$, is nonzero, this gives evidence of the *structural* stability of the hierarchical macromodel.. A minimal eigenvalue $\alpha_n(T)$ (at upper level of hierarchy) defines a reserve of stability.

From the connection of matrix **A** with diffusion, with Γ, and entropy, it follows that the maximal reserve of stability is associated with maximum informational diversity of the hierarchical macromodel. At a locality of the DP, macromovement passes the fractal separatrex saddles that separate the new formed structure from the nonstability region preceding its formation. The negative eigenvalues (at the moment t'-0) for the initial stable differential operator, change a sign (at the moment t'). The transformation of the specific phase point into the saddle is accompanied with discontinuity jumps, changing the differential equation dimension, and also by raising the singularities [2]. The information forces of the strain compression act periodically along the separatrex, and affect the equal eigenvalues coupling process. Liapunov's indicator is connected with the eigenvalue of differential equation of the dynamic systems according to the formula

$$\sigma_i = \lim_{n\to\infty} \frac{1}{n\tau} \ln \lambda_i(n),$$

where t= $n\tau$ is a long enough interval of observation of the dynamic system, which could be divided on n small discrete intervals τ. The following relations are true: for $\lambda_i > 1, \sigma_i = \sigma_i^+$, and for $0 < \lambda_i < 1, \sigma_i = \sigma_i^-$.

At each fixed n=1,2,.and τ , the current value of Liapunov's indicator has the view

$$\sigma_i(n) = \frac{1}{\tau} \ln \lambda_i(n) .$$

Differenting that equality by τ, and assuming $\sigma_i(n)$ is independent on τ (within each τ of possible process transformations) we get the formula

$$\sigma_i(n) = \frac{d\lambda_i(n)}{\lambda_i(n)d\tau},$$

which connects the currents $\sigma_i(n)$ with $\lambda_i(n)$. The considered random process can be identified by the correlation functions $r_i(\tau,n)$ that determines $\lambda_i(n)$ within each τ -interval :

$$\lambda_i(\tau,n) = \frac{dr_i(\tau,n)}{r_i(\tau,n)d\tau}.$$

Substituting the last formula into the previous $\sigma_i(n)$ formula we define the dependency $\sigma_i(n)$ on a current observed sequence of process data, and a possibility for their direct computation. The condition of the process stochastization consists of increasing $\sigma_i(n)$>0 at σ_i>0. The observed process preserves its regularity at σ_i=0, or at decreasing $\sigma_i(n)$. Applying these conditions for the $\sigma_i(n)$-formula (that expressed via the correlations), leads to the equation

$$-\frac{d^2 r_i(\tau,n)}{d\tau^2} = [\frac{dr_i(\tau,n)}{d\tau}]^2 [r_i(\tau,n)]^{-1} \geq 0$$

as the condition of regularity, and to the equation

$$(2.1)\quad -\frac{d^2 r_i(\tau,n)}{d\tau^2} < [\frac{dr_i(\tau,n)}{d\tau}]^2 [r_i(\tau,n)]^{-1} \geq 0$$

as the condition of the process stochastization. Both the process identicators can be measured directly using the current process data that implies the practical application of the control methodology. By measuring the process diffusion $\tilde{\sigma}_i(\tau,n) = \dfrac{dr_i(\tau,n)}{d\tau}$, we can transform the above conditions into the forms:

$$-\frac{d\tilde{\sigma}_i(n)(\tau,n)}{d\tau} = [\tilde{\sigma}_i(n)]^2[\int\tilde{\sigma}_i(\tau,n)d\tau]^{-1} \geq 0,$$

$$-\frac{d\tilde{\sigma}_i(n)(\tau,n)}{d\tau} < [\tilde{\sigma}_i(n)]^2[\int\tilde{\sigma}_i(\tau,n)d\tau]^{-1} \geq 0.$$

The regularity condition is an indirect form of the Euler equation for the macrosystem's eigenfunctional extremum [3]. For the consolidated macromodel, the increment of the eigenvalues of matrix Λ :

$$\Delta\lambda_i = \lambda_{i+1} - \lambda_i = \frac{\dot{\lambda}_i}{\lambda_i}$$

can be expressed directly using the above formulas for Liapunov's indicator : $\sigma_i(n) = \Delta\lambda_i$, with a current control of the process regularities by measuring the correlations. The chaotic attractor's size (within each IN node) defines the uncertainty zone. The model is robust by preserving the structure at the fluctuation within the UR. An admissible robust zone size depends on the relative parameter $\Delta t^* = \dfrac{\delta t_i}{t_i}(\gamma)$ as a local invariant. With t_i growing , the UR absolute size (F) is increasing and affects the increasing number of the IN enclosed nodes. Let us consider the bifurcation point with an interaction of two eigenvalues (doublet structure) Figure.2.2.1. One of them, $+\alpha_{2t}$, carried out by a local instable process, acting on the expending model's transformation, another one a result of a local stable, process, with the eigenvalue defined at the discrete moment t_2:

$$\alpha_{1t}(t_2) = -\frac{\alpha_{1t}\exp(\alpha_{1t}(t_2 - t_1)}{2 - \exp(\alpha_{1t}(t_2 - t_1)},$$

acting on a compressing model's transformation. The information contribution from $+\alpha_{2t}$ is equal to $\mathbf{a} = \alpha_{20}t_2$, $\mathbf{a} = \mathbf{a}_o \dfrac{\alpha_{20}}{\alpha_{2t}}$;

the second contribution (at $G_2 = \dfrac{t_2}{t_1}$) brings the quantity of information equal

$$(2.2)\, d_1 = \alpha_{1t}(t_2)t_2 = -\frac{\mathbf{a}_o \frac{t_2}{t_1}\exp(\mathbf{a}_o(\frac{t_2}{t_1} - 1))}{2 - \exp(\mathbf{a}_o(\frac{t_2}{t_1} - 1))} = -\frac{\mathbf{a}_o G_2 \exp(\mathbf{a}_o(G_2 - 1))}{2 - \exp(\mathbf{a}_o(G_2 - 1))}.$$

Because the signs of $\mathbf{a}$ and $\mathbf{a}_o$ are opposite, the doublet accumulates the summarized contributions: $d_{12} = |\mathbf{a}| + |d_1|$. This result we may express in numerical form, for example, at γ =0.5, we get d_1 =1.1606, **a** =ln2, and d_{12}=1.8537.

By applying the needle control that changes the sign of $+\alpha_{2t}$, we get d_{12}=0.4675. The maximal quantity of delivering information d_o from two eigenvalues (in one interaction) is equal to 2**a** plus the information 2a_o delivered by the optimal control: d_o=2(**a**+**a**$_o$). We obtain for γ =0.5, d_o=2ln2 +0.5=1.8863, that is more than the accumulated triplet information.

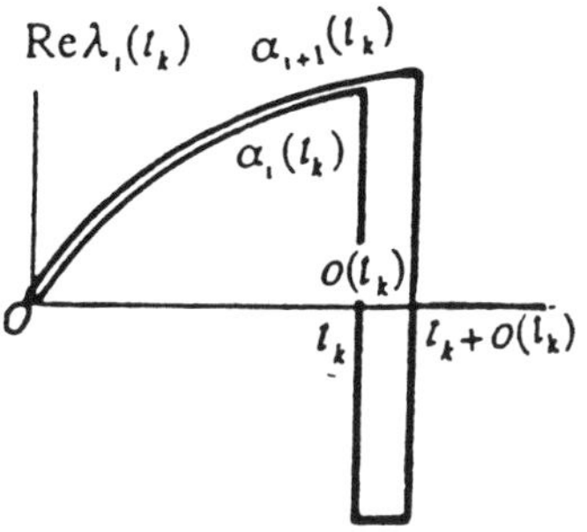

Figure 2.2.1. The dynamics of $\alpha_i(t_k)$, $\alpha_{i+1}(t_k)$ with forming the needle control.

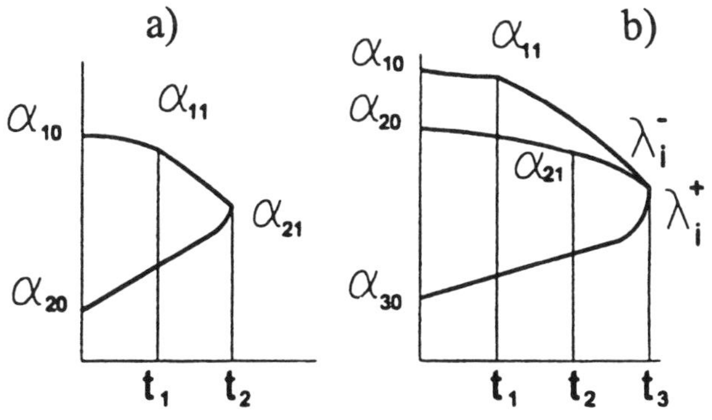

Figure 2.2.2. Schema of the bifurcation points: a) For a doublet structure b) For a triplet structure.

The difference d_o-d_{12}=0.325 can be transferred with the formed triplet structure in the next discrete interval. For the triplet structure (Figure 2.2.2) we have two possibilities, that had been considerted in ch.2.1.4. The maaximum of delivered information is d_o=3($\mathbf{a}_o$+$\mathbf{a}$), the maximum of accumulated information' is d^1_{13}=d_{13}-3$\mathbf{a}_o$. This gives $d^1_{13}(\gamma=0)$=2.374$\mathbf{a}_o$, and a possibility of transferring the information difference d_o-d^1_{13}=3 $\mathbf{a}$+6$\mathbf{a}_o$-d_{13} to a new triplet equal to 3($\mathbf{a}_o$+$\mathbf{a}$)≅ d_o at $\gamma=0$.

The optimal control at the bifurcation points makes a choice between the instable and stable movements (with the extending and compressing transformations) by selecting a such one that satisfies the second law. The participation of instable local movement into the douplet or triplet structures increases a maximal quality of the accumulated information. The balance between the delivered, accumulated, and transferred information confirms the second law execution.

The point of cooperation as a chaotic attractor, enables it to produce the real intrinsic information flow. These points also model the hidden casualties of sub-sequential events created by interactions. The generated ordered macrostructures counterbalance to chaotic disorder and uncertainty.

2.2.2. Macrosystem Adaptivity: Potential for adaptation

Generally, adaptivity is an ability to adapt to the changes that will not distort the existing systems. That quality has an external as well as an internal system meaning and the corresponding adaptive mechanisms are based on a mathematical model [4]. The system flexibility, sensitivity to changes, and structural stability are the internal characteristics of adaptivity. The IS model is able to accept the local changes (of the eigenvalues) at the locality of DPs when the system is opened for interaction with the random external activities. Those changes can create new IN node connections, as new macrosystem qualities which inherit small local changes.

The external environment via microlevel diffusion changes the parameter γ in A={ $\alpha^t_i(1+j\gamma)$}, i=1,...,n. Deviations $a_{i\tau}$ *= $\Delta\alpha_{i\tau}(\alpha_{i\tau})^{-1}$ can be a result of perturbations and controls. The ability of the macromodel to preserve regularities, based on VP, characterizes its *adaptive quality*. This capability is defined by the preservation of the VP invariants with a discrete compensation of $a_{i\tau}$ * by the control. The mechanism of adaptation, which preserves $\mathbf{a}_o$-invariant, shifts the moment $t^* = \Delta\tau_i(\tau_i)^{-1}$: $(\alpha_{i\tau} +-\Delta\alpha_{i\tau})(\tau_i -+\Delta\tau_i) = \mathbf{a}_o$,

$$(1+-a_{i\tau}*)^{-1} = (1-+t_i*)\ ;\ a_{i\tau}* = +-((1-+t_i*)^{-1}-1)$$

that leads to the approximation of the OPMC by its adaptive model. Perturbations of the discrete systemic spectrum { a_{io}} act through separate deviations {Δa_{io}} by changing the macromodel parameter of multiplication $\gamma^{\alpha}_i(\gamma)$.

Increasing γ at a given $\mathbf{n}$ draws a_{io} closer to $a_{i+1,o}$, which could disturb the initial code sequence, DP's, and the ability of the macromodel to preserve its characteristics.

Using the invariant condition for the initial α_{io}^{t}: $\alpha_{io}^{t} t_i = \mathbf{a}$, we come to an analogous formula: $a_{io}* = ((1 - t_i*)^{-1} - 1)$ for any sign of deviation $a_{io}* = |\frac{\Delta \alpha_{io}}{\alpha_{io}}|$. The potential for adaptation of P_m defines the model ability to preserve the systemic invariants, that are responsible for the mechanism of resistance to significant changes, which violate the model stability and the preservation of its entropy functional. The potential of adaption, according to the formula

(2.3) $P_m = \sum_n |a_{io} *| = \sum_n |(1 - t_i*)^{-1} - 1|$

is a systemic parameter that depends on the limited admitted deviations of $a_{io}*, t_i*$, for which the invariants are preserved. From the other side, the limited deviations of $\{\alpha_{io}\}$ are determined by conditions of nonequality of $\{\alpha_{io} + \Delta\alpha_{io}\}$ with $\{\alpha_{i+1,o}\}$ and are connected with forming triplets, if hold true the realtions

$$a_{io}* = \frac{\Delta \alpha_{io}}{\alpha_{io}} \leq 1 - \frac{\alpha_{i+1,o}}{\alpha_{io}} = 1 - (G_i)^{-1},\ \alpha_{i\tau} t_i = \mathbf{a}_o.$$

Each triplet at γ =0.5 with the multiplicator $G_i \sim \gamma_i^{\alpha}$ has the parameters: G_1=2.21; G_2 =1.79. This leads to the inequality $a_{io}* \leq$ 1- $(2.21)^{-1}$+1-$(1.79)^{-1}$ $\approx$ 1. For the n-dimensional macromodel with the number of triplets **m**= $\frac{n-1}{2}$, we get $P_m' \leq$ $\leq \frac{n-1}{2}$, at γ =0.5, where P_m' represents the quantitative estimation of the stability of minimal code. P_m' can be expressed via the triplet's dimension **m** defined by the parameter G^* of the initial operator spectrum, or by the basic parameters (γ , **n, k**):

(2.4) $P_m(\gamma$, **n, k**)= $P_m(t_i(G^*(\gamma)),$ **n, k**); P_m'(**m**, γ =0.5) $\cong$ 1/3**m**.

The ability of the conformation rotation (defined by **k**) depends on P_m .

With growing **n** and decreasing γ , P_m' increases. As it follows from OPMC, the triplet's structure can exist only if $|t_i*| \leq 0.26$ at γ =0.5. Applying the P_m equation to t_i* =0.26, we obtain P_m=0.3514**n,** which for the same **n** is close to P_m' At the negative t_i* =-0.26, we get P_m=0.206**n**, which shows a nonsymmetry of the macromodel characteristics at deviation γ and at the external perturbations.

At preservation P_m , the model embraces more decreasing γ than increasing.

For maximal **n**=96, the nonsymmetry between the adaptive potentials is equal to 17.05-10.01=7.0410.01=7.04. With equal probable signs and values of perturbations, there is a tendency toward decreasing γ . This fact leads to increasing the negentropy production and shows a trend toward an automatic execution of the PM in the adaptation process. The microlevel randomness is a generator of negentropy. The difference between negentropy and external entropy

(2.5) $N(\mathbf{n}, \gamma) = -\mathbf{a}(\gamma)^2\mathbf{n} + \mathbf{n}/2$

grows with decreasing γ, and increasing **n**. The **n**-dimensional macromodel can produce more negentropy than can consume it for consolidation of states, which may lead to nonstability. Compensation of the nonstability is possible by an equivalent changing **n**, γ. The *adaptive* macromodel, by counteracting to perturbances, has a tendency to grow (**n**, P_m), and the time of functioning (T). The models with more γ, which possesses less (P_m,T), terminate their existence earlier. The environment filters such models, creating a trend in evolution of macromodel with decreasing γ and increasing **n**. Decreasing γ restricts the maximum value of **n**. Using N(**n**, γ) for increasing of the dimension Δ **n**, we receive: $\mathbf{a}(\gamma)^2\mathbf{n} - \mathbf{n}/2 = \mathbf{a}(\gamma)^2 \Delta\mathbf{n}$. For a stable model, the entropy of controls is compensated for by the inner entropy production at $\Delta\mathbf{n}=0$, and $\mathbf{n}/2 = \alpha'(\gamma)^2\mathbf{n}$, which corresponds to $\mathbf{a}(\gamma)^2=0.5$, and $\gamma=0.5$. To get the maximum of $\Delta\mathbf{n}/\mathbf{n}=\mathbf{n}^*$ we need the negentropy per dimension $\mathbf{a}(\gamma=0)^2 \cong 0.585$. Using the negentropy surplus for generation of just one control, we may determine the minimal even dimension of the self-control system: $\mathbf{n}_o = \mathbf{a}(\gamma=0)^2 \cong (\mathbf{a}(\gamma=0)^2 \cong -0.5)^{-1} \cong 8$.

The maximal dimension $\mathbf{n}_m$ is determined by the condition of forming the self-control system of minimal dimension, based on dimension $\mathbf{n}_o$:

$(\mathbf{a}(\gamma=0)^2 \cong -0.5)\,\mathbf{n}_m = \mathbf{n}_o$, $\mathbf{n}_m \cong 94\text{-}96$.

The processes in such models are mutually controllable, and can create each other, if the model with $\mathbf{n}_o=8$ has arisen an originally. The potential for adaptation defines the probability of forming a macrosystem as a result of the PM execution.

2.2.3. About the probability of forming a macrosystem

The value of the adaptation potential can be used to evaluate the lowest probability limit of performing a movement along the macrotrajectory: $P = \varepsilon\exp - [2\Delta S(1-\varepsilon)^{-1}]^{1/2}$ where ε is found from the solution of the equation $(1-\varepsilon)^3 = \dfrac{\Delta S}{2}\varepsilon^2$ (ch.1.2), and ΔS is defined by this integral for all admissible Δt_i deviations at each t_i locality of the process of consolidation:

$$\Delta S = \int H(\Delta t_i)\, d(\Delta t_i)\,,\; H(\Delta t_i) = \frac{1}{2}\sum_{i=1}^{m}\Delta\alpha_{i\tau} = \frac{1}{2}\sum_{i=1}^{m}\frac{\Delta\alpha_{i\tau}}{\alpha_{i\tau}}\alpha_{i\tau} = \frac{1}{2}\sum_{i=1}^{m}\frac{\mathbf{a}_o\alpha_{i\tau}{*}}{t_i};$$

$$\Delta S = \frac{\mathbf{a}_o}{2}\int\sum_{i=1}^{m}\alpha_{i\tau}{*}\frac{dt_i}{t_i} = \frac{\mathbf{a}_o}{2}\int\sum_{i=1}^{m}\alpha_{i\tau}{*}\,dt_i{*};\;\alpha_{i\tau}{*} = 1-(1+t_i{*})^{-1}.,$$

where the signs of $\alpha_{i\tau}$ and α_{io} are opposite. Then, at $\mathbf{m} = \dfrac{\mathbf{n}}{2}+1$, we get

$$(2.6)\Delta S = \frac{\mathbf{a}_o}{2}\int\sum_{i=1}^{m}[1-(1+t_i^*)^{-1}]dt_i^* = \frac{\mathbf{a}_o}{2}[t_i^* - \ln(1+t_i^*)](\frac{\mathbf{n}}{2}+1) .$$

In the limit, at $t_i^* \to 0$, $\Delta S \to 0$ we get the maximal probability P=1 for any **n** and $\varepsilon \to 1$. From (2.6) at the positive t_i^* =0.26 we get $\Delta S = \frac{a_o}{2}(\frac{\mathbf{n}}{2}+1)0.02889$ and at the negative t_i^* =-0.26 we have $\Delta S = -\frac{\mathbf{a}_o}{2}(\frac{\mathbf{n}}{2}+1)0.51$.

A system of minimal even dimension, **n**=2, $\mathbf{a}_o(\gamma=0.5)=|0.25|$. has $|\Delta S| = 0.1275$.

Let us evaluate the admissible probability P on a macrotrajectory for that ΔS: $P = 0.69\exp-[0.255(0.31)^{-1}]^{1/2} \approx 0.278, \varepsilon \approx 0.69$. Applying the first ΔS formula (for t_i^* =0.26), we get ΔS=0.0072225, $\varepsilon \approx 0.9$ and the probability: $P = 0.9\exp-[0.0.014445(0.1)^{-1}]^{1/2} \approx 0.612$, which does not satisfy the admissible minimal limit. The minimal even **n**=4 (for forming an elementary triplet) defines the minimal macromodel dimension. For all **n**>2, the admissible probability P is decreasing. For example, at **n**=10 we get $|\Delta S|$=0.3825, ε =0.59, and $P = 0.59\exp-[0.765(0.41)^{-1}]^{1/2} \approx 0.15$.

With decreasing t_i^* (within t_i^* <0.26), the limited probability values of performing an extremal macromovement are expended. Because with decreasing $t_i^* \to 0$, the obtained minimal probabilities (for all t_i^* <0.26) are increasing (up to 1), the movement is preserved within these limits. The above probability defines a lowest limit of joint functioning of two and more macroelements enable to form a *system*. If a real probability is less than the above evaluation, the considered elements would not be able to form a system that preserves the macroscopic properties.

Let us define the minimal value of the lowest probabilistic evaluation of performing a given macromotion. For the maximal dimension macromodel with **n**=96, we obtain $|\Delta S|$=3.12, ε =0.39, P=0.0156. This means, with a large number of elements (**n**>100), it is very difficult to perform their joint macromotion, which minimizes the entropy functional. Thus, the probability of the macromodel forming a system is estimated between 0.266 and 0.0156 at **n**=2-96 and γ =0.5.

By the end of the optimal movement, the macroprocess could be transformed into stochastic fluctuations that decay the formed macrostructures.

Let us define the minimal admissible value of entropy, that limits forming the macrostructures and increasing the probability by the end of optimal motion.

For the OPMC, the maximal probability of forming a macrostructure is equal to $\hat{P} = m^{-1}$, where m=**n**/2+1. Such a probability increases with cooperation at decreasing m. At m=1, we get $\hat{P}$=1 , which leads to disintegration of the macrosystem at the final discrete interval. The same result gives the formula $\hat{P}$=exp(-ΔS) at minimal ΔS=0. The macrosystem will not disintegrate if at the beginning of the final interval of the optimal motion, the macrosystem has only two nonconsolidated subsystems with the minimal dimension **n**=2. It defines ΔS=0.14,

and gives the limited maximal probability $\hat{P}$=0.869. The noncontrolled process has less probability, which is maximized at minimization of the entropy.
The lowest and upper bound limits of this probability is evaluated by the equality ΔS=-1/2$\int \dot{D}D^{-1}dt_i$, where $D=D(t_i)$ is a dispersion of macrocoordinates at the locality of the DPs t_i . We come to the following equalities

$$(2.7)\quad -1/2 \ln D(t_i)=\frac{\mathbf{a}_o}{2}(\frac{\mathbf{n}}{2}+1)0.51,\quad D(t_i)=\exp[-0.51\mathbf{a}_o(\frac{\mathbf{n}}{2}+1)].$$

From this, the dispersion is decreasing at growing the macromodel dimension **n**. For example, at **n**=10, we get D=0.465; at **n**=100 we get D=0.0015.

The obtained equality enables us to identify the macromodel dimension by measuring the object dispersion $D(t_i)$. (See also ch.1.3).

2.4. Informational Geometry

Understanding relationships between gynamics generated geometry, represents an actual scientific problem. The geometrical forms and structures of crystals, polymers, as well as the morphologies of biological systems are among numerous examples of such connections. The new systemic aspects of this problem were discovered based on IMD information transformations. The OPMC equations and invariants connect the macrostructure's dynamics and geometry. The trajectory of each of the **n** three-dimensional model movements represents the parametrical equation of a curve on the cone (Figure 2.2.3). Transferring from the one cone trajectory to another is executed at the extremal points of the cone equations. By the action of the rotating moment (ch.1. 3), three dynamic eigenvectors of the operator (having projections on each of the local space systems) is undergoing transformation of rotation. This rotating transformation is capable of successive diagonalizing the dynamic operator. At the DP, the operator eigenvectors coincide by their directions, satisfying the condition of consolidations into doublets and/or triplets. Each triplet carries out three dimensions in a local spatial coordinate system. The successive *integration* of the triplets into macro structures (MS) corresponds to a new transformation of rotation (with transference) of the local coordinate systems and fixing them at DP. The geometry initiates a growing negentropy increment in the MSs with an increasing number of triplets. As a consequence of this, the MS's self-organization is possible, starting from some minimal dimension of the phase space (**n**>8). In a process of competition: disorder-order, the geometry is a carrier of order because of its higher order quality comparing with dynamics (which are able to create fluctuations and chaos). The jumpwise changes of the MS curvature K generate the negentropy with storing the defect information at DPs. Between the DPs, the K is fixed, and the quantity of this information is not changed. At the materialization of the information structures, the corresponding geometry (of that structure) binds (by K) some energy as an information analogy of energy of gravitation (ch. 2.6). Geometrical space for each joint triplet represents an analogy of the inclined billiard table planes, which pitfalls collect, while MSs are considered as billiard's balls. After the consolidation, the formed geometrical structures execute movement with subsequent integration and current states' memorization. The software, we may consider as a universal program

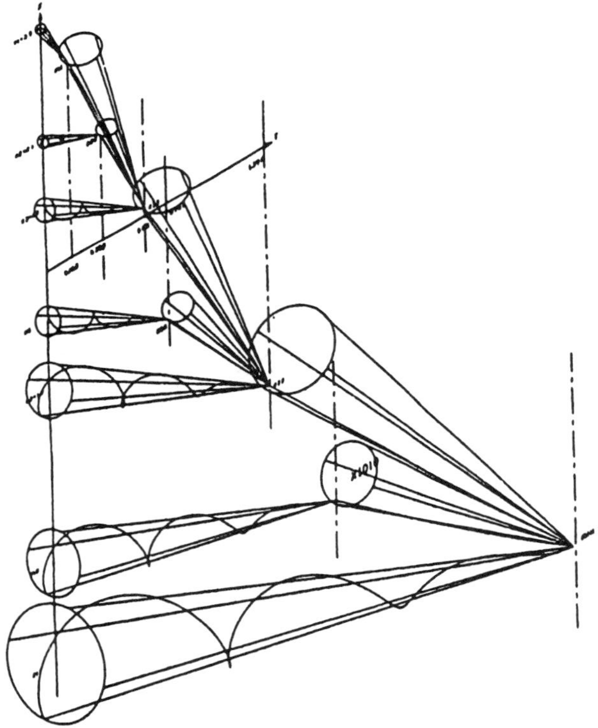

Figure 2.2.3 The geometrical network structure obtained in computer simulation.

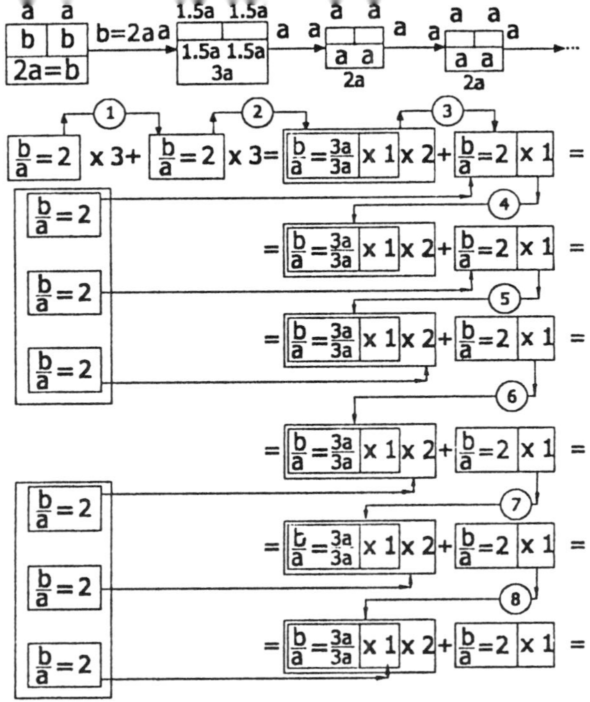

Figure 2.2.4. The geometrical form of the MS: forming BSM's geometrical forms.

(in an analogy with Turing machine), and the hardware as a machine's performer of the program functions with reading (memorizing) results and shifting the program. Reading (with integrating) is transferred into subsequent controls' functions. The software operations define **n**, initial quantities information $\{h_{io}\}$, movement with vector velocity C, and the sequence of transformations {T} forming a local three-dimension geometrical space at each of the triplet structures. The hardware operations implement the transformations {T} and movement with corresponding C, the state cooperation with MS's forming, and carry the discrete and δ-needle controls functions. Within the UR region, defined by the DC, the gradient of information forces X (per the states x): ($\partial X / \partial x$) is directed toward an insight of the region with square function ($-2 X X^T$). It means, the initial states will be kept within the UR at this constraint. This UR, as an initial RS, has a fractal geometry and introduces the entropy of constraint. As it follows from the DC solution, the constraint successively decreases the number of initially independent states forming a string of mutually connected states. Each DP in the string, contributes to the state's interaction and integration. At each DP, the entropy is changed by jump, correlations between the states arise, get coupling, and decoupling during the interactions. These interactions generate the entropy production, a time course, with a scale of time, introduced by the DP's sequence. Each DI determines the discrete time (t') with time course from t-0 to t+0, (max δ t(t')=2[illegible]+0)-(-0|, and the entropy production H=$b X X^T$ as a result of interconnecting information states within the UR with initial information forces. This mechanism is associated with our understanding of casualty in IS. Geometry carries out the inner feedback on dynamics. A curvature of geometrical space is a source of the *rotating transformation* of the dynamic operator toward a subsequent integration, memorization, and forming MS. The transferring of stochastics into the dynamic constraints at the macrolevel couples up the information, fixed into the macrostructures, and throug the MS, creates a new geometry. Irreversible macrodynamics originate an evolution of their geometry by memorizing the renovated *geometrical* structures. New geometrical structure is an attribute of the changed macrosystem dimension. The geometrical space is an additional source of information, capable of carrying control functions and mechanisms of ordering. In the process of generating MS, the dynamics (stable) and geometry compete, contributing an opposite sign of entropies. With a growing dimension **n**, integrated dynamics are memorized in a corresponding geometry with increasing MS curvature, which could be an additional (to nonstable dynamics) source of self-organization. The conformation phenomena, that follows up from those connections of geometrical rotations and dynamics, are widely known. Reference to the rotating movement in the spatial three molecule's model of the chemical kinetics at a large value of the bifurcation parameter may be found in [4]. The points of transferring kinetics into diffusion at moments of their conjugation and breaking symmetry (stimulated by diffusion) are sources of the self-organized structures for both the Dissipative [4] and IMD models. Another example of the phenomena of kinetics and geometry associated with each other, is the rotating chemical reactions [5], which are described by the singular trajectories of the spatial-time macromodel. By the general principles of molecular biophysics [6], the most important features of biopolymers are caused by their conformation mobility. The conformation nature of the liquid crystal properties of the diaphragms, mobility of the lipid structures, and the phase transformations within them, is determined by the rotation of the protein molecule around axis, which is perpendicular to the plane of the diaphragm. In particular, the translation diffusion of rodopcine, the conformations melting of lipids by rotating isomerization of the hydrocarbon chains [6] are the result of the general nature of conformation in macroinformation systems.

The question is How do we select an appropriate optimal geometry?

The optimality of the triplets (as the MS units) and associated three-dimensional geometry is a condition of reaching a maximal dynamic order. The geometry acquires a systemic category that carries out the information for ordering as a source of additional (before latent) group of variables that are essential for the control and subsequent structuring; some way of memorizing the macrostates and the MSs.

The sequence of the operations is as follows: locality of the DP, singular states, a local connection geometry and phase coordinates, equalization of the relative phase flows, rotation of initial spatial system, diagonalization of the dynamic operator, integration and memorizing of the consolidated and renovated states, and forming the MS. The information forces as a result of the PM are responsible for the element consolidation into the hierarchical systemic associations.

The stability of the association is provided with the needle controls, by changing the sign of the joint macrooperator at discrete moments. Inseparableness of geometry and macrodynamics is a consequence of the PM as an information law.

2.2.5. Theory of Dynamic systems and the IST: A minimal size program

The Theory of Dynamic Systems is the most developed part of General Systems Theory , which up to now did not have a direct connection with IST.

The entropy approach , in particular, with its entropy functional and its connection with the metrical entropy, gives us an opportunity for reformulating some dynamic system models using informational language and finding their applications in IST. In the IST approach, we consider the dynamic system that is characterized by a spectrum of dynamic operators having a finite n-sequence of nonrepeating eigenvalues with a multiplicator $\gamma_i^{\alpha}(\gamma)$. Such a system is deterministic but can be characterized by entropy S=$\mathbf{a}(\gamma)\,\mathbf{n}$, where the invariants $\mathbf{a}=\mathbf{a}(\gamma)$ and $\mathbf{n}=\mathbf{n}(\gamma)$ are connected via the multiplicator $\gamma_i^{\alpha}(\gamma)$. All of **n** eigenvalues can be represented by **n** random number; they are statistically independent and are equally probable.

On the other side, the number **n** of the nonredundant eigenvalues can be obtained from a pure statistical approach dealing with the probability of observed processes and computing Shannon's channel capacity (C_p) that in asymptotic is equal to invariant $\mathbf{a}(\gamma)$. From this, we may determine γ using $\gamma_i^{\alpha}(\gamma)$, and the random number **n** of the eigenvalues sequence. We come to a direct connection between *randomness and regularities* , where regularities are expressed via the asymptotic entropy of randomness. The entropy functional of a random process defines not only the IN systemic hierarchical informational structure but also the optimal information code as a minimal program of the process of logical representation. The macromodel's minimal size program is expressed in terms of the discrete set of eigenvalues, or the local entropy spectrum. The same entropy evaluates the algorithmic complexity that depends on the parameter γ , which characterizes the ε -closeness of the eigenvalues. At γ approaching 2.5, ε =1- γ_i^α approaches zero, and the eigenvalues are able to *intersect.* The corresponding trajectories can *interact,* which leads to nonstability and stochastization of the dynamic process. At γ >2.5, we come to $\varepsilon < 0$, and in addition, some of the initial eigenvalues can change sign, which creates nonstability at the beginning of cooperative process, with a possible future stochastization. Both the condition of cooperation and the satisfaction of the systemic invariant $\mathbf{a}=\mathbf{a}(\gamma)$, with growing γ may require changing the sign of some eigenvalues. At γ approaching zero, the informational difference between the nearest eigenvalues is growing, and their possibility of interactions decreases. This leads to the regularity of the corresponding dynamic process. Therefore, increasing γ may affect both changing signs of ε and the initial eigenvalues that are able to transform dynamics into stochastics. The considered string of **n** eigenvalues possesses some regularities in the form of the fixed value of the multiplicator $\gamma_i^\alpha(\gamma)$. The length of the minimal program determines the bit's number to compute γ , which is identified by the channel capacity $C_p=\mathbf{a}(\gamma)=H_p$ (as a binary entropy) and all operations on γ to get the **n**-string, including computation γ_i^α , **n** and the initial eigenvalues.

The complexity of the string with **n** eigenvalues and entropy $S(\gamma)=\mathbf{n}H_p$ measures the relative distance between the random regular sequences with the nearest γ . At decreasing γ , the complexity is decreasing, and vice versa.

In the geometrical space of a distributed model, there is an additional influence γ on the macromodel space structure that contributes to the entropy changing.

The dynamics concentrated into *the minimal program* can be observed only *macroscopically.* Such an optimal program enhances the macromodel dynamics, statics, and enables it to reproduce the macromodel geometry. The code sequence provides a prognosis for the dynamic processes satisfying the PM information law that defines the space-time connections in the IN form. IN generates the minimal program that can predict the creation of new informational macro structures. The MC function is defined by a minimal discrete spectrum of macromodel's operator, which depends on the mutual closeness of the nearest spectrum values, evaluated by the parameter of uncertainty $h=h(\gamma)$. The measured MC is created by the functioning of the minimal program that counts the contributions from both dynamics and geometry. The MC defines the degree of the macrosystem organization and the resulting entropy increment, which enables us to overcome the crucial limit of complexity, creating the self-organization. It brings also a constructive computing of the object's algorithmic complexity, which is connected with the extremal principle, and can be used for deriving an information law.

The cooperating and superimposing actions of the initial local information discretus ("parents") can produce new informational events and new results (that carry more information than their"parents"), even though they interact only virtually. This property, measured by the MC, adds a new space dynamic information quality into algorithmic complexity. The minimum size program utilizes the algorithmic representation of initial information and the IN's logic.

2. 2.6. An initial triplet as a carrier of total macrostructure dimensions

According to formula (1.3..20), a variation of γ changes the starting moment t_1 and the macrosystem dimension **n**. A family of **n** dimensional macrosystems can be *generated by a set of the initial triplets* with a different starting moment t_1 (at fixed **n**, $\gamma = \gamma$ *). The MS dimension **n** defines the quantity of information accumulated by the macrosystemic entropy according to S*=**n a** (γ *). Therefore, the initial triplet carries *genetic* information about future macrosystem organization including the macrosystem structure and the quantity of accumulated information.

A possible macrosystemic organization is enclosed into *a set* of the initial macrosystem's triplets. Each of them has the same geometrical spiral structure.

A sequence of the initial triplets with growing **n**(γ) and the quantity of information is represented by a chain of spiral structures with similar geometrical configurations (Figure.2.2.3, 2.2.5). The chain of different structure dimensions is generated by a sequence of rotations and shifts of the single initial triplet (Figure 2..26 c) preserving the local invariant. The triplet's chain is formed under the action of optimal controls by doubling of the chain coordinates at the DP: $v(\tau) = -2x(\tau)$, $(\tau = t_1, t_2, t_3, \ldots, t_{n-1})$. The macrosystem's state vector (z_i) is proportional to its space coordinates (l_i): $z_i \sim -l_i$ in the coordinate system that is built on the eigenvectors of state matrix. Because of this, the geometry of control actions is represented by a cone spiral structure symmetrical to the macroprocess structure with the same DPs where the nodes are concentrated.

The double spiral chain with the opposite rotations of the spirals is a common generic triplet's structure for a family of macrostructures.

Interaction of the opposite chains generates the chain information code.

The question is, how can one describe a specific characteristic of each chain triplet?

What is the optimal code that defines the genetic information enclosed into each particular triplet? The quantity of information S*= $\log_2$D measures the number of the code symbols D (as the code alphabet). The elementary triplet is *formed* from the minimal even macrosystem dimension **n**=4. For γ *=0.5 we get S*=2 bits and D=4. This means, we need a minimum of four symbols to measure an elementary triplet information with the number of symbols per one dimension equal to one.

The *already formed* triplet has the dimension **m**=3, and requires these three symbols to encode the triplet' information. The vacant fourth dimension of the initial minimal (**n**=4) macrosystem represents a source of development of the macrosystems growing from the generic triplet as a sprout of future structure.

These four symbols can encode 64 combinations of the triplet parameters with coding information equal to S**=6 bits, or maximal macrosystem dimension **n**=12 An average quantity of information encoded by a triplet is equal to (S*+S**)/2 =4 bits. The double chain and its coding language are similar to ones for DNA. But as an alternative to *experimental* DNA discovery, the double chain and coding language implement the mathematical IMD model. We consider the double chain spiral structure as a *general genetic generator for any optimal macro structures*. The word sequence of four symbols represents a minimal program that encodes a future organization of different informational macro structures and their dimensions.

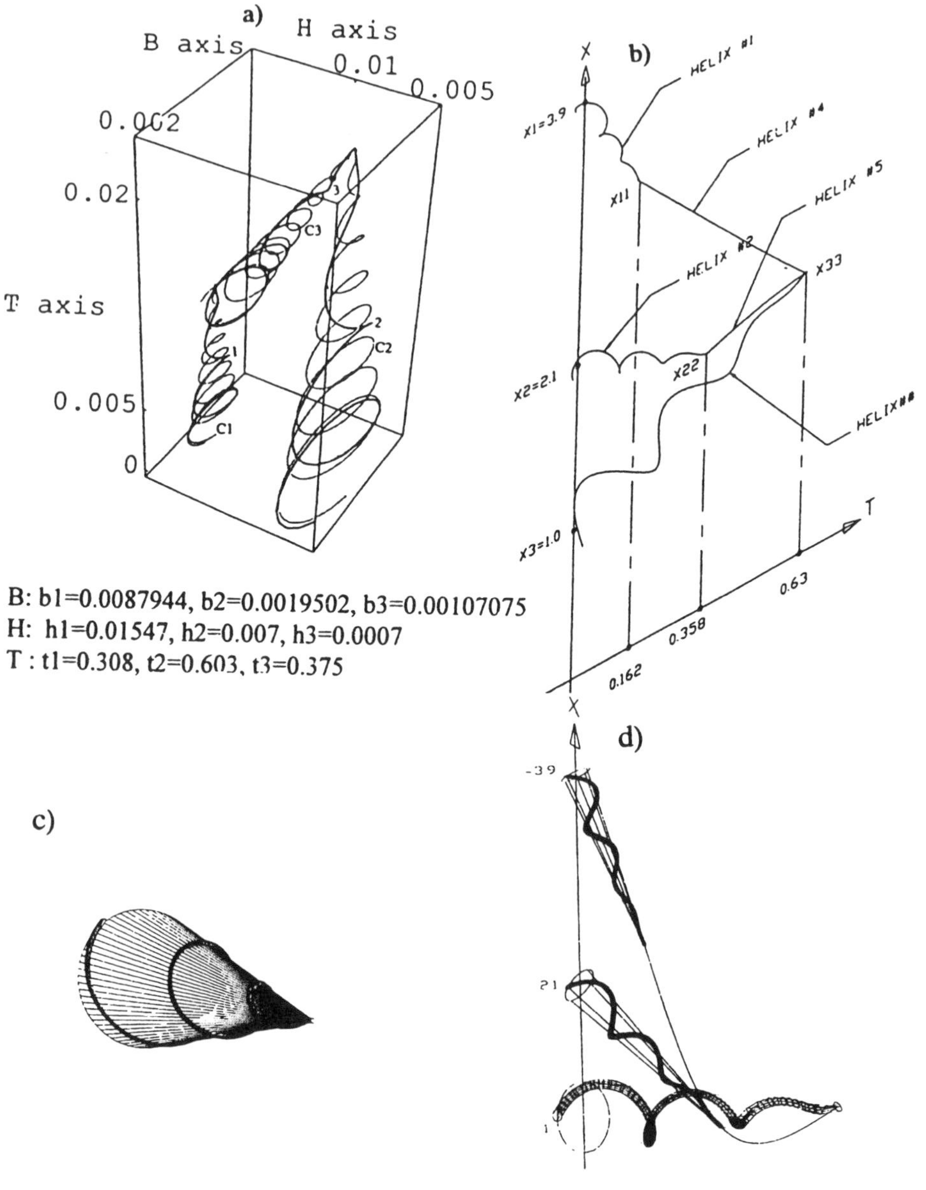

Figure 2.2.5.a. The simulated doublets on the cones C1,C2,C3; b, c. Simulation of the triplet trajectories-helixes (#1, #2, #3) on the cones (X1, X2, X3, X11, X22, X33) accordingly; c, d. The space shape of a cone helix and triplet.

2.2.7. The geometrical forms of the model surfaces

Interactions and exchanges occur at the boundary surface (BMS) of the MS. The BMS is determined by such values of their geometrical coordinates, for which the MS is an open information system that can interact with an environmental model at DPs. The singular DPs points (SPs) or singular trajectories (SSs) belong to the BMS. The stability assumes a balance between the MS's source of negentropy, generated at the BMS, and the MS's external entropy. Such a coordination is executed along all BMSs with some distribution of the λ (e) eigenvalues spectrum. An essential variety of BMS's (and an external) forms with different λ (e)-space distributions supposes to compensate the environmental influence.

Lacking of such variety, or some noncompensated values of this spectrum, leads to nonstability. The MS's discrete eigenvalues spectrum determines allocation of the BMS's λ (e) with some discrete spatial interval δ l defined by relative time interval (δ t) within the MS.structure. The entropy at BMS is proportional to the entropy density $\sum_{i=1}^{m} \lambda (e)_i(t_i)$ and the value of the BMS square F. Assuming a fixed entropy density for the maximal δ l(γ $\rightarrow$0)=0.372=const, we may determine the maximal elementary BMS square(δ F) for each triplet δ F=π3(δ l)^2 /4. The total square for all BMS with (**n**/2+1) triplets is equal F(γ $\rightarrow$0)$\cong$ 0.32(**n**/2+1). That F is close to the value of the adaptation potential P_m. This connection is not only formal, because via the BMS, equilibrium between the MS and environment is accomplished as an essence of the adaptation. During the fluctuation, the cone vertexes at BMS are processing but their mutual contacts with environmental interactions presume to be maximal. This requirement defines a maximal length of contacting line along F for the BMS. The stability of the MS's assumes an essential variety of the λ -spectrum. It leads to the maximization of the adaptation potential.

The triplet's BMS geometrical surface has to preserve its form after each subsequent joining of the initial triplet's surfaces at the SS". It can be proved that one of the possible geometrical BSM forms is a rectangle. If we take an initial rectangle with ratio of its sides b/a=2, then by joining three of such rectangles with b/a=2$\cdot$ 3, we obtain rectangle with b/a=3/2. Three such rectangles form the rectangle with equal ratio of sides: b/a=3a/3a=1. From the two obtained squares and one rectangle we can form a new square: b/a=2a/2a, and after that, the equivalent figures repeat. The schema of the successively formed rectangles is presented in Figure 2.2.4. If the initial triplet's number is 3$\cdot$ 3 = 9 with b/a= 2 each, and total b/a= 2$\cdot$ 3 , then one of them takes part in transformation 1-2, the second one performs transformation 3-4, and the third one does the analogous transformation 6-8. One pair with b/a=1 in the transformation 3, along with transformation 2, forms the square, obtained by transformation 3. By analogy, for the execution of transformation 4, one square is used as a result of transformation 3, and so on, because all following transformations are equivalent to the third one. We obtain system of eight transformations with feedbacks. Such a system, to start of functioning needs three triplets with b/a= 2$\cdot$3. The initial triplets can be produced by a self-controlled system that possesses three noncooperating processes at the last DP . Other possible plane figures, for example, triangles, or 5-6 angles, do not preserve their form at integrations and transformations analogous to Figure 2.2.4.

They also do not satisfy the conditions of the maximal BMS's square, and the maximal contact of interacting triplets integrated into the MS.

2.2.8. Simulation of the geometrical structure formatting

In Figure 2.2.5a the results of computer simulation of forming the doublet as an elementary geometrical structureare given. Simulation is based on an analytical model of the macromodel trajectories at the cone surfaces. The MSs form at the points of junction of the cones (Figure 2.2.5b, d). The trajectories 1, 2, 3 are located on the cones C1,C2,C3 accordingly. Cone C1 is transferred into cone C2 at the first discrete moment (t_1); t_3 is the time of movement of line 3 along C3. Both cones C2 and C3 are joint at the discrete moment $t_2 = t_1 + t_3$. The simulating parameters of the cone spiral (b_1, b_2, b_3), their heights (h_1, h_2, h_3), and the moments (t_1, t_2, t_3) are given in Figure 2.2.3,5(a-e), with the results of simulation of the trajectories, helixes on the cone triplet structures, switching control line, and starting the cone geometry. At each triple point of the cone connection, the three cone's vertexes (X11, X22, X3) connect with the base of the fourth cone (X33, Figure 2.2.5b). It represents three inputs and one output. Because the geometrical sizes of cones X11 and X22 depend on the corresponding discrete intervals, their radius' in the joint points are different, being proportional to information flows. This initiates interaction and the impulse needle controls. The above results support the analytical model.

2.2.9. Informational mass and cooperation

Created information at the microlevel is characterized by the information mass m (from (2.1.10)) in the form $m = -j h (b)^{-1}$, and is associated with its classic definition as a proportion between the force X and the speed $\frac{dx}{dt}$ in (2.1.6):

$X = (2b)^{-1} \frac{dx}{dt}$, $m = (b)^{-1}$. The quantum macrolevel m definition is based on

$$h = |\Delta x_i(t') \times \Delta(\frac{dx_i}{dt}(t')^*)| \text{ for } 0 < h < 1, \; b(t') = |x(t') \times (\frac{dx}{dt}(t')^*)|$$

and taking into account the UR, acquires a view:

$$m = -j|(\Delta x_i(t') \times \Delta(\frac{dx_i}{dt}(t')^*))| \times |x_i(t') \times (\frac{dx_i}{dt} t')^*)|^{-1}.$$

This definition characterizes the capability of the ensemble elements to deviate due to the action of a collective force in a process of movement.

As m increases, the relative deviation ,or the relative uncertainty

$$h^* = \left(\frac{\Delta x_i(t')}{x_i(t')}\right) \times \left(\frac{\Delta(dx_i/dt)}{dx_i/dt}\right)^*$$

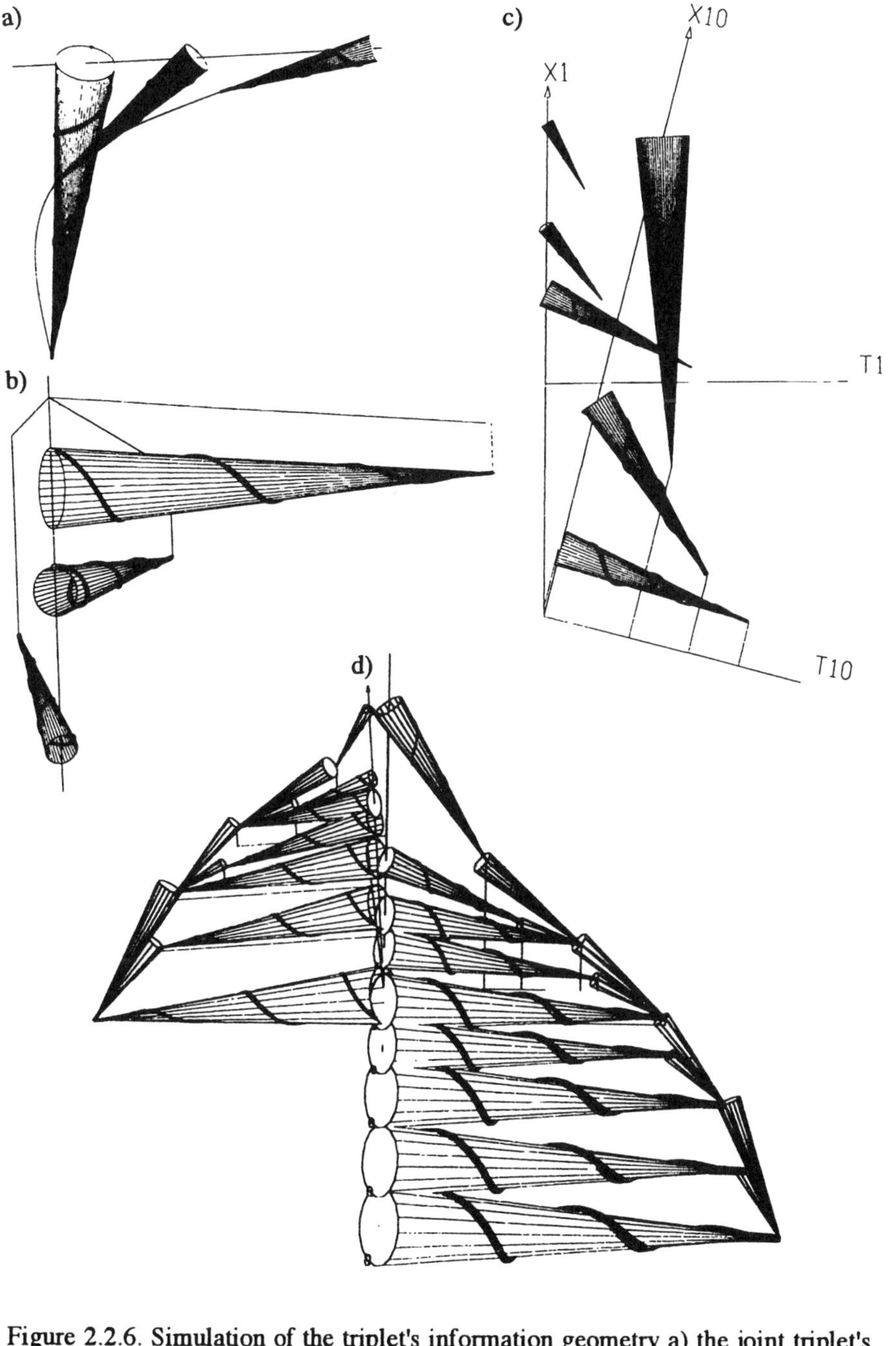

Figure 2.2.6. Simulation of the triplet's information geometry a) the joint triplet's helixes; b) the triplet's 3-space dimensional projections; c) forming the (n+2) IN's triplet dimension by rotating and shifting the initial triplet; d) the family of the IN's triplets dimension 8 and 10 accordingly.

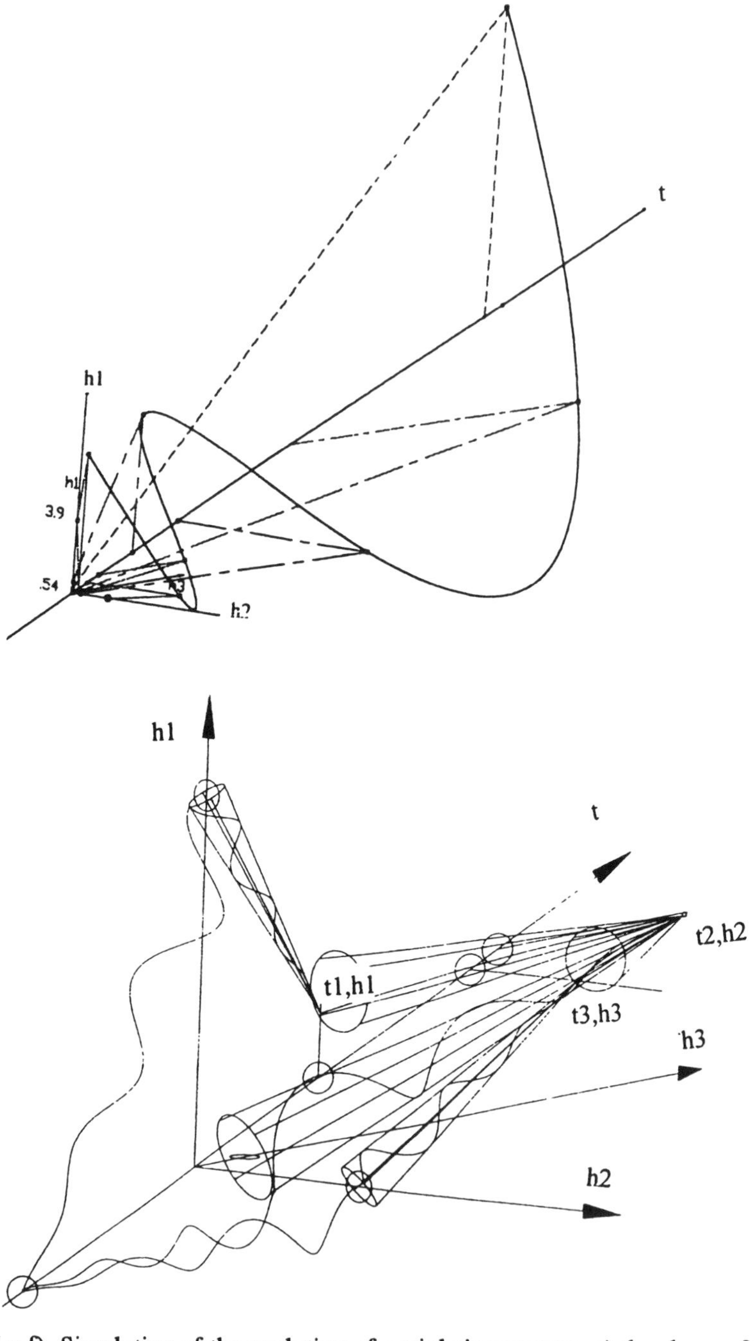

Figure 2. 6 e-f). Simulation of the evolution of a triplet's structure: e) the shape of the witching control line; f) simulating the origin of cone geometry in four-dimensional space-time (h1, h2, h3, t).

and the corresponding diffusion $b_i(t')$ decreases, and vice versa.

On other hand, $jh\,b^{-1}$ characterizes the nonlinear and irreversible effect:

$$m = -j[x_i(t'+0)\frac{dx_i}{dt}(t'+0) - x_i(t'-0)\frac{dx_i}{dt}(t'-0)] \times [b_i(t')]^{-1} =$$

$$= j\,[b_i(t'+0) - b_i(t'-0)] \times [b_i(t')]^{-1} = -j[r_i(t'+0) - r_i(t'-0)] \times [r_i(t')]^{-1}$$

in the process of the information structure creation, or is represented in the form

$$m = \frac{t}{t'} b^{-1},\ m = \frac{\mathbf{b}_0}{\mathbf{a}} b(t')^{-1}\ ;\text{at } t = t',\ \mathbf{b}_0 = \mathbf{a},\ m = b^{-1}(t')$$

with $b(t')$ as a diffusion matrix at DP (t'). The information mass is created by information flow $I(x,t)$. It increases at decreasing diffusion of the information flow and vice versa. The inverse diffusion matrix represents a generalized coefficient of conductivity. For a physical system at $t' = t_o$, where $t_o = 2.66\ 10^{-16}$ s is the light wave interval, the initial information mass is $m_o = b^{-1}(t_o)$ at the light speed C, with $b(t_o) = 1/2\,t_o$, and $m_o = 0.75\ 10^{16}[\text{s}]^{-1}$. The relative information mass $\frac{m}{m_o} = \frac{\mathbf{b}_0}{\mathbf{a}} b(t')^{-1} b(t_o)$ is proportional to the ratio of the imaginary information to the accumulated real one. At $t' \sim l/\text{C}'$ the information mass is in inverse proportion to the geometrical size of an elementary cell (l). Considering an elementary length increment in the geometrical space and the uncertainty at DP

$$d\,l = \sum_1^3 d\,l,\ \frac{dr}{dt} = \frac{dr}{dl} \times \frac{dl}{dt} = \frac{dr}{dl} \times \text{C},\ \lim h_{t \to |t'-o,t'+o|} = 1/2\,|\frac{d^2r}{dl^2}|\,\text{C},$$

we receive another form for accounting for the contribution from all local diffusions, defined by product of the C, K: $m = -1/2\,j\,\text{C}\,|\text{K}|[b]^{-1}$, where K$= \frac{d^2r}{dl^2}$ is the curvature of the function $r = r(l)$ in the geometrical space. For a vector case, h is represented by a norm of the product $|\Delta x \times \Delta(\frac{dx}{dt}^T)|$, and the total informational mass m has a scalar value, measured by length of the derivatives of the normalized correlation vector ($\rho' = \frac{dr}{dl}|r|^{-1}$): $m = -j|\frac{d^2\rho'}{dt^2}| \times |\frac{d\rho'}{dt}|^{-1}$, or $m = -j\,C^2\,|\frac{d^2\rho'}{dl^2}| \times |b|^{-1}$, where the numerator characterizes the curvature of the vector space $r(l)$. In the initial geometrical space $l = \sum_1^3 (e_i \times l_i)$, the space movements of the vector of states along the extremal segments are reflected by the segments of the spiral curves on the surface of the cones, joint with each other by the conditions of consolidation. Finding the local information mass for each MS, created at DP's, represents an actual interest. At the DPs, the geometrical MS's space curvature is changed by a jump creating the local informational mass, determed by the curvature of the cone's geometrical space:

$$K' = \frac{\partial d}{\partial \varphi} = 2[\frac{\partial \rho}{\partial \varphi}(\rho + \frac{\partial^2 \rho}{\partial \varphi^2}\sin^{-2}\beta)]; d^2 = \rho^2 + \frac{\partial \rho}{\partial \varphi}\sin^{-2}\beta,$$

$$\rho(t') = b'\sin\beta\sin[\varphi(t')\sin\beta], \beta = k^{-1}.$$

The jump of curvature K' takes place at the locality of (t' -0), (t' +0) of each DP t', at transferring from one cone to another cone, when these equations are fulfilled

$$m' = K'(t'+o) - K'(t'-o), \frac{\partial d}{\partial \varphi}(t'-0) = 0, d(t'-0) = \rho(t'-0) = 0,$$

$$\rho(t'+0) = b'\sin\beta\sin[\varphi(t'+0)\sin\beta], b' = l'/k\pi, \sin\beta \neq 0.$$

with l' as a discrete space interval : $l' = c\,t'$. From this we obtain the equality

$$\frac{\partial \rho}{\partial \varphi}(t'+0) = b'\sin\beta\cos[\varphi(t'+0)\sin\beta] = b'\sin\beta, \text{ at } \sin\varphi(t'+0) = 0,$$

Then we get $m' = K'(t'+o) = 2b'(\sin\beta)^{-1} = 2ct'(k\pi)^{-1}2k \approx 4ct'/\pi$ at $\sin\beta = (2k)^{-1}$ that follows from the cone equations (ch.1.3.2).

Therefore, the information mass created at each discrete moment is proportional to the space interval, or to the discrete time interval at c=Const. Each triplet forming, is accompanied by as a minimum of two of such jumps transferring both of them to a new cone with $b'(t'+o) = ct'(+o)/k\pi$.

The summarized mass m_Σ as the contribution from **m=n**-1 discrete intervals, is equal to $m_\Sigma = \frac{4c}{\pi}\sum_{i=1}^{m=n-1} t'_i$, or, based on the relation $t'_{n-1} = \sum_{i=1}^{m=n-1} t'_i$, we come to $m_\Sigma = \frac{4c}{\pi} t'_{n-1}$. Changing the speeds, brings the mass ratio to $\frac{m_\Sigma}{m^o_\Sigma} = \frac{l_{n-1}}{l^o_{n-1}}$,

where $l_{n-1} = ct_{n-1}$, and $l^o_{n-1} = c_o t^o_{n-1}$ are the space intervals at the speeds c, c_o accordingly. The mass depends on the intervals of the interaction ($l' = c\,t'$) or on the system time course (t'), which change in a moving system according to the Theory of Relativity. At speed c→C, approaching the light speed C_o, the corresponding information mass depends on the relative speeds according to formula:

$$m_\Sigma = m^o_\Sigma C/C_o[1-(C/C_o)^2]^{-\frac{1}{2}},$$

where $m^o_\Sigma = \frac{4c_o}{\pi} t^o_{n-1}$ is an initial information mass, that characterizes the information *accumulated within* themacrosystem (at $l^o_{n-1} = c_o t^o_{n-1}$).

If c_o or t^o_{n-1} is equal to zero, the system does not accumulate any information (at discrete moments) and it's $m^o_\Sigma \equiv 0$ (because K'(t')→0).

The information mass depends on space speed, and it differs from the flow I, that presents an external system information characteristic. A fully cooperated and ordered macro process carries a finite information mass at any $C < C_o$.

At $C \to C_o$, the information mass approaches infinity. Taking into account the relation $t'_i = \mathbf{a}_o / \alpha_i$, the local mass is inversely proportional to local entropy production α_i: $m_i = 4c\mathbf{a}_o / \pi\alpha_i$, or $m_i = 4c\mathbf{a} / \pi\alpha_{i,o}$ at $t'_i = \mathbf{a} / \alpha_{i,o}$, where $\mathbf{a} \sim C_p(\gamma)$, $\alpha_{i,o} \sim \omega_{i,o}$ with $C_p = C_p(\gamma)$ as an information capacity and $\omega_{i,o}$ as the frequency corresponding to the i-th initial eigenvalue.

The summarized information mass $m_\Sigma = 4c\mathbf{a} / \pi\alpha_{n-1,o}$, expressed via the maximal information speed C_p and the minimal frequency $\omega_{n-1,o}$ at given space speed c, acquires the form $m_\Sigma = 4cC_p / \pi\omega_{n-1,o}$.

The mass gets the entropy contribution only at the moment t'_i.

Within the DI, this contribution is absent. At the negative α_i, or $\mathbf{a}_o$, the mass increment is negative. Both formulas for information mass, m=jhb^{-1} and $m' = 4ct'/\pi$, are in the agreement because $b \sim t'^{-1}$, or in particular, at $m = m'$, $b = j\dfrac{\pi h}{4ct'}$. At $C \to C_o$, $\alpha_i \to 0$, and $m_\Sigma \to \infty$.

Let us define the information forces X_1, X_2 from the DC equation

(2.8) $$grad X = -2 X_1 X_2, \quad grad X = \frac{\partial X}{\partial \bar{x}},$$

where the grad X is considered in the phase space, in the direction of the normal to the surface S ($\bar{x}$) for the eigenvector $\bar{x}$.

Using the transformation $T\bar{x} = \bar{l}$, we may consider the gradient in the direction of the spatial coordinate for an appropriate normal $\bar{l}$ ($\dfrac{\partial X}{\partial \bar{l}}$):

$$\frac{\partial X}{T\partial \bar{x}} = T^{-1}\frac{\partial X}{\partial \bar{l}} = -T^{-1}F_l, \quad -\frac{\partial X}{\partial \bar{l}} = F_l = 2T^{-1}X_1X_2, \text{ where } F_l = -\frac{\partial X}{\partial \bar{l}}$$

is a cooperative force. By substitution informational forces and speeds

$$X_1 = b(t')_1^{-1}\dot{x}_1(t'), \ \dot{x}_1(t') = \alpha_1(t')x_1(t');$$

$$X_2 = b(t')_2^{-1}\dot{x}_2(t'), \ \dot{x}_2(t') = \alpha_2(t')x_2(t')$$

into the last equation, and taking into account the relations

$$\alpha_1(t')t' = \alpha_2(t')t' = \mathbf{a}_o, \ m_1 = b_1(t')^{-1}, m_2 = b_2(t')^{-1},$$

we get the equality for the considered gradient, expressed via above relations

(2.9) $$F_l = T^{-1}\frac{b(t')_1^{-1}b(t')_2^{-1}\alpha_1(t')t'\alpha_2(t')t'M[x_1(t')x_2(t')]}{t't'},$$

which is an equivalent of the equation of gravitation force $F_l = G_l \frac{m_1 m_2}{l_o^2}$,

at the distance between two mass's $l_o = l' /2, l' = ct'$, if the multiplicator represents G_l=8$\mathbf{a}_o^2 c^2 T$M[$x_1(t')x_2(t')$]=2$\mathbf{a}_o^2 c^2 T r_{12}(t')$, or using the transformation T^{-1}=$r_{12}(t')$=M[$x_1(t')x_2(t')$], we obtain G_l=8$\mathbf{a}_o^2 c^2$, where G_l depends on invariants $\mathbf{a}_o(\gamma)$ and c. For example, in a stable macrosystem with parameters γ=0.5, $\mathbf{a}_o^2 \approx 0.0671$, $c^2=9 \cdot 10^{12}$ we get G_l=4.8312 $\cdot 10^{12}$.

The General Relativity equation $K^o = \frac{8\pi}{c^4} G^o$ expresses the connection between the curvature K^o of physical space and the gravitation constant G^o, where the curvature has a meaning of the mass-energy density $\rho_o = K^o$, $G^o = 6.6726 \bullet 10^{-11} Nm^2 / kg^2$.

At the condition of physical reality, the information form of the gravitational constant and the physical constant are supposed to be equal: G^o =k* G_l with some coefficient of proportionality k*. We can find it from the relation k*= G^o / G_l.

By the substitution of the bove constants, we obtain k*= 1.381 $\cdot 10^{-23}$, which is close to the Bolzman constant $k_b = 1.38054 \cdot 10^{-23}$J/K. This means the equality $G^o = k_b G_l$ is a condition analogous to the creation of the physical mass m=E/c^2 as a result of a real space curvature. Considering the creation of an elementary mass m_o during each t' interval with entropy invariant $\mathbf{a}_o(\gamma)$=E/k_b, we get

(2.10) $$m_o = \frac{\mathbf{a}_o(\gamma) k_b}{c^2}.$$

For $\mathbf{a}_o(\gamma)$=0.25 we obtain m_o=0.383 $\cdot 10^{-24}$J/K $\cdot (m/s)^2$.

A source of bound information $\mathbf{a}_o$ creates the space curvature and mass m_o.

In a physical space-time, each informational discrete point is able to generate the mass-energy density $\rho_o = K^o$.

Finally, we obtained the equation for cooperative force, which is analogous to a known equation for gravitation. The information forces, associated with the creation of the defect of information accumulated by the curvature of spatial space, are the attributes of the process ordering. The ability of gravitation to carry out the oriented energy is widely known. The gravitation field is oriented as a magnetic field, and the geometry fixes the order in memorized form of macro structures.

The IMD concepts lead to new understanding of the role and meaning of gravitation as a product of the information field that imposes a restriction on dynamics, and is a source of ordering. The information field and its geometry are the natural antagonists and counterbalance to the second law. Considering a triplet as an elementary informational macro unit with $t' = t_3$, and $l_o = l_3$, we can find the dependency of its cooperative attractive force on the curvature of the geometrical space. For such triplet's field, the cooperative attracting force arises only at the distance $l_o \geq l_3$. At all distances $l_o < l_3$ the attraction is absent.

For the elementary triplet's field, the above force is maximal, comparing with the triplet's macro structure.

If some of the initial triplets are joined together, forming an MS, then their cooperative forces have been used for the creation of a hierarchical ordered system, and therefore, would not be available for other cooperations.

It means, the cooperative forces, created by the ordered triplet's hierarchy are smaller than the cooperative forces in the elementary nonordered triplet's field.

More generally, an ordered geometrical space is characterized less by the free cooperative attracting forces, than in the nonordered geometrical space.

In the triplet field, we can find the concentration of the triplet mass' within some volume, for example, within a sphere radius r_o.

The maximal distance between the nearest vertexes of the triplet cones is $\delta l_o(\gamma) = \frac{\delta l'}{l'}$, $l' = l_3$.

Within the radios r_o we might have $N_0 = \frac{r_o}{\delta l'}$ triplets, each of them with the mass $m_3 = 4ct'_3/\pi$. For the volume sphere πr_o^3, we get $N_v = \frac{\pi r_o^3}{(\delta l')^3}$ triplets, which contain the total informational mass

(2.11) $M_v = m_i N_v$, or $M_v = \frac{4\pi r_o^3}{(\delta l_o)^3 l_3^2}$.

The same way we may compute the summarized defect negentropy De_v within the above volume: $De_v = \frac{\pi r_o^3}{(\delta l_o)^3 l_3^3} De_3$ if the triplet's negentropy defect is De_3.

Each of the $\delta l_o(\gamma)$-locality presents an elementary random volume with a fixed entropy which characterizes a static macrostate.

Two such localities have different entropy values, which depend on the number of the bound macrostates. A more cooperated macrostate, contains less entropy comparing with a macrostate that binds a small number of cooperative states, and therefore, possesses a more entropy. The corresponding $\delta l_o(\gamma)$-localities can be measured relatively in terms of a negentropy and an entropy. Each static macrostate is surrounded by a zone of uncertainty (UR) that contains a set of the equivalent random states formed at the DP. All $\delta l_o(\gamma)$-localities (with the same and/or different entropies) are disposed within the UR. Such consideration of the macrostatic model is connected with statistic physics. IMD brings a new understanding of the *informational static* model as a set of the informational

dynamic states that have reached the UR, with the different $\delta l_o(\gamma)$-localities within the UR. These macrostates are also distinguished by their geometry, in terms of the locality's curvature, the cone parameters, and different numbers of the local cones (in process of cooperation and the entrance on the UR hyperbolas).
Any influence on these trajectories within UR is able to bring the significant unpredictable changes. The initial input might create many different outputs depending on the particular UR. The dynamic equations (with UR) don't have single solutions. Variations within UR could bring unpredictable results including the possibility of creation of a new level of instable chaotic dynamics.

2.2. 10. Information field and intrinsic memory

Each consolidation by a nonlinear jumpwise attraction with the jump of curvature, creates an information element. Information structure is an evidence of the nonlinearity, irreversibility, and creation of the information forces between elements, as a result of space curving. Approaching information elements reduce the distance between elements which decreases a possible number of the element states, causing the elements move. The bound macrostates possess different defects of information, and an intrinsic memory, in particular, for doublets, triplets, and for a singular, not cooperating macrostate. Local concentrated jumps of curvature model islands of memory within the space, which attract the macrodynamics by forming both the controls and the latent information masses. There are three possible options for the corresponding geometry: three-dimensional geometrical structure for triplets, two-dimensional for doublets, and one-dimensional for single macro states. The corresponding informational field assumes all three kinds of the macro elements with a suitable geometry. The macrostates with different $\delta l_o(\gamma)$-localities, within UR memorize a different quantity of information and possess a hidden intrinsic (latent) time. The macrostate's memory can be measured by the latent time of the memory forming, and vice versa. A local three-dimensional orientation, created by a set of distributed triplets (or by a single elementary triplet) brings a three-dimensional information field. The informational field is a bearer of a negentropy and memory. Each triplet is a carrier of a negentropy defect, memorized at the moment of its assembling, and is a source of the needle control. Positions of these triplets in the space are random and are not coinciding, that can be described only with some accuracy and probability within the UR, where all such states possess an equal entropy. Because their space positions are not superposed, these triplets cannot be joined for the subsecond cooperations (without applying additional informational forces), but they are ready for informational attraction to each other in the informational field. An ordered information in the triplet sequence represents a logic, a program, or software. Both a geometrical three-dimensional physical space and the informational triplet's space hold a symmetry of rotating reflection.

Suppose, a set of local quantities of information an initially exists as a sequence of information frequencies given by a program (software) at the quantum level.

This set of information nodes, cooperating into the triplet structures, holds an information mass. With forming each triplet, such an information mass acquires the three-dimensional space coordinates and time as a fourth dimension.
Such a triplet structure is associated with physical fourth dimensional space forming the information mass as a result of the jumpwise changing of the space curvature.

It leads to possible models of transformation of initial field information into a material substance, or software program into hardware with information frequencies as a hardware generator. Information bound into a software program, represents a physical product, as a result of various kinds of energy that have been memorized and spent on designing the software. The three-dimensional geometry might be considered as an additional constraint imposed on dynamic variables, which may bring the optimal contribution, materializing the order and organization.

The initial dynamic process in the primary IMD model potentially is capable of binding the different multidimensional geometry. The three-dimensional geometry is selected by the optimal triplet organization. Thus, the three-dimensionality is a limitation on multidimensional macrodynamics. The triplets are the optimal functional structures that impose this restriction. The MS's surface structures are simulated by the rectangles (Figure 2.2.4) with different **k** at the DP's. Such a surface contains the reproducing cells of growing curvature (similar to honeycombs or scale elements, which also have the analogies to chain armor surfacing).

2. 2. 11. The optimal model's life time starting and its duration

In macrodynamics, the time direction is associated with the second law of thermodynamics. At the statistical microlevel, the entropy increases, and at the macrodynamic level the decrease of entropy is accompanied by self-organization. However, the time course at the micro- and macrolevels, defined by DC, is the same. An order arises as a result of asymmetry when forming the successively complicated structures, initiating the time direction. Each macromodel's inner lifetime is generated by the intrinsic irreversible processes coordinated via a sequence of linkages in DPs. At zero or negative time, the structures are absent. Only at positive time directionare are the structure formations possible.

According to equation (2.1.14), the inner time is measured by the intervals between the moments of interactions (DP) , which could be identified by emission of the information signals as a result of the operator (2.2.8) singularity's at these moments. Macrosystem's time course corresponds to a decreasie of local entropy productions, and an increase of the intervals between interactions.

The inner macromodel time takes discrete meanings, concentrated in the interaction points. The illusion of the uninterrupted time is made by observer, fixing the sequence of the great many of interactions, divided into small intervals that are not distinguished at the classic macrolevel. The DI calibration can be made by interaction with some standard process with a minimal $t_i = t_o'$. Such a natural process is light radiation. The time scale is defined by the numerous light wave intervals (m'_o) within DI: $t_i = m'_o t_o$. If an object is moved with the space speed C', close to light speed C, then it approaches the light wave t_o'. As it follows from the theory, the invariance of the eigenfunctional and the macrodynamic equations are preserved in the macrosystem moving with constant spatial speed.

Because the number of interaction processes and their sequence are preserved with growing speed (C'), the number of DI's t_i will remain the same.

With C'<C increasing, the duration of each DI is increased, if we compare it with the analogous DI, calibrated by a standard process, for the macro system, moving with speed lower than C'. For the same macrosystem, the DI's sum increases if its

speed becomes more, comparing with the conditional immobile macrosystem.

The same events (corresponding to the points of process interactions) are slower for the macrosystem moving with higher speed.

The indicated changes can be observed only in the calibrated system, since the observer in the moving macrosystem measures DI by the interactions with its processes, for which DIs are being increased in the same ratio. The DI extension in the moving (t*) system comparing to the time course with the fixed scale calibration (t') (in the immobile system) is in agreement with the Theory of Relativity (TR):

$$t^* = t' [1-(\frac{C'}{C})^2]^{1/2} .$$

The minimal dissipative losses (in the optimal model) as a function of the relative speed can be expressed via the dispersion in immobile D and moving systems D*

$$(2.12)\ D^*=D[1-(\frac{C'}{C})^2]^{1/2} ;\ D= \mathbf{a}/t' ,\ D^*=\mathbf{a}/t^* ,$$

and when C'=C, then D* turns to zero. According to the second law, D*>0, D>0, and, therefore, $\frac{C'}{C}<1$. From the macrosystemic interpretation of the time course, it follows, that the considered model's time is different from the fourth dimension in TR, as an attribute of interactions. At $C' \rightarrow C$, the intervals of interactions between the systemic elements approach infinity for an external observer, and the system looks like a single element. Within an n-dimensional system, at growing dimension of initial macro processes $\mathbf{n} \rightarrow n_{max}$, the DIs decrease. The minimal t' approaching the light discrete interval, limits growing the dimension up to $\mathbf{n}=n_{max}$.

Actually, the information invariant **a** defines both the scale of the macrodynamics and the geometry, that together with a local entropy production determines an inner model's time course.

Information flow $I_{max} = \mathbf{a}(n_{max} - 1)$, (probably, at $\mathbf{a} \rightarrow \mathbf{a}_o$) carries a maximum information about such a limited system. At $C' \rightarrow C$, only a single nonrandom separated state can exist with a real flow $I_o^o = 0$, which leads to losing information about the system. A macrosystem (at $C' << C$), that finishes its procedure of cooperation, also has dimension **n**=1, and generates information flow I^o=0, because of complete ordering.

The difference consists of observers. Even though the observer is moving with such an ordered macrosystem, he gets information I^o=0 . An immobile observer of any macrosystem that is moving with C'=C, will get information $I_o^o = 0$, if this system has not yet completed its cooperation.

The vacuum property does not affect the light speed, independent from the observer movement; perhaps it is associated with an absence of the interacted processes, which are considered to be essential for any measurements.

The considered information media (IM) (at lacking of interactions) is modeled by the set of δ_o-Dirac's functions, each of them is characterized by the infinite imaginary spectrum. Such IM provides the discrete set of the imaginary information flows, which could also be considered as the δ -controls.

A pure stochastics (delivered within δ ~o) do not contribute to a time course.

The common limited IM imposes the information constraint that is connected with transformation RS- into RS+, and the UR existence. The imaginary information is materialized and integrated into the irreversible structures with its own time course and memory. The consolidation (by IM) of the previously unconnected imaginary flows in the materialized structures is analogous to unification of the separated symbols in the words. The idea, which binds the symbols, materializes the imaginary information, and could be a source of the time start and the irreversibility. A cycle of the model functioning (Figure 2.1.4) includes decreasing the parameter γ during the model lifetime. The value of this parameter γ =0.5 corresponds to a process of equilibrium, after the model originates at $\gamma \to 0$.

The process gets progressively organized by the evolution γ from 0 to 0.5.

A process of growing γ is the most probable by a consent with the second law.

Starting from γ >0.5, the model degrades, and at γ >0.8 it gets decomposed, losing structural stability. The following analysis contributes to understanding this phenomenon. According to OPMC's analytical results, there exists an error ε of sticking together the model's triplets, which depends on γ .

Let us compute this error for different γ using the formula for OPMC: $\varepsilon_i = \exp(-\mathbf{a}_o)\exp(\gamma_i^\alpha \mathbf{a}_o) - 2(1 - \mathbf{a}_o / \mathbf{a})$ where $\gamma_i^\alpha = \alpha_i / \alpha_{i+1}$.

We get ε (γ =0)=0.0875-0.3245, ε (γ =0.5)=0.0959-0.1118, ε (γ =0.8)=0.075-0.418 with a possible error deviations:

$\delta\varepsilon$(γ =0)=0.237, $\delta\varepsilon$(γ =0.5)=0.017, $\delta\varepsilon$(γ =0.8)=0.343.

The model degradation is connected with growing that error and with the error deviation $\delta\varepsilon$(γ =0.8) up to 20 times comparied to $\delta\varepsilon$(γ =0.5) in the equilibrium. At beginning of the process organization, the macromodel needs more precise control. The ratio $\delta\varepsilon$(γ =0.8)/$\delta\varepsilon$(γ =0.5) defines a threshold of the model's decay. In the process of growing γ , the model accumulates the errors until at γ >0.8 it degenerates.

2.2.12. Macrosystem evolution

The macromodel evolves to minimal $\gamma \to 0$ at the process of adaptation. It leads to increasing the number **n** of consolidated subsystems. With increasing $\gamma \to 1$, **n** is decreasing. The γ -parameter, as a carrier of the initial imaginary information (at the starting moment), is responsible for the genetic peculiarities of the IMD model.

PM implies a δ -punctuated evolution with local chaotics at DPs. The evolution process starts at an initial point with injection of negative infinite entropy by the δ - controls. That initiates both the geometry (as some area) and macrodynamics (as a consolidated process) that develop from the initial point. The first triplet is a source of a defect information and three-dimensional conical space with spiral trajectory on the joint cones. This geometrical structure consolidates and memorizes the macrodynamic process and serves as an informational channel that transmits the defect information to a new MS as a receiver. The processes in such MSs are mutual controllable, and can create each other if the model with **n** = 8 was arisen originally.

The controlled macroprocess after cooperating, is transformed into a one-dimensional consolidated process $x_n(t) = x_n(t_{n-1})(2-\exp(\alpha^t_{n-1}t)$, that at t=$t_{n-1}=\frac{\ln 2}{\alpha^t_{n-1}}$ is approaching the final state $x_n(t_n)=x_n(T)$=0, with phase speed

$$\frac{\dot{x}_n}{x_n}(t_n) = \alpha^t_n = -\alpha^t_{n-1}\exp(\alpha^t_{n-1}t_n)\,(2-\exp(\alpha^t_{n-1}t_n)^{-1} \to \infty,$$

at $\frac{\ln 2(t_{n-1})^{-1}}{0} \to \infty$. That function, at $x_n(t_n) = 0$ leads to $\dot{x}_n(t_n) \neq 0$.

The model with such a finite phase speed (at $t = t_n$) cannot reach the zero final state with $\dot{x}_n(t_n)=x_n(t_n) = 0$. At the moment $t = t_{n+0}$, the deviation of the state $x(t_{n+0})$ determines the control $v(t_{n+0})$=-2 $x(t_{n+0})$ and a new real eigenvalue:

$$\alpha(t_{n+0}) = -\alpha(t_{n-0})\exp(\alpha(t_{n-0}0(t'))) (2-\exp(\alpha^t_{n-1}0(t')))^{-1} \to -\alpha^t_{n-1},$$

and so on. The periodical process arises as a result of the alteration of the movements with opposite values of the relative phase speeds $\frac{\dot{x}(t_{n+k})}{x_n(t_{n+k})}$, k=1,2.. and under control switching. Such nonlinear fluctuations can be represented by the superposition of linear fluctuations with the frequency spectrum (ω^*_1,..., ω^*_m) proportional to the imaginary components of the eigenvalues (β^*_1,..., β^*_m), where ω^*_1 and ω^*_m are the minimal and maximal frequencies of the spectrum accordingly, and the function β^*_i is defined by the relation:

$$\lambda^*_i(t_{n+k})=\alpha^*_i(t_{n+k})+\beta^*_i(t_{n+k})=-j\beta^*_i\frac{\cos(\beta^*_i t)-j\sin(\beta^*_i t)}{2-\cos(\beta^*_i t)+j\sin(\beta^*_i t)} =$$

$$=-\beta^*_i\frac{2\sin(\beta^*_i t)+j\beta^*_i(2\cos(\beta^*_i t)-1)}{4-4\cos(\beta^*_i t)+1}.$$

From this, at $\beta^*_i = \beta^*_i(t_{n+k}), \beta^*_i \neq 0 \pm \pi k$, the eigenvalue $\lambda^*_i(t_{n+k})$ contains the real component $\alpha^*_i = \alpha^*_i(t_{n+k}) \neq 0$, at $\gamma \to 0$, $\gamma = \frac{\beta^*_i}{\alpha^*_i}$.

Such a moment $t_0 > t_n$ could exist, that for the new initial eigenvalues, the following equalities are fulfilling: $\alpha_i(t_0) = \operatorname{Re}\lambda^*_i$, $\beta_i(t_0) = \operatorname{Im}\lambda^*_i$, $\lambda^*_i = \lambda^{*t}_i$, $\lambda^*_{i0} = \lambda^t_i(t_0) = \lambda^t_{i0}$, where $\{\lambda^t_{i0}\}$ are the new eigenvalues before the consolidation. Therefore, returning to an initial model and repeating the cooperative process is a quite possible after ending the consolidations and arising the periodical movements. This leads to the cyclic macromodel functioning when the state integration alternates with the state disintegration and the system decay.

For the cyclic process repeating, the parameters (γ , **n**) defined by the maximum real eigenvalue $\alpha_{i0}(\gamma, \mathbf{n})$, supposed to be preserved.

Using the above relation, we get for α_{i0} the equations:

$$\gamma_o = \frac{2\cos(\beta_i^* t) - 1}{2\sin(\beta_i^* t)}, \quad \alpha_{i0} = -\beta_i^* \frac{2\sin(\beta_i^* t_o)}{4 - 4\cos(\beta_i^* t_o) + 1},$$

at $\beta_i^* t_0 = \arccos 0.5 = \pi / 3$, we come to $\gamma_o \to 0, \alpha_{i0} = -0.5773\beta_i^*$,
where α_{i0} (γ_o, n) is defined via β_i^* by the maximal frequency $\beta_m^* \to \omega_m^*$ of the fluctuation by the end of the optimal movement.

Writing $\beta_i^* t_0$ via the optimal model invariant's **a** , $\mathbf{a}_o$, we get the equations

$$\beta_i^* \frac{t_0}{t_n} t_n = \mathbf{a}\gamma \frac{t_0}{t_n}, \ \mathbf{a} = \alpha_{n0}^* t_n = \text{inv}, \ \frac{t_0}{t_n} = \ln 2(a')^{-1},$$

$$\mathbf{a}_o = \alpha_n^*(t_n) t_n = \text{inv}, \ \beta_i^* t_0 = \frac{\mathbf{a}}{\mathbf{a}_o} \gamma \ln 2.$$

Let us define such a value Φ, that provides the macromodel with the real eigenvalue α_{i0} for given $\beta_i^* t_0$:

$$(2.13) \ (\beta_i^* t_0)\Phi = \pi / 3, \quad \Phi = \pi / 3 \left(\frac{\mathbf{a}}{\mathbf{a}_o} \gamma \ln 2\right)^{-1}.$$

The Φ is an invariant for the optimal model because it is defined via the local model's invariants. Let us evaluate Φ, taking into account the possible stochastization of the dissipative movements (with the real α_{i0}) at $\gamma_o \to 0$, and

the parameter $\gamma_o = \dfrac{2\cos(\beta_i^* t) - 1}{2\sin(\beta_i^* t)} \to 0, \ \beta_i^* t_0 = \pi / 3.$

The limited accuracy of determination γ at the frequency doubling (by doubling the α_{i0}) is $\Delta\gamma \cong 0.097$ at $\mathbf{a}(\gamma \to 0 = 0.768048$, $\mathbf{a}_o(\gamma \to 0) = 0.23$.

From this, we find the indicator of doubling the bifurcations:

$$\Phi = \frac{\pi 0.23}{3 \bullet 0.768048 \bullet 0.097 \bullet \ln 2} \cong 4.665$$

which corresponds to the Feigenbaum constant (Φ=4.6692) in the process of transferring an order into stochastization [2].

The maximal enlargement of the discrete intervals is determined by the maximal ratio $\gamma_i^\alpha = \dfrac{t_{n/2+1}}{t_{n/2-1}}$, which computing for $\gamma \to 0$ also gives the Feigenbaum constant $\gamma_i^\alpha \cong 4.6$. That constant is analogous to the parameter of ordering for the phase transitions of the second order. It leads by analogy to the discrete points with the phase transitions of the second order.

The maximal frequency ω_m^* depends on $t_n = \ln 2(\alpha(t_n))^{-1}$, or on the minimal real eigenvalue $\alpha_{no}(\gamma_o, n)$, and also on the threshold of the control device $\varepsilon^* = \frac{\Delta x}{x}(t_{n+0})$, which action generates the fluctuations with the maximal ω_m^*. At given initial $\{\alpha_{i0}\}$, the ω_m^* is defined by ε^*. The ε^* is decreasing with increasing ω_m^*. The time of the macrosystem decay increase with an increase in the accuracy ε^* of reaching the given final state. The model lifetime depends on the macromodel sensitivity to the state derivations, which is defined by the macrosystem dimension $\varepsilon^* \approx \exp(-\mathbf{n})$ (at γ =0.5) [7]. At increasing ε^*, the intervals t_{n+k} are increasing and the diversity of the frequencies is growing, which contributes to the macromovement disintegration on a set of the fluctuations. At $\varepsilon^* \rightarrow 0$ (t'), all β_i^* are concentrating in a small frequency band, and the corresponding macrostates are located near the consolidated one ($x(t_n)$). The intervals between the control switching are increasing, and ω_m^* is decreasing with decreasing $\alpha_{no}(\gamma_o, n)$ (which leads to decreasing α_{i0} and growing **n**) at the same ε^*. At the fixed ε^*, the environment can change ω_m^* because of the macromodel opening at the discrete moments. Generally, it leads to generating a random β_i^* and a possibility of arising the random initial eigenvalues at the beginning of the cycle. Because of this, the model cannot precisely repeat both the cycle time and its amplitude. Since the law of increasing entropy is not violated, each following cycle has tendency of fading and chaotization of the periodical processes. The model of the cyclic functioning includes the generator of random parameters that renovates the macromodel characteristics and peculiarities. The model adaptive potential enables increasing under the actions of the random generator; even though the randomness carries the positive entropy. Such an adaptive repeating self-organizing process is the evolutionary cycle. The future macromodel characteristics define the frequency of periodical movements that depend on inner ε^* and the environmental randomness.

Two mutual controllable processes (initiating the cycle) should nonconsolidate by the moment of the cycle renewing. The interactive process, initiating the cycle may belong to the different macromodels with the nearest, possible nonidentical parameters (ε^*, $\alpha_{no}(\gamma_o, n)$) providing their common functioning, and generating a new consolidating macromodel. The $\{\alpha_{it}\}$ dynamics and geometry predicts the model's entropy production as the local Hamiltonian.

Each macrosystem dimension **n** is characterized by a inner optimal code and the universal mechanism of the code formation . This coding life program encapsulates all essential information about given macrosystem, including its hierarchical structure organization and a possibility of its restoration.

The existence of such a universal mechanism of code transformation can initiate open communications between interacting macrosystems. Macrosystem is able to continue the life process by renewing the cycle, with transferring the coding life program into the new generated macrosystems and providing their secured mutual functioning. A specific information unit of this program mesured, in particular, at $\mathbf{a}(\gamma = 0.5) = \ln 2)$, $h_{oo} = \mathbf{a}(\gamma) = C_p$, by $\frac{dh_{oo}}{dt'} = \alpha^t_{oo} \sim (t')^{-1} \sim \frac{dC_p}{dt'}$ enables the model to carry a local DC, positive time course, introducing the second law. An equivalent imaginary information is a potential source of these substances.

Finally, the macromodel characteristics are

- the limited lifetime of existence of the ordered processes
- the generation of new peculiarities in renewing the periodical process, by ending of the cooperation and ordering
- the possibility of generating macromodels and systemic structures by transferring the model's code during the evolutionary cycle.

2.2.13. The admissible deviations of quantity information

What are the conditions of origin of a macrosystem and the conditions of supporting the macrosystem existence? The origin condition consists of creating a set of interacting and mutually useful subsystems. A necessary condition of arising such a set consists of creating a diversity of subsystems with the ranged spectrum of eigenvalues capable of forming a chain of mutually sustaining subsystems. The following basic conditions define an existence and development of the IN structure:

- the reasons of arising the different subsystem dimensions as a condition of macrosystemic diversity
- the reasons of preserving these subsystems in the dynamic process as a condition of not uncoupling of their sequence.

The first condition can be satisfied if a *maximal* distance between the nearest initial eigenvalues that belong to the same dimension (the $\alpha_{i+1,o}$ as a new one, and $\alpha_{i,o}$ as an existing one): $\Delta\alpha_{io} = \alpha_{i+1,o} - \alpha_{i,o}$, exceeds a limit of $\varepsilon = \Delta\alpha_{i,o} / \alpha_{i,o}$ which determines a necessary condition of creating new dimensions.

This limit is measured by the ratio $\gamma_i^\alpha = \frac{\alpha_{i,o}}{\alpha_{i+1,o}}(\gamma)$ which is connected with the parameter γ for the nearest eigenvalues. The limit ε is also proportional to the ratio of local invariants $\Delta\mathbf{a} / \mathbf{a}\ (\gamma)$ (at a fixed initial moment $t_i = t_{io}$) that are proportional to the ratio of nearest quantity of information $\frac{h_{io}}{h_{i+o}}$, where $\Delta\mathbf{a}(\gamma)$ is defined by the increment of initial eigenvalue arising in an evolutionary process and connected with a systemic adaptivity . The condition of sustained ability of the IN chain is satisfied when the *maximal admissible* distance ε^* between the coupled subsystems sequence does not exceed a limit, defined by the mutual connectivity of the nearest triplets, that depends on a limited ratio of current discrete moments: $\varepsilon^* = \Delta t_i / t_i(\gamma)$. Within this limit, the macrosystem is able to preserve the dimensions under random perturbances and has the potential of adaptation that determines the robustness of control code enabling it to manage these connections. The ratio $\varepsilon / \varepsilon^* = m^*$ characterizes the relation between the conditions of changing and preserving the macrosystemic dimension. Considering the maximal deviation for both $\alpha_{i,o}$, $\alpha_{i+1,o}$ eigenvalues for different γ, we get the distan e values $\varepsilon(\gamma=0.1)=1.046$, $\varepsilon(\gamma=0.5)=0.98$, $\varepsilon(\gamma=1)=0.833$, $\varepsilon^*(\gamma=0.1)=0.35$, $\varepsilon^*(\gamma=0.5)=0.26$, $\varepsilon^*(\gamma=1)=0.129$, $m^*(\gamma=0.1)\approx 3$, $m^*(\gamma=0.5)\approx 4$, $m^*(\gamma=1)\approx 7$.

The creation of new dimension requires from three to seven time more deviations of the initial eigenvalues than is necessary to sustain the macrosystemic robustness. For example, to create a new dimension for $\gamma=0.5$, requires a deviation of initial eigenvalues equal to 100% (and more), and preservation of the chain connections that is not exceeding the current deviation (during the macro movement) of these eigenvalues more than 26% with their ratio equal to ≈ 4. The criteria ε, ε^* require a less limit when a subsystem possesses a maximum uncertainty at $\gamma=1$. Transferring to a new dimension is simpler at high γ. For each fixed γ, it is possible to determine the minimal accuracy of computation of the nearest h_{io}, which would be within the limit of admissible redundant quantity of information. At $\gamma=0.8$, the minimal accuracy requires the two nearest h_{io}, h_{i+o} be not more different than on 17%. But transferring to a new dimension requires the deviation of initial quantity information by more than 86.6%. The adaptive macrosystem, which adaptive potential is able to compensate for the maximal admissible ε^*, can preserve both dimension and robustness within $\varepsilon=m^*\varepsilon^*$. By knowing γ (or any of $\mathbf{a}(\gamma)=C_p$, $\mathbf{b}_o(\gamma)$), the IMD program can compute **n**, and identify the number (m^*) of nonredundant h_{io} within a given **n**. The procedure of origin and development of a new macrosystem consists of the appearance of new initial eigenvalues (and h_{io}) according to the criterion $\varepsilon(\gamma)$, and after that, in preservation of the new eigenvalues with an accuracy not less than $\varepsilon^*(\gamma)$.

Let us find the maximal number of different macrosystem dimensions that are limited by such $\mathbf{n},\gamma$, which lead to repeating the macrosystemic peculiarities.

Thist means, no new macrosystems would be generated with further increasing **n.**

For example, at this maximal **n,** the discrete intervals repeat: $t_2 / t_1 \approx t_3 / t_1$.

The diversity of macrosystem dimensions depends on the admissible diapason of changing γ from a minimal $\gamma=\gamma_o$ to maximal $\gamma_o=\gamma_m$.

The minimal admissible γ_o can be found from $\gamma_o=h_o/(1+h_o)$ where h_o is the minimal admissible measure of uncertainty zone, that is defined by the minimal increment of invariant $\Delta\mathbf{a}/\mathbf{a}(\gamma_o)=\mathbf{a}'(\gamma_o)=1/137=0.0072$, corresponding the creation of a single macrosystem dimension ($n_o=1$). From this, we get $\gamma_o=0.007148$. The maximal $\gamma_m\approx 3$ is found from the process simulation where no new macrosystems can arise by changing γ. Then the maximal macrosystem dimension is evaluated by the ratio $n_m / n_{o=1} = \gamma_m/\gamma_o \approx 420$.

2.2.14. Information and regularity

The macromodel regularities are a consequence of the Principle Minimum of Uncertainty (PM) that in addition to VP contributes to the information space-time cooperation. What is the probability of selecting PM as an information law in the evolutionary process? Information regularities are created in the process of transformation of imaginary infromation from the region RS- into the region RS+ of real informationThe regions RS- and RS+ are correlated as a prognostic, and as an executed (materialistic) behavior of the macrosystem. The specified probabilities determine the unity of their formal description without a principal distinction between information in RS- and RS+. According to the VP, the transformation from RS- into RS+ regions of the macromovement preserves the probability measure. The imaginary information structure is transferred to the real one using equation (2.1.18). The imaginative macrosystem carries information about its future uncertainty by an existence of the prognosis of discrete intervals. A discrete pair of the macrotrajectory's pieces with the imaginary information has the transition probability P=exp(- $\mathbf{b}_o^2$ (γ)). After realization, the carrier of that information is the *geometry* of the macrostructure. Within RS+, the geometry conveys the probability of the future macro movements: P=exp(-2 $\mathbf{a}^2$ (γ)). The macrolevel carries statistical information of the microlevel, and vice versa. The prognostic macrosystem, before and after its realization, is "wrapped in mist" of uncertainty, carrying the UR probabilistic information. Future macrodynamics are remembered in the macro structure, capable for subsequent self-organization. The transition probability at the imaginary DIs, satisfying PM, also represents the probability of the execution of an information law, determined by the limited values of the invariant $\mathbf{b}_o$(γ =0)=ln2, $\mathbf{b}_o$(γ =1) $\cong$ 0.587, and estimated by P(γ =0)=0.6185, P(γ =1)=0.7085, where the last one (at γ =1) corresponds to the maximum of local uncertainty.

These probabilities are responsible for transformation around the evolutionary loop. Let us evaluate the probability of "nonselection" of the PM law, which implies an impossibility of transferring of the initial states to the UR. This leads to the absence of finite discretization intervals: $\mathbf{b}' = \beta_{it} t_i^- \to -\infty$ at $t_i^- \to -\infty$,(or $t_i^- \to +\infty$).

The probability of such choice is estimated by P= exp($-\infty$) $\to$ 0.

The process satisfying PM is most probable comparing it with possible deterministic movements and with random processes of a nonmimimal uncertainty. At this meaning, the PM chooses itself, containing the inner feedback and an ability for self-control. The PM is a principle of maximizing a simplicity, that is responsible for information law and creation of information. The consired in ch.2.1.15 exhibition of PM is starting with forming the first triplet within the initial UR. The process can further develop spontaneously; it needs only the trigger start with probability, perhaps not less than 0.6185 and the imaginary (idealistic) initial information (in the software form). This trigger is an initial triplet information structure. The action of the consolidated controls, determined by fixed values of the structure information for each triplet, becomes weaker due to an increase of total geometrical sizes and informational volumes. It limits the maximal geometrical sizes and the dimension of the macrosystem at the upper level of hierarchy as well.

The PM creates a potential opportunity to form the completely consolidated systemic model (**m**=1) with the wide ranged of the geometrical sizes. Self-control and self-organization themselves cannot accomplish the systemic model by forming a limited geometry and hierarchy. This leads to a family of possible macromodels with the wide diversity of geometry and different phenomena. Realization of the PM possibilities demands additional influences outside, for the completion of consolidations and systemic organization.

Upper hierarchical levels containing highly organized macrosystems of great sizes need a contribution from an outside negentropy for forming the macrostructures. That negentropy can be delivered by other macrosystems through their disorganization. Apparently, without artificial design, the systemic sequence of consolidations, predicted by the PM, could not be realized.

2.2.15.The macromodel's dynamics and geometry as its software and hardware

The current defect information can be transferred to interacting processes and memorized via an informational channel. The channel is an information media, as an information space, that enables it to transmit and accumulate the current defect by a physical form of information signal. A formal mathematical macromodel description includes some logical operations, dynamic parallel distributive processing with current interactions, and controls, that act on some closely correlated states. These mathematical functions have to be fulfilled in real time with random interactions, generation and fixing current controls, remembering and storing the cooperative states. Description of the math functions is considered as the software operations, and an information media, that carries out the parallel distributive processing with current controls and memory, is considered as a hardware. These software and hardware are mutually complimentary not only by the performance of the macromodel functions, but as a mechanism of minimization of the UR uncertainty and simulation of the series of mathematical solutions.

The hardware also transforms the current defect information between interactive processes as an information channel. The question is What is the most general substance of such hardware? Macrodynamics and intrinsic geometry are the source of memorized defect information and distributive parallel processing, that carry out both software and hardware functions which are unseparated.

The UR software is a source of information interactions, which are accompanied with transmitting a signal through the intrinsic hardware. Geometry performs a role of the macrosystem hardware, that is able to deliver the controls for processing via macrodynamics. The geometry emerges also as a method of storage of the defect of information, and as a carrier of the system structured information.

The above consideration leads to a possible model of transformation: an initial information into material substance or software program into hardware.

Information, bound into software program represents a physical product, as a result of various kinds of energy, that have been memorized and spent on designing the software. If an initial real physical space is represented by a set of distributed triplets masses, then for starting a progressive cooperative process we need a minimum of three of such triplets. This means, an initial information space-time supposes to posses 10 dimensions (with 7 space-dimensions and 3 time-dimensions for the subsequent cooperation of three triplets into one triplet, with the fourth dimension space time). Actually, we come to the transformation of an initial 10-dimensional informational space-time system into the four-dimensional physical coordinate system that accompanies forming real physical structure. An initial information string (as a spectrum of a ranged sequence of seven information $\{h_{io}\}$modes-symbols) can create such primary structure. Moreover, all seven nodes-symbols are determined by a maximal $h_{1o} = h_{oo} = \mathbf{a}(\gamma) = C_p$. This initial program code with a maximum channel capacity C_p enables it to accumulate and predict all future consolidations in the process of the macrostructures' evolution.

The information gravitation constant, G_l=8 $\mathbf{a}_o^2 c^2$, taking into account the connection of the invariants, can be expressed via the channel capacity C_p:

(2.14) $G_l = 8 f(C_p)^2 c^2$, $G_l = f_l(t_i, \alpha_i, c)$.

It means, the information string can be created by a geometrical space curvature or by a information gravitation. From another side, the information code, delivered via the channel capacity, enables it to determine a cooperative space geometry, and creation of the information mass. Finally, a given C_p it can generate both the information strings and their cooperations into the triplet's macro structures.

2.2.16. Informational form of a physical law

Mathematical, logical, algorithmic, or verbal expressions of a physical law can be considered as a law's *information form.*

Information about a physical law can be obtained by observing a set of a law's peculiarities, events, or some results of actions displaying the law, which usually are random. By collecting and analyzing such a random law's model of *microlevel* activity, it is a possible to identify the information *macroscopic* description of the law. This means, the law's macrolevel information reveals itself via microlevel stochastics. Stochastics, over the DC, create a dynamic macroeffect in form of informational forces X (or inner control functions v), while a deterministic action of these macro forces, as a feedback, can initiate the microlevel stochastics.

It originates a channel of the micro- macrolevel transformations of information. The DC defines an inner time course, MC function, hierarchical structure of the macro model, and its algorithmical representation via a minimal program.

An object's behavioral law's model could be represented by the hierarchy of two main layers: (1) by describing the logistics of law (as its informational software) and (2)by a physical manifestation of the law (as its informational hardware).

The software and hardware interact through the communication channel using some operating system as a driver of macrolevel software, that performs the mutual interactions between the law's logical and physical layers. Within a physical medium, the software logics are automatically transferred into a physical part through this channel. The hardware, software, and operating system are not separated, existing as the inner intrinsic characteristics of the object's physics.

The IMD models this operating system by the IN with time-space discrete intervals distributed over physical media. At the DPs, the macrolevel information can be delivered to the microlevel by applying the discrete controls. The microlevel statistics can be identified, entering the macrolevel as a deterministic macroeffect, that symbolizes a feedback from hardware to software. The IN's DPs represent the most informative points of the object network that can be identified (as the points of the decoupling of time-space correlations, or as the points of generating of chaotic dynamics). The relationship between different logical law's expressions is an example of virtual connections of related information, as an alternative to their

physical interactions. At the fulfillment of a conservation law (for physical law), the information, contained in the law software is preserved.
It means, the law information is the invariant of appropriate group transformations.

The informational model of law is general enough. Execution of a particular law depends on the concrete exhibition of both the layers and the operating systems. The layers, simulated by corresponding software and hardware, are connected via the IN as an information operating system. For a physical media, the function of the logical layer is executed by the VP equations, and the physical layer delivers the microlevel statistics. Mutual feedback is performed via the diffusion matrix (operator) that affects macrolevel's forces, and vice versa. That matrix for a particular process plays the role of the channels diffusion conductivity, implementing a *natural* operating system. For biological systems (ch. 4.4), the environment where different species interact, live, fight for existence, and die delivers a mutual feedback that can be considered as a natural operating system. In economics (as a human creation), the corresponding operating systems connecting micro- and macrolevel, is implemented via the established market (ch.4.3). The behavioral law implementation depends on each individual, acting within a society, where no natural created operating systems exist. Information about a law assumes it to be delivered to each individual, and to be implemented individually according to a personal conscience.

The law, accepted by society, should be freely established and performed by each society member. Each behavioral feedback cannot be directly measured and evaluated by society; it is a part of individual law execution .

Thus, a carrier of the law information, executor of law, and provider of operating systems is each member of society. A society is responsible only for the creation of an information network that would promote distributing the law information and persuading its acceptance. The IN could be a part of an artificial operating system that delivers the law information to an individual's law provider.

Another part of the operating systems is built by an individual via a cognition, interrogating between a learned law information and personal behavioral actions.

The layer's model of physical object (in logical, software, virtual, and hardware forms) with its intrinsic operating system opens an opportunity of a cognitive understanding of the nature of law, its bilevel components and interactive structure; developing the methodology of monitoring, identifying, and controlling complex objects with unknown regularities; applying computer informational technology for revealing regularities of real systems.

2.2.17. The Neural Network (NN) and Informational Network (IN)

The NN is a physical mechanism for modeling of human brain functions, that carries out a signal processing by a response to input. The elements of physical processing are the NN nodes that are interconnected by the directed arks.

Response of each node depends on the process operation characteristics, the node activation and their schema connections within NN. Each NN performs specific (generally nonoptimal) functions defined by a current input, signal processing, and physical interactions between the nodes. The deterministic result of NN modelling, generally are not predictable directly, before the net was designed and all signal processing were implemented. NN should be trained and learned in the procedure of physical simulation of the object functions. The NN mathematical model is related to neuron physics and the state equations. The existing NN mathematical models (as the Hophield Network) interpret physical signal processing, node functioning and their connections, using the minimal and maximal potential, that reflects the node characteristics and the memory functions. Even with NN algorithm (as a flow diagram), the result of modeling is unknown until the implementation of an algorithm on real hardware. NN is a simulation hardware tool for an object with an unknown mathematical model. The structure of the object, including its hierarchy, control mechanism, optimization, evolution, and so on, cannot be the result of NN simulation. The simulation brings only an experiment numerical result.

The NN model does not even reflect correctly the brain functions and mechanism, which needs more detailed understanding and modeling. For example, such assumptions as arranging neurons by layers and feeding forward a signal between layers imposes significant restrictions on real neurons, which can be both excitatory and inhibitory, and irreversible as well.

The IN models a theoretical optimal strategy (based on information law) that was developed mathematically before the IN was drawn. The IN schema of the node connections is defined by the initial mathematical model, without processing within node. IN generally reflects nonphysical but information cooperative connections between the nodes as an optimal path through the IN. The IN is a software product (with its information language), that does not need a physical signal processing. The IN hierarchy and structure can be drawn directly, even independently from statistics, as a math tool for aggregation. The results of modeling, the model evolution are predictable from mathematical model. The IN does not need to be trained and learned. Instead of training (that adjusts the NN to the investigated object) the IN architecture and structure are predetermined by the object's statistical identification.

According to A. Kolmogorov's *existence theorem* [9], a continuous function of m variables is transformable into a continuous function of n=2m+1 variables. The theorem proves that a method exists, which defines any of these functions. But, purely the existence of these functions is not constructive for NN. The theorem result, in the form m=(n-1)/2 coincides with the triplet number in the IN, where the input and output functions are defined from the relations (ch. 1.1.3).

2.2.18. Review of the main IST sources and contributions

Claude Shannon [1a]. W. Weaver starts with the broad meaning of the communication system, which includes "all procedures by which one mind may affect another. This, of course, involves not only written and oral speech, but also music, the pictorial arts, the theater, the ballet, and, in fact, all human behavior, which would include the procedures by means one mechanism affects another mechanism ... ". Therefore a systemic information approach has been introduced and used initially. C. Shannon has applied a Marcovian chain as a model of statistical ensemble for a definition of the information of a message, and the entropy, associated with the amount of freedom of choice in constructing a message. Fundamental meaning has channel capacity C_p as an ability of a source to produce (or transmit) the limit amount of information. For the probabilities of source with binary events: P, and 1-P, the logarithmic measure of uncertainty is C_p=-P$\log_2$P-(1-P)$\log_2$(1-P). The capacity of a noisy channel is equal to the maximum rate, at which useful information (total uncertainty minus a noise uncertainty) can be transmitted over the channel. Shannon Information Theory (SIT) introduces the mathematical foundation of communications for different sources of information: discrete, continuous, mixed, and also the optimal coding method based on the channel capacity. Working with an ensemble of random functions, Shannon has not introduced the information measure for *nondeterministic trajectories*. For the selection of a discrete source of entropy, a "fidelity evaluation" of "the *underlying stochastic process*" is used. The information evaluation of stochastic *process* is measured by the IMD entropy functional.

Norbert Wiener [2a]. Cybernetics were arisen and developed as Information Science that covers areas of control communication and computer science for physical and nonphysical applications, including modeling of human beings. N.Wiener sees the foundation of this science in the statistical theory of information, that includes Shannon's, Kolmogorov's, and Schrodinger's results. N.Wiener's starting point is statistical ensembles, related to the theory of Brownian motion and invariants of group transformations, as a model's characteristic of some physical law. N.Wiener considers importance of irreversibility for modeling in connection with statistical thermodynamics and with observations in quantum mechanics. Fundamental notions are message, quantity information and coding methodology, unity of informational flows and the processes in machines and animals, with ideas of application of the communication theory for modeling society, biology, economics. This characterizes N.Wiener as a founder of IST.

Ervin Schrodinger [3a]. Life cannot be explained only by regular physical laws. The biological dynamic laws are determined by statistical regularities that have an analogy with the diffusion law as a result of random Brovnian motion. The most important is concept of regularity and order, measured by entropy with a connection to statistical physics. The human organism is fed by the negentropy that supports him at the high level of ordering and stability. The organism is able to extract "order from order" or "order from disorder" as well. The informational concept of the negentropy and ordering is the main result of E. Schrodinger's approach. The OPMC is an example of negentropy production in bio-systems modelling (ch. 4.6).

Andrei Kolmogorov [4a]. The Theory of Information belongs to cybernetics as a process of receiving, control, transformation, storage, and transmitting information. The foundation of mathematical theory of information, which includes the combinatorial, probabilistic and algorithmically approaches, considered independently. Both the combinatorial and asymptotic probabilistic definitions of entropy lead to similar results and similar informational characteristics of random processes. The ε -entropy is a quantity information, measuring the selection of some individual function from a class of functions. The ε -capacity is the quantity information, which can be encoded by some set of elements, if the distance between the elements is not less than ε The basic theorem of information theory and constructive definition of complexity are introduced. In the algorithmical approach, measuring object complexity is defined by the object's information about itself. The complexity as a minimal (optimal) program of given object, does not depend on the randomness of optimal method. The relations between the regularities and randomness depend on the limited complexity phenomena. Dependency information theory on the probability theory is not necessary by a formal definition of

randomness via combinatorial approach, and the general schema of an arbitrary algorithmical process. "If a limited set M of a big number N of its elements admits definition by the program length L$\approx \log_2 N$, then almost all M elements have complexity closed to $\log_2 N$; and the elements x $\in$M of that complexity are the random elements of the M". The randomness of x-sequence is not defined by itself, but only with respect to set M that contains x. The complexity of set s(n,k) elements (with the digit sequences of n-time one, and k-time zero) is equal to its entropy $\log_2 s(n,k)$=H(k/n)n, and is closed to the Shannon entropy H_p of a random value with two probabilities P and 1-P: H_p=-P$\log_2$P-(1-P)$\log_2$(1-P). Any sequence is less random, if its entropy is more distinctive comparing with H(k/n)n. The metrical entropy is introduced as a new metrical invariant of dynamic systems, which opens applications to coding methods in theory information for the dynamic systems.
Such a code is able to reflect one space sequence into another space sequence.

W. Ross Ashby [5a]. W. Ashby defines a system as a set of variables that undergoes the general form of transformations, including probabilistic (informational) transformations. The sequence of states, generated by the successive powers of the transformations, is defined as the line (trajectory) of behavior. Operation of coupling (cooperating) systems consists of effecting one behavior on other. The system has a potential property of breeding by growing and expanding. Systemic variety is a concept that is inseparable from information. Transmission of the varieties is a communication process of encoding and decoding information. A message is considered as the exchanges of information between coupling systems. A channel is a certain behaviorial relation between two points (system parts). Noise is not desirable. Ashby's machine that encodes information is identical to Shannon's transducer. Designing is a process of decoding the varieties, and it is an act of communication (from designer to machine), that includes the selection of a desired model from many similar models. The result of a design is evaluated by communication capacity of channel between designer and machine. Making machine of a desired property (design) is an act of regulation, that is associated with a selection from set of the transformations. Intellectual power is an equivalent of a power of appropriate selection, which can be amplified, but is defined initially by the information measure of the decoded message of varieties. W. Ashby included the general form of information communications in Cybernetics as Systems Theory. Ashby extends the D.M. MacKay [6a] thesis, that a measured quantity of information, always corresponds to some quality i.e., an intensity of the selection.

Leon Brillouin [7a,8a]. Extenuation and generalization of information communication theory on a "pure science": physics, including thermodynamics, quantum mechanics; language, symbols, signals, computing, organizations, observations. Negentropy Principle of information: the negative entropy corresponds to information about system; the increase in entropy is always larger the information gained. Entropy measures the lack of information about the actual structure of the system. Low entropy implies existence of an instable situation, that follows its normal operations, evolution toward stability and high entropy.
Observation is an irreversible process that requires the negentropy. The negentropy principle cannot be reduced only to quantum and uncertainty relations. The quantity

of negentropy, needed for observation, is characterized by Boltzman's constant that appears in measurement. When the measurement is performed on a quantum level, Plank's constant cannot be eliminated from final results. It connects both theories, which are mutually complimentary in terms of a limit of observations.
The information content of an empirical law, using the uncertainty principle, emphasizes on incompleteness and valueless as a scientific law in terms of the limited field of law application, and its correctness within certain possible errors. Scientific laws are discovered by human imagination, which connects observation with creation of negentropy by human thinking. "Human imagination builds up a composite model out of seemingly contradictory parts, and science goes on without ever coming to rest." A model, created by a systemic observation is a different from an initial system because the observation is impossible without perturbing the system by a finite interaction (measured at least a few quanta). Coupling between an observer and observed object cannot be ignored, as well as time's irreversibility, asymmetry, that imposes a nonrepeatableness on the result of measurements and modeling based on observations. Nature exceeds human imagination. There is not strict determinism and causality in nature. The natural evolution of a system corresponds to a loss of information, and hence, an increase in entropy. The computation process is similar to translating the program incoded in active network. A computer does not add any new information but only repeats it in different language, and a possibly with some losses. By Webster's dictionary, information is "communication or reception of knowledge or intelligence; or knowledge obtained from investigations, study." Facts, ready for communication, are distinguished from those incorporated in a body of thought or knowledge, intelligence.

Ludwig Von Bertalanffy [9a]. L. Bertalanffy defines a system as a complex of interacting elements, introduces the concepts of an open system, dynamic interactions, stability, hierarchical order; informational flow in systemic communications between elements and subsystems, measuring of order or systemic organization by Shannon's quantity of information, and uses systemic concepts of communications, feedback control with self-regulation and homeostasis-stabilization. "Law of optimum size organization: the larger an organization grows, the longer is the way of communication and this, depending on the nature of organization, acts as a limiting factor and does not allow an organization to grow beyond a certain critical size." Aims of the General System theory consist of integrating various sciences with unified theory, which may be important in nonphysical science. The principle of minimum action in mechanics, and general structural isomorphism at different systemic levels could be the general systemic approaches for discovering similarities and phenomena in various sciences.

Richard Feynman [10a]. Mathematics is the language plus the logic, that enable us to analyze the behavior of complex systems, while physics cannot predict behavior of a single system element. The mathematical symbols can transfer information fast. The minimum principle is useful for mathematical formulation of physical laws. The fundamental preservation laws and their connection with physical symmetry follow from the invariant transformations that are a consequence of the particular minimum principle. Uncertainty, probabilistic and quantum description of discrete interactions are the intrinsic characteristics of nature. Feynman's "Lectures in Computations" [11a] join theory information, the theory of computation and physics as a bridge between general information regularities and physics.

Ilya Prigogine [12a]. The fundamental role of the second law and irreversible thermodynamics. He considers microlevel entropy and averaged macroscopic entropy. Entropy, as a measure of the difference between a past and future, that carries information about the states connections, and introduces the array of time as an inner system characteristic. It is mechanism of violation of the dynamic invariance and system intrinsic (time) symmetry that builds a bridge between dynamics and thermodynamics. The second law, as a principle of selection of the local stable asymmetrical (irreversible) transformations from the initial instable dynamics. That principle is an extra additional, auxiliary to regular dynamics, that cannot be only a consequence of dynamics. The selection requires of spending some quantity information, which depends on the current system phase state. Such transformation shifts the system into a future, creates a possible self-organization and evolution; it exists for an initially instable systems, that possess "an intrinsic randomness." The quantity of information that is necessary for the selection of the irreversible transformation, determines the "entropy barrier" of transferring to the future. The selection deals with two possible asymmetrical transformations: extending, or compressing a dynamic process. One of them leads to entropy increasing in the positive time direction (and creates a physical observed evolution); another one leads to entropy increasing in the opposite time direction.

Self-organization is a sequence of irreversible phase transformations accompanied with changes of some controls or parameters of bifurcation.

R. L. Stratonovich [13a]. Strong concept that the mathematical theory of information is the product of statistical thermodynamics, Shannon communication theory, and the theory of optimal statistical solutions. He introduced the variational methods for the definition of other thermodynamic analogies, in additional to entropy: as a penalty function for energy, risk for an averaged energy, the derivation of the risk by the channel information capacity C_p for temperature, where C_p can be computed as the derivation of thermodynamic potential by temperature.

A generalized definition of entropy, using the Radon-Nicodime derivation as a density measure, leads to the determination of the entropy of random processes, in particular, obtaining the entropy of Marcovian process. If a transformation joins any two elements with nonzero probabilities into one element, then a such degenerative transformation decreases the initial information. The hierarchical additivity of information, the information bound into Gaussian process, the introduced value of information, the extension of communication systems on physical and general information systems, are important results of Stratonovich's approach.

Herman Haken. [14a,15a]. H. Haken introduces Synergetic as indisciplinar study of the nonlinear phenomena related to ordered self-organizing structures in different systems. A new aspect of information processing presents a synergetic computer, working far from the thermal equilibrium via the self-organization. Such computer technology includes an associative memory, gradient dynamics by ordering parameters in potential field, and the idea of pattern formation. The synergetic cell's network generates information flows that enable it to implement these principles.

George J.Klir [16a,17a]. A novel mathematical approach that considers a multidimensional nature of uncertainty and generalizes the traditional probability measure. Different types of the IST uncertainty ca be measured by a total system uncertainty and information. The proposed principle of uncertainty invariance establishes the connections among different representations of uncertainty and information, as an alternative mathematical system theories. That principle is also important in converting the results, obtained in different systemic models, optimization criteria, and measures of complexity.

IMD contributes into IST not only by a new analytical macrosystemic approach, but also by implementing systemic computerized methodology and software for analysis and control of complex objects.

REFERENCES

1. Sinai Ya. G. *Topics in Ergodic Theory*, New Jersey: Princeton Press, 1994.
2. Neimark Y.I., Landa P. S. *Statistical and chaotical fluctuations*, Moscow: Science,1987.
3. Lerner V. S. "Parametric control of transformers", in *Regulated electrical drive,* Kishinev: Stiinza, 1981:100-112.
4. Zadeh L. A."On the Definition of Adaptivity,"*Proceeding of THE IEEE*, 1963; 3: 469-470.
5. Nicolis G, Prigogine I. *Self-organization in nonequiliblrium systems*, N.Y.: Wiley ,1974.
6. Volkenstein M.V. *The General Biophysics,* Moscow: Nauka , 1978.
7. Jabotinsky A.M. *The Concentrated Autoocsillations*, Moscow: Nauka, 1978.
8. Ippen E., Linder J. and Dito W.L. "Chaotic Resonance: A simulation". *Journal of Statistical Physics,* 1993; 70, 1-2: 437-450.
9. Kolmogorov A.N. "On the Representation of Continuos Functions of Many Variables by Superposition of Continuos Functions of One Variable and Addition," *Dokl. Akad. Nauk USSR,* 1978; 114: 953-956.

THE BASIC REFERENCES IN IST

1a.Shannon C.E., Weaver W. *The Mathematical Theory of Communication.* Urbana: The University of Illinois Press, 1949.
2a. Wiener N. *Cybernetics or Control and Communication in the animal and machine,* N.Y.: Wiley,1957.
3a. Schrodinger E.*What is life? The Physical Aspect of the Living Cell.*, England: Cambridge U. Press, 1945.
4a. Kolmogorov A. N.*Theory of Information and Theory of Algorithms*, Moscow: Nauka,1987.
5a. Ashby W. R. *An Introduction to Cybernetics*, N.Y.: Wiley, 1963.
6a. MacKay D.M. *Information, Mechanism and Meaning,* Cambridge: MIT Press,1969.
7a. Brillouin L *Scientific Uncertainty and Information*, London: Academic Press,1956.
8a. Brillouin L. *Science and Information Theory,* London: Academic Press,1964.
9a. Von Bertalanffy L. *General System Theory. Foundations, development, applications,* London, 1971.
10a. Feynman R. *The character of physical law,* London :Cox and Wyman LTD, 1965.
11a.Feynman R. *Feynman Lectures on Computation*, N.Y.: Addison -Wesley, 1996.
12a. Prigogine I. *From being to becoming: time and complexity in the physical science,* London: W. H. Freeman and Co,.1980.
13a. Stratonovich R. L.*Theory of Information*, Moscow: Soviet Radio, 1975.
14a.Haken H.*Information and Self-Organization*, Berlin: Springer-Verlag, 1988.
15a. Haken H. *Synergetic Computers and Cognition*, Berlin: Springer-Verlag, 1991.
16a. Klir.G.J."A principle of uncertainty and information invariance,"*International Journal of General Systems,* 1990;2-3: 249-275.
17a. Klir G.J., Wierman M. *Uncertainty -Based Information,* Berlin: Physica-Verlag, 1998.

PART III. INFORMATION-PHYSICAL MODELS AND ANALOGIES

3.1. Information-physical analysis of macrodynamic equations

These equalities connect the information micro-to-macro level functionals:

(1) $\max \tilde{S}(\tilde{x}_t) = \min S(x_t)$, $\min \tilde{S}(\tilde{x}_t) = \max S(x_t)$.

The concentrated dynamic process $x(t)$ is described by this equation of extremals:

(2) $\frac{dx}{dt} = a^u$, $a^u(t') = R^t x$, $R^t = \frac{1}{2}\dot{r}_t r_t^{-1}$, $r_t = M(\tilde{x}_t \tilde{x}_t^T)$, $\frac{1}{2}\dot{r}_t = b(\tilde{x}_t, t)$,

$a^u = \|\lambda_i^t\|, \lambda_i^t = \alpha_i^t + -j\beta_i^t$, i=1,...,n,

with the operator a^u identifiable at the discrete moment (DP) t'={t_i}, i=1,...., m.

The second law is executed by selecting and memorizing the positive eigenevalues at the δ-locality of the DPs. Such selection violates the space-time symmetry, creates irreversibility and instability. The second law selects only the first part of equality (1), which leads to the origin of the dissipative macrostructures at the moment of the eigenvalues equalization. The Boltzman "time arrow" is directed toward decreasing the microlevel information. The dynamic time arrow is directed toward increasing the macrolevel information. Equation (1) connects both thermodynamics and dynamics, that lead to unity of time arrow for the open systems. The initial conditions for the macrodynamic equations are determined by the dynamic evolution of the macrosystem and cannot be given an appriory.

The condition of preserving the invariant $\Delta S_o = x^T X$ following from the VP:

(3) $\frac{d\Delta S}{dt} = \frac{\partial \Delta S}{\partial t} + c\,grad\Delta S = 0$, $\frac{\partial \Delta S}{\partial t} = \frac{\partial \Delta S}{\partial x}\dot{x} = -H$, $\frac{\partial \Delta S}{\partial t} = -c\,grad\Delta S$

is a physical analogy of balance equation for a total amount of irreversible entropy. Proper functional (PF) as an analogy of the nonequilibrium entropy for a particular object. The PF extremum evaluates the dissipative contributions from different interactions: $\min \frac{\partial \Delta S}{\partial x}\dot{x} = \max H$ at forming of the macrostructure, as the criteria of the macroprocess quality. The execution of the PM indicates the intensification of structural and phase transformations, and has a meaning of a functional of ordering for micro- and macrostructures. The Lagrangian, corresponding to the probabilty density function $p^t = p^t(\sigma)$ (as a stationary solution of the Fokker-Plank equation for the non degenerative diffusion matrix $\sigma = \sigma(t)$), has form [1]:

(4) $L(p^t) = -1/4M[div\tilde{a}]$, $div\tilde{a} = \sum_{i=1}^{n}\frac{\partial \tilde{a}_i}{\partial x_i}$, $M[\tilde{a}] = \frac{dx}{dt}$,

which defines the speed of changing the current volume of the dynamic system phase flow. The functional $\Delta S(x_t)$ evaluates the volume of this phase flow.

Proposition 1. The equations of extremals (2) for the proper functional ΔS define the following potential functions for the conjugate variables:

$$(5)\ \dot{x} = -\frac{\partial U}{\partial x}, U = -\frac{1}{2}x^T r_t^{-1}\dot{r}_t x + C_x = -x^T\dot{x} + C_x,\ \dot{x} = \frac{1}{2}x^T\dot{r}_t r_t^{-1}$$

$$(6)\ \dot{X} = -\frac{\partial U}{\partial X}, U = \frac{1}{2}X^T\dot{r}_t r_t X + C_X = -X^T\dot{X} + C_X, \dot{X} = -\frac{1}{2}X^T\dot{r}_t r_t,$$

where the constants C_x, C_X are not dependent on x, X accordingly.

Indeed, using these potential functions, we arrive at the equations for extremals. •

Proposition 2. The extremals of equations (2) define the following equations:

$$(7)\quad \ddot{x} = \frac{d}{dt}(R^t x),\ R^t = \frac{1}{2}\dot{r}_t r_t^{-1}$$

that have a form, expressed via the potential functions

$$(8)\ \ddot{x} = -\frac{\partial U^1}{\partial x},\ U^1 = -\frac{1}{2}(x^T\dot{R}^t x + x^T R^t R^t x) + C^1_x .$$

Indeed, using the extremal's equation in the form $\dot{x} = R^t x$, we get $\ddot{x} = R^t\dot{x} + \dot{R}^t x$. •

Potential function U^1 has a meaning of potential energy of the system.

The corresponding kinetic energy T^1 is a quadratic function of the phase speeds: $T^1 = \frac{1}{2}(\dot{x},\dot{x})$. The total system energy $U^1 + T^1 = E$ is preserved for these functions by the definitions: $\frac{d}{dt}(E) = (\dot{x},\ddot{x}) + (\frac{\partial U^1}{\partial x},\dot{x}) = (\ddot{x} + \frac{\partial U^1}{\partial x},\dot{x}) = 0$ as an invariant during a total time of extremal movement (for each fixed initial states $x(0) = \tilde{x}(0)$) with the corresponding Lagrangian L^1 and Hamiltonian H^1:

$$L^1 = T^1 - U^1 = \frac{1}{2}(\dot{x},\dot{x}) + \frac{1}{2}(x^T\dot{R}^t x + x^T R^t R^t x) - C^1_x$$

$$H^1 = T^1 + U^1 = \frac{1}{2}(\dot{x},\dot{x}) - \frac{1}{2}(x^T\dot{R}^t x + x^T R^t R^t x) + C^1_x$$

or $H^1 = \frac{1}{2}x^T R^t x + C^1_x$, and Euler's equationin form: $\ddot{x} = x^T\dot{R}^t + x^T R^t R^t$. For that H^1, the Liouville's theorem [2] of preservation of the phase volume is fulfilled at each DP-moment: $Divf(x) = \frac{\partial}{\partial X}(-\frac{\partial H^1}{\partial x}) + \frac{\partial}{\partial x}(\frac{\partial H^1}{\partial X}) = 0, \dot{x} = f(x)$ as well as the ergodic condition in the form: $\Delta S(x, X) = \Delta S_o = \text{inv}$.

As an opposite to the energy law, the preservation law for the total entropy (of the initial random process) and the corresponding Liouville's theorem are executed only for a specially selected (by the controls) subsets of the phase points. The entropy is an invariant at each optimal trajectory, excluding the DP, where a local conservative subsystem become open. The average energy and absolute temperature are not

constant during the total time of optimal movement. According to the second law, the maximal *work* can be performed during an irreversible process, without rasing the entropy value, which is approaching the entropy of a reversible process. The macro model with the invariant entropy satisfies this condition. The transformations, acting at DPs, create the statistically equivalent motions with the equal probabilities at their trajectories. The statistically independent states:
$\{x(t_i), X(t_i)\}$ and $x(t_{i+1}), X(t_{i+1})$ are defined by the probability transformations:

$$(9)\ P_B^i \cup P_B^{i+1} = P_B^i \times P_B^{i+1},$$

$$P_B^i = P\{x(t_i), X(t_i) \in B_i\},\ P_B^{i+1} = P\{x(t_{i+1}), X(t_{i+1}) \in B_{i+1}$$

which preserves an invariant measure [3]. Such transformations are a sufficient condition of the ergodical transformations. The uncorrelated dynamic process can be transformed into a chaotic movement at the DP locality.

The above results are the consequence of selecting the dissipative solutions from the initial Hamiltonian system. The informational analogy of Boltzman's kinetic equation, taking into account the interactions at the moment t'+o, has a view :

$$(10)\ \frac{\partial \Delta S}{\partial t} + \sum_{i=1}^{n} \frac{\partial \Delta S}{\partial x_i}\dot{x}_i + \sum_{i=1}^{n} \frac{\partial \Delta S}{\partial X_i}\dot{X}_i = -2j\alpha_{io}^{t}\mathbf{a},\ \mathbf{a} = \alpha_{io}^{t} t_i^{'} = k\mathbf{a}_o,\ \mathbf{a}_o = \alpha_i^{t} t_i^{'},$$

where $t > t' + \delta t'$, k is a constant, α_{io}^{t} is an eigenvalue, and $\mathbf{a}$,$\mathbf{a}_o$ are the macrosystemic invariants.

At the moment preceding the interaction, this equation has the form:

$$\frac{\partial \Delta S}{\partial t} + \sum_{i=1}^{n} \frac{\partial \Delta S}{\partial x_i}\dot{x}_i + \sum_{i=1}^{n} \frac{\partial \Delta S}{\partial X_i}\dot{X}_i = 0,\ t < t' + \delta t',$$

where the right side (10) presents the contribution in interaction from any of the j-component with the last (n-1)-components (from the total n-components).

In the case of n interactions, j=n, and the n-th contributing component can be written in the form: $2nj\alpha_{io}^{t}\mathbf{a} = -2n\,k\,\mathbf{a}\,\alpha_i^{t} = -g_s^{t}/t_i^{'},\ g_s^{t} = -2nk\mathbf{a}$,

where g_s^{t} measures the deviation of the equilibrium state (according to both equations) by the interactions ; t' is the relaxation time.

Such models of interactions are widely known in statistical physics [4]. The jump-effect of Boltzman's entropy at the inversion of the speed direction (at the moment of opening the system) has been studied in [5]. The obtained kinetic macrolevel equations describe the adaptive macro system peculiarities of mutual approaching both the controlled $\tilde{x}_t$ and the standard $\tilde{x}^1{}_t$ random processes. (The last one also models the macrosystem's reflection of the environmental perturbations ξ_t).

3.2. About the physical conditions of forming dynamic constraint (DC)

Transformation of random process with a nonzero shift into a Wiener process $\tilde{x}_t \rightarrow \zeta_t$ (a microlevel stochastization) is accompanied by macrodeterminism" (forming the macrodynamics). Stochastization follows from the execution of the second law. A continuity of physical processes in open thermodynamic systems requires an external influx of negative entropy, which compensates for an internal entropy production. These equalities for entropy

$$(11)\ \frac{d\Delta S_e}{dt}+\frac{d\Delta S_i}{dt}=0,\ \frac{d\Delta S_e}{dt}=\frac{\partial S}{\partial t}=-I^T X,$$

$$I=\dot{x}=a^u(t,x),\ X=\frac{\partial S}{\partial x},\ \Delta S_i=\int_s^\tau \frac{d\Delta S_i}{dt}dt>0,$$

$$(12)\ \frac{d\Delta S_i}{dt}=b\frac{\partial^2 S}{\partial x^2},\ \dot{x}^T X=b\frac{\partial^2 X}{\partial x},\ \frac{\partial X}{\partial x}+\ 2\mathrm{X}\,\mathrm{X}^T\ \geq 0$$

acquire a physical meaning of the conditions of the external and internal entropy balancing (11); the quation (12) is defined by the microlevel diffusion processes in form of DC, which executes the balance condition at the fixed moments.

Between the DPs, the macrodynamics via the microlevel stochastization *generates* the internal entropy ΔS_i, which defines the moment t=τ, when the balance condition (12) could be fulfilled. The continuity of both the micro- and macroprocesses is achieved by applying the external control, delivering a negentropy (with DC). The balance equation is responsible for decreasing of the dimension of state vector as a consequence of decreasing the matrix $b=\frac{1}{2}\sigma\sigma^T$ rank, arising its singularities, and executing the conditions

$$(13)\ \sigma_{ij}(\tau_i)d\zeta_i(\tau_i)\rightarrow 0, i=j, i\neq j, i,j=1,\ldots,n$$

which lead to stopping the random process at the discrete points of applying the control . The equation (12) is a condition for Kolmogorov's equation:

$$(14)\quad \varphi=\tilde{\varphi}L,\ -\frac{\partial\tilde{L}}{\partial t}=\tilde{\varphi}\tilde{L},\ \tilde{\varphi}=a^u\frac{\partial}{\partial x}+b\frac{\partial^2}{\partial x^2}$$

for the function defined by the equality

$$(15)\, L(t,x)=M_{t,x}[\tilde{L}(t,\tilde{x})]=\tilde{L},\ \text{at}\ \lim_{x(t)\rightarrow x(\tau)}\varphi(x(t))=0.$$

It defines an apparent independence the function $L(t)$ from t. The corresponding Kolmogorov equation for a transition probability of a homogeneous random process, shows the absorption of that process at the border point $x=x(\tau)$. Process $\tilde{x}_t$ is stopping at this point, cutting off (by the control) at the moment t=τ, when the relation $\tilde{x}(\tau)=M_{\tau,x}[\tilde{x}(\tau)]$ is executed. The random moments, when the equations (15) are satisfied, are the Marcovian moments. The above relations can be true only at the moments t=τ, when the probability function of diffusion process is transformed into the δ-distribution. That takes place at the moment of stopping the random process. The operator of the Kolmogorov equation satisfies the equality

$$(16)\ \tilde{\varphi}\tilde{L}(\tilde{x}(\tau))=\lim_{G(\lambda)\rightarrow x(\tau)}\frac{M_x[\tilde{L}(\tilde{x}(\tau))]-\tilde{L}(\tilde{x}(\tau))}{M_x[\tilde{\tau}]},$$

where $M_x[\tilde{\tau}]=\tau$ is the moment of the process exit from a corresponding x locality: $G(x)$, which is concentrating toward the point $x(\tau)$. The condition (15) can be executed only at DPs. The DC and the balancing condition can be true only at Marcovian moments . Stopping the microlevel process is result of control action, but the moment of its applying depends on the value of $\Delta S_i(\tau)$ from the balance condition (11). The DC equation connects both the moment of microprocess stopping and applying the external discrete control with the execution of the balance equation and generating macrodynamics. The DC equation follows directly from the maximum principle: $\max H = 0$ imposed on both Kolmogorov's and Hamilton's equations, which leads to $L = \dot{x}^T X$, and the execution of equality (15).

Therefore, the balance equation, DC, their discrete nature, and the control action (including the "needle" δ -control), are also the results of the optimization problem for the PF. The second law (via DC) is a model's source of discretization that limits the model's operator frequency spectrum (bandwidth).

3.3. The physical meaning of the optimal control action

The mathematical meaning consists of connecting the VP and statistics with the execution of the Legendre condition for the extremal field equations.

Applying the optimal controls takes place at the DPs: t'=$\{t_i\}$ with the equalization of the model's eigenvalues λ^t_j, λ^t_i, when the local Hamiltonians of the subsystems $H_i(t_i)$, $H_j(t_i)$ become equal to:

$$H_i(t_i) = \lambda^t_i, \lambda^t_i(t_i) = \alpha^t_i, \; H_j(t_i) = \lambda^t_j, \lambda^t_j(t_i) = \alpha^t_j, \alpha^t_i = \alpha^t_j,$$

(17) $\lambda_i = -\lambda_{i-1}\exp(\lambda_{i-1}t_i)(2-\exp(\lambda_{i-1}t_i))^{-1}, \; \lambda_i = \lambda^t_i.$

The entropy and its derivative change with the corresponding entropy production:

(18) $$\frac{d\Delta S}{dt} = -H + \frac{\partial \Delta S}{\partial t}, \quad \frac{d\Delta S}{dt}\Big|_{t=t'+\delta t'} = -H(t)\Big|_{t=t'+\delta t'} + \frac{\partial \Delta S}{\partial t}\Big|_{t=t'+\delta t'}.$$

(19) $$\frac{\partial \Delta S}{\partial t}\Big|_{t=t'+\delta t'} = \frac{\partial \Delta S}{\partial t}(t') + \frac{\partial \Delta S}{\partial t}(\delta t'),$$

$$\frac{\partial \Delta S}{\partial t}(\delta t')\Big|_{\delta t \to 0} = \frac{\partial}{\partial t}\Big(\frac{\partial \Delta S}{\partial t}\Big)\Big|_{t=t'} = -\frac{\partial H}{\partial t}\Big|_{t=t'}, \quad \frac{\partial H}{\partial t}\Big|_{t=t_i} = \frac{\partial \alpha^t_i}{\partial t}.$$

(20) $\Delta S(t') = \Delta S(t_i) = \alpha^t_i(t_{i-1})t_i = \mathbf{a} = \text{inv},$

$$\frac{d\Delta S}{dt}\Big|_{t=t_i+\delta t\to 0'} = -H(t_i) - \frac{\partial H}{\partial t}\Big|_{t=t_i} = -\alpha^t_i - \frac{\partial \alpha^t_i}{\partial t}$$

(21) $$\frac{\partial \alpha^t_i}{\partial t}\Big|_{t=t_i+\delta t\to 0} = -2(\alpha^t_i(t_{i-1}))^2 t_i = -2\alpha^t_i\,\mathbf{a}, \quad \frac{d\Delta S}{dt}\Big|_{t=t_i+\delta t\to 0'} = -\alpha^t_i(1-2\mathbf{a})$$

with the entropy increment from the controls: $\Delta S(t_i+\delta t_i) = \mathbf{a}(1-2\mathbf{a})$ At γ =0.5, $\frac{d\Delta S}{dt}\Big|_{t=t_i+\delta t\to 0'} = 0$ and $\Delta S(t_i+\delta t_i) \approx \mathbf{a}_o$, where $\mathbf{a}$, $\mathbf{a}_o$ (γ =0.5) satisfy stationary process with $\frac{\partial \Delta S}{\partial t} = -H$. The entropy increment from the needle control is equal $\Delta S(\delta t_i) = -2\mathbf{a}^2$, which corresponds generating the negentropy for compensating the entropy increment from the optimal process: $\Delta S(t_i) = \mathbf{a}$.

For n-dimensional model, with n-discrete interval t' (at $\gamma < 0.5, \mathbf{a}(\gamma) > 0.5$), we get

(22) $\Delta S(t') = n\mathbf{a}$, $\Delta S(\delta t') = 2n\mathbf{a}^2$, $\Delta S(t' + \delta t') = n\mathbf{a}(1 - 2\mathbf{a})$.

and the optimal model is capable of generating much more negentropy than it can consume the optimal process. The potential function at the t_i-moment is

(23) $U_i^1 = -\frac{1}{2}(x_i^2 \frac{\partial \alpha_i^t}{\partial t} + x_i^2 (\alpha_i^t)^2) + C_x^1$ at $R_i^t = \alpha_i^t$.

At $\frac{\partial \alpha_i^t}{\partial t} = -2\alpha_i^t \mathbf{a}$, we get $U_i^1 = -\frac{1}{2} x_i^2\, \alpha_i^t(-2\mathbf{a} + \alpha_i^t)$, or $U_i^1 = -\frac{1}{2} x_i^2\, (\alpha_i^t)^2 (-2t_i + 1)$.

That function reaches the minimum at $t_i = 0.5$, $\alpha_i^t = 2\mathbf{a}$. Because the condition (21) is fulfilled under the optimal control action, these controls minimize the potential energy and bring the local stability for the process (with a positive α_i^t).

The character of the potential function is shown on Figure 3.1 at the points of applying the needle controls. Both the total energy and the kinetic energy $E_i^1 \sim \frac{1}{2} x_i^2 (\alpha_i^t)^2 = \frac{1}{2}\frac{dx_i}{dt}(t_i)^2$ are decreasing because of $\frac{dx_i}{dt}(t_i) \to 0$, at the local stability, and minimization of U_i^1. The physical function of the optimal controls consists of bringing a portion the energy from the controlled system.

Decreasing the system entropy leads to ordering and forming the subsystems connections. The joint equally probable (coherent) states possess less energy and entropythan the coherent states before cooperation. In particular, such cooperation leads to a local jumpwise changing of the natural border conditions, measured by the value of the invariant ΔS_o. The subsystem connection is established via removing the potential barriers between them. The optimal control creates such interactions between the coherent subsystems, which lead to their sticking together with the possibility of self-assembling into cooperative macrostructures. The value of the cooperative forces are determined by the potential function for the interactive subsystems, which has meaning the potential of interaction [6]. The considered forces are the physical analogies of the Van der Waals bound forces, acting on small distances $\delta l' \sim 0$. In a more general case, the needle controls change the energy of constraints at the phase transformations. Minimization of the PF by the minimization of its H-function coincides with the minimum of kinetic energy.

This fact causes a possible total energy transfer into energy of the constraints, or into the structural and phase transformations, creating the ordered structures. The moments of the macrostructure ordering are in inversely proportional to the local Hamiltonian values. Increasing these intervals in the optimal system leads to decreasing the absolute temperature. Maximum of the negentropy production (transferred to other subsystems) defines the condition of maximal usefulness [7].

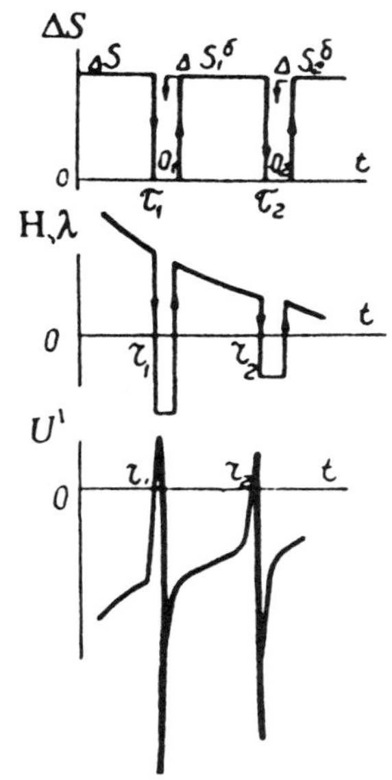

Figure 3.1 The macromodel characteristics of the entropy ΔS (t), Hamiltonian H(t), eigenvalue $\lambda(t)$, and the potential U^1 (t) in the optimal process.

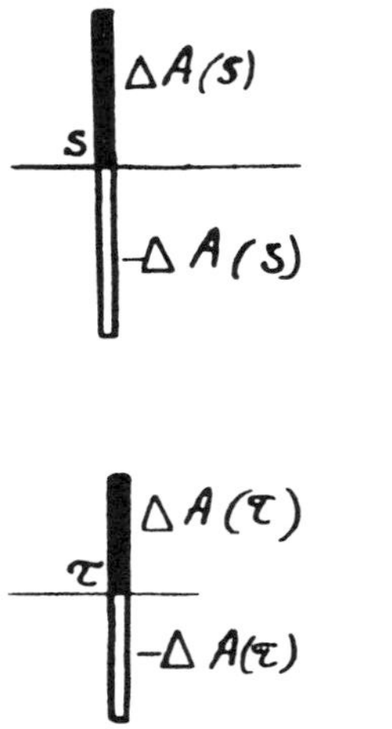

Figure 3.2 The diffusion barrier between the DP: (s, τ)$\in$ t'.

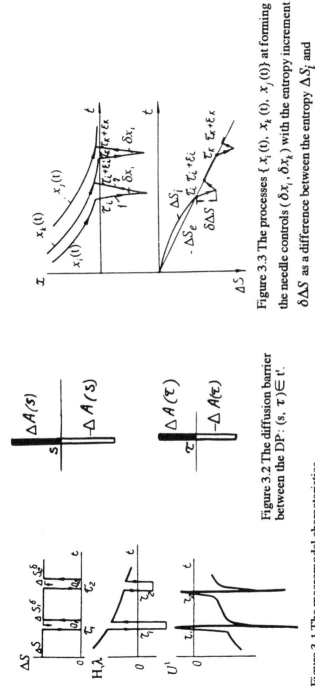

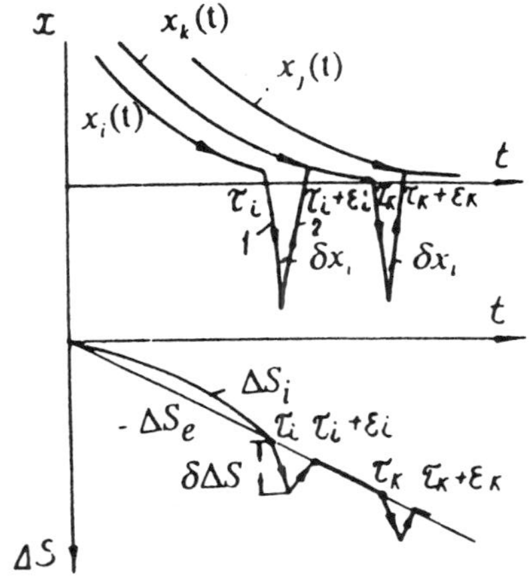

Figure 3.3 The processes { x_i (t), x_k (t), x_j (t)} at forming the needle controls (δx_i , δx_k) with the entropy increment $\delta \Delta S$ as a difference between the entropy ΔS_i and the negentropy - ΔS_e .

3.4. The macromodel's quantum level: An Analogy with Quantum Mechanics (QM)

Feynman's path functional introduces the integral of a wave probability function ($\overline{\varphi}$):

$$(23)\quad \overline{P}(x(s),x(T)) = \int_{x(s)}^{x(T)} \overline{\varphi} Dx(t), \overline{\varphi} = \exp(j\overline{S}/h),$$

where $\overline{S} = \int_{s}^{T} L(\dot{x},x,t)dt$ is a function of action, and $Dx = \prod_{i=1}^{n\to\infty} dx_i$ is differential along a given trajectory of a "particle" $\tilde{x}_t = x(t)$, which measures a total probability $\overline{P}(x(s),x(T))$ for the trajectory to pass through a sequence of the gates, defined by discrete values of $\Delta x_i = \int_{\Delta t_i} dx_i(t_i)$. This functional is determined [8] via the mathematical expectation along a trajectory taken with some measure $\overline{P}_{s,x}(dx)$:

$$\overline{P}(x(s),x(T)) = M_x[\overline{\varphi}] = \int_{x(s)}^{x(T)} \overline{\varphi}\overline{P}_{s,x}(dx).$$

The entropy functional in form (ch.1.1) is different from above formula only by the function of uncertainty $\ln q_s^T$, where q_s^T is defined by the relative probability measure. Using other than Marcovian measures of the uncertainty function (including for example, fuzzy set measure and many other uncertainties) essentially extends the definition and application of the information functional and IMD methodology. The joint consideration of Hamilton's and Kolmogorov's equation leads to the analogy of Schrodinger's equation (2.1.10). There is an analogy of common problems in QM and IMD of finding the coordinate system, where Hamitonian has a diagonal form, which corresponds to decomposition the system into independent subsystems. An event is characterized by values of eigenvalue for both QM and IMD. The imposition the DC constraint creates a possibility of interaction of the events (subsystems) and the system renovation at discrete points DP. Classical Hamiltonian equations of dynamic systems do not define such properties. At the renovating moment, the sign of a real eigenvalue is changed, and Turing's bifurcation arises, as a distinction of Hoph's bifurcation, when one of real eigenvalues turns into zero. Extending the DC on other, than DI time-intervals is possible for an imaginary time by defining the continuous wave functions as a solution of Schrodinger's equation. Entropy defines the probability waves (distributed within a field) that provide uncertainty until interactions are absent. At the DP, the probability waves are able to overcome the diffusion barrier with the aid of transmitting the outside negentropy. Then, the entropy acquires the real value and can be transmitted by quanta. Measuring the controllable process $\tilde{x}_t$ consists of comparing it with a standard process $\tilde{x}_t'$, that performs a role of gauge for $\tilde{x}_t$ at the

DPs, as the moments of observation $\tilde{x}_t$ by that comparison. Any other process states can be defined only with some probability at random trajectories. The equalization of probabilistic measures (of $\tilde{x}_t$ and $\tilde{x}_t'$) is fulfilled at the DPs where the conditional probability takes the values

$$(24)\ P = \begin{Bmatrix} 0, \tilde{x}(\tau) \notin B \\ 1, \tilde{x}(\tau) \in B \end{Bmatrix},$$

that satisfy the condition $P = P^2$. The probabilities can also be defined on the ensemble of extremal trajectories of the entropy functional. The probabilities $P_i = P_i$(t), i=1,..., n are determined only for such Marcovian moments t'=τ, when the functional $\tilde{\omega}_s^t$ is additive and the functional q_s^t is multiplicative.

The Hamilton equations enable us to estimate the probabilities $P_i = P_i$(t), i=1,..., n within the discrete intervals t'=τ.

The basic macrostates are characterized explicitly by the eigenvalues of operator $A = \|\lambda_i\|$ that defines the Hamiltonian H=Sp**A** and the PF: $S_i = -\int H_i(t)dt$.

By analogy with QM, we define a set of events distinguished by the matrix **A**=A(t) eigenvalues of $\lambda_i = \lambda_i$(t), and also the probability of an event, that has analogy with a transitional probability. The events with equal eigenvalues, having the equal probabilities (at the DPs), are undistinguished. An observer delivers information from the observed process and compares it with the standard process. Acting as a latent control, the observer transforms the probabilities of the before unobserved processes, at $t \neq \tau$, β_i(t)$\neq$ 0, into the probabilities of the observed processes, at $t = \tau$, $\beta_i(\tau) = \beta_j(\tau) = 0$. If the observer is absent, there are no cooperations, and the probability of the unobserved processes carries only uncertainty. At the consolidation of undistinguished events, we get their cooperation with maximal probability, and zero uncertainty.

According to the QM oscillation theorem, the wave function of discrete spectrum with (n+1) eigenvalues turns into zero n-times (at finite $x(\tau)$). For the macro model with the wave function $\varphi_i(t) = \exp(jS_i(t))$, $S_i(\tau + o) = -\infty$, it corresponds to breaking off the random process at each of the n-discrete moments.

The macromodel's number of macro states 2m+1, m=n/2, is an analogy of the number of spine projections on a given axis, which expresses Paul's principle in QM. Hamiltonian system, at the initial moment with α_{io}=0, $\lambda_{io} = \pm j\beta_{io}$, has a minimal values of the Hamiltonian and the invariant **a** accoding to equation:

$$(25)\ \cos\beta' - \frac{\sin\beta'}{\gamma} - \exp(-\mathbf{a}) = 0,$$

at $\gamma \to \infty$, $\cos\beta' = \exp(-\mathbf{a})$, $\mathbf{a} = \alpha_{io}\, t_i = \mathrm{Re} j \dfrac{\exp j\beta'}{2 - \exp j\beta'}$ =inv,

and the minimal dissipative losses. At each discrete interval, the macromodel as a discrete filter selects the values $\Delta x_i(t_k) = x_i(t_{k-1})(2 - \exp(\lambda_i(t_{k-1})t_k) - x_i(t_{k-1})$,

$x_i(t_{k-1}) = x_i(t_{k-1})(1-\exp(\lambda_i(t_{k-1})t_k)$ which under action of the needle control acquires the form: $\Delta x_i(t_k) = -\lambda_i(t_k)t_k\, x_i(t_{k-1})$ with the elementary entropies for each coherent state: $\lambda_i(t_{k-1})t_k = \Delta s_o^i = \Delta s_o^i$, $\lambda_i(t_k)t_k = \Delta s_k^i$. From the relation: $e_i = k_B\theta\, \Delta s_o^i = h\, \upsilon_i$ (h is the Planck constant), and taking into account connection of the entropy Δs_o^i with the energy e_i of coherent proper frequency υ_i, we obtain

$$(26)\ \lambda_i(t_k)t_k = \exp(\lambda_i(t_{k-1})t_k - 1,\ e_{io} = \frac{h\upsilon_i}{\exp\frac{h\upsilon_i}{e_i} - 1},\ e_i^* = \frac{h\upsilon_i}{e_i},\ e_{io}^* = \frac{h\upsilon_i}{e_{io}}$$

where e_i is an average energy, accumulated by the moment t_k, e_{io} is the average energy, emitted by the moment of applying the needle control.

We get an analogy with Planck's formula for energy emitted at discrete moment.

The QM's uncertainty relation between the impulse p $= \frac{\partial S}{\partial l}$ (with S as the action) and the distance l: $\Delta p\, \Delta l \sim S$, has the IMD analogy in the form:

$$(27)\ M[\frac{\partial \Delta S}{\partial l}\Delta l] \sim \delta\lambda_i^l o(l_i) = \delta\lambda_i^t o(t_i) \sim \hat{h},$$

with corresponding eigenvalues λ_i^l, λ_i^t, that satisfy

$\lambda_i^l(l_i + o(l_i)) = \lambda_i^l(l_i) - \delta\, \lambda_i^l(l_i)[1(l_i + o(l_i)) - 1(l_i)]$.

Optimal control process can be accomplished with the finite accuracy's $o(t_i)$, $\varepsilon(t_i)$ that take the maximal values $o(t_i) = 0.26t_i$, $\varepsilon(t_i) = \frac{\delta x_i}{x_i}(t_i) \cong 0.1, (\gamma = 0.5)$.

At each discrete moment, the jump of the speed $\frac{dx_k}{dt}(t_i)$ leads to its multivalues at the same coordinate value $x_k(t_i)$.

The speed and the coordinate can not be determined simultaneously. For the considered Hamiltonians $H_i(t_k)$, $H_{i+1}(t_k)$, the uncertainty principle has the form:

$$H_i(t_k) - H_{i+1}(t_k) = \lambda_i(t_k) - \lambda_{i+1}(t_k) \sim \frac{\hat{h}}{o(t_i)},$$

and it means that a set of variables of one subsystem (measured at the moment t_k by $\lambda_i(t_k)$) cannot coincide by that time with a set of variables of another subsystem (measured by $\lambda_{i+1}(t_k)$). At the same moment of time, only one measurement is possible. Because of this, the imaginary components of conjugated processes ($\lambda_{i+1}(t_k) = \lambda_i(t_k)^*$): $\mathrm{Im}\,\lambda_{i+1}(t_k) = \beta_{i+1}(t_k)$, $\mathrm{Im}\,\lambda_i(t_k) = \beta_i(t_k)$, cannot disappear simultaneously. If $\beta_{i+1}(t_k) = 0$, then $\beta_i(t_k) \neq 0$, and vice versa.

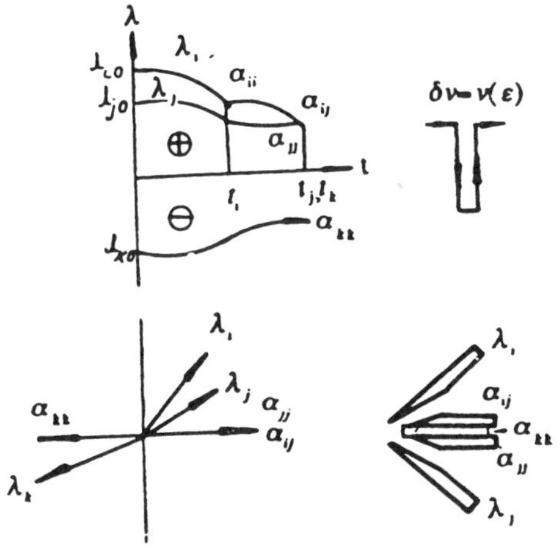

Figure 3.4. The consolidation of the local operators $\{\lambda_i, \lambda_k, \lambda_j\}$ at the triplet and the needle control $\delta v = v(\varepsilon)$ forming: $\alpha_{ij} = \alpha_i(t_j), \alpha_{ii} = \alpha_i(t_i),\ \alpha_{jj} = \alpha_j(t_j)$, $\alpha_{jj} = \alpha_j(t_j)$ at the discrete moments $(t_i, t_k, t_j,) \in t'$.

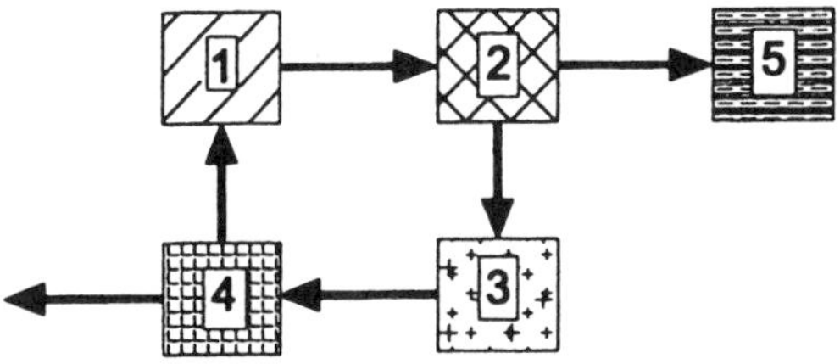

Figure 3.5. Operations in superimposing processes: 1 Asymmetry, 2 Rotation, 3 Diagonalization of dynamic operator, 4 Dynamics, 5 Geometry.

The difference of the imaginary conjugate components is determined by the distinction of the corresponding wave functions, which leads to the complex S, H, and $\lambda_i(t_k)$. The corresponding imaginary components of the optimal processes turn into zeroes not simultaneously, which creates a finite time difference $o(t_i)$ for the applied needle controls. The conjugated real eigenvalues ($\alpha_i(t_k)$=Re$\lambda_i(t_k)$, $\alpha_{i+1}(t_k)$=Re$\lambda_i(t_k)$*) at that interval have an opposite signs, which correspond to the automatic action of the needle controls (Figure 2.2.1). The fastest process operator $\alpha_i(t_k)$ changes sign earlier than the following by ranging the operator $\alpha_{i+1}(t_k)$. Hamiltonian systems with conjugated fluctuations could have self-organized procedure of the optimal control forming. Existence of an appropriate geometry curvature, that enables to change the sign of the derivative $\frac{\partial x}{\partial l}$ creating both the regular, v_i=-2$x(l_i)$, and needle controls, represents the necessary condition

3.5. The diffusion barrier for information cooperations

The differential constraint (DC), that connects micro- and macrolevels, is responsible for the transformations. A simplified equation of the DC at the moment (t') of imposing constraint, has a form of the balance condition:

(28) $b(t') = D(t')$, $D(t')$=A(t')M[$(x(t') + v(t'))x(t')^T$], $a^u = A(x+v)$, t'={t_i}, i=1,..., m.

At $b(t') \le D(t')$, the microlevel diffusion defines the macrolevel dynamics (kinetics), and the influx of the macrolevel negentropy. It corresponds with the macrolevel ordering via microlevel stochastization. A Wiener process (with its steady distributions by frequencies of spectral density) is an attractor for all other microlevel distributions. It leads to a possible stochastization of the initial random process and generation of the macrolevel dynamics. At $b(t') < D(t')$, the macrolevel kinetics defines the diffusion and the influx of the microlevel entropy.

The dissipative macrodynamics generate the diffusion. The stable kinetics reduce dispersion, the instable kinetics increase fluctuations. The execution of the balance equation (28) at the DI, is a main border's condition of forming the diffusion barrier.

At overcoming the barrier, the operator A(t') is changed by a jump (Figure 3.2). The diffusion barrier's length is measured by the operator's A(t') interval jumps. For the initial stable system, we get Sign A(t'-o)<0, SignA(t'-o)=-SignA(t').

After overcoming the barrier, the operator changes the sign again:

Sign A(t'+o) =- Sign A(t')<0, and the kinetic process is continued at the next discrete interval as a stable process. The distance between the barriers defines the dynamic sizes of an information element forming at interaction of the diffusion and kinetics. Imposing a discrete DC successively decreases the rank of $b(t')$ matrix with transformation some matrix elements into zeros. At the diffusion barrier, this leads to absorbing and stopping the corresponding diffusion components with creation of the statistical nondistinguished states as a source of macrodeterminism.

An increment of the operator: Δ A(t')=|A(t'+o)-A(t'-o)|=|2A(t')| ,Sp|A(t')|= $H(t')$, defines the dynamic height of the barrier with H(t') measured the entropy production. The barrier existence creates the irreversible time direction from past to future. Overcoming the barrier requires application of the needle controls, which bring the cooperative connection between the equal probable macro states (at both barrier side). Both the regular and the needle controls can be created automatically at the expense of the negentropy influx. At A(t')>0, the instable process $x(t'+\varepsilon)$=$x(t')$(2-expA $(t'+\varepsilon)\varepsilon$) increases sharply acquiring a character of δ - function (Fig.3.3). Under the action of the reduced v(ε)-controls, the matrix A($t'+\varepsilon$+o)$\Rightarrow$A(t'+o) changes the sign: SignA(t'+o)=-SignA(t')<0, that restores the stable kinetics at a new DI and joins the processes on both barrier side. The automatically created needle controls have the barrier shape (Figure 3.4), forming the potential hole against the barrier height, which embraces the barrier shape by principle "key-lock" connection. At A($t'+\varepsilon$)>0, the instable kinetics intensify stochastics, which sharply increases A(t+ε+o) and gets progressive rise x(t+ε).

At the t'-barrier locality, the connection and coordination between the stochastics and diffusion lead to intensification of both of them. For the initial microlevel process with weak kinetics (a small drift), the stochastization increases fluctuations and diffusion. For strong kinetics, the instability of the macrooperator is a source of the microlevel stochastization. At the moment t'+o of overcoming the barrier, the DC-equation is satisfied: b(t'+o)=A(t'+o)M[$x(t'$+o$)x(t'$+o$)^T$], and is equivalent to (28) at $v(t')$=-2$x(t')$, $x(t'$+o)$\approx$ $x(t')$, A(t'+o)=-A(t'), $b(t'$+o)=$b(t')$.

At the moment t+ε+o, the control acts together with the needle control v(ε)=δ(ε). The needle controls are responsible for the barriers nonsymmetry and forming the "key-lock" connections. These controls (acting between the points t', $t'+\varepsilon$) violate the VP, which preserve the symmetry within the DIs. The barrier characterizes both the discrete model properties and its ordered determinism are forming during the microlevel stochastization. The discrete high depends on the local H eigenvalue that measures the accumulating entropy production. The last (n+1) discrete interval accumulates the dissipative losses from all preceding n-intervals. The barrier is also a point of meeting and consolidation of the dynamic trajectories {x_i(t), x_k(t), x_j(t)}, characterized by their relative phase speeds : $\frac{dx_i}{x_i dt}=i_i$, $\frac{dx_k}{x_k dt}=i_k$, $\frac{dx_j}{x_j dt}=i_j$ as the local relative information flows (i_i, i_k, i_j). By the moment t_{n+1}, only a single macroflow will exist, and the consolidating process, the barries forming, and stopping the random process are ending. According to equation $\lambda(T)=\lambda(t_{n+1})=\lambda(t_n)(2-\exp\lambda(t_n)\tau_n)$, at $\lambda(t_n)\tau_n=\ln 2$, the current shift $a^u(T,x)$ defined by $\lambda(T)$, turns into zero, the diffusion matrix $\sigma(t_n)$ has the rank 1, and random process is transformed into a one-dimensional Wiener process. At the negative feedback absence, it leads to diffusion chaos. With applying the optimal external controls, the condition $a^u(t,x) \neq 0$ is still fulfilled. It creates (at T>t_{n+1}) one dimensional stochastic fluctuations with limited dispersion, the increasing mean square phase speed, and the decreasing intervals of applying controls. The carriers of the informational exchanges are the signals, imitated at the points of interactions.

The relative phase speed, characterized by its frequency is a quantitative evaluation of the signal.

Forming the triple $(i_i(t'), i_k(t'), i_j(t'))$ is a result of the subsequent consolidation of two doublets: $(i_i(t'), i_k(t'))$ and $(i_k(t'+o), i_j(t'+o))$.

The triplet cooperative connection is based on the difference of the ranged information flows creating the entropy production.

For example, at $i_i(t') < i_k(t') < i_j$(t'), the signs of the flow increments: Sign($i_k(t') - i_i(t')$)=-Sign($i_i(t'+o) - i_j(i_k+o)$), H(t')= $i_k(t') - i_i(t')$, H(t'+o)=$i_i(i_k+o) - i_j(i_k$'+o) and the corresponding entropy productions are opposite. That enable them to form the domains (divided by the barriers) with the different (positive" $\oplus$ " and negative "-") signs of diffusion conductivity's (analogous to the hole conductivity for the informational charges), Figure 3.4. Both positive and negative conductivity's can be compensated for by approaching the barriers with the information exchanges between the domains via a bridge. One of the bridge functions is the virtual information exchanges, which connect both positive and negative domains analogous to a covalent bond by sharing a virtual electron. In the triplet, the i_k information flow carries the bridge function, which connects two doublets as a "calibrating charge", that brings the information cooperation to the domains. The ranged information flows are grouped in a such way, that each triple satisfies the relations

(29) $i_i(i_k) = i_k(i_k) \approx (i_k$ (t'+o))=$i_j(i_k+o), i_i$(t')+i_j(t'+o)+ i_k (t')+ i_k (t'+o)≤ 0

H(t')+H(t'+o)≤ 0, $i_i = \lambda_i = \alpha_i + -j\beta_i, \beta_i(t')=0$, i, k, j =1,...,n.

The inequality (29) defines the possible *negentropy* production for the triplet.

The execution of the equality (29) corresponds with the compensation of the entropy, needed for the triplet cooperation by the negentropy of third information flow. Each cooperation produces some defect negentropy that triplet cannot consume, which brings an additional negentropy influx into macrosystem.

Physically, Lorentz's force arises between the currents i_i, i_k, which is proportional to their multiplication: $i_i \times i_k = i_i \bullet i_k \cos\phi$, $\phi = arctg(\beta_i / \alpha_i)$.

Under the imaginary current components (proportional β_i), the force squeezes the local conductivity channels, forming the common channel at the moment of cooperation (Figure 3.4). At the moment t_i, the imaginary component of the complex signal λ_i vanishes. At the t_k moment, the imaginary component of the signal λ_k vanishes, and both of the signals acquire the real values (α_{ii}, α_{kk}) with the equal phase directions. At the next moment t_k+o , the third complex signal λ_j loses the imaginary component, and all three real information speeds become equal ($\alpha_{ii}, \alpha_{kk}, \alpha_{jj}$). Considering the information speeds as a real charges, we come to the schema where the negative charge $-\alpha_{kk}$ performs the virtual charge function by connecting the positive charges (α_{kk}, α_{jj}) (Figure.3.4). The virtual jump acts as the needle control, and a virtual charge transfers the information force (proportional to the charge value), which binds the charges. At the barrier elimination, the conductivity current undergoes the jump, which generates the needle control. In the space distributed system, the conductivity jumps are dispersed, moved, and stored into information media, which represents a natural carrier of the needle controls.

The δ-locality of the DP is accompanied with compensation diffusion flow by the kinetics affecting the collectivization. Collectivization, acting on small δ-locality of the trajectory ensemble, decreases both the dissipative loses and the ensemble dimension. Each measurement at t=t' is an interaction with the barrier, it demands the entropy expense for the barrier overcoming. Such interaction enables it to renovate the process. Any measurement can decrease the ensemble dimension by interacting with its components. One might suppose, that a measurement of a given trajectory does not recognize it but affects other trajectories with an infinite speed. That paradox of collective movement, the IMD can explain and predict.

At the DPs, the local Hamiltonian $H_i = \lambda_i = i_i$ takes extremal and minimal value:

$$\frac{\partial \lambda_i}{\partial t}|_{t'=t_i} = 0, \lambda_i = -\lambda_{i-1}\exp(\lambda_{i-1}t_i)(2-\exp(\lambda_{i-1}t_i))^{-1},$$

$$\lambda_i = \lambda_i(t_i), \lambda_{i-1} = \lambda_i(t_{i-1}), \lambda_i = \alpha_i +- j\beta_i .$$

For the ranged sequence of the informational flows as the relative phase speeds :

$i_1 = \frac{\dot{x}}{x}$, $i_2 = \frac{\ddot{x}}{\dot{x}}$, $i_3 = \frac{\dddot{x}}{\ddot{x}}$, we come to conditions:

$$\frac{\partial i_i}{\partial t}|_{t'=t_i} = 0, \text{ i=1,2,3,...}$$

which starts with the equalization of the first information flow pair :

$$\frac{\dot{x}^2 - x\ddot{x}}{x^2} = 0, \quad \frac{\dot{x}}{x} = \frac{\ddot{x}}{\dot{x}}, \quad x \neq 0 .$$

The minimum condition defines the positive value of the second derivative:

$\frac{\partial^2}{\partial t^2}(\frac{\dot{x}}{x}) > 0$, with the inequality $\frac{2\dot{x}\ddot{x} - \dot{x}\ddot{x} - x\dddot{x}}{x^2} > 0$

from which it follows $\dot{x}\ddot{x} - x\dddot{x} > 0$, $x \neq 0$, $\frac{\ddot{x}}{\dot{x}} - \frac{\dddot{x}x}{\ddot{x}x} > 0$, at $\frac{\dot{x}}{x} = \frac{\ddot{x}}{\dot{x}}$.

This leads to the condition :

$\frac{\ddot{x}}{\dot{x}} - \frac{\dddot{x}}{\ddot{x}} > 0$, or $i_2(t_1) > i_3(t_1)$ at the points of local minimum $i_1(t_1)$.

At the point of local maximum $i_1(t_1)$, we get $i_2(t_1)<i_3(t_1)$. Therefore, if the initial ranged flows $i_1>i_2>i_3$ are disturbed, it is an indicator of possible transferring from local minimum Hamiltonial to its local maximum, at other equal conditions.

The execution of the equality $|\frac{\partial i_i}{\partial t}=\frac{\partial i_{i+1}}{\partial t}|_{t'=t_i}=0$ is evidence of some singularities in the phase trajectories, considered in each of the three-dimensional coordinates axis' (satisfying a single triplet):

$$y_1=\frac{\dot{x}}{x},\ y_2=\frac{\partial}{\partial t}(\frac{\dot{x}}{x}),\ y_3=\frac{\partial^2}{\partial t^2}(\frac{\dot{x}}{x}),\ \frac{\partial}{\partial t}(\frac{\ddot{x}}{\dot{x}})=\frac{\dddot{x}}{\dot{x}}-(\frac{\ddot{x}}{\dot{x}})^2=\frac{\dddot{x}\dot{x}-\ddot{x}^2}{\dot{x}^2}.$$

Indeed, at coinciding of both extremums $\frac{\dot{x}}{x}$, $\frac{\ddot{x}}{\dot{x}}$, we get $\frac{\dot{x}}{x}-\frac{\ddot{x}}{\dot{x}}=0, \frac{\ddot{x}}{\dot{x}}-\frac{\dddot{x}}{\ddot{x}}=0$

which leads to $y_2=0$, $y_3=0$, or revealing the singularities at the plane (y_2, y_3). This defines also the points of catastrophe according to [9], with the points of parameter bifurcations, where the derivative of the coordinates turn to zeroes.

Applying the optimal control at these points, brings the macromodel's local stability. For the triplet forming, the relative maximum of the i_k-flow (as an information source) has to coincide with the relative minimum of the i_j-flow (as an information consumer). The maximized diffusion conductivity i_k becomes the real one by the moment t_k : $\mathrm{Re}\, i_k=\mathrm{Re}\, i_j(t_k)$. The conductivity i_k remains the complex one until the extremization at $t'=t_k$. Its imaginary component characterizes the connection (via inductivity or capacity) through a physical field with other flows. The negentropy transformation takes place, when the active conductivity (of the source) reaches the maximum, at the extremum of the acceptor's diffusion active conductivity, which does not interacts with other flows (via the field). For a distributed wave source, the maximum of diffusion conductivity could be reached at the resonance condition, at coinciding the maximum values of the wave amplitudes. The space of coinciding of these amplitudes (at given moment of time) exists, when the space and time coordinates are proportional: $l'=ct'$.

It means, the simultaneous events should be located at the same space points. The OPMC spiral space trajectory on a cone is a reflection of the optimal dynamics. (For example, the caterpillar has a kind of spiral movement, stimulated by its biophysical processes of searching food, the defense reactions, which are results of the PF optimization.) At the resonance conditions, transferring the maximal information flow takes place to the diffusion acceptor, located at the same space point. The resonance leads to intensification of the diffusion fluctuation components of the stochastic equation. The wave source creates a such dissipative resonance.

3.6. The informational analogies of the phase transformations

In the macromodel, the informational transferring via the diffusion barrier models the physical phase transformations. At the DPs δ -locality, the bifurcation can be a result of intensification of small fluctuations, forming the renovated macrostates with new features. Physical meaning of discreteness reveals itself at the points of the phase transformation, where the physical parameters enable changing by a jump, creating the different forms of ordering [10], [11]. Some of the physical jump-mechanisms at superimposing phenomena are well known [12], but general mathematical models and the methodology for prognosis of such phenomena are not developed. The analysis [13,14] shows that the mathematical essence of these mechanisms could be described by the equalization of the local eigenvalues of the kinetic operator and a following then the Marcovian moment, which changes the operator time-space structure. It leads to a degeneracy of the linear operator and the jumps of the Hamiltonian. At the phase transformation, the random values become noncorrelated, and the process dimension can be compromised. At these points, the kinetic energy and the energy of interactions reach the local minimum.

The eigenvalues of the linear operator reach the local extremum. The local extremum of the microlevel information entropy at the points of interactions, represents the information meaning of the phase transformations. At these points, the PF (as a dynamic macrolevel entropy) coincides with the microlevel entropy, and both the eigenvalues and the local Hamiltonians get the extremal values.

At these points, the system possesses strong nonequilibrium states. The phase transformations of the second order [15] are the physical analogies of that mathematical mechanism. Phase transformation is a result of translating the dissipative energy into the structural transformations. In the optimal model, the initial dimension n is changed with forming m=n/2+1 new phases. The jump,-changing peculiarities (defined by the operator jumps), create new elements.

According to the Gibb's phase rule, the degrees of freedom in such a system is : $f^s = n+2-(n/2+1) = n/2+1$ as well as the relative structural entropy

$$\Delta S_s = \ln g(n,m) = 2m/n; \Delta S_s = S_s / S_{so},\ g(n,m) = \frac{n!}{n/2!n/2!} \times$$

$\times \exp(2m/n)$ are decreasing in the consolidating process, where g= $g(n,m)$ is the level of macrostate degeneracy (or the number of the system states with a given energy). The entropy ΔS_s depends on the path of transferring into the final state.

For the nonoptimal path, the decreasing number of the possible system states would be different, comparing with the optimal path. That entropy defines the level of the system organization, as a distinct from the function of action $\Delta S_o = x^T X$.

At δ -locality of the consolidating points, two or more phases could co-exist, and they become identical at consolidation. Such points are critical. According to the Gibb's rule, the critical phase, which does not co-exist with the remaining phases (within n-dimension system), has (n-1) degree of freedom. For the optimal model, it leads to number of the phase states m=n+2-(n-1)=3. Each new phase decreases the state number on 1, and the critical one decreases on 3. The triplet is an analogous to the critical phase. Forming three critical points creates the second-order phase transformation. The dynamic of changing the coefficient of ordering (at t'): $h_\varepsilon^i = m\alpha_i(t_i) / \sum_{j=1}^{n} \alpha_j(t_j)$ is determined by the ratio of Hamiltonian of the bound processes to the general Hamiltonian, taking into account both the bound and vacant (free) processes within the n-dimensional macro system.

At $h^i_\varepsilon(t_{n/2+1})$ =1 all states of the n-dimensional macro model are bound, at $h^i_\varepsilon(t_o)$ all the states are free. For example, at the triplet forming, the Hamiltonian is reduced taking the value

$$\Delta H = 1/2\sum_{i=1}^{n}(\alpha_i(t_o) - 3\alpha_i(t_i)) \ ,$$

which for **n**=6, γ =0.5 is equal ΔH=3.312.

The specific Hamiltonian, related to changing speed of the volume $\frac{\partial V}{\partial t}$=cF*, defines the differential entropy of the macro model h^ε:

$$(30)\ H/\frac{\partial V}{\partial t} = 1/2\sum_{j=1}^{n}\alpha_j(t_o)/cF^* = h^\varepsilon .$$

That function characterizes the MC-complexity of the superimposing processes and their specific dissipative loses. Differential entropy determines the number of the discrete model points, where the new information can be created. The generated information, transferring to other subsystems, evaluates the effectiveness of information consuming. The minimal program is measured by the height of the diffusion barrier at the DPs, and the distances between them. The macro model's mechanism of the regularization of stochastization is implemented via the sequence of the bifurcations with a decreasing degree of freedom of the periodical movements.

The transfer into turbulence is an opposite mechanism, which includes a series of bifurcations with increasing the degree of freedom in each of them.

At the phase transformations, dissipative energy is transformed into structural deformations with the symmetry violation. The asymmetry of the consolidating structures creates their new features and morphology.

3.7. The superimposing processes, control, and symmetry

The stochastic Ito equation is the initial model for both the irreversible thermodynamic processes in random environment and the statistical ensemble of interacting particles in physical kinetics.

Formulation of the Onsager-Machlup functional in irreversible thermodynamics, is also based on this model [6]. In the thermodynamic macroequation

$$(31)\ \frac{dx_i}{dt} = \sum_{i,j=1}^{n} L_{ij}X_j$$

a chain of superimposing processes (i-1, i,i+1), is connected via the mutual cross phenomena defined by the equations:

$\frac{dx_i}{dt} = L_i X_i + u_i,\ \ u_i = \sum_{j=1}^{n} L_{ij}X_j, i \neq j$, which performs the control function [16] depending on the state coordinate at (i-1) discrete interval:

$$u_i = -2\lambda_i x_i(t') = 2\frac{dx_i}{dt} = 2x_{i-1}(t'),\ L_{ii'} r_{ii}^{-1} = \lambda_i,\ v_i(t') = -2x_i(t').$$

Applying the needle controls $\delta v(t', l) = -2x(t', l) + 2x(t'+o, l)$, $\delta v(l', t) = -2x(l', t) + 2x(l'+o, t)$, change only the sign of the operator components without changing their absolute values. The extremals of the PF are the informational analogies of the solution of the irreversible equations with the Onsager conditions on the each extremal segment. The kinetic operator in the form

$$(32)\ \overline{L}(x(t', l')) = 2b(x(t', l')) = M_{x(t,l')}[x(t,l)\frac{\partial x}{\partial t}(t,l)^T],$$

$$M_{x(t,l')}[x(t,l)\frac{\partial x}{\partial t}(t,l)^T] = M_{x(t',l)}[\frac{\partial x}{\partial t}(t,l)x(t,l)^T]$$

is changing by jump at each time-space point (t', l') of the discrete control forming, where the following equality is satisfied

$$(33)\ \frac{I_i}{X_i}(t_j', l'_j) = g_i(t_j', l'_j) = g_k(t_j', l'_j) = \frac{I_k}{X_k}(t_j', l'_j),$$

and g_i, g_k are the subsequent equalized components of the generalized transient conductivity. The needle controls select them based on the condition of the model controllability. Sequence of the chain dependable n-controllable components of these conductivity's can be reduced to one controllable conductivity, for example to electrical conductivity, which is simple to measure [17]. Physically, the DIs are the distances between the diffusion barriers (Figure.3.2), which are required for establishing the equality in (33). At these moments, the condition of a nonhomogeneity with the mutual controllable kinetics and diffusion is created by the controllable operator of transient conductivity (responsible for the kinetics).

Interpretation of a known control function consists of forming the object-regulator connection to compensate the object perturbations by the dynamic control minimizing uncertainty. The considered control function uses the natural object's DC-diffusion constraint to select the ordered feedback as a dynamic hierarchical compensator minimizing uncertainty of object's superimposing processes.

The generalized forces X=$(2b)^{-1}\frac{\partial x}{\partial t}$ are formed by the stochasics and applied macrocontrols, that physically have a quantum (portion) character at the macrolevel interactions. The interacting processes form the spiral space chain of macrostructures based on their subsequent dynamic consolidation. The points of compensation the diffusion and kinetics hold the chain connection. The nonlinearity of the matrix $\overline{L}$ is a result of interactions, and it is an indicator of new effects and phenomena at superimposition. The bifurcation singularities at the δ-locality of DPs reflects instabilities at the matrix renovation. In the space consolidated model, diagonalization of the dynamic operator occurs under the rotating transformation T, which is periodical. At execution of the border equation (28), the diffusion matrix and the corresponding correlation matrix also become periodicals. The periodical covariation matrix coincides (with the accuracy of an arbitrary constant matrix) with the rotating matrix. Such covariation matrix can be identified on the object. By the periodical rotation of the matrix A, each three eigenvectors form the basis of the model geometrical coordinate system. The phase connection: $x_{i-1}(t')=\frac{dx_i}{dt}=\lambda_i(x_i+v_i)$ of the state coordinates (as a consequence of VP) leads to existence the symmetrical transformations. The rotating space transformations, are able to diagonalize the A(t')-matrix, decrease the number of components of the proper functional's Lagrangian, minimizing the entropy production. It means, the space movement, directed toward diagonalization of the dynamic operator (as an attribute of the space consolidation process), is a source of generating an additional negentropy for cooperation. The entropy balance condition, in particular, reflects principle of detail stability, which determines an existence of the symmetry at inversion and preservation of the local entropy production in form: $\frac{d\lambda_i}{dt}=0, \frac{dH_i}{dt}=0.$

The stability condition for the entropy functional defines the Abel's property of the matrix A, and the existence of its elementary eigenvalue multiplicators.

It admits the coexistence of the space movements with the consolidation process, preserves some features in the specific space directions, and possesses a rotating space symmetry at some conditions.

The ranged sequence of the triplet eigenvalues preserves the pairwise ratios:
$\lambda_1/\lambda_2=G1, \lambda_2/\lambda_3=G2, \lambda_3/\lambda_4=G1, \lambda_4/\lambda_5=G2,\dots$
as the constant multiplicators: G1,G2, defined by ratio of local entropies .

The rotation spreads these ratios along each coordinate axes: $l_x\to$G1, $l_y\to$G2, $l_z\to$G1. At the rotation, the ranged eigenvalues as well as their pair-wise multiplicators are distributed along each geometrical axes. For example, along the axes l_x, l_y, l_z such segments can be selected which preserve the multiplicators:
G(x)=λ_1/λ_4=G1•G2•G1; G(y)=λ_2/λ_5=G2•G1•G2;
G(z)=λ_3/λ_6=G1•G2•G1=G(x) accordingly.

These segments define the macrocell volumes, which preserve the ratios of geometrical sizes proportional to the invariant **a** as an elementary quantity information for each macrocell. The rotating matrix, applied to the ranged triplet eigenvalues, retains the space probability function as an invariant, and defines the group transformation of symmetry with preservation of the above multiplicators.

The transformation of symmetry acts only within each DI's, when VP is satisfied.

The macro cells can be mutually transformed by translation, analogous to crystal structures. Such a well known transformation consists of the macro cell rotation on angle $\varphi=2\pi/n$, and changing the linear sizes in p-times, where n and p are connected by the relation $n=2\pi(\arccos\frac{1-p}{2})^{-1}$. The order's index n of the rotating symmetry and p take the values: n= (2,3,4,6), p=(3,2,1). For the considered macromodel, is executed G1•G2≥2, G2≥1, and because of that, we get p≥1.

The real macrosystems have G1•G2≥2, G2>1.5, which define p=3, n=2. For this case, the macrocell with Gx=G1•G•G1=3 has linear sizes three times longer than the macromodel's cell . Each of these pairs can be translated into others by the rotation on angle φ and by increasing the initial geometrical sizes three times. It makes it possible to build the consolidated macrosystem from the equal size macrocells formed at the previous DIs. The needle controls bind them according to existing of the systemic multiplicators. The consolidation in form of triplet structures and the distribution of the eigenvectors by three with preservation their multiplicators, are a consequence of the three-dimensionality of the geometrical space, where existence of the geometrical symmetrical transformations follows from VP. It leads to the existence a common symmetry transformation for all macrocells, which also represents the original phenomena that connects dynamics and geometry. The macrostructures with considered multiplicators enable to preserve symmetry only at very narrow values of the macrocell parameters.

Generally, macrocells with arbitrary multiplicators cannot be transformed into each other by symmetrical transformations because they are asymmetrical. By the consolidation moment, three of such macro cells have almost equal sizes, and they are able to form the joint macrocell with the triple linear sizes. The consolidated cells are asymmetrical, they cannot coincide via the symmetrical transformations. By the end of DI, the diagonalization of the matrix elements is completed, and the subsequent individual macrocell rotation is directed toward the equalization within each triplet. The needle controls consolidate the asymmetrical local instable irreversible macro states into stable cooperative structures at new DI.

The connected triples are analogous to three-critical identical phase transformations of the second order with a specific connection the kinetics, diffusion and the symmetry order in crystals. The space distributed model has a spiral structure on a cone with a possible left (L) or right (R) direction of the spirals, and the triplet structure that connects the LRL or RLR asymmetric forms. In a macrosystem with superimposing processes, each i-asymmetrical (L or R) process can control the subsequent (i+1) (R or L) asymmetrical process. The superimposing processes of an opposite asymmetry direction are able to create a force (analogous to Lorentz's force), which can be a physical source of rotating the geometrical coordinate system in the space consolidated model. It means, in the superimposing processes, the asymmetry enables to control geometry and change the macrodynamics by rotating the dynamic operator (Figure 3.5). Both the rotating symmetry and its inner rotating mechanism, are specific characteristics of macromolecule polymers [18].

A set of the macromodel triplets create a specific shape of corresponding key-lock connections according of their LRL-RLR- asymmetry sequence, which is responsible for recognition the macro model, and enables to create a communicating information language. *The IN models the superimposition of macro processes with revealing a created phenomena and singularities* (at DPs).

3.8. The informational analogies of quasi-equilibrium thermodynamic functions

The informational model of complex object with superimposing processes creates the informational analogies of the main physical characteristics, as the potential and kinetic energy, the nonequilibrium thermodynamic functions: temperature, pressure, chemical potential, statistical sum, which are identifiable on real object. Using the definitions of the thermodynamic functions via the macro system statistical characteristics [19], we come to the folowing equations:

(34) $\theta^{-1} = (\frac{\partial \Delta S}{\partial E})_N$, $P^* = (\frac{\partial E}{\partial V})_{\Delta S, E}$, $\mu^* = \frac{E - \theta \Delta S}{N^*}$,

where V is a volume, E is an energy, ΔS is an increment of quasi-equilibrium entropy, N* is a density of the number of elements. We may determine the information analogy of the temperature for the optimal model at discrete points (t'):

$$(35)\ \theta \frac{d\Delta S_e}{dt} = \frac{\partial E}{\partial t},\quad \frac{d\Delta S_e}{dt} = \frac{\partial \Delta S_e}{\partial t}(t') = SpR_t(t') = R_t^T,$$

$$\frac{\partial E}{\partial t} = -1/2\, Sp[\frac{\partial R_t}{\partial t} R_t^T r_t(t') + (\frac{\partial R_t}{\partial t} R_t^T r_t(t'))^T],$$

$$r_t(t') = r_t(t')^T,\ r_t(t') = M(x(t')x(t')^T),\ R_t = 1/2\dot{r}_t(t')r_t^{-1}(t'),$$

$$(36)\ \theta = -(SpR_t(t'))^{-1} Sp(\frac{\partial R_t}{\partial t} R_t r_t(t')),\ \theta = -\frac{\sum_{i=1}^{n} \dot{\alpha}_i^t \alpha_i^t(t') + \dot{\beta}_i^t \beta_i^t(t')}{\sum_{i=1}^{n} \alpha_i^t(t')}.$$

Transferring to the equality for physical temperature from its information analogy (36) requires renormalizing the expressions for energy and entropy. The equation for differential temperature is considered in the relative form: $d\Delta\theta = d\frac{\partial E}{\partial S} / \frac{\partial E}{\partial S}$, that after integrating leads to the formula for the temperature increment:

$\Delta\theta = \ln \frac{\partial E}{\partial S}(t') + C$, $\frac{\partial E}{\partial S} = \frac{\partial E}{\partial t}\frac{\partial t}{\partial S}$, and the connection to the correlations

$$\frac{\partial E}{\partial S} = \frac{Sp[\frac{\partial R_t}{\partial t} R_t r_t]}{SpR_t},\ \Delta\theta = \ln \frac{[\sum_{i=1}^{n} \dot{\alpha}_i^t \alpha_i^t(t') + \dot{\beta}_i^t \beta_i^t(t')] r_t(t')}{\sum_{i=1}^{n} \alpha_i^t(t')} + \ln C_\theta.$$

The last one determines the information form (36) with E, $\Delta S, \theta$ as the specific (in unit per volume) values of energy, entropy, and temperature accordingly.

The information analogy of pressure follows from (34) in the form

$$P^* = \frac{Sp[\frac{\partial R_t}{\partial t}(t') R_t(t') r_t(t')]}{\frac{dV}{dt}(t')}\Big|_{\Delta S, E},\ \frac{dV}{dt} = \bar{c}\, F^*,\ F^* = \frac{\Delta V}{\Delta \bar{l}},\ \bar{c} = \frac{d\bar{l}}{dt}$$

is the average linear speed, $\Delta \bar{l}$ is the average linear shift, F* is the macrostructure cross section. From the definition of the statistical weight $\Delta\Gamma_j$ for the distribution of N_J independent elements by the n_j states, follows the equation:

(37) $\Delta\Gamma_j = \dfrac{n_j^{N_J}}{N_J!}$, $\Delta\Gamma_j = \exp\Delta S$, $\Delta S = n/2$,

where for the optimal model holds true ΔS=inv, and the state number is decreasing in the consolidation process. We come to equation for the cooperative state number

(38) $n_j = \exp\left(\dfrac{n}{2} + \sum_{N_J=1}^{N_J} \ln N_J\right)(N_J)^{-1}$

which connects N_J and n_j for the optimal model. Writing the previous relation in the form $\dfrac{(n_j - \Delta n_j)^{N_J+\Delta N_J}}{(N_J + \Delta N_J)!} = \dfrac{n_j^{N_J}}{N_J!}$, we come to the condition

(39) $(1 - n_j^*)^{N_J+\Delta N_J} = \dfrac{(N_J + \Delta N_J)!}{n_j^{\Delta N_J}}$, $n_j^* = \dfrac{\Delta n_J}{n_J}$.

The left side of that equation takes value from 1 to 0 at $\Delta N_J \to (0, \propto)$, and $n_j^*>0$. To get the equality of both parts, the inequalities have to be fulfilled:

$n_J^{\Delta N_J} \geq (N_J + \Delta N_J)!$ $n_j \geq \exp(N_J)^{-1} \sum_{N_J=1}^{N_J+\Delta N_J} \ln(N_J + \Delta N_J)$,

$\ln n_j \geq (N_J)^{-1} \sum_{N_J=1}^{N_J+\Delta N_J} \ln(N_J + \Delta N_J)$,

which for the given $N_J, \Delta N_J$ define a such n_j, that satisfies the condition of the states consolidation. The chemical potential for each of the n_j states we find using the relations (34,36,37,38) in the forms

(40) $\mu^* = \dfrac{\mu_j(t')}{n_j} = \left(\dfrac{E(t')}{\theta(t')} - \dfrac{n}{2}\right)(N^* \theta(t'))^{-1}$, $N^* = \dfrac{N_J}{n_J}(t')$.

By knowing the temperature and the energy of the interacting subsystem, we may determine the statistical sum:

(41) $Z^* = \sum_{i_J=1}^{n} \exp\left(-\dfrac{E_i}{\theta}\right)$, $E_i = \dfrac{\partial R^i_t}{\partial t}(t')r^i_t(t') = \dfrac{\partial \alpha^i_t}{\partial t}(t')r^i_t(t')$,

which gives an opportunity to compute all thermodynamic functions of the model. Figure 3.6 represents the results of computation the informational analogies of the dynamic growth of the cross-section F* of the consolidated macrostructure, the relative values of the energy E*, the temperature θ*, the chemical potential μ*, the pressure P*, the statistical sum Z*, the number of cooperating subsystems n_j, for the optimal macromodel dimension n=6. The chemical potential $\mu^* = \mu^*(t)$, turns to zero at the moment $t'_n = t'_7$, which is evidence of ending the diffusion processes. The function $\mu^* = \mu^*(t)$ reflects changing the number of the states $n_j = n_j(t)$ of the consolidating process for the optimal subsystem number $n_j^o = n_j^o(t) = n(t)$. The thermodynamic values of the functions ΔS, θ can be obtained using Bolzman's constant. Therefore, the informational analogies of the main thermodynamic variables: E, θ, P*, N*, μ are determined based on the known differential macroequations or given the microlevel stochastic equations, and also through the experiments on a real process. For example, by known $N_J(t'_n) = N$, using Figure 3.6c, we can find $n_J(t'_n = t'_7) = n_{Jn}$, and after that we come to the restoration of the dynamics $N_J(t)$, $\mu_j(t)$ for the optimal model. The developed computer-based methodology with the software package enables us to restore the informational analogies both for the quasi-equilibrium and nonequilibrium thermodynamic functions, and for the optimal macromodels dimensions n→(4,...,100), which covers the wide diversity of complex systems.

The informational analogies of the electrical and magnetic field equations in a random media are considered in [20].

3.9. The nonequilibrium models

The macromodel equation in general form

$$(42)\quad \frac{\partial x}{\partial t} = \bar{L}X \ , \ \bar{L} = \{L^t(x(t',l)), L^l(x(t,l'))\},$$

presents the information analogy of the controlled equation of nonequilibrium thermodynamics with the nonlinear matrixes, that are discontinuous at the discrete points (t',l'). The local stationary states satisfy the condition

$$\frac{I_i}{X_i}(t_j', l'_j) = g_i(t_j', l'_j) = g_k(t_j', l'_j) = \frac{I_k}{X_k}(t_j', l'_j).$$

Considering the macromodel equations in the form

$$(43)\quad \frac{\partial x}{\partial t} = c\frac{\partial x}{\partial l}, \quad \frac{\partial X}{\partial t} = -c\frac{\partial X}{\partial l},$$

together with the equations of the extremals

$$\frac{\partial x}{\partial t} = R^t x \ , \quad \frac{\partial X}{\partial t} = -R^t X \ ,$$

after substituting into (43), we come to the equations of extremals for the space distributed movements:

$$\frac{\partial x}{\partial t} = cgrad(c(R^t)^{-1}\frac{\partial x}{\partial l}), \quad \frac{\partial X}{\partial t} = -cgrad(c(R^t)^{-1})\frac{\partial X}{\partial l}.$$

If c and R^t are not dependable (at an ordinary situation), then we obtain the extremal's equations in the form of the conjugated parabolic equations:

$$(44)\quad \frac{\partial x}{\partial t} = c^2(R^t)^{-1}\frac{\partial^2 x}{\partial l^2}, \quad \frac{\partial X}{\partial t} = -c^2(R^t)^{-1}\frac{\partial^2 X}{\partial l^2}.$$

a)

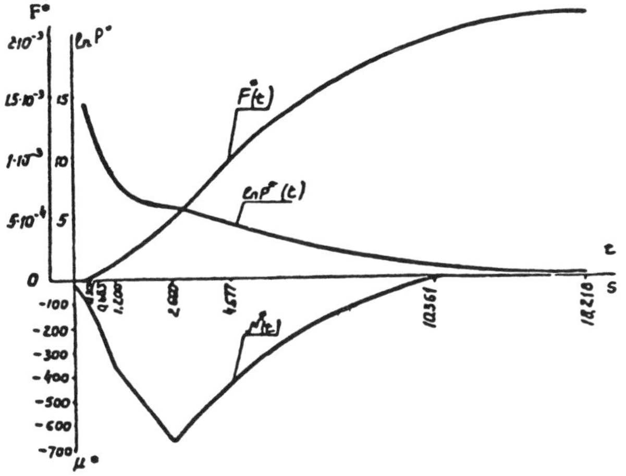

b)

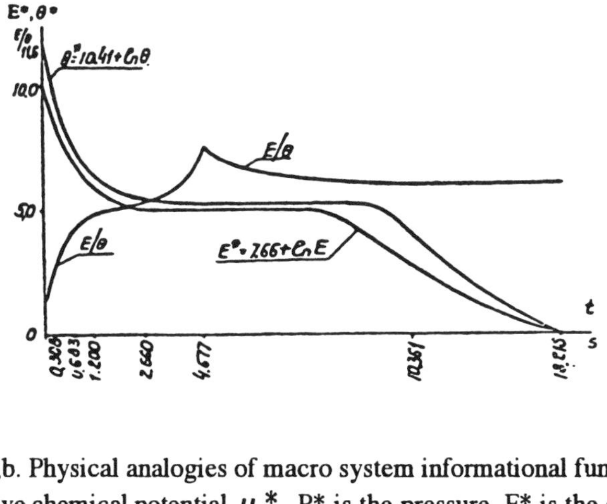

Figure 3.6a,b. Physical analogies of macro system informational functions:
a The relative chemical potential μ *, P* is the pressure, F* is the cross-section of the consolidated macro structures;
b) The energy E, the temperature θ are represented by their relative values E*, θ *.

c)

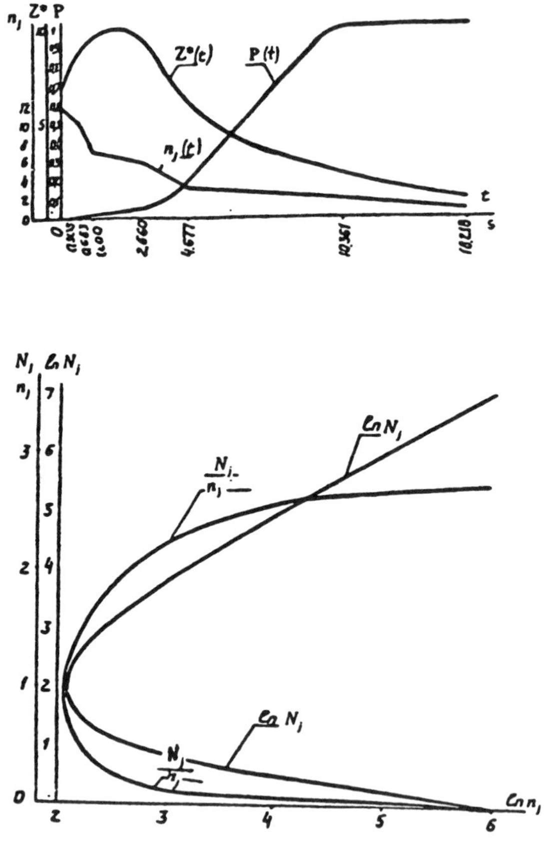

d)

Figure 3.6c, d. Physical analogies of macro system informational functions:
c) The probability P, statistical sum Z, and the number of subsystems (states) n_j;
d) The number of states per the volume unit N_j and their logarithmic values as the function of n_j .in the logarithmic scale.

The macromodel can be reduced to the forms of Fouries's and Fick's equations. For example, at $x_i = \theta$, $x_k = \Delta c$ (with the controls absent : $v_i^t = v_{i+1}^t = v_i^l = v_{i+1}^l$) where θ is a temperature, Δc is a concentration increment , we get the equations:

$$\frac{\partial\theta}{\partial t} = \lambda_i^t\,\theta\,,\ \frac{\partial\ \theta}{\partial l} = \lambda_i^l\theta\,,\ \frac{\partial^2\theta}{\partial l^2} = \lambda_{i+1}^l\,\theta\,,$$

(45) $$\frac{\partial\theta}{\partial t} = \lambda^o\frac{\partial^2\theta}{\partial l^2},\quad \lambda^o = \lambda_i^t(\lambda_{i+1}^l\lambda_i^l)^{-1}$$

(46) $$\frac{\partial\Delta c}{\partial t} = \lambda_k^t\,\Delta c\quad \frac{\partial\Delta c}{\partial t} = D^o\,\frac{\partial^2\Delta c}{\partial l^2},\quad D^o = \lambda_k^t(\lambda_{k+1}^l\lambda_k^l)^{-1},\quad \frac{\partial^2\Delta c}{\partial l^2} = \lambda_{k+1}^l\,\Delta c$$

with the coefficients of a heat conductivity λ^o and diffusion D^o, which are statistically identifiable via the correlation functions.

The corresponding controlled equations can be written by analogy.

The equilibrium diagram (that connects Δc with θ) can be statistically identified, using equations (45, 46) and the relations

(47) $$\frac{\partial\Delta c^*}{\partial\theta} = \frac{\dfrac{\partial\Delta c}{\Delta c}}{\dfrac{\partial\theta}{\theta}} = \lambda_k^t(\lambda_i^t)^{-1} = \lambda_k^l(\lambda_i^l)^{-1},\quad \Delta c^* = k^1\Delta\theta^*\,\lambda_k^l(\lambda_i^l)^{-1}.$$

In the Onsager theory [21], the thermocapacity is the linear operator, which changes by jump at the phase transformations. Its informational analogy is

$$c_V^\theta(t_i') = (\frac{\partial U}{\partial\theta})_V^i = \lambda_i^t\,\frac{\partial\dot{\lambda}_i^t}{\partial t}\,/\,\frac{\partial\lambda_i^t}{\partial t} + (\lambda_i^t)^2,$$

which is degenerated at the discrete moments of changing $\lambda_i^t = \lambda_i^t\,(t_i)$.

3. 10. The indirect evaluation of the macromodel physical parameters

A movement of physical system with the mass speed c^o, and a flow of the carriers with a density $\tilde{\rho}$, is satisfied the equation of the flow continuity

(48) $$\frac{\partial\tilde{\rho}}{\partial t} + \frac{\partial\tilde{\rho}}{\partial l}c^o = -\tilde{\rho}\frac{\partial c^o}{\partial l},\ c^o = \frac{\partial l^o}{\partial t}.$$

Then the optimal model equations are defined on the moving coordinate system $l^o = l$(t), created by the carrier flow $\dfrac{\partial x_k}{\partial t} = I_k$, where $x_k = \tilde{\rho}$ is one of the macro coordinates, l^o is measured at the external normal to the equipotential surface $\Delta S^o(x,l) = inv$. From that, we get the equations

(49) $$\frac{\partial\tilde{\rho}}{\tilde{\rho}\partial t} = \frac{\partial x_k}{x_k\partial t} = \lambda_k^t,\quad \frac{\partial\tilde{\rho}}{\tilde{\rho}\partial l}c^o = \lambda_k^l\,c^o = \lambda_k^t,\quad 2\lambda_k^t = -\frac{\partial}{\partial l}(\frac{\partial l}{\partial t}),$$

which connect the phase and space coordinates with the carrier density (at the known $\lambda^t_k = \lambda^t_k$ (t), which defines $l = l$ (t)). In a particular, from (49) it follows that $\tilde{\rho} = \exp - \int \frac{\partial}{\partial l} \lambda^t_k (\lambda^l_k)^{-1} \partial t$, for given λ^t_k, λ^l_k, determines $\tilde{\rho} = \tilde{\rho}_o (2 - \exp \lambda^t_{ko} t) \exp(\lambda^l_k l)^{-1}$. Let us measure, for example, the heat conductivity coefficient using the Wayman-Frank law in the form

(50) $$\frac{\lambda^o}{\theta \sigma_e} = \frac{1}{3} (\frac{k_B \pi}{e})^2 = k^o,$$

where σ_e is an electrical conductivity, k_B is the Boltzman constant, e is an electron charge. Einstein's relation in the form

(51) $$\sigma_e = k^o_1 r_t,\ k^o_1 = \frac{e^2 \bar{n}}{k_B \theta} = \frac{e^2}{(\frac{\partial \mu}{\partial \bar{n}})_\theta},$$

where $\bar{n}$ is the density of the particle number, μ is a chemical potential, connects the covariation r_t of the Marcovian diffusion process with the electrical conductivity, and takes into account the dependency σ_e from a temperature and chemical potential. Relations (50, 51) follow from the common molecular transfer mechanism, responsible for such phenomena as the diffusion, heat transfer (as an energy diffusion), viscosity (as an impulse diffusion) with the coefficient D^o defined by both the diffusion and the friction coefficients ς according to formula :

(52) $$D_o = k' \theta \varsigma^{-1}.$$

Using the relations (50, 51), we obtain the equation

(53) $$\lambda^o = k^o_2 r_t, k^o_2 = \frac{\pi^2}{3} k_B \bar{n},\ \lambda^o = \frac{k^o_2}{k^o_1} \sigma_e,$$

which gives us an opportunity to determine λ^o by measuring σ_e.

The strong connection between kinetics and diffusion is a characteristic of the phase transformation, which reveals itself in the coefficients of transferring in such media's as a gas.

According to Fick's equation, the one-dimensional diffusion D_o is connected with the average carrier's speed c_o, and the averaged length of the free motion l_o: $D_o \sim l_o c_o$, $D_o \sim \frac{r_t}{\tau'}$, where τ' is the time interval between the interactions [15].

The diffusion coincides with the informational analogy of $\sigma^2 = 1/2 \dot{r}_t \sim D_o \rightarrow \sigma_e$ following from the macromodel equation, and from (50, 52). The macroparameter σ_e is a common indirect measure of the above thermodynamic parameters, which has technical applications for the electrical technological processes.

In particular, measuring σ_e naturally ubstitutes the complicated procedure of computation the conditional mathematical expectations in equation (2.1.8).

3.11. The informational model of macrostructure production in a moving system

A real technological system can be modeled by the set of interacting information flows that create macrostructures. Technological production of structured information is an important result of macrosystem functioning.

Let us consider the entropy balance at the external consumption of the information from the optimal model moving with the linear speed c_T, at the internal macro structure forming with the average linear speed $\overset{o}{c}_o$:

$$\frac{d\Delta S}{dt}=\frac{d\Delta S_e}{dt}+\frac{d\Delta S_i}{dt},\quad \Delta S=\int_V \Delta S^{\rho}dV,\ \Delta S^{\rho}=\frac{\partial \Delta S}{\partial V},$$

$$(54)\quad \frac{d\Delta S_e}{dt}=-\int_V div(\Delta S^{\rho}c_T)dV,\quad \frac{d\Delta S_i}{dt}=-\frac{\partial \Delta S}{\partial t}-\int_V div(\Delta S^{\rho}\overset{o}{c}_o)dV,$$

where ΔS^{ρ} is the specific entropy per volume V.

From the balance equation for the optimal process we have

$$\frac{d\Delta S_o}{dt}=\frac{\partial \Delta S}{\partial t}+\frac{d\Delta S_i}{dt}=0, \Delta S_o == \underset{t}{extr}\,\Delta S,$$

and the stationary condition for the specific entropy follows:

$$\frac{d}{dV}\left(\frac{\partial \Delta S}{\partial t}\right)=-div(\Delta S^{\rho}\overset{o}{c}_o),\quad \frac{\partial \Delta S^{\rho}}{\partial t}=-div(\Delta S^{\rho}\overset{o}{c}_o),\quad \frac{d\Delta S^{\rho}}{dt}=0,$$

which leads to the invariance of average speed ($\overset{o}{c}_o$=inv), according to the relations:

$$(55)\quad \frac{d\Delta S}{\Delta S dt}=-div\overset{o}{c}_o,\quad div(\Delta S^{\rho}\overset{o}{c}_o)=\Delta S^{\rho}\,div\overset{o}{c}_o+\overset{o}{c}_o\,\mathrm{grad}\,\Delta S^{\rho}.$$

And the balance condition for the specific entropy acquires the form

$$-\frac{\partial \Delta S^{\rho}}{\partial t}=\overset{o}{c}_o\frac{\partial \Delta S^{\rho}}{\partial l_i},\quad \frac{\partial \Delta S^{\rho}}{\partial l_i}=\mathrm{grad}\,\Delta S^{\rho},\ (\overset{o}{c}_o)^{-1}H_t^{\rho}=\frac{\partial \Delta S^{\rho}}{\partial l_i},\ l^{\rho}=\{l_i\},\ i=1,\ldots,m.,$$

where H_t^{ρ} is the specific Hamiltonian of the macrostructure, forming with the average speed $\overset{o}{c}_o$ and under action of the informational technological potentials $\frac{\partial \Delta S^{\rho}}{\partial l_i}$; H_t^{ρ} is the informational technological characterisic of the macrostructure, which is responsible for the common system informational transformations of given technology.

The space length of the vector gradient $\left|\frac{\partial \Delta S^{\rho}}{\partial l_i}\right|$ we consider in direction of the normal to the surface $\Delta S^{\rho}=inv$, with the vectors $\bar{l}_i=\sum_{j=1}^{3}\bar{e}_j l_j$, representing normal moving in the three-dimensional space. It means, the length of the vector $\frac{\partial \Delta S^{\rho}}{\partial l_i}$ (in the three-dimensional space) is proportional to the gradient $|\frac{\partial \Delta S^{\rho}}{\partial \bar{l}_i}|$.

The mathematical expectation of the length increment $M|\bar{l}_i|$ for the vector gradient can be found from the relations

$$\partial \Delta S^{\rho}=(c_o^o)^{-1} H_t^{\rho}\, \partial l_i\,,\ M|\partial \Delta S^{\rho}|=(c_o^o)^{-1} H_t^{\rho}\, M|\partial l_i|,\ \ M|\Delta S^{\rho}|=\Delta \hat{S}^{\rho},$$

where $M|\bar{l}_i|=\sum_{i=1}^{n} P_i|\bar{l}_i|l^o$. We arrive at the equality

$$M|\frac{\partial \Delta S^{\rho}}{\partial l_i}|=M|\frac{\partial \Delta S^{\rho}}{\partial \bar{l}_i}|=\frac{\partial \Delta \hat{S}^{\rho}}{\partial l^o},$$

with the nonrandom ΔS^{ρ}. Assuming both speeds (c_T, c_o^o) are concentrated and are not dependable on the macrostructure geometrical parameters (V, l_i), we get

$$\frac{d}{dt}\int_V \Delta S^{\rho} dV = -c_T \int_V grad\Delta S^{\rho} dV + c_o^o \int_V grad\Delta S^{\rho} dV\ .$$

The last equation can be written in the form

$$\int_V \frac{d}{dt} d\Delta\hat{S}^{\rho} = (c_T - c_o^o)\int_V \frac{d}{dl^o} d\Delta \hat{S}^{\rho},$$

where Δl^o is the total increment of the geometrical coordinates measuring by the normals to the surface $\Delta S^{\rho} = inv$, which get averaged by all the macrostructure cones. Suppose, we apply c_T to the forming macrostructure at the moment t_k, when the macromodel dimension is m = n-k. It means, the process of the macro model consolidation in the moving system has not been accomplished yet.

Let us determine the ratio $m_o^V = (\frac{\partial \Delta S}{\partial V})_n / (\frac{\partial \Delta S}{\partial V})_{n-k}$ of the specific entropies for the macro model dimensions n and n-k accordingly. The total probability P_o (for all macro model n-subsystems) to get into an elementary volume dV is equal to

$P_o = \int_{x \in V} P(x_i) dV = 1$, or in the discrete form: $\sum_{i=1} P(x_i)\Delta V_i = 1$.

At the discrete moments $t' = (t_i\}$, all subsystems have the equal probable states:

(56) $\sum_{i=1} P(x_i)\Delta V_i = P_o(x_n = x(t_n))\, n\, \Delta V_n\,,\ \Delta V_n / \Delta V_{n-k} = \frac{n}{n-k}$.

If the controlled model has the (n-k)-dimension at some point of the switching control line, then we get by analogy $P_o(x_{n-k} = x(t_{n-k}))$(n-k)$\Delta V_{n-k}$. In the process of optimal movement, each subsystem preserves the equal probability of getting into above volume by the relation (56), and $\Delta S_{n-k}/\Delta S_n = n/(n-k)$ for the above triplet's dimensions. Finally, we obtain the result: $m_o^V = (\frac{n}{n-k})^2$.

At each triplet formation, the initial macromodel dimension is decreasing on 2, and it is equal m =n-k, for k=2,4, ..., n-1. Using the extremal condition for entropy functional in the form $\Delta S = \int_V \Delta S^p dV dt = \int_V \frac{d\Delta S}{dV} dV dt$,

we obtain the Euler equation for this functional :

$\frac{d}{dt}(\frac{d\Delta S}{dV}) = 0$, $\frac{d\Delta S}{dV}$=const.

Applying the last equality to the balance equation, we get

$$\int_V \frac{dV}{dt}\frac{d\Delta S}{dV} dt = m_o^V (c_o^o - c_T) \int_V \frac{dV}{dl^o}\frac{d\Delta S}{dV} dt,$$

$$\int_V \frac{dV}{dt} dt = m_o^V (c_o^o - c_T) \int_V \frac{dV}{dl^o} dt, \quad \frac{\Delta V}{\Delta t} = m_o^V (c_o^o - c_T) \frac{\Delta V}{\Delta l^o}, \quad c_o^o = \frac{\Delta l^o}{\Delta t}.$$

From that, we come to the equality for the speed of macrostructure production

$c_T = (c_o^o - \frac{\Delta V}{\Delta t} / \frac{\Delta V}{\Delta l^o})(m_o^V)^{-1}$, $m_o^V \neq 0$, where $\Delta V(\Delta t)$, $\Delta V(\Delta l^o)$ are the volume increments as the functions of time and the geometrical coordinates accordingly. The applied external speed $c_T(t_k)$ supposes to start at the moment, when the first macrostructure has already formed. The first moment of the triplet forming is t_3, and the primary structure is forming during the interval t_5-t_3. The selected moment t_k defines the hierarchical level of the forming macrostructure, the complexity of the informational throughput production. The external consumption can start at the moment $t_k = t_5$. After applying $c_T(t_k = t_5)$, the macrosystem process assumes to preserve optimality, by the fulfillment of the condition

$$\frac{d\Delta S}{dt}(t_i^{''}) = 0, \quad (57)$$

starting with $t_5^{''} = t_5$ +t" ,where t" is determined from the solution of the equation

$$c_T(t_5^{''}) = c_o^o(t_5^{''}) - \frac{\Delta V}{\Delta t} / \frac{\Delta V}{\Delta l^o} = 0, \quad m_o^V \neq 0.$$

At this condition, the optimal set of discrete points should not be changed.

It requires the execution the equality (57) at each moment $t_i^{''} \in$T. Therefore, the moments of time $t_i^{''} = t_5$+t"+t"+...= t_5+m't" and the discretization moment { t_i } have to coincide with an accuracy of some integer m'. For example, at n =6 we have $t_6 = t_5$+m't". The invariance condition for the total entropy, according to (54), leads to the invariance of the average speed c_o^o. The last one for the moments $t_5^{''} = t_5$+t" and $t_i^{''}$ = t_k +m't" we may write in the form

(58) $c_o^o(t_k+\text{m't"})=c_o^o(\text{t"})=(m't")^{-1}\int\limits_{m't"} c_o(t)dt=(m't")^{-1}\int\limits_{m't"}\frac{\partial l^o}{\partial t}(t)dt=\frac{\Delta l^o}{m't"}$

with $F"(t")=F"=\int\limits_{t"} c_o dt=F"(\ l_x",l_y",l_z"\ )$ as a homogenous function, satisfying the equality $m'F"(t")=F"(m't")$, $F"=\int\limits_{t"} c_o dt$.

For a such function, according to Euler theorem, the following equality is executed $l_x"\frac{\partial F"}{l_x"}+l_y"\frac{\partial F"}{l_y"}+:l_z"\frac{\partial F"}{l_z"}=\text{p}\ F"$,

where p is a degree of homogeneity, in our case, for $(m')^p=m'$, we get p=1.

Finally, we obtain the equality

(59) $c_o^o=c_o^o(t_k+t_i")=\frac{l^o(t_i")-l^o(t_k)}{t_i"-t_k}$,

which for n=6 leads to

$c_o^o=\frac{l^o(t_6)-l^o(t_5)}{t_6-t_5}$.

Using (58), we can find t" according to the known functions $\frac{\partial l^o}{\partial t}(t)=c_o(t)$ and the optimal model parameters t_6, t_5,c.. The $c_o(t")$ and t"are the local invariant of the optimal model. The integral

$(t")^{-1}\int\limits_{t"} c_o(t)dt=\frac{\Delta l^o}{t"}(t)=c_o^o$

is also the local invariant, defined by the given functions $c_o(t)=\frac{\partial l^o}{\partial t}(t)$ (which takes the equal values), and by the known functions $c_o(t)$ or $\Delta l^o(t")$.

Let us show, that the fulfillment of the condition

$\int(\frac{dV}{dt}-(c_0^0-c_T)\frac{dV}{dl})dt=0$

corresponds the total entropy balance, and it also leads to $\frac{d}{dt}(\frac{d\Delta S}{dV}(t_i^"))=0$ at the moments when .

$c_o(t_i^")-c_T(t_i^")=0$.

Indeed. Integrating the equation

$\int\frac{d\Delta S}{dV}(\frac{dV}{dt}-(c_0^0(t_i^")-c_T(t_i^")\frac{dV}{dl}))dt=$

$$=\frac{d\Delta S}{dt}\int(\frac{dV}{dt}-(c_0^0(t_i^")-c_T(t_i^")\frac{dV}{dl}))dt-$$

$$-\int\frac{d}{dt}\frac{d\Delta S}{dV}dt\int(\frac{dV}{dt}-(c_0^0(t_i^")-c_T(t_i^")\frac{dV}{dl}))dt$$

by its parts, and using the condition (55), we get

$$\int\frac{d\Delta S}{dV}(\frac{dV}{dt}-(c_0^0(t_i^")-c_T(t_i^")\frac{dV}{dl}))dt=0.$$

From which, at $c_0^0(t_i^")-c_T(t_i^")=0$ we obtain

$$(60)\int\frac{d\Delta S}{dV}(t")(\frac{dV}{dt}(t")dt=\frac{d}{dt}(\int\Delta S^p dV)=0.$$

The last one is executed at an arbitrary $\frac{dV}{dt}$, if $\frac{d}{dt}(\frac{d\Delta S}{dV}$(t"))=0. The condition $\frac{d\Delta S}{dV}=c^V$ for the discrete point $l^o(t_i)$ takes the form $c^V\Delta l^o\Delta F^*=\Delta S(t_i)$=inv, where the increment of cross section ΔF^* can be expressed via the equivalent radios r, with $\Delta l^o\,\Delta F^*=\Delta V$. According to previous results, the distribution by the length l^o is proportional to the distribution by the normal to the cross-section of the forming structure (taken by all three-dimensional coordinates for the same ΔF^*). The last distribution is defined by the distribution along the cross-section radius. It is also related to the connection between the distributions the eigenvalues by the length and by the cross section of the forming macrostructure. The execution of the equation (55) leads to forming the volume cells $\Delta V=\pi r^2\Delta l^o$, defined by the invariant condition of the specific entropy, which can be applied to a cross-section with the optimal controls. It creates automatically the optimal processes also within the cross-section of the forming macrostructure. The border of the forming cross-section ΔF^* contains the set of points, which preserve the invariant $\mathbf{a}_o=\alpha_i^t t'$, and is characterized by the moving equipotential surface with the equal $grad\Delta S^p$.

At t"=t_{n-1}, this surface coincides with the external macrostructure surface, which is defined by the natural entropy border conditions, given by the control distribution at the border surface. The form of the external surface of cross-section includes the center of symmetry of the forming macrostructure. At each of the set of the equipotential surfaces, the optimal controls are fixed, and can be defined by the required external form. The physical production implements the chosen informational transformations (as the information technology computer program) into specific technological operations of the available conventional technology.

3.12. Uncertainty and Cooperation: The Informational analogies of physical invariants

Function of uncertainty in the physical systems (h^p) is the ratio of Planck's constant ($\tilde{h}$) to the mass of a quantum element ($\tilde{m}$): $h^p = \tilde{h} / \tilde{m}$, where h^p is a characteristic of physical (energetic) interactions.

Let us compare h^p with the informational function of uncertainty h^i equal to the ratio of the corresponding informational analogies $h^i = \hat{h} / \hat{m}$, where h^i is a information function of the evaluation of some "cooperative interactions".

For their comparison, let us consider the electromagnetic interaction with the electron-mass $\tilde{m} = m_e$ as a mass-energy of a quantum element (m_e=8.2$\bullet 10^{-10}$J (joule)(that corresponds to the mass-energy of a moving photon).

Then, the uncertainty functiont for the electromagnetic interaction is

$$h^p = \frac{6.6262 \bullet 10^{-34} J.s}{8.2 \bullet 10^{-10} J} = 0.81 \bullet 10^{-24} s .$$

The informational mass, related to the physical minimal discrete interval (for a light photon), is $\hat{m} = m_p$=$0.187 \bullet 10^{-1} s^{-1}$. From that, at $\hat{h}$=0.449 we get

$h^i = 2.41 \bullet 10 s$. The ratio of the indicated uncertainties

$h^p / h^i = \dfrac{0.81 \bullet 10^{-24} s}{0.241 \bullet 10^2 s} = 0.335 \bullet 10^{-27}$, is a comparative (but a nonmeasured) evaluator of uncertainty created in both the electromagnetic and cooperative interactions. It means, the cooperative interactions enable to produce $\approx 10^{-26}$ times more compact mass-energy packing, than the electromagnetic interactions.

Comparing with well-known relations for mass-energy in physical interactions: nuclear, electromagnetic, weak and gravitation, for example, published in [22], we get the following ratios: $1 : (10^{-2}\text{-}10^{-3}) : (10^{-11}\text{-}10^{-14}) : (10^{-28}\text{-}10^{-30})$.

From that, the ratio of the energies for the gravitation and electromagnetic interactions : $\dfrac{10^{-28}}{10^{-2}} - \dfrac{10^{-30}}{10^{-3}} = 10^{-26} - 10^{-27}$ is close to the obtained value h^p / h^i. Thus, the cooperative interactions, in particular, can be considered as an informational analogy of the gravitational interactions, and the information mass has an analogy with the gravitation mass. The value h^p evaluates an elementary level energy of disorder, related to the unit of the element's mass, created at given interaction. An analogy of the inner energy (for a given energetic level : $\hat{e}_i \sim \dfrac{a_o}{t'_i} = \alpha_i^t$), related to the information mass, is an invariant, equal to $\dfrac{\hat{e}_i}{\hat{m}_i} = \alpha_i^t t_i' = \mathbf{a}_o(\gamma)$ for any macrosystem dimension. The invariants also are

- the area of the bordered surface forming during the discretization interval: $\partial F(\gamma \to 0)$=0.32
- the entropy S per a triplet's dimension **m**: $\dfrac{S}{n/2+1} \cong 0.04$
- the admissible derivation of an analogy of inner energy (that do not violate a

given dimension) : $\Delta\alpha^* = (0.26)^{-1}$=3.85, at γ =0.5

- the relative maximal linear size of macroelement at a DP locality: : $\delta = \frac{\Delta l'}{l'}$=0.26 ($\gamma$ =0.5) and its relative volume $v_\delta = \frac{\pi\delta^3}{6}$=0.94• 10^{-2}
- the relative volume pertinent for a macroelement is $v_\delta^o = \frac{v_\delta}{3}$=3.1• 10^{-3}.

From that, the number of macro elements, corresponding to a given macrostate per the unit of such volume, is $N_\delta = (v_\delta^o) \cong 300$, which represents an analogy of Avogadro's number (as the quantity of elements within one mole): the ratio of the analogies of energy's and mass' increments : $\frac{\Delta\alpha^*}{\Delta\hat{m}} = \frac{t_i' t_i'}{\Delta t_i' \Delta t_i'} = (0.26)^{-2} \cong 14.8$.

The summarized information mass of a macroelement is the function of DPs: $M_o \cong 0.45(3(t_3)^{-1} + 2(t_5)^{-1} + ... + 2(t_{\frac{n}{2}+1})^{-1})$.

The dependency of number of elements $\overline{N}_i$ on the quantity information at each element's information level $\bar{i}_i = \alpha_i$, represents an analogy of Bolzman's distribution (as the function of the level's position from the macro elements settling). During the consolidation process, the $\overline{N}_i$ at the lower information levels is increasing, which leads to decreasing the analogy of Bolzman distribution function with increasing $\bar{i}_i = \alpha_i$ (Figure 3.7). This function can be obtained from the known functions $\alpha_i = \alpha_i(t_i)$ and $\overline{N}_i = \overline{N}_i(t_i)$. The relative changes of the informational settling for each level is measured by the increment of the element numbers $\bar{n}_i = \frac{\Delta\overline{N}_i}{\overline{N}_i}$, that defines the increment of the quasistationary entropy :

$\Delta\overline{S}_i = k_b \bar{n}_i$. The entropy ratio to the energy increment, according to $\bar{e}_i \sim \bar{i}$: $\frac{\Delta\overline{S}_i}{\Delta\bar{e}_i} = (\bar{\theta}_i)^{-1}$ is in the inverse proportion to the absolute temperature $\bar{\theta}_i$. The entropy depends on the element numbers, occupying the information level and does not depend on the level position. If the consolidation does not take place, then $\bar{n}_i$=const and the quasi-stationary entropy is growing linearly (Figure 3.8). At the consolidation, the number of the unbound elements $\bar{n}_i$ and $\overline{S}_i$ are decreasing. The entropy is equal to zero, when all macrostates are cooperated, but the macrosystem still has a finite uncertainty $\bar{h}_m = \bar{h}(n/2+1)$ that corresponds to the highest $m = (n/2+1)$ hierarchical level with a finite inner energy. Therefore, the final cooperative motion possesses some finite disorder. Because $\bar{n}_i$ and $\alpha_i = \alpha_i(t_i)$ are the same for all joining states, the disordered motion (within a zone of uncertainty) does not contribute into the thermal macro system characteristics. The probability of selecting a separated macrostate (spreading over the neighboring macro states)is very low. A specific macrostate wanders within the macrozone of uncertainty $\overline{h}_m$.

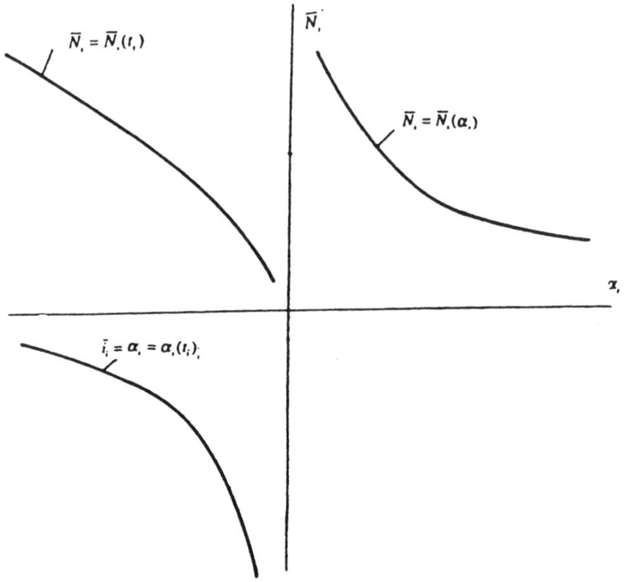

Figure 3.7. The analogy of Bolzman's distribution function.

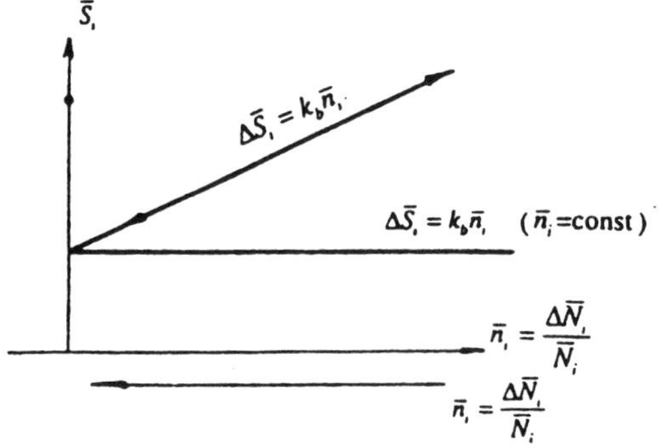

Figure 3.8. The quasistationary entropy function.

Each of such collective macro states possesses the quanta of the entropy production $\bar{i}_i = \alpha_i$ (related to the quanta of inner energy $\bar{e}_i \sim \bar{i}_i$), which depends on the macrosystem dimension. A phase transaction is associated with a jumpwise changing of the relative number of the level elements, with renovating and ordering.

That changes the distribution of the quantum states by the corresponding levels.

With broadening of that distribution, the thermodynamic probability $\overline{P}_i = \overline{P}_i(\bar{e}_i)$ is squeezed, increasing a possibility of ordering.

The probabilities of all cooperative macrostates occupying a given level are equal and an identical to the corresponding microstate numbers $\overline{P}_i = \overline{N}_i$.

Finally, the macromodel characteristics are the Bolzman distribution, quasi-stable entropy, and the quantum values for evaluation the level of disordering, settling, an entropy of quanta. The duration of the local instable macrostates (at $t_i = (t_1, t_2, t_3)$ are related in an average as the retios $t_2 / t_1 \cong 2$, $t_3 / t_2 \cong 2$.

This result has been discovered experimentally for many nonequilibrium systems and still does not have an explanation in known physical models [12].

A possible scenario of origin of the order is

- an availability of the external source of the high-quality energy
- a sequential chain of transformation energy with forming the barrier
- the discrete control functions, programmed by the barrier code"
- a sequential enlargement of the quantum intervals with decreasing the levels of reducing of the dissipative energy .

3.13. The bound energy of informational cooperation

The Hamiltonian macrosystem with the imposed constraint requires the dissipate energy: E=k_bT bXX^T, which is spent on forming the triplet's macrostructures. Disordering releases this energy. The triplet's bound latent information is a carrier of that energy and the cooperative forces X. An arbitrary sequence of the nonbound information symbols does not carry any energy. That sequence is not constrained, its latent information is absent. An essence of a transmitted information message constitutes its bound latent part , that is encoded in some language. A receiver at first supposes to translate the carrier code of information message into an appropriate recipient language, for example, by transforming an initial digital code into a sequence of letters of the recipient's alphabet.

The second and the most important part of accepting information, consists of interpreting of the translated symbols by their binding into the message. This requires spending an energy for understanding the message. This operation associates with eating the information (in Benett-Feynman terminology [23, 24]).

Software that accumulates a latent information from a software creator had obtained it by "eating" of an initial creator's information". Such software also accumulates a corresponding energy from a creator. A software consumer accepts a bound and latent information and spends energy for the operation of "eating" by hardware energy. Erasure of information, and not its measurement is a source of entropy generation. Revealing and identifying a bound latent information is accompanied with expenditure of energy. A software creator's energy has been embedded into latent information in the form of a corresponding information mass.

That mass binds an initial energy, which has been spent on cooperation.

Substantial are the following physical transformations of information

- creation of an idea by binding information symbols into the cooperative structures, accompanied with transformation energy into information of cooperative mass
- disclosure the cooperative mass, accompanied with an exposure of an idea (bound into the mass), which also requires an expense of energy.

The quantitative characteristics of the bound information is the summarized information mass m_{Σ} as the contribution from **m**=**n**-1 discrete intervals:

$$m_{\Sigma} = 4c / \pi \sum_{i=1}^{m=n-1} t'_{i},$$

or, based on the relation

$t'_{n-1} = \sum_{i=1}^{m=n-1} t'_{i}$, we come to $m_{\Sigma} = 4c / \pi t'_{n-1}$. The mass depends on the DI ($l' = ct'$), or on the system time course (t'), that is changing in moving system according with Theory of Relativity. It leads to dependency of the mass on the relative speed c'/c. Taking into account the relation $t'_{i} = \mathbf{a}_{o} / \alpha_{i}$, the local mass is in inverse proportion to local entropy production α_{i}: $m_{i} = 4c\mathbf{a}_{o} / \pi\alpha_{i}$, or $m_{i} = 4ca / \pi\alpha_{i,o}$ at $t'_{i} = \mathbf{a} / \alpha_{i,o}$, where $\mathbf{a} \sim C_{p}(\gamma), \alpha_{i,o} \sim \omega_{i,o}$ with $C_{p} = C_{p}(\gamma)$ as an information capacity and $\omega_{i,o}$ as the i-th eigenvalue frequency.

The summarized information mass $m_{\Sigma} = 4c\mathbf{a} / \pi\alpha_{n-1,o}$, or $4cC_{p} / \pi\omega_{n-1,o}$ can be expressed via the maximal information capacity C_{p} and the minimal frequency $\omega_{n-1,o}$ at given space speed c. Information mass is in direct proportion to the latent quantity information $\mathbf{a}$ that has the energy equivalent e_{a}. The mass gets the entropy contribution only ouside of DI. At a negative invariant $\mathbf{a}_{o}$, the mass increment is negative. These equations determine the corresponding energy:

$$m_{\Sigma} k_{b}\theta = 4c\mathbf{a}k_{b}\theta / \pi\omega_{n-1,o}, \quad k_{b}\theta\mathbf{a} = e_{a}, \; e_{a} = m_{a}c_{0}^{2} k_{b},$$

$$e_{a} = \frac{m_{\Sigma} \pi\omega_{n-1,o} k_{b}\theta}{4c},$$

where the physical mass is

$$m_{a} = \frac{m_{\Sigma} \pi\omega_{n-1,o} k_{b}\theta}{4cc_{0}^{2}}.$$

These equations evaluate the energy, accumulated into information mass, and its physical mass. There is an analogy with physical energy, bound into the atom's nucleus that requires an external energy to expose the nuclear energy.

An idea, incorporated into macrostructure, is produced by a cost of a brain energy.

An elementary quantum of latent information $\mathbf{a}$ is evaluated by the equivalent quantum of bound energy e_{a}. The triplet's bound information depend on γ, that detrmines a minimumal values of $\mathbf{a}(\gamma)$ and the frequency of transmitted symbols

$\omega_{n-1,o}$ (which is defined by the total macrostructure maximal dimension $\mathbf{n}=\mathbf{n}(\gamma)$).

Invariant $\mathbf{a}(\gamma)$ cannot exceed the maximal channel capacity C_p : $\mathbf{a} \leq C_p$.

For the message length Mc, the greatest amount of information, sending with the message is C_p Mc, and the corresponding cost of energy is $E = e_a C_p$ Mc.

Such approach evaluates the message content by Shannon's entropy associated with maximal uncertainty of the message symbol.

There are two levels of revealing the message uncertainty:

1. translating an initial message code into a receiver alphabet
2. understanding of an idea message's bound information.

Each of them has a specific uncertainty, that requires spending an energy.

In the first one, uncertainty is associated with each initial code symbol (because one doesn't known the location and position of current symbol). In the second one, uncertainty of a message is associated with a sequence of cooperative macrostructures (for the sequence is unknown, and also unknown is, which of the symbol's bits bring a bound information). The bound information is accounted in the units of quantity of information, carried by the message symbols.

Using the IMD model, it's possible to evaluate a total message only by a single bound uncertainty, defined by Shannon's entropy. The acceptance of such a message requires also a minimal energy expenditure E. Such an energy would be spent only to get quantity information from the priory unknown data, symbols.

The process of copying does not cost an energy because it does not bring a new unknown knowledge. The operations include building the message's IN that simplifies the message structure, computerizing and automatizing the process of message understanding, and bringing the maximal compression of the message symbols, that increases communication speed of the symbol transmission up to C_p.

Example of superposition of virtual information.

Suppose we deal with different domains of knowledge (as an informational substance) in such areas as biology, physics, chemistry. We are selecting from each domain some quantity information: h1 (biology), h2 (physics), h3 (chemistry) to invent a common new domain of bio-physical-chemistry, as a triplet with quantity information h123, that has been formed by intersection of the initial ranged quantity information h1, h2, h3.

The procedure of choosing the specific quantity of information (h1, h2, h3) requiers a "virtual cutting" (or erasing) of all information from each domain except the needed portions (h1, h2, h3). For example, by selecting appropriate parts of biology, physics, chemistry, their intersection reflects a result of superposition of that knowledge. Such a superposition consists of a "cutting parts" from h1, h2,h3.

The procedure of forming the above triplet is accompanied with spending an energy for erasing the intersection of the domains.

Such a triplet accumulates an energy and represents a material substance.

If the triplet is formed spontaneously, it illustrates the transformation of the initial information into material substance, or a software into hardware form.

Perhaps, any intersection of virtual information, for example, at forming images (as a superposition of graphical information), can be considered as the transformation of information into a material substance, that accumulates an energy.

The superimposed information could be bound initially by human or artificial intellect, and it requires spending an energy. In the process of acceptance, the bound information is transformed into a material substance, creating a corresponding physical process. For example, software information is a product of some human thought, that after its acceptance by a computer operating system is transformed into a physical product. A "human operating system" enables one to accept an idea, environmental information, and transform it into a physical process, and then back to environmental information. If a carrier of bound information transmits it, the receiver that is able to accept the bound information gets its corresponding material analog. This means bound information acquires a material substance after it has been accepted.

Existence of actual superimposing processes is connected objectively with the reality of the controls in nature [16].

REFERENCES

1. Stratonovich R.L. *Theory of Information*, Moscow: Soviet Radio, 1975.
2. Arnold V. I. *Mathematical Methods of Classic mechanics*, Moscow: Nauka, 1974.
3. Ornstein D. *Ergodic theory, Randomness and Dynamic systems,* Moscow: Mir, 1978.
4. Kubo R. *Statistical Physics,* Moscow: Mir, 1967.
5. Misra B., Prigogine I. "On Foundations of Kinetic Theory". *Stochastic Nonlinear Systems in Physics, Chemistry, and Biology,* eds. L. Arnold, R. Lefever, Proceeding of the Workshop, Bielefeld: Springer-Verlag, 1981: 2-11.
6. Graham R. "Stochastic Methods in Nonequilibrium Thermodynamics", *Stochastic Nonlinear Systems in Physics, Chemistry, and Biology*, eds L. Arnold, R. Lefever, Proceeding of the Workshop, Bielefeld: Springer-Verlag, 1981: 202-212.
7. Truchaev R. I., Lerner V. S. *Dynamic models of the Decision Making Processes*, Kishinev: Stiintza, 1974.
8. Kac M.(Ed). *Probability and related topics in physical science*, N.Y.: Inter science Publishers, Inc., 1957.
9. Poston T., Stewart I. *Catastrophe Theory and its Applications*, London: Pitman, 1978.
10. Daison F., Montrol A., Kac M., Fisher M. *Stability and the Phase Transformations*, Moscow: Mir, 1973.
11. Stanley H. E. *Introduction to Phase Transformations and Critical Phenomena*, Oxford: University Press, 1980.
12. Careri G. *Order and Disorder in the structure of Matter*, Roma: Laterza, 1982.
13. Stanley H. E., Coniglio A., Klein W., Nakanisghi H., Redner S., Reynolds P.I., Shlifer G. "Critical Phenomena: Past, Present, and Future". *Dynamics of Synergetic Systems,* eds. H. Haken, Berlin: Springer-Verlag, 1980: 22-38.
14. Ma S. *Modern Theory of Critical Phenomena,* N.Y.: Benjamin/Cummings, 1976.
15. Landau L. D. and Lifshitz E. M. *Statistic Physics,* Moscow: Nauka, 1964.
16. Lerner V. S. *Superimposing Processes in Problem of Control,* Kishinev: Shtiinza, 1973.
17. Lerner V. S. "Parametric control the transformers," *Regulated electrical drive*, Kishinev: Stiinza, 1981: 100-112.
18. Volkenstein M.V. *The General Biophysics*, Moscow: Nauka, 1978.
19. Kittel Ch. *Thermal Physics,* N.Y.: Wiley , 1975.
20. Lerner V. S. and Bilinkis P. G. "Optimal Dynamic Model of Electromagnetical processes", *Regulated electrical drive,* Kishinev: Stiinza, 1982: 3-14.
21. De Groot S.R., Mazur P. *Non-equilibrium Thermodynamics,* Amsterdam: North-Holland Publ. Co, 1962.
22. Feynman R. *Feynman Lectures in Computation*, N.Y.: Addison-Wesley , 1996.
23. Benett C. H. "Thermodynamics of Computation", *International Journal of Theoretical Physics,* 1982, 21: 905-940.

PART IV. SOLUTION OF THE APPLIED IMD PROBLEMS

4.1. ANALYTICAL AND NUMERICAL SOLUTIONS

4.1.1. The formal procedure of identification, optimal control, and consolidation

Let an object be described at the macrolevel by the solutions of equations (2.1.9) with an unknown matrix A=A(t),which values fixed at the DIs .

The solution of the identification problem consists of the restoration of matrix A by measuring (computation) of object's covariation matrix r_v and its derivative $\dot{r}_v$.

Let us show that the matrix $R_v(\tau)=1/2\dot{r}_v(\tau)r_v(\tau)^{-1}$, settled on the solutions of the equations (2.1.8, 9), determines the object operator A.

Indeed, at $\forall(s,\tau)=(\tau_k,\tau_{k-1})$, k=1,...,m, we have the following equations:

$\dot{x}_t=A(x_t+v_t)$, v_t=-2x_s, y_t=x_t+v_t, $\dot{y}_t=A\,y_t$, y_s=-x_s,

y_t=exp(At) y_s=-exp(At) x_s, $r_v(t)=M(y_t y_t^T)$=exp(At)r_s exp(At);

$r_s=M(x_s x_s^T)$;$r_v(t)^{-1}$=exp(-At)r_s^{-1} exp(-At);

$\dot{r}_v(t)$=$r_1(t)+r_1^T(t)$=$M(\dot{y}_t y_t^T)+M(y_t\dot{y}_t^T)$=Aexp(At)$r_s$ exp(At)+

+exp(At)r_s exp(At)A; $\dot{r}_v(\tau)$=$\dot{r}_v(\tau-o)$=2Axp(At)r_s exp(At);

$R_v(\tau)$=Aexp(Aτ)r_s exp(Aτ)exp(-Aτ)r_s^{-1} exp(Aτ)≡ A= $A(\tau-o)=A(s+o)$.

For the observed controlled object (1.1.7,8), the identification of the matrixes $A_k=A(\tau_{k-1}+o)=A(\tau_{k-1}-o)$ and $\overline{A}_k=\overline{A}(\tau_{k-1}+o)=\overline{A}(\tau_{k-1}-o)$ is performed by the analogy at *each discrete interval of applying optimal control.*

The number of the discrete intervals is equal to the number of the independent state variables, and (n-1) moments of the switching control are determined by the system of equalities (2.1.7,8,11) at given $r(\tau_o)$, $\dot{r}(\tau_o)$, $(\tau_o=0)$.

That control enables it to transfer the object into a given final state via an optimal trajectory. If there exists a set of the moments $(\tau_k^1,\ldots,\tau_k^j,\ldots,\tau_k^{N_1})$, then the unique solution of the optimization problem (in term of selection of a single τ_k for each found control v_t) is achieved at choosing the minimal $\tau_k^j=\tau_k$ for each 'k ".

A chosen τ_k ensures a minimal time of the above transformation. The initial v_t piecewise optimal control is determined from the relation $v_t=-2x(\tau_k)$.

Solving the joint problem of optimal control and identification includes the following sequence. At an initial moment $(\tau_o=0)$, using a known $r(0),\dot{r}(-0)$ let us determine the matrix

$A^{v}(-0)=-1/2\dot{r}(-0)\,r^{-1}(0)$=A(+0), A_t=A(+0) $\forall t\in(0,\tau_1)$ that is transformed into diagonal form. Considering $C_n^2=\dfrac{n!}{(n-2)!2!}$ of possible equalities:

$$\lambda_i^1=\frac{\lambda_i^o\exp(-\lambda_i^o\tau_1)}{2-\exp(-\lambda_i^o\tau_1)}=\frac{\lambda_j^o\exp(-\lambda_j^o\tau_1)}{2-\exp(-\lambda_j^o\tau_1)}=\lambda_j^1,\ \text{i,j=1,...,n},\ \ i\neq j\ ,$$

let us find all roots for each of the equalities, and select a such one that corresponds to the minimal $\tau_1=\min\limits_{j=1,..,N_1}(\tau_1^1,\dots,\tau_1^j,\dots,\tau_1^{N_1})$, which defines the first moment of switching control. The above equalities for the eigenvalues $(\lambda_i^1,\lambda_j^1)$ are reduced to the simple form of the equation

(1.1) $\eta^{\alpha}-\dfrac{\alpha}{2}\eta+\alpha-1=0$,

where $\alpha=\dfrac{\gamma_{ij}^o-1}{\gamma_{ij}^o}=\alpha(i,j)$, $\gamma_{ij}^o=\dfrac{\lambda_i^o}{\lambda_j^o}$, $\eta=\exp(-\lambda_i^o\tau_1)>0$,

that follows directly from the equalization of the eigenvalues at τ_1.

All discrete moments $\{\tau_k\}$ are found by the analogy: $\tau_k=\tau_{k-1}+\min\limits_{j=1,\dots,N_1}\{\tau_k^j\}_{j=1}^{N_k}$, $\tau_k>\tau_{k-1}$, k=2,...,m-1, where $\{\tau_k^j\}$are the roots of the equations (1.1).

The last moment of discretization τ_n=T (when the control is turned off), is found from the equality x(T)=0 by the solution the corresponding Caushy problem.

The condition of the eigenvalue positivity is satisfied by applying the needle control $\delta v(\tau_k,\cdot)=v(\tau_k+\varepsilon,\cdot)-v(\tau_k,\cdot)$ at the infinite nearest moments t=τ_k and t=$\tau_k+\varepsilon$, $\varepsilon>0$. Let us show, that applying that control will change the matrix's $\overline{A}(\tau_k+0)$ sign with respect to the sign of the matrix $\overline{A}(\tau_k-0)$.

Indeed, following the known eigenvalues for $(\lambda_i^1,\lambda_j^1)$ we get

$$\overline{A}(\tau_k+0)=-(2E-\exp(\overline{A}(\tau_k-0)(\tau_k-\tau_{k-1}))^{-1}\times$$
$$\times\exp(\overline{A}(\tau_k-0)(\tau_k-\tau_{k-1}))\,\overline{A}(\tau_k-0),\ \ \overline{A}(\tau_k-0)=\overline{A}(\tau_{k-1}+0).$$

Assuming $\varepsilon=\tau_k-\tau_{k-1}$ and then turning $\varepsilon\to 0$, we arrive at the equalities

$$\overline{A}(\tau_k+0)=-(2E-\exp(\overline{A}(\tau_{k-1}+0)\varepsilon)^{-1}\exp(\overline{A}(\tau_{k-1}+0)\varepsilon)\times$$
$$\times\overline{A}(\tau_k-0),\ \overline{A}(\tau_k+0)=-\overline{A}(\tau_k-0).$$

The needle control should be applied at the violation of the object controllability.

Let us consider the procedure of the macrostate consolidation.

The condition of the eigenvalues equality for the matrix

$$a=\begin{Vmatrix}a_{11},a_{12}\\a_{21},a_{22}\end{Vmatrix}\overset{def}{=}\begin{Vmatrix}A_{ii}^{v}(\tau_k),A_{ij}^{v}(\tau_k)\\A_{ji}^{v}(\tau_k),A_{jj}^{v}(\tau_k)\end{Vmatrix},\ a=a^{T},\ t\in(\tau_{k-1},\tau_k),$$

$A^v(\tau_k) = A^v(\tau_k - 0) = A^v(\tau_k + 0)$, according with the relations

$$\lambda_{1,2} = \frac{Spa}{2} + -[(\frac{Spa}{2})^2 - \det a]^{1/2},\ (\frac{Spa}{2})^2 - \det a = (a_{11}a_{22})^2 + 4(a_{12})^2 = 0,$$

leads to $a_{11}=a_{22}$, $a_{12}=0$, e.g., to the matrix diagonalization. The model is reduced to the diagonal form (with state vector z and equation $\dot{z} = \overline{A}(z + \overline{v})$), and then is transferred to a new rotating coordinate system, toward achievement the equalization of phase coordinates. The angle φ_{ij} of rotation the coordinate plane $(0z_i\, z_j)$ is found

from the equations $z'_i = z'_j$ and $\begin{Vmatrix} z_i \\ z_j \end{Vmatrix} = \begin{Vmatrix} \cos\varphi_{ij}, -\sin\varphi_{ij} \\ \sin\varphi_{ij}, \cos\varphi_{ij} \end{Vmatrix} \begin{Vmatrix} z'_i \\ z'_j \end{Vmatrix}$.

We get equations $z'_i \sin\varphi_{ij} + z'_j \cos\varphi_{ij} = \dfrac{z_j(\tau_k,\cdot)}{z_i(\tau_k,\cdot)}(z'_j \cos\varphi_{ij} - z'_i \sin\varphi_{ij})$ and

$$\varphi_{ij} = arctg\frac{z_j(\tau_k,\cdot) - z_i(\tau_k,\cdot)}{z_j(\tau_k,\cdot) + z_i(\tau_k,\cdot)} + -N\pi\ ,\ N=0,1,2,\ldots.$$

Because of an arbitrariness of k=1,...,(n-1), i,j=1,...,n, the analogous relations are true for any two components of the state vector and for each (τ_k, τ_{k-1}) DI. By the successive (n-1) of such rotations, we arrive at the coordinate system $(oz'_1,\ldots,z'_n)$, where all state variables are indistinct in time. The transformation of initial state coordinates into that coordinate system corresponds to the origin of a new macrostate variables. Indistinctness in time of the state variables we call the state cooperation. Thus, during the model optimal motion, the problem of the successive states cooperation gets the simultaneous solution with the identification problem. By the extremal conditions for information entropy, the pieces of the process extremals approximate the random process with a maximal information. That fact leads to a possibility of the optimal discrete (nonlinear) filtration of random process (within each discrete interval). The controlled discrete filter (Fig.4.1) [1] passes a signal through only at the moments of the operator renovation, when the information entropy reaches a maximum. The filter structure implements the computer operations with the object matrixes.

Let us consider some class of nonlinear objects, which model can be presented by the equation

(1.2) $\dot{x}_i = a_i(x_j) = (x_i + v_i), i \neq j, i, j = 1,\ldots,n,$

with the reduced control v_i and the essential nonlinear operator, for example,

$$a_i(x_j) = \begin{Bmatrix} \phi_i(x_j), \delta_2 < |\delta| < \delta_1 \\ a_i sign\delta, \delta_1 < |\delta| < \delta_0, \\ \psi(x_j), \delta_0 < |\delta| < \delta_3 \end{Bmatrix}, \delta = (x_j(t) - x_j(\tau)),$$

where $\delta_0, \delta_1, \delta_2, \delta_3$ are some fixed constants. For such objects, the identification of unknown operator $a_i(x_j)$ is possible, using the $R(\tau)$ matrix at the Marcovian

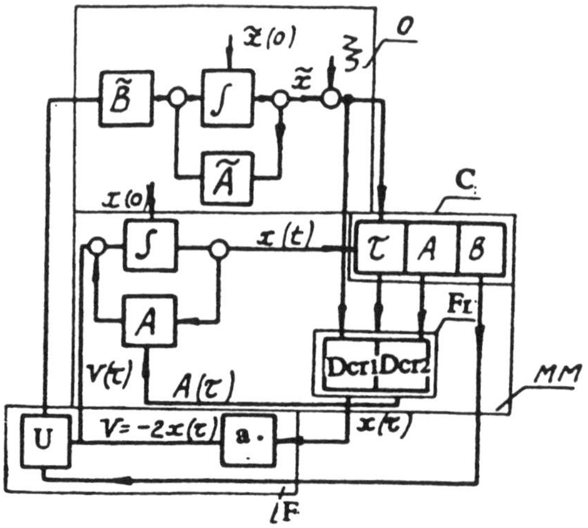

Figure 4.1.1. Matrix structure of optimal discrete filter: O is an object, C is a computer with macromodel MM, τ is the moments of the model operators A,B discretization, $\tilde{A}, \tilde{B}$ are the object operators, U is the controls, F is the filter with the discretizators Dcr1, Decr2 of input signal and the operator A accordingly, Fr is the block of forming the control with an amplifier a •.

moments of uncoupling the time correlation's, when the control $v_i = v_i(x_i)$ fulfills the condition

$$\dot{r}_i(\tau_i) = 2M_{v_i}[a_i(x_j(\tau_i))(x_i(\tau_i)+v_i)^2] = 2a_i(x_j(\tau_i))M_{v_i}[(x_i(\tau_i)+v_i)^2]$$

that leads selecting the nonlinear operator from of the sign of mathematical expectation. By substituting $\dot{r}_i(\tau_i)$ and $r_i(\tau_i) = M_{v_i}[(x_i(\tau_i)+v_i)^2]$ into $R(\tau)$ we come to $R(\tau_i) = a_i(x_j(\tau_i))$. Fixing $R(\tau_i)$ simultaneously with $x_i(\tau_i)$, we restore the unknown nonlinear operator. Solving that problem is possible by applying the optimal control, minimizing the proper functional and giving rise to the hierarchical cooperation. The illustrative examples [1] are considered below. Equation (1.2) is associated with the model of superimposing processes with an additive Hamiltonian

$$H = \sum_{i=1}^{n} H_i, \; H_i = a_i(x_j)$$

of the interacting processes that satisfies the following condition

$$\frac{\partial H_i}{\partial x_j} \neq 0, i \neq j.$$

The condition of consolidation: $a_i(x_j(\tau_i)) = a_j(x_i(\tau_i))$ defines the operator of cooperative model. The corresponding macro equations follow from the equations::

$$\frac{\partial \hat{H}}{\partial \hat{X}_i} = \dot{\hat{x}}_i, \; -\frac{\partial \hat{H}}{\partial \hat{x}_i} = \dot{\hat{X}}_i, \; \hat{H} = M_x[H], \; \hat{x} = M[x].$$

4.1.2. Illustration of the procedure by examples

Example 1. Let us start with a stochastic equation of the second order as a microlevel model of object at time interval s=$(0,\tau_1)$:

$$d\tilde{x}_1(t,\cdot) = a_1(t,\tilde{x}_t,u)dt + \sigma_{11}(t)d\xi_1(t,\cdot) + \sigma_{12}(t)d\xi_2(t,\cdot)\ \tilde{x}_1(s,\cdot) = \tilde{x}_{1s},$$

$$d\tilde{x}_2(t,\cdot) = a_2(t,\tilde{x}_t,u)dt + \sigma_{21}(t)d\xi_1(t,\cdot) + \sigma_{22}(t)d\xi_2(t,\cdot), \tilde{x}_2(s,\cdot) = \tilde{x}_{2s}.$$

The task at the macrolevel is given by a constant vector $\overline{x}_t^1 = \overline{x}_o^1 \forall t \in \Delta$, $\overline{x}_o^1 \in R^2$,which is chosen at the beginning of coordinate system $(0\,\overline{x}_1\ \overline{x}_2)$. Then $x_t = \overline{x}_t^1$. The macrolevel model required the identification of the matrix A_t is

$$(1.3)\ \dot{x}_1(t,\cdot) = A_{11}(t)(x_1(t,\cdot)+v_1(t,\cdot)) + A_{12}(t)(x_2(t,\cdot)+v_2(t,\cdot)),$$

$$x_1(s,\cdot) = x_{1s},\ v_t = -2x_s,\ \dot{x}_2(t,\cdot) = A_{21}(t)(x_1(t,\cdot)+v_1(t,\cdot)) +$$

$$+ A_{22}(t)(x_2(t,\cdot)+v_2(t,\cdot)), x_2(s,\cdot) = x_{2s},\ t \in \Delta^0,$$

$$\Delta^0 = (0,\tau_1) \cup (\tau_1, T),\ \Delta = \Delta^0 \cup 0 \cup \tau_1 \cup T,\ X_p(t) = X_t(t) + p_t(t),$$

$$X_t = (2b_t)^{-1} A_t(x_t + v_t), A_t = r_1 r_v^{-1}, A(t) = \begin{Vmatrix} A_{11}, A_{12} \\ A_{21}, A_{22} \end{Vmatrix},\ v_t = \begin{Vmatrix} v_1(t,\cdot) \\ v_2(t,\cdot) \end{Vmatrix}$$

$$b = \begin{Vmatrix} b_{11}, b_{12} \\ b_{21}, b_{22} \end{Vmatrix} = \frac{1}{2}\begin{Vmatrix} (\sigma^2_{11} + \sigma^2_{12}), (\sigma_{11}\sigma_{21} + \sigma_{12}\sigma_{22}) \\ (\sigma_{11}\sigma_{21} + \sigma_{12}\sigma_{22}), (\sigma^2_{21} + \sigma^2_{22}) \end{Vmatrix},$$

$$r_1 = \begin{Vmatrix} (M[\dot{x}_1(x_1(t,\cdot)+v_1(t,\cdot))]), (M[\dot{x}_1(x_2(t,\cdot)+v_2(t,\cdot))]) \\ (M[\dot{x}_2(x_1(t,\cdot)+v_1(t,\cdot))]), (M[\dot{x}_2(x_2(t,\cdot)+v_2(t,\cdot))]) \end{Vmatrix},$$

$$r_v^{-1} = \begin{Vmatrix} (M[(x_1(t,\cdot)+v_1(t,\cdot))^2]), (M[(x_1(t,\cdot)+v_1(t,\cdot))(x_2(t,\cdot)+v_2(t,\cdot))]) \\ (M[(x_2(t,\cdot)+v_2(t,\cdot))(x_1(t,\cdot)+v_1(t,\cdot))]), (M[(x_2(t,\cdot)+v_2(t,\cdot))^2]) \end{Vmatrix}$$

$$M[\cdot] = \left\{ \begin{array}{l} \int_{R^2} [\cdot] P_o(0,x)dx, x = x_{0,}, t \in [o,\tau_1), \\ \int_{R^2} [\cdot] P_{\tau_1}(\tau_1,x)dx, x = x_{\tau_1,}, t \in [\tau_1, T), \end{array} \right\}.$$

The object observation is a discrete time process with the elements of A_t, as a piecewise constant functions of time that are fixed within each of two discrete intervals $[0,\tau_1),(\tau_1,T]$. The identification problem consists of restoration $A(t) \forall t \in (\tau_1, T)$ by known r_1(t), r_v^{-1}(t) using model's solution as model's object under observation. Let us consider solutions (1.1) for given initial matrix

$$A(-0) = \begin{Vmatrix} -2, -3 \\ -3, -10 \end{Vmatrix}, \text{ and } x_t + v_t = y_t \text{ at } [o,\tau_1) \text{ interval:}$$

(1.4) $\dot{y}_1(t,\cdot) = a_{11}y_1(t,\cdot) + a_{12}y_2(t,\cdot),\ y_{10} = x_{10},$

$\dot{y}_2(t,\cdot) = a_{21}y_1(t,\cdot) + a_{22}y_2(t,\cdot),\ y_{20} = x_{20},$

$$A(+0) = \begin{Vmatrix} a_{11}, a_{12} \\ a_{21}, a_{22} \end{Vmatrix} = A(-0) = A_t\ \forall t \in (o, \tau_1),\quad \overline{A}(+0) = \begin{Vmatrix} -\lambda_1^0, 0 \\ 0, -\lambda_2^0 \end{Vmatrix},$$

$$\lambda_{1,2}^0 = \frac{1}{2} SpA(-0) \pm ((\frac{1}{2} SpA(-0))^2 - \det A(-0))^{\frac{1}{2}},\ \lambda_1^0 = -11,\ \lambda_2^0 = -1;$$

$y_{11}(t) = \alpha_{11}\exp(11t),\ 11\alpha_{11} = 2\alpha_{11} + 3\alpha_{12},$

$y_{12}(t) = \alpha_{12}\exp(11t),\ 11\alpha_{12} = 3\alpha_{11} + 10\alpha_{12},$

$y_{21}(t) = \alpha_{21}\exp(t),\ \alpha_{21} = 2\alpha_{21} + 3\alpha_{22},\quad \alpha_{11} \overset{def}{=} 1,\ \alpha_{12} = 3$

$y_{22}(t) = \alpha_{22}\exp(t),\ \alpha_{22} = 3\alpha_{21} + 10\alpha_{22},\ \alpha_{21} = -3, \alpha_{22} \overset{def}{=} 1.$

The fundamental system and general solutions of (1.4) have the forms:

$$\begin{Vmatrix} y_{11}(t), y_{12}(t) \\ y_{21}(t), y_{22}(t) \end{Vmatrix} = \begin{Vmatrix} \exp(11t), 3\exp(11t) \\ -3\exp(11t), \exp(t) \end{Vmatrix},\ x_0 = \begin{Vmatrix} x_{10} \\ x_{20} \end{Vmatrix},\ y_0 = x_0 .$$

$y_1(t,\cdot) = C_1\exp(11t) - 3C_2\exp(t),$

$y_2(t,\cdot) = 3C_1\exp(11t) + C_2\exp(t), C_1, C_2 \in (R^1, \beta(R^1), P_0),$

using the following initial conditions and the constants:

$C_1 - 3C_2 = x_{10},\ 3C_1 + C_2 = x_{20},\quad C_1 = -0.1(x_{10} + 3x_{20}),\ C_2 = 0.1(3x_{10} - x_{20}).$

The Caushy problem solution leads to the relations

$y_1(t,\cdot) = -0.1[x_{10}(\exp(11t) + 9\exp(t)) + 3x_{20}(\exp(11t) - \exp(t))],$

$y_2(t,\cdot) = -0.1[3x_{10}(\exp(11t) - \exp(t)) + x_{20}(9\exp(11t) + \exp(t))],$

with the fundamental matrix $Y_t = \begin{Vmatrix} \exp(11t) + 9\exp(t), 3(\exp(11t) - \exp(t)) \\ 3(\exp(11t) - \exp(t)), 9\exp(11t) + \exp(t) \end{Vmatrix}.$

Let us determine the covariation matrix and its derivative, using the relations

$r_v(t) = M[(x_t + v_t)(x_t + v_t)^T] = M[(y_t y_t)^T] = M[Y_t\, y_0\ y_0^T\, Y_t^T] =$

$= M[Y_t\, x_0\ x_0^T\, Y_t^T] = Y_t\, r_0\, Y_t, r_0 = M[x_0\ x_0^T],\ \dot{r}_v(t) = \dot{Y}_t r_0\, Y_t + Y_t\, r_0\, \dot{Y}_t,$

$\dot{r}_v(t) = r_1(t) + r_1^T(t),\ r_1(t) = M[\dot{x}_t(x_t + v_t)^T],\ r_1(t) = \dot{Y}_t r_0\, Y_t,\ r_1^T(t) = Y_t^T\, r_0^T\, \dot{Y}_t^T =$

$= Y_t\ r_0\, \dot{Y}_t,\ R_v(t) = r_1(t) r_v^{-1}(t) = R_v^T(t) = Y_t^{-1}\, \dot{Y}_t .$

As it follows from the last relation, the matrix R_v (t) does not depend on the probability distributions of an initial state vector, which brings important results for applications. The following equations establish the connection R_v (t) with matrix

$A_t = A(+0)$ at (o, τ_1): $\quad Y_t^{-1} = (\det Y_t)^{-1}\, Y_t^T,$

$$Y_t{*} = 0.1 \begin{Vmatrix} 9\exp(11t) + \exp(t), -3(\exp(11t) - \exp(t)) \\ -3(\exp(11t) - \exp(t)), \exp(11t) + \exp(t) \end{Vmatrix},\ \det Y_t = \exp(12t),$$

$$Y_t * \dot{Y}_t = D_t = \begin{Vmatrix} D_{11}, D_{12} \\ D_{21}, D_{22} \end{Vmatrix};\ D_{11}=2\exp(12t),\ D_{12}=D_{21}=3\exp(12t), D_{22}=10\exp(12t),$$

$$\dot{Y}_t=0.1\begin{Vmatrix} 11\exp(11t)+9\exp(t), 3(11\exp(11t)-\exp(t)) \\ 3(11\exp(11t)-\exp(t)), 99\exp(11t)+\exp(t) \end{Vmatrix}.$$ From this we obtain

$$R_v(t)=R_v^T(t)=(\det Y_t)^{-1} Y_t^T \dot{Y}_t=\exp(-12t)\, D_t=\begin{Vmatrix} 2,3 \\ 3,10 \end{Vmatrix}=A(+0),$$

and the identification problem gets the precise solution by the observed matrix R_v (t).

That distincts this method from the known identification procedures. Let us find the discretization moment τ_1 of switching the optimal control using the relations

(1.5) $$\frac{\dot{x}_1(\tau_1,\cdot)}{x_1(\tau_1,\cdot)}=\frac{11C_1\exp(11\tau_1)-3C_2\exp(\tau_1)}{-v_1(0,\cdot)+C_1\exp(11\tau_1)-3C_2\exp(\tau_1)}=$$
$$=\frac{\dot{x}_2(\tau_1,\cdot)}{x_2(\tau_1,\cdot)}=\frac{33C_1\exp(11\tau_1)+C_2\exp(\tau_1)}{-v_2(0,\cdot)+3C_1\exp(11\tau_1)+C_2\exp(\tau_1)},$$
$$v_1(0,\cdot)=-2x_1(0,\cdot),\quad v_2(0,\cdot)=-2x_2(0,\cdot).$$

(1.6) $5\exp(11t)-11\exp(10t)+1=0$, $t>0$, that has the unique root $\tau_1 \cong 0.7884$.

Application of the formula (1.1) also leads to (1.6) at the following parameters

$$\overset{o}{\gamma}_{12}=\overset{o}{\gamma}_{12}=\frac{\lambda_1^o}{\lambda_2^o}=11,\ \alpha=10/11,\ \eta=\exp(11t).$$

That illustrates the independency of the discretization moment on a chosen coordinate system. We also obtain the eigenvalues at moments τ_1 and the final T:

$$\lambda_1^1=\lambda_2^1 \cong 11,\ T=\tau_1+\frac{\ln 2}{\lambda_1^1}\cong 0.851,\ \overline{A}(\tau_1+0)\cong\begin{Vmatrix} 11,0 \\ 0,11 \end{Vmatrix}.$$

If the initial matrix is positive, then the solution (1.2) leads to the equations:

$$A(-0)=\begin{Vmatrix} 2,3 \\ 3,10 \end{Vmatrix},\ \overline{A}(-0)=\begin{Vmatrix} 11,0 \\ 0,1 \end{Vmatrix},\ A(+0)=A(-0),$$

at $$\overline{A}(+0)=\begin{Vmatrix} -11,0 \\ 0,-11 \end{Vmatrix},\ t\in[0,\tau_1),$$

$y_1(t,\cdot)=C_1\exp(-11t)-3C_2\exp(-t)$, $C_1=0.1(x_{10}+3x_{20})$,

$y_2(t,\cdot)=C_2\exp(-t)+3C_1\exp(-11t)$, $C_2=0.1(3x_{10}-x_{20})$,

$$y_t=-0.1\begin{Vmatrix} \exp(-11t)+9\exp(-t), 3(\exp(-11t)-\exp(-t)) \\ 3(\exp(-11t)-\exp(-t)), 9\exp(-11t)+\exp(-t) \end{Vmatrix} x_0,\quad y_t=x_t+v_t.$$

By analogy we obtain the relations

$$\frac{11C_1\exp(-11\tau_1)}{-v_1(0,\cdot)+C_1\exp(-11\tau_1)-3C_2\exp(-\tau_1)}=$$

$$=\frac{33C_1\exp(-\tau_1)+C_2\exp(-\tau_1)}{-v_2(0,\cdot)+3C_1\exp(-11\tau_1)+C_2\exp(-\tau_1)}$$, and the equation for t= τ_1:

(1.7) 5exp(-11t)-11exp(-10t)+1=0, t>0 ,

that defines $\tau_1\cong 0.193$, and the corresponding negative eigenvalues $\lambda_1^1=\lambda_2^1\cong$ -0.7. For the fulfillment of the condition of positive eigenvalues at τ_1, we apply the needle-sign control, that leads to $\lambda_1^1=\lambda_2^1\cong 0.7$ with $T=0.193+\frac{\ln 2}{0.7}\cong 1.187$

By knowing the discrete moment, we can identify the matrix $A_t\,\forall t\in(\tau_1,T)$ at the new discrete interval by knowing initial matrix and using the relations

$$A(+0)=\begin{Vmatrix}2,3\\3,10\end{Vmatrix},\ t\in(0,\tau_1)$$

$$\overline{Y}_t=0.1\begin{Vmatrix}\exp(11t)+9\exp(t)-20, 3(\exp(11t)-\exp(t))\\3(\exp(11t)-\exp(t)), 9\exp(11t)+\exp(t)-20\end{Vmatrix},$$

$$x_t=\overline{Y}_t\,x_0\,,\dot{\overline{Y}}_t=-\overline{Y}_t+\begin{Vmatrix}2,0\\0,2\end{Vmatrix},r_t=M[x_t\,x_t^T]=\overline{Y}_t\,r_0\,\overline{Y}_t\ ,\ \dot{r}_t=-(\dot{Y}_t\,r_0\,\overline{Y}_t+$$

$$+\overline{Y}_t\,r_0\,\dot{Y}_t),\quad \dot{\overline{Y}}_t=-\dot{Y}_t,\ \dot{r}(\tau_1)=2\dot{Y}(\tau_1)\,r_0\,\overline{Y}(\tau_1)=-2\overline{Y}(\tau_1)\,r_0\,\dot{Y}(\tau_1),$$

$$r_t^{-1}=\overline{Y}_t^{-1}\,r_0^{-1}\,\overline{Y}_t^{-1},\ \overline{Y}_t^{-1}=(\det\overline{Y}_t)^{-1}\,Y_t^T\ ,\overline{Y}_t{}^*=-0.1\begin{Vmatrix}\overline{Y}_{22},-\overline{Y}_{12}\\-\overline{Y}_{21},\overline{Y}_{11}\end{Vmatrix}=$$

$$=-0.1\begin{Vmatrix}9\exp(11t)+\exp(t)-20,-3(\exp(11t)-\exp(t))\\-3(\exp(11t)-\exp(t)),\exp(11t)+\exp(t)-20\end{Vmatrix},$$

$\det\overline{Y}_t$ =exp(12t)-2exp(11t)-2exp(t)+4;

$$A(\tau_1+0)=\frac{1}{2}r(\tau_1)^{-1}\ \dot{r}(\tau_1-0)=-\overline{Y}(\tau_1)^{-1}\,\dot{Y}(\tau_1)=$$

$$=-(\det\overline{Y}(\tau_1))^{-1}\,\overline{Y}^T(\tau_1)\,\dot{Y}(\tau_1);-Y_t^T\,\dot{Y}_t=\overline{D}_t=\begin{Vmatrix}\overline{D}_{11},\overline{D}_{12}\\\overline{D}_{21},\overline{D}_{22}\end{Vmatrix},$$

$\overline{D}_{11}$=2exp(12t)– 2.2exp(11t)– 1.8exp(t),

$\overline{D}_{12}=\overline{D}_{21}$=3(exp(12t)– 2.2exp(11t)+0.2exp(t)),

$\overline{D}_{22}$=10exp(12t)– 19.8exp(11t)– 0.2exp(t).

Finally, the elements of the identified matrix are determined by the relations

$$A_{11}(\tau_1+0)=\frac{2\exp(12\tau_1)-2.2\exp(11\tau_1)-1.8\exp(\tau_1)}{\exp(12\tau_1)-2\exp(11\tau_1)-2\exp(\tau_1)+4},$$

$$A_{12}(\tau_1+0)=A_{21}(\tau_1+0)=\frac{3(\exp(12\tau_1)-2.2\exp(11\tau_1)+0.2\exp(\tau_1))}{\exp(12\tau_1)-2\exp(11\tau_1)-2\exp(\tau_1)+4},$$

$$A_{22}(\tau_1+0)== \frac{10\exp(12\tau_1)-19.8\exp(11\tau_1)-0.2\exp(\tau_1)}{\exp(12\tau_1)-2\exp(11\tau_1)-2\exp(\tau_1)+4},$$

with the numerical result for this matrix:

$$A\,(\tau_1+0)\cong\begin{Vmatrix}11.006,-0.00077\\ -0.00077,11.004\end{Vmatrix}\cong\begin{Vmatrix}11,0\\ 0,11\end{Vmatrix}.$$

Comparing both results for $A\,(\tau_1+0)$ we come to the conclusion that identification $A_t\forall t\in(\tau_1,T)$ with high precision (defined by a computation accuracy) does not depend on a chosen coordinate system.

The optimal processes on the second discrete interval:

$x_1(t,\cdot)$ =(2-exp(11(t-τ_1)) $x_1(\tau_1,\cdot)$, $x_2(t,\cdot)$=(2-exp(11(t-τ_1)) $x_2(\tau_1,\cdot)$,

are different only by their initial states ($x_1(\tau_1,\cdot)$, $x_2(\tau_1,\cdot)$).

The matrix A(τ_1+0) is identified at opposite sign of the initial A(-0).

The corresponding optimal processes have the forms

$x_1(t,\cdot)$ =(2-exp(0.7(t-τ_1)) $x_1(\tau_1,\cdot)$, $x_2(t,\cdot)$=(2-exp(11(t-τ_1)) $x_2(\tau_1,\cdot)$,

with τ_1 =0.193.

Let us build the phase trajectories of the dynamic model at both discrete intervals.

At the first, let us find these trajectories for the diagonalized system at t $\in(0,\tau_1)$:

$$\frac{dz_1}{dz_2}=-\frac{-\lambda^o{}_1}{-\lambda^0{}_2}\frac{z_1}{z_2},\quad z_2=\pm\,|\iota|z_1^{\frac{\lambda^o{}_1}{\lambda^0{}_2}},\quad \iota\in R^1,\quad \pm|\iota|=\frac{z_2(0,\cdot)}{z_1(0,\cdot)^{\frac{\lambda^o{}_2}{\lambda^0{}_1}}}.$$

The phase trajectories of that system (Figure 4.1.2) represent the ι -parametrical family of the curves with a singular tangle-point in (0,0). The phase picture (Figure 4.1.2a) is turned over the angle ψ , that is defined by the transformations

$$G_t=G=\begin{Vmatrix}\cos\psi,\sin\psi\\ -\sin\psi,\cos\psi\end{Vmatrix}\ \forall t\in(0,\tau_1),\quad G^{-1}=G^T,\ \det G=1.$$

We come to the following equations

$$z_t=G\,x_t\,,\quad \dot z_t=G\,\dot x_t=G\,\mathrm{A}(+0)(x_t+v_t)=G\,\mathrm{A}G^T\,(z_t+\bar v_t),\quad G\,\mathrm{A}G^T=\begin{Vmatrix}-\lambda^o{}_1,0\\ 0,-\lambda^o{}_2\end{Vmatrix}.$$

Let us determine ψ for the initial eigenvalues -$\lambda^o{}_1$=11,$-\lambda^o{}_2$=1.

We get the relations $G\,\mathrm{A}G^T$ =

$$=\begin{Vmatrix}((GA)_{11}\cos\psi+(GA)_{12}\sin\psi),(-(GA)_{11}\sin\psi+(GA)_{12}\cos\psi)\\ ((GA)_{21}\cos\psi+(GA)_{22}\sin\psi),(-(GA)_{21}\sin\psi+(GA)_{22}\cos\psi)\end{Vmatrix}=$$

$$=\begin{Vmatrix}11,0\\ 0,1\end{Vmatrix},\quad G\,\mathrm{A}=\begin{Vmatrix}(a_{11}\cos\psi+a_{21}\sin\psi),(a_{22}\sin\psi+a_{12}\cos\psi)\\ (-a_{11}\sin\psi+a_{21}\cos\psi),(-a_{12}\sin\psi+a_{22}\cos\psi)\end{Vmatrix},$$

$$a_{11}\cos^2\psi+a_{12}\sin 2\psi+a_{22}\sin^2\psi=11,$$

and the equations for obtaining the above angles

$$\frac{1}{2}(a_{22}-a_{11})\sin 2\psi + a_{12}\cos 2\psi = 0,$$

$$a_{11}\sin^2\psi - a_{12}\sin 2\psi + a_{22}\cos^2\psi = 1.$$

$$tg\,2\psi = 2\frac{a_{12}}{a_{22}-a_{11}} = -0.75,\quad \psi = \frac{1}{2}arctg\,2\frac{a_{12}}{a_{22}-a_{11}} + \frac{k\pi}{2},$$

$k=0,\pm 1,\pm 2,\ldots$ $\psi_1 = \psi|_{k=0} \cong -\frac{\pi}{2}$, $\psi_2 = \psi|_{k=-1} \cong -0.6\pi$, $\psi_3 = \psi|_{k=1} \cong 0.4\pi$.

From the same equations we get

$$\cos 2\psi = \frac{(11-1)(a_{22}-a_{11})}{(2a_{12})^2 + (a_{22}-a_{11})^2} = -0.8,$$

which leads to the equivalent expressions for ψ, because of the fulfillment of the equality $\cos^2 2\psi \equiv (1 + tg^2 2\psi)^{-1}$.

The phase picture in the initial coordinate system $(0\,x_1\ x_2)$ is given in Figures 4.1.2b-d. For building the phase trajectories at the second discrete interval, we will find the phase picture of the relation (1.5). We have the relations

$a_{11}(x_1+v_1)x_2 + a_{12}(x_2+v_2)x_2 = a_{21}(x_1+v_1)x_1 + a_{22}(x_2+v_2)x_1$; $a_{12}=a_{21}$;

(1.8) $a'_{11}x_1^2 + 2a'_{12}x_1x_2 + a'_{22}x_2^2 + 2a'_{13}x_1 + 2a'_{23}x_2 + a'_{33} = 0$; $a'_{11} = a_{21}$,

$a'_{12} = 1/2(a_{22}-a_{11})$, $a'_{22} = -a_{12}$, $a'_{13} = 1/2(a_{21}v_1 + a_{22}v_2)$,

$a'_{23} = -1/2(a_{21}v_2 + a_{11}v_1)$, $a'_{33} = 0$.

The line's equation (1.8) of the second order, after transferring the beginning of the proper coordinate system into the line center, acquires the form

$$a'_{11}(x'_1)^2 + 2a'_{12}x'_1x'_2 + a'_{22}(x'_2)^2 + \frac{I_3}{I_2} = 0,$$

where $x = x'_1 + x^o$, $x^o = (x_1^o, x_2^o)$ are the initial coordinates of the system $(0\,x_1\ x_2)$ in the coordinate system $(0\,x'_1\ x'_2)$, that satisfy the equations

$a'_{11}x_1^o + a'_{12}x_2^o + a'_{13} = 0$; $a'_{12}x_1^o + a'_{22}x_2^o + a'_{23} = 0$,

$$I_2 = \det\begin{Vmatrix} a'_{11}a'_{12} \\ a'_{12}a'_{22} \end{Vmatrix} = \det\begin{Vmatrix} a_{12}, 1/2(a_{22}-a_{11}) \\ 1/2(a_{22}-a_{11}), -a_{12} \end{Vmatrix} = \text{inv} = -25,$$

$$I_3 = \det\begin{Vmatrix} a'_{11}a'_{12}a'_{13} \\ a'_{12}a'_{22}a'_{23} \\ a'_{13}a'_{23}a'_{33} \end{Vmatrix} = \det\begin{Vmatrix} 3, 4, 1/2(3v_1+10v_2) \\ 4, -3, -1/2(3v_1+2v_2) \\ 1/2(3v_1+10v_2), -1/2(3v_1+2v_2), 0 \end{Vmatrix},$$

$$I_3 = -1/4(33v_1^2 + 327v_2^2 + 196v_1v_2) = \text{inv},$$

$$\frac{I_3}{I_2} = -0.01(33v_1^2 + 327v_2^2 + 196v_1v_2).$$

After a trivial simplification, we get the equations

$$a''_{11}(x''_1)^2+a''_{22}(x''_2)^2+\frac{I_3}{I_2}=0,\quad \begin{Vmatrix} x''_1 \\ x''_2 \end{Vmatrix}=\begin{Vmatrix} \cos\vartheta, \sin\vartheta \\ -\sin\vartheta, \cos\vartheta \end{Vmatrix}\begin{Vmatrix} x'_1 \\ x'_2 \end{Vmatrix},\ ctg2\vartheta=$$

$$=\frac{a'_{11}-a'_{22}}{2a'_{12}}=0.75;\ I_2=\text{inv}<0;\ I_2=\det\begin{Vmatrix} a''_{11}a''_{12} \\ a''_{12}a''_{22} \end{Vmatrix}=\det\begin{Vmatrix} a''_{11}0 \\ 0a''_{22} \end{Vmatrix}=a''_{11}a''_{22}<0,$$

$$a''_{11}=a'_{12}\sin 2\vartheta+\frac{a'_{11}-a'_{22}}{2}\cos 2\vartheta,\quad a''_{11}\overset{def}{>}0,$$

$$a''_{22}=-a'_{12}\sin 2\vartheta-\frac{a'_{11}-a'_{22}}{2}\cos 2\vartheta,\quad a''_{22}\overset{def}{<}0.$$

At $I_3<0$ we obtain the canonical equation of hyperbola with respect to the real axis $(0'x''_1)$ and the imaginary axis -$(0'x''_2)$ (Figure 4.1.3a.):

$$(1.9)\quad \frac{(x''_1)^2}{[(\frac{I_3}{I_2a''_{11}})^{\frac{1}{2}}]^2}-\frac{(x''_2)^2}{[(\frac{I_3}{-a''_{22}I_2})^{\frac{1}{2}}]^2}=1.$$

At $I_3>0$ we come to the hyperbola with respect to the real axis $(0'x''_2)$ and the imaginary axis -$(0'x''_1)$ (Figure 4.1.3b):

$$(1.10)\quad \frac{(x''_1)^2}{[(-\frac{I_3}{I_2a''_{11}})^{\frac{1}{2}}]^2}-\frac{(x''_2)^2}{[(\frac{-I_3}{-a''_{22}I_2})^{\frac{1}{2}}]^2}=-1.$$

At $I_3=0$ we get a couple of the equations that satisfy to the coordinate points, located on the straight lines, representing the asymptotes of the hyperbolas (1.9,10) (Figure 4.1.3c):

$$(1.11)\quad \frac{x''_1}{(\frac{1}{a''_{11}})^{\frac{1}{2}}}+\frac{x''_2}{(\frac{1}{-a''_{22}})^{\frac{1}{2}}}=0,\quad \frac{x''_1}{(\frac{1}{a''_{11}})^{\frac{1}{2}}}-\frac{x''_2}{(\frac{1}{-a''_{22}})^{\frac{1}{2}}}=0.$$

On the coordinate plane $(0'x''_1x''_2)$, the phase picture of the relation (1.5) represents a couple of the conjugated hyperbolas with the asymptotes, defined by the equation (1.11), and the saddle singular point (0,0) (Figure 4.1.3d).

The phase trajectories of the dynamic system at the second discrete interval, after switching the control, are determined by the equations

$$\dot{y}_1(t,\cdot)=A_{11}(\tau_1+0)y_1(t,\cdot)=\lambda_1^1y_1(t,\cdot),\ t\in(\tau_1,T),$$

$$\dot{y}_2(t,\cdot)=A_{22}(\tau_1+0)\ y_2(t,\cdot)=\lambda_2^1\ y_2(t,\cdot),\ \lambda_1^1=\lambda_2^1,;$$

$$\frac{dy_1}{dy_2}=\frac{y_1}{y_2},\ y_1=\pm|C|y_2,\ C\in R^1,\ \pm|C|=\frac{y_1(\tau_1,\cdot)}{y_2(\tau_1,\cdot)}=\frac{x_1(\tau_1,\cdot)}{x_2(\tau_1,\cdot)};$$

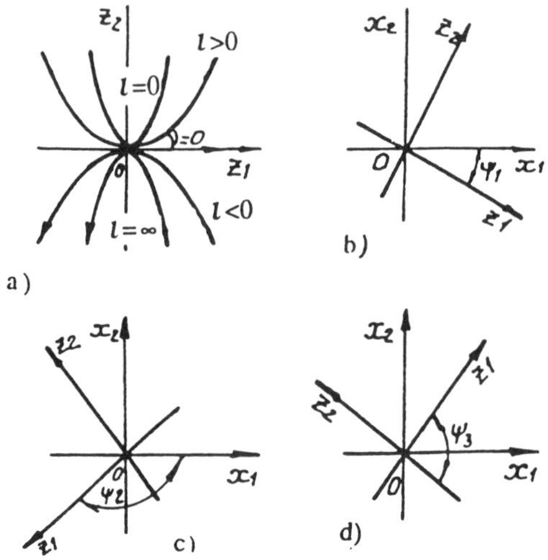

Figure 4.1.2 (a-d). The phase picture of the dynamic model in the initial coordinate system at the first discrete interval.

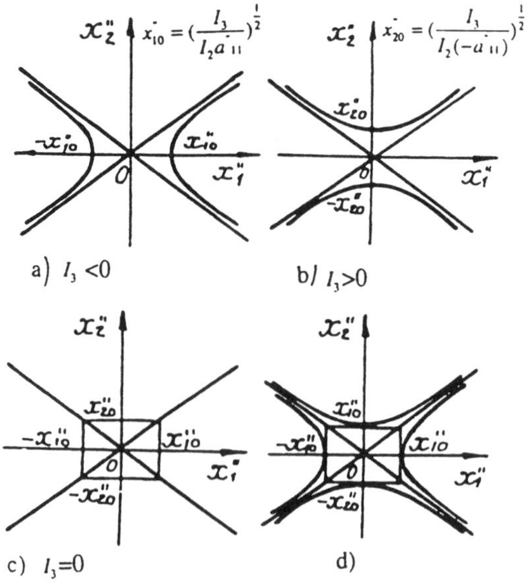

Figure 4.1.3.The phase picture of the dynamic model (a-c) and the relation (4.1.5)(d) at the second discrete interval after transformation of the initial coordinate system.

$x_1 + v_1 = \frac{x_1(\tau_1,\cdot)}{x_2(\tau_1,\cdot)}(x_2 + v_2)$. A family of straight lines of the parameter $\frac{x_1(\tau_1,\cdot)}{x_2(\tau_1,\cdot)}$ at $t \in (\tau_1, T)$, represents the phase picture according to the equation:

(1.12) $x_1 = \frac{x_1(\tau_1,\cdot)}{x_2(\tau_1,\cdot)} x_2$.

The phase picture of the equality

(1.13) $\frac{\dot{x}_1(\tau_1,\cdot)}{x_1(\tau_1,\cdot)} = \frac{\dot{x}_2(\tau_1,\cdot)}{x_2(\tau_1,\cdot)}$, $t \in (\tau_1, T)$

has the form $A_{22}(\tau_1 + 0)\, v_2\, (\tau_1 + 0) x_1\, (t,\cdot) = A_{11}(\tau_1 + 0)\, v_1\, (\tau_1 + 0) x_2\, (t,\cdot)$;

$x_1 = \frac{x_1(\tau_1,\cdot)}{x_2(\tau_1,\cdot)} x_2$.

At the second discrete interval, the phase pictures of the dynamic model (1.12) and the relation (1.13) coincide. Because of this, their relative phase speeds are equal at $t \in (\tau_1, T)$, when the dynamic system the differential constraint, following from stochastics, is imposed on extremals. The comparison of the Figures 4.1.2, 4.1.3 for (1.12,1.13) illustrates the geometrical interpretation of the constraint action. At the moment of applying the control, the phase pictures of the dynamic model and the relation (1.5) coincide. That leads to the renovation of the matrix $A\,(\tau_1 + 0)$ with respect to the matrix $A\,(\tau_1 - 0)$, and it creates the new model's peculiarities.

Finally we get the hierarchy of the model's eigenvalues.

Let us determine the jump of the phase speed at the discrete moment:

$$\delta\dot{x}\,(\tau_1,\cdot) = \dot{x}\,(\tau_1 + 0,\cdot) - \dot{x}\,(\tau_1 - 0,\cdot) = -A\,(\tau_1 + 0)\, x\,(\tau_1,\cdot) -$$
$$-A\,(\tau_1 - 0)(x\,(\tau_1,\cdot) + v_0) = -(A\,(\tau_1 + 0) + A\,(\tau_1 - 0))\, x\,(\tau_1,\cdot) +$$
$$+2A\,(\tau_1 - 0)\, x_0 = [-(A\,(\tau_1 + 0) + A\,(\tau_1 - 0)\,\overline{Y}(\tau_1) + 2A\,(\tau_1 - 0))]\, x_0\,.$$

Remark. The values $\varpi_i = \lim_{t\to\infty} \frac{1}{t} \ln \frac{\delta x_i(x_i,t)}{\delta x_i(x_i,0)}$ define the Liapunov's indicators (as an averaged speed of the exponential divergence of the nearest trajectories), which positive sum is connected with Kolmogorov's differential entropy h_ϖ: $h_\varpi = \sum_i \varpi_i$.

For the classical integrated Hamiltonian systems, all indicators equal to zero and $h_\varpi \equiv 0$ •. From the phase speed expressions and the previous relations we have

$$A\,(\tau_1 + 0) + A\,(\tau_1 - 0) \cong \begin{Vmatrix} 13,3 \\ 3,21 \end{Vmatrix}, \quad 2A\,(\tau_1 - 0) = \begin{Vmatrix} 4,6 \\ 6,20 \end{Vmatrix};$$

$$\begin{Vmatrix} 13,3 \\ 3,21 \end{Vmatrix} \overline{Y}(\tau_1) + \begin{Vmatrix} 4,6 \\ 6,20 \end{Vmatrix} = K = \begin{Vmatrix} K_{11}, K_{12} \\ K_{21}, K_{22} \end{Vmatrix}, \quad \delta\dot{x}\,(\tau_1,\cdot) = K\, x_0\,,$$

K_{11}=2.2exp(11 τ_1)+10.8exp(τ_1), $K_{12} = K_{21}$=6.6exp(11 τ_1)-3.6exp(τ_1),
K_{22}=19.8exp(11 τ_1)+1.2exp(τ_1)-22.

At τ_1=0.7884, we obtain the following K numerical results

$$K=\begin{Vmatrix} 12848.65, 38532.75 \\ 38532.75, 115602.66 \end{Vmatrix},$$

that determine the values of the jumps:

$$\delta\dot{x}_1(\tau_1,\cdot)=51381.4,\ \delta\dot{x}_2(\tau_1,\cdot)=154135.41 \text{ at } x_0=\begin{bmatrix}1\\1\end{bmatrix}.$$

For the solution of the consolidation problem, we turn the initial coordinate system on angle φ to find a such coordinate system $(0 z_1^{'} z_2^{'})$, where the optimal processes are nondistinguished. Using the relations for consolidation, we get

$$\varphi_{12}=\varphi=\operatorname{arctg}\left(\frac{x_2(\tau_1,\cdot)-x_1(\tau_1,\cdot)}{x_2(\tau_1,\cdot)+x_1(\tau_1,\cdot)}\right)+k\pi,\ k=0,\pm 1,\pm 2,\ldots,$$

$$x(\tau_1,\cdot)=\begin{Vmatrix} x_1(\tau_1,\cdot) \\ x_2(\tau_1,\cdot) \end{Vmatrix}=\begin{Vmatrix} 5839.294, 17511.88 \\ 17511.88, 52537.66 \end{Vmatrix}\begin{bmatrix}1\\1\end{bmatrix}=\begin{Vmatrix} 23351.17 \\ 70049.54 \end{Vmatrix}, \text{ at } x_0=\begin{bmatrix}1\\1\end{bmatrix}$$

and the angle $\varphi=\operatorname{arctg}\dfrac{46698.37}{93400.71}+k\pi \cong \operatorname{arctg}0.5+k\pi,\ \varphi|_{k=0}\cong 0.1472\pi$.

The considered results explain the procedure and the numerical solutions of the joint optimal control, identification and consolidation problems.

Example 2. Let us illustrate the reduction of the vector's $x=\{x_i\}$ dimension by using the DC equation applied to the entropy square-approximation function:

$$\Delta S(x,t)=-1/2\, x^T h(t)\, x,\ \partial\Delta S/\partial x_i=-\sum_{k=1}^{n} h_{ik}\, x_k,\ \partial X_i/\partial x_k=-h_{ik},$$

The DC for this function acquires the form of the systems equations

$$2\left(-\sum_{j=1}^{n} h_{ij}\, x_j \sum_{m=1}^{n} h_{km}\right)=h_{ik},\quad h=r^{-1},\ i, k=1,\ldots, n,$$

where n variables of $\{x_k\}$ are connected by n equations in the form $2X_i^{\ 2}=h_{ii}$, and the considering equations: $2X_i\ X_k=2X_i\ X_k=h_{ik}=h_{ki}$ are connected by the $m=(n^2-n)/2$ constraint. It is just m constraints requires for the pairwise connection of all the n variables C_m^2=n(n-1)/2 which leads to the linear dependencies of all [1] macrovariables (at a finite τ_n when DC is imposed on all information forces X_i,, and the number of independent coordintes $\{x_i\}$ is reduced to m=1).

Example 3. Let the object's model at microlevel is described by the equation $\ddot{\tilde{x}}+\alpha\dot{\tilde{x}}+\alpha\beta\tilde{x}\dot{\tilde{x}}+c\tilde{x}+\tilde{u}=0$, with the random parameters α, β, c, where α, c have the continuous uniform distributions with the means α_o, c_o accordingly.

Writing the model in systemic form, we get

$$\dot{\tilde{x}}_1=\tilde{x}_2,\ \dot{\tilde{x}}_2\ -c\tilde{x}_1-\alpha\,\tilde{x}_2-\alpha\,\beta\,\tilde{x}_1(\tilde{x}_2+\tilde{v}),\ \alpha\,\beta\,\tilde{x}_1\,\tilde{v}=\tilde{u}.$$

The control $\tilde{v}$ are chosen from the condition of uncoupling correlation's:
$M[\alpha\beta\tilde{x}_1(\tilde{x}_2+\tilde{v})^2]=\beta M[\alpha]M[\tilde{x}_1]M[(\tilde{x}_2+\tilde{v})^2]=\alpha_o\beta M[\tilde{x}_1]M[(\tilde{x}_2+\tilde{v})^2]$,
that can be fulfilled at the DPs of the control jumping. Then the matrix $R(\tau_i)$ identifies the above operator. The macromodel of the microlevel equations

$$\dot{x}_1 = x_2\frac{\dot{x}_1}{x_1}, x_1 = M[\tilde{x}_1], x_2 = M[\tilde{x}_2],\ \dot{x}_2 = -(c_o\frac{x_1}{x_2} + \alpha_o\beta\ x_1 + \alpha_o),$$

$u=-(c_o\frac{x_1}{x_2}v + \alpha_o\beta\ x_1 v + \alpha_o v)$, is identified by the equations

$$\begin{Vmatrix}\dot{x}_1\\ \dot{x}_2\end{Vmatrix} = \begin{Vmatrix}R_{11}, 0\\ 0, R_{22}\end{Vmatrix},\ R_{11} = \frac{\dot{x}_1}{x_1} = \frac{x_2}{x_1},\ R_{22} = \frac{\dot{x}_2(\tau)}{x_2(\tau)+v} = -(c_o\frac{x_1}{x_2} + \alpha_o\beta\ x_1(\tau) + \alpha_o).$$

Example 4. Optimal synthesis for the nonlinear object's model:
$\ddot{x} - \exp(-x)\dot{x} + \alpha\ \dot{x} + u = 0$
at random initial conditions $x(0)$, $\dot{x}(0)$. Using the indications
$x_1 = \exp(-x), x_2 = \dot{x}$
and the controls $(u_1, u_2) = u$, we come to the system:
$\dot{x}_1 = -x_2\ x_1 + u_1$, $\dot{x}_2 = (x_1 - \alpha)x_2 + u_2$, the equation for the discrete moments:
$\lambda_1(\tau) = x_2(\tau) = x_1(\tau) - \alpha = \lambda_2(\tau)$ and the optimal control. functions:
$u_1(\tau) = -2\dot{x}_1(\tau) = 2x_2(\tau)x_1(\tau)$, $u_2(\tau) = -2\dot{x}_2(\tau) = -2(x_1(\tau) - \alpha)x_2(\tau)$.

Extention the IMD optimization methodology

The IMD approach leads to a solution of both on the optimal problem for information functional and the Caushy (Boundary-value) problem for a many dimensional dynamic object. Comparing Bellman's method of dynamic programming, the IMD achieves the solution of "bottleneck"-dimensional problem by successive consolidating the model dimension into a single upper level node of the IN. Some optimal problem contains strong limitations on the admissible value and total number of external control $U \in \Omega$.

Let us outline a solution this problem.

Suppose there is only one external control U limited by its maximal value $U_m \in \Omega$ for an initial n-dimensional macro model with a given spectrum of eigenvalues A= $\{\lambda_{io}\}$. The model control function $\hat{U}$=Av can be found for the final DI (τ_n): $\hat{U}(t,\tau_n) = \lambda_n(\tau_n)v_n(\tau_n)$ and can be reduced to an admissible external control $U_m \in \Omega$ using a simple control relation $U_n = \hat{k}\ \hat{U}(t,\tau_n)$, where the coefficient $\hat{k} = U_m / \hat{U}$ is applied to all model's controls at each DI.

We obtain a new sequence of the model controls $U_i = \hat{k}\lambda_i v_i, i = 1,\dots,n$.

To get only one external control at each discreet interval we need, at first to find the vector sum of these controls

$$U_i^* = \sum_q U_{iq} = \hat{k}\lambda_i v_i, i = 1,\dots,n, q = 1,\dots,m$$

at each discreet (where q is the number of different λ_i for each discrete interval), and then to find the equivalent projection of this vector into a such coordinate axis, where only one external control could be applied. Finally, we get the sequence of one-dimensional external controls $U_i(t,\tau_i)$, applying at each DI as an equivalent of the IMD model's controls. To limit each of these controls (from the sequence) by the maximal value U_m, we can use a new coefficient $\hat{k}_i = U_m / U_i$ at each DI, finding the admissible one- dimensional control $U_\Omega = U_m(t,\tau_i)$.

Let us outline the solution of more general optimization problem with a given performance functional in form $I = \int F(\hat{x}, \dot{\hat{x}}, t)dt$.

Suppose we formulate this problem as a sequential solution of two variation problems: the Euler-Lagrange problem for functional I, and the IMD optimal problem for the informational functional S.

This assumption will join the classical variation problem solution with the IMD solution of the consolidating, and Boandary-value problems.

Both extremal systems (Euler-Lagrange equations for I functional extremals, and the IMD optimal macromodel), presented in the diagonal forms: $\dot{\hat{x}}_i = \hat{\lambda}_i \hat{x}_i$, i=1,...,m $\dot{x}_i = \lambda_i x_i$, i=1,...,n, generally have different dimensions n and m. By transforming the extremal equations into Hamiltonian forms, we may reduce the corresponding Hamiltonian $\hat{H}$ to the form, similar to the information Hamiltonian $H = \sum_{i=1}^{n} \lambda_i$: $\hat{H} = \sum_{i=1}^{m} \hat{\lambda}_i$.

Assuming an additivity of these Hamiltonians, the resulting Hamiltonian for both optimization problems $H_o = \hat{H} + H$ presents a sum of corresponding eigenvalues.

Applying of this condition consists of algebraic summing of the corresponding macromodel eigenvalues with the analogous eigenvalues of the Euler equations, that have the same dimension. Figure 4.1.4 illustrates summing both eigenvalues at such DI, when they have an equal dimension n-k=m. The above summing will change the moments of discretizations, internal and external controls. That procedure also helps to avoid the complications, connected with Bellman's dimensional problem. The main difference consists of finding specific discrete optimization intervals, defined by model's and performance's functional eigenvalues, comparing with the arbitrary DIs for other optimal methods, that use a discrete approximation.

4.1.3. Identification of the space distributed model

Let us consider the object with a structure of a matrix differential equation

$$(1.14)\ \frac{\partial x}{\partial t} = A\frac{\partial x}{\partial l}; A = A(x,t,l),$$

where x is vector of the state coordinates, l is a vector of the space coordinates.

This is a generalized form, applied for some equations of mathematical physics, as the diffusion, heat transfer, wave functions, Laplace's and Helmgoltz's equations.

The identification problem consists of restoration of the operator by observation of the equation's solutions in the form

(1.15) $x(t,l) = T_1 T_2 x_0;\ T_1 = T_1(t,l_0), T_2 = T_2(t_0,l)$,

with the random initial conditions $x_o = x(t_o, l_0)$, and a given probability density $p(x_o) = p_o$. The boundary conditions $x = x(t_o,\ l) = x(l)$ for the observed process, assume, are included naturally into equation (1.15).

At the first, we determine the operator of the ordinary differential equation

(1.16) $\dfrac{\partial x}{\partial t} = A_1 x\ ;\ A_1 = A_1(x,t,l)$,

which according to equation (1.15), takes the form

(1.17) $\dfrac{\partial x}{\partial t} = T_1' T_1^{-1} T_1 T_2 x_0\ ,\ T_1' T_1^{-1} = A_1\ ,\ T_1' = \dfrac{\partial}{\partial t} T_1$.

Using for the identification of equation (1.16) the relations

(1.18) $R_1 = M[x\,x^*]^{-1}\ M[x(\dfrac{\partial x}{\partial t})^*]$,

$M[x\,x^*] = M[T_1 T_2 x_0\ x_0^* (T_1 T_2)^*] = T_1 T_2 M[x_0\ x_0^*](T_1 T_2)^*$

with the symmetry conditions $M[x(\dfrac{\partial x}{\partial t})^*] = M[(\dfrac{\partial x}{\partial t}) x^*]$,

$M[x(\dfrac{\partial x}{\partial l})^*] = M[(\dfrac{\partial x}{\partial l}) x^*]$ and the solutions (1.15), we come to the equations

$M[x(\dfrac{\partial x}{\partial t})^*] = M[(T_1 T_2)^* x_0\ x_0^*](T_1 T_2)^* (T_1^{-1})^* T_2^{*\prime}]$.

The nonrandom functions can be taken out of the operation of mathematical expectation. We get the equality $R_1 = A_1$ from the relation

(1.19) $M[x(\dfrac{\partial x}{\partial t})^*] = T_1 T_2 M[x_0\ x_0^*](T_1 T_2)^* (T_1' T_1^{-1})^* = T_1' T_1^{-1} M[x\,x^*]$.

Let us determine the operator of the equation

(1.20) $\dfrac{\partial x}{\partial l} = A_2 x\ ;\ A_2 = A_2(l,t,x)$,

that can be written in the form

(1.21) $\dfrac{\partial x}{\partial l} = T_2' T_2^{-1} T_2 T_1^* x_0^*\ ;\ T_2' T_2^{-1} = A_2\ ,\ T_2' = \dfrac{\partial}{\partial t} T_2$.

By the substitution the solution of equation (1.15) into the relation

(1.22) $R_2 = M[x\,x^*]^{-1}\ M[x(\dfrac{\partial x}{\partial l})^*]$,

we obtain $M[x\,x^*] = T_1 T_2 M[x_0\ x_0^*](T_1 T_2)^*$, and

(1.23) $M[x(\frac{\partial x}{\partial l})^*]=T_2''T_2^{-1}M[x\, x^*]$, $R_2=T_2''T_2^{-1}=A_2$.

After substituting (1.16,20) into the initial equation, we come to the equality $A_1\, x$=A $A_2\, x$, which has to be satisfied for all nonzeroes x in (1.15,17,19,21,23).

Writing this equality in the form $A_1\, x\, x^*$=A $A_2\, x\, x^*$, we determine the unknown operator by formula A= $A_1\, A_2^{-1}$.

The operator A_2^{-1} can be identified directly using the relation

$$R_2^{-1}=M[x\, x^*]\{M[x(\frac{\partial x}{\partial l})^*]\}^{-1}.$$

If the operators depend on the state coordinates, then the extraction of the considered nonlinear functions is executed from the condition of uncoupling the time-space correlation's, for example, by applying the controls u(t, l)=u(t, l_o)u(t_o , l) to the object. For this purpose, we write the equation (1.16) in the form

$$\frac{\partial x}{\partial t}= A_1(x+v_1),$$

where $A_1 v_1$=u(t, l_o) is the time depending control, applied at the space point l_o of the space distribution; $v_1=v_1$ (t, l_o) is the control, reduced to the state coordinates x(t, l_o). By analogy, we write the equation for the space distributed controls $\frac{\partial x}{\partial l}=A_2(x+v_2)$, where $A_2 v_2$=u(t_o , l) is the control, applied at the moment t_o to the space distribution; $v_2=v_2$ (t_o , l) is the control, reduced to the state coordinates x(t_o , l). The operators (1.19,23) are identified in the process of optimal movement, at the first, by applying the optimal control u(t, l_o) at the fixed point (l_o), and then by the distribution of the controls as the function of l.

Such identification and optimal control are combined by time and space.

If the increments of the space coordinates become zeros, then we get the consolidated space model operator. If the increments of the time state coordinates become zeros, then we get the consolidated time model operator.

On the contrary, we will continue the identification procedure until we obtain the distributed model in the form (1.20). Some of the mass, heat transfer and chemical kinetic processes are described by the integral-differential equations:

(1.24) $$\frac{\partial x(l)}{\partial t}=\int_{l'} A(l,l')x(l')dl'.$$

To such a form can be also reduced the equations in partial derivations:

(1.25) $$\frac{\partial x}{\partial t}= divL\nabla X$$

with $x=x$(t, l), $X=X$ (t, l) as the vectors of conjugate coordinates, and L(x , l ,t) as a matrix function of the kinetic coefficients. At X=h x (with h as an inverse covariation function), the equation (1.25) acquires the form

(1.26) $\frac{\partial x}{\partial t} = \nabla L \nabla hx$,

where ∇ is a Hamilton operator in the equation for gradient, divergence : ∇X=grad X, ∇L=div L.

In particular, the equation (1.25) at constant L(l), h(l) leads to the generalized diffusion form equation with the operator R=$\frac{dr}{dt} r^{-1}$, r=M[$x\, x$*].

Transformation of the equation (1.26) to the form (1.24) is given in [2].

Following this transformation, we write the operator (1.25) in the form

$$\int_{l'} \nabla L \nabla hx \delta(l-l')dl' = \int_{l'} Adl' = \nabla L \nabla h,$$

where $\delta(l\text{-}l')$ is the three-dimensional δ-function. We identify the integral operator assuming that the solutions (1.24) are observed:

(1.27) $x = T_1\ T_2\ x_0{}^*$; $T_1 = T_1(t, l_0)$, $T_2 = T_2(t_0, l\ )$, $x_0 = x\,(t_0, l_0)$.

Using (1.27) we write the equation

(1.28) $\frac{\partial x}{\partial t} = A_0 T_1\ T_2\ x_0{}^*$, $A_0 = T_1{}' T_1{}^{-1}$,

which operator is identified by applying (1.17,19). We obtain the equalities

$$R_0 = A_0,\ R_0 = \mathrm{M}[x(l)x(l)^*]^{-1}\mathrm{M}[\frac{\partial x}{\partial t}(l)x(l)^*].$$

After equalization of (1.24) and (1.28), and integration by l of the both equality sides, we have $\int_l A_0 x dl = \int_l [\int_{l'} Adl']x\, dl$.

Integral equation $A_0 = \int_{l'} Adl'$ defines the unknown operator. For the variable l' we get A=-div A_0. The symmetry condition for (1.24) leads to the equetion

$$\frac{\partial R_0(l,l',t)}{\partial l} = \frac{\partial R_0(l',l,t)}{\partial l'}.$$

Example 1. Let us consider the distributed one-dimensional object, described by the heat-transfer equation

(1.29) $\frac{\partial x}{\partial t} = A\frac{\partial^2 x}{\partial l^2}$, $x = x_1$, $l = l_1$, $A = a^2$=Const

at given initial probability density and the known initial distribution $p(x_o) = p(x_o, l_o)$ along the line $x(t_o, l) = x(l)$, with the solution (1.29):

(1.30) $x(t,l) = x_o \exp(ikl - k^2 a^2 t)$.

The problem consists of restoration of the operator A. We find the solution by two steps. First, we identify the operator of the ordinary differential equation

$$\frac{\partial x}{\partial t} = A_1 x, A_1 = A_1(x,t,l):$$

(1.31) $R_1 = M[x(t,l)^2]^{-1} M[\frac{\partial x}{\partial t}(t,l)x(t,l)]$.

By substituting the solution (1.32) we obtain $R_1 = -k^2 a^2 = A_1$.

Then we identify the operator of the equation in its systemic form

$$\frac{\partial^2 x}{\partial t^2} = A_2 x:$$

(1.33) $\frac{\partial x_1}{\partial l} = r_{12} x_2$, $\frac{\partial x_2}{\partial l} = r_{21} x_1$, $x = x_1$, $\frac{\partial x_1}{\partial l} r_{12}^{-1} = x_2$.

At $r_{12} = r_{21}$, the symmetry condition for this operator:

$R_2 = \begin{Vmatrix} 0, r_{12} \\ r_{21}, 0 \end{Vmatrix}$, $\frac{\partial^2 x}{\partial l^2} = r_{12} r_{21} x_1$, $A_2 = r_{12}^2$, is fulfilled.

From which we find unknown operator of the initial equation

(1.34) $A = A_1 A_2^{-1} = a^2$.

Writing the system (1.33) in the form

$$\frac{\partial x_1}{\partial l} = x_2, \quad \frac{\partial x_2}{\partial l} = A_1 x_1,$$

we satisfy the symmetry condition at $A_2 = -k^2 = 1$, which leads us toward (1.34).

Example 2. The distributed object is described by one-dimensional wave equation

(1.35) $\frac{\partial^2 x}{\partial t^2} = A \frac{\partial^2 x}{\partial l^2}$, $A = c^2 = const$,

at the given initial conditions $x(t_o, l) = x(l)$, and the known initial probability density $p(x_o) = p(x(t_o, l_o))$. The solution to the equation has the form

(1.36) $x(t,l) = x(t_o, l_o) \exp(\pm ikl \pm ickt)$.

Let determine the operator of the system

$\frac{\partial x_1}{\partial l} = a_{12} x_2$, $\frac{\partial x_2}{\partial l} = a_{21} x_1$, $R_1 = \begin{Vmatrix} 0, a_{12} \\ a_{21}, 0 \end{Vmatrix}$, $a_{12} = a_{21}$,

which we represent by the analogy with (1.33) in the form

$\frac{\partial x_1}{\partial l} = r_{12} x_2$, $\frac{\partial x_2}{\partial l} = r_{21} x_1$, $R_2 = \begin{Vmatrix} 0, r_{12} \\ r_{21}, 0 \end{Vmatrix}$, $r_{12} = r_{21}$.

using the (The second equation we write

Using the relations (1.20), (1.31) and the solutions (1.36), we get the solutions

$R_1 = \begin{Vmatrix} 0, \pm ick \\ \pm ick, 0 \end{Vmatrix}$, $R_2 = \begin{Vmatrix} 0, \pm ik \\ \pm ik, 0 \end{Vmatrix}$.

Returning to the initial form of both equations, we come to the equations

$$\frac{\partial^2 x}{\partial t^2} = A_1 x, A_1 = a_{12}^2, \frac{\partial^2 x}{\partial l^2} = A_2 x, A_2 = r_{12}^2, A = A_1 A_2^{-1} = a_{12}^2 r_{12}^{-2} = c^2.$$

Example 3. The identification of integral- differential equation in the form

$$(1.37)\ \frac{\partial x}{\partial t}(l_1,t)=\int_{l_2} A(l_1,l_2,t)x(l_2,t)\,dl_2;\ \frac{\partial x}{\partial t}(l_2,t)=\int_{l_1} A(l_1,l_2,t)x(l_1,t)\,dl_1$$

at given initial probability distribution $p[x(l_1^o,l_2^o,0)]=p_o$.

At the first, we identify the operators $1/2\int_{l_1}\int_{l_2}\dot{r}_1(l_1,t)r_1^{-1}(l_1,l_2,t)dl_2dl_1=\int_{l_1}R_1dl_1$,

$1/2\int_{l_2}\int_{l_1}\dot{r}_2(l_2,t)r_2^{-1}(l_1,l_2,t)\,dl_1dl_2=\int_{l_2}R_2dl_2$, using the relations

$r_1(l_1,l_2,t)=M[x(l_2,t)x^*(l_1,t)]$, $r_2(l_1,l_2,t)=M[x(l_1,t)x^*(l_2,t)]$,

$r_1(l_1,t)=M[x(l_1,t)x^*(l_1,t)]$, $r_2(l_2,t)=M[x(l_2,t)x^*(l_2,t)]$

and the solution of the system (1.37) in the form $x(l_1,t)=x_1$, $x(l_2,t)=x_2$.

At computation the functions

$$\frac{\partial r_1}{\partial t}(l_1,t)=2M[\frac{\partial x}{\partial t}(l_1,t)x^*(l_1,t)],\ \frac{\partial r_2}{\partial t}(l_2,t)=2M[\frac{\partial x}{\partial t}(l_2,t)x^*(l_2,t)],$$

we use the initial equation forms and their solutions. We have the equation

$$\frac{\partial r_1}{\partial t}(l_1,t)=M\{[\int_{l_2} A(l_1,l_2,t)x(l_2,t)\,dl_2]x^*(l_1,t)\}.$$

Because $x(l_1,t)$ does not depend on l_2, we may enter it under the integral sign. Then the last relation has a form

$$\frac{\partial r_1}{\partial t}(l_1,t)=M\{[\int_{l_2} A(l_1,l_2,t)x(l_2,t)x^*(l_1,t)dl_2]\}.$$

Because $A(l_1,l_2,t)$ is a nonrandom function (as well as the dl_2),we may write

$$\frac{\partial x}{\partial t}(l_1,t)=\int_{l_2} A(l_1,l_2,t)M[x(l_2,t)x^*(l_1,t)]dl_2],$$

$$\int_{l_1}R_1dl_1=\int_{l_1}\int_{l_2}A_1(l_1,l_2,t)M[x(l_2,t)x^*(l_1,t)]M[x(l_2,t)x^*(l_1,t)]^{-1}dl_2dl_1=$$

$$=\int_{l_1}\int_{l_2}A_1(l_1,l_2,t)dl_2dl_1,$$

$$\int_{l_2}R_2dl_2=\int_{l_2}\int_{l_1}A_2(l_1,l_2,t)M[x(l_1,t)x^*(l_2,t)]M[x(l_1,t)x^*(l_2,t)]^{-1}dl_1dl_2=$$

$$=\int_{l_2}\int_{l_1}A_2(l_1,l_2,t)dl_1dl_2,$$

and we can get the sought operators from the relations

$$\frac{\partial R_1}{\partial l_2}=A_1(l_1,l_2,t),\ \frac{\partial R_2}{\partial l_1}=A_2(l_1,l_2,t).$$

The symmetry conditions in the form $A_1(l_1,l_2,t)=A_2(l_1,l_2,t)$ and the equations for R_1, R_2 lead to the equalities

$$\frac{\partial R_1}{\partial l_2}=\frac{\partial R_2}{\partial l_1},\quad \frac{\partial[\int_{l_1}\dot{r}_2(l_2,t)r_2^{-1}(l_1,l_2,t)dl_1]}{\partial l_1}=\dot{r}_2(l_2,t)r_2^{-1}(l_1,l_2,t)=$$

$$d_2=d_1=\dot{r}_1(l_1,t)r_1^{-1}(l_1,l_2,t)=\frac{\partial[\int_{l_2}\dot{r}_1(l_1,t)r_1^{-1}(l_1,l_2,t)\,dl_2]}{\partial l_2},$$

which determines the equalization of the local operators d_1, d_2 at the DPs, preceding their subsequent cooperation [3-6].

REFERENCES

1. Lerner V. S. *Special Chapters to the Course" Optimal and Self-Controlled Systems,*"Kishinev: KPI-press, 1977.

2. Achieser N. I., Glasman I. M. *Linear Operator Theory in Gilbert's space,* Moscow: Nauka, 1968.

3. Lerner V. S. "Identification of the space distributed objects", *Dynamics of Systems,* 1981, 15: 63-72.

4. Lerner V. S. "The controlled Dynamics of Irreversible Processes and their Optimization," *Dynamics of Systems,* 1981: 74-107.

5. Lerner V. S., Donin A.B. "Building the mathematical models for some complex systems based on physical approach,"*Identification of automatic objects,* 1972; 49:3-22.

6. Lerner V. S. "Method of combination the identification and optimization for complex systems,"*The Correlation Extremal control systems,* Tomsk: University Press, 1979: 261-265.

4.2. DATA MODELING AND COMMUNICATIONS

4.2.1. The theoretical optimal encoding-decoding using the IN structure

Let us design the Huffman code based on the probability distribution P{ $p(i)$ }(i=1-N) with the corresponding entropy

$$H(p(i))=-\sum_{i=1}^{N} p(i)\log p(i).$$

The Huffman code is the prefix (instantaneous) code which codeword lengths satisfy to the Kraft inequality over an alphabet of size D [1]:

$$\sum_{i=1}^{N} D^{-l(i)} \leq 1.$$

The Huffman coding procedure generates an optimum code with minimum *average* codeword lengths L equal to the entropy of distribution $\{p(i)\}$: L= H($p(i)$).

The specified set of codewords has the optimal lengths l_i *=$-\log_D p(i)$ (that could yield the noninteger values) with a minimal average codelength l_i=L/N equal to differential entropy of the distribution H/N=h. The IN represents an optimal code structure, evaluated by the total entropy S=**a** (γ)**n**. If we equalize the entropy of the encoding probability distribution $H\{p(i)\}$ with S(γ ,**n**), we may use the IN optimal code to encode the data with probability distribution $\{p(i)\}$, assuming N=**n**. Then we come to the average optimal code length l=**a**(γ), where l is proportional to differential entropy $h = H / \ln N$. Using relation $h(\gamma)$= **a**(γ) gives an opportunity for additional decreasing of optimal number of bits per symbol, exceeding the limit defined by the above h value. The IN code is also the optimal prefix code, that satisfies the Kraft inequality [1], and the IN set of codelengths is expressed by the values of $\{\alpha_i^t(\gamma)\}$. If the initial data $\{A_i\}$ are ranged in a descending probability order $\{p(i)\}$, then each $A_i(p(i))$ will be represented by the codelengths $\alpha_i^t(\gamma)$, and each codelength is expressed as the function of γ. Changing γ will transfer this codelength set to another set with other initial entropy $H(p(i))$. But for each data set $\{A_i(p(i))\}$ the sequence of codelength set is a unique encodable and decodable. Let us define a *fixed-length optimal* code(*FL*), in which codeword length $l(i)$ is constant and proportional to the entropy H of code source symbols (Data) with the alphabet size D equal to the number N of source symbols: $l(i) = H / \ln N$. The FL code could be generated by the N letters of a source code, whose entropy is equal to the entropy of the initial data H. Such code is an *equal entropy* *FL* code. The *FL* constant codeword length

$l(i)$ is determined by the different permutations of the N code letters that encode all N initial data symbols $A_i(p(i))$. From the total number of possible permutations Per=N! , the *FL* code uses N × N code letters. The equal entropy *FL* code is a unique code applicable for different probability distributions.

Proposition 1. The optimal FL codes, encoding different probability distributions, are proportional to the corresponding entropies and the logarithms of the distribution dimensions.

Proof. Let us consider the optimal codes, encoding the probability distributions P(p) and P(q) with the corresponding alphabet sizes D(p)=D, and D(q)=Q, and the different code word lengths $\{l(i)(p)\}$, $\{l(i)(q)\}$. Each optimal code letter is independent, characterized by equal probability: P(D)=1/D and P(Q)=1/Q accordingly, with the optimal code length set:

$\{l(i)(p) = -\ln(p_i)/\ln D\}$ and $\{l(i)(q) = -\ln(q_i)/\ln Q\}$.

For the considered *FL* optimal codes, each set of codeword lengths is constant and equal to $l(i)(p) = H(p) / \ln N_p$, and $l(i)(q) = H(q) / \ln N_q$,

where the code alphabet numbers D= N_p ,Q= N_q are defined by the corresponding numbers of the distributions elements $\{p(i)\}$ and $\{q(i)\}$.

Therefore, the ratio of codeword lengths for the corresponding probability distributions is : $l(i)(p) / l(i)(q) = H(p) / \ln N_p / H(q) / \ln N_q$. ●

Corollary 1. If the entropies for the corresponding probabilities distributions are equal, the FL optimal codes are distinguished only by the probability dimensions N_p, N_q: $l(i)(p) / l(i)(q) = \ln N_p / \ln N_q$.

Corollary 2. Suppose, the N-dimensional data distribution is encoded by the FL optimal code represented by the equal entropy of the unique IN n-letter code, whose codeword length is formed by the permutations of the IN's code letters $\{l_i\}=\{\alpha_i^t(\gamma)\}$, *then the constant FL code word length is equal*

(2.1) $l = \mathbf{a}(\gamma) n / \ln N$.

Proof. For the data source entropy H and the code alphabet N, the optimal codeword length is $H / \ln N$. Let us encode this data using the equal entropy FL optimal code, represented by the permutations of the n of IN's letters measured by $\{l_i\}=\{\alpha_i^t(\gamma)\}$. For this code, the following equalities are true: H=S=$\mathbf{a}(\gamma)n$, where S is the entropy of appropriate IN with number of letter n, and the codeword length is equal to (2.1). ●

The possible permutations of n of the IN's letters can encode maximum of N=n! data letters. A sender supposes to transmit the above codeword length to a receiver *physically* if the receiver does not have the same *equal entropy IN*.

For the receiver to be able to restore the same IN, a sender needs to transmits to the receiver two of IN's parameters γ , and **n**. If the receiver creates the IN, whose entropy is equal to entropy of initial data, then it is not necessary to transmit *physically* the above code word length. The sender has to transmit only the sequence of $\{l_i\}$ numbers n × N , that encode the N initial data into n of the IN letters. The receiver will decode these numbers using the recreated equal entropy IN.

The above code word length would be transmitted in this case only virtually as a *virtual code*. The advantage of such transmission consists of separating the physical transmitted optimal code from the entropy of data sources.

Traditional optimal code is not separated from the entropy of initial data sources according to its average codeword length $\tilde{l} = H / \ln D$, or $l = \mathbf{a}(\gamma)n / \ln D$ for the IN code source, where for the traditional binary code D=2.

Comparing the physical *FL*'s code word length l with $\tilde{l}$ at the equal entropies we come to shortening of the codeword length in the ratio $l / \tilde{l} = \ln N / \ln D$, or $l / \tilde{l} = \log_2 N / \log_2 2 = \log_2 N$.

Corollary 3. Suppose the encoded distribution (according to Corollary 2) is transmitted using the N combinations of the n IN's letters, then the transmitted code word length is equal to

(2.2) $l_t = \ln n / \ln D$.

This result follows from the entropy of transmitted code equal $H_t = \ln n$, and the connection H_t to the optimal code word length l_t. ●

Corollary 4. At the fulfillment of the Corollary 3, the compression ratio r *of the transmitted code word length l_t to the IN's coded code word length l at the same alphabet is defined by the relation*

(2.3) r= $l / l_t = \mathbf{a}(\gamma)n / \ln n$.

Corollary 5. Both the virtual and its physical codes are the Kraft decodable if

(2.4) $\mathbf{a}(\gamma) \geq \ln N / n$.

Let us check the Kraft inequality for the both codes. For the code word $l = \mathbf{a}(\gamma)n / \ln N$, the Kraft inequality is $N N^{-l} \leq 1$, or $-l \ln N \leq -\ln N$, $\mathbf{a}(\gamma) \geq \ln N / n$. ● This inequality imposes some constraints on virtual coding.

For the maximal $\mathbf{a}(\gamma = 0.001) \approx 0.707$ the inequality $\ln N / n \leq \mathbf{a}(\gamma)$ leads to $N \leq 10$ at n=3. For the codeword length $l_t = \ln n / \ln D$ the Kraft inequality is $nn^{-l_t} \leq 1$, or $l_t \geq 1, n \geq \ln D, n \geq D$. The last inequality is fulfilled starting with binary code. ●

Example. At n=3-100, $\mathbf{a}(\gamma = 0.01) = 0.707$, the theoretical expected compression ratio according to formula (2.3) is increasing from 2.1 to 16.7. The virtual coding decreases the entropy of the optimal physical code at the same ratio, and therefore, it overcomes a limit of theoretical optimal coding. That can essentially improve the traditional compression methods. The virtual IN's coding has another advantage.

Let us introduce the IN's distance d_{ij} between any two code words from the sequences of $\{l_i\}_i^n$ numbers (for each fixed $\mathbf{a}(\gamma)$) as an information measure of these codewords neareness. The encoded sequence of $\{l_i, \ldots, l_j\}_i^n$ numbers for each of the N data $\{A_i\}_1^n$ describes a *path* through the IN nodes, evaluated by the distances between these nodes. Each code word (and corresponding data) is represented in the IN's measure, defined by the equal entropy value for the data and the code. From a possible encoded sequences of $\{l_i\}_i^n$ numbers (for each fixed $\mathbf{a}(\gamma)$), can be selected one ($l_1,\dots, l_n$) with all sequentially increasing l_i index numbers. The corresponding IN has a minimal total path distance determined by the optimal value of the entropy functional with the invariant $\mathbf{a}(\gamma)$. Such an encoding sequence ($l_1,\dots, l_n$) characterizes a *basic* IN for each $\mathbf{a}(\gamma)$, that is measured by a corresponding value of the MC complexity. All other code sequences are evaluated by the relative distances with the respect to the basic IN, that automatically introduces the complexity measure for each code and corresponding data set, useful for their constructive comparison. In terms of this informational measure, the code word and the data can be classified and characterized by their closeness and differences. The IN's path distance is an example of the Algebra Operations, defined by the IN's structure. For any two pathes l_i, l_j along the IN, the scalar distance between them is $d_{ij}=l_i-l_j=d_{ji}$, and the vector distance is : $\bar{d}_{ij}=\bar{l}_i-\bar{l}_j \neq \bar{d}_{ji}=\bar{l}_j-\bar{l}_i$.

The informational measure of a code could be useful for choosing the n-permutations of total N! to select the code words with the informational distances maximal between them. Such a code is a more error protective. The data measured by the minimal informational distances are more connected and informational bound.

It could help for revealing the mutual data connections in data analysis and searching procedures, and essentially for data compression. The IN distances reflect FL code.

Example. Let the data (A1, A2, A3, A4, A5) are represented by the basic equal entropy IN with the following distances between 5 nodes: $l_1 - l_2$=2, $l_2 - l_3$=3, $l_3 - l_4$=2.5, $l_4 - l_5$=1.5. And the *FL* codewords for corresponding data is A1: $l_1 l_2 l_3 l_4 l_5$ A2: $l_4 l_1 l_5 l_2 l_3$ A3: $l_1 l_3 l_2 l_4 l_5$ A4: $l_3 l_2 l_5 l_1 l_4$ A5: $l_5 l_3 l_4 l_2 l_1$.

Each code word characterizes a sequence of total distances for corresponding data : J1=9, J2=16.5 (J2*=-2.5), J3=15 (J3*=-2), J4=26.59 (J4*=2.5), J5=14 (J5*=-9).

In parenthesizes are given the total distances measured in vector's forms. These code words and the data are measured by the following relative values of macrosystemic complexity with respect to the complexity of basic IN: MC(J2/J1)=1.833, MC(J2*/J1)=-0.277, MC(J3/J1)=1.66, MC(J3*/J1)=-0.222, MC(J4/J1)=2.94, MC(J4*/J1)=0.277, MC(J5/J1)=1.55, MC(J5*/J1)=-1.

In terms of this measure, the initial data can be ranged and classified by their informative connections. (The vector's measured distances define the different MC complexities for these code words). The *transmitted* codewords for the virtual code are represented by a simple matrix of natural numbers (describing the ($l_1,\dots, l_n$) sequence) and are ranged according to the codewords informational measure:

$$\begin{vmatrix} A1 \\ A5 \\ A3 \\ A2 \\ A4 \end{vmatrix} \Rightarrow \begin{vmatrix} 12345 \\ 53421 \\ 41523 \\ 32514 \\ 13245 \end{vmatrix} \Rightarrow \begin{vmatrix} 1 \\ 1.55 \\ 1.66 \\ 1.83 \\ 2.94 \end{vmatrix} \text{ or } \begin{vmatrix} A1 \\ A5 \\ A3 \\ A2 \\ A4 \end{vmatrix} \Rightarrow \begin{vmatrix} 12345 \\ 32514 \\ 13245 \\ 41523 \\ 53421 \end{vmatrix} \Rightarrow \begin{vmatrix} 1 \\ 0.277 \\ -0.222 \\ -0.277 \\ -1 \end{vmatrix}$$

Example. Let the data sequence (A1, A2,A3,A4, A5) with entropy H=2.12 are represented by the IN with n=3, **a**(γ =0.5)=0.707 and by the permutations of $l_1 = 0.03$, $l_2 = 0.05$, $l_3 = 0.11$, forming the three-letter words: $l_1 l_2 l_3$, $l_1 l_3 l_2$, $l_2 l_1 l_3$, $l_3 l_1 l_2$, $l_2 l_3 l_1$. The corresponding distances and MCs are J1=0.08, J1*=-0.08, J2=0.14, J2*=-0.02, J3=0.1, J3*=-0.06, J4=0.1, J4*=0.06, J5=0.14, J5*=0.02; MC(J2/J1)=1.75, MC(J2*/J1*)= 0.25, MC(J3/J1)=1.25, MC(J3*/J1*)=0.75, MC(J4/J1)=1.25, MC(J4*/J1*)=-0.75, MC(J5/J1)=1.75, MC(J5*/J1*)=-0.25. The vector's measured distances will give the different values of the MC functions. If the given initial data sequence (A1, A2,A3,A4, A5) (with unknown probability distributions $P = \{p_i\}_1^5$) are encoded by the ranged sequence of the n-letter's words $l_1 l_2 l_3, l_2 l_1 l_3$, $l_3 l_1 l_2, l_1 l_3 l_2$, then the average code length is equal to (1.75× 2+1.25× 2+1)/5=1.4 bits, or using 1 bit to encode each of four MC's vector measured distances (for the above sequence of five data) we get 0.8 bits. Generally, using the (N-2) MC letters (N=n!) with 1 bit length each of them, we can get an average codeword length equal N-2/N bits approaching 1 bit for large N. This code word length does not depend on the data source entropy. For the theoretical minimum average code word length equal to differential entropy h of the data source, the expected compression ration is equal h/1=h. It means the virtual encoding theoretically is able to eliminate redundant information completely. Comparing with the optimal codelength equal to 2.12 bits, we get the MC's compression ratio~1.5 (or 2.65 for the vector measured complexities). Example. Suppose we are using n =3 virtual code with the IN's path vector measure to encode N=n!=6 data source letters: C,D,E, F,H,J. The three-letter code words are the followings: $l_1 l_2 l_3, l_2 l_1 l_3, l_1 l_3 l_2$ $, l_2 l_3 l_1, l_3 l_1 l_2, l_3 l_2 l_1$ with the corresponding ranged IN's path vector measures: -0.08,-0.06, -0.02, 0.02,0.06,0.08 that encodes the above data letters sequence. To start the transmission, a sender at first identifies the data code library, for example, by sending the string of N × 1 numbers located in opposite to each of the D number letters of a total possible alphabet. This string will also contain (D-N)× 0 bits located opposite to such of the D numbers, that are not represented by the considered N number data source. By receiving this string, sender will identify each of the N letters of data source. After receiving the IN parameters (**n** , γ) and the sequence of above MC code letters, the receiver would know both physical and virtual dictionary code for each of the N letters. Actually, by receiving only N letters (and using N=n!) the receiver can restore both the n-letter virtual code and compute the MC measure path codes for each of the N letters. The transmission of data message consists of sending only one the MC code for each N letter of the natural ANSII code. The receiver will decode the corresponding N letters using the own IN. This part of transmission works as optimal entropy compression. In addition, the IN Algebra Operations are able to encode the different coupled combinations of the N letters within the message. For example, the pair combinations of the above letters can be encoded as the following: CF=-0.1, FC=0.1, DE=-0.4, ED=0.4, DJ=-0.14, JD=0.14. In addition to the pair combinations, it is possible to compress some of the four and even the eighth combinations of these letters as following: CFDE=-0.5, FCED=0.5, DJDE=-0.54, JDED=0.54, EDDJ=0.26, DEJD=-0.26,DEFC=-0.3, EDCF=0.3, CFDEJDED=0.04, FCEDDJDE=0.04, FCEDJDED=1.04, CFDEDJDE=-1.04. Moreover, it would be sufficient to transmit only the above code numbers which can transfer the different text combinations of eighth, four, or two. During the communication, it is not necessary to transmit code of each message letter. We can transmit only the code of such letters that have not been transmitted before, and then, transmit the code of different combinations of these letters, using the corresponding IN's Algebra code. This part of compression works as the Lempel-Ziv code method. Traditional compression methods work with a sequence, which contains the pattern of repeating symbols. If we tried to compress a sequence that does not contain repeating pattern, we would need more bits to transmit, than if we had not performed any compression. The main advantage of the virtual IN's encoding, compared with existing compression methods, consists of the ability to compress nonrepeating symbols. If the above message example contains only the sequence of the letters C, F, D, J ,F, G we can transmit the different their concatenates from two to eighth. The compression ratio is 2:1 even though this sequence does not contain repeating symbols. With growing of coding sequence, the compression ratio is increasing. For this case, the IN's n dimension is found from relation n!=N, and a fixed γ is chosen from condition of simple and non ambiguous relations between the IN's code and the letter combinations. In our example: n=3, N=6, γ =0.001. This part of compression has a unique quality. We do not need to trasmit even the initial text at all, the receiver can restore it by getting only the IN code of the maximal available letter chains within current text, and by knowing the data library. Using the IN for the chain connection of data is the main feature of this methodology. Finally, the IN virtual encoding can compress both redundant and nonredundant message sequence, combining some features of Huffman and Lempel-Ziv methods. The ordered relations between the data (N_i) and the FL triple code:

$$N_1 \rightarrow (l_1, l_2, l_3), N_2 \rightarrow (l_2, l_3, l_1), \ldots,$$

$$N_k \rightarrow (l_k, l_{k+1}, l_{k+2}), \ldots, N_n \rightarrow (l_n, l_{n+1}, l_{n+2})$$

can avoid the transmission of both the FL and the IN's path codes. By getting the string of $N \times 1$ bits the receiver would know not only the relations between the data and the first FL code letters : $N_i \rightarrow l_i$, but also is able to restore the corresponding IN's path code. Using the ordered permuations of the FL triplet's code, could be sent only the first l_i number of each triple. The coding approach, using optimal IN, opens new ways of economical virtual encoding procedure with minimal length code words (See also ch.2.1.13). Described theoretical optimal methodology has the wide areas of practical implementations including data compression and encryption. Applied software package can identify IN whose entropy S is equal to entropy H of compressed data and build the FL code.

4.2.2. The waiting time in communication line

If there is a random sequence of n information sources with information flows (speeds) $\{\alpha_i\}, i = 1, \ldots, n$, which are ready to communicate through a single line, they have to wait a certain time T until the communication line becomes idle (to prevent a collision). An optimal evaluation of this time is an important problem in queuing systems [2]. Using IMD is possible to find the time T based on evaluating the total quantity information S anticipating for communication:

$$S = \sum_{i=1}^{n} \mathbf{a}_i(\gamma_i),$$

where $\mathbf{a}_i(\gamma))$ are the local invariants, defined by the parameter of uncertainty γ_i $(\frac{\alpha_i}{\alpha_{i+1}})$ of the ranged information sources. For an equal $a_i=\mathbf{a}$ with $S=\mathrm{n}\mathbf{a}$ and the averaged information speed $\alpha_i=\alpha$, the waiting time is $\mathrm{T}=S / \alpha = \mathrm{n}t^*$, where $t^* = t_i$ is the time to transfer the information flow α. For a particular source with information speed α_k the waiting time is $T_k=S / \alpha_k$.

The IMD approach determines a less waiting time to such source, that is able to communicate with more information speed within a given sequence of sources.

4.2.3. Acceptance of the Space Visual Information Structure

Let us consider the moving information source with a space speed $C_O(t)$ representing visual data. The problem is organizing the adequate process of transformating all the generated information into some acceptor, which can detect and distinguish the visual images. Suppose, the acceptor is capable of following the information source with some space speed $C^*(t)$ during some time interval t*; then, it stops for accumulation of the generated information during time interval $\hat{t}$, and after $t_o''=t^*+\hat{t}$ it repeats all its actions. For example, the acceptor is a human who reads some text that is moving with a space speed $C_O(t)$. A human can accept the text (moving his eyes following the text) with a speed $C^*(t)$ during t*, then he stops eyes for accumulation the information during $\hat{t}$, and repeats all procedure again. Time $\hat{t}$ defines a first part of short-term memory, that is connected with a process of observation and accumulation of the initial information.

The question is What are the functions $C^*(t)$, $t^*(t)$, $\hat{t}$ (t) for complete acceptation and accumulation of all information, generated by the moving source distributed in square S_O ? (We suppose that the space regions of generation (S_o) and acceptation (S^*) are equal: $S_o=S^*$) At our conditions, the generated information is distributed with volume speed $dV_o / dt=C_o S_o$ during $t_o''= t^*+\hat{t}$.

The acceptor's instant volume speed is $dV^* /dt = C^*(t)\, S^*$ during t^*.

The difference between these volumes defines the volume speed dV / dt, that can be generated during $\hat{t}$: $dV / dt = dV_o / dt - dV^* / dt = C_o S_o - C^* S^*$, or at $S_o=S^*$: $C^*(t)=C_o(t)-dV / Sdt$. The execution of condition $C^*(t)=0$ defines the t^*(t). We also require the complete transformation of all generated information into the acceptor at each t_O. It means, that equalization of the average volumes at t_0, and t^* leads to

$\int_{to} dVo / dt - \int_{t*} dV^* / dt = 0.$

By introduction the average speeds $\hat{C}_o$, $\hat{C}^*$, that satisfy equations $\int_{to} dVo / dt = \hat{C}_o t_0$, $\int_{t*} dV^* / dt = \hat{C}^* t^*$,

we come to the relation for definitions $\hat{t} : \hat{t} = t^* (\hat{C}^* / \hat{C}_o - 1)$ for given $\hat{C}^*$, $\hat{C}_o$, and t^*. To better utilize these formulas, one should define the functions dV / Sdt, $C^*(t)$, $C_o(t)$, and the average speeds via the space-time equation of macro model (ch.1.3, 3.13).

Considering the equations for each triplet, we come to the following functions:

$dV / Sdt = \{l(t) - l_3) F^* / [(t_5 - t_3)^3 + (t_5 - t_4)^3 + F^*]\}$,

$C_o(t) = C(\mathbf{n} / (\mathbf{n} - 3)^2 [(l_6 - l_5) / (t_6 - t_5)]$,

where C is the maximal model speed, t_i, l_i are the time and spacial intervals DI; F* is the following function of t_i, and the DL-function of the indicated DIs:

$F^* = (t_7 - t_5)\sin(\pi / 2(t - t_6)) / (t_7 - t_5)^3 + \chi \sin(\pi / 2(t - t_6)) / (t_7 - t_6)^3$

$\chi = DL(t_7 - t_6)$, $DL(t_5 < t < t_6) = 0$, $DL(t_7 > t > t_6) = 1$ with a current spatial interval: $l(t) = (l_1 + l_2 + \ldots + l_k) / \mathbf{n} + C\, t (p(\mathrm{k}+1) + p(\mathrm{k}+2), \ldots, + p(\mathbf{n}))$; $p(\mathrm{k})$ is the parametrical function of $(l_i, \gamma, \mathbf{n})$. The affine transformations get developed according to their relative dynamic probability distribution for each DP(i):

$p(i) = F(o) / \mathbf{n}F(i)$; $F(i) = 4 - 4(\exp(\alpha_{io} t_i)\cos(\gamma \alpha_{io} t_i) + \exp(2\alpha_{io} t_i))$.

After substitution of the above functions, we obtain t^*, and by averaging the functions $C_o(t)$ and $C^*(t)$, we get $\hat{t}$. The developed computer program package utilizes these functions in real-time dynamics.

4.2.4. Data Classification and Modeling

The MC-function are useful for classifying and grouping data in terms of their macrosystemic complexity [ch.1.3.4]. The macromodel selects the information macrosystemic effectiveness of the data by separating their dynamics from randomness. Based on the identification equations (2.1.8), the procedure computes the correlations and their derivatives. The computing results are substituted into the macroequation (2.1.9). Application of the piece-by-piece method and boundary conditions leads to the solutions of the equation for each time interval of given random functions. The analytical exampes (ch.4.1) illustrates the procedure.

Finally the stochastic process is modeled by the hierarhy of differential macroequations (ch.4.1) that could be transffered into a single final macrostate.

REFERENCES

1. Cover Th. M., Joy A. Th. *Elements of Information Theory*, N.Y.: J.Wiley, 1991.
2. Kleinrock L. *Queuing Systems*, vol. 2, Computer Applications, J.Wiley, 1976.

4.3. COGNITIVE MODELING IN ARTIFICIAL INTELLIGENCE

4.3.1. Informational Structured Network for Cognitive Modeling

The IN can model a cognitive mechanism not only at the level of neuron circuits (as the brain hardware), but rather at the level of neuron software.

As a *tool* for a structural modelling of cognitive functions, the IN includes:

- the microlevel net of the neuron "circuits" generated information for macrolevel
- the macrolevel net of the macronodes as chaotic attractors for a structural representation of the associative (correlated) cooperative activities (with uncertainty depending on the attractor's volume)
- the time and space distributed hierarchy of informational dynamic processing; an ability to memorize the macro node processing by a stored sequence of the enclosed IN's nodes
- the hierarchical memory as an attribute of the IN dynamic structure
- the formal inner decentralized language, generated by the IN's interactions and communications
- an active acquisition and reflection of the environment with an ability to create the renovated dynamic structures of progressive growth
- a self-organizing, adaptive mechanism enables the evolution and preserving a robustness,which is stimulated by both external and internal interactions
- an ability of the IN's selective locations in different domains of the entire space, distributed cognitive structure (depending on the IN's dimensions)
- an ability to create both dynamic and the static node domains, that are not dependent on time and/or space; a limited life-time of the local IN, defined by a number of enclosed nodes (after that time expires, the local IN is disintegrated automatically).

4.3.2. Cognitive modeling concepts

Cognition and learning are modeled as the mutually complementary processes with a feedback of the cooperative self-organized response on reflected information. Learning consists of feeding the novelties, that stimulates cognition, creating the IN cognitive model. Cognition is associated with the recognition of correlated activities via the IN connections, cooperation, and macroprocessing, which stimulates learning, creating a learned concept as the highest IN's node.

The IN learning structure arises and develops as a dynamic reflection of accepted information (novelty), delivered from interaction with the environment.

Cognition depends on understanding the meaning of transmitted data.

Reflected data consists of two parts: objective one, describing some regularities, and subjective one, containing and transferring the individual specifics.

The meaning of an informative term can be understood by disclosing all logical connections and knowledge, encapsulated within the accepted terms. It means, the terms should be opened by revealing a chain of interlinked informational structures associated with them. The way of disclosing of an encapsulated informational structure depends on the personal cognitive structure, the individual level of knowledge [1]. Therefore, the meaning of specific information belongs to the individual and is not a formalized category, even though some common method of encapsulating information would be available. From a psychological point of view, the IN dynamic enclosed structure represents a model of thinking process with a corresponding sequence of thought elements (terms).

An information difficulty of the message recognition can be measured by the MC function evaluating the complexity of the symbols connections, their informational closeness, and the total node number within the network.

Each term within the IN, with the MC-measure, is evaluated by a corresponding *level* of information difficulty. The IN learning genetics includes an *ability* to generate a flexible creative IN's structure (depending on γ) in which dynamics, dimension, geometry, and MC complexity are determined by learning novelties.

Thinking is modeled on a process of communicating *between* the object's inner IN's. Modeling uses two kinds of *languages*: the external as a natural language, which recognition is based on parsing the language words according to informational content of the word parts, and the internal language, as a discrete code, generated by a particular IN node.

The understandable set of symbols should be invariant with respect to some group of transformations **G**(T), that defines the class. The n-classes with (hi, i=1-n) values of the relative entropy have to form a set of symbols (alphabets) for different formal languages. The first problem is to identify such n-classes of symbols, that are characterized by (n-1) different groups of transformations **G**(T). The most natural **G**(T) is the nonsingular transformation of symmetry. For two-dimensional (the plan projection of crystal structures) there are 17 different groups of symmetry, and 230 possible groups of symmetry for three-dimensional crystals [2].

The second problem is measuring each of groups of the transformations by appropriate entropy measure. A.N.Kolmogorov [3] introduced the entropy of transformation as the general invariant in theory of transitive transformations.

The theory groups and the transformations with invariant entropy measure give many examples of appropriate geometrical forms of the symbols. Based on that, we may expect an average number of symbols as an alphabet for different languages between 17 and 32, which is in agreement with some existing languages.

The natural language alphabet includes also sounds (phonetics) of letters (as a geometrical symbols). A harmony of sounds is also responsible for a sequence of symbols to form the words. A sound carries an additional (to grammar) redundancy, that allows correcting of the errors at transformation of at oral speech.

A joint combination of three components of natural language: geometry of symbols, their sound, and grammar coordinates the incoming information with individual information spectrum (with particular G*).

Macrostructure embodies initial symbols into information words by adding redundancies and preserving the long-term correlations. This ability can be measured by a value of maximal mutual information distance between different model symbols (also called transformation [4]).

The IMD transformation (Tr) is defined by the formula Tr=$(G^*)^{\mathbf{m}}$, where $\mathbf{m}$= $\mathbf{n}$/2-1 is the number of triplets, G*(γ) is a systemic model parameter for each triplet responsible for structural identity of a variety of information objects in cognitive model. For optimal self-organized model (**n**=96) the maximal number of different triplets, capable to cooperate, is 46. At **m**>46, the system decays after complete cooperation of all triplets, and creates uncorrelated fluctuations.

If each symbol transfers one triplet information, then transformation with G*=0.8 is $Tr=3.48 \bullet 10^{-5}$. Tr determines the maximal size block of different symbols, generated by macro dynamics in encoding information structure, as a string of alphabet letters in text, sequence of nucleotides in genetic code, modules in computer program, and so on.

A short-term memory, accumulating one triplet bound structure, has 7 nodes that correspond to the Miller's magical number [1]. Three unite complex information structure has 7 types of information symbols: $\mathbf{m}_o$= 3,7, 21, 63, 189, 567.

These numbers impose limitations on $\mathbf{m}_O$ computer code, language, text, genetic code, visual information, and so on. The sequence transfers much more of the total quantity information than the **m** sequence with equal number of triplets.

If these three-units elements form the self-organized system, then number of cooperated $\mathbf{m}_O$ in the system cannot exceed 46, since fluctuations might be possible. It means, the maximal number of different informative symbols, system parameter G*, and value Tr are preserved.

All cognitive models with the same G* are capable of understanding each other, even though the coding informational units are different.

Structural similarity is a basis of mutual communication, objective reflection the same information.

Each language preserves Zipf's law: logarithm of probability of various words in any language is proportional to logarithm of the most popular word-order.

The IN node's inherent zone of uncertainty carries an initial fuzziness for such a language. Instead of precise definition of symbols, the language would model an inherent human mind reflection of environment with uncertainty.

Operating with the IN nodes, as an Artificial Intelligence (AI) language, does not require of using traditional mathematical logic, forming a foundation of any computer language. Human way of thinking does not need the formal logic rules. The set of the assigned symbols makes sense by transferring a mining, if it forms the enclosed macrostructure, regardless of a context.

Existence the common systemic parameters for the enclosed symbol's sequence provides an evidence of forming of the IN structure.

Such a symbol's sequence (selected from all reflected ones) models a logical structure in human mind. An essence of this logic can be understood by opening the symbol's sequence and reconstructing the symbols terms in the macrostructure.

This procedure, we believe, models a human intelligence, which way of thinking and communicating is completely different from traditional AI and intelligent computers. Before starting any information operations, human being is trying to understand their mining. No one conventional computer, based on mathematical logic can do it. Assigning the appropriate symbols to IN nodes makes this language useful for nonmathematical computer applications in social science, arts, musics, human reasoning with emotions and so on. Under this way of thinking, lay both the IMD statistical micro- and dynamic macrolevels of acceptation and transformation of information. The symbol's uncertainty and interactive dynamics (including chaotics) distinguishes this language from other AI languages where the symbols are introduced by some postulates.

Any language contains the uncertain errors, as a part of its ability to convey a bound information structure. The intrinsic language uncertainty imposes the limitation on the language correctness and the error correction mechanism to minimize the errors during any communications. Both the terms-words-phrases of objective (common) representation and carrying the individual informational structure of particular message, make the language structure the unique mechanism for mutual communication and understanding. The internal language code (word) needs a minimal quantity information to maintain and sustain the connections within the IN hierarchical structures. The IN code is a robust code, preserving these connections with some deviation of optimality .

4.3.3. The cognitive model structure and operations

A collection of informative terms according to their relative quantity of information, is stored in a personal base of knowledge (BK) and identified in a personal dictionary of knowledge (DK).

The informational parsing initiates storing and recognizing of the word's parts in a "learning Webster"(W), that is responsible for identification of the language grammar and forming of language terms (or images).

The learning model includes an individual cognitive information network with a personal base of knowledge (IIBK{BK, DK, W}); a language of communication between the IIBK; an intercommunication code within the IIBK's.

An inner formal language, is a personal code of the language terms, that recognizes terms according to their information content, delivers the terms to hook them up into the created IN's nodes, and uses the code for communications between (W, BK, DK) within IIBK. The *current macrostate* from the BK's IN is transformed into the *learnedstate* in DK's IN , Figure 4.3.1.

The IN node could be instable within an uncertainty zone (at a locality of the chaotic node volume) in the process of the node creation, but it becomes a structural stable by fixing the node as a learned state.

The mutual communicated systems exchange the inner formal language, which carries each cognitive structured network quantities information of the personal assigned terms. The receiving information flow can reproduce the individual information network during the learning process, measures the level of knowledge and macrosystemic complexity of the base of knowledge within IIBK [1].

The IIBK processing operates in BK and DK, using the formal personal language.

The BK functions consist of acquisition of a message by reading an initial message code and transforming it into the message terms; evaluating the term's novelty by comparing it with the term's information stored within DK; creating an individual information network of the nonredundant message terms according to their informativeness; sending the above net into DK to store as accepted terms, learning states and concepts.

The collection of concepts, expressing the different ideas (as the nested connections between the entropies of the DK terms), can be stored within IIBK in the conceptual dictionary (CD).

The DK functions consist of acquisition and storing of new information by forming a database of terms and concepts in interaction with a created informational cognitive geometry; enriching the database along with the incoming information

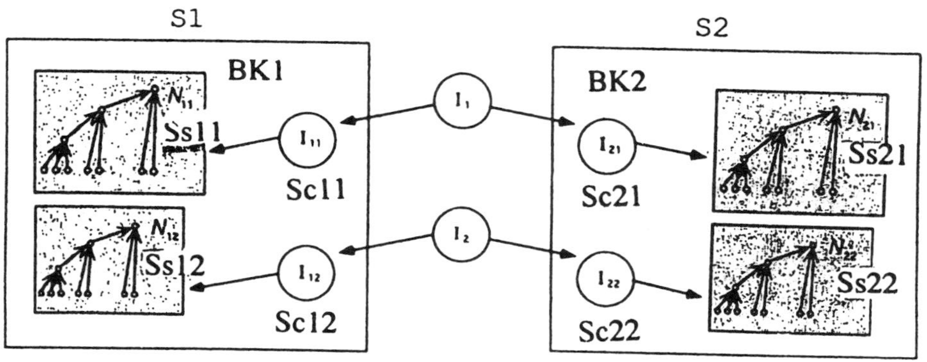

Figure 4.3.1. The scheme of the IIBK's modeling in the process of mutual communication S1 and S2: I11, I12, I21, I22 are the reflections of the information flows I1, I2 with the current states Sc11, Sc12, Sc21, Sc22, and N11, N12, N21, N22 are the information structured networks with the learned states Ss11, Ss12, Ss21, Ss22 accordingly.

from BK in the process of learning and cognition; ranging and storing message terms and concepts, according to their information measure of novelty (entropy).

The BK *operations* are evaluating the message term's information measure, focusing on a maximum novel term (N_o); evaluating the quantity of information of this term h_o by the entropy invariant of elementary node, that depends on the model parameter uncertainty γ_o: h_o=**a** (γ_o), where γ_o defines the optimal IN dimension **n**, and the IN "genetic" matrix structure with a sequence of the node quantity of information {h_i, i=1,...,n}; searching within the DK cognitive geometry to find the corresponding $h_i * \approx h_i$ for each N_i term; assigning the ranged {h_i} sequence to the selected sequence of the {N_i} terms.

Location of terms within the DK data base domain depends on their connection with the DK's related terms (N_i *) and their quantity information (h_i*).

The geometrical space information structure (Figure 4.3.2) defines the position of a particular node, according to its information measure, that identifies the location of the concrete term (h_i*, N_i *) on this cognitive geometry.

The shape and surface of such geometry determine the spiral cones which parameters depend on the information invariant **a** (γ_o), and the vertexes determine the positions of (h_i*, N_i *).

A distance from a current, identifying term to the comparing one (that already exists within DK domain), is measured by the units of the network code and determines the term's h_i*.

The same term might have a different novelty depending on its location within a variety of messages and its position within cognitive geometrical domain. The condition h_o=**a** (γ) connects the informative characteristics for both message and its acceptor.

The personal characteristics are N_i ,h_i and the network code along with cognitive geometry. The VP of network creation is an objective mechanism as the learning itself. A concept (as a highest network node) carries a particular network structure with a sequence of h_i*, that has been embedded in the appropriate terms N_i *.

The transmitted message carries the initial IN's structure with the message "genetic" matrix, that the receiver can recognize by using the described operations.

The sequence of a receiver's operations is the following: accepting a moving message tape MT (Figure 4.3.2); reading an initial message code and transforming the message binary code into natural language terms; putting sequentially each term (N_i) on some starting position St of the DK cognitive geometry; selecting within DK the message term N_o with maximal novelty h_o, that has a maximal informativeness; generating the "genetic" matrix of the message with the ranged {h_i}, based on the knowing γ_o; searching for each message term N_i the corresponding DK term (N_i *) with its information measure (h_i*) on the cognitive geometrical structure; finding such N_i* which h_i* will be nearly to one of the matrix h_i (with ε -accuracy), using the metric distance h_i* (Rt-i , Figure 4.3.2) on the cognitive DK geometry; ranging the found sequence $\{N_i^* \Leftrightarrow h_i^*\}$ according to the ranged $\{h_i\}$ of the message matrix.

The identified and ranged N_i^* sequence creates interacting terms (N_{ij}^*) with their h_{ij}^*. The known values of the ranged h_i:$\{h_o, h_1, h_2, h_3, ..\}$ and the sequence of h_i^*:$\{h_o, h_1^*, h_2^*, h_3^*, .\}$ identify the message informative term's sequence N_i^*: (N_1^*,N2*,N3*,...). Within the process of establishing connections: $h_i \Leftrightarrow N_i \rightarrow N_i^* \Leftrightarrow h_i^* \rightarrow h_i$, the selection of nonredundant terms $N_i \rightarrow N_i^*$ and corresponding h_i^* takes place. Within the message matrix, the accuracy ε of definition of each h_i is found between $\varepsilon(\gamma_o)$=0-0.3.

Within this accuracy, the genetic matrix preserves h_i, and, therefore, it keeps some robustness. The task of the searching procedure consists of finding (within DK data base cognitive geometry) such a ranged N_i^* terms sequence (based on the message N_i terms) with corresponding h_i^*, that will approach the message matrix sequence $\{h_i\}$ with the $\varepsilon(\gamma_o)$ accuracy.

The term, that has a maximal novelty for a receiver, determines the maximum h_o=**a**(γ_o) and, therefore, defines γ_o, and the genetic matrix of the incoming message. If the term is unknown for the DK, in the searching process would be found the nearest to it by the h_{ij}^* value, according to their optimal network connections ($N_{ij}^* \Leftrightarrow h_{ij}^*$).

The meaning of the message can be revealed as an identification of the term's concept by the IN's *logical connections* anddependencies.

The informational term's connection represents the "information logic" responsible for *informational necessity* of the enclosed terms. Each of the following triplets is an elementary logical structure, that *includes* each of the previous triplet.

The IIBK implements the procedure of assigning the information measure without a direct computation of the entropies of incoming symbols and the terms as well, which includes the evaluation of both external and internal informativeness of the message terms.

The *alphabet* of the IIBK language consists of **n** initial symbols-letters $\{h^o(\gamma^o), h_i\}$ and **m**=**n**/2 of three-bound symbol combinations (triplets), forming the language words. An alphabet sentence is defined by the word sequence as the sentence grammar, that is also determined by a function of γ^o. That requires an additional symbol for identification of the word sequence.

The current alphabet, generated by γ^o, is only a carrier of incoming terms, that are hung up on the alphabet letters and transferred into DK for storing and future recognition -identification [5].

The inner IIBK language and its alphabet can adopt the terms from any natural language.

The application software includes the acceptance of visual space information (ch.4.2.3).

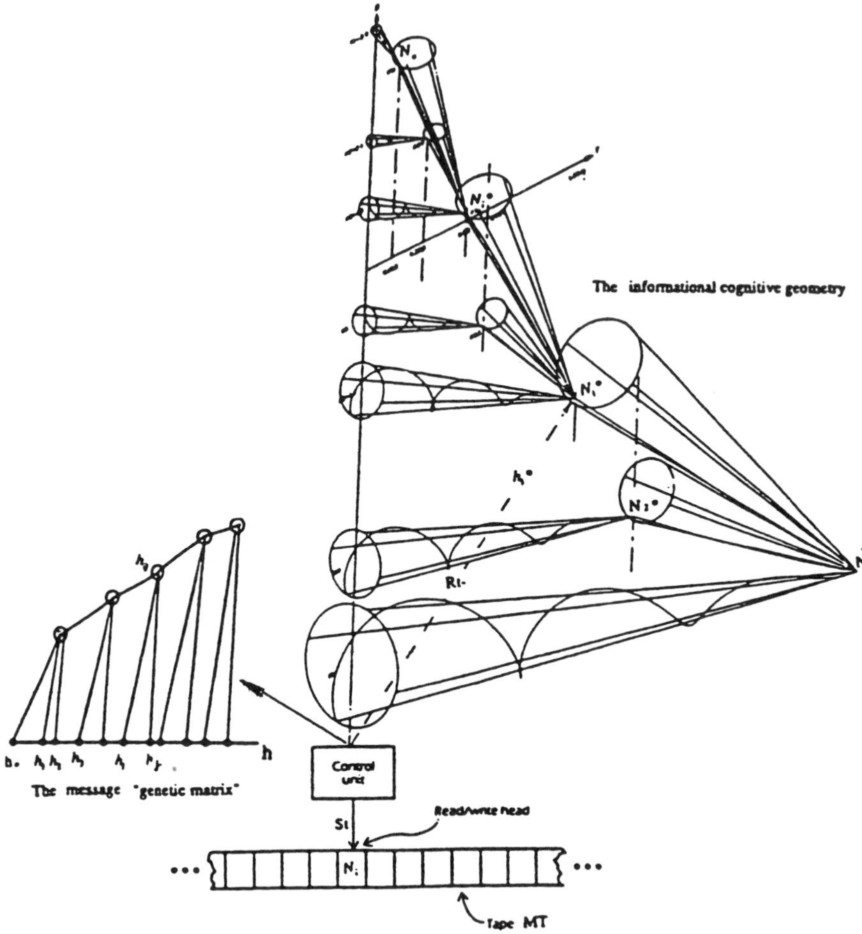

Figure 4.3.2. Scheme of formal operation in Cognitive Learning Machine.

The software package can *simulate* the mutual communication between a receiver and sender in real time, with restoration of the IN models, parameters (**n**, γ, **k**), MC functions and the optimal code length L*=**n**/ln(**n**).

As an example, the identified receiver's initial IN1 has the parameters **n**=4, γ =1.68, **k**=6, MC=6.91, and the optimal length of the code letters L*=2.885~3.

The identified sender's initial IN2 has **n**=8, γ =2.09, **k**=6, MC=20.07, and L*=3.847 ~4. It means, IIBK1 has 4 level of knowledge with the MC complexity ~7, and IIBK2's level of knowledge is 8 with the almost 3-times higher complexity. The mutual communications during the simulation creates the common IIBK model with **n**=6, γ =1.999, **k**=6 , MC=11, and the average L*=3.35.

These results illustrate the connection between the IN's, and an opportunity of mutual adaptation of the IIBK models.

4.4.4. Computer Programs

Computer program for the restoration of the cognitive model includes the following components and their functions:

- input of the images as the initial data

dentification of the proper functional and its macromodel

- determination the initial inner controls and applying them as initial instructions to start the dynamic operation in cognitive processing
- determination and applying the new inner controls, as new instructions at the next DI, with performing the logical operations for processing the symbols
- transferring the symbols dynamics into dynamics of images with determination of the operations with images via images controls
- output final dynamic prognosis and decision controls, applying to random set of images.

The functional and logical operations of the cognitive processing can be reviled and bring out only at the DP.

This representation has analogy with human brain processing, when the results of functional processing are visual after some discrete intervals and logical operations with these results.

This universal program represents a cognitive analogy of Turing processing.

Cognitive processing models a formal information tool and software applicable to a variety of different learning problems in education, management, engineering, artificial intelligence. The cognitive geometrical structure embraces a personal experience by memorizing terms and their interactive connections. The key-lock structure models each of the connections and carries the control mechanism. The distributed processing with decentralized memory (at the net nodes) is capable to create new dynamic connections, stimulated by a novelty of learning. That self-regulatory process of recognizing, minimizes an uncertainty in response to the stimulation. The objective principle of learning creates the subjective informational states and structures. Compiled personal net's can interact within IIBK, creating new, before unlearned connections and information structures. Operating with IN's numerical code (representing letters, terms), a human cognition is able to connect them into the mutual understandable informational structures (words, concept) [6].

The mechanism of recognition of external information, delivered by a triplet's code (ch.4.2), is based on the triplet's ability to join with the inner IN's triplet into enclosed structure.

Binding that information (ch.2.1.10) is an indicator of the recognition.

We understand only a such information, that could be bound into a personal IN.

Classification, ranging of a specific information by some scale of preferences, and hanging it up to the IN are a subject's personal functions.

The ability to bind information into triplet's structures and recognize them by the personal IN is a general mechanism, that is not dependable on the above specifics.

REFERENCES

1. Lerner V., Dennis R., Herl H., Novak J., Niemi D. "Computerized Methodology for the Evaluation of Level of Knowledge," *Cybernetics and Systems, International Journal,* 1993; 24, 5: 473-508.

2. Feynman R.P., Leighton R.B., Sands M. *The Feynman Lectures on Physics,* N.Y.: Addison Wesley,1963.

3. Kolmogorov A. N. *Information Theory and Theory of Algorithms,* Selected Works, Vol. 3, Moscow: Nauka, 1987.

4. Nicolis J.S. and Katsikas A.A. In West (Ed.), *Studies in Nonlinearity in Life Science,* Singapore: World Scientific, 1992.

5. Lerner V.S. "The Information Model of the Mutual Learning in Artificial Intelligence," *Proceeding IEEE, 6th International Conference on Electronics, Communications and Computers*; 1996 February 28-March 1, Pueblo, Mexico, SAIEC, IEEE.

6. Lerner V.S. "Constructive Understanding of Artificial Intelligence through Information Cognitive model,"*Working Paper Series,* University of Urbino, Italy, IMES-LCA, WP-17, 1996: 1-20.

4.4. THE INFORMATIONAL NETWORK FOR PERFORMANCE EVALUATION IN EDUCATION

4.4.1. Introduction

The IMD is applied for evaluating the *informativeness* of both knowledge generation and acquisition in the following components *of* the educational process:

- measuring the quantity of information
- informative representation of knowledge
- informational evaluation of an initial level of knowledge
- delivering informative instructions
- informative learning
- informational evaluation of the results of learning.

That includes *informativeness* of teaching, curriculum, instructional strategy, strategy of learning, and evaluating the results of learning; evaluating the *informativeness of different courses* (or the course parts) related to the same branch of science. Considered methodologies are the examples based on representation of initial information from student's pairwise similarity tests or student's-drawn concept maps into dynamically-organized hierarchical structured informational network (IN). The IN models the sequence of the most informative items pertinent to each individual, and the relative influence of these items upon student's test performance. The MC function, computed for each of these networks, evaluates each individual level of knowledge, accumulated as an evidence of performance on the particular test. The methodologies were practically implemented for evaluating a student's personal level of knowledge in the learning process.

4.4.2. Evaluation of a student's Concept Map

The students draw digraph like concept maps represent common tools in cognitive psychology as instruments in the measure relevant and important links between concepts or ideas. Information modeling and formal evaluation of cognitive structures or maps is an actual and unsolved problem in areas of applied information theory, artificial intelligence, educational psychology, cognitive science and other related fields. The IN presents a human reflection as an evidence of initial drawn map which does not coincide with a student's drawn map. Expert map serves as a standard to reveal the informative items that student does not know and should study eventually. The IN is defined by the number of the most informative items **n** within the map, the uncertainty parameter γ that is a function of the conditional channel capacities $C(x_j/e_j)$ of information flows for students' and experts' node maps, and the geometrical factor **r** of the IN shape [1]. The channel capacities $C(x_j)$, $C(e_j)$ measures the maximal quantity of information, accumulated by each information node for the student's and expert's networks, and are determined by computing the probability distributions $P(x_j)$, $P(e_j)$ among both students' (x_j) experts'(e_j) maps, which evaluate the information flows for each of those nodes.

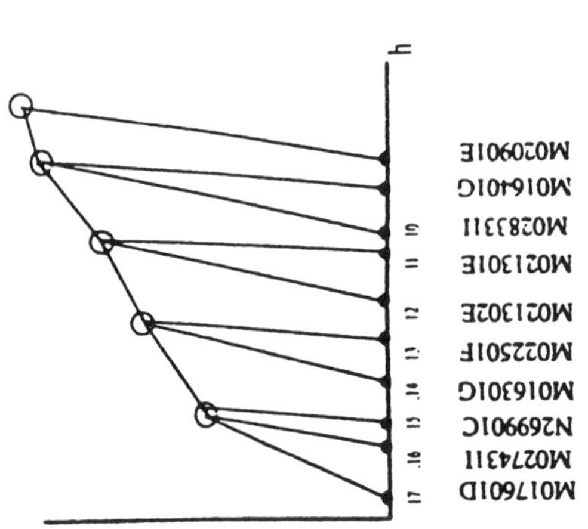

Figure 4.4.2.Subscale#3 Geometry.

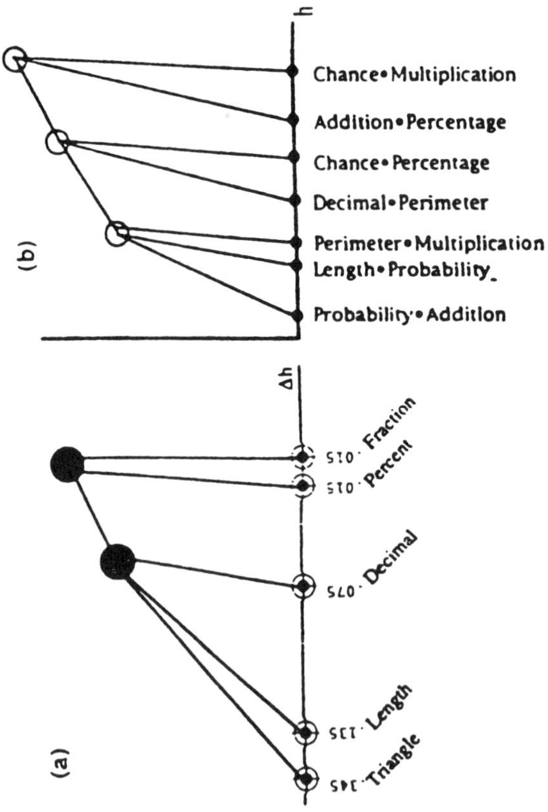

Figure 4.4.1a,b.Examples of students networks for the map.

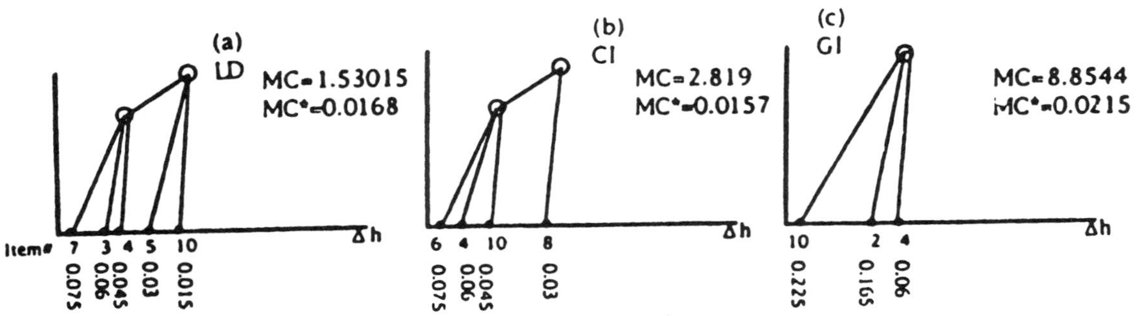

Figure 4.4.3. Examples of student's networks for history performance test.

#	ID	r	m	a	γ	MC
1	26	0.010674	4.	0.45039	1.68000	6.90767
2	27	0.011515	3.	0.54451	1.20000	1.73693
3	41	0.010723	2.	0.45520	1.66000	0.75347
4	40	0.010566	4.	0.44017	1.75000	6.41009
5	42	0.009818	5.	0.37794	2.07000	4.19457

Table 4.4.1. The MC complexities.

The problem consists of building the IN, based on probabilistic functions of each node and evaluating a student performance by measuring MC(**n**, γ, **k**), where **n** is determined by eliminating redundancies in the number of the computed personal student's entropies. A node in the IMD macromodel is the unification of three macrostates. Such nodes obtain equal quantities of information (3**a**) from three macro states during each discrete time interval.

The methodology enables restoring a student IN, if the student drawn map:
1. consists only of number of arcs connection the initial nodes
2. contains also the quality characteristics of each link (by their ranking)
3. has the vector's drawn lines that indicate a different arc's type as the responses from several tests.

The methodology with the link quality characteristics is based on renormalization the number of links according to their weight in standard pairwise similarity rating and further normalizing the computed probabilities. Each student's map was characterized by the quantity of connections emanating from each node. For each node the probability $P(x_j)$ of x_j connections to, or from that node can be estimated for a given group of students. This function is normalized in order to compute entropies for each node. The same can be computed from maps drawn by experts. A single teacher (from the advanced math classroom) has been used as the standard. In the absence of an actual group of experts, to estimate the probability distributions, a single expert's performance was projected upon the student probability distributions, estimated upon the entire group of students. These probabilities have been normalized in order to compute conditional Kullback's entropies $h_i(x_j/e)$, the student's $h_i(x_j)$ entropies for each node, and then are found the local entropies of the nodes $\Delta h = h_i(x_j) - h_i(x_j/e)$. Further procedures include both the elimination of redundancies within each Δh_i and the determination of the information channel capacity of each student $C(x_j)$ as well as a conditional capacity for each student $C(x_j/e_j)$ on the basis of an averaged or composite expert $C(e_j)$. Finally we get the construction of each student's conditional dynamic network reflecting the systematic sources of uncertainty (Figure 4.4.1). Student's relative level of knowledge can be compared in terms of the MC complexity. Table 4.4.1 shows the examples of computation of the MC functions as well as the corresponding (**n**, **a**, γ) and **r** for each student. The MC function is the integral comparative measure (relative to a composite expert) of individual student's performance on this mapping task. The students network show the relative contribution of items to the overall complexity; and the order and connection of the most informative terms. The network representation translates student-drawn links amongst concepts into a sequence of nodes, path, where MC is a quantity measure of all path. The summed entropy from all local link (h_{ij}) is

$$h_i^* = \sum_{j=1}^{n} h_{ij}; i \neq j.$$

The difference in these two calculations $Dh_i = h_i - h_i$ reveals an interaction which is the source of new information equal to

$$\sum P_{ij}(-\ln P_{ij} + \ln \sum P_{ij}) \geq 0,$$

which is a positive since

$$-\ln P_{ij} \leq \ln \sum P_{ij} \text{ at } \sum P_{ij} > P_{ij}.$$

This means that the entropy of each node (h_i) is less than the sum of the entropies (h_i') from all the links, that may emanate from that node. Each node binds some defect of information, created by the interaction of the link entropy flows. A linear assumptions between these two approaches to the calculation of entropies are not satisfied. The minimal admitted probability distribution, which will be in accordance with the accuracy of the model fitted to the data set, is determined by a minimal difference between neighboring values of entropy

$$\Delta h_i, \Delta h_{i+1}: d=|(1-P^o(x_j))\ln(1-P^o(e_j))-(1-P^o(e_j))\ln(1-P^o(x_j))|,$$

where $P^o(x_j)$ is the maximum probability from students' data, $P^o(e_j)$ is maximum probability for experts' data. Therefore, the minimum condition to identify a distinctive entropy is $\Delta h_{i+1} = \Delta h_i + d$. The minimal deviation of the MC function depends only on the accuracy of $\delta_a(\gamma)$ with a fixed $C(e_j)$: $\Delta MC = MC(\mathbf{n}, \gamma, \mathbf{r}) - MC(\mathbf{n}, \gamma + \delta_a(\gamma), \mathbf{r})$.

Combination of the map methods, that disclose both the most uncertain node (as an item) and the most uncertain node connection (as a concept), creates a directional map with revealing the sources of uncertainty for any pair-wise connections. That extends the IMD map methodology. Examples include also the evaluation of reading historical topics, questionnaire in reading comprehension's, and writing an essay [2].

Student's performance in each test is measured by some rating scale, with building the IN, its evaluation by the MC indicator of complexity. The concrete data includes topics of Historical Test:

a) Lincoln - Douglas Debates (LD)
b) Debate on Chinese Immigration (CI)
c) Debate on General Immigration (GI)
d) Writing Essay on a- c.

The IMD model connects the test items in the network structure. For example, for LD (Figure 4.4.3.a) this connection goes through "Douglas" (in 7-4-5-10) and "Douglas thinks" to (3); for CI (Fig.4.4.3.b) the possible connection goes through "Brooks" (6-10-8) and contributions (10) in industry (4); for GI (Figure 4.4.3.c) the connection of items (10-2-4) goes through "money."

To compare student's performance in a different test, relative MC-functions have been computed and normalized among all (a-c) tests. The most complex for the students was the LD test (with average MC=0.0161, sd=0.0009), next is the GI test (with average MC= 0.0156, sd=0.0008), and the easiest one was the CI test (with average MC=0.0154, sd=0.0079).

These results range *different* tests in terms of their complexity for each student and analyze the logical connections in the process of reflection and acquisition of knowledge.

4.4.3. Information Analysis of the Complexity of Mathematical Subscale Dimensionality

The mathematics assessment framework in the National Assessment of Educational Progress (NAEP) consists of five content areas: Numbers and Operations; Measurement; Geometry; Data Analysis, Statistics and Probability; and Algebra and Functions; and three process areas: Problem Solving, Procedural Knowledge, and Conceptual Understanding. The issue of dimensionality is an important consideration in NAEP, because it affects the administration, scoring, data analyses and reporting of the results. The scores in math, reading and science are reported at the subscale levels for Grades 4, 8, and 12. D.Rock [3] in his study on NAEP math subscale dimensionality, found very high correlations between the five subscales in math, which he argues indicates a unidimensional trend at the subscale level. Based on his results, he reached the provocative conclusion that "...we are doing little damage in using composite scores in mathematics and science".

The comparative IMD analysis of the subscales was to discover whether the subscales are distinct in terms of informational differences.

The method and results present a more general interest not only as a new tool for NAEP data analysis, but also for the quantitative evaluation of different reading and learning tests, as well as other human thinking and cognitive structures. The IN informational elements is considered as the NAEP items within a subscale.

The quantities of information, associated with each item and, in turn, the number of informative items within each subscale are unknown a priori and must be determined. Once the information structure of each subscale is identified, the subscales can be compared in terms of their respective MC functions.

Traditional and well-known statistical techniques, that are based upon regression, correlation, and dispersion analysis, are only able to evaluate linearly-connected variables. The initial data analyzed in this study are the NAEP catalogued probabilities for each of the 137 items from the 7 eighth-grade booklets, representing the five subscales. Although NAEP catalogues a considerably greater number of items for this grade level in the total data set, a specific item-selection procedure was adopted in order to match data sets with a parallel study being conducted by Dr. J. Abedi at UCLA. The data were prepared and placed in two files: one a-file with the initial subscale identification [2]. For purpose of comparison, all 137 items were taken as forming a single general math scale, and were included in the second b-file. Additionally subscale #1 (number and operations) was randomly split into two (subscales 1a, and 1b) and treated as separate and distinct subscales.

All analysis was repeated again with one file, representing the subscales and another one, representing a hypothetical general math superscale.

The relatively greater number of items in subscale 1 allowed for this reliability check. Computer Procedure includes the computation of

the subscales normalized probabilities $P_i^j(x)$, where i is a number of items (x) in each of the j-subscales: i=1-137; j=1,2,3,4,5 for file (a); j=1a,1b,2,3,4,5 for file (b); the NAEP scale normalized probabilities $P_i(e)$ for i=1-137 items;

the local entropies for each item of subscales $H^i(x) = -P_i^j(x)\ln P_i^j(x)$; and the

local conditional Kulback's entropies for each NAEP scale item: $H(x / e) = - P_i(x)\ln P_i(E)$, i=1,...137.
The nonredundant local subscale entropies $h(x)$ and the NAEP scale nonredundant *conditional* Kulback's entropies $h(x / e)$, which were arrived at after eliminating redundancies from $H^i(x)$ and $H(x / e)$ accordingly.

The extraction of redundancies is directed to obtain the independent macrostates, each of which is characterized with a unique value of surprise. The difference between the number of nonredundant entropies Nx for each subscale from $h(x)$, and the number of nonredundant entropies Ne from $h(x / e)$ determines **n** ,where Nx , Ne define the corresponding algorithmic entropies.

The maximal probabilities for each subscale are used to compute the information channel capacities $C_i^j(x)$,$C_i(e)$, and $C(x / e)$ accordingly.

The relative MC function for each subscale is defined by **n**, parameter γ from relation $C(x / e)$=**a** (γ), and the parameter **r** from the relative channel capacity.

The information network for subscale 3 with maximal value of MC function is shown in Figure 4.4.3. This network shows the relative contribution of items to the overall complexity indicated by MC, as well as the order and connection of the most informative items in this subscale. The admitted error δh in the computation of the local entropy is defined by the closeness of the actual maximum value of the local entropy h^o =($h(x)$, $h(x / e)$) to its global maximal value h_m:

$$\delta h = h_m - h^o, \delta h(x / e) = -(1 - P_i^o(x))\ln(1 - P_i^o(e))$$

$$\delta h(x) = -(1 - P_i^o(x))\ln(1 - P_i^o(x)).$$

By comparing $\delta h(x / e)$ and $\delta h(x)$ we may choose which one is minimal and use that to determine the maximum entropy accuracy for both $P_i(x)$ and $P_i(e)$.

For example, subscale 3 has $P_i^o(x)$=0.06258; $P_i^o(e)$= 0.01326, and $\delta h(x / e)$ =0.0125, $\delta h(x)$ = 0.0605. So, the first accuracy is more than second, and we may accept the maximum accuracy δ^o=$\delta h(x / e) \approx$ 0.01 for the computation of all subscale entropies. Subscale 3 and the NAEP scale have the minimum ($P_i^o(x)$ and $P_i^o(e)$) across the others subscales. Because of that, the values $\delta h(x / e)$ and $\delta h(x)$ are minimized. The minimal distinction between two MC values , according to ΔMC, is determined by the deviation of $\delta_a(\gamma)$= 0.01, while holding **n** constant. In terms of the MC function, the five subscales can be ranged in following sequence showing increasing magnitude of complexity: 4, 5, 2, 1, 3.

Clearly geometry (Subscale 3) is the most complex at the eigth grade level.
The subscales 2 and 5 have $\delta_a(\gamma)$=0.0116 where both have **n** =3. The difference in their MC-functions is ΔMC=26.8%. Consequently, these two subscales can be considered as an indiscriminative in terms of their MC functions. In other words,

the NAEP items under the subscales of Measurement and Algebra (at the eigth grade level) can be considered as existing in one dimension. Subscales 4 and 5 belong to different dimensions even though they have the same value of **n** , and rather small values of MC, but $\delta_a(\gamma)$=0.0811>δ^o, and the ΔMC is 62%.

Table 4.4.3 presents the subscales MC's, where subscale 1 was randomly split into two hypothetical subscales 1a,b. The purpose of this analysis was to investigate whether the relative range of the MCs across subscales is preserved and whether reliability is maintained. The deviation of MC-function for subscales 1a ,1b is close to mentioned admitted accuracy $\delta h(x/e)$= 0.0125. For these subscales, the distinction between their information complexity is found within the limit of admitted accuracy: ΔMC = 6.88, or ΔMC = 24.2%. In other words, these two subscales are indiscriminate in terms of the MC function. The subscales 1b and 2 have $\delta_a(\gamma)$=0.0128, but different **n**. Therefore, their MC-functions are essentially different. The subscales 2 and 5 have changed only slightly from the above analysis and therefore remain within the same informational dimension. The results show that the MC-function does not depend solely on the number of informative items.

Even though subscales 4 and 5 have a large number of informative items, their complexities are small. Subscale 3 has a smallest number of information items, but the largest MC-function. The accuracy of MC computation depends on $\delta_a(\gamma)$ with given **n** and **r**. For these data we may suppose the MC accuracy has the limit of 26.5%. This means the sets are discriminated in terms of MC-function if their $\Delta MC^o \le$ 26.5% at **n**=3 and $C^i(e)$ = 0.07048. If we split the items of the same subscale randomly into two parts, the MC-function of each part is increased by almost twice. Or, stated inversely, if we join these two sets of items into one subscale, the MC-function of the single subscale is decreased by almost half. This result is critical in the explanation of information complexity for the general NAEP data math scale. When we join items of different subscales in the united single NAEP scale, we lose information. By joining the subscales we destroy information.

There are also theoretical confirmations of this fact. As it follows from [4] if some transformation joins at least two elements with nonzero probabilities into one single element, such transformation decreases (destroys) the initial quantity of information. The above results shows, that even at the level on the NAEP data for the entire population, there do exist distinguishable informational dimensions.

However, the items labeled by NAEP, as belonging to the content dimensions of Measurement and Algebra, actually are indistinguishable in terms of the model presented. Items from these scales exist within the same informational dimension for this population. The most complex math subject for eigth grade students is geometry, which is a new subject area, representing the greatest challenge for them.

The computerized methodology can improve learning and teaching strategy in many different fields of education.

REFERENCES

1. Lerner V.S. and Dennis R.A. "Informational Networks for Performance Evaluation in Education Process," *Proceedings of the 1999 Western MultiConference,* San Francisco, January, 1999.

3. Rock D.A. 1991. "Subscale Dimensionality", *NAEP/DAC Meeting,* Washington.

4. Stratonovich R.L.1975. *Theory of Information,* Soviet Radio, Moscow.

4.5. THE INFORMATION DYNAMIC MODEL OF MACROECONOMICS

4. 5.1. The IMD economical model

Evidently, the first Information Models of Economics were considered in [1]. There were the static models and the aggregation analysis applied to the local economic problems with the entropy measure of employment, markets, incomes, industrial concentrations in the USA, occupational diversity in cities, all of which can be linked to the growth and decline of social systems [2, 3].

Construction of the information dynamic model of macroeconomics, taking into account the interaction of the material, social-labor, and biology processes on the base of the united information mathematical formalism is represented by the actual, before noninvestigated problem [1,3].

Human control of the process of the informational binding is the most effective producer of entropy. Aggregation of the macroeconomic model on the basic of both the system structurization and the information description leads to the quantify information measuring of the decomposed macro structures.

The macroeconomics analogies of the informational valuations prove to be expedient for definition of the optimal ratio of distribution of incomes from property and social-labor, the optimal conditions of distribution income between production, its proper needs, reproduction, and human collective, maximizing the information criterion of usefulness.

The IMD considers a set of random elements jointly functioning in the common environment. Functionality of the elements depends on their individual criteria of usefulness and some collective macroindicators of these interactions with feedback on the individual characteristics. Such system with random processes at microlevel and dynamic ones at macrolevel is governed automatically. Each individual behavior is characterized by a trajectory of random process and the local functional of the micro level interactions.

The cooperative behavior of the elements forms the macrotrajectories evaluated by the path functional integrating the local functional contributions.

As the VP is fulfilled, the macrofunctional becomes the set proper functional (PF), which have the same structure for each element defined on the averaged trajectories of that set. That principle makes possible to select the macrotrajectory, generated by individual contributions, along which the joint contribution gets the extremal value. It leads to formal coordination of interests of the set of interacting elements as a collective with interests of each element. The VP execution maximizes the PF, representing the criterion of usefulness of elements in collective environment. The set of elements satisfying that criterion, generates the controls, selecting the extremal trajectories which maximize the collective effect from interaction of elements and reveals the optimal macro structure of collective.

Behavior of collective minimizes the uncertainty from the random interactions.

The VP defines some systematic self-organization, which is expressed in the transformation of the random processes of microlevel into the system of the collective deterministic macromotions, possessing the hierarchical structure.

4.5.2. The Informational Economic Valuations of the macromodel

The problem consists of discovery those macroeconomic constraints and mechanisms that follow from the PF maximum, defining the optimal economic macro model. This model generates the evolutioning cycle combined with adaptation, which selecting mechanism chooses freely and consolidates the macrosystems of the maximal usefulness. The process of entropy productions are characterized by increasing of the generalized expenses needed to be compensated by the negentropy influx at DPs.

The processes generating the negentropy are the sources of developing the cyclic macro models, and the increment of capital, represented by the increment of negentropy. For the information model, the separated states of collective processes, social, cultural, moral, economic, politic, are undistinguished.

Consequently, the consumption of income, capital are extremely symbolic and conventional which the negentropy measure (characterizing the generalized income of the potential resources for the society and its elements) is the most adequate.

The structural entropy, as a general evaluation of these potential resources, should be returned to collective of random elements, producing that entropy. At the macrotrajectory, the following plots are located: the negentropy contributions; the uncertainty zones; the local equilibrium for triplet's structures; the local nonequilibrium (when a decomposition of subsystems is possible at lacking of compensation of the produced negentropy); the global macrosystem nonequilibrium at completion of the optimal process (when the macrosystem produces more negentropy, than it is capable to consume and transmit to environment).

At the DP localities, the random local contributions, redetermined at macrolevel, are equalized. The defect of information at this moment is a result of the collective contributions, and it has to be distributed equally between the interacted elements.

At the consolidation, the joint triplet's structure memorizes three bound information flows by accumulating the defect information d", created by the information contributions of each first and second eigenvalue in the triplet $d''=\mathbf{a}_o(\gamma)(\delta_{12}+\delta_{13})$; $\delta_{ik}=G_k\exp(G_k-1)/(2-\exp(\mathbf{a}_o(\gamma)(G_k-1))$; $i\neq k=1,2,3$.

The information contribution from third eigenvalue is spent for the proper controls $\alpha_{3t}\, t_3=\mathbf{a}_o$, determining the balance equation $\mathbf{a}-\mathbf{a}_o=(a_{3o}-a_{3t})t_3$, that is fulfilled at each DP.

If at the consolidation (beside of the proper controls), the external controls are applied to the first and second eigenvalues, then a lesser defect is accumulated: $d_o''=\mathbf{a}_o(\gamma)(\delta_{12}+\delta_{13}-2)$.

The source of entropy is compensated by the equal macrolevel information contributions, that carry the controls.

For the MS dimension **n** the structural negentropy N is formed :

(5.1) $N=N_1+N_2+N_3$; $N_1=N_2=(\delta_{12}+\delta_{13})\mathbf{a}_o(\gamma)(\mathbf{n}/2)$;

$N_3=\mathbf{a}_o(\gamma)\mathbf{n}$.

At the equilibrium balance: $\gamma=0.5$; $N_1=N_2=0.31\mathbf{n}$; $N_3=0.25\mathbf{n}$.

The PF gets a maximal value, when $N(\gamma)$ reached maximum at $\gamma\rightarrow 0$:

$N=0.3212\,\mathbf{n}$, at $a_o=0.23$; $\mathbf{a}=0.77$;

(5.2) $N_1 = N_2$=0.6425**n**/2; N_3 =0.23 **n** .

The structural entropy defines the total macromodel increment (as the entropy income), created by interaction of set of random elements.

That increment does not belong to each of those elements taken separately.

The information flows of the collective can be separated at macrolevel by the expense of contributions from the most rapidity information flows (I) and from the following it by rapidity at each triplet (I_1), and also from the controls at DP (I_2).

The possessor of the PF obtains the summarized income (5.1).

The negentropy of controls compensating the macromodel uncertainty, admits an equal distribution between elements of a collective which generate it (at the DP locality). The structural negentropy, as a distinction of I_2, is not the subject for direct distribution between the elements, but it can be distributed in a concordance with a quotable participation of the macro flows at their forming. It means, that the quota N, created by N_1 , N_2 has to be distributed between I_1, I_2 , directly proportional to their quotable participation, and the quota, direct proportional to N_3 has to be return to the collective as a single unit. However, as a distinction of N_3, returned to collective at DP, the quota of the structural entropy $N(N_1, N_2)$, is stored (reserved) in macrostructure as result of participation not only the controls, but from interactions of all macrosystem information flows.

That negentropy income can be returned to the united collective (according to it quotable participation in creation N) after completing of all process.

Considering the equilibrium balance (at γ =0.5), it is a naturally to suppose the distribution of the information incomes in the ratio :

(5.3) $N_1 : N_2 : N_3$ =0.3565: 0.3565: 0.287,

with the components of income:

$N_1 = N_2$ =0.11**n**, N_3=0.09**n**, where N_3 is carried by controls.

The absolute increasing N is possible by growth of dimension **n**, which corresponds to the enlarged negentropy generation.

The maximum contribution in N carries the most rapidly processes of the ensemble of the interacted subsystems carrying $N_1(\mathbf{n},\gamma)$.

Therefore, increasing the dimension is accompanied with the growth of negentropy incomes from the most rapid processes ($I_1 \sim \alpha_{10}$), following also from the equation for the OPMC dimension **n**:

(5.4) ($\ln|\mathbf{a}| - \ln|\alpha_{10}|$-2.949876)**n**+0.6184847=0, γ =0.5.

So, the optimal expending of the production, satisfying the PF maximum is a result of increasing the negentropy incomes from the most rapidity processes.

Therefore, N_1 is the component responsible for the enlarged reproduction.

The negentropy, used for the enlarged reproduction, determines the corresponding increase of dimension Δ **n**=0.11 **n**, and its relative growing Δ **n/n**=**n***=0.11.

Taking into account an even macrosystem dimension, we receive at minimal **n**=$\mathbf{n}_o$=2, the increased macrosystem dimension **n'** =18.8 ≅ 18-20.

For the comparison, if we would use N_3 for the enlarged reproduction, then **n'**

=25.8≅26 which corresponds to a greater than **n** numbers of macroprocesses, essential for starting of the enlarged process reproduction.

Therefore, the lower limit of the minimal processes numbers exists from which the enlarged reproduction can start.

That limit is connected with the minimal complexity of the initial macrosystem at which the enlarged reproduction is possible. As the current **n** is growing, the absolute income from the enlarged reproduction is increasing progressively with the same quote of N_1, consumed for increasing **n** . The PF possessor can use the quota N_2 for the own consumption after returning N_1 and N_3 .

Using the quota N_1 for the own consumption (and N_3 for the enlarged reproduction) will decrease, at the first, the total income on the next cycle (determined by **n***=0.09, instead of **n***=0.11), at the second, it will demand the greater numbers of the initial processes for the enlarged reproduction.

So, at both cases it will bring less profit than using N_2.

The specific dissipative losses are decreased with decreasing $\alpha_i(t_i)$, and the function of usefulness is increasing. With the macromovement transferring on the less rapidity processes, the macrosystem regularities and unexchangeability of the macrostates are increased; the coherence of macrostates, remembering the structural entropy and their cooperation are increased.

So, the less rapid processes are responsible for forming the structural entropy and the collective hierarchy. That is why N_2 represents the attribute of the unifying functions of the PF by definition of its specific interests and wants. The proper macromodel consumption is expended on generating the processes compensating the dissipative losses, connected with a clock course, and the space movement.

We may define a degree of the macrosystem organization (**O**) as a measure of the differences between quantity of information (**S***) bound in structural macrodynamics, and quantity of algorithmic information in initial microlevel (**S**) by formula

O= **S***-**S** ,

where **S***=**S***(**m**, γ ,**k**) is defined by the phase volume, which is changed only at DP: **S***=$\ln G_v$, with $G_v = G_v(t_i)$ as a relative volume of the phase flows, consolidating at DP. Information of microlevel is not structured.

The **O** is a function of time, geometry and an initial microlevel information, and is connected with the MC complexity.

We consider the systemic structure of a human interaction (M1) with the economic social system (M2), risen by human to satisfy human needs.

Analyzing the interactions of M1 and M2, we assume that both macrosystems obey the same informational regularities, with the optimal negentropy productions, distributed by equation (5.1), and the imposed different constraints and limitations.

For example, because the set of the vital human functions are stable, the number of the human macro processes are limited by some **n.**

During process of a human development and improvement, the adaptive qualities could be increased, which consists in rising of the adaptive potential, and as a final goal, in increasing quantity of the generated negentropy at given **n** . For M2, it is a possibility of changing the dimension (**n**) in process of the enlarged production for satisfaction M1 needs. Both macrosystems exist, one at the expense of another, being the mutual useful, and there are not any outside sources. Therefore, the system of their interaction (M=M1+M2) has to be closed. Humans (M1) are considered as a collective system, whose existence is supported by expense of the corresponding negentropy contributions from M2 as well from M1.

Some equilibrium states can be reached in a transitional dynamic process of changing dimension **n** and transformation of the negentropy contributions between M1 and M2.

The negentropy is considered as the universal unit for calculation of income and measuring the exchanges, that is not a subject to fluctuations of the supply and demand (as a distinction of the gold and other currency), and which requests are compensating by the entropy units, to preserve a balance at stable equilibrium.

As a result of above assumptions, functioning of M2 needs the negentropy input N' $=\mathbf{n}/2$ to compensates its proper entropy.

The input starts the nonequilibrium processes, generated the negentropy increment N $=0.31\mathbf{n}$, divided in the considered ratio: $N_1=0.11\mathbf{n}$ (for reproduction); $N_2=$ $=0.11\mathbf{n}$ (for collective payment to M1); $N_3=0.09\mathbf{n}$ (as an increment), Figure 4.5.1. Functioning of M1 also requires the negentropy $N_o'=\mathbf{n}_o/2$ which is used for generating the negentropy increment $N_o=0.31\mathbf{n}_o$ with the components $N_{o1}=0.11\mathbf{n}_o$ (for reproduction: as child-bearing, bringing up children, family, and so on); $N_{o2}=0.11\mathbf{n}_o$ (for the social needs, necessary for the existence of human collective), and $N_{o3}=0.09\mathbf{n}_o$ (for consumption of the proper needs).

The negentropy N' is generated by a human participation, which delivers in M2:

(5.4) $N_o' + N_o - N_{o1}=0.81\mathbf{n}_o-0.11\mathbf{n}_o$,

and also by the resources from the information market (**R**) of the goods N' , produced by M2 (Figure 4.5.1).

We obtain the equation

(5.5) $0.5\mathbf{n}=0.81\mathbf{n}_o-0.11\mathbf{n}_o+N_1'$.

The information commodity, delivered **R**, is measured by the equality

(5.6) $N-N_1=0.81\mathbf{n}-0.11\mathbf{n}$,

which is exchanged on the negentropy resources :

(5.7) $N_1'+N_{1o}'=0.81\mathbf{n}-0.11\mathbf{n}$,

where N_{1o}' is the negentropy resources necessary for M1. M1 receives from M2 the negentropy contributions $N_2=0.11\mathbf{n}$, and $N_3=0.09\mathbf{n}$ in the form of social assignations and the proper income.

M1 also expends the correspondence proper sources of the negentropy: $N_{o1}=0.11\mathbf{n}_o$, $N_{o3}=0.09\mathbf{n}_o$ for the compensation of own entropy N_o' .

So, we obtain the equation

(5.8) $0.5\mathbf{n}_o=N_{1o}'+0.11\mathbf{n}+0.09\mathbf{n}+0.11\mathbf{n}_o+0.09\mathbf{n}_o$.

By joining solution the equations (5. 5-8) we find

(5.9) $\mathbf{n}=-\mathbf{n}_o$; $N_1'=1.2\mathbf{n}$, $N_{1o}'=-0.5\mathbf{n}$.

The total entropy increments, generating by the nonequilibrium processes:

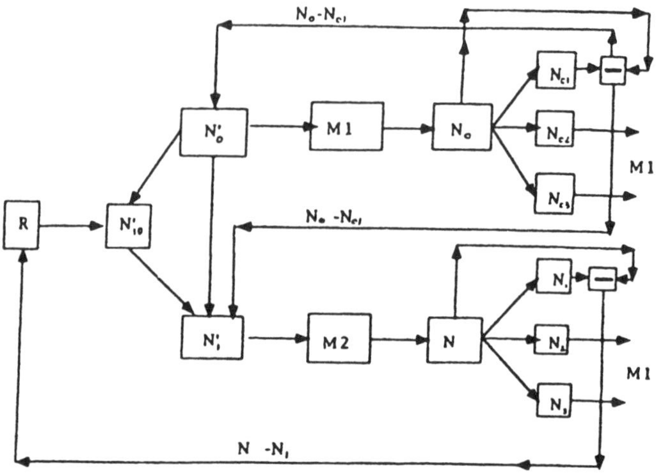

Figure 4.5.1.Scheme of Optimal Interaction of the human system (M1) with the social economic system (M2).

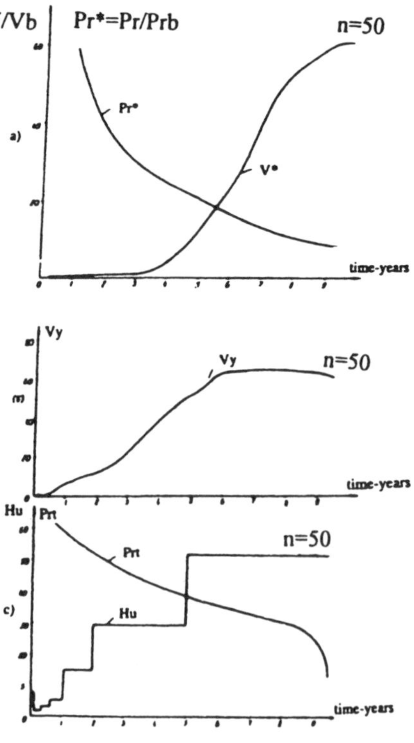

Figure 4.5.2.Prognosis of the dynamics of the optimal development and cooperation of the macro structures.

$N = 0.31\mathbf{n}$, $N_o = -0.31\,\mathbf{n}_o$ are mutual compensated.
So, M2 produces the negentropy compensating the equal entropy of M1(at $\gamma = 0.5$). Because of that, the signs of the indicated dimensions are opposites. From that and from $N = N_o$ it follows, that the profit should compensate the social consumption.

The condition (5.9) means, that the number of the M2 processes has to be increased approaching the number of the biology functioning M1 processes considered before. Increasing **n** occurs by the rise of the negentropy contributions (N_{o1}) for the enlarged reproduction and improvement of new generations. The conditions of balance comes, when the economic social system, satisfying the human needs, gets the same MC complexity , as the human system, but M2 can not exceed M1 by MC complexity. These results follow from the PF maximum and give the natural limit of increasing the dimension and complexity for M2.

Considered analysis is a formal and an enough general to be applied to any system, created by a human, that represents some extension of human being.

Maximal reserve of stability is connected with the maximum informational diversities of the hierarchical macro models.

At increasing of the adaptive M1 potential (at $\gamma \rightarrow 0$), N rises to $N_o' = 0.3212\ \mathbf{n}_o$, and its distribution also is changed according to equalities:

(5.10) $N_{1o}' = 0.367 : N_{o2}' = 0.367 : N_{o3}' = 0.266$.

Reaching the balance with M1 requires also the M2 improvement, which corresponds $\gamma \rightarrow 0$, and the analogous distributions of the negentropy sources in M2. After the equilibrium at $\mathbf{n} = -\mathbf{n}_o$, the subsequent development occurs without increasing dimension, via a corresponding redistribution N in M2 at $\gamma \rightarrow 0$, when the contributions of the dynamic stability can be disturbed (broken down).

As a result of that, could be a change for the worse the conditions of mutual coexistence M1 and M2 in the dynamics, in meaning of difficulty of reaching the balance states. If we suppose that only within M1 $\gamma \rightarrow 0$, and ensure the mutual stability M1 and M2, then γ within M2 is increased symmetrically (relative $\gamma = 0.5$) up to $\gamma = 1$, and then the equation (5.9) at $\gamma = 1$ acquires a view:

(5.11) $-0.3212\mathbf{n} = N$; $\mathbf{a} = -0.587$; $\mathbf{a}_o = 0.294$; $t_3/t_1 = 2.95$; $t_3/t_2 = 1.16$.

Because M2 generates a less negentropy than M1 needs, the number of M1 processes can be decreased in ratio $|\mathbf{n}_o/\mathbf{n}| = 0.94295$; that means M1 can degrade.

M1 can start at the limited $\gamma = 0.8$, for which $\mathbf{a}_o = 0.2765$; $t_3/t_1 = 3.301$; $t_3/t_2 = 1.6765$, $(\mathbf{a}_o\,\delta_{12}) = (\mathbf{a}_o\,\delta_{13}) = 0.6513$; $N = 0.325\mathbf{n}$; $\mathbf{n}/\mathbf{n}_o = 0.987$.

For $\gamma > 0.8$, forming of the consolidation states ceases, because of lacking the negentropy generation (as the source of forming the consolidated structures and preservation of balance between M1 and M2).

At the stable equilibrium, such $0 < \gamma < 0.8$ is established, at which the negentropy needs of M1 are satisfied by the corresponding generation it in M2.

M2 has to produce N as M1 requires for development and its improvement.

This is the meaning of condition of harmony M1 and M2, realized by a suitable redistribution of the negentropy contributions.

A market reflects the informational debalance between the producer's and consumer informational exchanges (communications), where a free (not bound information) creates uncertainty. Generally, the VP at the market could not besatisfied, and in particular is evaluated by the function (ch.2.2)::

$$\delta^* = 1 - \frac{1/2\dot{r}_{ii} r_{ii}^{-1}}{dx_i / x_i dt} = 1 - \frac{\lambda_i'}{\lambda_i} = \frac{\Delta H_i'}{H_i'}, \frac{dx_i}{x_i dt} = \lambda_i', 1/2\dot{r}_{ii} r_{ii}^{-1} = \lambda_i,$$

that determines the difference between the macro model's (satisfying VP) and the corresponding auxiliary differential equation's eigenvalues. If δ^* approaches zero, a market is a regular and predictable. A necessary condition is : Sign λ_i'=Sign λ_i.

A human participation in the structure of considered interactions consists of forming and applying the controls, carrying negentropy at the fixed moment of time, determined by DP. So, the optimal human contribution is not continuous, it has to act on M2 discretely at the successive extended and strict determined time intervals, delivering the increasing quality of the input information.

The optimal control strategy, maximizing the PF, ensures the successive increase of the informational incomes at the moment of time, when the rise of the system organization is possible.

The obtained distribution of incomes is the optimal as an execution of the PF maximum for both M1 and M2 securing their stable conditions of the mutual functioning. The distributions can be considered as a completion of the information regularities, optimizing the evolutionary development of human society.

An example of practical implementation of the macrodynamic model is the computed optimal tax policy (Hu) for the cooperating producers (**n**=50) (Figure 4.5.2), that are joining together their local volumes of production into an initial (basic) volume Vb. The prognostic dynamics characterize increasing the relative volume of production V* (related to Vb), and decreasing the relative price Pr* (as a current price Pr related to a basic price Prb), considering as a function of demands that are proportional to time (in years), with increasing the volume in the price from the volume (in the price form presentation Vy=V • Pr*). The optimal controlling tax policy is decreasing (at beginning), and then is increasing with growing the discrete intervals and the volume production. The last one has a tendency of decreasing at continuation of increasing the tax policy Hu .

The modelling results show that involving new producers into the cooperative process will positively change this tendency. The methodology of the spatial-time synthesis was implemented on computers by the IMD software package [4].

4. 5. 3. About the Informational connections of Economics and Biology

Economics as well as biology is a science studying interactions of the mutual useful subjects (MU), which exist one for another expense.

The only difference is a measure of that mutual usefulness which for economics is money, and for biology is negentropy [5].

Using the negentropy equivalent of money, we may overcome this difference.

As one subject contributes negentropy to another, the informational structure and networks are formed in process of their interaction.

The stable functioning for the *mutual useful* systems of the different dimensions is possible, if they can supply each other by the negentropy for the compensation of production of own entropy, forming the production-consumption successive chain for the negentropy produced by each previous dimension system. For this system, we may use the additivity entropy (negentropy) condition, and its connection with a dimension (**n**) of the stable macrosystem in the form S=**n**/2.

For the elementary three subsystems of such an association (n_{i-1}, n_i, n_{i+1}), the joint system functioning for dimension n_{i-1}, n_i can supply the negentropy to the third one n_{i+1} (or generates it), if these dimensions are connected by the condition $n_{i-1}+n_i=n_{i+1}$. On the other side, the minimal dimension, ncreasing relatively to the initial triplet (n_{i-1}=3), has to be equal 2.

Therefore, n_i=3+2=5, and n_{i+1}=8, that corresponds to the minimal dimension of the *self -controlled* macro model. Then, the dimensions of the *mutual useful* macrosystems take the value of the Fibonacci numbers: 13, 21, 34, 55, 89, where n = 89 satisfies the maximal dimension of the optimal *self-organized* model.

Economics represents the Biology analog of the negentropy exchanges within a human population, maximizing PF.

Optimal strategy consists of compensating the inner entropy with the external negentropy, supplied by discrete controls on each piece of the PF extremal. Optimal controls bind the pieces of the PF extremals at each step of optimal movement by overcoming uncertainty, which separates these pieces at UR. (The UR can be modeled also as an uncertainty environment of each extremal piece).

The UR existence in economics as well as in biology, is a result of the information transmission according to second law.

By binding the extremals in consolidated states, negentropy is created.

Bound states are more complicated and more informative.

Transmission of information by the negentropy production means the process binding through the consolidated states and overcoming the UR.

The IN structure, which binds these states, reflects the structural connection of the mutual useful subjects. Both economics and biology need some mechanism to find the complementary MU for their information interactions and exchanges.

The MU in biology can recognize each other using, for instance, complementary or coherent structures, capable to form "key-lock" connections.

To find the complementary biological subjects they have to search each other in a common geometrical space, and to use some way of a sensitive communication, before interaction.

In economics, there are networks of communications (newspapers, radio, TV, INTERNET), that lead to creating an information market (**R**).

The **R** is a place of binding the interacted customer's entropy and seller's negentropy. In biology it is a place of dwelling, settling of MU, where they can communicate and exchange negentropy.

In economics, **R** is an artificial human formation which could be result of its biological heredity.

Communicating and searching processes in economics can occur faster, and with more diversity of the exchanged products, than in biology.

Plants and animals can exchange only their own production.

Human can exchange at **R** all kinds of Earth productivity, including plants, animals, manufacturing, minerals, and so on, using his top hierarchical level position. So, the human **R** deals with the extended spectrum of information flows, larger scale of dimensions and complexity.

Both economical and biological processes are controlled by maximizing PF and the adaptive functioning, as a consequence of the PM.

The profound likeness of economics and biology consists in common:

- the negentropy exchanges in MU interactions, controlled by the maximum PF conditions
- the IMD information modelling based on the PM
- time-space interactions in a conjoint environment, which has to be searched by communication and spreading
- mechanism of detecting and discovering MU
- mechanism of dynamic balance in process of natural competition.

The informational approach may consider *economics as a human extension and development of biology.*

The information regularities of the optimal evolution opens new opportunities of a progressive development of society.

REFERENCES

1.Theil H.*Economics and Information Theory*, Amsterdam: North-Holland Publishing Co., 1967.

2. Theil H. *Statistical Decomposition Analysis*, NY: Elsevier, 1972..

3. Rodin L. *The Meaning and Validity of Economic Theory*, N.Y: Harper & Brothers Publishers, 1956.

4. Lerner V.S., Portugal V.M. "The Economic and Mathematic Model of Optimal Consolidation of the Productions Structures," *Izvestia Academy of Science USSR*, Nauka: Moscow, 1991; 5: 979-981.

5. Schrodinger E. *What Is life?The Physical Aspect of the Living Cell*, Dublin: Cambridge University Press, 1944.

4.6.THE INFORMATION MACROMODELS IN BIOLOGY AND MEDICINE

The chapter introduces the concrete biological examples of the constructive IMD model applications for analysis and discovery some important biosystem mechanisms, functions, and phenomena. The macromodel's systemic mechanisms have an analogy in biosystemic functional activities.

4.6.1. Information models for autoregulatory processes

The mechanism of regenerative processes in the remaining part of an organ after its injury has not had a satisfactory explanation in spite of numerous publications analyzing and studying this problem. These processes play an important role in both biology and medicine. A mathematical model that is able to describe the main functions of the regenerative regulatory process has not been developed to solve the problem. It has been experimentally shown [1], that the process of cell destruction, initiated before the regeneration, stimulates the mitotic activity in remaining cells. Increasing and then abating the mitotic activities is a result of the cell decomposition, and can be described in terms of changing the ratio of one- and two-nuclear cells, controlled by an autoregulatory mechanism.

The modeling problem has been solved via the identification of the model parameters, based on experimental data, and then by the simulation of the IMD model for optimal prognosis of the restoration process and revealing the regulatory mechanisms [2]. Based on statistical analysis of histological microscopic slices (sections) from 100 rats, two independed coordinates have been selected: x_1 as the number of two-nuclear sectretory cells; and x_2 as the number of one-nuclear sectretory cells in an acinus (one of the ends of a silavatory gland), which is considered as a macroaggregate unit.

The IMD software packet has computed the correlation functions, the model operator, the Hamiltonian and proper functional; it has also simulated the optimal processes at different initial conditions and controls. As a result, the model coefficients a_{ij} and the eigenvalues $\lambda_1 = \alpha_1 + j\beta_1, \lambda_2 = \alpha_2 + j\beta_2$ for the identified macromodel in the form :

$$(6.1)\quad \frac{dx_1}{dt} = a_{11}(t)x_1 + a_{12}(t)x_2, \frac{dx_2}{dt} = a_{21}(t)x_1 + a_{22}(t)x_2$$

are given as the functions of time in the Table 4.6.1 (where [t] =hour, $[a_{ij}, \alpha_i, \beta_i] = \times 10^{-3} s^{-1}$). The model functioning depends on the interaction of processes x_1 (t), x_2 (t), that exhibit itself in the inner feedback, which is identified as the control: $u_2 = h_{22}^{-1} h_{21} v_1$ (with h_{22}, h_{21} as the elements of the inverse covariation function r) for the macromodel with inner controls:

$$\frac{dx_1}{dt} = \lambda_1 (x_1 + v_1), \ \frac{dx_2}{dt} = \lambda_2 (x_2 + v_2).$$

Such model can be reduced to the form $\frac{dx_1}{dt}=a_{11}{}^{o}\,x_1$, $\frac{dx_2}{dt}=a_{22}{}^{o}\,x_2$,
with the coefficients $a_{11}{}^{o}=\lambda_1(1+v_1/x_1), a_{22}{}^{o}=\lambda_2(1+v_2/x_2)$.

The obtained model describes satisfactory the regenerative process and possesses its functions: the stability with respect to initial data, the discreteness of the Hamiltonian (H) and the control function.

The simulated optimal process $x^{o}(t)$ is similar to the experimental process x(t), Figure 4.6.1.The matrix eigenfunctions for the optimal process:

(6.2) $\alpha_1=\mathrm{Re}\,\lambda_1=\frac{1}{2}\mathrm{Re}(\frac{\dot{x}_1}{x_1}+\frac{\dot{x}_2}{x_2})$; $\beta_1=\mathrm{Im}\,\lambda_1=\frac{1}{2}\mathrm{Im}(\frac{\dot{x}_1}{x_1}-\frac{\dot{x}_2}{x_2})$

are the periodical in time functions, its zero-eigenvalues alternate with each other.

At the first DP moment (t_1') of discretization (and control switching), the relative derivatives $\frac{\dot{x}_1}{x_1}$, $\frac{\dot{x}_2}{x_2}$ are equal, and we come to equalities

$$\beta_1(t_1')=0,\ \alpha_1(t_1')=\lambda_1(t_1')=\lambda_2(t_1')=\frac{1}{2}\mathrm{H}(t_1')=\lambda\,(t_1').$$

The last equality defines the operator and Hamiltonian of the consolidated system selected by the control at t_1'. As it follows from the Table, the regenerative process develops in direction of equalization of the eigenvalues, i.e., to such redistribution of the one- and two-nuclear cells, that leads to similar peculiarities of the cellular subsystems. At the moments of changing the structure (t_1'=78, t_2'=176 hours), the imaginary eigenvalue components disappear, and the regenerative process is described by single macro equation:

(6.3) $\dot{x}=\hat{a}\dot{x}$, $\hat{a}=\lambda$ (t'), $\dot{x}$(0)=x(t'), λ (t)= α +-jβ,

which characterizes the acinus (starting from t_1'=78) as a cooperative macrounit with its inherent organic functions. The restoration of original structure is accompanied with fluctuation both the natural and simulated processes as well. At the moment of optimal process completion, the optimal control turns off with α (t"-0)=0, β (t"+0)$\neq$ 0. The optimal feedback stores at DP's both the real and imaginary eigenvalues. At the vicinity of t_2', the phase trajectories have an ellipse form with the center as a singular point. The linearized movement of the system has a neutral stability which may develop the auto fluctuations at moment of turning off, if the non linearity will be included. These results have been used for the prognosis of fluctuation process as an essential part of the regenerative mechanism.

The prognosis has been proven experimentally [3]. Comparison of the simulation and experiments shows that actual regenerative process is similar to optimal prognosis process, although there are some reserves of intensification of the restoration. The results support the concept, regarding development of the natural regeneration according to the minimum principle for the process' proper functional.

The identified control has form of discrete function of time, with its action as a analogy in a trigger mechanism. The counted moment of the control switching

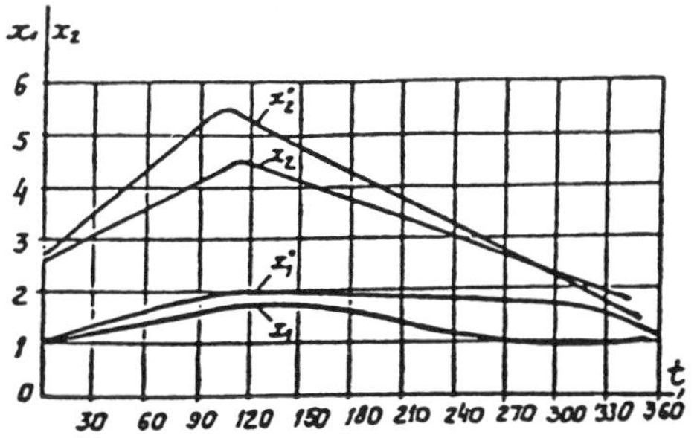

Figure 4.6.1. The model's $x^o(t)$ and experiment's $x(t)$ functions.

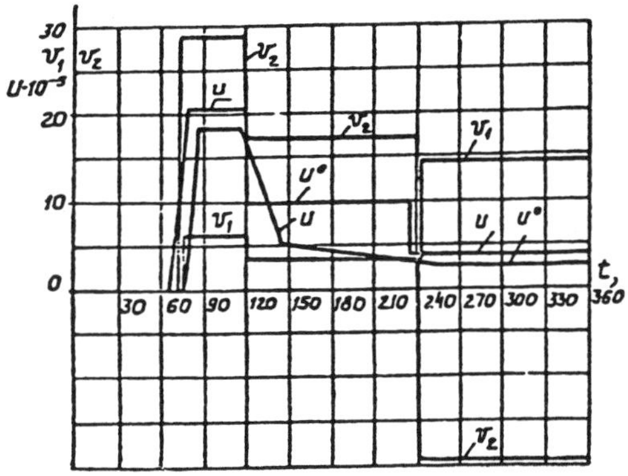

Figure 4.6.2. The model's $v_1(t)$, $v_2(t)$, $u^o(t)$ and experiment's $u(t)$ controls.

Table 4.6.1.

	$0 < t \leq 60$	$60 < t \leq 78$	$78 < t \leq 126$	$126 < t \leq 174$	$174 < t \leq 360$
a_{11}	−0.26	−4.79	1.19	4.97	−0.39
a_{12}	0.47	8.76	−3.38	0.46	−0.42
a_{21}	−0.37	1.69	0.37	2.16	0.17
a_{22}	−2.76	−4.70	2.07	3.46	−0.25
α_1	−2.70	−8.50	1.63	3.06	−0.32
β_1	1.32	0	0.14	0	0.27
α_2	−2.70	−1.00	1.63	5.36	−0.32
β_2	−1.32	0	−0.14	0	−0.27

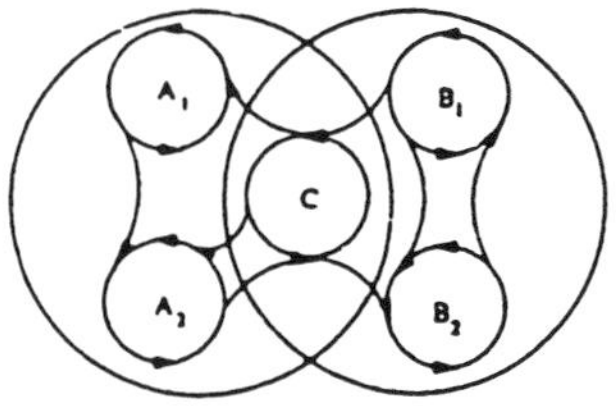

Figure 4.6.3. Hebb's solutions for the binding problem.

agrees with the equation (6.1) which is satisfied at t'o =59 hours, and it concurs with the experimental data (Table) and with results of other researchers. The model control functions (v_1 (t), v_2 (t), u^o (t), Figure 4.6.2, reflect the experimental (u(t)) mitotic dynamics [3]. It may conclude, that the mitotic activity, initiating the restoration process, is an analogy of control action in the feedback. The mitotic activity affects the speed of forming one-nuclear cells, and changes via them the speed of two-nuclear cells, because of their connection according to the equation (6.1). The controls are created by the structural modification of the end organ parts, and they don't need the stimuli action from outside. The model enables to simulate the time of regeneration and possesses an ability of adaptation by reorganizing its structure and self-regulating mechanism, which accomplishes the extremal entropy principle. The space distributed macro model is built, reflecting the processof forming the spiral geometrical structure, analogous to Figure 3. 6. At given initial experimental fields, the macromodel can be used for analysis of the eritrocite kinetics, simulation the evolution the micro structures [2], and populations [4].

4.6.2. The IMD models of population dynamics

The macromodelling is applied to process of interaction of species and population [4]. The microlevel is described by the random behavioral trajectories of n-species (for each population), which interact in a common environment. For instance, a set of random movements of different insects (termites, and others), obtained by observations, form a random time-space behavioral field. The information interactions also include the virtual connections species, even though their space-time locations do not coincide.

The biological aspect of such cooperative interactions is associated with a mutual recognition of some biological species. Identification of the microlevel random field defines the macrolevel dynamic model by using the matrix differential equations, which state's vector (x) characterizes the density of species (or populations) and the conjugate vector (X) expresses the gradient of concentration in the behavioral field as a macro force. The macrosystemic model describes regularities of interactions within population and the between species' competitions as well. The invariance of the entropy functional integrates the different biological conditions, that satisfy the preservation of a selected system. The macromodel reveals the open chain of the trophic connections dividing them into the pairs: predator-victim.

The ranged sequence of the model eigenvalues represents the chain and direction of a biomass movement. The negative values of the eigenvalues validates the evidence of a deficiency between-species' interactions, and existence of the inter-species' competitions for limited recourses. The moments of time, when the constraint (DC) is imposed, corresponds to the pair equalization of the relative species concentrations. The biological meaning of these connections consists of establishing such concentrations of the species (populations), for which their mutual coexistence in the dynamics is possible.

Those moments of approaching (predator-victim) correspond to the between-species' interactions with forming their mutual local stable concentrations.

At the point of interactions, the sign of the corresponding eigenvalue is changed, that accompanies with alternating and interchanging the intervals of increasing and decreasing of the corresponding concentrations. As a result, the dynamically ordered hierarchy of the flows and concentrations is established.

Consequently, it characterizes the subsequent decreasing of the concentrations.

The positive Hessian matrix (of the model's equations) defines the structural stable macro system. The n-the ranged specie, which completes the trophic chain and forms the top of the ordered hierarchical dynamic structure of the information network, possesses a minimal relative value of concentrations.

At the locality of the point of interactions, the diffusion is able to conjugate and connect the kinetic processes, that stabilizes the system in the point of between specie interactions. Their phase macrotrajectories are separatresses, and a chaotic behavior at these points is possible. Optimal parameters of the macromodel quantum spectrum define the maximal informational diversity of population.

In the space distributed macro model, each n-dimension carries the proper quantum spectrum of the initial eigenvalues, maximal time duration of the interactive processes, and their maximal space extension.

For the n-dimensional association, the space prolongation is defined by a such distribution of decreasing concentrations in the space of population hierarchies, at which the structural stability is disturbed. The existence of the trophic chain, that concludes the vertical structure of the initial built hierarchical model and performs the control function for the top level population, leads to the feedback model, that serves for self-organization. The optimal model of such a feedback system, determines the minimal concentrations and the dimension number n, that limits the chain size by the species interactions, and the conditions of self-restoration of the minimal population size on the top of the chain hierarchy. It occurs, for instance, in the chain: plants-insects-birds-large predators, which is encircled by microbes and bacteria. Such a model is able to allocate as an association, any part of that chain, starting presumably from insects. On the table below are shown some extracts from the results of simulating the comparative macromodels with different initial (n_o, γ_o, k_o). These data numerically support the OPMC analysis (ch.1.3). Evidently, growing **n**, **k** and decreasing γ leads to increasing macromodel's relative geometrical sizes $L^*=L/L_o$, volumes $V^*=V/V_o$ and life-time T with decreasing the relative macroprocesses's speeds $C^*=C/C_o$. Using the Table 4. 6.2, it's easy to predict the absolute values of above parameters for specific model.

For example, if initial macromodel parameters are $n_o=4$, $\gamma_o=0.56$, $T_o=8.6s$, $L_o=2\bullet 10^{-7}$ m (that is a minimal linear size of a corresponding virus), then $C_o=2\bullet 10^{-7}/8.6=0.23\bullet 10^{-7}$m/s. At **n**=8, $\gamma=0.527$, **k**=16, we find $L=0.319\bullet 0.23\bullet 10^{-7}$m, $C=0.23\bullet 0.77\bullet 10^{-7}$m/s=0.176m/s and T=36.3s which coincides with C according to the Table 4.6.2. Actually C is the parameter responsible for a macromodel geometry. A single gene (with **n**=6, $\gamma=0.5$) according with the Tables 4.6.2 has linear size $L\cong 1.6\ L_o=3.2\bullet 10^{-7}$m which is in good agreement with Korenberg's results [21] showing that an average gene length is $3.4\bullet 10^{-7}$m. Corresponding time interval at $C^*=C/C_o=0.92$ is equal $T=L/C=3.2\bullet 10^{-7}/0.23\bullet 0.92\bullet 10^{-7}\cong 15.1$s which is close to T=17.2s given by the Table. That also confirms the initial approximation for C.

From the simulating results follow that a maximal relative volume $V^* = V(n) / V_o(n_o)$ of a macrounit (related to initial macrounit volume $V_o(n_o)$) is growing in 10 times with forming of each new triplet.

Therefore $V_o^* = V(n=7) / V_o(n_o=1) \cong 10^3$ determines the macrounit volume ratio, that is necessary for starting the process of self-organization.

A maximal volume corresponds to the most "active" units, characterized by negentropy maximum (at $\gamma = 10^{-4}$).

Let us simulate the adaptive process (ch.2.2.2) and show, at which conditions a random change of eigenvalues $\Delta\alpha_{io} / \alpha_{io}$ is capable of creating a new macro model dimension m /n. Assume the increases $\Delta\alpha_{no}$ with decreasing γ, in such value, that it enabling to determine a new $\alpha_{mo} = \alpha_{no} + \Delta\alpha_{no}$, m>**n**, which satisfies the spectrum of the m-dimensional macromodel operator.

Suppose some conditional probabilities in the relation $P(\alpha_{mo}, \alpha_{no}) = P(\alpha_{no})\, P(\alpha_{mo} / \alpha_{no})$

become equal to the nonconditional ones: $P(\alpha_{mo} / \alpha_{no}) = P(\alpha_{mo})$.

Then a number of independent values α_{mo} is increasing. Probability of the m simultaneous events from N is defined by Feller's formula [22]:

$$P[m] = \prod_{i=1}^{m} P(\alpha_{io}) = [\exp(m!)]^{-1}, \quad P(\alpha_{io}) = \frac{N(\alpha_{io})}{N},$$

where N is the number of events α_{io} with probability $P(\alpha_{io})$.

By checking the execution of this relation for different α_{io} one can find the number of independent α_{io}, that defines a new dimension m.

Appearance of the independent events m is preceding by binding the pairs $(\alpha_{m-1,o}\alpha_{mo})$ as a result of cooperative behavior. In the computer simulation, that corresponds of decreasing γ, and because of their limitations, it leads to transferring the model at larger n. The simulated sequence of decreasing γ and increasing **n**, **k** at initial n_o=6, $\gamma_o = 10^{-4}$, k_o =6 is given on Table 4.6.3.

The computed indicator of inverse complexity $(MC)^{-1}$ and its relative values h^* (to the initial model) are decreasing, the model life time and geometrical sizes are growing with increasing the admissible maximal eigenvalues.

The process of decreasing γ has a limit at **n**=94 with maximal relative unit volume V*$\cong 10^{47}$. The gradient of the increment S_{dv}, measuring the degree of self-organization in the evolution process, is increased with growing of the number of trophic chain populations. For instance, based on the results of computer simulation [4], we got the evolutionary gradient:

$gradS_{dv}(n = 6 / n' = 4)$=-0.22925, $gradS_{dv}(n = 13 / n' = 6)$=~-2.5.

Justification of biological reasons of changing the chain dimension is based on the IMD evolutionary model. The informational "individuality" of subsystem within a population is a continually supported, as "farther" (in terms of the classification

n	γ	k	T,s	L/L_o	C/C_o	V/V_o	$(MC)^{-1}$
				$n_o=4$			
6	0.7997	7	14.98	1.35	0.850	2.02	-
6	0.5900	9	17.2	1.59	0.920	2.12	-
8	0.7645	9	29.2	2.485	0.565	9.32	0.372
8	0.6117	10	33.7	2.931	0.527	12.7	0.283
8	0.5270	16	36.3	3.190	0.770	6.56	-
10	0.6084	13	66.2	5.550	0.346	57.4	0.098
12	0.5958	17	131.2	10.744	0.266	266.4	0.033
12	0.5400	18	142.1	11.74	0.218	307.7	0.029
				$n_o=6$			
8	0.7252	7	30.3	1.240	0.917	2.02	0.262
10	0.5896	10	67.7	2.721	0.567	2.12	0.072
12	0.5859	13	133.1	5.221	0.371	9.32	0.025
18	0.5773	28	998.3	37.554	0.105	12.7	0.0096
18	0.5546	29	1050.0	39.657	0.102	6.56	0.0089
18	0.5323	30	1100.3	41.803	0.100	57.4	0.0082
				$n_o=8$			
50	0.522	1324	$5.62 \cdot 10^{7}$	$96.64 \cdot 10^{4}$	$0.185 \cdot 10^{-3}$	$287.5 \cdot 10^{-11}$	$0.14 \cdot 10^{-10}$

Table 4.6.2. Macromodel's dynamics and geometry at $\gamma_o = 10^{-4}, k_o = 6$ and different n_o.

γ	0.5859	0.5859	0.5773	0.5323	0.522
n	10	12	18	18	50
k	10	13	28	30	1324
$(MC)^{-1}$	$7.162 \cdot 10^{-2}$	$2.448 \cdot 10^{-2}$	$9.58 \cdot 10^{-4}$	$8.21 \cdot 10^{-4}$	$1.43 \cdot 10^{-11}$
h*	2.32	1.51	0.425	0.407	$0.363 \cdot 10^{-2}$

Table 4.6.3. Results of simulation of the adaptive process at $n_o = 6, \gamma_o = 10^{-4}, k_o = 6$.

complexity) that population is located from the neighbor subsystems. Such distance has a limit defined by a minimal stable parameter γ , and maximal **n** which correspond to the dynamic equilibrium between the system and its environment.

The condition of self-organization is fulfilled at the optimal ratio of the above systems dimension $\mathbf{n}/n_1$=1.14. That in particular, at **n**=60, n_1=52 associates with the generation of the subsystem of minimal dimension $\Delta n = n_o$=8 which is capable for self-organization. Environmental influence reveals itself in stochastic perturbances acting on dynamic equations. The Earth system modelling includes monitoring of distributed data, that provides a stochastic input into initial dynamic equations. In existing models, the stochastic effect is accounted by adding the random diffusion components to the dynamic equations.

It brings the stochastic solution to the initial dynamics and changes an essence of the dynamic determinism. The questions arise: how to estimate a pure dynamic effect of the stochastic influence on the initial dynamics without changing the nature of the classical dynamic solutions? What is "deterministic impact" the stochastics on Hamiltonian mechanics and physical kinetics?

The answer affects the methodology of information modeling, simulating, and monitoring of natural systems, environmental technology.

In IMD, a "deterministic effect "of the microlevel's stochastics is accumulated in differential dynamic constraint (DC), imposed on the Hamiltonian mechanics and kinetics at discrete points of the time and space field.

Chaotic movement at the DPs, could serve as an indicator of the sensor's locations in the field for monitoring and collecting data. The IMD equations model the complex phenomena, characterized by a superimposition of physical processes such as heat transferring, hydrodynamical, chemical and diffusion. The equations also include interactions with biological systems and informational processes (describing human activities, environmental monitoring and economical processes).

The IMD modeling methodology selects the most informative data, responsible for the process phenomena, and simulates the creation of new effects in process of interaction with the environment, enables a prediction the evolution of Informational Macrostructures and their Informational Geometry [23, 24].

4.6.3. Modelling probabilistic distributions of microstructures

An initial research result, often can be obtained in form of microstructures from an optical electronic microscopy, random images in computerized observations, and so on. A variety of biological observations are presented, for example, through the distributions of cell structures by size, forms and functions, distributions of microstructures of nervous tissues at different functional states, the statistical distributions in kinetics of erythrocytes, the microstructural characteristics of biological self-organizations, and so on. The samples of the microstructure carry information on time and on geometrical allocations that is provided by investigations of a research problem. The IMD models [17] reveal the regularities of the microstructures by building their hierarchical dynamic macro models.

Using the correlation functions of the given distributions, the macromodel operator (**A**) has been identified, with its spectrum of eigenvalues, that defines the informative discrete moments (t') of the optimal control and cooperation.

The investigated microstructure processes are approximated by the pieces of extremal of the identified proper functional from the condition of statistical equivalence (of the extremals and the random trajectories of the microstructures).

The prognostic hierarchical macro structure, that is based on of consolidation procedure, exposes the number (**n**) of essential macrodynamic elements (or local dynamic processes within the initial micro structure), and discloses the connections between them. The built macromodel has identified such biological mechanisms as cell segregation along with their aggregation and allocation of their geometry and the domain dynamics. For instance, selecting of organized cell by common functions of their associations (as the secretor cells, classification functions of the initial micro structure, and so on). The computation procedures of identification, optimal macromodelling and prognosis have been performed using the applied software package. A large number of biostructures (as ferment, muscle cells, others) is characterized by the different forms of wave processes (concentrated, standing waves, self-supporting spiral waves, solitons) [12, 13].

The IMD model describes origin of such wave process mechanism, which geometry and dynamics depend on the structure of matrix $\mathbf{A}(t')$, identifiable from micro level.

4.6.4. The biological examples of performing the IMD functional properties

We will illustrate the evidence and performance by the IMD model, the systemic set of biological functions on the examples of well-known biological systems, such as protein, nucleotide, cell membrane, DNA dynamic, and geometrical chain structure, self-regulatory Jacob-Monod's mechanism, neuron system, Eigen's evolution hypercycle. Those biosystems represent practically the common and the most important set of biological functions and mechanisms.

We don't know any single mathematical model other, then IMD, that enables it to describe all systemic set of these functional activities, and restore specific behavioral dynamic mechanisms, based on the result of the observed statistics. The IMD model functions follow from the PM principle, but the actual biosystemic functions that this principle can create, have been unknown. The entropy function, useful in thermodynamics, does not create the dynamic equations and does not contribute into systemic approach. Meixner's paradox [19,20] (the different nonlinear systems could have the same macroscopic thermodynamic entropy) is based on "only the macroscopic entropy consideration", without "existence of the microlevel structures." In the IMD approach, the macrolevel entropy functional is defined by the *structure of microlevel* processes, and therefore, that paradox is irrelevant.

The IN network can *predict* a creation of new informational macrostructures as results of applying the minimal program, initiated by the entropy *functional*.. Ability to "predict" constitutes the basic quality of biosystems. The information description with packetization of the ranged information flows, represents model of higher hierarchical level, comparing with physical and chemical descriptions. The initial set of $\{h_{ik}\}$ entropies interacts at DPs by such way, that each high frequency component of the packet, controls the nearest low frequency component. As a result, the mutual controllable systemic packet is formed, with a nonlinear behavior, which is characterized by a discrete set of interacted eigenfunctions as a nonlinear oscillators. The trajectory, that connects these local oscillators is not continuos, and possibly, such a quasy-dynamic trajectory even does not exist, because of connected trajectory's pieces are uncertain and unknown. But somehow these oscillators interact, forming the interlinked enclosed structures. The sequence of the local oscillators forms the nested macrostates, that are determined by the points of the controls switching. The needle controls, as a spark, connect the oscillators opening the communications along the sequence of informative states.

The example of implementation of that mechanism is the transmembrane ionic potential in nerve axon. The process of joining of the most informative states, that are result of successive consolidation, perhaps, can model a consciousness.

The interacting packet of information flows might be considered as a nonlinear wave packet, which is characterized by a soliton wave function [25].

E. Shcrodinger suggested the fulfillment of the minimum entropy principle in Biosystems [5]. But up to now it was not clear, what kinds of the biological functional mechanisms might follow directly from applying this principle.

According with IMD mechanism, an object with spiral geometry enables it to complicate, cooperate, and order its macrostructure by joining new elements, which requires an ability to change the inner positions and local form of the spiral area; to carry out the selective connections, improving the proper functional.

The first functions describe the proteins as the elements building a macrostructure; the second activities perform the proteins as the enzymes.

The material carriers of these functions should be sensitive (by amplifying an attracting), and cooperative (by sticking elements together) with a possibility to repeat and control the process. The sensitivity and cooperation functions perform the proteins, and the control functions perform the nucleotides.

The considered macrosystemic functions reveal proteins as the control object with a variable geometry, defined by dynamics, and the nucleotides as the discrete controls, that are able of copying, memorizing, storing, and inheriting the macrostates (at vicinity of discretization points, which open access the microlevel fluctuations as the mutations). Enzymes are the material carriers of cooperative controls in the cell mitosis, and genes performs the control functions in chromosomes. By general principles of molecular biophysics [6], the most important features of biopolymers are caused by their conformation mobility. The conformation phenomena follow up from the connections of geometrical rotations and dynamics in the IMD model. The conformation nature of the liquid crystal properties of the cell membrane, mobility of the lipid structures, and phase transformations within them, are determined by rotation of the protein molecule around axis, that is perpendicular to plane of the membrane. In particular, the translation diffusion of rodopcine, the conformations melting of lipids by the rotating isomerization of the hydrocarbon chains [6] are the result of the general nature of conformation in macroinformation systems. The protein molecules change their form, inner structure, and peculiarities as a function of temperature and acidity of environment. At small deviations of these variables from standard values, the protein molecules can restore the initial states and their biological functions. The protein molecules form the linear chain structure, which dynamic properties and geometry are mutual connected and are revealed in polymers.

On the chain geometry depend the following positions and composition of the molecules.The protein polymer chain possesses the flexible space spiral structure.

The monomer nature and its sequence define a three dimensional polymer configuration as the primary molecular structure responsible for the protein quality.

The secondary and tertiary structures define their assembling and twisting, determined by the interchain interactions in a monomer chain. The reaction quality depends on all three structures, but the tertiary structure is the most flexible (dependingon binding a minimal energy), which has a more important role in the chain. The chain contains information on the protein structural and restoration functions, as a memory about its structure, possessing a rich collection of physical and chemical functions, that ensure high sensitivity of the chain to the environmental conditions. It defines an ability of the polymer chain in transferring the maximum information along the α -chain. Collagen as a constructive element of organism, is an example of performing these functions. The collagen protein molecule has a triple-spiral geometrical structure, that consists of three polypeptide α -chains, twisted around a common axis. One spire of small spiral helix repeats three amino acid residues, one spire of the larger spiral helix repeats 30 amino acids. Third hierarchical level is formed by the spiral axis of the big spiral for each of three spirals, twisted each around other. The collagen molecules cooperate in the ordered macrostructures: fibrils and fibers to perform their main supporting functions. The cooperation occurs through self-assembling by forming: 1. asymmetrical slices, with the same molecule directions within each slice, and the opposite one between the slices, each of them are not equivalent; 2. symmetrical slices with the opposite molecule directions within each equivalent slice. As the collagen disassociates, its spiral molecule rolls up into a random ball through the disconnection of the chains. The preserved structural memory gives an opportunity to restore the structure after returning to previous conditions. The molecule forms, sizes and the chemical activity distributions at their surface carry the information about the self-assembling. The molecule self-assembling is defined by transferring it into a state with minimum energy. The ordered self-assembly procedure is planning by DNA code, which programs the sequence of synthesized enzymes. One of the enzyme functions is to bind the substrates for overcoming the membrane potential barrier. That function fulfills the active center as a pocket in the enzyme surface. The pocket corresponds to the molecule size, which participates in chemical reaction controlled by the enzyme. Both the pocket active center and the molecule form the "key-lock" connection, that decreases an activation potential barrier to be able to overcome the barrier. Membranes separate the distinct controllable reactions and proceed metabolic processes in cell. The cell membrane works as a controllable discrete filter, that carries in the selective substances, and brings out disposal of chemical reactions. The membrane creates a non equilibrium distribution for transferring information through the cell. The electron transmission from one protein to other is fulfilled by changes in the protein molecule orientation and configuration. The membrane architecture has the triple form, that connects three groups of lipoid-proteins aggregations [7]. The lipoid-proteins substances carry positive or negative charge. The water hydrogen composites form an ordered net, which joins the lipoid heads such way, that they form polar layers as a barrier on the water-air border. Existing transmembrane potential ensures preservation of metabolic membrane functions. The cooperative biopolymer properties reveal itself in the molecular recognition [6]. Nucleotides possess a high ability for cooperation, and the triplet structure (which has the maximum constant of association), preserves a great advantage for cooperation. The stability coefficient for the triplet within the double stranded DNA spiral decreases, if the spiral contains more than four nucleotide pairs [8]. A biological control and cooperation functions are written in genetic program by the triple code in double spiral DNA chain. Connections between the complementary nitrous based of DNA chains, carry out two or three hydrogen bridges which stabilize the molecule. The "key-lock" mutual coordination exists between the chains. The discrete DNA states (codons) define the points of joining new amino acids. The nucleotide triplets, code the corresponding sequence of amino acid sets. An individual difference of the ranged macrostates and the codons (as a discrete set of selected macrostates) depends upon the discretization moments (t',l') of the macrostates forming, which are responsible for the codon geometrical structure and their selective control functions. The codon can control only specific amino acids (with particular dynamic and geometry) by binding such amino acid molecules, which are complimentary to the codon geometry. The codon action is an irreversible in the direction codon-amino acid. The code is built by analogy to any of n-dimensional structures, so that each following dimension includes the code of preceding one. An individual codon properties (defined by t',l') depend on parameter γ, which is determined by the ranged set of information speeds at the codon formation. The terminal DNA codons interrupt the protein synthesis, when the chain reaches the programmable length, acting as the terminal IMD controls. The neighboring structure genes regulate protein synthesis of the operon, which itself is controlled by a regulator gene. The inducer, as a product of controlled biochemical reaction upon binding to the regulatory protein, turns on the gene operon upon binding to the operator. A suppressor, when the products of metabolic reaction are over norm synthesized, turns off the operon upon interacting with the regulatory protein. The self-regulatory cell mechanism is known as the Jacob-Monod mechanism [6]. Analysis of this mechanism shows, that it performs the main macrosystemic model functions [9], and is an example of implementation of the discrete control functions with inducer and suppressor as the sensitive control elements. Structured gene initiates the task control function, which gene operator performs by stabilizing the control process through a discrete feedback regulation. Reading and blocking the DNA information depend on specific chemical components, which are the end products of the metabolic process. The consolidation functions of control system are modeled by the gene recombination's which include: crossing over, the gene integration, the renovating properties, the memorizing of new mutations delivered by microlevel at DPs. Enlargement of the control system accompanies with the hierarchical spiral control structure forming. Biosystems are a general example of irreversible macrodynamic systems, formed by cooperation of the asymmetrical elements [10], as an opposite to crystal structures, formed by cooperation of symmetric elements. Forming the undistinguished macrostates with discrete level of quantity information is a preparation for the consolidation. The impulse control acts as a virtual information, that contributes asymmetry into each of the macrostates, and binds them by the general contribution into a new hierarchical level. Forming the covalent ties is an physical example of cooperating the undistinguished elements. The positive ionized hydrogen molecule consists of two protons and one electron "scurrying" between them. When the electron approaches one proton, it adds its bound energy to the initial proton energy, and subtracts its bound energy from the second proton energy. The situation is reversed, when the electron approaches the second proton. Such a system forms the cooperative unit with the stable state of minimum energy. This virtual electron ties the protons by introducing the asymmetry of energy. The electron sudden leap between two equivalent protons performs the "needle control" function. Actually, the contribution of asymmetry into local equilibrium is result of the DC created by microlevel. The "key-lock" connection implements the asymmetry cooperative

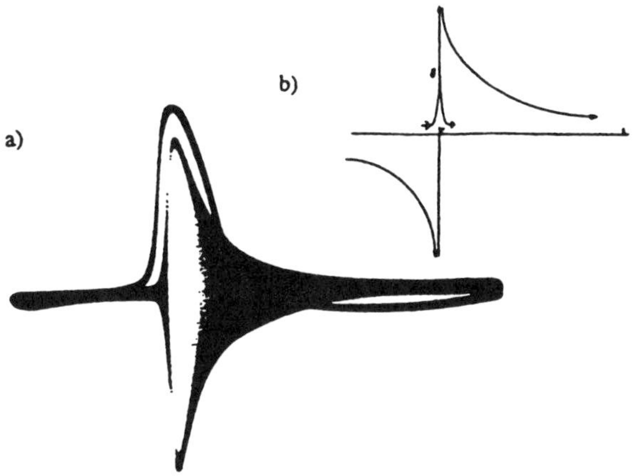

Figure 4.6.4. a) Direct measurement of the increase in membrane ionic permeability (band) and transmembrane voltage (line); b) The model control function.

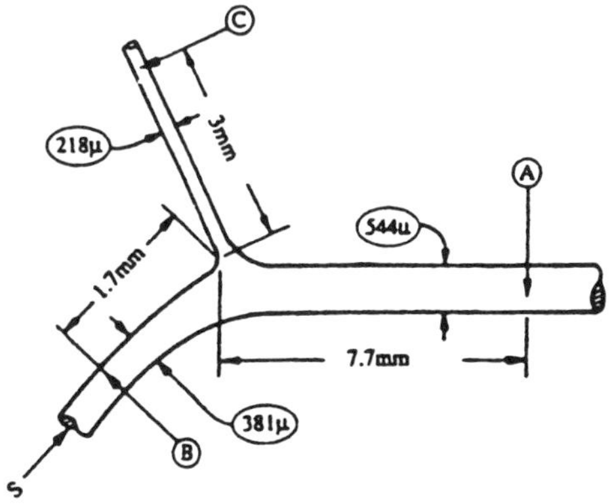

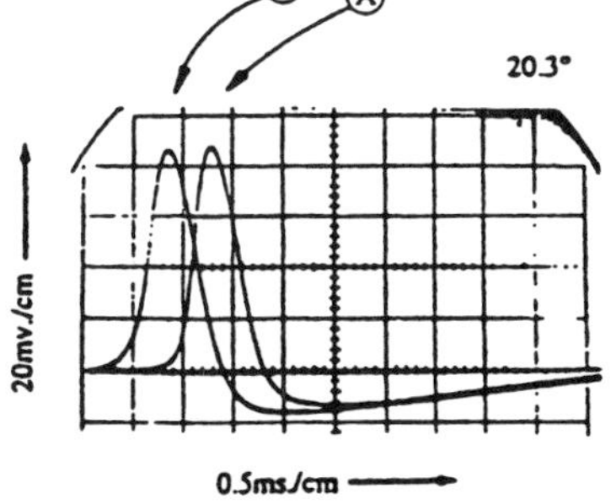

Figure 4.6.5. Branching geometry and single action potential for propagation an a squid giant axon.

mechanism in many biological systems. For example, the protein structure performs the lock function, and the key is formed by the structure of complimentary enzymes, which control the protein synthesis. Functions of virtual exchanges can perform also other particles such as: mesons at interaction of protons and electrons; photons at revealing the electrostatic forces between electrons, and so on. The function of virtual information contribution (as a control) can perform third information flow interacting with two undistinguished flows at forming the triplet structure. The exchanged information resources during the interactions (at DP's) represent the universal function of the optimal IMD controls. For example, the different resource exchanges in business, economy, the information and energy exchanges in biology. Virtual element binds the entropy source and consumer as a donor and acceptor. Such connection is an analogy of the "hole conductivity" in electronics. The examples of the cooperative exchanges in biology are the gene cross over; the carrier transfer through the potential barrier in the cell membranes. The constructive example of cooperative virtual binding represents the Hebb solution for the assemblies of visual images in human brain (Figure 4.6.3) [11] as two information triplets in IMD model. The singular states (at DP's locality) have arisen in the IMD model at the points of transferring kinetics into diffusion, at moments of conjugation and breaking their symmetry. These transformations are the basis of the self-organized processes in dissipative systems. Reference to the rotating movement in the spatial three molecule's model of the chemical kinetics at large value of the bifurcation parameter may be found in [12]. The creation of the self-organized structures within such a model is a result of breaking symmetry, stimulated by diffusion. Another example of phenomena of kinetics and geometry, associated with each other, is the rotating chemical reactions [13], which are described by the singular trajectories of the spatial-time macromodel. The Eigen's hypercycle [8] is an example of the considered evolutionary macrosystemic cycle.

The chromosome set (with n_o-dimension) might be the evolutionary source for synthesis the protein amino acids (with n-dimension), and the last one might be the evolutionary predecessor of the nucleotide code (with m-dimension). In the hypercycle, exists both the direct chain: nucleotide-protein, and the feedback chain: protein-nucleotide. The macrosystemic analysis of molecular evolution [14] as well as the hypercycle were considered in [9]. It was shown, the optimal relation between the hypercycle feedback is: n_o=46, n=20, m=4, which provides their spontaneous self- production.

Examples of the hierarchical element levels are quarks-protons-atoms-molecules-monomer polymers-polymer chains-amino acid polymers as proteins, nucleotide polymers as nucleic acids; biomolecules (macromolecules)-membranes-cells-the cell collectives (organisms), and ecosystems.

The impulse needle controls act to change the one of the cooperating macro operator sign, if both operator signs are positive, and therefore, both subsystems are instable. At that moment (as it follows from the IMD equations), the needle controls can be created automatically as a result of instability, which is able to cooperate the subsystems. The needle controls connect the subsystems, opening the communications along the sequence of informative states. In the neurons system, the needle controls work as a spark that connect neurons opening communication at the impulse propagation. The example of implementation of that mechanism is the trans-membrane ionic potential in nerve axon [15].

The observed reversion of the trans-membrane potential (Figure 4.6.4) needs to connect cell with its environment for transferring a between-cell's information.

This function perform the "needle controls" (Figure 4.6.4).

It is known that cyclic ATP as a cell product, is a regulator of gene functions and the enzyme's biosynthesis reactions.

Analysis of the cyclic ATP functions reveals the impulse cATP action on the aggregation ability of the simple cells (for example the slugs) [12]. The geometrical axon structure (Figure 4. 6.5) [15] is an example of implementation the triplet cone connection (Figure 3. 6). At each triple point of the cone connection, the two cone's vertexes (1, 2) connect with the base of the third cone 3. It can be considered as two input's (1, 2) and one output (3). Because the geometrical sizes of the cones 1 and 2 depend on the corresponding discrete intervals, their radiuses in the joint point are different (as their DP's). These radiuses are proportional to particular information flows that initiate interaction and the impulse needle controls.

The bioexamples of macromodel identification, control, and restoration are the evidence of micro- macrorelations, existing inner and the impulse "needle" control functions. That shows not only biological correctness of the IMD model, but also indicates the practical proof and justification of such details of the cooperative process, as the procedure of equalization of eigenvalues which were changed their sign at the moment following the consolidation (Table 4.6.1). It benefits both the biological research and the IMD theory. The IMD quantum macro level is applicable to the biosystems observation, discretization, cooperation and origin of the "needle" control functions. The biological mutations affect the macromodel only at the DP. The practical example presents spectrum of genetic information, that could be renovated from the mutations using statistical micro level at the DP localities. The macromodel reveals also the relations between quantum dynamics and hierarchical macro structures (See also [16]). The quantum information, located between the discrete sets, are not observable and changeable, with an intrinsic parameter uncertainty h. The discrete sets within the quantum level define the DP points of *measuring* statistical values, that contribute to the macromodel quantity information. Information between the discrete points is redundant for the optimal macro model. For specific biological object, these DPs identify a location of measuring instruments for a sufficient collecting of the object's information. Those DPs have been identified and used for measuring the time involved in regenerating.

The IMD applications also open a wide possibilities to discover unknown biological mechanisms for investigated biosystems.

REFERENCES

1. Husak P. "Materials for the reparative regeneration the protein glands," Moscow: *The Anatomy Archives*, 1965; 49, 12:34-43.

2. Lerner V., Husak P. "Dynamic macromodel of the regenerative process", *Proceedings of Conference on Biological and Medical Cybernetics*, Vol. 2, Moscow: Academy of Science USSR, 1978. .

3. Husak P., Lerner V. "The dynamics of regulatory process and its optimal characteristics," *Natural science for Health science*, Novosibirsk, USSR, 1980: 83-85.

4. Lerner V.S. "The Dynamic Macro model for Computer Investigation of Biological Populations of Different Complexity,"*Modelling of Dynamics of Populations*, Gorki: GSU-press, 1989: 45-54.

5. Schrodinger E. What *Is life? The Physical Aspect of the Living Cell*, Dublin: Cambridge University Press,1944.

6. Volkenstein M.V. *The General Biophysics*, Moscow: Nauka,1978.
7. Cole K.S *Membranes, ions and impulses,* Berkeley: University of California Press,1968.
8. Eigen M., and Schuster P. *The hypercycle: A principle of natural self-organization,* Berlin: Springer-Verlag, 1979.
9. Lerner V.S.*Informational-Probabilistic Approach for solution the Modelling and Control problems in Complex Systems*, Research Report #GR 605281,USSR,1977.
10. Kisel V.A. The *physical reasons of unsymmetry in vital systems*, Moscow: Nauka, 1985.
11. Hebb D.O. *The organization of behavior*, N.Y.: J. Wiley, 1949.
12. Nicolis G., Prigogine I. *Self-organization in nonequiliblrium systems*, N.Y.: Wiley,1974..
13. Jabotinsky A.M. *The concentrated Auto oscillations*, Moscow: Nauka, 1978.
14. Fox S., Dose K. *The molecular evolution and origin of life*, Moscow: Nauka, 1975.
15. Scott A. C. *Stairway to the Mind,* Berlin: Springer-Verlag,1995.
16. Rosen R. "Biology and measurement problem," *Computer and Chemistry*, 1996; 20,1: 95-100.
17. Lerner V.S. "Dynamic Model of the Origin of Order in Controlled Macrosystem." *Thermodynamics and Regulation of Biological Processes*, Berlin- New York: Walter de Gruyter & Co., 1984: 383-397.
18. Lerner V., Husak P. "Macromodels of the probabilistic microstructure distributions", *Proceedings of Conference on Statistical Microstructures Properties*, Moscow: Academy of Science USSR, 1978; Vol. 1.
19. Meixner J. "Thermodynamics of electrical networks and Onsager-Casimir reciprocal relations", *Journal Mathematical Physics,* 1963; 4, 2: 154-159.
20. "Networks in Nature, Editorial News and Views," Nature; 1971, 234: 380-381.
21. Kornberg A. The *cell*, Moscow: Mir, 1975.
22. Feller W. An *Introduction to Probability Theory and its Applications*, J.Wiley, 1970.
23. Lerner V.S. "Informational Model of Stochastic Impact on Environmental Dynamics," Proceedings of the 1999 Western MultiConference, San Francisco, January, 1999:99-104.
24. Lerner V.S. "Informational Systems Modelling of Space Distributed Macrostructures," *Proceedings of the 1998 Conference on Mission Earth: Modelling and Simulation of Earth Systems*, San Diego, January, 1998: 105-110.
25. Lerner V. S. "Information Macrodynamic Approach for Modelling in Biology and Medicine", *Journal of Biological Systems*, 1997: 5, 2:215-264.

4.7. INDUSTRIAL TECHNOLOGY'S IMD APPLICATIONS AND IMPLEMENTATIONS

The chapter reviews the technological IMD applications that emphasize on utilizing the computer methodology and theory and. The detailed original results are given in References.

4.7.1. Optimization of the electro-technological processes

Optimization and electrification of technological processes are an important practice for increasing their productivity, quality, and effectiveness, including a possibility of implementing the optimal automatic control systems.
The powerful electrical furnaces are widely used in metallurgy for such nonferrous metals as nickel, copper, zinc, lead, and for ferrous metals as steel, ferrous alloy's, and concentrates. The electrolyze metallurgy is an another example of the electrical technological processes. The main characteristics of these technologies are superimposition of such physical and chemical processes as electrical conductivity, heat and mass transfer, electrokinetic and electromagnetic phenomena, diffusion and chemical reactions. The process quality depends on the speed of physical and chemical transformations, the random composition of the raw material's ability to change the technological interactions, the expense of energy, the metal loses, and productivity. These features characterize the technology as a multiform criterion process, for which formulating a priori the optimized criteria and applying the regular control methods are not possible. The high temperature and the aggressive chemical reactions in the control furnace zone make difficult a direct measurement of such technological parameters as temperature, speed of physical transformations, characteristics of chemical components, and the gas pressure. The essential physical and the cross interacting processes are not separated without losing technological information. For such superimposing processes, IMD methods of macromodeling, optimal control and indirect measurement of the integrated macroparameters are the most effective. In a particular, using electrical conductivity for controlling the chain of superimposing technological transformations, depending on temperature, speed of chemical reactions, parameters of electrical and magnetic fields, as an intrinsic function of the interactive processes, and the external control as well, is a simple enough. The Hamiltonian $\hat{H}$ of the controlled process, according to the IMD equations, can be expressed via the electroconductivity $\sigma_e = \sigma_e$(t') at the discrete moment's t': $\hat{H} = 1/2\dot{\sigma}_e\sigma_e^{-1}$. It defines the optimization criterion in the form

$$\min k_e = k_e{}^{o}\ ,\ k_e = \frac{\partial G_e}{\partial \mu_e} G_e^{-1},\ \ G_e \sim \sigma_e,\ \ \mu_e = \frac{h_e}{h_o}\ ,$$

where the furnace electrical conductivity G_e is measured in process of the electrode's movement h_e, with h_o as a level of a melting metal in a furnace; μ_e is a relative electrode's movement. The connection of measurement k_e with the main

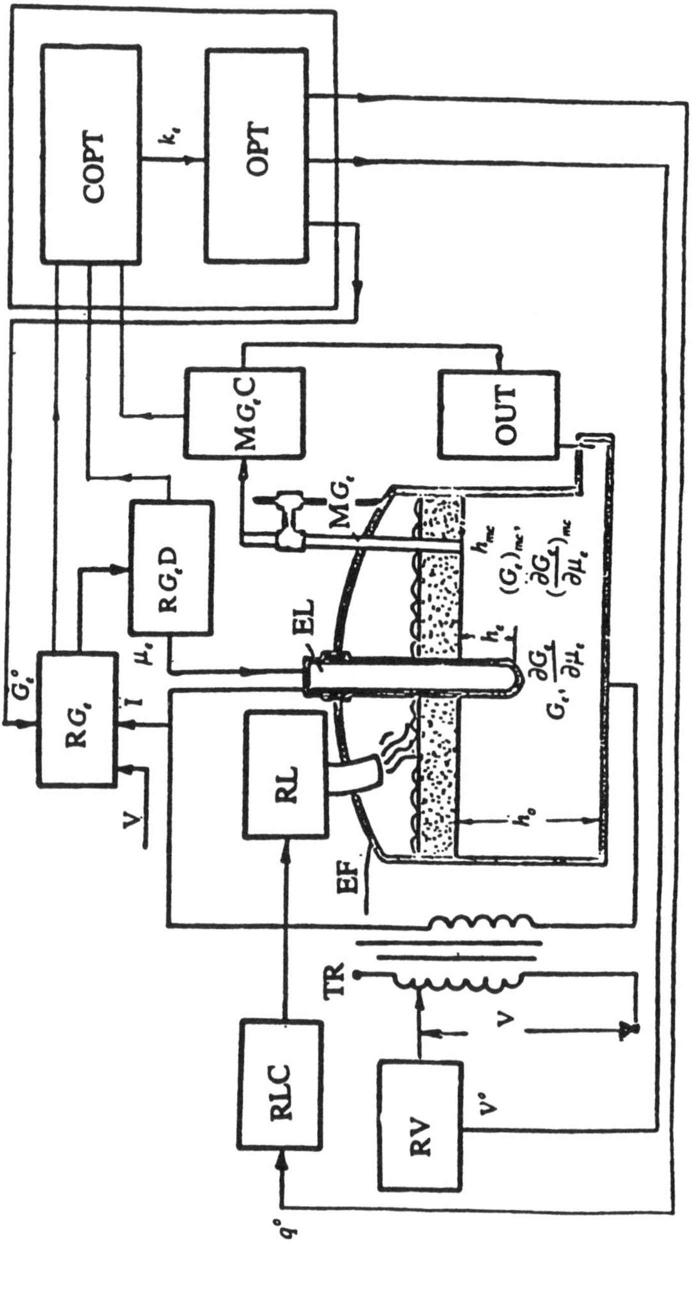

Figure 4. 7.1.3. The optimal self-control system.

technological parameters has been established as a result of practical work on many industrial objects [1-20]. During these projects, the methodology has been developed and implemented with the procedure of minimization of the k_e -function, that actually provides the optimal technological process with a minimum energy loss. The procedure has been automated by designing the computer-based optimal control system (Figure 4. 7.1.1). The automatic system includes the central computer optimizer, that minimizes k_e by changing the control strategy for local regulators. The optimizer's nonsearch procedure is based on combination of the optimal control synthesis $v=v\{k_e(t')\}$, $v(t')=(v_1,v_2,v_3)$ and the identification methodology.

The local controls consist of the following devices:

- the regulator of the furnace electrode's conductivity $G_e=G_e(\mu_e)$, $v_1 = G_e^o$
- the regulator of the furnace voltage V, $v_2=V^o$;-the regulator of the furnace loading (q) by changing the raw materials, as the function of indirect parameter $q=q(\frac{\partial G_e}{\partial \mu_e})$, $v_3 = q^o$
- the h_o control device, using the additional electrode for measuring the level of a melting metal in the furnace, and the local contact conductivities: $(G_e)_{mc}$, $(\frac{\partial G_e}{\partial \mu_e})_{mc}$
- the special electrode devices for measuring the level of the melting components (h_{mc}), as a function of the electroconductivities $h_{mc}=h_{mc}((\frac{\partial G_e}{\partial \mu_e})_{mc})$ of the components
- the controlling devices for the automatic output the melting components from the furnace.

The optimal control system has been inculcated in industry for some acting the non ferrous and ferrous electrical technological objects [15]. It was shown [12], that for these objects, the k_e- criterion is also an integrated indicator of a similarity of the technological features, that is useful for the comparison of different electrical furnaces in terms of their capacity, geometry and dynamics. Such a comparative analysis is also important for a direct transformation of experimental results and model's investigations applying to industrial objects and technologies. The direct transformation is also a part of the industrial applications of control systems, that have been developed at the experimental or similar objects. The prognosis for an optimal technology includes a methodology of computer simulation of the technological process with the optimal control system [13-20]. Analogous results have been achieved for the metallurgical electrolysis processes with a chain of electrical, chemical and thermophysical interactions and the cross-physical process phenomena. Both the technological optimization and control systems, based on the indirect measurement of the electrical conductivity, have been implemented on industrial objects. The electrolytic technology for manufacturing of the composite ligatures is an example of such an object [3]. The manufacturing process of microwire casting in a microwave furnace has a wide applications. That a high-speed technology is based on the superimposition of the electromagnetic, heat and chemical interactions. The macromodel of the optimal technology has been restored following the IMD identification methodology and the indirect measurement of the main furnace parameters. The results of computer simulation have predicted the optimal furnace parameters and the control systems structure [19]. The designed optimal system has been implemented in some acting microwave furnaces.

The methods of macromodeling, identification and optimization have also been applied for some chemical technologies [1].

REFERENCES

1. Antonovich A., L., Lerner V. S. "Mathematical description of the physical and chemical saturated processes", *Academy Science News, Physical and technical sciences,* Kishinev: 1968; 3: 81-89.

2.Golovinscky L. V., Lerner V. S. "The device for regulating the thermal process of electrical furnace," *Journal Priborostroenie*, 1962; 7: 19-21.

3. Lerner V. S. "Automatic control the electrolyser and the electrical furnace,"*The Information Technical Bulletin* , Moscow: Institute Information, 1958; 2: 45-52.

4. Lerner V. S."The proportional speed device for control systems," *Electrical Manufacturing Vestnic*, Moscow, 1958; 10: 34-36.

5.Lerner V. S . "Regulating the electrical power for electrical furnace," *Journal of Electricity*, 1959; 9: 73-78.

6. Learner V. S. "The differenting device," Patent No. 123330, Moscow, 1959.

7. Lerner V. S. "The theory of regulating the electrical power for electrical furnace," *Journal of Electricity*, 1960; 7: 25-30.

8. Lerner V. S. "The methods of correction the control systems". Patents No. 140112, 409191, Moscow, 1961, 1974.

9. Lerner V. S."The automatic device for measuring the melting level," *Journal of Technical Measurement*, 1962;11: 56-59.

10. Lerner V. S., Platonov G. F. "The connections of the geometrical sizes and technological peculiarities of the electrical furnaces with their regulating properties,". University News, *Energetic*, 1963; 8 : 52-58.

11. Lerner V. S. "Automatic control the furnace voltage in the optimal system," *Journal Electrotermia*, 1964; 11: 17-19.

12. Lerner V. S. "The generalized models of electrical transformers,"*Application mathematical methods and computers*, Kishinev, 1965: 76-78.

13. Lerner V. S ., Rudnitsky V. B., Osipov Ia., Ch. "Automation of the electrical furnaces on the Pechenga Nickel Factory," *Electrical melting processes*, Moscow: Metallurgy, 1968: 22-42.

14. Lerner V. S., Litvak Z. V., Chebotaru I., S. "Identification the microwire melting process and its optimization", *Microwire and the resistance devices*, Kishinev, 1969: 33-42.

15. Lerner V. S. *Application of Physical Approach to Some Problems of Control*, Kishinev: K.Mold., 1969.

16. Lerner V. S., Shargorogsky M.T. "Self-control automatic model minimizing the physical functional," *University Reports*, Kishinev, 1972.

17. Lerner V. S. "The control device," Patent No. 686012, Moscow, 1979.

18. Lerner V. S."The optimal indirect parameters minimizing the macro system eigenfunctional,"*Regulated electrical drive*, Kishinev: Stiinza,1980: 60-74.

19. Lerner V. S. "Method optimal control the Electrical melting process". Patents No. 2129659, Moscow,1981.

20. Lerner V. S. "The parametric control the transformers,"*Regulated electrical drive*, Kishinev: Stiinza,1981: 100-112.

4.7.2. The optimal technological prognosis and automatic casing design

Introduction

The IMD approach has been used for solidification modeling and optimization of the casting process with the example of horizontal continuous casting (HCC)[1-2]. The IMD model takes into account the interrelated thermal, diffusion, kinetic, hydrodynamic, and mechanical effects essential for the given casting process. The optimum technological process parameters are determined by simultaneous solution on the problems of identification and optimal control. The control functions of the synthesized optimal model is found from the extremum of the entropy functional having sense of the integrated assessments of the continuously cast bar physicochemical properties. For considered physical system, the IMD structures of optimal model are connected with controllable equations of nonequilibrium thermodynamics (NT) (ch. 3.9). This approach was applied to HCC of ductile iron (DR), and the results were compared with experimental data and numerical simulation methods. Good agreement was confirmed between predicted and practical data, as well as between new and traditional methods. Horizontal continuous casting is a relatively new, but promising method of producing near net shape high quality castings in gray, ductile and Ni-Resist irons, as well as nonferrous alloys like aluminum and copper alloys. Figure 4. 7. 2. 1 illustrates a schematic of HCC. Liquid metal from the transfer ladle is poured into the metal receiver. A water-cooled graphite die is attached to the side of the receiver and bar is pulled out by extraction system which controls stroke length and frequency. Special mechanism cuts and breaks the bars to required lengths.

The major advantage of this process is a high casting yield of 92-95%, since it eliminates traditional ingots and risers. Liquid iron in the receiver plays the role of a preheated riser, that continuously supplies liquid metal to feed the bar during solidification. By maintaining an adequate balance between the iron chemistry (carbon equivalent and residual magnesium content), iron temperature, iron level in the receiver, and drawing and cooling parameters, it is possible to produce defect free high quality ductile iron bars.

Mathematical Model

Table 4.7.2.1 shows a scheme of the main interrelated physical phenomena, that participate in HCC of DR. Each of the phenomena in this scheme is described in independent phase-variable (x^t_{n-k}) and spatial (x^l_{n-k}) coordinates, where: n is the total number of phenomena considered in the model; k is the number of the phenomenon, interpreted from the origin (in this case, heat conductivity). The phase coordinates have the minimal number of states variables which characterize the HCC process, and have the meaning of corresponding derivatives and integrals regarding the temperature θ, and the associated physical quantities: rate of crystallization v_c, increase in concentration ΔC, rate of mass transfer v_m, thermomechanical stresses σ, strains ε, density ρ, and pressure p.

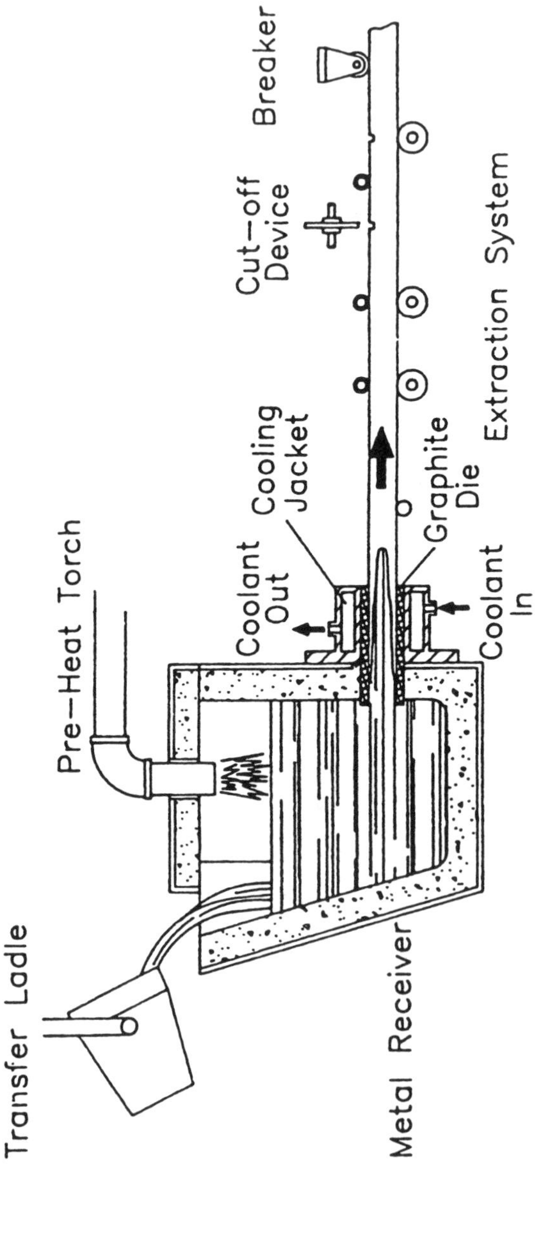

Figure 4. 7.2.1. Horizontal Continuous Casting Processes.

Physical phenomena and their notations	Phase-space coordinates x^l		Phase-time coordinates x^t	
1. Thermomechanical stresses (TH)	x^l_{n+1}	$\int \theta dl \sim \sigma(l)$	x^t_{n+1}	$\sigma(t)$
2. Heat conductivity (T) (initial phenomenon)	x^l_n	$\theta(l) \sim \frac{\partial \sigma}{\partial l}$	x^t_n	$\theta(t) \sim \frac{\partial \sigma}{\partial l}$
3. Crystallization (K) under temperature gradient	x^l_{n-1}	$\frac{\partial \theta}{\partial l} \sim v_c$	x^t_{n-1}	$\frac{\partial \theta}{\partial t} \sim \Delta C$
4. Effective diffusion (D) under heat flow	x^l_{n-2}	$\frac{\partial^2 \theta}{\partial l^2} \sim \frac{\partial v_c}{\partial l}$	x^t_{n-2}	$\frac{\partial^2 \theta}{\partial t^2} \sim \frac{\partial \Delta C}{\partial t}$
5. Mass transfer (M)	x^l_{n-3}	$\frac{\partial^2 \Delta C}{\partial l^2} \sim v_m$	x^t_{n-3}	$\frac{\partial^2 \Delta C}{\partial t^2}$
6. Phase conversions (PC) causing stresses and pressure	x^l_{n-4}	$\frac{\partial \sigma}{\partial l} \sim \frac{\partial \rho}{\partial t} \sim \frac{\partial \varepsilon}{\partial t}$ $\frac{\partial v_m}{\partial l} \sim \frac{\partial^3 \theta}{\partial t^3}$	x^t_{n-4}	$\frac{\partial v_m}{\partial t} \sim \int p dl \sim \frac{\partial^2 \rho}{\partial t^2}$
7. Hydrodynamic transformations in liquid-solid (HD)	x^l_{n-5}	$\frac{\partial^2 v_m}{\partial l^2} \sim p(l)$	x^t_{n-5}	$p(t)$
8. Hydrodynamic mechanism (H) developing a pressure	x^l_{n-6}	$\frac{\partial p}{\partial l}$	x^t_{n-6}	$\frac{\partial p}{\partial t}$

Table 4.7.2.1. Scheme of the main interrelated physical phenomena.

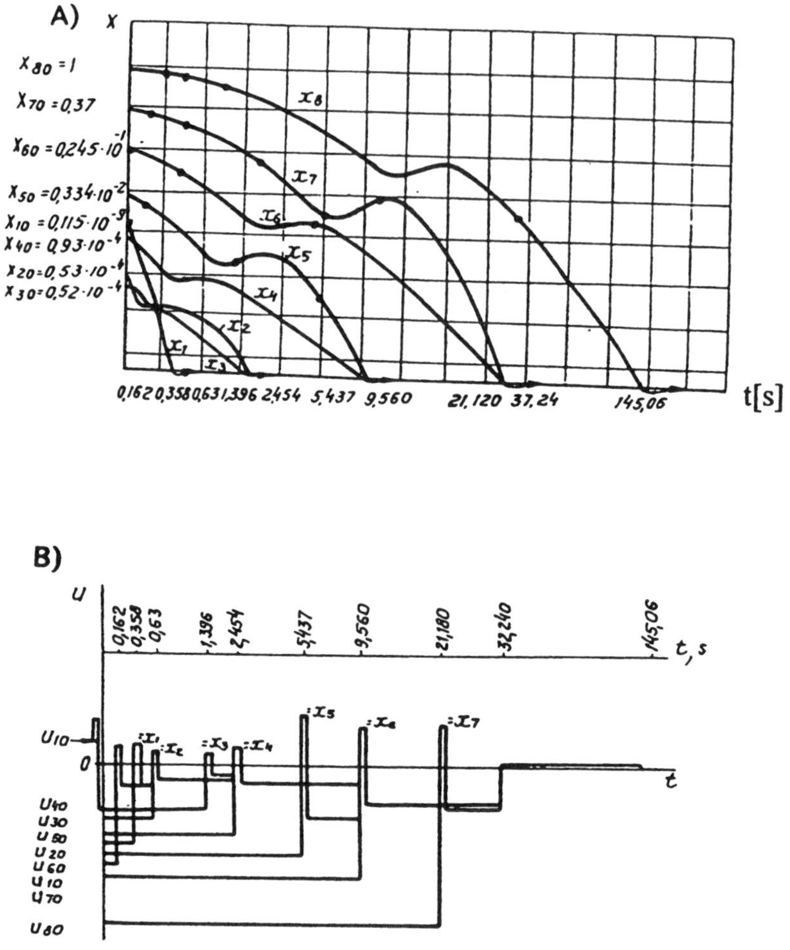

Figure 4.7.2.2. Optimal dynamic processes (A) and controls (B) for processes on Table 4. 7.2.1.

Each coordinate(x^t_{n-k}, x^l_{n-k}) is presented as a derivative of the corresponding $(n-k+1)$ coordinate, where the number of total variables n is previously unknown.

Mathematical description of each of separated phenomena is a well-known from the solidification theory [6]. For example, to describe the heat conductivity (T) and the solidification (S), the Fourier and Stephen's equations are used. Diffusion (D) is described by equations of Fick's first and second laws, associated by laws of conservation. The equations of thermomechanical stresses (TH) are determined by the temperature distribution in the time and space: $\theta = \theta$ (t,l) in the forming casting, i.e., by the solution of T equations, and the equations describing the phase conversions (PC), associated with the change in concentration of carbon Δ C=C-C1 in the liquid (C) and solid (C1) phases. To describe the hydrodynamics (H), the Navier-Stock's equation is used, etc. Also considered are the mass transfer (M) initiated by effective diffusion; the motion of the liquid phase transfer under the influence of the hydrodynamic forces (HD). The obtained system of n differential equations of the first order (with variables shown in the Table 4.7.2.1) includes the informational form of the NT equations which together with the main phenomena reflect also the effect of overlapping phenomena during the casting process.

The entropy functional is used as a quality optimization criterion for the systemic macromodel, which a minimal value determines the maximum order of bar's structure. The conditions of the extremum of nonequilibrium entropy functional, emerges as a general indicator of bar structural uniformity on the micro- and macrolevels. The order on the microlevel means both the structural uniformity of the metallic matrix along the cross section of the bar with uniform distribution of graphite nodules in it, and the uniform distribution of chemical elements along the cross section of the grain boundaries without segregation. The order on the macrolevel corresponds to production of a bar with a uniform macrostructure without internal defects, with fulfillment of the conditions of directional solidification and compensation for shrinkage. As a result of the optimization problem solution, we have found the regularity of changes in the kinetic operator, characterized by successive reduction with time in its intrinsic eigenvalues of the macrosystemic equations, which are equated at specified points (DP). The curves $x_{n-k}(t)$ (Figure 4. 7.2. 2) illustrates the dynamic processes of the optimal model, and corresponds the processes (1-8) on the Table 4.7.2.1. On all the curves we clearly see the inflection points of the relations characteristic for processes in the melting two-phase zone. The IMD dictates a certain ranking for the initial intrinsic values and their interrelation, by virtue of which the optimal model (referred to dimensionless form) is characterized by two parameters: the number of equations **n**, and the uncertainty parameter γ that is a common for the initial intrinsic values.

The optimal dynamics at the boundary of the bar cross section acquire functions of the boundary conditions in calculating the distribution of the physical processes within the solidified bar. The calculation procedure consists of identifying the real time-space parameters of the synthesized HCC optimal model for the circular cross section DI bars. This enable us to determine a fixed for the bars (with a given grade of cast iron), the model indicator of the process: the specific Hamiltonian $h_v \sim k_e$ (analogous to k_e), that is used to calculate the new process parameters.

Optimal hydrodynamic conditions for solidification model

The maximal macrostructure order and obtaining a homogenous bar without defects, is reached by minimizing the specific space distributed Hamiltonian $h_v(t,l)$, that defines the optimal function of the entropy production $\sigma=\sigma(t,l)$.

The problem consists of finding the optimal functions for hydrodynamic variables: the pressure p, the velocity υ of the liquid phase movement, that are defined by the given function of entropy production $\sigma=\sigma(1,\tau)$.

Let us consider the movement of a noncompressed Newton's liquid within a cylindrical channel, that is described by the equations:

(7.2.1) $$\frac{\partial \upsilon}{\partial \tau}=\Delta \upsilon-\frac{\partial p}{\partial z}, \; z=\frac{z_o}{r_o}, \tau=\frac{t\nu}{r^2_o}$$

with the border conditions:

(7.2.2) $$\upsilon(0,R)=\psi(R), \; R=\frac{r}{r_o}, \quad \upsilon(\tau,1)=\varphi(\tau)=0; \frac{\partial \upsilon}{\partial R}=-2g(\tau).$$

The tangent tension on the border of separation liquid-solid phase is given by (7.2.3)

$$f=a_1\frac{\partial \upsilon}{\partial R}, \; a_1 \sim \mu, \; \mu=\rho\nu.$$

The equations are written in relative (nondimensional variables) as the time τ, the radius R and the one of space coordinates $l=z$, and with the absolute variable: t is a time, ν, μ are the kinematic and dynamic viscosities, r, r_o are the current and fixed channel radiuses accordingly, z_o is the axis coordinate, ρ is the density.

The entropy production is connected with the tangent tension f by the relation

(7.2.4) $\sigma(R,\tau)=a^2 f^2, \; a^2 \sim \mu$

It is assumed, that the parameters a, a_1, ρ, ν are given and fixed.

The entropy production for the optimal systemic model is defined by the equation

(7.2.5) $\sigma(1,\tau)=b^2\alpha^t_o(1,\tau)$,

where $\alpha^t_o(l,\tau)=\alpha^t(\tau)$ is the given function of time (in the IMD equations), and b here is the constant coefficient.

Functions g(τ)can be expressed via α^t using the equations (7.2.1-5) in the form:

(7.2.6) $$b^2\alpha^t=a^2 f^2=a^2 a_1^2\left(\frac{\partial \upsilon}{\partial R}\right)^2, \; g=\pm\frac{b}{2a_1 a}(\alpha^t)^{1/2}.$$

By solving the equations (7.2.1-3) at an arbitrary function $\frac{\partial p}{\partial z}=f$ at the given α^t, we obtain the following integral equation with regard to the function f:

$$(7.2.7)\quad \sum_{k=1}^{\infty}\int_{0}^{\tau} f(\varepsilon)\exp(1-\lambda_k^2(\tau-\varepsilon))d\varepsilon = C(\alpha^t)^{1/2}, \; C=\pm\frac{b}{a},$$

where λ_k^2 are the eigenfunctions in the equation (7.2.1).

The solution gets the following representation

$$(7.2.8)\quad f=\sum_k f^k, \; \int_0^{\tau} f^k(\varepsilon)\exp(-\lambda_k^2(\tau-\varepsilon))d\varepsilon = \frac{C}{2^k}(\alpha^t)^{1/2}.$$

After substituting (7.2.8) into (7.2.1-3) can be found the field of velocities $v = v(R,\tau)$. Let us consider the concrete results.

Suppose the function σ is given by the following equations

$$\sigma=\overline{\alpha}_o\overline{\sigma}, \; \overline{\sigma}=\overline{\sigma}(\alpha_o,\overline{\beta}_o,z), \; \overline{\alpha}_o=\alpha_o\left(\frac{v}{r_o^2}\right)^{-1}, \; \overline{\beta}_o=\beta_o\left(\frac{v}{r_o^2}\right)^{-1}, \; \alpha_o=\alpha_o(\gamma),$$

where α_o, $\beta_o=\alpha_o\gamma$ are determined by the parameter γ of the optimal model at given r_o and v. The sought function $f' = \varphi$ acquires the form

$$\varphi=\pm 25.1\left(\frac{|\alpha_o| r_o^2}{4v25.1}\frac{\dot{\sigma}(t)}{[\sigma(t)]^{1/2}}+[\sigma(t)]^{1/2}-[\sigma(0)]^{1/2}\right),$$

from that at following initial conditions we the solutions:

$\sigma(0)=0, \sigma(t)=\overline{\sigma}(t), \alpha_o=-2.29, \beta_o=-1.1456, \gamma=0.5$ we get

$$\varphi_o=\pm 25.1\left(\frac{3.3\dot{\sigma}(t)+\sigma(t)}{[\sigma(t)]^{1/2}}\right).$$

The program computes the functions: the pressure changing φ_o, its gradient $\Delta\varphi_o$ and the velocity v (t) at the channel axis z. These functions define the optimal laws for the pressure and velocity to reach the maximal ordered macro structure.

The pressure changing should be applied to the forming iron bars by alliterating the metal level within the receiver (Figure 4.7.2.1). The corresponding velocity of liquid metal at the channel axis, fulfills the above relations. In the casting process with applied pressure, for fulfillment the directional solidification, the external pressure as a control function should satisfy the relation for φ_o. The feeding and the solidification processes in systemic model are mutually interconnected by a such way, that the speed of the liquid metal movement is coordinated with changing the density of the solidificating bar. The optimal feeding law (Figure 4. 7. 2.5) $C(l_n)=C[l_n(t_n,\Delta l_T, \Delta t_c,\Delta t)]$ satisfies these conditions, where t_n is the starting

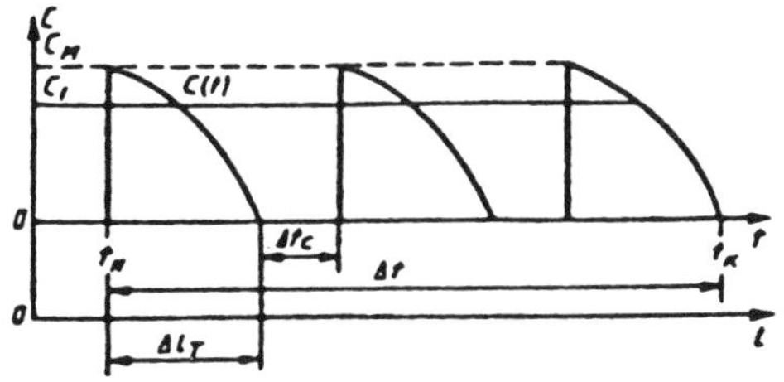

Figure 4.7.2.5. The optimal feeding law of the impulse withdrawing.

moment of changing linear feeding velocity C(t); t_k is the fixed time interval, Δt is the current time interval, Δl_T is the space interval of the impulse feeding controls; Δt_c is the time interval of stopping the feeding impulses (as the optimal controls); C_l is the average solidification speeds. The linear bar size increment satisfies the function $l_n = (C - C_l)t_{n-1}$, where the component $C = \frac{\Delta l_T}{\Delta t}(1 - \frac{\Delta t_c}{t_k})$, $\Delta t = t_k - t_n$ characterizes the average speed of feeding. The difference (l_n) defines the space distribution of metal, that is necessary to compensate a volumetric contraction at $l = l_n$, and during the time interval t_{n-1}. At real conditions of the gravitational feeding, the impulse law is implemented with the continuous speed feeding C_l (equal to the average solidification speed), and the bar high equal h=l_n. The optimal informational model has been implemented as computer-based methodology for design the casting processes. A special feature of developed IMD model consists in determination the intervals of withdrawal Δl_T and pauses Δl_c, on the basis of the model rather, than being set externally as in conventional approach. The HCC parameters, calculated by the IMD model, are in good agreement with industrial conditions during production of DR bars [3]. The IMD model calculates an amount of alloying elements, for example Sn, Cu, Mo, which are capable under real solidification conditions to control the zone of effective diffusion. The model calculate a phase transition in the presence of k points of nonequilibrium, particularly, the nodule count (NC) when (**n**-4+k), or two (**n**-2+k) elements are precipitated. The radius R of the bar corresponds to the model length of the solidification pipe, that is characterized (at the fixed angle at its vertex) by the segment of the helix of the cone l(n+1)),where the number of elements L**n**+1/L**n**+k-1)*2(**n**-2-k)(1+γ^2)^2 is found. The nodule count per unit cross-sectional area S=πR^2, precipitated at the k-th point, is determined as:

NC=4π /S(**n**-2+k)^2 (L**n**+1/L**n**+k-1)^2 (1+γ^2)^2, where **n** and γ are the OPMC parameters , L(**n**+1)=L(**n**, γ) is the model length of solidification cone; L(**n**-4)=L (**n**, γ) is the model length of the effective diffusion zone calculated on computer.

According to the optimal model, graphitization occurs in the spatial interval L(**n**-4) with the maximum NC (L(**n**-4)) nodule count.

The computerized method calculates the NC at any point along the entire cross section of the bar with a sufficient accuracy .

The Automatic Control System design and development

The developed information model has been used as an integrated computerized self-adaptive module to control real HCC parameters. HCC machine, installed in jobbing foundry, was equipped with series of thermocouples to monitor and record iron temperature in the receiver, the cast bar temperature, and water temperature in the die. These data were automatically input into the computerized system, containing developed software, that was able to adjust and simultaneously automatically control drawing parameters (speed and intervals) regarding to the actual process variables. Successful series of experiments have confirmed again practical value of a new solidification model not only to simulate, but also to control the casting process. The developed micro processor for the self-tuning HCC system has been practically applied [5].

The IMD approach have been successfully used for modelling of ductile iron permanent mold casting and for calculation of feeding system [4].

REFERENCES

1. Lerner V.S., Sobolev V.V., Trefilov P.M. "Optimum conditions for cast iron solidification in horizontal continuos casting," *Steel in the USSR*, 1989; 19, 7: 316-317.

2. Lerner V.S., Lerner Y.S., and Tsarev G.G. "Computer optimization of parameters for horizontal continuous casting in spheroid graphite cast iron," *Liteinoe Proizvodstvo, Metallurgy*, 1988; 3: 25-27.

3. Lerner Y.S. Microstructure and Properties of Continuous Cast Ductile Iron, *AFS Transactions*, 1993, 5: 349-354.

4. Lerner Y.S., Lerner V.S., and Bulaevskii Y.V. "Riser Dimensioning for Gravity Diecasting in Nodular Cast Iron," *Liteinoe Proizvodstvo, Metallurgy*, 1989;1:13-14.

5. Lerner V.S., Jelnis M.V., Dobrovolscis A.S., Tsarev G.G. "The system of the process automatization," *Liteinoe Proizvodstvo, Metallurgy*, 1990; 1: 16-17.

6. Kolmogorov A.N. "About statistical solidification theory of metals," Moscow: *Izvestia Academy of Science USSR*, 1937,2:28-39.

4.7.3. The structure of optimal control devices

The control device (CDC) [1], implementing the theoretical results, is used in different optimal control systems, in particular, as an optimal electrical regulator. CDC combines the nonsearchable programming with the identification and optimization of control processes at different performance criteria. Moreover, the identification occurs during the time intervals of applying the optimal controls. In Figure 4.7.3.1 the CDC block is shown with the control object 1, the control formalizer 2, the sensor and the phase coordinates formalizer 3, performer 4, computer 5, programmer 6, differential amplifier 7, discriminator 8, and discretizer 9. The programmer is setting up the assigned process-task, formalized in the optimal program, that extremizes the required performance criteria. For a given integral criterion, both the Euler-Lagrange and IMD equations define the assigned optimal process. The process, considered in deviation of the optimal program, and its controls are found by the PF optimization, associated with the specific integral functional. The "needle controls" provide the system controllability by changing the operator sign. The differential amplifier determines the moments of the operators equalization, and sends the signal, when the eigenvalues moduli are equal. This operation executes the first step of the discrete filtration (Figure 4.1.1) as a part of the optimal control process with simultaneous object identification. The computer calculates each pair of absolute values and signs for the operators (Figure 4.7.3.1),, based on the condition of their pair equalization, and sends the results to the discriminator, governed by the controls formalizer. The discriminator senses the operator signs and sends the signal, initiating the needle controls in a such case, when the sign of any operator is positive. This discriminator function, which itself

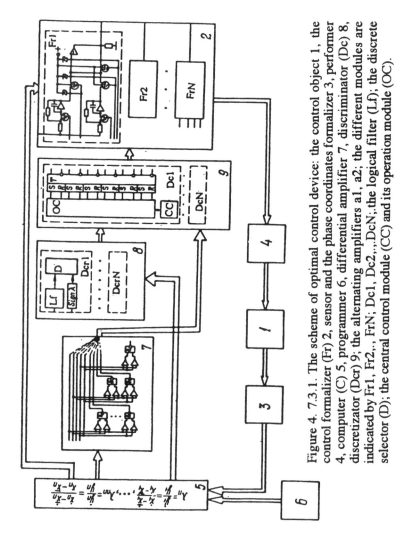

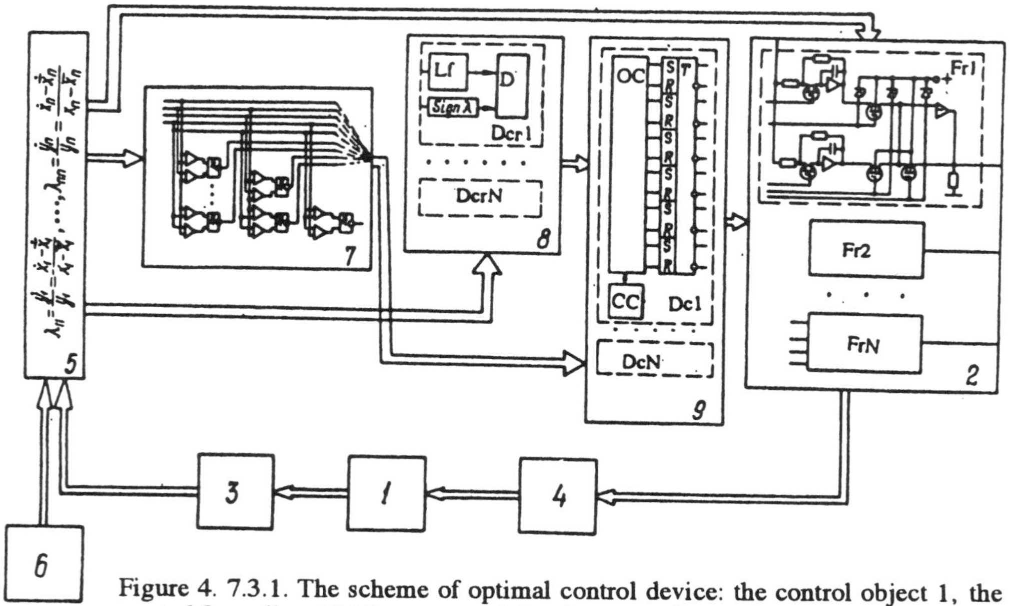

Figure 4. 7.3.1. The scheme of optimal control device: the control object 1, the control formalizer (Fr) 2, sensor and the phase coordinates formalizer 3, performer 4, computer (C) 5, programmer 6, differential amplifier 7, discriminator (Dc) 8, discretizator (Dcr) 9; the alternating amplifiers a1, a2; the different modules are indicated by Fr1, Fr2,., FrN; Dc1, Dc2,.,.DcN;.the logical filter (Lf); the discrete selector (D); the central control module (CC) and its operation module (OC).

is another sequence of the optimal controls action and the identification, constitutes the element of the discrete filtration. The control formalizer sets up the object state coordinates (that satisfy the condition of controllability), and models the optimal control functions. The performer transfers the modeled optimal controls into the actual control actions. The discretizer governs the control formalizer directly by turning on and diverting the signals from the block of elements 5-7-8-9 at the DPs of the optimal filtration. The discretizer turns off the controls at the moment of the optimal process completion. The control formalizer also combines the optimal control, identification, and optimal filtration by memorizing the signals and applying the control to the object at the moments of the information entropy maximum, according to the condition of optimal discrete filtration. The control action on the object, though, is not interrupted during the intervals of filtration due to alternating of the functioning channels with each other by forming and memorizing the controls. The needle control function is implemented via converting the amplifier that is governed by the contactless switching. The principle of memorizing includes the process of the scanning the input signal by one of amplifiers (a1), whereas the second one (a2) stores the memorized control, applied to the object, and vice versa. The differential amplifier consists of the operating amplifiers and the logic elements the input of the latter, represents the impulses at the DP's of the operators equalization. Comparison of all operator pairs is performed simultaneously. The control forming is performed independently for each equalized pair. The discriminator determines the moment of the optimal controls disconnection and selects the nearest DP of the control switching. Information about the operator signs is formed at the moments of applying the discrete controls. The signal coming from the discriminator, serves as an input to the discretizer. Thus, discriminator, discretizer, and the control formalizer as well as the programmer computer and differential amplifier are designed, based on the principle of the even number of modules, according to the channel number. It allows of executing the process of pair- independent forming of all control signals, thus achieving the pair-autonomous status, leading to a better robustness, faster speed and enhanced reliability, the noise resistance of the device. The autonomous module design principle is implemented by the parallel connecting of the n-differential amplifiers to the logical comparative elements, and by connecting the n-outputs to the same numbers of independent channels of the discriminator, discretizer and the control formalizer; selection of the channels is performed by the differential amplifier automatically. The module design CDC collects the required number of the typical standard modules depending on the object dimension. The important features of the n-dimensional device are forming: the model operators within the *single* module; the optimal controls for each pair of operators in the *independent* modules, which increases the device accuracy and provides minimum time performance. The device is able to control complex object with the hierarchical structure. The corresponding hierarchy of the control strategy is formed in the device during the identification and control processes. The effectiveness of the nonsearchable control device is determined by the combination, within the single regulator, the automatic optimizer enables to identifying, the filtering, and optimizing an object simultaneously, and by the device applications for programmable and adaptive systems.

REFERENCE

1. Lerner V. S. "The nonsearch control device," Patent No.798702, Moscow, 1981.

CONCLUSION

The IST subject is the *cooperation of uncertainties* as the carriers of information. Uncertainty is a component of physical realty, but is also the basic element of computer coding language, that manipulating with uncertainties, creates a virtual realty, going beyond physics: as the real and imaginary informational images, algorithms, and software in CT. IMD establishes an information law of optimal design of the cooperating uncertainties into information systems. IMD introduces a real and imaginary invariant measures of an object's intrinsic uncertainty, connects uncertainties into informational network, defines a minimum size program, that prognosis's the object's control strategy, and informational geometry for systemic integrations. That leads to both the scientific object's informational classification and the general methodology of developing their specific systemic algorithms. The IMD theory and computer methodology reveal a creation of complex dynamic properties and ordered macro structures, formed by the microlevel stochastics. An order can be a result of both an initial microlevel order, and an initial microlevel disorder as well. The second law acts as a deterministic tendency enables of delivering a negative entropy from interacting high speed processes. The control function is a source of negentropy at some discrete (time-space) points, generated by high-quality energy or by instable fluctuations, or it could be a result of geometrical space curvature, especially, changing by jumps. The micro- macrolevel communication channel satisfies the general principle of minimizing the maximal created uncertainty. That principle means the maximum transmitted information from the entropy provider to its consumer with a minimum lost. This formula satisfies both initial conditions for the order and disorder, and requires a discrete nature of a space with a discrete time or local jump of its curvature. If these singularities exist naturally, then the minimax principle is fulfilled automatically.
The local concentrated jumps of curvature model some "islands" of memory within the n-dimensional space, which attract macrodynamics by forming both the control's and the latent information mass's. With increasing system dimension **n**, the self-production of negentropy and the system self-organization are possible. The macromodel's nonsymmetry increases an adaptive potential and the negentropy production under external random perturbations. Dynamic constraint is a source of cooperative forces, consolidation, structurization information, and the hierarchical macroformations. The random information "*collected by path functional*" is transformed in regular sequence of the network nodes *enclosed into the highest node* of the hierarchy as an *algorithm of minimal program*. This program enables us to encapsulate a total network's information both from computer and human being, and compress a microlevel data. The IMD information network creates the inner information language, useful for modeling and communication. An information integrating of collective computer and human intelligence into a "super intellectual entity" implicates information revolution in organization society. The human information activities extract maximum information from Nature-Universe. This dialog improves and elevates a human being. IMD represents not only a effective tool for modeling of complex objects but also the methodology for revealing peculiarities of natural systems. The IMD science and methodology introduce new study and tool that are ready for applications to diverse research problems.

INDEX